Remember Who ʏou Are

Remember 'where' you are and where you 'come' from

Remember ...

David Icke Books

First published in January 2012

 David Icke Books Ltd
185a High Street
Ryde
Isle of Wight
PO33 2PN
UK

Tel/fax: +44 (0) 1983 566002
email: info@davidickebooks.co.uk

Cover illustration and design by Neil Hague
and political art by David Dees

British Library Cataloguing-in
Publication Data
A catalogue record for this book is
available from the British Library

ISBN 978-0-9559973-3-4

Printed and bound in India by Thomson Press India Ltd

Remember Who You Are

Remember 'where' you are and where you 'come' from

Remember ...

David Icke

What is happening to the world?
Read on...

Original Illustrations in this book are by
Neil Hague

Neil is a British artist, illustrator and visionary, whose
work is dedicated to the 'truth vibrations'.
For over 16 years Neil's work has appeared on book covers
all over the world and he has had numerous exhibitions
of his highly individual and imaginative paintings across the UK.
Those that have seen Neil lecture have often described
his work as neo-shamanic, healing and from the heart.

He has also written three books including his first
Illustrated Graphic Novel
Kokoro - The New Jerusalem & the Rise of the True Human Being
For more information about his books, lectures, prints, workshops
and original paintings found in this book visit

www.neilhague.com

Dedication

To Linda, Kerry, Gareth, Jaymie, Carol Clarke, Neil Hague, Mike Lambert, Linda Smith, Regina and Scott Meredith, Monnica Sepulveda, Credo Mutwa, Stewart and Janet Swerdlow and all who have given me such unwavering support through so many challenging years.

To Jason of Jay4louise – fantastic work, mate, fantastic – an example to all who say 'but what can I do?'

Other books and DVDs by David Icke

Books

Human Race Get Off Your *Knees* - The Lion Sleeps No More

The David Icke Guide to the Global Conspiracy (and how to end it)

Infinite Love is the Only Truth, *Everything* Else is Illusion

Tales from the Time Loop

Alice in Wonderland and the World Trade Center Disaster

Children Of The Matrix

The Biggest Secret

I Am Me • I Am Free

… And The Truth Shall Set You Free – 21st century edition

Lifting The Veil

The Robots' Rebellion

Heal the World

Truth Vibrations

It Doesn't Have To Be Like This

DVDs

The Lion Sleeps No More

Beyond the Cutting Edge – Exposing the Dreamworld We Believe to be Real

Freedom or Fascism: the Time to Choose

Secrets of the Matrix

From Prison to Paradise

Turning Of The Tide

The Freedom Road

Revelations Of A Mother Goddess

Speaking Out

The Reptilian Agenda

*Details of availability at the back of this book
and through the website* ***www.davidicke.com***

Contents

What the *hell* is going on?

How often I hear this question in its many variations, from the polite and genteel: 'What the goodness is going on?' ... through: 'What on earth is going on?'... to the more 'of the street', though very expressive and effective: 'What the *fuck* is going on?'

The latter captures the energy of the question rather well, although it might upset those who have been programmed to recoil at the use of such a word because it is 'naughty'. Well, it depends on how it's used, really. It can be used abusively and aggressively, but then so can lots of other words that are perfectly acceptable to 'moral society'; and I defy anyone to come up with a better response to hitting their thumb with a hammer than: '*Fuuuuuuuuucccccckkkkkkkkkkkkkkk!!!*' It's a sort of verbal painkiller. It makes *me* feel better, anyway. And what if, by some twist of fate, the slang word for sexual intercourse had turned out to be, say, 'sandwich', and the word for something eaten between two slices of bread had passed from the Latin through the Greek, with some Outer Mongolian influence, to become 'fuck'? We would now be asking for a cheese and tomato fuck, heavy on the mayo, and no one would flicker an eyelash. But ask for a 'sandwiching fuck' and we would be asked to leave the shop. Humans are so funny. So much moralising about a word while at the same time thinking it perfectly 'moral' to pepper-bomb cities full of people to protect them from violence. Media organisations in the United States can be fined ludicrous amounts of money if anyone says the word 'shit' on the radio, yet it's fine to broadcast the US President announcing that he is going to bomb more children with brown faces to protect their freedom, while asking the people to 'support our troops' in doing that. Well, support the live troops who can still serve the mass slaughter and exploitation. Forget about the dead and maimed troops. They're really bad for selling the next war and recruiting more bomb fodder. What a distorted sense of 'morality' it all is – and there is a reason for that. We *live* in a 'distortion'. But more of that later. Anyway, where was I? Yes, back to the point. I mean, what is '*going on*'? I'll settle for: 'What the *hell* is going on?' as a sort of middle ground, still just on the right side of 'naughty', yet still a little risqué to the moral extremists – 'Don't you say that word in this house or I'll get the soap,' and all that stuff. I am sorry if I upset such people with my use of the word 'hell', but, if I do, well, fuck it! The time is over for pussyfooting around, talking around the point and desperately trying to avert our eyes so that we can't see the elephant in the living room; or it had

Figure 1: How we got into this mess

better be if we want to live in a world in any way connected to another and far more important 'f'-word – Freedom. We need to wake up and grow up lightning fast and heads and sand need to part company, along with sofas and arses just as quickly (Fig 1). The world is being bombarded with so many shocks – economic, political, military, geological and so on, and we are hurtling towards, at least at the moment, a global centralised fascist/communist dictatorship in which the very few are dictating the increasingly fine details of the lives of the very many. And we have seen nothing yet if heads and sand, sofas and arses continue in their current relationship. This is what is 'going on', but even that is only a part of what we need to know.

Remember, remember, *remember*

The world appears to be so bewilderingly complex that most people find it impossible to make sense of it. Instead they give up, switch off and concede their potential uniqueness to the tramlines of programmed convention. Most don't even try to make sense of it. They leave the womb and head for the tram station, encouraged by a global system specifically designed to hijack their sense of self and reality, and by parents who had the same done to them long ago. The blind led by the very partially sighted (Fig 2). The apparently complex is just that – *apparently*. What is 'going on' and why nothing is as complex as it seems at its core is very simple. Well, let's say simple with one addition. It is simple when you open your mind and become truly *conscious*. To the closed and programmed mind, forget that I said anything about simple. To those in such prisons of perception, there *is* no simple. Everything appears complex when you can't see how the

Figure 2: You are feeling sleeeepy – baa, baa, baa

random is the planned and the strand is just a part of the tapestry. Put this book down now and don't waste your time if your mind can conceive only of individual 'things' with 'empty' space in between, and can't perceive that the cutting edge of possibility is way ahead of anything we are told is possible. But, if you are opening your mind to *consciousness* and opening your eyes to truly 'see', or you are prepared to give it a try, then what lies between these covers could change your life in ways you never thought possible. *I* will not change your life – the information will. *You will.* You already know all this anyway; you have just forgotten. It is not a case of new knowledge – only *remembering* what the system has purposely blanked out.

Remember, remember, who you really are. I have written the best part of 20 books, and I never know where they are necessarily going to take me when I sit down to start. They take on a life of their own as I write them, and new insights and leads come as the process unfolds. The big books – and some are *really* big – can take nine months from start to finish; but I am writing this in the little more than a few weeks between two major speaking tours around the world, and so I know already that this one is not going to be *really* big. This also fits with what I am feeling sitting here on day one, and with the reason for writing this at all. I have been consciously doing what I do now for well over two decades. The journey has taken me to more than 50 countries and put before me a mountain of multi-levelled, multi-subject information from endless sources and personal experiences, some nice and some not so nice. This has been communicated in a series of very detailed books, all-day presentations across the world, DVDs, my website: www.davidicke.com, Smartphone 'applications' and in hundreds of videos and interviews circulating on the Internet. There are an estimated 250 million websites and, in 2011, Davidicke.com entered the top 5,000 most visited in the United States and the top 6,500 in the world. The interest in this information is now fantastic, not least because ever more people are feeling extremely uneasy about the world and where it is going. They are rejecting the official explanations that once made sense, but no longer do, and they are looking elsewhere for a fix on what is, well, *'going on'*. So what I am setting out to do here is connect the dots of this apparently complex – and certainly crazy – world to explain what is happening today and how a stream of events, organisations and people that appear to have nothing to do with each other are, in fact, fundamentally connected. Only when these connections are made will the apparently complex take on a far simpler persona. The book is aimed at people new to this information to expand the global numbers who can see through the multi-faceted illusions; but those who have been with me for years will find so much for them, too, as the cutting edge is moved by a gigantic leap.

The adventure begins

I'll briefly summarise for those new readers how this all started for me and how it plays out to this day. It's important to know how the information has been coming to me for more than 20 years before you choose what to accept or not. I was born in the city of Leicester in the English Midlands on April 29th, 1952. You would say that we were a poor family, but I never felt deprived because everyone around me was pretty much the same. As a young boy, I would walk with my mother around the back of the factory where my father worked to pick up his wages on Thursday lunchtimes to pay for that night's dinner. This is how tight things were. On many occasions I hid behind the sofa with my mother when the rent man knocked on the door for money we just didn't have. He would look through the front window when no-one answered, and we'd stay behind the sofa until she gave the all-clear. As a boy, I was a 'loner' and I'd spend long periods of time by myself, playing, lost in my own little world (Fig 3). I wasn't academically successful at school and I

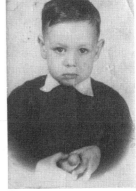

Figure 3: So glad to be here. Earth's a shitty place, I wanna go home

didn't concentrate very well. School, for me, was something to get through. The only nice thing about it was playing for the football team (or 'soccer' as they call the game in the United States). I was a goalkeeper – a position that suited my nature. I was part of a team, yes, but with a very different role to play. Football gave me the confidence to mix with people more, and I decided at a very early age that I wanted to be a professional. This looked highly unlikely, until a series of 'coincidences' and 'lucky breaks' put me in the right place, in the right team, at the right time, to sign as a professional with

Figure 4: The footballer. Smiling through the daily agony

Coventry City Football Club. I left school at 15, having not taken, never mind passed, any of the major academic exams (thank you, God). I had felt through much of my childhood that I had come here to do something in particular, something 'different'. But, what? I could never put words to it. There was just *something*. When I signed for Coventry City I thought *that* must be it – I have come here to be a footballer. But, no. Nothing like. I developed what was later diagnosed as rheumatoid arthritis within six months of starting my 'new life' in professional football. I wasn't going to give up my dream even with the arthritis, and I played for six seasons as a professional footballer with ever-worsening pain as it picked off joint after joint. It's staggering when I look back. In my last two years in the game, every daily training session was agonising until my joints had warmed up. In the final year I was in a then successful team called Hereford United, and my will just drove me on despite the pain (Fig 4). The club had no idea how bad my condition really was. They would have been looking for another goalkeeper had they been aware of the progressing discomfort that I was in. The end (and there had to *be* an end as the arthritis spread) came very suddenly when I had just turned 21. I awoke one morning, in that state of sensory crossover half-sleep, and I realised that I couldn't breathe. I tried to wake my wife, Linda (the most important person in my life to this day), and I realised that I couldn't move my body either. I was in a sort of frozen state, unable to move in any way or to breathe. It was like my consciousness was not in my body. I thought: this is it – I am going to die. Finally, I gasped a breath and my body kicked into life. Well, kind of. Once I breathed and became 'unfrozen', I was hit by excruciating pain in every joint in my body – even the ones unaffected this far. I went to bed a professional footballer and woke up never to play again. A fun time.

The 'Pattern'

I see footballers today earning huge amounts of money – the top ones the best part of £200,000 a *week* – but the most I ever earned as a basic weekly wage in football was £33. Linda and I were holding on for dear life financially when my career ended and the money stopped. It was to stay that way for many more years as I pursued my next ambition – journalism. I was interviewed on a live television programme about the end of my football career, and I was so taken by the buzz and the atmosphere that I said to Linda that night, 'This is for me.' I was told that the way into television news was via newspaper journalism, and I managed to get a job on a tiny weekly newspaper ... in my home town of Leicester of all places. The paper was so awful that no-one else wanted to work there. It was called *The Leicester Advertiser*, and I am pleased to say that it has long since been put out of its misery. I progressed very quickly through bigger newspapers, to radio, to regional and national television (Fig 5). When I say 'very quickly', this was a time when I first began to wonder, here and there, not often, if there was some sort of destiny playing out here. But *what?* I had decided that I wanted to be a professional footballer, and a series of 'coincidences', and thereby opportunities, arose to allow that to happen. In my despair when my football career

Figure 5: Hello, good evening and welcome

ended, I had decided that I wanted to be a television news and sports presenter and, again, a series of 'coincidences', and thereby opportunities, arose to allow that to happen. I had noticed the pattern, but I gave it only brief attention and carried on. But 'the pattern' could no longer be ignored when I decided to enter politics with a then little-known party called the Green Party. Another string of 'coincidences' led to me becoming the joint national spokesman within *weeks* of joining the party as a local member on the Isle of Wight – off the south coast of England – where I live. It was *insane* that this should happen in that timescale – totally ridiculous – but it did. I was asking seriously by now what was happening with my life. This was crazy! I have described the details of these endless 'coincidences' in other books, but it was as though something was opening and closing doors to guide me through the 'maze' of life in a very particular way. But again, what? And why? The answer to the question of 'why' would arrive about a couple of years later; the 'what' would take longer. My appointment as a national Green Party spokesman coincided with a lot of mainstream television programmes in Britain highlighting the gathering damage to wildlife and environmental systems in the late 1980s, and this played a major role in securing the biggest vote in the party's history at the European elections of 1989. Two million people voted for the Green Party – something absolutely unheard of before. The morning after the result, I found myself facing a packed room of mainstream journalists and cameramen at a news conference, and I was all over the television news as a politician (Fig 6). I pondered again about what was happening to me. I had dreamed my way

through school with minimal focus and yet, by the age of 37, I had already been a professional footballer, a newspaper journalist, a radio journalist, a national television news and sports presenter, and now a national politician. *What?* How could this be? There was a clear pattern. I would decide that I wanted to do something and the 'coincidences' and opportunities then began until it happened. I started to wonder for the first time at this point if 'I', the conscious 'me', was deciding what I wanted to do; or was something *else* going on here? As Morpheus said to Neo in *The*

Figure 6: The politician – but not for long, thank goodness

Matrix movie: 'The answers are coming.' They duly began to arrive in March 1990.

The 'Presence'

Throughout 1989, something very strange had begun to happen as I went about my work for BBC television and the Green Party. Whenever I was alone in a room it felt like I was *not* alone. There was a 'presence' in the room. This became ever more tangible and, one evening in 1990 as I was staying at the Kensington Hilton Hotel near the BBC headquarters in London, the presence in the room was so obvious that I actually said out loud: 'If there is anybody here, will you please contact me because you are driving me up the wall!' A few days later, I was with my son, Gareth, at a newspaper shop about five minutes from my home. He's now a big, strapping singer- songwriter and radio host, but he was only a little boy then. Gareth was inside the shop looking at railway books while I was chatting to somebody outside. I went to the door to tell Gareth we were leaving, when the soles of my feet suddenly started to feel incredibly hot. I also had the sense of them being pulled downwards, as if magnets were in the floor. My feet wouldn't move, and, as I stood there utterly bewildered, I heard a 'voice', or a very powerful thought, pass through my mind. It said: 'Go and look at the books on the far side.' I guess, when I think about it, the scene was a bit like Morpheus in *The Matrix* movie talking to Neo at his workplace, only without the phone! What was happening? I didn't know. I just instinctively felt to go with this and see if it led anywhere. My feet were freed when I moved towards 'the books on the far side' which I knew were almost entirely made up of cheesy romantic novels. But, in among the tales of tall, dark handsome men and perfectly-formed English Roses, there was one book that was so different it caught my eye immediately. It was called *Mind to Mind* and was written by a lady called Betty Shine, whose picture was on the front cover (Fig 7). I turned it over to read the blurb and I saw the word 'psychic'. Betty was a professional psychic and 'hands-on' healer who wrote a series of books. I wondered immediately if she might 'pick up' on the 'presence' that I had been sensing around me for the past year. I bought the book, and, after reading it quickly, I contacted Betty and arranged to meet her. I told her nothing about the presence. I said that I wanted to see if her healing technique could help my arthritis. 'Hands-on' healing is the exchange and balancing of

Figure 7: Betty Shine: The face in the newspaper shop

energy, and not at all the 'mumbo jumbo' that it is derided to be by the deeply ignorant and academically programmed. Betty knew nothing about what was happening to me – only that I wanted to try her healing.

I visited Betty four times in all. Nothing happened on the first two occasions except that she did her healing and we chatted about other dimensions of reality. This is from where genuine psychics glean their information. They tune in to frequencies of reality that are not accessible to the five senses. The five senses only connect with a tiny band of frequencies that we call 'visible light' – the 'world' that we see, hear, touch, taste and smell. People look through their eyes (or think they do, as we shall explore) and they believe they are seeing all that there is to see in the 'space' they are observing. But they're not. We *see* only an infinitesimal fraction of what exists – the frequency range known as 'visible light'. The electromagnetic spectrum represents about *0.005 per cent* of the energy and 'matter' that exists in the Universe, according to some in mainstream science. Others put it higher, but not by much. Visible light, the only frequency range that our decoding system can currently 'see', is *a fraction even of that* (Fig 8). Within the same space that we live and perceive is

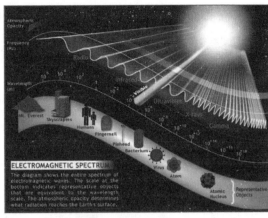

Figure 8: The tiny frequency band of human perception within the electromagnetic spectrum

also Infinity – all existence – and this interpenetrates our 'world' in the same way that radio stations share the same space without interfering with each other (unless they are very close on the dial). If you tune a radio to, say, Radio 1, that's what you get. When you move the dial to Radio 2 you hear – perceive – that station instead. But Radio 1 doesn't stop broadcasting when you are no longer tuned in to it. It goes on broadcasting – existing – in the same space in which you are now listening to Radio 2. It is the same

with our reality. The body's five senses and its entire genetic structure is a decoding system. It picks up frequencies within a certain very narrow band and we perceive that band as the world that we 'live in'. But all the other 'worlds' and expressions of infinite existence are sharing the same space. We can't see them because they are resonating to frequencies that the five senses cannot pick up, just as you can't hear Radio 1 when you are tuned to Radio 2 (Fig 9). I said all this on a British television programme in 1991, during a time of enormous ridicule for me, and, 17 years later, in 2008, the famous American physicist, Dr Michio Kaku, said the same, virtually word for word. You can see the comparison on *YouTube* in a video headed: 'Michio Kaku Confirms Icke To Be Correct'. It is crucial to appreciate the nature of our reality to understand what is 'going on'. Different frequencies don't normally interfere with each other unless they are close on the dial, and it is the same with the frequency 'worlds' of Creation. People experience 'interference' from frequencies close to ours in the form of 'ghosts', for instance, and other 'paranormal' phenomena. The 'ghosts' mostly don't look 'solid' to us because we are not on their 'station'. Interference from another radio station frequency is not

Figure 9: Creation is an infinite range of interpenetrating frequency 'worlds', and the frequency range that we decode becomes our sense of reality. But all the other 'worlds' share the same 'space', just like radio stations and analogue television channels

Illustration by Neil Hague (www.neilhague.com)

Figure 10: Other 'worlds', or ranges of frequency, can be contacted by genuine psychics by attuning their minds, or consciousness, to another 'station'

sharp and clear. The 'ghosts' would look as solid as you and I if we were on the same frequency (not that we *are* solid, but that's for later). It is possible for entities in other frequency worlds to move in and out of ours using technology, and, for the even more advanced, simply through the power of consciousness. Non-human entities and 'UFOs' can appear 'out of nowhere' and disappear 'into nowhere', or at least it seems that way to the human observer. What actually happens is they enter the frequency range of the human five senses and suddenly appear to our sight; and when they leave our frequency range they suddenly 'disappear' in our perception. In fact, they have just dipped into the range of frequencies that we are able to decode, and therefore perceive, and have then left again. Genuine psychics, as opposed to those who claim to be, but aren't, can tune their higher senses to other frequencies of reality and communicate with sources of information that are 'not of this world' (Fig 10). This includes those expressions of consciousness that have departed this reality for frequencies new at what we call 'death'. There *is* no death in terms of the real 'us' – consciousness, awareness – only the demise of the body, which is the vehicle that allows us to experience this range of frequencies that we call our everyday reality.

We have contact

My third visit to Betty Shine changed my life and set me on a journey that I would never have thought possible. But it has happened, and continues to happen ever more profoundly. I was sitting up on a medical-type couch while Betty was doing energy healing near my left knee. I suddenly felt like a spider's web was touching my face, and I immediately recalled reading in her book that when 'spirits' or other dimensions are trying to make contact it can feel like a spider's web touching you. I now know that what I was feeling was electromagnetic energy – the same thing that happens in a large excited crowd when people feel the hairs on their neck stand up. This is caused by the accumulation of electromagnetic energy generated by the crowd. The 'spider's web' was an electromagnetic connection being locked in between different frequency ranges of reality, although I had no idea about that at the time. I didn't say anything to Betty about what I was feeling, but 10–15 seconds later she threw her head back and said, 'Wow! This is powerful. I'll have to close my eyes for this one!' I was sitting there wondering what I had gotten myself into, but I was about to understand why I had felt the 'presence' around me for the last year. Betty said that she was seeing a figure in her mind which was asking her to communicate information to me. 'They' said they knew that I wanted them to contact me, but the time had not been right. This was a reference to me sitting on the bed at the Kensington Hilton Hotel saying: 'If there is anybody here, will you please contact me because you are driving me up the wall!' But Betty knew nothing about that. There followed a series of messages that seemed bizarre and crazy at the time, but more than two decades later the ones relating directly to me have all happened or are happening. These are some of them:

- He is a healer who is here to heal the Earth and he will be world famous.
- He will face enormous opposition, but we will always be there to protect him.
- He is still a child, spiritually, but he will be given the spiritual riches.
- Sometimes he will say things and wonder where they came from. They will be our words.
- Knowledge will be put into his mind and at other times he will be led to knowledge. He was chosen as a youngster for his courage. He has been tested and has passed all the tests.
- He was led into football to learn discipline, but when that was learned it was time to move on. He also had to learn how to cope with disappointment, experience all the emotions, and how to get up and get on with it. The spiritual way is tough and no-one makes it easy.
- He will always have what he needs [this could have been 'wants'], but no more.

A week later, I went back to Betty and more information came through:

- One man cannot change the world, but one man can communicate the message that will change the world.
- Don't try to do it all alone. Go hand in hand with others, so you can pick each other up as you fall.
- He will write five books in three years.
- Politics is not for him. He is too spiritual. Politics is anti-spiritual and will make him very unhappy.
- He will leave politics. He doesn't have to do anything. It will happen gradually over a year.
- There will be a different kind of flying machine, very different from the aircraft of today.
- Time will have no meaning. Where you want to be, you will be.

The figure that communicated these words (a projection from another frequency range into Betty's mind) took a Chinese form and said that 'Socrates is with me'. Socrates (469–399 BC) was the Greek philosopher who taught Plato, and at the age of 70 he was charged with heresy and corruption of local youth. He carried out his own death sentence by drinking hemlock. There is a long list of great quotes by Socrates, including one that is perfect for this book and my work in general: 'Wisdom is knowing how little we know.' These messages were communicated electromagnetically to Betty Shine, who, like all true psychics, decoded the information into words. An English psychic decodes into English, an Italian into Italian, and so on. The communications are not sent in words, but in electromagnetic 'thought-form'. This is decoded like a radio or an analogue television decodes information encoded in broadcast frequencies into: 'Hello, you are listening to Radio ABK,' and: 'Good evening, here is the news,' or whatever. The process is so simple, but it is dismissed by the deeply controlled and ignorant mainstream of what passes for 'science' which is utterly clueless about the real nature of our reality that I will be explaining in these pages.

Bye bye, 'real' world

So here I was, a national television presenter with the BBC and spokesman for the Green Party, being told that I was going out onto a world stage amid great opposition and 'They', whoever 'They' were, would always be there to protect me. It was all very confusing. What did 'healing the Earth' mean? And I would 'write five books in three years' about *what* exactly? But something within me just knew I had to go with this and see where it led. Things soon began to move very quickly. A few months later, my contract with the BBC was not renewed, and I stepped back from my work with the Green Party. I knew that one day I would go public with all this and I didn't want to cause them damage with a programmed electorate. I also knew by now that politics was irrelevant, anyway. I told a handful of people in the Green Party what had happened to me and 'David's gone crazy!' rumours began to circulate. So much for the 'different' and 'enlightened' Green politics. I can tell you from experience that it is only the old politics under another name, and its obsession with selling and exploiting the manipulated nonsense about human-caused 'global warming' (renamed 'climate change' after temperatures began to fall) will ultimately destroy its credibility altogether. My life became an amazing series of synchronistic 'coincidences', experiences and happenings from the time of the first communications in March 1990. This was leading me to knowledge and information in the form of people, books, documents, a few more psychics, and personal experiences. An unseen force was handing me pieces to a vast puzzle, and I am still learning how truly colossal it is more than 20 years later. The puzzle is still expanding, today faster than ever, and, as they say, the rabbit hole goes very deep. The scale of interconnected information is so mind-blowingly enormous, the story so seemingly endless, and the subject areas so numerous, that the communication of the 'clues' has had to be done in a systematic way. Layer has been added to layer as I have gone deeper and deeper into the rabbit hole. The themes have been consistent all along, but the detail has changed here and there, and has been added to and tweaked, as my mind has expanded and more detail has been put before me with the passage of what we call 'time'. There are so many smokescreens of false information to steer through, too. In the end, the themes are more important than the fine detail. People can forget detail, but remember themes. To understand and do something about what we are facing does not require us to know someone's collar size or coffee preference. My challenge has been to keep my mind open to all possibility and not to dismiss information or insight simply because it is way outside of the 'norm'; and to have the determination to communicate that information knowing the ridicule and abuse that I would face, at least at first, from the public and brainless media. But that hasn't really been much of a 'challenge' in the sense that I have never dismissed anything throughout my life purely on the basis of it being different from what most people can believe.

What was about to happen has since helped me to ignore ridicule and abuse – it is now water off a duck's rear end. I spent the rest of 1990 travelling and writing my first book. I called it *Truth Vibrations* after a vibrational change that 'They' told me was coming that would transform life on Earth and the human perception of reality. I will explain more about this as we go along, but essentially I was told that the Truth Vibrations, a fundamental change in the vibrational construct of our reality, would have three main effects: (1) They would act like an alarm clock, or a click of the hypnotist's fingers to ease, sometimes snap, humanity out of its trance-like state, its amnesia. People would remember what they had been manipulated to forget about the true nature of self and the 'world'; (2) All that had been hidden from humanity in terms of what has been happening without their knowledge would be revealed. We would see behind the 'wizard's curtain', as in the highly symbolic *Wizard of Oz*; (3) The Earth's energy fields and vibrational structure would have to synchronise, as with humans', with the changing energetic resonance of the reality, and this would bring an increase in severe weather and geological activity such as earthquakes and volcanoes. We should always keep in mind, however, that the technology exists to manipulate the weather and geological activity, as I will be explaining. Far from all extreme weather and geological happenings are 'natural'. There was no evidence whatsoever when I was told all this in 1990 that there was going to be some mass 'awakening'; or that what has been going on with regard to a Hidden Hand controlling world events throughout history was coming to light. But it is clear today that both are happening, and on an increasingly global scale. It was a very lonely road when I started out, but there has been an explosion in recent years of conspiracy researchers and research material; and incredible numbers of people are opening their minds to a new perception of self and the world compared with just a few years ago, let alone in 1990 when I was told all this was coming. What's more, it is growing by the day.

Figure 11: Sillustani in Peru. As I walked around the ruins, I had no idea that the clock was counting down to a 'new' David with an incredible experience in a stone circle close by. Talk about 'life changing'. *Everything* changed.

Plugged in to the 'mains'

I finished writing *Truth Vibrations* by the end of that year and, when it went off to be printed and published, I suddenly had a tremendous urge to go to Peru. I didn't know anything about Peru, except that I had seen the football team play in the World Cup a few times; but there was this feeling of 'I must go to Peru'. I was seeing 'Peru' crop up again and again in a variety of places, from travel agency window displays, bookshops and television documentaries to name a few. I *had* to go there. I knew that. I had no idea why, though. I have described in detail in other books what happened to me there, but, in short, I had an incredible series of daily experiences and 'coincidences' that eventually led me to a place called Sillustani, an ancient Inca site in the countryside about 80 minutes' drive from the city of Puno (Fig 11). It is on a hill with a lagoon on three sides and the area is encircled by mountains way off in the distance.

Figure 12: The stone circle where it all happened

My Peruvian guide who was showing me around the country had booked us into a hotel in Puno called The Sillustani. It had pictures of the place all over the walls and as soon as I saw them I knew I had to go – the intuitive urge was so great. I hired a little tourist bus with the guide and a driver, and off we went. Sillustani is beautiful and I enjoyed looking around the ruins and seeing the magnificent views, but when it came time to leave I was disappointed. As lovely as it was, my experience there did not even nearly match the urge I'd had to go. I returned to the bus and headed back for Puno, but not for long. I was gazing through the window in a semi-daydream state. A few minutes down the road, a small hill, or mound, to my right, caught my attention. All I could hear in my head as I looked was: 'Come to me, come to me, come to me.' Now a bloody *hill* was talking to me! *Whatever next?* I asked the driver to stop and said I wanted to walk up the hill for a minute or two. It turned out to be rather longer. When I reached the top, I found myself looking at an ancient stone circle which I hadn't been able to see from the road (Fig 12). I walked into the centre under a sunny, cloudless sky and looked back to Sillustani and the distant mountains. Suddenly, my feet began to feel incredibly hot again as they had in the newspaper shop near my home almost a year earlier, only this time with far greater intensity. It felt once more like magnets were pulling my feet to the ground. A drill-like sensation started in the top of my head and I felt energy flow down from my head through my feet to the ground. Another flow was coming the other way. My arms stretched out at 45 degrees either side of my head although I had made no conscious decision to do that. They would stay there for something like an hour, although time did not exist in my reality from now until it was over. A 'voice' (a decoded electromagnetic communication) passed through my mind very clearly that said: 'They will be talking about this moment a hundred years from now'; and then: 'It will be over when you feel the rain.' The latter seemed ridiculous given that a piercingly hot sun shone from a sky without a single cloud. The energy passing through me increased and increased until my body was shaking. It felt like an incredibly powerful electrical force was zipping through me in each direction – which I now know it was. I kept moving in and out of my conscious mind, as you do when you are driving a car and you can't remember where the last few miles went. The subconscious has been doing the driving. When I came back to conscious awareness on one occasion, I noticed a light grey mist over the distant mountains, and the mist soon grew darker. Clearly it was raining quite heavily over there and I watched the storm move towards me very quickly. Weather forecasters talk about a 'front' coming over. Well, this was a 'front' of billowing clouds with the rain moving towards me in an almost perfect straight line. It was like a curtain was being drawn across the sky. Eventually, the clouds obscured the sun and, in the end, I watched the wall of stair-rod rain coming towards me. People would understandably say that it was too far-fetched if you included a scene like this in a story or movie. But it happened. I was instantly drenched as the rain hit me and the energy flow immediately stopped. I had not felt the pain from holding my arms aloft continuously up to this point, but now my shoulders started to feel the painful consequences. My legs were like those of a newly-born giraffe. Energy was pouring from my hands and feet. I was like a walking, talking column of electricity. I went back to the bus and held a big quartz crystal to diffuse the energy a little, but it was to resonate from my feet for the next 24 hours.

Kundalini Kid

I had no idea at the time what had happened to me in that stone circle. But I do now. Many things happened in fact. The energy burst the

Figure 13: The major human 'chakras', or vortices, which resonate to different colour frequencies and connect the 'physical' body to other levels of self and the wider reality

energy/consciousness bubble that most people live in, for reasons I will be explaining. An electromagnetic communication channel was also established between me and 'They'. Information, concepts and insights from other levels of reality began to pour through that connection into my 'human' mind. There followed a seriously challenging transitional period of about three or four months, from February to May 1991, when I didn't know what was going on. With hindsight, I can see that it was like pressing too many keys on a computer too quickly and the computer 'freezes'. It can't process so much data at one time. I was struck by a tidal wave of information when the connection was made and everything had to settle down before I could start to process the data. It was akin to a dam bursting, causing great upheaval and turbulence until the water settles into its new situation. This was what was basically happening in my mind. I now know that what happened in the stone circle triggered an absolutely enormous 'Kundalini' experience and my 'chakra' system burst open for all that information to come flooding in. It was like trying to ride a mental and emotional version of a bucking bronco. 'Chakra' is an ancient Sanskrit word meaning 'wheel of light'. Chakras are vortices that connect the body to other levels of mind and awareness in what is called the 'auric field' (Fig 13). These are the seven main chakras: (1) The crown chakra is on top of the head, and it was through here that the energy came and went during my experience in the stone circle. (2) The third-eye chakra is in the centre of the forehead and connects to the pineal and pituitary glands in the brain that comprise the 'third eye' or 'psychic sight'. (3) The throat chakra is the vortex for creativity and communication. (4) The heart chakra is in the centre of the chest and if this vortex is open it connects us to far higher levels of awareness. (5) The solar plexus chakra is located in the 'belly' and is directly connected to feelings and emotions. This is why we feel strong emotions such as fear and dread in this area. (6) The sacral chakra is located just beneath the navel and relates to sexuality and reproduction. (7) The base chakra is at the base of the spine, and it grounds us in this reality as well as being the location of the kundalini, or 'coiled snake'. This is the energy which, when released, shoots up the central nervous system opening all the vortex points and pours through the top of the head to connect us with 'enlightenment', or far more advanced levels of awareness. This is what happened to me during my experience in Peru, and this is why I didn't know what day it was for a while.

Mass ridicule

Unfortunately, or rather *fortunately* from the point of view of my own development, soon after I returned to Britain in this 'transitional state', my book, *Truth Vibrations*, was published and I was interviewed by the national media. I was subjected to fantastic levels of ridicule that few people could have experienced at such ongoing intensity. This reached a peak when I appeared on a live prime-time television chat show hosted by Terry Wogan, the best-known television personality in Britain at the time. I was dressed in turquoise – a colour I had an urge to wear all the time at this point – and around 15 minutes later all bridges to my old life were burned and trashed (Fig 14). There was no going back now. Not that, for a second, I wanted to go back, despite the way my life was falling apart. My life was crashing so that a new one could emerge, although I didn't know that then. Terry Wogan didn't cover himself in glory the way he played to a laughing audience to enhance his own perceived image, but, to be fair, he was faced with a guy going through the most monumental transformative experience. Even I didn't know what was happening to me and I am not surprised that Wogan didn't, especially as he's not the most open minded of people. He interviewed me again many years later and the outcome was very different. You can see both interviews on *YouTube*. When faced with the scale of public ridicule that came my way for years after the Wogan show – and still does from the juvenile mainstream media – you can either run away and hide or come back stronger. What doesn't kill you makes you stronger, as they say. The title of one of my early books, *I Am Me, I Am Free*, sums up the way I chose to

go. Mass ridicule was an experience that set me free from the fear and, therefore, the lifetime limitations of the mind and emotional prison that the overwhelming majority of people live in worldwide: *the fear of what other people think*. The masses that succumb to this psychological fascism are not living or speaking their own unique truth or expressing their own unique self. They are living within prison walls built by what they believe is acceptable to those around them – their parents, schoolmates, friends, colleagues, people down the pub, or, if they are a public figure, the 'media'. Sod that! I was not having it, and if people have a problem with what I am then that describes the situation perfectly. They have the problem. I don't. The irony of the ridicule in the years that followed the Wogan show is that they have been ridiculing 'someone' who only existed for three or four months in 1991. The computer

Figure 14: 'Er, what's my name, where am I?'

'unfroze' when that transitional period was over and people I knew were saying to me: 'I thought you were supposed to have gone mad – you are just the bloke I used to know.' Well, it may have seemed like that, but I wasn't. Yes, 'David' was 'back', but it wasn't the same David. I saw the world in a totally different way and what I couldn't see before was now blindingly obvious. My conscious journey had begun, and there would be many more 'Davids' as the layers of the onion have been peeled and programs deleted. I"m sure there will be many more, too.

All meant to be

I can see from today's perspective that my life has been perfect right from the start as a preparation for what I came here to do. What seemed like random events before the conscious 'activation' in 1990 were giving me the experiences and skills that I would need for what my conscious mind did not know was coming. But 'They' did, and so did subconscious levels of my multi-levelled awareness. My experience in football demanded dedication to reach a target, and playing most of my career with the constant pain of rheumatoid arthritis triggered a never-give-up determination to go on, no matter what. Journalism gave me the skills to write succinctly and to present the apparently complex in simple ways. It also showed me that any connection between the mainstream media and telling the truth about the world is purely coincidental most of the time. If you saw the average newsroom at work in newspapers, radio or television,

Figure 15: Different essential steps on the *same* journey

you would never believe a word they told you ever again. Television showed me what a lie factory that is, too, and gave me a public profile so that when I said what I did after Peru it would not be ignored – a vital aspect of the story when you are communicating suppressed information. My period in the Green Party showed me that politics is an irrelevance to changing anything for the better and that different names and colours do not mean different political methods of operation. The Green Party is a classic example. It also allowed me to see that politicians who appear to be opposing each other in public are doing anything but in private. The mass ridicule after the Wogan show cleared me of any fear of what other people thought of me, and so freed me to go with the information and not censor and tailor it for conventional belief. This was essential. It does rather help not to care what people think or say about you when you are talking about shape-shifting reptilian entities and saying the Moon is not 'real' in the sense of it being a 'natural body' (Fig 15). When people look at their own lives they will see patterns that connect the apparently unconnected. Life is not as random as they think it is. When the patterns reveal continually-repeating cycles of behaviour and experience they are telling you something very important: You are in a mind-prison. Once you know that, acknowledge that and decide you don't want to be there anymore, you can do something about the cause – you. One of the messages that I was given through a psychic in 1990 said:

> Arduous seeking is not necessary. The path is already mapped out. You only have to follow the clues ... We are guiding you along a set path. It was all arranged before you incarnated.

This is what I have clearly experienced since I was a child, and when I look at the 'parts' of my life I can see that they are all the same seamless journey. That includes both the experiences I have liked and those I have not liked at all. Life often gives us our greatest gifts brilliantly disguised as our worst nightmares. These experiences might not be very pleasant, but they can make us wiser and more knowledgeable. I had two people come into my life at virtually the same time who together have been a horror story, and quite the biggest challenge that I have had to my work, health, emotions and finances while both claim to be the very epitome of 'love, peace, and kindness'. But the experience made me stronger, wiser and more aware of many things, not least to see into the 'mind' of the heart-closed, empathy-deleted, me, me, me mentality that operates at every level of human society. I saw in their self-obsession the attitudes that make the world what it has become. So it wasn't a 'mistake'; it was the gift of experience. These two people had an experience in the same way that they can potentially employ to discover what it takes to be kind, unselfish, have empathy, wisdom and a sense of fairness. I won't be holding my breath with this pair, but, hey, life is forever, and the opportunity to change is forever. Two other messages that I was given by 'They' in 1990 have played out down to the letter: 'Sometimes he will say things and wonder where they came from ... They will be our words'; and: 'Knowledge will be put into his mind and at other times he will be led to knowledge.' This has been happening since the moment I heard those words in Betty Shine's front room. First, an insight comes to me and then solid 'five sense' information starts to flow my way in the form of people, experiences and information from endless sources. I now know the process very well. I have long since learned to trust it after what I was told would happen *did* happen. It has reached the point where what I have written in my books over the years is now playing out on the television news. Few were interested in what I had to say for a long time, and I would speak to mostly empty rooms. In 1996, I travelled America for three months researching and talking to handfuls of people. Just eight turned up when I spoke near Chicago, and I travelled to New England to speak in someone's lounge to even fewer. There were many times when I wondered why I bothered and where it was all going. What was the point? But something inside drove me on despite all the frustrations and the many financial challenges that came. I was aware of this 'something' when the human 'me' was dying inside during the first Wogan interview. I heard a 'voice' speaking to me while I was sitting there on live television. It was saying: 'Don't worry, everything's fine; this is leading somewhere.' And it has. You can't *un*hear something, and it is so important to speak your truth no matter what the reaction of others. If what you say has validity it will eventually be shown to be so; but that process cannot

Figure 16: A tough journey but, oh, so worth the pain and effort. Speaking in Times Square, New York, in 2010

happen if you stay silent out of fear of the consequences. From the turn of this century, and especially after 9/11, the interest in my work has soared. People all over the world are starting to see through the lies told to justify wars of conquest and mass slaughter, and impose a global Orwellian State. I have gone from talking to next to no-one to addressing audiences of thousands. This is so even when what I say has to be simultaneously translated into another language over the eight or nine hours that I am connecting the dots and revealing the picture. I still have to pinch myself now and then to believe that it is happening; but it is precisely what I was told would happen in 1990. There is so much more to come, too (Fig 16). The awakening I was told was coming is beginning to impact on the perception of multi-millions, and it is going to progress faster and faster as the Truth Vibrations tease open human minds. It is not the majority yet, or even nearly so, but compared with when I started out the numbers are incredible and I know it is a global phenomenon from my almost constant travel around the world.

The 'future' is here

Ever more people are looking at the world anew in the light of the extraordinary levels of control and imposition that I have been saying were coming for over two decades. Detailed surveillance of human life is gathered from satellites in space; from cameras all over our towns, cities and road systems; from remotely-controlled flying cameras; from mobile phones and computers; from credit cards and 'loyalty' cards; from iris scanning; and from many other methods we don't even know about yet. Our food and drink is poisoned with chemical cocktails known as 'additives' – and food and drink aimed at children is the worst of all. We have genetically-modified food that is designed to genetically modify *us*, and poisonous fluoride in our drinking water, which re-wires the

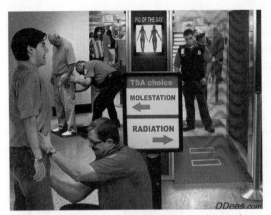

Figure 17: What are we doing allowing ourselves and our children to be either irradiated or sexually molested before we board a plane

brain just as food 'additives' do. Fluoride was put into the drinking water at the Nazi concentration camps to make the inmates docile. Little children are being subjected to up to 30 (and growing) vaccinations before the age of two while their immune systems are still forming. Their natural defences will never be what they were meant to be once that happens. The British government is talking about adding yet another vaccine for hepatitis B to all the others. The Hidden Hand-controlled World Health Organization and British Medical Association say this should happen without delay. I bet they do. Adults, too, are being subjected to an ever-increasing array of toxic chemical shite called vaccinations which damage them mentally, emotionally and physically. Compulsory vaccinations are on the agenda of the Control System. The police are becoming more like the military every day with the ever-expanding use of guns and Tasers that give often moronic people in uniform the chance to unleash 55,000 volts of electricity at targets who are no threat to them. Peaceful protestors are being scattered by excruciatingly painful sound technology, while governments doing this say they must bomb other countries to protect the right to protest peacefully. Children are being born in those bombed countries with severe birth defects because of all the depleted uranium on the land and in the air from the weapons dropped on or fired at them. We are being subjected to multiple sources of radiation that are increasing all the time and this is not by coincidence, but by design. There are mobile phones and communication masts; the wireless Internet; microwave cookers; irradiated food with 'safe' levels (they never were) continually being raised. 'Low-energy' lightbulbs are being forced upon people as bans of the alternatives are justified by the Big Lie about human- caused 'global warming'. Scientists, never mind personal experience, have confirmed that they give off toxic chemicals and dangerous levels of radiation. Boarding a plane increasingly involves the choice of being irradiated or sexually molested. Frequent flyers going through full-body scanners are going to pay dearly for the cumulative effect (Fig 17). Then there are the nuclear disasters like the one at Fukushima in Japan which has been pouring catastrophic amounts of radiation into the seas and global atmosphere. At the same time, holes are being punched into the ionosphere, in the upper atmosphere, by the weather-changing, earthquake-causing technology known as HAARP. This is controlled by the American military in Alaska and connects with similar technology around the world. Those holes are allowing cosmic radiation to breach the Earth's defences that would normally protect us. The food chain is being hijacked by a few controlled-by-the-same-people corporations while small farmers, and even back-yard food growers, are being targeted to give the food and biotech cabal a monopoly on where we get our food and drink and what is in it. A sinister scam called Codex Alimentarius (Latin for 'food book' or 'food code') was set up by Nazis jailed for war

Figure 18: 'Hey, teacher – leave those kids alone'

crimes and the aim is to stop the effective use of food supplements and natural medicines by those who have a mind of their own. The 'education' system has always been there to program the minds of children and young people with a perception of self and the world that suits the agenda of the global controllers; but the programming is getting ever more extreme to dumb down the younger generations who are being prepared for life as tomorrow's adult slaves (Fig 18). The extraordinary use of mind-altering drugs on young people at younger and younger ages is designed to suppress any independent thought. Most of the time the 'problems' they are supposed to be 'treating', as with the bogus 'Attention Deficit Disorder', display precisely the same behaviour symptoms as those caused by food and drink additives. Of course they do. One is causing the other. 'Go on dear, drink your Coke.'

We are also being deluged by constantly-passed legislation to dictate the very detail of our lives – what we can do, say, even think. Much of this is coming from centralised and dictatorial non-elected dark-suits such as the European Commission and the faceless handlers of the US President (it doesn't matter which one; it's the same with all of them). They are seeking, as I write, to give the president, even narcissistic idiots like Boy Bush and Obama, the right to declare war on anyone, at any time, without the already muted and neutered rabble on Capitol Hill having any say at all. We are back to Caesar in ancient Rome, and that's very appropriate as we shall see. We have also had the creation of a 'Super Committee', or 'Super Congress', a small group of politicians usurping what is left (little) of American 'democracy'. It consists of six Democrats and six Republicans with the president having the deciding vote and, in effect, this makes the rest of Capitol Hill irrelevant to the decision-making process. Obama has established a panel of ten state governors – the 'Council of Governors' – which *he* selects to 'review' the National Guard, homeland defense and the coordination and *integration* of state and federal military activities in the United States. For the latter, read the military taking over domestic law enforcement. The centralisation of power is now incredible – especially in the hands of the president. America calls itself a 'free' country (it's not) and a 'democracy' (which doesn't mean freedom) and yet it gives astonishing power over its affairs to one man, the president, who is, himself, always controlled by the Hidden Hand that I have been exposing all these years. We have 'FEMA Camps' in the United States run by the Federal Emergency Management Agency, and these are nothing less than concentration camps waiting for the dissidents and the 'listed' if we allow the global military takeover to happen. The same programme is happening in other countries. Anyone who thinks I am making this up – I wish I was. Put 'United States', 'FEMA Camps' and 'concentration camps' into a search engine and see the pictures and official documents that you can find on the Internet. The banking cartel, or 'Big Banking', is controlled by the same people that control Big Government, Big Media, Big

Biotech, Big Food, Big Oil, and so on, and it has crashed the world economy while paying itself stupendous bonuses. This happens despite the fact that taxpayers who bailed out the banking system are now losing their homes and basic financial necessities to the same banks that caused the problem and to governments imposing vicious austerity programmes because, they say, of what they have given to the banks. In comes the International Monetary Fund (IMF) or the European Central Bank (ECB) when governments get into a financial mess for bailing the banks. They offer the governments even more debt to bail *them* out and, in effect, take control of the country. It is worth noting, therefore, as I have been showing in my books for so long, that the IMF, ECB and other institutions of control such as the World Bank, World Trade Organization and World Health Organization, are controlled, and were indeed created, by the same network of families. These very much include the House of Rothschild and the Rockefellers, and they own and control Big Banking, Big Government, Big Media, Big Biotech, Big Food, Big Oil ... you get the picture. These same families engineer wars and lend governments the 'money' (non-existent 'money' called 'credit') to fight them by purchasing weapons from armament companies which they also own. They then lend more 'money' (credit) to rebuild the devastated infrastructure caused by the war and to re-arm for the next one. This has been going on for centuries and, in this way and others, they have secured ownership of the world. That includes governments and nations which we are told are controlled by 'the people'. When I say 'families', I am actually talking about a network of ancient *bloodlines* that have weaved themselves through history under different names. They have different genetics and origin to the rest of humanity, as I will be explaining. The bloodlines manipulate and control through a global secret-society network that many collectively call the 'Illuminati', or 'Illuminated Ones' – illuminated into knowledge that they are desperate to keep from the rest of us. This is who I mean when I refer to the 'Illuminati bloodlines'. It was these same bloodline families, through their agencies in government and the military, such as the CIA, British Intelligence and the Israeli (Rothschild) Mossad, who were behind the engineered terrorist attacks on 9/11. This, in turn, was used to advance and justify their agenda for wars of acquisition in Afghanistan and Iraq, and to target other countries on their wish-list using their age-old technique of demonise and invade.

The mainstream media is also owned by the same cabal. Its role is to tell the public the version of events that the owners of the media want people to believe, in order to hide what is really happening. These lies and fake cover stories issue from the lips of the power structure through puppets like Bush and Obama, and the lies are then repeated as truth by 'journalists' who are employed because they are deeply uninformed and don't know their arse from the middle of their arm when it comes to what is really happening in the world they are supposed to be 'reporting'. The official (cover) story about 9/11 could be taken apart by a moron it's so ridiculous. But there has been no investigation of the facts worth the name by the mainstream media *worldwide*. The authorities release the cover stories and the media repeats them unquestioned. They become official history through constant repetition while any real journalists that expose the lies are dismissed by the anything-but-journalists as 'conspiracy theorists'. This is how people like Piers Morgan, Larry King and their ilk get the big jobs with organisations like CNN. They are safe because they are clueless about the way the world works and so they don't ask the telling questions of those in power. Morgan claims to have been a journalist for 25 years, when he hasn't been a real one for 25 seconds. CNN sacked presenter, Lou Dobbs, when he began asking highly pertinent questions about what was happening in America. Cenk Uygur, a presenter with cable news channel MSNBC, left his job after efforts to suppress his right to challenge the government. An executive told him: 'People in Washington are concerned about your tone.' The executive said that 'outsiders are cool, but we're not outsiders, we're insiders. We are the establishment'. Cooperation between major media organisations and the CIA has been well documented over the years and the same happens in the UK and other countries, with the media working in concert with intelligence agencies. Watergate journalist Carl Bernstein wrote an article for *Rolling Stone* in 1977 entitled 'The CIA and the Media'. He said:

> Among the executives who lent their cooperation to the Agency were William Paley of the Columbia Broadcasting System, Henry Luce of Time Inc., Arthur Hays Sulzberger of the New York Times, Barry Bingham Sr. of the Louisville Courier-Journal, and James Copley of the Copley News Services.

> Other organizations which cooperated with the CIA include the American Broadcasting Company, the National Broadcasting Company, the Associated Press, United Press International, Reuters, Hearst Newspapers, Scripps-Howard, Newsweek magazine, the Mutual Broadcasting System, the Miami Herald and the old Saturday Evening Post and New York Herald-Tribune. By far the most valuable of these associations, according to CIA officials, have been with the New York Times, CBS and Time Inc.

The BBC is a fundamentally controlled organisation with a long line of editorial censorship and strict rules on stories being 'signed off' before being allowed to air. This includes an 'Editorial Policy' that goes under the Orwellian name of 'EdPol'. All BBC staff and independent production companies working for the BBC are forced to undergo mandatory 'EdPol' training. Even when the outrageous lies about weapons of mass destruction in Iraq, and so many others, are exposed by events, the zombie media goes on repeating the next lie as truth with no questioning or investigation. What a head-shaker it was to see the truly, truly ludicrous story about the long-dead Osama bin Laden being killed *again* in the 'US raid on the compound' in Pakistan in 2011. Excuse me, where's the body? Er, immediately buried at sea. Where are the pictures of the body? Er, too gruesome to release. And so it went on, lie after lie after lie. But what did the 'journalistic' Piers Morgans do? Repeated the official story as if it was true. 'Pathetic' is not the word (Fig 19).

This is what is *'going on'*. What appear to be random events and changes in society

Figure 19: Look into my screeeeeen

are actually part of a gigantic conspiracy to enslave humanity in a global fascist/communist Orwellian nightmare. The bloodlines want to impose a world government, a world central bank, a single world electronic currency, and a world army forcing its will upon a drugged, mind-controlled and microchipped race of human robots and computer terminals that have every facet of their lives under constant control and surveillance. Not possible? It could never happen? It *is* happening – minute by minute every day all over the world as this hidden agenda plays out. It is exactly what I was told would happen at the turn of the 1990s and I have been guided to uncover and expose ever since. The European Union, a new Soviet Union, is the most advanced of the second layer of global control that is planned to include an American Union, Pacific Union and African Union (already in place); and nation states are due to end and be divided into regions to dilute any unified challenge to the power structure above them.

Oh, but there's more

Even this is only one level of what is 'going on'. The pieces in the puzzle handed to me in the early years after Peru were all about the five-sense level of the conspiracy – the realm that we consciously experience every day. It was about the plan to impose world control and a global police state, and that information continues to come to me all the time. But from the latter part of the 1990s another level was added – the fact that this network of 'human' bloodline families are actually the middle men and women for non-human masters taking reptilian and other forms that operate mostly beyond the human frequency range. People need to open their minds big-time. They will never get close to seeing what is 'going on' if they stay within the extreme limitations of perception and possibility that human society is systematically programmed to accept. Possibility is actually infinite, and humans have been encased by design in a sense of the possible the size of a pea. Suppressing the *sense* of the possible becomes the suppression of the *experience* of the possible. What we don't believe is possible we don't try to do, and it also opens the way for mass control using technology and other techniques that those subjected to such control and manipulation deny can be happening because 'that's not possible'. Oh, but it *is*. Human potential operating inside the 'pea' can't do it, but others can and they *are*. The world is not just a little bit different to what humanity thinks it is – it is *nothing* like they think it is. The puzzle pieces added another level soon after the start of the new century – the illusory nature of 'physical' reality. It was now that pennies dropped by the million as I saw how the rabbit hole fits together from this perspective. While I was writing my recent book, *Human Race Get Off Your Knees*, I was led to realise that the Moon is not a natural satellite of the Earth and that it is broadcasting frequencies at this planet which are acting as a frequency *fence* to limit the range of reality we can perceive, in much the same way that the Chinese computer system is firewalled to stop the people accessing large parts of the Internet that the rest of us can see (at least for now). Frequencies beamed at us from the Moon are also feeding us a fake reality that is the same in principle as the one symbolised in *The Matrix* movie trilogy. This means that we are not seeing things that we would otherwise see and we are seeing things that aren't really there. I call this fake reality the Moon Matrix, and since my last book was published the synchronicity of experience and information has pointed me powerfully towards Saturn and its influence on life on Earth in league with what the Moon is doing. Saturn is the key, and I will be putting the pieces together as we proceed. The compelling research about the – at least on one level – electrical nature of the Universe has provided many answers to how information is communicated and how it can be 'hacked' in the way I have described.

You really do need a very open and fluid mind – or rather *Consciousness* – if you are to 'get it'. Fortunately that is happening with a fast-increasing number of people. We are seeing an exponential curve of 'enlightenment' emerge from the depths of intergenerational ignorance, and the suppression and control of our perception. The Truth Vibrations, which artist Neil Hague and I symbolise as a lion, are doing what I was told they would do, and we are indeed living in extraordinary times (Fig 20). The 'masters' of a dying epoch of control and exploitation seek to retain their power in the face of a mass awakening that they knew was coming and have long prepared for – hence we are seeing the extreme levels of control and

Figure 20: A new energy is being 'breathed' into the world to break up the density, fear and ignorance on which the Control System depends

imposition at the very time humanity is emerging from its Big Sleep. There are going to be amazing happenings at every level – on Earth, the Sun and in the 'Heavens' in general. Most of all, however, there are going to be amazing happenings in the human heart and mind. Expect the unexpected is the story of the years to come. Many of these events are going to be very challenging and many will be wonderful. In the end it will all be wonderful. We are at the cusp of a transition from an epoch of control, limitation and oppression to one of vastly expanded awareness and potential that will manifest a world that we can currently only dream of. Dream the dream – it's *coming*. The Control System of the ages will not go quietly, or immediately. *Go*, however, it will, for its very informational/vibrational foundations are eroding by the day. The vibrational sands are shifting; the vibration is quickening; and, to mix my metaphors, the house of cards is coming down once we realise that *we* are the ones holding it up.

So, there you go. There is so much to tell about what is 'going on', but the themes are essentially quite simple. I am going to tell the story in the pages that follow that I have been guided to uncover and communicate since 1990. It is a story that I clearly came here to tell on April 29th, 1952. I am not going to go into the endless detail. I have done that in other books, and *Human Race Get Off Your Knees* runs to 355,000 words, 650 pages and has hundreds of illustrations. What I am setting out to do here is connect the essential dots across a great swathe of interconnected subjects which often do not appear to be connected at first sight. It is an encapsulation of all that I have learned since I walked through the psychic's door all those years ago.

This is not the end of the story. There is *always* so much more to know. But at this time of great change and upheaval, when people across the world are getting more and more uneasy about the events that they see, this book will provide an urgently-needed road map or SatNav for what is *'going on'*.

What people make of it, of course, is entirely up to them, and so it should be.

2

The 'world' is in your 'head'

We cannot grasp what is happening in our lives or the world until we understand at least the themes and foundations of reality itself. What is 'reality'? Who are we? Where are we? Where do we 'come' from?

How few people ask these big questions compared with those who ask what time does the game show or the football start. Shocking numbers of people are so mesmerised by the five-sense movie that they live their lives like moths staring wide-eyed at a light on the porch, never seeing the guy with the swatter creeping up behind to smack 'em on the bum. This has been the human plight for thousands of years, and then some. Ask most people to explain Life and the World and they will likely quote you from the religion they have been programmed to believe in, or from the official scientific 'norm'. But religions are prisons of the mind – yes *all* of them, even the 'enlightened' ones like Buddhism. How does a shaven head make you more 'spiritual'? Or, as with Sikhs, not cutting your hair at all? The 'New Age' is a religion in its own way, while at the same time it dismisses religion. Why would a religion want to tell you the truth about reality when it only survives by you not knowing that truth? They are going to sell you a dogma that suits the men in frocks by maintaining you in a state of ignorance. Those who are awake enough to see who and what we really are would never follow a religion. It is a case of cause and effect. 'Hey, terrible news, bishop, rabbi, Imam, guru – the people are not stupid anymore and the tills have stopped ringing.' Cause and effect. But surely mainstream science can tell us about reality and how we are interacting with it. I mean, they're *scientists*, so they must be clever. Actually, that's not a cause and effect. What we call 'science' is a mass of different disciplines that rarely talk to each other and compete for funding and prominence. They focus on the various 'dots', but never connect them. Scientists have the image of being very knowledgeable, but most know a lot about a little and unless you connect the 'littles' you'll never see the bigger picture. They also have a song sheet called the 'scientific consensus' from which most dare not deviate for fear of losing funding, jobs and perceived 'prestige'. Most 'scientists' are working to produce new technology, drugs, food additives and suchlike – not investigating the nature of reality. The overwhelming majority are followers and advocates of a religion called 'Scientism' which, like all religions, is founded on fiercely imposed dogma that must be obeyed. Science is, like the New Age, a religion that dismisses religion.

One of the most vocal in this, and in the condemnation and ridicule of alternative methods of healing and explaining the Universe, is a bloke in Britain called Richard Dawkins. Dogma Dawkins would be more appropriate. But, hey, he's a professor at Oxford University. He must be clever and highly intelligent, right? Well, I have seen him in action at close hand and, er, how can I put it? Let's just say that this wasn't my experience. Dogma Dawkins, a man who looks very ill at ease in his own skin, lays into religion and yet he is an evangelist for his own – Scientism – which is as dogmatic and ignorant as all the rest when it comes to explaining 'Life'. Those of the Dogma Dawkins' mentality live in prisons of the mind, like all religious fanatics. Mainstream 'science' is a joke. There *are* real scientists who seek truth and understanding and not fancy titles or grants with strings attached from corporations; but they work outside of the mainstream which would otherwise suffocate their zest for genuine inquiry. What we call 'Science' is deeply manipulated and controlled and it will never uncover and tell us the truth about reality when those manipulating and controlling, not least through funding, don't want us to know who we are, where we are and where we come from. This ignorance is, after all, their prime means of human control. Those in the inner sanctums of the global secret-society network know about reality and how we interact with it. Their power would be gone if the target population also knew. The bottom line for the Hidden Hand is to stop us from knowing who we are and where we are, and so it must control science and suppress genuine scientific investigation. We now have thousands of mainstream television channels across the world; but how many programmes do you ever see exploring reality outside the norms of religion and 'science', or even exploring reality at all? Hardly any. But then the global media is owned by the same cabal of families and secret societies that own or control science, religion, politics, banking and the major corporations. The lack of discussion about reality almost anywhere in the media tells you something very profound about how badly they want to keep us in ignorance of this most basic area of understanding from which everything else comes.

So here is what they don't want you to know ...

The Cosmic Internet

Most people think that we live in a 'physical' world, and I grant you that certainly *appears* to be the case. But it's not, because we don't. There is no 'physical'. It's all an illusion. We are infinite, eternal Consciousness having an experience in a tiny range of frequencies that we *call* the 'physical world', but that isn't. We are not our name, body, occupation, family background, race, colour or income bracket. They are our current *experience*; they are not who we *are*. We are Consciousness – infinite, eternal Awareness. We have no form in our core state; we are just awareness, and an expression of Infinite Awareness. Hence, it is said that we are 'all One'. Yes, one Infinite Awareness having different experiences from different points of observation – different *levels* of awareness and perception. Our true nature was described very well by a Central American shaman (you know, those who the Dogma Dawkins' of this world would dismiss as primitive and ignorant): 'We are perceivers, we are awareness; we are not objects; we have no solidity ... We are boundless ... We, or rather our reason [programming] forget this, and thus entrap the totality of ourselves in a vicious circle from which we rarely emerge in our lifetime.' The aim of the Control System is to keep it that way for the entire journey

Figure 21: The human body is the vehicle that allows the real us – Consciousness – to experience this range of frequencies.

Figure 22: The body is like a 'lens' that focuses our attention on a specific range of frequency which then becomes our sense of who we are and where we are

from womb to tomb. Albert Einstein said that reality is an illusion, albeit a persistent one. It is 'persistent' because we are living in a virtual-reality universe that we decode into (illusory) 'physical' form from an *information* construct that is the same in theme as the wireless Internet. The information is encoded in waveform or energetic vibration/resonance, and the mind–body is an incredibly advanced biological computer system which decodes that information and allows our Infinite Awareness to interact with this range of frequencies that we call the 'world' (Fig 21). The mind–body computer is the vehicle for the real *us* – Consciousness – to interact with this range of frequencies. I could not tap this keyboard and you could not hold this book, or anything else, unless we had an outer 'shell' resonating within the frequency range that we wish to experience. Consciousness, our core self, is vibrating way faster than anything within visible light. If we didn't have the body then never the twain would meet, in the same way that Radio 1 doesn't interact with Radio 2. They are resonating to different frequencies. People who have had 'near death experiences', where their body has died and then been revived, describe the out-of-body state as dramatically different to the reality they perceived from 'inside' the body. They have fantastically expanded awareness and they are able to 'see' even though they have no eyes. They are experiencing the real self, undiminished by the limitations of mind–body. I was sitting in the bath one day when a series of clear pictures appeared in my 'head'. The first was billowing energy, which I immediately took to represent Consciousness. Then an eye appeared in the Consciousness and in front of that came a telescope. The Earth and our reality appeared at the other end of the telescope and the final movement was for the telescope to morph into a human body. I asked Neil Hague to paint a representation of what I saw (Fig 22). This is what mind–body is – a lens for Consciousness to experience this reality. But humanity has been systematically manipulated to self-identify with the lens and not the real self. We talk about people dying, but 'they' don't die and cannot die. It is their body, their 'operating system', that 'dies', not 'them' – *Consciousness*. 'Dying' is merely our Consciousness putting down the telescope when it has ceased to function. I make the clear and important distinction between what I call 'Mind' or 'mind–body' and what I call 'Consciousness'. You can symbolise the difference very well if you think of Consciousness as the infinite free-flowing ocean, and mind– body as more like frozen water. It is far more dense and limited (Fig 23). Ramana Maharshi,

Figure 23: Everything is the same Infinite Awareness, but there are limitless expressions of this same 'Oneness'. Consciousness is expanded awareness, like a flowing ocean, while Mind is like frozen water, or the white crest of an infinite wave – far more limited in its ability to perceive

who spent most of his life meditating on a mountain in India, described it very well when he said: 'Mind is consciousness which has put on limitations. You are originally unlimited and perfect. Later you take on limitations and become the mind.'

Understanding this difference between mind–body and Consciousness is crucial to having any idea about what is happening in the world (Fig 24). We live in what I term the 'Cosmic Internet', which is, as I say, the same in theme as the wireless Internet. You can't see the wireless Internet because the information exists in the unseen beyond the frequency range of human sight. Most people would be denying its existence if they didn't *know* that it was there – 'Don't be stupid, I can't see it, hear it, touch it, taste it or smell it, so it can't exist. I told you that Icke was crazy!' But we *know* it exists from the fact that when we go to a computer and 'log on' to the wireless Internet we see a whole global collective reality appearing on the screen – the World Wide Web. It is the *same* collective reality that can be accessed by people in the Americas, Europe, Africa, Asia and Australia. In fact, by anyone who has a computer, except in places like China where the computer system is firewalled to deny access to much of the Web. They block information that the authorities don't want the people to see with their

Figure 24: When we enter the 'physical' world and retain our connection to Consciousness, we have everything we need. We have the mind–body computer interface that allows us to experience this reality, and we have Consciousness feeding us the bigger picture – an awareness of a greater reality. But when we become disconnected from Consciousness we have only the limitations of mind–body to give us a fix on who we are and where we are. The Control System's media and 'education' then seek to programme the sense of reality of 'isolated' mind–body to produce ignorant, bewildered slaves and system-fodder

Figure 25: The foundation of the Universe is waveform information and the human mind–body biological computer decodes this into electrical, digital and holographic information that we perceive as the 'physical world'

'Great Firewall of China'. Something very much like that is happening to humanity in general through what I call the 'Saturn-Moon Matrix', and other related manipulations – but that's for later. The point is that the base construct of the Universe is waveform information encoded as vibrational resonance. I will call this waveform information construct the 'Metaphysical Universe' and it contains the information fields from which everything manifests. We decode this information through the mind–body computer system into the illusory 'solid' world that we think we are experiencing daily. It is no more 'solid' than the figures in a virtual-reality game on your computer screen. They are only information in waveform on the software disk being decoded into that apparently 'solid' state. The brain and the genetic structure of the mind–body computer transform vibrational information in the same way from the waveform 'Metaphysical Universe' into electrical and other information on the 'screen' in our 'heads'. We then experience this as the 'physical world' (Figs 25 and 26).The brain is in total darkness, but we see light. How? By decoding waveform information. The inside of a computer is dark, but we see lights and colours on the screen. The Cosmic Internet is an interactive 'game'. We receive information from the waveform Metaphysical Universe, but we also 'post' with our thoughts, emotions and perceptions. Information goes both ways. Reality can change us, and we can change reality.

'Seeing' is decoding

We say that *we* are 'going on the Internet', but we don't go on the Internet. The computer does. We *observe* the Internet and interact with it *through* the computer. Mind–body is a 'computer' for our Consciousness and the means through which we 'go on', or 'log on', to the waveform information construct – the Cosmic Internet. The human five senses decode vibrational information into electrical information which is transmitted to the brain, and ultimately the entire genetic structure, to be decoded into the digital and holographic information that we experience as the 'physical' world. I'll explain more about the holographic and digital levels of reality in a moment. These various forms are all the same information being passed on in different forms. The vehicles for the information may look very different, as with a woman in a red dress who hands information to a man in a blue T-shirt who gives it to a bloke in a grey suit.

But it is the *same* information, and so it is when the vibrational becomes the electrical, digital and holographic. There is no 'world' *outside* of us; it only appears to be like that because of the way we decode reality. 'Physical' reality is *within* us and what we experience is what we have chosen, consciously or unconsciously, to decode from the Cosmic Internet. We can only 'physically' see and experience the world that we think we live 'in' when we decode waveform information into the electrical, digital and holographic. Everything else in the Universe remains in the unseen waveform unless we do that. A few more open-minded scientists have postulated over the years that the world that we see and experience only exists in that form when it is *observed*. Change 'observed' to *decoded* and that is correct. When you put

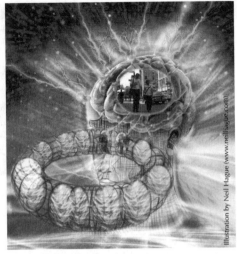

Figure 26: The 'world' appears to be 'outside' of us when it is all decoded waveform information in our head, heart and genetic structure

an information disk into a computer you don't see all the information on the screen at the same time. You only see that part of the disk that is being read – decoded – at any moment. The rest remains in a waveform state. So it is with our reality. I'll give you a wonderful example of what I mean. American author, Michael Talbot, wrote an excellent book called *The Holographic Universe* (HarperCollins; New Edition, 1996) and he told the story of an experience he had when a stage hypnotist was asked to attend a party to entertain the guests. A man called Tom was 'put under' and the hypnotist told him that when he returned to an awakened state he would not be able to see his daughter. The hypnotist then led the daughter to stand right in front her sitting father. He was looking straight into her belly. Tom was brought 'back' and the hypnotist asked him if he could see his daughter. 'No,' he said, she wasn't there. Actually, she was right in front of him. The hypnotist went behind the daughter and put his hand in the small of her back. 'I am holding something, Tom,' he said. 'Can you see it?' Tom immediately answered: 'Yes, it's a watch,' It was so clear to him, despite the little matter of his daughter standing between him and the watch. He was asked if he could read an inscription on the watch, which he did. Now, if you told that story to most people, especially a Dogma Dawkins in the scientific arena, they would say this was impossible and could not have happened. But it is not impossible at all. It is very simple and logical once you know how reality works. The base form of everything in this Universe, including the human body, is a waveform information field resonating beyond the digital/holographic realm that were can see, hear, touch, taste and smell. If any of those information fields are not decoded onto our brain/genetic 'screens' into a digital/holographic state then we are not going to be able to see them. The hypnotic implant, in the case of Tom, blocked or firewalled his brain and stopped it decoding his daughter's waveform field. He didn't decode her into a digital/holographic state that his conscious mind could see. He therefore saw what was behind her – the watch – because in his decoded 'physical' reality she wasn't there (Fig 27). Everyone else in the

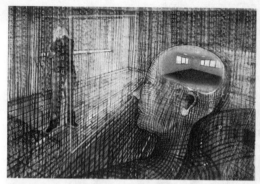

Figure 27: Waveform is the prime reality in the Universe, and what we do not decode through into the holographic, or 'physical', does not exist in our experienced perception. Therefore, 'Tom's' daughter could be seen by everyone in the room – except him

room could see her. They had not been subject to the hypnotic firewall and they decoded the daughter's waveform through to the 'physical'. A profound truth was being spoken when the child in *The Matrix* said, 'There is no spoon – it is not the spoon that bends; it is only yourself.' There is no 'spoon' or *anything else* in a physical sense. How can there be when there is no physical? It is all about the way we decode reality. We can see this when people walk barefoot across hot coals and don't get burned. They enter another state of awareness that decodes reality differently to the norm, which would otherwise decode: '*Aaaaaaaaaagggggghhhhh!!!!* Call an ambulance.' An illusion can only burn an illusion if you believe it can and so decode that reality. There are no miracles, only a greater understanding of how it all works. We only feel pain when the brain decodes the communication from the source of the pain. If that doesn't happen – no pain. We can now see that this scene from the first *Matrix* movie was perfectly accurate:

Neo: 'This isn't real?'
Morpheus: 'What is real? How do you define 'real'? If you're talking about what you can feel, what you can smell, taste and see, then 'real' is simply electrical signals interpreted by your brain.'

So it is, and this has profound consequences for the way humanity is controlled. The simplest way to censor the Cosmic Internet is to target the body–computer to limit the range of information – insight, understanding – that it can decode. This is done by programming perception in the same way that a stage hypnotist is programming the perception of the stooges on the stage. The idea is to ensure that we decode reality (like 'Tom') in line with the hypnotic implants (beliefs) that the hypnotist downloads into our minds. I went to a number of these hypnotist stage shows for my research and I watched people see, hear, touch, taste and smell things that were not there, except in their programmed *perception* of reality. I saw others that didn't see things that *were* there. I saw people eating a potato while believing it was an apple. The potato tasted like an apple to them after the hypnotist had implanted the belief that this is what it was. When the tongue communicated electrical information from the potato to the brain, this was decoded as apple. The decoding system had been 'hacked' by the hypnotist. Think about the potential for individual and mass programming in the light of this when a handful of interbreeding families have control of the major sources of information that people are seeing and hearing throughout their lives. Humanity as a whole is being programmed to decode reality in the desired way – desired by the controllers – by having beliefs and perceptions implanted through 'education' (yeah, right), the media, religion, doctors, scientists, politicians, and so on. The overwhelming majority are not even doing it knowingly. They are themselves programmed to program others. Scientists can affect the outcomes of their own experiments for the same reason – through belief or disbelief (another form of belief!). Our mind–body decoding system is also being systematically imbalanced and destabilised through chemical additives in food and drink, fluoride and other shite in the water supplies, and ever-gathering forms of electrical, electromagnetic and radiation pollution.

Everything has awareness

Mind–body is an electrochemical organism on one level and so, of course, it can be distorted electrochemically – and it is. The 'physical' level of the body is some 60 to 70 per cent water, and this is highly significant when you think that water has been shown to have a memory that retains *information*. The Aerospace Institute in Stuttgart, Germany, developed a means of making the structure of water visible. This allowed them to see that every drop of water has it own unique structure. I have been using the analogy for a long time of how we are like droplets of water in the ocean. We are unique in ourselves, but all part of the same whole. The findings of this German Institute confirm that the analogy is extremely appropriate. Researchers ran an experiment in which people were asked to put droplets from the same bowl of water into separate containers. You would think that all the droplets must have looked the same. But, no. The drops delivered by each person were unique to that person. Drops that involved person number one all looked the same; drops involving person number two all looked the same, but different from person one, and so on (Fig 28). The water had retained the memory, or information, relating to each individual. Researchers have put different flowers in the water and then found the image of the same flower in *every* droplet of that water. Of course water has a memory. *Everything* is the interaction of awareness and information, and *everything* has a form of memory – which is what? The

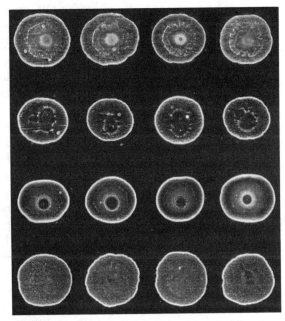

Figure 28: Each line of water droplets relates to a different person who took the droplets from the same container of water. Their unique information was retained by the water, because it is a form of consciousness and so has a 'memory'

ability to store and retain information. Scientists can't find the source of the human memory because they are looking in the wrong place. It is not in the brain; it is in the entire genetic structure which is only a projection of waveform information, anyway. The foundation of memory is information retained at the waveform level of reality. The healing technique of Homeopathy is based on this fact. Mainstream science arrogantly dismisses Homeopathy by saying that the ingredients in its potions are so diluted that nothing is left except water. Yes, water carrying the *information* of the ingredients in its *memory*. One of the Aerospace Institute researchers said that their findings reveal that rivers and seas are constantly absorbing information. He said that if you drink water at the mouth of the River Rhine, you will be drinking more information than if you drank it at the source. But what *kind* of information would that be, given that rivers are now so polluted? What is pollution and radiation? Rogue *information*, like a computer virus. This is the prime reason why the bloodline Control System is pouring pollution and radiation into the seas and rivers. Look at Fukushima and the oil disaster in the Gulf of Mexico alone. They are purposely distorting the information harmony of the planet for reasons I will be explaining. The bloodline families are desperate to suppress this knowledge that everything is connected and everything has awareness. The late Jacques Benveniste, a French immunologist, was savaged by the ignorant prostitutes of the 'scientific' mainstream when he realised in the 1980s that water had a memory. *Nature*, the prestigious, but ludicrous 'scientific journal' in Britain, led the character assassination of Benveniste. The attack was joined by James Randi, the 'magician' and professional 'debunker' of anything that threatens the scientific song sheet. The editor of *Nature* at the time, John Maddox, who called for at least one book challenging mainstream dogma to be 'burned', said that Benveniste's findings appeared to have no 'physical basis'. There we go – the five sense 'scientific' jailbird again. There is no 'physical', mate. Get used to it! *Nature* ran an editorial saying that if Benveniste was right 'much of modern science would have to be junked'. *Oh my God!* Call security, call the police, call the fire service, call anyone. *Aaaaaaaaaagggggghhhhh!!!!* The deeply unpleasant John Maddox died in 2009. I bet he feels a right prat now.

Holograms within holograms

'Physical' reality is an illusion that only exists on a symbolic 'screen' in our brain and genetic structure. The world looks and feels solid, that's for sure, and if you bang your head against a wall, it hurts. But if you walk through fire in a 'normal' state of mind you'll get burned, while others, in an altered state, will not. What we experience as 'solid' is only resistance between two different electromagnetic (waveform information) states. The world cannot be solid. Scientists tell us 'matter' is made up of atoms, but atoms have *no solidity*. They are just packets of energy with electrons orbiting a nucleus, and

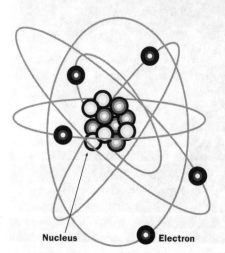

Nucleus   **Electron**

Figure 29: Empty atoms. How can they be the structure of a 'solid' world? They can't, and they don't need to be. The 'world' is not solid

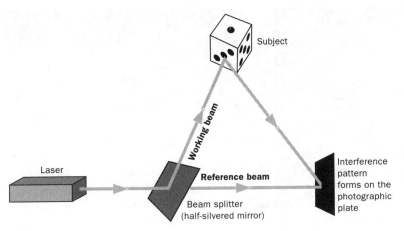

Figure 30: Holograms are created by directing two parts of the same laser on to a film. One part goes directly to the film, and the other carries the vibrational image of the subject. The two parts collide on the film to create an 'interference pattern', and when a laser 'reads' this pattern an apparently three-dimensional image appears

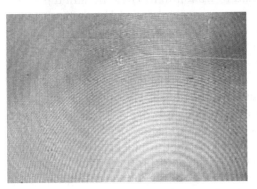

Figure 31: A holographic interference pattern. This is waveform information waiting to be read into an illusory three-dimensional form – and the same principle applies to the way we decode the metaphysical waveform Universe into illusory 'solidity'

the electrons and nucleus aren't solid either – *nothing* is. There is no 'matter'. The proportions in Figure 29 are not the true distances inside an atom. The true scale would be far too big to put in a book. One writer used a telling analogy: 'If an atom was the size of a cathedral, the nucleus would be the size of a ten cent piece.' How can 'empty' atoms make a solid 'physical' world? They can't, and they don't need to. The world is not 'solid'. It is *holographic* – illusory 'solid'. What scientists identify as atoms are part of the energetic process that takes place as vibrational waveform information is decoded through the electrical to the digital and holographic. Holograms that you can buy in shops are made by diverting two parts of a laser onto a photographic print. One part, the 'reference beam', goes pretty much directly onto the print while the other, the 'working beam', encodes the vibrational image of the object being photographed. It then collides on the print with the reference beam (Fig 30). This creates what they call in holographics an 'interference pattern'. What is that? Information in *waveform* (Fig 31). It is like dropping two stones into a pond and watching the waves expand and collide to create a wave pattern *information* construct of where the stones dropped, how fast, and so on. The holographic interference pattern is a waveform information construct of the object being photographed, and when you direct a laser at that pattern an amazing thing happens. An apparently three-dimensional projection of the object appears before you, and the best of them can look as solid as you and I (Figs 32 to 35). Holograms are being used more and more in exhibitions and suchlike, and they are now developing digital holograms that are even closer to the reality we experience daily. A mainstream news report said: 'And they look real – so real that when Ford used a [digital] hologram to show off a car concept model people

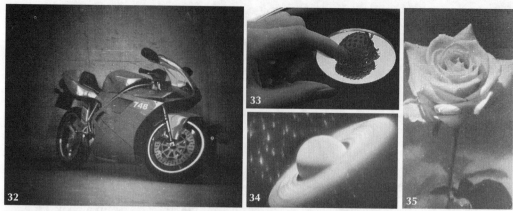

Figures 32 to 35: These images are all holograms and the best of them can look as 'solid' as you and me; but you could put your hand through any of them. Their solidity is an illusion. (See my previous books for other images)

Pictures: 'Strawberry' Mirage - 3D Hologram Generator, http://www.eyetricks.com/mirage • 'Rose'courtesy of Holography Studio, All-Russian Exhibition Center, Moscow, see www.holography.ru • Picture 'Saturn' courtesy of Royal Holographic Art Gallery, see www.holograms.bc.ca

Figure 36: The man on the left is on a stage in Adelaide, Australia, and the one on the right is a hologram projected from Melbourne

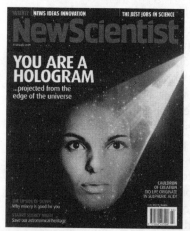

Figure 37: Even some mainstream scientists are looking at the possibility that our reality is holographic. It *is*
© Courtesy of Tim Graystock

stopped, afraid to walk into it. They thought the holographic car was really there ...' The motorcycle in Figure 32 is a digital hologram and not at all 'solid'. The man on the right in Figure 36 is in Melbourne, Australia, but he has been projected as a hologram onto a stage in Adelaide. I have been writing and talking about how the 'physical' world is holographic for a long time now and so I was very interested to see a copy of the mainstream science magazine, *New Scientist*, as I was walking through Heathrow Airport in 2009. The front cover said: 'You are a hologram ... projected from the edge of the universe' (Fig 37). It was an article featuring a scientist who was investigating the possibility that the Universe is a hologram. It didn't tell us very much, really, but at least some scientists are beginning to see that this is the direction in which they need to go. The holograms are not projected from the edge of the Universe; they are decoded from information in the waveform construct that I am calling the Metaphysical Universe. Scientists have been baffled at experiments that show that what they call a particle can be a waveform at the same time. But let's think about this from the holographic point of view. The interference pattern, or waveform print, is the information from which the hologram is 'read'. Without the waveform information there is no '3D' hologram, which is only a projection from the waveform information field. So not only *can* the waveform and the hologram exist at the same time

– they *have* to. One is only an expression of
the other. Take away the waveform
information and you take away the
hologram. Oh yes, one other thing. What
happens when the information on the
waveform print is not being decoded,
'observed', by the laser? It remains only in
waveform, exactly as our 'physical' reality
only exists when we decode it.

Another highly significant characteristic
of a hologram is that every part is a smaller
version of the whole. If you cut a
holographic print into four pieces and fire
the laser at them you would not get a
quarter of the picture. You would get a
quarter-sized version of the *whole* picture
(Fig 38). This explains many 'mysteries',
including how healing methods dismissed
as mumbo jumbo by the Dogma Dawkins
brigade have a very logical basis.
Reflexology, acupuncture and other
alternative practices say that they can treat
the whole body working with specific
points in the ear, foot etc. There are points
in every part of the body that relate to the
organs, and to the body in general (Fig 39).
But, *of course* that must be the case. The
body is a *hologram* and so every part must
be a smaller version of the whole. All the
parts are interconnected. You treat the
heart itself when you treat an area of the
foot holographically relating to the heart.
The holographic nature of 'physical' reality
explains why the human auric field and
the Earth's magnetic field look the same,
and why brain activity mirrors activity in
the Universe (Figs 40 and 41). This is also
the basis of practices such as palmistry. The
hand contains information about the whole
body. The term 'as above, so below' is
describing the holographic universe,
although most people who use the phrase
don't realise that. Harvey Bigelsen M.D., a
friend of mine in California, has even
written a book about the way blood is
holographic – see *Holographic Blood* at:

Figure 38: Every part of a hologram is a smaller
version of the whole

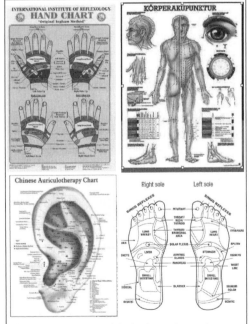

Figure 39: Every part of the body can be used to treat
the *whole* body, because it is a hologram; and so
every part is a smaller version of the whole

Figure 40:
The human energy
field and the Earth's
energy field. As above,
so below

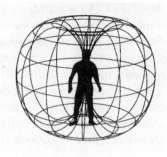

www.drbigelsen.com. This means that, even at the body–hologram level, we are *the Earth and the Universe* (what I call the 'Super Hologram'). Every expression of form is a smaller version of the whole. It is not only at the holographic level that we are all 'one'. It is the same with the digital, electrical and waveform levels, too. It has to be – the holographic is only a projection of the waveform and everything in 'between'. My goodness, we are already a long way from 'Little Me', I am just my name, job, and all that stuff. No, we are *everything*. We have just forgotten. Physicist Alain Aspect at the University of Paris discovered in 1982 that subatomic particles can instantaneously communicate with each other no matter if they are an inch or 100 billion miles apart.

The discovery demolished Albert Einstein's contention that nothing can surpass the speed of light (nonsense) and perplexed mainstream science. But this 'mystery' is easily explained when you realise that everything is *One* and that we live in a holographic reality. The 'particles' are only a holographic expression of a seamless waveform information field – the Metaphysical Universe. At that level, the particles can communicate instantly because they are *each other*.

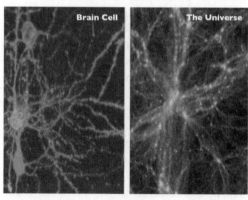

Figure 41: Human brain cell activity and electrical activity in the Cosmos. As above, so below

The digital level of experienced reality explains why number sequences and mathematical proportions keep repeating, such as the Golden Section (Pi, Phi), and the Fibonacci sequence in which the last two numbers are added together to get the next one, as in 1, 1, 2, 3, 5, 8, 13, 21 ... The sequence can be found throughout nature in everything from the way plants and shells grow to the proportions of the human body (Figs 42 and 43). This must be so when what we call Nature is a vast tapestry of digital holographic forms. Numerology is the reading of the digital

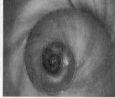

Figure 42   **Figure 43**
The Fibonacci sequence of numbers can be found in the way plants grow, shells form and in the proportions of the human face

level of reality, and so is the Chinese 'I Ching' and other methods and techniques. The numbers running down the computer screens in *The Matrix*, and the way that Neo saw everything as digital when his mind opened to Consciousness, were based on fact. Numbers are digital expressions of vibrational waveform information. When the same numbers continually recur, they are signs of something recurring in the waveform information fields. Ancient initiates and secret societies who had this understanding built their temples and other buildings to certain geometrical and mathematical proportions. They knew that this would automatically connect the building to the vibrational fields that the numbers digitally represented. The Illuminati bloodline families and their secret-society network plan dates for their events and manipulations in great detail so that they happen at a time and place that gives them the best chance of success from their point of view. Those in power who publically dismiss and ridicule practices such as numerology and astrology are using them in very detailed ways behind the scenes. Was the date of 9/11, the emergency telephone number in the United States, only a coincidence? Is even having 911 as the emergency number a coincidence? You must be joking.

Disconnecting mind from consciousness

Vital for the Control System (the very few) to make slaves of the people (the enormous many) is to ensure that the people perceive and decode reality only through the lens of mind–body, and maintain a lifetime disconnection from the influence of their true and eternal self – Consciousness. You have everything you need when you retain a connection between mind–body (the computer) and Consciousness (the one at the desk with the mouse and keyboard) – see Figure 44. Mind–body 'logs' you on to the Cosmic Internet and this allows you to interact with its frequency range; but Consciousness gives you the bigger picture and the wider perspective that the five senses cannot perceive. You are, in short, 'in' this world, in the sense that you are experiencing it, but

not 'of' this world in terms of your entire perspective of reality. Take Consciousness away and you are left with mind–body and the realm of the five senses. This is like a computer now deciding where you go on the Internet and what you think about it. Mind–body can do this because it has awareness. Everything does. Mind– body is a *biological* computer, as they are called, which not only reacts to data as programmed to do so, but can also assess that data and make decisions about what to do with it. The immune system is doing this

Illustration by Neil Hague (www.neilhague.com)

Figure 44: Consciousness is symbolically sitting with the keyboard and the mouse observing the Cosmic Internet through the computer interface of body–mind. The problem starts when body–mind no longer responds to the tapping keys and clicking mouse and decides where to go and what to do from an extremely limited sense of perception all the time. But mind–body is supposed to be a vehicle for Consciousness to experience this reality – not to be the governor of the reality that it decodes. This, however, is where the great majority of humanity is still at, although it is changing, thank goodness. Humans are imprisoned in the mind–body computer. And what are computers designed to do? Be *programmed*. Here you have the reason why people are so predictable in their responses and behaviour patterns. They are running the same software called programmed beliefs and perceptions which, like the potato and the apple and the guy who couldn't see his daughter, decode reality to fit the beliefs and perceptions. It's a feedback loop. You become a computer terminal on an information grid once Consciousness is out of the picture. People are told what to believe, and the belief programs the decoding process to manifest what they think they see and hear. Most of this programming is done via the oblong hypnotist in almost every home called the television. This presents to you something that sums it up perfectly – *programmes*.

The foundation of the global conspiracy of the ages is to disconnect mind–body from Consciousness and then program mind–body with the sense of reality that suits the Control System. This is the perception of limitation, Little Me, and, I can't. This is further underpinned by fear, worry, anxiety and an overall sense of powerlessness. Religion, mainstream media, song-sheet science, medicine and 'education' were all invented and imposed as vehicles for mass perception programming. They are there to program mind–body with a reality of Little Me and subordination to belief systems (hypnotic implants and firewalls) designed to imprison people in a pea-sized perception of self and events. The world is 'mad', because it is *asleep*. It is no good getting angry and frustrated at those who can't see the bloody obvious (obvious to Consciousness). They are simply not conscious enough to compute and decode the bloody obvious. But they can make the choice to do so whenever they decide to open their minds. The controllers are even more insane, but not quite as asleep in the same way. They have worked for aeons to manipulate humanity into a smaller box than they are in. As the saying goes: 'In the land of the blind, the one-eyed man is king.' The controllers are the 'one-eyed man' and so no match for two-eyed, third-eyed Consciousness once we awaken to it. The entire structure of mainstream human society is designed to hold people in a hypnotic, amnesic state, believing that their body, name, job, etc., is what they *are*. Only then can the very few control everyone else in the way that they currently do (but won't for too much longer). All this explains why humans can be so stupid and the world so insane.

Consciousness doesn't fight, for example. It knows that we are all the same Infinite Awareness – *Mind–body* fights because it sees only apartness and separation in the 'physical' world of daily experience. It is through these illusory fault-lines of perceived separation that we have individual conflict, wars and the belief that we need to constantly compete with other expressions of separation. But there is no separation, except in our own distorted perception. Albert Einstein rightly said: 'A human being is a part of the whole called by us "Universe", a part limited in time and space. He experiences himself, his thoughts and feelings as something separated from the rest, a kind of optical delusion of his consciousness.' This optical delusion is the mind–body. Whenever you see troops in uniform with guns in their hands, or dropping bombs from their flying virtual-reality machines, you are looking at the unconscious playing out the programmed and computerised illusions and delusions of mind–body. These minds in uniform are sent to war by minds in dark suits. The weapons they use are made by minds in white coats and overalls in the centres of 'science' and technology. They are sold to minds in government by minds in armament companies and paid for by the minds in government borrowing non-existent money called 'credit' from minds that run the banks; and all of this is reported inaccurately by minds in the media. There is no *Consciousness* to be seen in this panorama of mind that runs the world. How can 'journalists' imprisoned in mind accurately report events that need Consciousness to see them in their true light? The conspiracy is a mind game in

Figure 45: The isolated mind that controls mainstream science, media, politics, 'education', religion etc., etc

every sense. The isolated mind, seen in Figure 45, is the whole source of the problem. It is the village idiot compared with Consciousness. This is why the world is as it is. To open your mind to Consciousness means to let go of the programs of mind, fears of mind, including the fear of what other people think. It means doing what you *know* (Consciousness) to be right, rather than what you *think* (Mind) is right for you in the moment. It means losing the fear of *doing* what you know to be right. As Morpheus said in *The Matrix*: 'You have to let it all go, Neo. Fear, doubt and disbelief. Free your mind.' Even better – free yourself *from* mind. Let Consciousness in with all the challenges in being accepted and understood in a world of mind. Opening minds to Consciousness will not only support the revolution of human society. It *is* the revolution of human society.

Still, silent, sensational

There is much to open up to ... an infinity of all possibility. This is who we are – All Possibility having an experience of some possibilities. In 2003, the synchronicity of my life took me to the Brazilian rainforest not far from the northern city of Manaus. I went to a centre in the forest to speak to a gathering of people over several days, and to take a rainforest brew called Ayahuasca, which can expand your awareness and enable you to access higher levels of consciousness. You drink it in a small glass and it tastes a bit like liquorice. Some people have a bad time on it. I had a life-changing experience over two nights. I could have taken it four times, but I only did it twice. I got what I needed and I have never felt the need to do it again. I found myself saying the words: 'I am love'; and then, 'I am everything and everything is me; I am infinite possibility,' as I entered an altered state on the first evening. When I did so, an extraordinary energy began to pour from the centre of my chest and fill the room. I was lying on a mattress in the pitch dark, but first one and then three striplights on the ceiling came on without anyone touching the switch. The switch would have turned them all on, anyway. The music player began to turn on and off, triggered by the electromagnetic energy surging out of me. It is electromagnetic energy projected from another reality which is the source of many 'ghostly' and 'paranormal' happenings that often include electrical equipment turning

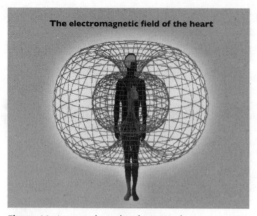

The electromagnetic field of the heart

Figure 46: An open heart has fantastic electromagnetic power – much greater than the brain

on and off. The centre of the chest is the location of the 'heart chakra', the balance centre of the seven major vortex points, or 'chakras', which I described earlier. This is the real origin of the association between the heart and 'love'. The symbol of the 'physical' heart is used today, but it is the energetic heart that expresses love and much else. The 'physical' heart is highly significant, too, and not only for pumping blood around the body. The energetic heart is the source of our intuitive *knowing*, which is a far more advanced state of awareness than thinking, and the heart is far more intelligent and 'enlightened' than the brain when it is given a chance to impact upon our perception. Researchers at the Institute of HeartMath in the United States have established that the heart has its own energy field which encircles the body (Fig 46). The heart generates 60 times and more the electrical amplitude than the brain and it was going some this night in Brazil. I felt the energy pouring from my heart chakra in an arc to the 'third eye', a source of psychic connection on my forehead. The heart is a gland as well as an organ and secretes hormones that connect with the pineal and pituitary glands in the brain which are part of the third eye. The sensation was like someone was tightly gripping my forehead. I then began to speak about how humanity had become disconnected from Infinite Oneness and how this was the reason for the world that we see.

On the second night, as I moved through altered states of awareness, a loud and lovely female voice spoke to me. 'David,' the voice began, 'we are going to take you to where you come from, so that you can remember who you are.' Where I 'went' was a state of incredible bliss where everything was *One*. 'This is the Infinite, David' the voice said. 'This is where you come from and this is where you shall return.' There was no 'time'; no 'place'; no divisions; no us and them. I was at *One* with all existence and no existence; but I still retained my sense of individuality. We transfer our point of attention to different realities. The mind–body focuses our attention on this tiny frequency range that we are experiencing called 'visible light', and so we perceive only this. It is only a point of focus – *attention* – and infinity awaits us beyond the illusory 'walls' of that perception. The voice said that all I really needed to know is that 'Infinite Love is the only truth – *everything* else is illusion.' The words were repeated over and over. 'Infinite Love is the only truth – *everything* else is illusion.' Put another way, Infinite Consciousness is the only truth – everything else is the imagination of that Consciousness made manifest in infinite forms. I call the 'place' that I experienced All Possibility. This is the still and silent *everything* and I can tell you that it is *LOVE*. I don"t mean the 'physical' and chemical attraction that I dub 'mind love'. I have met many people subjected to horrific government mind-control projects who were programmed to fall in (mind) love with someone who was programmed to (mind) love them. All you have to do is stimulate certain chemicals in the brain and you can get people to 'love' someone they wouldn't look twice at without the engineered attraction. Most people in this reality who say they are in love are in mind love. When the chemical attraction subsides they either break up or move into real love. We have to call this 'unconditional love', or, as I do, 'heart love', to make clear the difference. With heart love there can be no, 'I don't love you anymore because ...' Heart love says I just love you. It doesn't say that I am 'in' love with you. This implies the possibility of one day being 'out' of love. Heart love is simply, I love you. That's it. No escape clauses necessary. This is the love that I felt in that still and silent heart of the All That Is – All Possibility, or what some call 'The Void' (Fig 47). It may sound strange to say that something that I experienced as still and silent can be All That Is, and All Possibility. I understand that. It appears to mind that still and silent = nothing. Surely, only with movement, form or sound do we have a 'something', never mind an 'everything'. The opposite is the case as usual in our suppressed and bewildered world. Stillness and silence is All Possibility waiting to manifest. It is, therefore, everything and nothing; it is and it isn't; it is everywhere and nowhere. You can't have everything and nothing? It must be or not be? You can't be everywhere and nowhere? Oh, yes you can. Everything *must* be possible with All Possibility; and nothing. When you experience silence and stillness you are experiencing the All That Is waiting to manifest. When people meditate deeply they go into a state of stillness and silence. This is the core of our being – all being, and not being. Sit quietly for a moment and feel the silence. Do it for long enough and you'll *hear* the silence even in a noisy location. You move your point of *attention* away from the realm of the five senses and into the All That Is. If you sit quietly

Figure 47: The still and silent All That Is; All Possibility; All Knowing

Figure 48: 'Worlds' of form (ranges of frequency) are created out of All Possibility using information encoded in waveform vibration (thought, sound)

for a moment and then start talking, the words are one possibility manifesting out of All Possibility. When you stop talking, that possibility returns to the silence of All Possibility. This is what happens when a 'physical' form 'dies' and returns to pure energy. The 'worlds' of illusory form and vibration emerge from the still and silent All That Is. This is what we call 'Creation'. These 'worlds', or realities, are made manifest by what you might describe as sound vibration, although it is more than that. The vibration, or waveform, is encoded with information generated by various expressions of 'thought', but again this is not the same as thought as we perceive it. I prefer to use the word 'imagination'. It is the creative imagination of the All That Is which brings these worlds of vibration into being, and then other manifestations of the All That Is experience them and play with them (Fig 48). These are the virtual-reality worlds which resonate to different frequencies and they can exist in the same 'space' as each other, as do radio stations.

Also, just to mark the card of the Dogma Dawkins mentality, the infinite 'body' forms which emerge from All Possibility do not all look like humans do. *Staggering*, isn't it? If anyone doubts that vibration can create form then go to *YouTube* and enter the word 'Cymatics'. You will see random particles on a plate (All Possibility waiting to manifest), and when sound is played the particles assemble to create incredible geometrical and other patterns. As the sound changes, so the pattern changes. What I have described here explains why the voice in Brazil told me: 'If it vibrates, it is illusion.'

Yes, the illusion of 'physical' Creation.

3

Playing the Game

Virtual-reality games are getting ever more sophisticated and 'real', and the day is coming when you will not be able to tell them apart from the virtual reality that we call the Universe. Technology is mirroring our experienced reality and also giving us the tools and analogies to explain it.

The most sophisticated of these games, when you wear special gloves and goggles, can already make false realities look and feel 'real'. And what is this technology doing? It is hacking in to the five senses and manipulating them to decode a different reality to the one they normally would. This can be so effective that some hospitals connect burns patients to virtual-reality technology while nurses are changing their dressings. It reduces the pain by tricking the brain into constructing another reality. People learn to fly aircraft to a large extent and do many other things by working with this same technology. Virtual-reality games communicate electrical information to goggles and gloves, and the brain decodes this into pictures and sensations. The five senses communicate information to the brain in the same way for brain and body to construct 'physical' reality. They decode vibrational information into electrical information. The most obvious example is the ears, which pick up sound vibration and send it in electrical form to the brain which then 'hears'; but all five senses are doing the same. A mainstream news report said:

> Researchers have been able to translate brain signals into speech using sensors attached to the surface of the brain for the first time. The breakthrough, which is up to 90 per cent accurate, offers a way to communicate for paralysed patients who cannot speak and could eventually lead to being able to read anyone's thoughts.

There you go. The technology now exists to decode electrical signals in the brain into speech, and this is what the brain does naturally. What we call 'speech' is vibrational information generated by the vocal chords that our ears translate into electrical information for the brain to turn into the 'speech' that we recognise as language. There is no language until the brain has constructed it, and so, as I said earlier, an Italian psychic will 'hear' (decode) waveform information in Italian and an English one in English. Even 'physical movement' is a decoded illusion. There are brain malfunctions, for example, that cause some people to see tea pouring into a cup as a still 'freeze frame'; or, one moment they see a car in the distance and the next it is flying past them with nothing in between. I cannot stress enough that the 'physical' world is an illusion and those behind the human Control System *know* this. They just don't want us to know, when the manipulation potential of us not knowing is limitless. The Universe is information, and information decoding information. You put information into a computer in the form of a disk or data stick, and other information – the computer – decodes that information. It is all encoding and decoding, encoding and decoding. Speaking and hearing is a simple example.

Programming perception

We don't see, hear, feel, taste or smell until the brain decodes that information and constructs that reality. This is how a hypnotist can make somebody eating a potato taste an apple, and why the brain is the 'stadium' in which human life and the whole conspiracy to enslave humanity is played out (Fig 49). Not only the brain, however, also the heart and the DNA/genetic structure in general. The Control System is constantly seeking to program the mind–body through what we see and hear, to decode reality in ways that suit its agenda (Fig 50). The brain is very easy to trick. We can see this with optical illusions and with hypnotism; and the brain wave state when we are watching television is the same as that which hypnotists use to implant perception programs. Is this yet *another* coincidence?

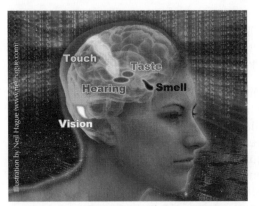

Figure 49: Those behind the Control System know how we construct reality, and we are constantly being manipulated to decode the perceptions that advance the agenda for human enslavement

Not a chance. Television is communicating far more than the pictures we see and the words that we hear. People are told what to watch, eat, wear, think and 'be'. They are told what to believe is success (money and fame) and failure (not having money and fame). The most powerful forms of suggestion are subliminal or 'below threshold' and they bypass the conscious mind. Later they seep into the conscious mind from the subconscious as apparently the person's own thoughts, desires and ideas. I wonder how many people actually have any original thoughts and perceptions that have not been implanted through the endless sources available to the system. Many of these sources will not even be known outside of the secret

Figure 50: The mainstream media in all its forms along with 'education' is the prime means of perception programming

research projects and the inner circle elite. Advertising, with all its subliminal
techniques, is an obvious example of manipulating perception, but my goodness so is
television, radio and print 'news'. It spews out the official (lying) version of everything
and it is especially effective in programming perception with one of the major forms of
mind control – *repetition*. The official story is given by those in power to the mainstream
media which then repeats it for all time as the true story of events. The official story
becomes official history in this way – not through fact, but through repetition. Tell most
people enough times and they will believe that 19 Muslim terrorists were responsible
for 9/11 on the orders of Osama bin Laden from a cave in Afghanistan, and that an
already dead Osama bin Laden has been killed again. Their perception of reality will
have been re-programmed even though both stories are blatant nonsense. It becomes an
'everybody knows that'. Everybody who has been programmed to *believe* that, would be
far more accurate. No-one's perception is programmed more powerfully than most
'journalists'. Steven J M Jones made this point in an article for the website:
www.globalresearch.ca:

> Media has become a mirror of the disconnected state that humanity finds itself in [and a creator
> of it]. News, current affairs, even the dramas and reality TV shows that entertain us serve to
> exacerbate the religion of polarity being reflected back to us in all its forms – materialism,
> hatred, killing, idolization and separation. Almost all television, be it sagas and melodramas or
> daily news, is as addictive as any drug. This single dimensional 'pulpit' from which media
> preaches to us (often in the centre of our living rooms) actually seeds many of our negative
> behavior patterns in day-to-day life.
>
> Dramas and melodramas aside, we have been led to believe that the news and current affairs
> programs we watch are true, unbiased, fair. Often this is anything but the case. News is
> provided, increasingly, by a select few. Those who have views outside what the owners of
> global media want us to hear and see have found themselves without a platform from which to
> present their knowledge and opinions.
>
> Governments ensure that only the very powerful are able to access our living rooms by staking
> ownership and guardianship of the airwaves through licensing priced well outside the reach of
> ordinary people. As a result, the news we see in all developed countries, particularly those of
> Anglo–Saxon ethnicity, is exactly the same, word for word, picture for picture. There is purpose
> behind this; it ensures that the now global corporate empires of media become bigger and
> more powerful, gobbling up any small players along the way. A select few controlling interests
> effectively distort democracy by shaping public opinion through deception on a grand scale.

This monopoly of the media by a few corporations, ultimately owned by the same
families, is not primarily about money. It is about programming the perceptions of the
population so that we perceive self and the world in the way that suits them and their
aims.

Biological computer
I talk about the mind–body computer, but I am, of course, describing something
extraordinarily more advanced than computers that we know. However, the basic

Figure 51: A computer virus is rogue information and so are the attacks on the human mind– body computer

principles are the same. A serious virus in your desktop computer can damage the operating system to the point where it will not even switch on. What do we say? 'My computer is dead.' In other words, it is no longer able to function and process electrical power and information. The computer might be dead, but the chap with the keyboard and the mouse is still very much alive. He must now go in search of another computer (reincarnation) if he wants to continue to experience the Internet. The same thing happens when our bodies die. Drop a computer from a great height and it won't work anymore. Fall off a cliff and ... *exactly*. Computers go into sleep mode when they tick over on minimum energy. So does the human body. Computers have anti-virus technology to protect the operating system from viruses, and the human body–computer has a fantastic expression of that called the immune system. A desktop computer can be devastated by a new virus that the software is not programmed to deal with. The worst of them can 'kill' the computer. We see this with the immune system. Native Americans died in large numbers when Europeans took smallpox to smallpox-free America. Their immune systems did not have the 'software' to meet a challenge it had not experienced before. Computer viruses are rogue *information* which distorts the information harmony and balance of the operating system and creates chaos (Fig 51). The same is true of the human body. I am going to emphasise quite a lot that the foundation construct of the Universe is waveform information and the electrical, digital and holographic levels are only projections of that. It is so important to hold that thought throughout to appreciate how it all works. We see disharmony in our 'physical' (holographic) reality that we call illness or *dis- ease*. But this is only a reflection – a projection – of vibrational / waveform disharmony. An illness, a poison, or whatever, is a decoded distortion at the waveform information level which undermines the operating system – the body–computer – in much the same way, in principle, as a virus undermines the one on your desk. We see a drug, for example, but that is a decoded information field that can either harmonise or – most likely with pharmaceutical drugs – imbalance the information field that is the body. We refer to this drug-induced vibrational mayhem as 'side effects' when they are simply 'effects'. There is nothing 'side' about them. They are as much an effect of the drug as the one they say will be good for you in all the drug advertisements that pay for American television. Appropriate, really, given that the pharmaceutical cartel, or Big Pharma, is owned by the same families and secret societies that own the American TV networks. The cabal-owned Big Biotech and Big 'Food' corporations are feeding rogue information to the body–computer operating system in the form of genetically-modified 'food' and chemical additives to limit and distort the way we decode reality.

Computers have a motherboard, and so does the body. This is the network of energy lines known as 'meridians' which are the basis of the ancient healing art of acupuncture.

The picture on the left in Figure 52 is an enhanced image taken during a French hospital study in which a tracer dye was injected into specific points on the meridians known as, not surprisingly, acupuncture points. You can see in the picture where the dye travelled. The word that came to me immediately when I saw it was 'motherboard'. They have found that when what acupuncture calls 'chi' energy is passing along the meridians too slowly or too quickly, or if there is a blockage anywhere, this manifests as some form of 'physical', mental or emotional problem. The reason for this is simple. The chi energy is actually *information* and the meridian network is a major part of the process, along with the

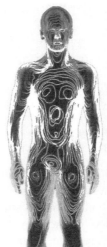

Figure 52: The meridian system of *chi* energy is the body–computer 'motherboard'

brain and the heart, of interacting with the Cosmic Internet. The body cannot accurately decode and encode this information when the chi is blocked, or is circulating too slowly or too quickly, and the operating system starts to malfunction. The insertion of hair-like needles, and other acupuncture techniques, seeks to balance the flow and remove any blockages to allow optimum communication to be restored. We can see the same principle in desktop computers. The first thing we usually notice when a computer is infected by a virus is that 'my computer is running so slow today'. It is slow because the virus is affecting the speed at which the information is being communicated. People laugh and scoff at the suggestion that acupuncture can cure a headache with a needle in the foot, because they are, well, ignorant. Meridian lines of energy flow all around the body and if one connected to the head is blocked where it passes through the foot it would not do the headache much good to stick a needle in the head, would it? My great friend, Mike Lambert, from the Shen Clinic on the Isle of Wight, says: 'The location of the symptom is rarely the location of the cause.' The human brain is what computer people call the Central Processing Unit, or CPU. It is, like the CPU, a main, but far from the only, processor of information traffic. The brain receives information from the rest of the body system and the Cosmic Internet, and transmits its decoded response. 'Physical', mental or emotional imbalances once again ensue when this communication breaks down. Parts of the brain work on the binary system of on–off electrical charges represented by 0 and 1, the way computers do. The brain also employs the trinary system that some research projects around the world are introducing to computers. The added mode is coded as minus 1, and would allow computers to ignore information when necessary just as the brain can ignore your surroundings while you are concentrating on something. Another vital aspect of reality decoding is that of the heart, and I will be coming to that.

Having a chat with my DNA

DNA, or deoxyribonucleic acid, is the hard drive of the body–computer, and *so much*

```
CCCAACACCCAAATATGGCTCGAGAAGGGCAGCGACATTCCTGCGGGGTGGCGCGGAGGGAATGCCC
GCGGGCTATATAAAACCTGAGCAGAGGGACAAGCGGCCACCGCAGCGGACAGCGCCAAGTGAAGCCT
CGCTTCCCCTCCGCGGCGACCAGGGCCCGAGCCGAGAGTAGCAGTTGTAGCTACCCGCCCAGGTAGG
GCAGGAGTTGGGAGGGGACAGGGGGACAGGGCACTACCGAGGGGAACCTGAAGGACTCCGGGGCAGA
ACCCAGTCGGTTCACCTGGTCAGCCCCAGGCCTCGCCCTGAGCGCTGTGCCTCGTCTCCGGAGCCAC
ACGCGCTTTAAAAAGGAGGCAAGACAGTCAGCCTCTGGAAATTAGACTTCTCCAAATTTTTCTCTAG
CCCTTTGGGCTCCTTTACCTGGCATGTAGGATGTGCCTAGGGAGATAAACGGTTTTGCTTTAGTTGT
CGCCAAGGCAGTTCCCTTCCAAACTAGCGCTAGAGCGAATGAGCGAGCAGCCAGGACCACCATTCTG
GGTTTCCAACAGGCGAAAAGGCCCTTTCTGAGTTTGAAATGTCACAGGGTTCCTAACAGGCCACTCT
TCCCTGGATGGGGTGCCAACGCCTTTCCCATGGGCATCTCCTTCCACCCTCACGCTGGCCCAGCAAG
CAGGCAGTGCTGAGGCCTTATCTCCCTAGGTGACAGATGTGGTCAGGGAGGCGCAGAGAGGATGGGC
ACTAGCGTCCAGCTCCTGGAACAGGTGTCAGGCAGGGAGGGCAGACAGGTCTTGGGAACATGTTCCC
CTGGCTATGTGGACAGAGGACTTCTCAGTGGGTCTCGCGACCCTGTGCCCCTTTTCCTGGTTCAGGG
CAGCCTTAGCCGGGGCAAAGGTCGAGAAAGAAACCCCTGGTCGCCGCCCTGGCAGAATTTGAGTGGC
TCCGGCAGGAGATGTCCCTAGGTTCCTGGGGAGGGAGGACGTCGGGGGCCAGCCAGGCTTACCCCCCC
CTGCCGCTGAGACTTCTGCGCTGATGCACCGCGCCTCTTCGCGGTCTCCCTGTCCTTGCAGAAACTA
GACACAATGTGCGACGAAGACGAGACCACCGCCCTCGTGTGCGACAATGGCTCCGGCCTGGTGAAAG
CCGGCTTCGCCGGGGATGACGCCCCTAGGGCCGTGTTCCCGTCCTCCATCGTGGGCCGCCCCGACACCA
GGTCAGGCTGCCCCTCCGCAGAGGGAGCCGGCTCGGGGTCCCCGCGTAAGCCAGCCTGGTGCCACC
```

Figure 53: The arrangement of DNA codes dictates the physical form

more. It consists of codes known as A, G, C and T (Adenine, Guanine, Cytosine, Thymine). How the codes are arranged in relation to each other decides if something manifests as a human, mouse or virus, for instance. The differences in code arrangement can by very small compared with the differences in form (Fig 53). Rats have something like 90 per cent of the DNA found in humans. DNA code sequences look a little like the digital codes seen in *The Matrix* movie series, and that is no surprise when DNA is digital in nature on one level. DNA is a software program that offers Consciousness a particular experience called 'being human'. An article in *The San Francisco Chronicle* said: 'DNA is a universal software code. From bacteria to humans, the basic instructions for life are written with the same language.' Knowing this will be very important when I come to describe the genetic software of the families that seek to control us. We are aware of the holographic expression of DNA, but in its base form it is an information field. It is also a receiver–transmitter which interacts with the Cosmic Internet and can connect us with many dimensions of frequency outside the tiny frequency range of visible light. You would expect a receiver–transmitter to involve crystals in some way, and it turns out that the human body is basically a liquid crystal. DNA, or deoxyribonucleic acid, is crystalline, and the membrane of every one of our some 70 trillion cells is a liquid crystal. Earth is vastly crystalline, because it is also receiving and transmitting. DNA is a monumental receiver–transmitter of information, as this Internet article pointed out:

> From the characteristic form of this giant molecule – a wound double helix – the DNA represents an ideal electromagnetic antenna. On one hand it is elongated and thus a blade which can take up very well electrical pulses. On the other hand, seen from above, it has the form of a ring and thus is a very magnetical antenna.

We connect to the Cosmic Internet vibrationally, electrically, digitally and holographically. DNA is at the heart of this and it has been described as a 'biological Internet'. Mainstream science ridiculously labels between 90 and 97 per cent of DNA (depending on who you talk to) 'junk DNA'. They do this because they have no idea what it does and, from their version of reality, it appears to serve no function. I would say that there are two main reasons for 'junk DNA'. One is that some of it has been purposely 'switched off' for reasons I will get to later in the book. The second is that large swathes of 'junk DNA' are interacting with other realities and also following a pre-programmed software code which, again, I will explain in due course. Russian scientists have discovered that DNA can create magnetised 'wormholes' – tunnels of communication with other levels of the Universe beyond what we call space and time. Pjotr Garjajev, a Russian biophysicist and molecular biologist, has done some great work in this field. He and his associates across many disciplines have established that DNA is involved with data storage and communication as well as its genetic functions.

It is a superconductor able to operate at body temperature and not at the extremely low temperatures necessary for the artificial variety. Superconductors can carry very large amounts of electricity for a very long time without losing energy in the form of heat. I read an article on superconductors that said: 'The future of superconductivity research is to find materials that can become superconductors at room temperature. Once this happens, the whole world of electronics, power and transportation will be revolutionized.' DNA does exactly that, but this knowledge has been suppressed around the world to stop *human awareness* being revolutionised. The Russians confirmed that DNA can be reprogrammed by words and frequencies. These are really the same thing. Words are frequencies. The Russian team discovered that DNA follows similar patterns of grammar and rules to those found in human languages and that this could be the origin of language communication. Experiments showed that DNA can be healed simply through vibrations and words. But that *must* be so. DNA is a crystalline receiver–transmitter and its base form is vibrational, as with everything in the Universe. The ability to change DNA by vibrational means will all be seriously relevant later when I explain how the Control System works from the depths of the rabbit hole where, to my knowledge, no one has ever been before.

The Russian team says that this greater understanding of DNA's role as a receiver–transmitter can explain intuition, clairvoyance, telepathy, spontaneous healing and self-healing, and how humans can influence the weather and each other. These are all phenomena of DNA either receiving or transmitting as it interacts with the multi-levelled Cosmic Internet. The team realised that living DNA chromosomes 'function just like solitonic/holographic computers using ... DNA laser radiation'. *Yessssss.* Exactly! I have known all this since 2003 from the information that came to me on the subject in many forms following my experience with the 'voice' in Brazil. 'Solitonic' refers to a pulse-like wave that 'does not dissipate and can travel long distances with little loss of energy or structure'. In short, we are looking at a holographic biological and waveform receiver–transmitter computer system. The Russian research group successfully transmitted information patterns from one DNA to another and changed the form it was manifesting. They transformed frog embryos to salamander embryos in one experiment by transmitting salamander DNA information patterns. This will be very significant when I come to the subject of 'shapeshifing' and the manipulation of human genetics. We can communicate with our DNA and heal ourselves. This is where the theme of 'mind over matter' comes from. There is no matter so there is no need to have your mind over it. We only need to use Consciousness to communicate on the right frequency with another form of Consciousness – DNA. The Hidden Hand behind human affairs knows all of this. DNA is being targeted by all manner of means to enslave us in the vibrational box of five-sense ignorance when we should be so much more. DNA is being influenced by the words that we hear, and by radiation. Mothers are giving birth to babies with horrific genetic defects after being subjected to the depleted uranium in American, British and NATO bombs and missiles dropped on their countries. The radiation has scrambled their DNA. The cumulative effect of exposure to radiation in all its forms, including full-body scanners, mobile phones and nuclear 'accidents' like the one at Fukushima in Japan can be devastating to DNA, and therefore to our health. But, on the other hand, the reality-transforming potential of DNA is incredible when it is allowed to function in anything like its natural state.

Time's up

Most people are obsessed and controlled by what is known as 'time'. 'What's the time?' 'Is that the time?' 'I'm running out of time.' 'I have time on my hands.' 'The time has flown.' But, like 'space', there is no 'time'. It is simply information encoded into the waveform fabric of the Universe which we *decode* as time. The way we decode it dictates how fast or slow 'time' appears to 'pass'. Information on a software disk can appear on the computer screen as pictures that seem to have space and time. The sequence moves from stage to stage and it seems like 'time' is moving forward. The scenes appear to have distance and perspective. But all of this is only information on a disk being read by the computer. This is what we do with regard to 'space' and 'time'. When scientists talk about 'space–time' or the 'space–time continuum', they are talking about something akin to a computer game being decoded to *appear* as 'space' and 'time'. It's all illusion. We perceive

Figure 54: What we call 'clock-time' is an illusory construct and yet it dominates the lives of billions

almost unimaginable 'distances' between stars and planets when we look at the night sky when the whole scene exists only in our decoding system. There is no 'distance' or 'space' – only one infinite *everything* in which infinity and a pin head are the same. How can time as we measure it be 'real' when you can pass an invisible line in the ocean and go into tomorrow; or go the other way and enter yesterday? The so-called 'international dateline' is not even straight. It wanders all over the place to accommodate locations that wish to be in yesterday or tomorrow (Fig 54). The Gregorian calendar that most people use to chart 'time' throughout the 'year' is a joke. It is only there because Pope Gregory XIII signed a decree in 1582 that decided this would be. They had to follow September 2nd with September 14th to make it all fit when it was first introduced. Eleven days just disappeared!

There is only one moment – what is known as the NOW. Everything happens in that moment. There is no other. Most people would see the NOW as the 'present' on the journey from 'past' to 'future'. But there is no past and future; there is only the NOW. 'Oh, but' people cry, 'there *must* be a past and future.' Okay, when we talk about the 'past', where are we? In the NOW. When we talk about the 'future', where are we? In the NOW. Everything happens, and can only happen, in the NOW. But our power to impact upon the NOW is constantly diluted by living mentally and emotionally in the 'past' (regret, resentment, guilt, even nostalgia) and the 'future' (ambition, anxiety, fear of what is to 'come'). 'Past' and 'future' are states of mind and emotion, not states of 'fact'. People have a very different relationship with reality when they go into any form of deep meditation and move beyond the realm of perceived 'time'. This happened to me in the stone circle in Peru, in the rainforest in Brazil and on endless occasions since. Another important point here is that while body–mind operates in illusory 'time', Consciousness is a state of no-time – the NOW. This alone can massively contribute to the disconnection of communication and awareness between body–mind and Consciousness, and this is a major reason why human society is founded in so many ways on clock-watching. I am not saying that people should ignore clock 'time' and date 'time' if they need to interact with others welded to the existence of 'time'. I am saying that when people make a date to 'meet at four o'clock', they are aware that it is an illusory moment and just another term for the NOW. Acknowledging the illusion for what it is loosens its grip upon your sense of reality. The NOW is the only moment that we can meet anyone whether we call it four o'clock or twenty-past six. I was told through psychic, Betty Shine, in 1990 that time as we perceive it would eventually appear to move so quickly that it would be frightening; and there are certainly many people now who are feeling that 'time' is speeding up.

Figure 55: 'Time' is like watching a DVD – our sense of the 'present' is only where the disc is being read at that moment; but this also dictates our sense of the 'past' (the scenes we have watched) and the 'future' (the scenes we have yet to watch)

Illustration by Neil Hague (www.neilhague.com)

I have written extensively over the years about something that I call the 'Time Loop' and I even wrote a book called *Tales from the Time Loop*. The term describes the circular way that the Universe, as we experience it, 'moves' through a sequence and returns pretty much back to the start. We don't realise this when we only experience a small section of the 'loop' called a 'lifetime'. We seem to be moving from 'past' to 'future'. Ancient societies such as those in Asia, and the Mayan people in Central America, believed that 'time' goes around in a circle involving different periods, epochs or 'yugas', in which the life experience is very different. They say that some epochs/yugas allow for great expansion of awareness and are often referred to as the 'Golden Age'. Others are 'dark' periods of oppression, suppression and ignorance, according to this view. They each offer different experiences, and Consciousness chooses where it wishes to join the 'ride', or at least that is the way it seems. I will, however, be adding a 'Big *But*' to this towards the end of the book. Those of us 'here' today have chosen to experience the cusp of an enormous transformation of awareness among many other things. You might see a contradiction in saying that time is illusory and yet also circular, but there is no paradox here. The 'Time Loop' is the holographic level of perception as we decode information in the NOW into an apparent sequence of events. It would look like a 'loop' if you could see the whole thing in the holographic realm. But the holographic is only a decoded projection of the waveform information construct and this information does not 'move' in a circle; it vibrates in the NOW. It goes through a *vibrational* sequence of changing *information*, and as we decode that into holographic reality we appear to be moving from past to future. But we're not. The 'Time Loop' is, once again, an illusion created by the way we decode and experience reality. Every part of the 'loop', whether you call it an epoch or yuga exists in the same NOW. 'Time' is like viewing a movie on DVD (Fig 55). The scene you are watching (experiencing) is your perception of the 'present'; those you have watched are your sense of the 'past'; and

THE TIME LOOP

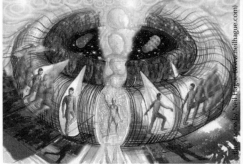

Figures 56 and 57: The Time Loop when we retain a connection to Consciousness is a very different experience compared with when we don't

those you have yet to watch are the 'future'. But the *whole movie* exists at the same 'time' – NOW. Your fix on 'where' you are 'in time' is dictated by the information the laser is decoding at any point. The Time Loop is the same, but it is an *interactive* virtual-reality 'game'. We can change reality when we interact with it, as it can change us. If we retain a connection to Consciousness we can access far greater insight into what is happening in the Time Loop. If we are entrapped in mind–body we can become lost and bewildered in a strange and crazy 'world' in which we don't know who we are, where we are, or what the hell we are actually experiencing (Figs 56 and 57).

If you think all that is far-out, get this: Nothing is made, built or constructed in the way that we perceive it with a series of actions or events taking place that lead to an outcome – a car, house or strawberry yoghurt. The car, house and strawberry yoghurt are created *first* and the *apparent* sequence of actions and events that *appear* to 'make' them in our perception of reality comes *after* they are manifested by thought in their completed form in the unseen realms of waveform – the 'Metaphysical Universe'. I say 'after', but it is really all happening in the same infinite NOW. The mind-body computer and human programmed perception cannot understand, decode or know that level of awareness and potential when something can be manifested in a flash from the power of thought, imagination and Consciousness. So we decode a sequence of actions and events that lead us through the process of 'physical' (holographic) creation through car factories, house builders, dairies, and so on. 'Here is a car' becomes '*build* me a car'. The same applies to personal experiences. The 'outcome' has already happened and the sequence to 'get' there (the 'time-frame') is constructed by mind-body to satisfy the limits of its sense of the possible and our belief in the literal existence of 'time'. We are also encouraged to do this 'time-framing' by the human Control System and DNA programs in ways that I will come to later in the book. Deep, eh? But that is how far we are in daily human perception from understanding – *remembering* – the true nature of self and reality. When I say it is all an illusion – I *mean* illusion.

Whole brain or pea-brain?

We cannot understand human society and the way we decode this prison reality without an awareness of the two 'personalities', or hemispheres, of the brain and how they function. We have the left-brain and the right-brain with a bridge called the corpus callosum connecting the two. This bridge is supposed to allow the two hemispheres to 'talk' to each other, work together and make us 'whole-brained' (Figs 58 and 59). Most people are not, however. The structure and nature of human society is specifically directed at preventing that. The functions of the two

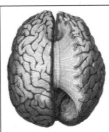

Figures 58 and 59: The two hemispheres of the brain with the corpus callosum 'bridge'; and Neil Hague's symbolic portrayal of their very different natures

sides of the brain are very different. The left-brain is 'logical and rational' in its definition of logical and rational. It decodes information in the NOW into a sequence. This is basically where 'time' comes from. The quicker the left-brain advances this sequence, the faster time seems to pass, and vice versa. The left hemisphere is 'analytical and objective' (it only exists if I can see it, hear it, touch it, taste it or smell it). Crucially, it decodes reality as *parts* rather than as a single *whole*. The left-brain gives us the perception of everything being apart from everything else with 'space' in between. It creates structures – *loves 'em* – and decodes language. I have just described the world as it is currently 'lived'. We live in a left-brain reality and this has been manipulated to be so. In the right-brain lives the maverick – the random and intuitive, the artist and creative inspiration of all kinds. The right-brain brings everything together. It perceives 'wholes', not parts. The left-brain sees individual dots, but the right brain can see how they fit together. Left-brain-dominated people control science, academia, medicine, politics, big business, religion, media and the military. These, in turn, act as the soldiers at the gate to the collective left-brain and work to keep right-brain reality at bay. Left-brain rules, OK? Neil Hague's excellent portrayal of the left-brain 'firewall' in Figure 60 captures the essence of how most of humanity, and certainly the overwhelming majority of those in positions of influence and power, are entrapped in the left hemisphere. This is the realm of apartness, structure, language and what passes for 'logic'. This is where the Control System wants us. They don't want human right-brains connecting the dots and seeing the picture; or expressing spontaneity and uniqueness when uniformity and conformity are essential to the mass control of the many by the few. Look at how large numbers of sheep are kept in order through daily conformity by a single shepherd (authority) and a sheepdog (fear). The sheep would be uncontrollable in this way if they expressed their uniqueness and spontaneity. Instead, they just repeat the same behaviour.

Human society is structured specifically to enslave us in the left side of the brain by rewarding the left-brainers and marginalising the right-brainers. This is so obvious with 'education'. We are now seeing even pre-school children being introduced to academic-type information to stimulate the left-brain and to reduce the period of ad-lib play that

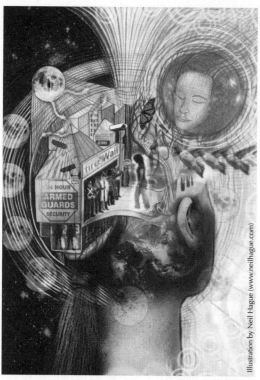

Illustration by Neil Hague (www.neilhague.com)

Figure 60: The Control System has guards at the gate to stop right-brain reality awakening the left-brain prison. We call these 'guards' teachers, journalists, scientists, doctors, politicians and peer pressure

opens the imagination and stimulates the right side of the brain. 'Education' targets the left-brain with academic information (much of it plain wrong) and then demands that the child or student repeats on the exam paper what the system has told them is 'real'. If you can do this very well, you pass your examinations (examination of your perception of reality). This qualifies you to attend college or university to put you in debt for most of your life to pay back the fees. The same process of left-brain information repeated on exam papers now ensues at a 'higher' level (of programming). Then you go off into the world with your 'good grades' and 'degree' (degree of programming) and you could choose to be a scientist, doctor, teacher or a professor like Dogma Dawkins. This involves still more memorising of the system's version of reality in the left side of the brain, and still more examinations to check how deeply your sense of reality has been hijacked. The vast majority of people who have been through this sausage machine are imprisoned in the left-brain for the rest of their lives. These same left-brain prisoners are appointed to run and direct the administration of the institutions of science, medicine and government etc., to maintain and expand the left-brain-prison society. Politics is dominated by left-brainers; so is science, medicine and the media. Most 'journalists' are no more than left-brain jailbirds reporting the beliefs, decisions and actions of their fellow inmates. Mainstream scientists are never going to grasp the nature of reality through their left-brain lenses or microscopes when what they really need to see is that everything is connected to everything else. The left-brain can't grasp (decode) that. How can left- brain 'journalists' tell us what is really going on in the world when you need to see wholes and not only parts to understand how the dots connect? Religions are structures of the left-brain with their hierarchy and dogma. The left and right hemispheres are not 'good guy' and 'bad guy'. They should be working together so we have the best of both. You see far-out creative people who are so dominated by right-brain reality that they cannot function in left-brain society. The right hemisphere is also open to hypnotic suggestion and programming. This is not about one or the other, but *both* working in unison. This is the last thing the Control System wants. There are people known as 'autistic savants' who can achieve extraordinary feats of the mind. Well, extraordinary to those who see human potential in such limited terms. Stephen Wiltshire, an 'autistic savant' in the UK, is famous for drawing whole cities from the air after only a short time looking out from a helicopter window. In 1987, when he was only 12, the BBC flew him over London for half an hour and he was not allowed to make notes or take photographs. He came down and drew London from the air in incredible detail that included 200 buildings (Fig 61). Their hundreds of windows were accurately portrayed even though his autism meant that he couldn't count. You can see Stephen's work at:

Figure 61: Stephen Wiltshire and his amazing artwork

www.stephenwiltshire.co.uk. Daniel Tammet is another British 'autistic savant' capable of exceptional mental abilities. He can process mathematical calculations at computer-like speed and learns languages, even the most challenging ones, amazingly quickly. He was once challenged by a television programme to learn Icelandic in a week – and he did. His language teacher described him as a 'genius' and 'not human'. Ah, but he is human. He is the human we once were and will be again when those who have genetically, mentally and emotionally enslaved us get their backsides out of here. The foundation of these apparently extraordinary abilities is they take a right-brain picture of a scene or language as one *whole*. While left-brain people are breaking a language down into syllables or trying to remember individual buildings, these guys just go 'click-gotcha'.

From experience

Jill Bolte Taylor is an American brain scientist, or 'neuroanatomist' who had an experience in 1996 that confirmed many of the concepts and explanations I am talking about. She woke up one morning feeling not too well, but she decided to work through her malaise and headed for the exercise machine. Jill looked at her hands gripping the bar and they appeared to be 'primitive claws'. Her whole body began to look very different. She said that it felt as if her consciousness had shifted away from her 'normal' reality, in which she was the one having the experience, into another perception in which she was a witness *observing* that experience. She later realised that she was having a stroke in the left side of her brain, which, as it malfunctioned, was no longer decoding reality into the world she thought she was living 'in'. Look at what she said. She changed from being the one *having* the experience to becoming the one *witnessing* the experience. Remember what I said about Consciousness observing through the body–computer in the same way that we observe and interact with the Internet through a desktop computer? Jill said that she could no longer define where her body ended and the rest of the room began. 'The atoms and the molecules of my arm blended with the atoms and molecules of the wall, she said. 'All I could detect was this energy.' What she called her 'brain chatter' then went silent: 'It was like someone had taken a remote control and pushed the mute button.' This is an important point. Most people have this chatter and gossip running through their minds. It constructs scenarios that cause worry, anxiety or anger when they will never actually happen. But most of this constant blah, blah, blah is not YOU – *Consciousness*. It is the mind–body biological computer which literally has a mind of its own. Stop for a moment and mentally detach from the chatter and simply observe it. The observer is who you are. Everything else, including the brain chatter, is the *experience*. The Infinite is all-knowing, still and silent All Possibility, and Jill Bolte Taylor found that her new world of silence was a wonderful place to be:

> I was immediately captivated by the magnificence of energy around me. And because I could no longer identify the boundaries of my body, I felt enormous and expansive. I felt at one with all the energy that was, and it was beautiful there ...

> ... Imagine what it would be like to be totally disconnected from your brain chatter that connects you to the external world. So here I am in this space and any stress related to me, to my job, it was gone. And I felt lighter in my body. And imagine all of the relationships in the external world and the many stressors related to any of those, they were gone. I felt a sense of peacefulness ...

> ... Because I could not identify the position of my body in space, I felt enormous and expansive, like a genie just liberated from her bottle. And my spirit soared free like a great whale gliding through the sea of silent euphoria. Nirvana, I found Nirvana. I remember thinking there's no way I would ever be able to squeeze the enormousness of myself back inside this tiny little body.

Jill was experiencing reality beyond the left-brain decoding system, but when she returned from what she called 'La La Land' she realised that she had a big problem and she needed to deal with it. She couldn"t remember the telephone number at work, so she searched for a business card. As she thumbed through a pile of cards, she could not see the 'physical' level of them – only pixels. Yes, *pixels*, the smallest single components in a *digital* image. The malfunction in her left-brain had caused her decoding system to malfunction. She was now seeing the digital level of reality. Craig Hogan, an American physicist, said in the *New Scientist* article about holograms that at a certain level of magnification 'the fabric of space–time becomes grainy and is ultimately made of tiny units rather like pixels ...' It took Jill 45 minutes to relate the pixel squiggles on the card to those on the phone and that was only possible because of 'brief waves of clarity'. The rest of the time 'the pixels of the words on the business cards blended with pixels of the background and the pixels of the symbols'. She dialled the number and a work colleague answered, but all Jill heard was 'whoo, whoo, whoo'. She replied, or thought she did, with, 'This is Jill! I need help!' But again all she heard was 'whoo, whoo, whoo'. She said they both sounded like a 'golden retriever'. The left-brain decodes language and the haemorrhage was preventing it from doing so. This gave Jill her 'silent mind' and the inability to hear (decode) language. There *is* no language or sound until the brain decodes them from vibrational information. Jill lost consciousness, but survived, and it was an experience that changed her life. Well it would, wouldn't it? She said:

> If I have found Nirvana and I'm still alive, then everyone who is alive can find Nirvana. And I picture a world filled with beautiful, peaceful, compassionate, loving people who knew that they could come to this space at any time.

One other major observation from Jill Bolte Taylor's experience: emotion. She said: '... imagine what it would feel like to lose 37 years of emotional baggage! I felt euphoria. Euphoria was beautiful.' It is not only the constant brain chatter that isn't 'us'. Most human 'emotion' isn't 'us' either. You can dramatically change someone's emotional state with chemicals in drugs and food additives. So how can those emotions be 'us'? Emotional disturbance can be seen in children who eat and drink this crap and have all the countless vaccinations. More than 40 years ago a British woman descended into extreme depression after having a large number of mercury tooth fillings. The media reported her miraculous recovery four decades later after she had the fillings removed and embarked on a mercury detoxification programme. If you had asked her during those years who 'she' was, she would have said that she was a clinical depressive. But she wasn't. The mind–body computer had been imbalanced by the toxic mercury (a vibrational distortion at its base level) and caused a distortion in the way it decoded reality. We also talk about being men and women, or being 'human'. But these are our current *experience*, not our true self. How can 'we' be men and women when chemical influence can change you from one to the other? People in Britain might remember the story in the media about Freaky the chicken. 'She' started out life as a hen laying eggs, but then an explosion of testosterone made 'her' a 'him'. Freaky grew a comb, began crowing at dawn and chasing the hens. 'Men' and 'women' are a *software program*. Did someone stroll up to Freaky and say, 'Hey, mate, you're a man now – you have to crow when the sun comes up.'? No, he just did it. He was now decoding the male chicken program in the same way that we decode the human program and its sub-divisions known as races and cultures. *We* are not 'human'. *We* are Consciousness having a human experience. People who have been released from the lens of body–mind know too well that this is the case. I have read extensively over the years about those who have had 'near death' experiences and what happened when they were freed from the limitations of the mind–body computer. The common themes are extremely compelling and this one encapsulates all that I have been saying here:

> ... everything from the beginning, my birth, my ancestors, my children, my wife, everything comes together simultaneously. I saw everything about me, and about everyone who was around me. I saw everything they were thinking now, what they thought then, what was happening before, what was happening now. There is no time; there is no sequence of events, no such thing as limitation, of distance, of period, of time, of place. I could be anywhere I wanted to be simultaneously.

That is who you are, *and so much more*. That is what we all are, and so much more. This is what the families and secret societies of the Control System don't want us to know or remember. They want us to believe that we are just a little 'person' with no power to impact significantly upon our own reality and experience. Too bad, fellahs. Those days are drawing to an end. The near-death or out-of-body experience described here also confirms what I have said about the perceived 'sequence' of 'creating' a product or outcome when they already exist – '*There is no time; there is no sequence of events*'.

Heart is the key

There is one more absolutely pivotal point to make before we move on. This is about the central importance of the heart. Most people think the heart is only an electrical pump that ensures that blood (information) circulates around the body, but it is so much more than that. Research in recent years by the Institute of HeartMath in the United States, and from other sources, has established that the heart is fundamental to stabilising or destabilising emotions and to harmonising or disharmonising the interaction between itself, the nervous system and the brain. This is the trinity of heart, mind and emotions. When they are out of sync, so are we. The heart has now been shown to have its own innate intelligence (far more than the brain); its own nervous system, called the 'heart brain'; and it has been found to be a sensory organ that *decodes and encodes information*. There are more nerves going from the heart to the brain than going the other way. The heart is constantly communicating to the brain and the whole body through the nervous system, electromagnetic fields, hormones and other chemical reactions and blood pressure waves. The heart is also an endocrine gland secreting hormones that can cure many diseases, including cancer. David Vesely, M.D. PhD, chief of endocrinology, diabetes and metabolism at the James A. Haley VA Hospital in Tampa and a professor of medicine, molecular pharmacology and physiology at the University of South Florida, found that heart hormones killed up to *97 per cent* of all cancers in cell cultures within 24 hours. We have come a long way from the heart being just an electrical pump. We feel intuition – intuitive *knowing* – through the heart and heart chakra vortex. The brain *thinks*; the heart *knows*. When we have intuition about something we don't need to sit down and use the mind to *think* it through. We just *know*. If you have the intuitive knowing that you need to be in a certain place tomorrow, you don't have to ponder on the pros and cons, the ifs and buts. You just *know* you have to be there. The mind has to think and try to work everything out, because it *doesn't* know. The heart generates 60 times the electrical output of the brain, and connects us, through the heart chakra vortex, to far higher levels of awareness. This is why intuition *knows*. People are pressured not to 'trust' their intuition and to go instead with their head; but that leads only to enslavement to the patterns of conformity and repeating behaviour. The heart is a real genius of our decoding system and a connection to even greater genius. The Control System has manipulated human perception so that the heart has been usurped by worship of the brain, the mind. A mind society looks like the one that we are experiencing, but a *heart* society would be one of love, respect, peace, harmony, incredible levels of intelligence and with a daily tidal wave of creativity and insight. People rightly talk about the 'wisdom of the heart'.

My heart has been the foundation of everything I have done since I began to awaken in 1990. It has been the source of insights galore into what is happening in the world; the reason that I will go with information A and reject information B; why I will drop everything and go somewhere purely on intuition only to find that there was a significant reason to be there at that moment. My brain/mind would be kicking and cussing and telling me at first all the reasons why I should not do any of these things; but there came a moment soon after I began my great adventure when my 'head' had observed enough times that when you follow your intuitive heart it all works out, despite some challenges along the way. This was the moment when my head and my heart became *one*. Head and heart have moved as one unit since then. My heart says, 'I feel to do this,' and my head says, 'Okay, let's go.' What I intuitively feel – *know* – and what I think, are the same. There is a war within most people between their head and their heart, and the head normally wins. It is time to change that, and in doing so change the world from a prison to a paradise. The Control System targets the heart more than anything else. The manipulators work to suppress the connection to heart intelligence, wisdom and knowing. This is vital if they are to imprison humanity in the 'head' – five-sense reality. One of the ways

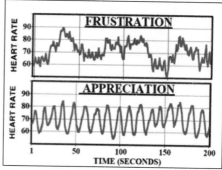

Figure 62: The very different electrical heart rhythms generated by incoherent and coherent emotional states

they do this is by manipulating events to trigger states of low-vibrational, imbalanced emotion. They want us angry, frustrated, fearful, resentful, depressed and irritable. They want us to close our heart and make it a bystander in the process of decoding reality and perception. Considerable research has shown that these emotional states generate incoherent – imbalanced – heart rhythm patterns. This, in turn, distorts the relationship between the heart, nervous system and brain, and all hell can break lose mentally, emotionally and 'physically'. Now we can see why heart disease is one of the biggest killers on Planet Earth – heart rhythm incoherence. The heart can only take so much before it's up and out of here. This is how stress and other emotions causes heart attacks and why people *do* die from a 'broken heart' when the emotional impact of a trauma or shock triggers severe heart rhythm incoherence. This is also what causes 'heartache'. Love, compassion, caring and appreciation have been shown to do the opposite. They lead to *coherent* heart rhythm patterns (Fig 62). The Institute of HeartMath has developed techniques through which the power of the heart, in its electrical output alone, can be used to bring emotional balance to the body and to work in harmony with the rest of our being. I can recommend a book called *Transforming Anger* (Raincoast Books 2003) which is authored by Doc Childre and Deborah Rozman.

I have talked in this chapter about how we decode reality and perception through the brain and genetic structure from the vibrational to the holographic. It is therefore appropriate that I end it by emphasising that the key to this process is the heart. This must be allowed to play its crucial role in decoding a new reality – one of love, peace, harmony and, yes, true, innate intelligence way beyond anything that the programmed brain can deliver. The further we go in this book the more obvious that will be.

4

The Schism

I have been explaining how the Universe is made manifest from a waveform information construct that is expressed electrically, digitally and holographically. Everything in the Universe is the same, be they stars, planets, people, flowers or trees.

A growing band of *real* scientists and researchers have been working for many years to identity the electrical level of the Universe. I am not saying that they accept the existence of the vibrational, digital and holographic realities that I am talking about, but they have done some magnificent work to highlight how the Universe operates electrically. Two leading researchers in this field are David Talbott and Wallace Thornhill. They have produced two excellent books, *The Electric Universe* and *Thunderbolts of the Gods*, which I thoroughly recommend. The Universe, on one level, is clearly a seething mass of electricity and electromagnetic fields. We are all familiar with lightning and we know that this is caused by electricity, not least because it's blindingly obvious (Fig 63). But there is far more to lightning than we think. People see electrical flashes and forks in the sky and they believe this is as far as it goes. What we don't see are the electrical connections from the lightning near the ground going up through Earth's atmosphere to connect with the cosmic electrical field that pervades the Universe. Virtually simultaneous with a lightning strike that we see are electrical flashes at higher altitudes that have been dubbed 'elves', 'sprites', 'gnomes' and 'jets' (Fig 64). The evidence is that this electrical circuit continues into the ionosphere in the upper region of the atmosphere and on to the solar field and the wider cosmos. Joseph Dwyer of the Florida Institute of Technology wrote in *The Geophysical Review* in 2003: 'The conventional view of how lightning is produced is wrong, and so the true origin of lightning remains a mystery.' Well, it does if you don't realise that the Universe is pervaded by electricity and electromagnetic fields and

Figure 63: Lightning is the most obvious expression of the Electric Universe

that in certain circumstances currents are discharged. The planet works like a capacitor used in electronics to gather and store electrical charge. Earth stores electricity between its surface and the ionosphere in the upper atmosphere, and when the charge build-up gets too powerful the pressure has to be released. We call this 'lightning'. Tornadoes are electrical phenomena and result from rapidly-rotating electrical charges. This is the reason why tornadoes are associated with electrical storms. The Aurora Borealis, or Northern Lights, is also an electrical phenomenon (Fig 65). So much is explained once you see that we are interacting with an electrical universe. We don't see the electrical web most of the time unless it reaches certain states of charge and discharge, but it is an organising and communication fabric of our experienced reality. Mainstream science has denied that electricity exists out in 'space' and says that celestial bodies are electrically neutral and move through a vacuum. But they accept at the same time the existence of electromagnetic fields in space. This is extraordinary when you can't have electromagnetic fields without electricity. But protecting dogma and fixed positions is far more important to the Dogma Dawkins' than opening their minds to the blatantly obvious. Talbott and Thornhill rightly say in *The Electric Universe*: 'It has been said that the greatest obstacle to discovery is not ignorance, but the illusion of knowledge.' This is also a form of ignorance, but the point is taken. The mainstreamers talk about the 'vacuum' of space and say everything is driven by gravity. I weigh about 16 stone, or 224 pounds, but I can still jump in the air very easily. Crikey, this gravity is powerful isn't it? Talbott and Thornhill point out that the electrical force is about a thousand trillion, trillion, trillion times more powerful than gravity. It is electrical and electromagnetic forces that hold everything 'together' and secure planets in their repeating orbits around the Sun – *not gravity*, which is a far weaker

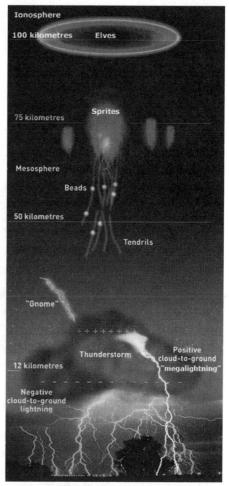

Figure 64: There is far more to lightning than the electrical flashes we see near the ground. It continues upwards into the cosmos

Figure 65: The Aurora Borealis, or Northern Lights

form of magnetism. These electrical forces, as with everything else, are information. The human brain receives and communicates through electrical information, and the heart beats electrically. We are interacting with the Cosmic Internet on one level through the electric Universe.

Conscious plasma

The observable Universe is 99.999 per cent plasma. This is a unique substance sometimes known as 'the fourth state of matter'. American Nobel laureate, Irving Langmuir (1881–1957), coined the term 'plasma' because of its life-like ability to self-organise as the electrical environment changes. It reminded him of blood plasma in that

Figure 66: The plasma ball – a symbol for the Electric Universe

electrical forces are carried in cosmic plasma in much the same way as red and white blood corpuscles are carried in blood plasma. Cosmic plasma is 'life-like' because it is an expression of *Consciousness*. We have all seen those plasma balls with the currents spiking out from the centre, and they give us a feel for the most crucial contribution of plasma in manifesting our reality (Fig 66). Plasma is a near-perfect medium for electricity and electromagnetic fields. When electrical currents pass through plasma, the interaction makes them spiral around each other. This creates filaments known as 'Birkeland currents', named after Kristian Olaf Birkeland (1867– 1917). He was a brilliant Norwegian scientist and a pioneer researcher of the electrical universe. These currents are flowing throughout the electrical/plasma universe and some are light years across while others are tiny. You can see in Figure 67 how the currents rotate around each other like a corkscrew and they are held apart by the very electromagnetic fields that their interaction creates. This is something known as the 'plasma pinch'. Brilliant. The same image can clearly be seen in the Double Helix Nebula near the centre of our galaxy. And what does it remind you of? *Human DNA* (Fig 68). This is not a coincidence. We are back to 'as above, so below' – the

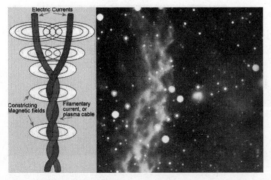

Figure 67: The Plasma pinch and its expression in the Double Helix Nebula

hologram. We are the Universe and the Universe is us. We are *everything* and everything is us. Compare again the similarity between human brain activity and electrical activity in the Universe (Fig 69). The human auric field has 'Birkeland currents', too, in the form of the meridians that carry the 'chi' energy around the body. The chi is *information* from many sources, including the electrical level of the Universe. Kundalini energy flowing from the base of the spine up through the main chakra

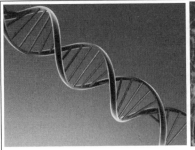 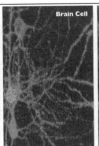 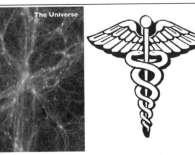

Figure 68: The similarity between the effect of the 'plasma pinch' and DNA is no coincidence

Figure 69: Electrical brain – electrical Universe

Figure 70: The kundalini caduceus

system and out through the top of the head also spirals in the same way. Kundalini has been depicted since ancient times as two intertwining snakes in a symbol called the caduceus (Fig 70). The central nervous system, a holographic expression of the kundalini/chakra system, is also electrical. We are communicating electrically with the Universe and with each other without knowing that we are doing so (Fig 71). DNA, and the genetic structure as a whole, is fundamentally involved with this interaction and I have emphasised that our reality is not decoded only by the brain. Humans have a meridian network carrying the chi, and the planet has the same with the network of meridians known as 'ley lines'. They form a communication and interaction grid between Earth and the electrical and vibrational universe. Massive vortices of electrical and vibrational energy (information) are created where many of these ley lines intersect. Ancient initiates

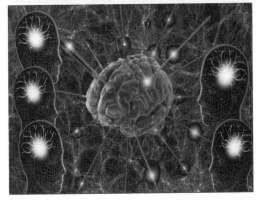

Figure 71: The electrical levels of mind-body connect with the electrical levels of the Universe

who had this knowledge located stone circles, temples and 'special' buildings at the major vortex points. Crystalline stones were used, because their role was to receive, transmit and amplify information (Fig 72). Crystalline DNA does the same. David Talbott and Wallace Thornhill write in *Thunderbolts of the Gods*:

From the smallest particle to the largest galactic formation, a web of electrical circuitry connects and unifies all of nature, organizing galaxies, energizing stars, giving birth to planets and, on our own world, controlling weather and animating biological organisms. There are no isolated islands in an electric universe.

The electrical expression of the Universe connects with the waveform, digital and holographic levels. Everything is a tapestry of interconnectedness – *Oneness*. When plasma infused with one kind of electrical charge meets plasma of a different charge, a

Figure 72: Stone circles were placed at major vortex points to interact with vibrational and electrical sources of cosmic communication

Figure 73: The Earth's magnetosphere is created by the 'Langmuir sheath' which is formed where two differently-charged plasma fields meet. © SOHO/EIT/LASCO

barrier is formed between the two. This is called a 'Langmuir sheath', named after scientist Irving Langmuir. These 'sheaths' form the planetary energy fields. Planets and stars are also electrical, and their very presence charges the plasma in a certain way. A sheath or barrier has been formed, for example, where plasma charged by the Earth meets differently-charged plasma out in 'space'. We call our side of that barrier the Earth's energy field or magnetosphere (Fig 73), but electrically-charged 'plasmasphere' would be far more accurate. This protects Earth and its inhabitants from dangerous radiation. The Sun has its own 'Langmuir sheath' called the 'heliosphere', and this is further protection for the Solar System from what would be highly destructive solar emissions. It is all a work of genius. Do we think that all this happened by some cosmic 'accident'? Or is it not rather more credible that it was made to be this way by some extraordinarily advanced 'software' programmer? Humans have their own 'magnetosphere' known as the 'auric field'. This operates with the same basic principles. Our electrical presence charges plasma around us differently to the Earth field. We talk about people having a 'powerful aura' or a 'weak aura'. This is related to the power of the charge – electromagnetic energy – that we are generating or tapping into. The Control System can disconnect us from the greater reality by manipulating our auric fields into energetic states that are very different to the fields that we are interacting with. This puts us not so much in a 'box', but in a 'bubble'. We have to understand at least the basics of how reality works before we can truly understand the nature of human control. It goes way beyond the five senses.

Electrical Sun

The Sun is also made of plasma and operates very differently to what is claimed by the scientific mainstream (Fig 74). Song-sheet scientists will tell you that the Sun is a gigantic nuclear reactor that generates heat and light from its core. But that is patent nonsense when you observe the evidence. The same goes for the idea that the Sun is heading for destruction through the process of producing heat and light from internal nuclear reactions. But it's not. They have next to nothing to support these claims and the evidence points another way. No matter. This unscientific mainstream crap goes on

being taught as fact in schools and
universities the world over. American
engineer and electric universe researcher,
Ralph Juergens, said: 'The modern
astrophysical concept that ascribes the
sun's energy to thermonuclear reactions
deep in the solar interior is contradicted by
nearly every observable aspect of the sun.'
I can tell you after researching so many
interrelated subjects since 1990 that if
mainstream science tells you *anything at all*
– check it, big-time. The Sun is an electrical

Figure 74: The plasma ball electrical Sun

transformer, and any nuclear reactions happen on its surface – not at its core. The Sun
transforms electricity in the cosmic plasma field (the Sun is 99 per cent plasma itself)
into what we call 'light' (a particular type of information). This is the same principle as
an electric lightbulb, which receives electricity and transforms it into light. The Sun goes
through cycles of higher and lower solar activity, just as electricity in the fabric of the
galaxy goes through cycles of high 'voltage' and low 'voltage' (Fig 75). The X-ray level
of the Sun dims when solar activity falls and this is the result of reduced *electrical*
activity. Think of a light on a dimmer switch. When you turn the electricity down, the
light gets weaker. The Sun is not producing light from inside itself; it is taking electricity
from the cosmic grid and transforming that into 'light'. The surface of the Sun is
relatively cool compared with the immense temperatures in the upper atmosphere. The

Figure 75: The electrical sun cycle

Figure 76: You only have to look at the Sun to see its electrical nature

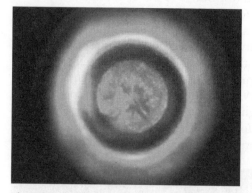

Figure 77: The Sun torus, or 'plasma doughnut'

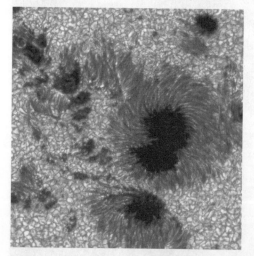

Figure 78: Sunspots are not created by internal activity, but by external strikes by massive charges of electricity

hottest part of the Sun is the corona – way out from the surface. The corona is the bright light that we see around the moon at the time of a total eclipse. The difference in temperature is enormous. The temperature is less than 5,000 degrees Kelvin three hundred miles from the surface, rising to *200 million* degrees at higher altitudes. It should be the other way around if the heat and light were being generated from within the Sun. But it all makes sense when you realise that the Sun is processing electricity sourced from the cosmos. We know that different parts of the Sun rotate at different speeds like a series of interacting electrical motors, and, well, *just look at it* (Fig 76). The Sun is a plasma ball processing *electricity*. Solar flares behave like lightning does. A 'plasma doughnut', or 'torus', can be clearly seen circling the solar equator when the Sun is photographed at the ultraviolet level (Fig 77). This is precisely what happens with plasma experiments in the laboratory. The torus draws in and accumulates cosmic electricity and this is released in the form of flares and what are called 'coronal mass ejections'. These strike the Sun's surface and punch holes that we know as sunspots (Fig 78). We are told that these are caused by ejections from within the Sun – but the opposite is true. More energy is obviously accumulated and released at the high end of the cosmic electrical cycle and so more flares punch more 'holes', or sunspots. Thus, the number of sunspots is an indicator of increased solar (electrical) activity. The Sun appears to change size in different phases of the cycle, because its plasma 'Langmuir sheath' shrinks and expands in line with electrical changes. We are also warned from time to time (and will be more so in the period ahead) that solar flares which project bursts of solar energy towards Earth could disrupt electrical technology, computer and satellite systems. Why would that happen? Because of the *electrical* effect on those *electrical* systems. Even NASA had to accept in 2007 that electromagnetic fields were the cause of the Aurora Borealis. It was reported that:

> New data from NASA's Themis mission ... found that the energy comes from charged particles from the Sun following like a current through twisted bundles of electromagnetic fields connecting Earth's upper atmosphere to the Sun.

They are describing the workings of the electric Universe.

'It's the electricity, stupid!'

Electrical energy processed by the Sun is the same energy flowing through the Milky Way galaxy and causing it to spiral. As it does so, it becomes a vast disc motor which, itself, produces electricity (Fig 79). The phenomenon of swirling galaxies can be reproduced in the laboratory by using plasma and electricity, as can other manifestations in the heavens, including nebulas (Fig 80). Mainstream 'scientific' dogma about the workings of the Universe cannot be reproduced in this way, and there is a good reason for that: the dogma is nonsense. We see comets with their long tails of light, and this is the interaction of the comet's electrical field with the electrically-charged plasma field. Mainstream scientists tell some long-winded story about comets being made of dust and ice that wasn't used in the formation of planets. They say that the tail is caused by the effect of solar heat on the 'ice'. Anything will do as long as they don't use that naughty word 'electricity'. The science establishment says that comets are gathered together in something called the 'Oort cloud' from which they enter the Solar System from time to time. This 'Oort cloud' has never been observed, because it doesn't exist. Or maybe it's just hiding. You can't trust these comets. They're very sneaky. 'Quick, someone's coming – act like you're the asteroid belt.' Great swathes of scientific 'fact' are just a compendium of fairy tales, and the system is structured and funded to make it so. The Control System doesn't want us to know about the reality we are

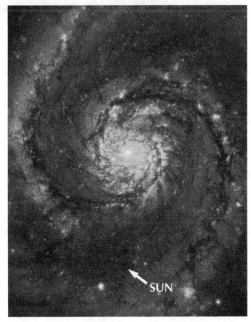

Figure 79: The Milky Way galaxy – a vast disc motor powered by electrical currents

experiencing. It wants us to live our lives ignorant, confused and bewildered in order to make control so much easier. The claim that the Universe started with the 'Big Bang' is a classic example of a constantly repeated theory becoming a constantly repeated 'fact' that is taught to each generation of children and students as 'this is how it is'. The theory goes that around 13.7 billion years ago, give or take a day or two, what we now call the Universe was compressed into the nucleus of an atom. They call this the

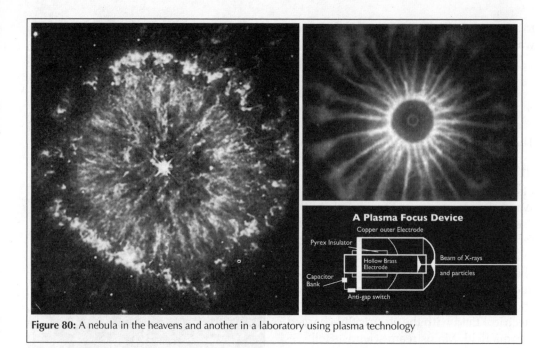

Figure 80: A nebula in the heavens and another in a laboratory using plasma technology

'singularity', and it is supposed to have happened before space and time existed (they still don't, except in their decoded form). Then came an explosion generating temperatures of trillions of degrees ('You can turn the heating off now, Ethel') and this 'Big Bang' created subatomic particles, energy, matter, space and time. Eventually, planets and stars were formed in a Universe that is still expanding from the force of the said 'Big Bang'. The theory was first postulated in 1927 by a Catholic priest, Georges Lemaître (1894–1966), at the Catholic University of Louvain. He was educated partly by the Jesuit Order, one of the premier secret societies in the global web. Lemaître called his Big Bang theory the 'hypothesis of the primeval atom'. A hypothesis since taught as fact. It has no credibility to anyone who looks at the evidence with an open mind. One of the main 'confirmations' that the Universe is still expanding from some 'Big Bang' is something called 'redshift' which, to put it simply, is the belief that celestial bodies appear to be red in the light spectrum when they are moving away due to the effect of frequency waves. The scientific establishment confidently gave us the date of their Big Bang – 13.7 billion years ago – from redshift calculations. But Edwin Hubble, the man credited with discovering redshift, said: 'It seems likely that redshift may not be due to an expanding universe, and much of the speculation on the structure of the universe may require re-examination.' Turns out he was right. The official cause of redshift is just another assumption, and not confirmation, that the Universe is expanding in line with, and in support of, the Big Bang theory. The redshift assumption also distorts by a fantastic degree the alleged distances between celestial bodies. How can you go on maintaining dogmatic 'norms' when you have been proved so spectacularly wrong so many times? The official explanation of Life and the Universe is in tatters wherever you look. The theory of black holes, as postulated by mainstream science, is also out of the window when you start to understand the electrical forces at work. I have used the term 'black holes' here and there, but in a completely different context to the 'scientific' mainstream. I am talking about connection and communication channels between realities – not something that gobbles up everything including light and denies it any escape. Interdimensional gateways or doorways would be a better way of putting it, like the principle of wormholes, through which energies and vibrational information can be exchanged. We are going to realise that these connecting gateways can profoundly impact upon this reality in terms of vibrational information. They can be found throughout the Universe.

Astrology is a science

The medical establishment, and those who live in the 'real world' (left-brain), wave aside any suggestion that you can treat a headache with a needle in the toe, or affect an organ by what you do to a specific point on the foot or the ear. They are so ignorant that they think they're intelligent, but they have no idea what the body really is. It's the same with astrology, or the ancient art of 'reading the stars'. Astrology is not an exact science, and cannot be when there is so much more to know about what is 'out there' and how it influences human personality. But it is a science when practised at a deep level. Nothing operates in electrical isolation in the electrical universe or its vibration foundation, the Metaphysical Universe. Planets and stars are electrical in nature and they impact, and are impacted upon, by interaction with the electrically-charged plasma field. We see the 'physical' (holographic) visible-light frequencies of planets and stars; but they are also electrical and vibrational information fields. They are interacting with the cosmic electrical and vibrational fields as they orbit the Sun and they are changing, and being changed by, the information in those fields. The impact is multiplied many times when they come together in certain alignments, or 'aspects'. We connect with the cosmic electrical energy and vibrational fields the moment we are born (some say conceived). The information in those fields at that moment dictates our 'star sign' and many more detailed astrological influences. Our astrological energy field – how the universe was when we were born/conceived – interacts throughout our lives with the ever-changing cosmic information grids in a different way to someone conceived or born at another point in the annual cycle. You often find clusters of people born in a certain (information) period who have similar gifts, abilities and personalities. Astrologically, an outcome can be more favourable if planned to coincide with certain positions of the planets and the stars (astro-logical). In the same way, we can experience resistance if the planetary positions are not taken into consideration should they be disharmonious. The Illuminati bloodline families and their secret society networks *know* this, while they pooh-pooh astrology in public. They plan everything they do with these universal forces in mind, vibrationally, electrically and digitally, through astrology, numerology and surfing energetic cycles. It wasn't coincidence that they launched the war in Libya in 2011 on the same vernal equinox that they invaded Iraq in 2003. There is another aspect to astrology, too. The Universe is a hologram in which everything is a smaller version of the whole, and so the movements and alignments of planets are happening within our own holographic field (Fig 81). As above, so below. We are very significantly affected and influenced by astrological forces, but, as ever, Consciousness can overcome them if it chooses to. Astrological readings that I have had throughout my life have shown me how much my journey for a long time was locked into an astrological path that was worked out in great detail before I arrived. It was part of the 'tramlines' that kept me 'on track'. It is the same with all of us, but there comes a time when we need to break through astrological patterns – with Consciousness. I am finding that astrological influences are less and less relevant to me. Not irrelevant, just not *as* relevant. I was told by an astrologer that the date of my speaking event in Times Square, New York, in 2010 was the worst possible day for me to do that. But the event was brilliant, the audience was brilliant, and I had a ball.

Worlds in Collision

Planets are maintained in their orbits by electrical and electromagnetic forces – not by 'gravity'. Anything that disrupts or distorts those forces is going to cause mayhem and likely catastrophe as the planets go 'walkabout'. This has certainly happened many times in our part of the Universe. There have been a series of cataclysmic events in the Solar System,

Figure 81: The holographic nature of 'physical' reality means that the human mind–body is a smaller version of the Solar System and the Universe

including one that affected the entire galaxy. It seems that our Milky Way galaxy 'collided' with its nearest large and separate galaxy neighbour, Andromeda, which is today, apparently, the farthest object that can be seen with the naked eye. Most people will dismiss the idea of galaxies colliding, but in 1994 astronomers discovered that what they call a 'dwarf galaxy' is colliding with the Milky Way now. The Andromeda collision was way back beyond any 'time' recorded by humans, and the Earth and the Solar System were not even where they are now before all this happened. The waveform construct of the galaxy was imbalanced by what happened and the 'clean-up' and 'clear-up' began by the creator-consciousness that established the 'game'. Worlds were repaired and species reseeded. This was not done by 'physical' means, but by reprogramming the 'game' at the *waveform* level of the information construct. Waveform realities (the 'Cosmic Internet') are beamed from the centre of the galaxy and 'picked up' by receivers in sync with the different ranges of frequency. The main 'receivers' and 'decoders' are the suns, and their broadcasts are picked up by planets, people, animals, plant life and so on. A galaxy and a universe have to be observed (decoded) into a holographic state like everything else. Vibrational/electrical upheavals delivered into this Solar System some 'outsiders', including Jupiter and Saturn. These are not planets, but a form of *star* or *sun* known as 'brown dwarfs'. There are many types of dwarf stars – some 'light up' and some don't. Saturn and Jupiter are made up of the elements hydrogen and helium – just like the Sun. Some scientists have described brown dwarfs as 'failed stars' and I suppose you could say they are in a kind of middle category between a planet and a fully-fledged sun or star. I will refer to them as 'suns' to keep it simple because they are much closer to that than a planet. Brown dwarfs were only discovered in 1995 and scientists have suggested that there may be as many brown dwarf stars as there are stars as we know them. So it is no big deal to have at least two in our vicinity. I know that scientists and astronomers will say that Saturn and Jupiter don't quite fit their criteria of a brown dwarf, but they only confirmed the existence of brown dwarfs well under 20 years ago and they are going to have to widen their criteria to encompass more bodies than they currently do. It is important to remember that knowledge of the Universe is still in its infancy. Scientists and astronomers believed not long ago that the Milky Way was the *only galaxy* in the Universe. It was only as recently as the 1920s that astronomer, Edwin Hubble, showed this to be outrageously inaccurate. People think they are looking at a stable and unchanging solar system when this is not the case at all. The Universe and everything in it is constantly changing. Galaxies attract dwarf galaxies and eventually absorb them into their own system. The Milky Way is orbited by two dwarf galaxies and we are closer to the centre of one of them, the Canis Major dwarf galaxy, than we are to our own. I have seen reports that the red supergiant star, Betelgeuse, in the constellation of Orion, is due to explode into what is called a 'supernova' and will appear from Earth as a second sun. I mentioned Betelgeuse in *Human Race Get Off Your Knees* with regard to Zulu legends about its place in human history. The Universe is always in a state of transition, movement and change. Our solar system is a real mish-mash or hodgepodge that came together as a result of many catastrophic events, and the Earth is not originally from 'these parts', either.

Russian–American scholar, Immanuel Velikovsky, and more recently American researcher, David Talbott, have provided new insights into what has happened in the Solar System in relatively recent times. Talbott was inspired onto this path by the late Velikovsky's pioneering work. They have both combined scientific research with ploughing through reams and reams of ancient accounts from every part of the world about the time, to quote the title of one book on the subject, when the Earth nearly died. The Solar System was very different to the one that we know today before these cataclysmic events. Velikovsky wrote a series of books starting in the 1950s, including *Worlds in Collision; Ages in Chaos;* and *Earth in Upheaval.* He didn't get everything right – who does? But I'm sure that his themes and those of David Talbott are correct. I might disagree on exactly when it happened, and other detail, but the fact that something of great enormity *did* happen is patently obvious. I have been writing about this for nearly the last two decades and it was one of the first subject areas that came to me soon after my experience with Betty Shine in 1990. Velikovsky deserves our respect and congratulations for his trailblazing 60 years ago, and for sticking with it amid merciless ridicule and dismissal. I know the feeling. I'll stay with the themes rather than get bogged down with differing views of the detail. Mars, Venus, Jupiter and Saturn were much closer before the cataclysms than they are today and they appeared as giant bodies to people on Earth. Saturn was a *sun,* or brown dwarf star, and did not have the rings that we see today. I'll explain how I am saying they came to be a little later. I have come across a number of accounts over the years of the 'two-sun' solar system, and more than 80 per cent of known solar systems have multiple suns. The Ancient Greeks said that Earth once had two suns, and they had two words for 'sun': *Theos* and *Helios* – which did not refer to the same body. The concept was featured in the *Star Wars* movie

Figure 82: Two suns rise in the *Star Wars* series.

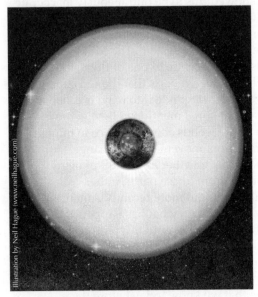

illustration by Neil Hague (www.neilhague.com)

Figure 83: David Talbott's view of how Saturn, Venus and Mars would have looked when viewed from the Earth in the solar system before the cataclysms

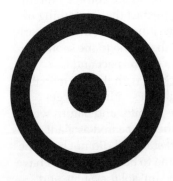

Figure 84: David Talbott suggests that this sun symbol relates to the sun Saturn, rather than the sun we are familiar with

series produced by Illuminati insider, George Lucas (Fig 82). I have also suggested in other books, such as *The Biggest Secret*, that at least many people of the white, or Caucasian, race have historical connections with Mars. An 'insider' who worked on many secret science programmes told me that he had been taken to an underground extraterrestrial base on Mars and that the entities looked virtually identical to humans. He said that he'd had to look closely before he could see minor differences. David Talbott's research concludes that Venus, Earth, Mars, Jupiter and Saturn orbited our sun together in a straight line. This made it appear from Earth that Venus was in the centre of the sun – the Saturn sun (Fig 83). Talbott suggests that the ancient symbol of the sun, a circle at the centre of a much larger circle, derives from this (Fig 84). He says that Mars appeared to be in the centre of Venus when viewed from Earth and that Jupiter was obscured by Saturn. Talbott produced a DVD outlining his ideas called *Remembering the End of the World* and you can currently get a copy at: www.thunderbolts.info. The cutting edge has moved on since this was made and he began to study the electrical nature of the Universe; but all the foundation themes are there. Saturn didn't appear to move from the perspective of Earth and so it was called the 'Steadfast One'. Talbott says that something happened that caused Mars to move in a vertical line closer to Earth and then go back the other way. Mars eventually came so close that stupendous electrical discharges were exchanged with the Earth – the thunderbolts of the gods recorded universally in ancient myth and legend (Fig 85). Mars became forever known as the 'god of War'. Electromagnetic stability was now electromagnetic chaos and Venus, Mars, Jupiter and Saturn went their separate ways. Venus is recorded as a comet-like body with 'long hair' – the result of the electrical interaction between an out-of-control Venus and the plasma field. It is possible

Figure 85: Neil Hague's portrayal of the Earth-Mars 'thunderbolts of the gods' © Neil Hague 2011

that images like the one in Figure 86 from ancient Egypt may be symbolising what was seen in the sky.

'Fallen' Earth

The Earth, too, was devastated, and all of this is recorded in ancient myths and legends across the world. They describe a time before the cataclysm of a 'Golden Age' of harmony when there was no discord or war, no reference to time, and no seasons. It was like an eternal spring of constant abundance.

Many legends speak of Atlantis and Mu, or Lemuria, as great continents in the Atlantic and Pacific that sank beneath the sea amid enormous geological upheavals leaving only remnants such as the Pacific islands and even the massive landmass of Australia. It is clear from the geological and biological record that there were earthquakes, volcanoes and tidal waves on a scale we could not imagine today. A period that keeps recurring with regard to this is between 11,500 and 13,000 years ago, but there has been far more than just one case of planetary upheaval. The biblical 'Great Flood' story is repeated across the world using different names for the heroes and

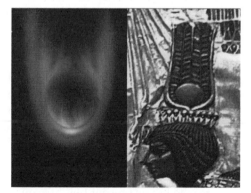

Figure 86: A portrayal of the electrical cosmos interacting with the atmosphere of Venus and the crown of Ankhsunamun's 'comet' on the throne of Tutankhamun © (esa/c. Carreau)

gods, and the story of Noah is a re-write of much older stories from ancient Sumer and Babylon, now Iraq. The Sumerian version tells how extraterrestrial 'gods', the Anunna, or Anunnaki, decided to destroy humanity; but one of them, called Enki, warned the priest-king Ziusudra of the coming flood. He told Ziusudra to build a great ship and take aboard 'beasts and birds'. The same story was told in the later Babylon, where the 'Noah' figure was called Atrahasis; and we can also find The Flood story in Egypt, Assyria, Chaldea, Greece, Arcadia, Rome, Scandinavia, Germany, Lithuania, Transylvania, Turkey, Persia, China, New Zealand, Siberia, Burma, Korea, Taiwan, Philippines, Sumatra, in Islam and in Celtic lore, and among native peoples throughout North, South and Central America, Africa, Asia, Australia and the Pacific. They tell of a great heat that boiled the sea; mountains breathing fire; the disappearance of the Sun and Moon, and the darkness that followed; the raining down of blood, ice and rock; the Earth flipping over; the sky falling; the rising and sinking of land; the loss of great continents; and the coming of the ice. They nearly all tell of a wall of water, a gigantic tsunami that swept across the planet. I read a book a long time ago by two researchers, D S Allan and J B Delair, called *When the Earth Nearly Died*. They compared ancient accounts with the biological and geological record and one supported and confirmed the other. Anthony L Peratt is one of the world's leading research scientists on high-energy plasma discharges. He made a remarkable discovery when he compared laboratory-repeated plasma discharges that would have been generated by the events that I have described with cave paintings, or petroglyphs, recorded by nearly all races in every part of the world. The image of 'Squatter Man' or 'Stick Man' is game, set and match when compared with how one form of plasma discharge would have looked in the sky. I wanted to include the comparison in the book here, but I could not get permission from Anthony L Peratt. However, if you put 'Plasma Squatter Man' into Google images you can see it there.

Most people have no idea how relatively-recently extraordinary events happened. The islands of the Azores are on the Mid-Atlantic Ridge, which is connected to a fracture line that continues for a distance of 40,000 miles. It is one of the most active regions for earthquakes and volcanoes such as those more recently in Iceland that have disrupted air travel. The Eurasian, African, North American and Caribbean tectonic plates meet here and so it can be extremely unstable. The Azores are said by some to be a remnant of Atlantis; and the ancient Greek philosopher, Plato (427–347 BC), seems to suggest in his writings that the end of Atlantis was about 11,000 years ago. Tachylite lava disintegrates in seawater within 15,000 years, but it is still found on the seabed around the Azores. Beach-sand gathered from depths of 10,500 to 18,440 feet shows that the seabed in this region must have been above sea level in geologically recent times. Oceanographer, Maurice Ewing, wrote in *National Geographic*: 'Either the land must have sunk two or three miles, or the sea must once have been two or three miles lower than now. Either conclusion is startling.' The Appalachia land mass, which connected today's Europe, North America, Iceland and Greenland, appears to have broken up in the same period as the upheavals around the Azores. The Himalayas, Alps and Andes only reached their present height around 11,000 to 13,000 years ago. Lake Titicaca on the Peruvian–Bolivian border is now said to be the highest navigable lake in the world at some 13,000 feet; but around 13,000 years ago much of that region was at sea level. Fish fossils are found high up in mountain ranges, supporting the legends of mountains being split apart and others surging from the Earth. Does anyone still seriously believe that the Grand Canyon in Arizona was scored away by the Colorado River? You would laugh at the very thought if you stood at the edge of that canyon and looked down at the tiny river way in the distance. I have been there a few times and it still makes me chuckle. How ludicrous! A tidal wave of the magnitude universally described would have generated pressures on the Earth's surface of two tonnes per square inch – the kind of pressure that creates artificial stone today. It would have caused things to fossilise within hours and caused the formation of mountains. This explains why still intact trees have been found fossilised. This could never have happened unless it was done amazingly quickly. Parts of the Earth were instantly frozen, and mammoths have been found in ice still standing up in the process of eating, with undigested food still in their stomachs. Random rocks and stones scattered across the Earth are the result of the global tsunami and it also explains why botanist, Nikolai Ivanovich Vavilov, studied more than 50,000 wild plants and found that they originated in only eight different areas – all of them high up in mountains. Plato wrote that agriculture began at high elevations after the lowlands were covered by a flood. All these accounts with their common themes that support each other were written off as the fiction of a primitive people, but they are now being taken far more seriously as the geological and biological record gives them ever more credence. There is further support, too, from the emerging understanding of the electrical/plasma universe. We can see that if something seriously distorts the balance of the electromagnetic forces that maintain the spheres in a stable orbit then they will hit the road.

The Earth took a long time to recover, and life here has never been the same since in far more than just a 'physical' or holographic sense. The foundation construct of our experienced reality is waveform information, and what happened caused a serious distortion – or what I call 'the Schism' – in the waveform information fabric of our part of the Universe. The human mind is connected to this information source and so the Schism also affected humanity's mental and emotional balance. This continues today in the distortions in the way that people view self, life and each other. The timeless Golden Age was over. Time as we know it was about to imprison human perception through the manipulation that I will be describing. Emotions like *hate* and *greed* appeared in a world that had not known them in the period of the Golden Age. The few humans that survived and those that followed were cast into a dark and merciless age of ignorance and suppression from which we now have the opportunity to emerge.

5

Hijacked Earth

We are now entering territory where only really open minds will go. We have been there already, really, with the cosmic catastrophe, but if you think that is strange and hard to believe – 'Fasten your seat belt, Dorothy, 'cause Kansas is going bye-bye', as the chap said in *The Matrix*.

The Earth was a scene of devastation; most of humanity was no more and everything had to start over. The belief in what people call 'evolution' implies a constant advancement of a species from ignorance to ever greater knowledge and potential. But that is not the case in reality. Earth has been home to endless civilisations that have come and gone over a period (in decoded 'time') that is far longer than the human history perceived by mainstream science. American author and researcher, Michael Cremo, has spent years studying the evidence for human existence way before the official version says human life began. He said that he embarked on his research after reading dozens of original scientific reports describing human bones and artefacts millions of years old that were never included in text books. Some of these Earth civilisations have been far more advanced than ours is today and others have been extremely primitive. The throttle goes both ways as they say in motorcycle racing, and so does 'evolution'. An advanced people can become primitive within minutes when the planet is struck by the type of events that I am talking about. Look at what happens in the aftermath of major earthquakes or disasters such as Hurricane Katrina. The 'modern world' is over in a flash until rescue teams arrive and rebuilding begins. What if there *were* no rescue workers or rebuilding because the same was happening all over the world? I made the point in *Human Race Get Off Your Knees* that it would immediately become a dog-eat-dog, everyone-for-themselves, find-your-own food, shelter and warmth free-for-all among those who survived. Memories of today's technological world would rapidly fade over the thousands of years it took for the planet to recover, and its existence would only be preserved in stories and myths that would be dismissed as fantasy and figments of the imagination. They would laugh at the very idea that such a world could have been here on Earth long before. They would employ the 'if-we-can't-do-it–it-can't-be-done' mentality that once scoffed at the very idea that craft could be built to even fly never mind go into space. We are looking at precisely such a scenario with the cataclysmic demise of the Golden Age and the passage through history of the legends and myths that tell of its existence and its end. My view is that the real Golden

Age of human consciousness expansion ended *well* in excess of 200,000 years ago (as we decode 'time'). This is what *some* Golden Age myths are really talking about, while others refer to what *appeared* to be a 'Golden Age' in far more recent times when compared with the world that followed its demise amid those great geological events. I will refer to the much earlier period as the *Real Golden Age* to make it clear what I mean.

Okay, it's deep-breath time if this is the first book of mine that you've ever read. Humanity had been interacting with non-human races for very a long period before the catastrophe. Some were benevolent and others not so, and the latter eventually took over. There are accounts that say these 'gods' in some way *caused* the cataclysms and this is a theme of the Great Flood stories when the gods – or in the monotheist religions, a single 'God' – decided to wipe out humanity and start again. I have already mentioned the Sumerian version which says that the Anunna, or Anunnaki, made the decision to destroy humanity; but one of them, known as Enki, warned the priest-king Ziusudra of the coming flood and told him to get a ship sorted pretty damn quick. The *Genesis* version has God saying to Noah: 'I am going to put an end to all people, for the earth is filled with violence because of them. I am surely going to destroy both them and the earth' ... 'I am going to bring floodwaters on the earth to destroy all life under the heavens, every creature that has the breath of life in it. Everything on earth will perish.' Nice bloke, 'God'. There are indications in the Sumerian story of the Anunnaki that humanity was targeted after a rebellion against the 'gods' and their desire to control and enslave. I suggest that the 'gods' were an alliance of non-human races dominated by a group taking reptilian form, but also including some of what are known as the ant-like 'Greys' and some that look virtually human. There may well be others, too, and I will call it the 'Reptilian Alliance' with the scaly guys very much at the forefront. It sounds fantastic, but almost everything outside the daily 'norms' seems to be 'fantastic', 'ridiculous' and 'not possible' to the solidified left-brain mind. It has a perception of possibility that can only be viewed through a microscope, so, of course, it sounds hard to believe; but is it really so 'fantastic'? Look at the extraordinary varieties of form among animals, insects, sea-life and nature in general. Come to that, look at the variety of human forms – black, brown, white and so on; and look at the difference in appearance between someone from the Far East compared with the black and white races. Then remember that this is only what exists on one planet within the incredibly narrow band of frequencies that we can 'see' – visible light. What the heck must there be in varieties of form in the infinity beyond that? When you look at it from this perspective it would be more 'fantastic' if intelligent life expressed through reptilian genetics did not exist. Ancient Mesopotamian tablets say that the Anunnaki came hundreds of thousands of years ago. They brought an end to what I am calling the Real Golden Age and turned Earth people into their slave race. The Reptilian Alliance (Anunnaki) have since then periodically caused global catastrophe to delete their genetic programs when they cease to be acquiescent slaves. This allows them to start again with, if necessary, an 'upgraded' human body–computer system. By upgraded, I mean more controllable. My jury is out on exactly when the Reptilians arrived, but there were certainly big and sudden changes in human genetics 200,000 years ago and 35,000 years ago. They are planning to do the same again now and we need to open our minds very fast to what is happening. Some say that the Reptilians have only been here for a few thousand years, but I think it is far, far longer although the nature of the

Illustration by Neil Hague (www.neilhague.com)

Figure 87: There is no physical shift in a shapeshift, because there is no physical. It all happens in the observer's mind

manipulation has changed in that period. The Reptilians appear to have connections to the Orion and Draco constellations, but not necessarily as we perceive them, and not necessarily in the frequency range of visible light. Planets and stars are multi-dimensional like everything else and there are dimensions of celestial bodies, constellations and galaxies that are very different to the range of frequency that we 'see'. Saturn and the Earth's 'moon' are at the heart of this story and I will come to that in the next chapter. Information about the Reptilian hijack began to come into my life from just after the mid-1990s when I began to meet people in the most synchronistic way around the world who told me of experiences with reptilian entities. I was introduced to the subject here and there in earlier years and I put it on the 'back burner' to see where it led. I don't just hear something and start shouting about it. This obviously sounded very weird and I needed to hear a lot more before I would pursue this, but I didn't dismiss it either. Information really started to flow over a 15-day period in 1997, as I travelled the United States going from place to place each day on a speaking tour. Well, sort of. I was speaking and touring, but not many were listening. But I did meet 12 unconnected people over those 15 days who told me the same basic story about the existence of a reptilian race. Several of them said they had seen people (often in positions of power, though not always) suddenly 'shapeshift' from human to reptilian form and back again. Remember that this is not a 'physical' shift. There is no 'physical'. It is a waveform *energetic* shift, and what appears to be a 'physical shift' only happens in the decoding process of the observer's mind (Fig 87). This appears as the illusion of someone changing physical shape when the two information fields shift and a different hologram is decoded by the observer. I have explained in detail in other books how information about the 'Reptilians' began to come at me from all angles after those 15 days in America. You can read this at length in books like *The Biggest Secret; Children of the Matrix; Tales from the Time Loop*; and the two mega-works, *The David Icke Guide to the Global Conspiracy*; and *Human Race Get Off Your Knees*. I am writing this book to outline the basic story for those now asking the question: 'What's going on?' But I have produced many very detailed works if you want to go deeper.

Ancient and modern confirmation

I was contacted by Credo Mutwa, a Zulu high shaman, or 'Sanusi', in South Africa when I first went public with the Reptilian story in *The Biggest Secret* in 1998. He gave me reams of information about the 'Chitauri' – the 'Children of the Serpent' or 'Children of the Python' in Zulu legend. These are what I call the 'Reptilians'. Credo was to become a great friend. He has just passed his 90th birthday as I write this – and what an incredible man he is. Credo is an example to everyone with his tenacity and refusal to give up, whatever the odds (Fig 88). He told me how black African secret societies had been created at the time of the European invasion led by people like the House of Rothschild agent, Cecil Rhodes, who established gold and diamond mines for his masters. Rhodesia, now Zimbabwe and Zambia, was named after him. Credo said that British colonialists, like Rhodes and others, sought to destroy the ancient African knowledge and version of human history passed down through the generations. They set out to replace this with Christian dogma that would demonise African beliefs and history. This happened all over the world with the expansion of colonialism, most notably by Britain. The idea was to delete the ancient accounts, legends and myths, and impose a fake history that would suppress what really happened and, therefore, what is happening. Secret societies were established in Africa to keep the knowledge alive, and Credo was initiated into some of them more than 60 years ago. It was then that he first heard about the 'Chitauri', which is spelled differently in various African languages. The story he told me about the Chitauri takeover of Planet Earth confirmed and supported what I had compiled from, by then, endless people around the world, ancient and modern sources, and Illuminati insiders that don't agree with its agenda. (There are many people working on the 'inside' against their will.) Compelling common themes about the Reptilian race were there whatever the source.

Figure 88: The great Credo Mutwa

Credo showed me an incredible ancient artefact called the *Necklace of the Mysteries* – since stolen – that is mentioned in accounts 500 years ago, and Credo reckons it is at least another 500 years older than that (Figs 89 and 90). The 'necklace' rests on the shoulders and it is extremely heavy. He said it was made to last, because they wanted the knowledge that it symbolises to survive as long as possible. Large symbols hang

Figure 89: The Necklace of the Mysteries

Figure 90: The human woman and the non-human male and a mass of symbols on the hand, including the six-pointed star (Saturn), the all-seeing eye and the constellation of Orion

Figure 91: The Illuminati symbol of the all-seeing eye on the dollar bill and the reverse of the Great Seal of the United States

Figure 92: One of the reptilian mother-and-baby figurines found in graves from the Ubaid period (around 6500 to 3800 BC) which preceded the Sumerians in Mesopotamia. Could the child be symbolic of the 'new' humanity?

from the big copper ring, and they are used to tell the story of African and human history since the Reptilian 'hijack'. A symbol of a hand is covered in other symbols, including a depiction of the Orion constellation and a six-pointed star, or 'Star of David', the symbol of the House of Rothschild that we see on the flag of the Rothschild fiefdom, Israel, and also a symbol of Saturn. There is also an eye, symbolic of the non-human 'Watchers', as the ancients called them. This is a theme that you find all over the world. The eye, or all-seeing eye, is a major symbol of the Illuminati bloodlines and can be seen on the dollar bill and on the reverse of the Great Seal of the United States which was first revealed publically in 1782 (Fig 91). This was designed by the Freemasonic cabal behind the American War of Independence. There is also a flying-saucer-type symbol on the necklace which is said to be the craft that the Chitauri used to come to Earth from their 'mothership'. The more I know, the more I feel that this could have originally symbolised Saturn for reasons that I will come to in the next chapter. Saturn has also been symbolised as an eye. I know that the rings of Saturn were not officially discovered until Galileo looked through his telescope in 1610, but I am well aware after all these years that ancient knowledge, myth and legend is often well ahead of scientific discovery. The two figures at the front of the necklace represent a human woman and a Chitauri reptilian male; well, it's pretty obvious he's a male, really. This symbolises the interbreeding of the Chitauri with humans, which I will develop further in a second. The penis is made of copper, but this replaced a golden one after it was stolen. This is the same as the story at the heart of ancient Egyptian mythology about the golden penis of their god, Osiris. A similar version was told in Babylon and elsewhere. You find universal stories throughout the ancient world using different names and locations. The golden penis is symbolic of what the Reptilians believe is their 'super seed'; and so is another prime Illuminati bloodline symbol – the lighted torch. Credo said that the Chitauri male doesn't look reptilian, because people were told not to depict them as they really looked. Many of their images are largely symbolic for this reason. They are depicted as clearly not human, but not as they really are, although you do still find literal, or at least reptilian, representations in many cultures (Fig 92). Credo

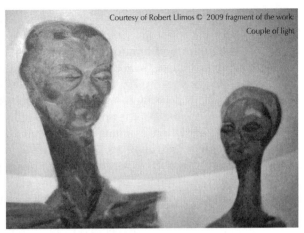

Courtesy of Robert Llimos © 2009 fragment of the work:
Couple of light

Figure 93:　　　　　　　　　　　**Figure 94:**
A Reptilian worker male painted by Credo Mutwa from ancient and modern descriptions; and two of the reptilian figures painted by Robert Llimos in Brazil in 2009 © www.robertllimos.es

painted a picture of one species of Reptilian/Chitauri (there are many) from ancient and modern accounts, which you can see in Figure 93. The picture alongside that looks remarkably similar was painted much more recently by Robert Llimos, a Spanish artist who I met when I spoke at an event in Barcelona, Spain, in 2010 (Fig 94). Robert's girlfriend is Brazilian and on a trip there in 2009 he went out alone into the countryside to paint the landscape. He was not interested in any of this information before then and wasn't even aware of my existence, let alone what I was saying. But his experience was to change all that. As he

Figure 95: The ship that appeared to Robert Llimos in the Brazilian countryside
Courtesy of Robert Llimos © 2009 Title: Spaceship scanning

stood with his brush and easel, painting away in the countryside, he said that a spacecraft, some 50 metres wide, descended in front him and stayed for two hours (Fig 95). Robert told me that he doesn't know if he was taken on board the craft, but he has no memory of that. He painted what he was seeing while two reptilian figures stared at him from the only window that was open. The left-brain media (of course) and much of the public thought that it was hilarious when I started talking and writing about the Reptilian manipulation of human society; but I didn't, and don't, give a damn. They are just water to my duck's arse. People can scoff and laugh as much as they like. These entities *exist* and they are fundamentally impacting upon human life. I have produced an enormous amount of detailed information and evidence in other books, but if people don't want to accept that, or even look at the possibility with an open mind, well, they will just have to do the other thing then. It's all the same to me. I am communicating suppressed information, not telling anyone what to believe.

Serpent Worship

The oldest known form of religious worship is the worship of the serpent. Sheila Coulson, an archaeologist from the University of Oslo, in Norway, has documented evidence of python worship 70,000 years ago in the Tsodilo Hills of the Kalahari Desert in South Africa. This is home to the world's biggest known concentration of rock paintings. The mythology of the ancient San people, also known as 'Bushmen', says that the Tsodilo Hills are where humans were created when the giant python went there with a 'bag of eggs'. Zulu shaman, Credo Mutwa, told me that 'Africa' comes from the ancient word, 'Wafirika'. This means 'the first people on Earth', or 'the first people here'. The word 'Zulu' itself means 'people from the stars'. They say they were seeded by a race that came from beyond the Earth. Rebecca Cann, Assistant Professor of Genetics at the University of Hawaii, co-authored a study in 1987 in the journal, *Nature*, suggesting that all modern humans are descended from a single mother who lived in Africa in about 200,000 BC. She said the connection was through the mitochondrial DNA, which passes down through the female. Human brain capacity apparently expanded at an increasingly rapid rate over millions of years, but this expansion suddenly stopped and went into reverse about 200,000 years ago. Mesopotamian accounts about the Anunnaki say that humans rebelled more than 200,000 years ago and they decided to produce a 'new human' that could be more easily controlled. A man called Reverend John Bathurst Deane published a study in the 1930s about the history of serpent worship all over the world. He traced its origins to Sumer and Babylon, now Iraq, a very significant land in the story I am telling. It's also known as Mesopotamia. Reverend Deane charted the expansion of serpent worship out of this region and into Egypt; Persia; Asia Minor (now Turkey); Phoenicia; Arabia and the Middle East; India and Asia; China; Japan; Ethiopia and the rest of Africa; Mexico; Great Britain; Scandinavia; Italy; Greece; Crete; Rhodes; Cyprus; Sri Lanka; Northern and Western Europe; and North, South and Central America. Well, virtually *everywhere*, in fact. The Mayan people, in what is now Mexico, say their ancestors were 'the people of the serpent'. They talked about a reptilian race that came from the sky to take over their civilisation and demand human sacrifice. The latter is a common theme. The reptilian race and their other non-human associates were perceived as 'gods' because of their technological capabilities. Hopi Indians in the United States talk of their 'snake brothers', the 'sky gods', who bred with their women. Indian accounts tell of a reptilian race called the 'Sharpa' that founded civilisation and were the originators of the shockingly racist Hindu caste system. This is a version of the strictly-imposed Reptilian genetic hierarchy. These guys are obsessed with genetics and hierarchy. The Illuminati bloodlines' genetic hierarchy originates from the same source. Indian accounts of the reptilian race also say that they demanded human sacrifice. Chinese mythology says that a 'Serpent Queen' interbred with men. The existence of a reptilian race, the demand for human sacrifice and the interbreeding with humans are universal themes. John Bathurst Deane produced the book *The Worship of the Serpent* (BibioBazaar; 2009, first published 1933) in which he says that 'the mystic serpent entered into the mythology of every nation; consecrated almost every temple; symbolized almost every deity; was imagined in the heavens, stamped upon the earth, and ruled in the realms of everlasting sorrow'. He said the serpent was the main symbol of mythology and the 'only common object of superstitious terror throughout the habitable world'. This was the book's conclusion:

> It appears, then, that no nations were so geographically remote, or so religiously discordant, but that one – and only one – superstitious characteristic was common to all: that the most civilized and the most barbarous bowed down with the same devotion to the same engrossing deity; and that this deity either was, or was represented by, the same sacred serpent. It appears also that in most, if not all, of the civilized countries where this serpent was worshipped, some fable or tradition which involved his history, directly or indirectly, alluded to the Fall of Man in Paradise, in which the serpent was concerned. What follows, then, but that the most ancient account respecting the cause and nature of this seduction must be the one from which all the rest are derived which represent the victorious serpent – victorious over man in a state of innocence, and subduing his soul in a state of sin, into the most abject veneration and adoration of himself.

Now some of this will have originated from serpent-like plasma discharges in the sky, which electrical-universe researchers say would have been produced during the cataclysmic events in the heavens. This is especially true with the myths about 'fire-breathing dragons'. But the correlation between global serpent worship and the ancient and modern confirmation of the existence of reptilian entities, or 'gods', is far too obvious and compelling to say that the universal worship of the serpent comes *only* from plasma images in the ancient skies. Anyway, documented serpent worship goes back many tens of thousands of years before the proposed time of the 'Saturn catastrophe' described in the last chapter. The challenge is to identify which are memories of the 'serpent plasma', and which symbolise the Reptilian 'gods'. The other thing we need to remember across the whole swathe of symbolism is that what the symbols mean to people can change over the countless generations. A goddess that began as a symbol for Venus, for example, can later be used to symbolise the Moon. A long list of symbols, buildings and imagery went through this metamorphosis when Pagan Rome embraced the closet Pagan religion of Christianity.

The Great Switch-Off

Humanity has been through a genetic metamorphosis as the Reptilian Alliance tampered with human genetics, deleted programs with Earth catastrophes and introduced new ones. Other racial groups within this alliance were also involved to some extent and this is one reason for different races on Earth. The Reptilian interlopers are master geneticists and they have designed the human mind/body–computer specifically for the purpose of enslavement. This genetic manipulation has had two major effects: (1) It drastically reduced the range of frequencies that humans could access and decode, leaving us with a tiny range of perception that we call 'visible light'; (2) The mind/body–computer was tuned into a false reality – the 'Matrix' – and I will explain how this is done later. (Strap in for that one!) The illusory reality portrayed in *The Matrix* movie series was very accurate with regard to how humans are 'plugged in' to experience a 'world' that isn't what it appears to be. Genetic manipulation explains part of the reason why scientists refer to between 90 and 97 per cent of human DNA as 'junk' DNA, because it does not seem to serve any purpose. In fact, a lot of this 'junk' DNA potential has been 'switched off' and other parts are interacting with other realities and programs. I read that the idea that we use less than 10 per cent of the brain is an urban legend, but they are talking about *areas* of the brain. If they knew the brain's true potential compared with what humans currently use they would realise that we are operating with a fraction of the brain's capacity. This is another consequence of genetic manipulation. There is clear evidence of gene splicing in the human body, a process that geneticists use today. Gene splicing is like cutting frames from a film and putting them back in at another place; or taking frames from two movies and editing them together to create a hybrid of the two. Lloyd Pye, an American researcher and writer, has made a detailed study of human origins. He says that human DNA has more than 4,000 defects, while only a few hundred are found in chimpanzees and gorillas. Pye says there is 'evidence of gene segments that have been cut, flipped and reinserted upside down back into the genome', and chromosomes in humans have also been fused together (a process seen only in laboratories) to leave us with apparently two fewer than chimpanzees and gorillas. Even mainstream science has noted there were sudden changes in human genetics around 200,000 years ago, and again about 35,000 years ago. Researchers involved with the Human Genome Project say they believe that the more than 90 per cent of non-coding DNA – 'junk' DNA – is the genetic code of extraterrestrial life forms. I think some of it definitely is and it is designed to attach us to their collective mind, as I will be explaining. Other sections of 'junk' DNA have simply been switched off to prevent them from connecting us to a far greater scale of decoded reality. The group's leader, Professor Sam Chang, says that the overwhelming majority of human DNA is of 'off-world' origin and the 'extraterrestrial junk genes' merely 'enjoy the ride' with hard-working active genes passed through the generations. Professor Chang worked with other scientists, computer programmers, mathematicians and scholars, to consider if 'junk' DNA was created by some kind of 'extraterrestrial programmer'. It *was*, and this will be massively important later in the book when I come to how technology is manipulating the perceptions of the human population. Professor Chang says that the 'alien' parts of 'junk' DNA have 'their own veins, arteries, and immune system that vigorously resists all our anti-cancer drugs'. He concludes:

> Our hypothesis is that a higher extraterrestrial life form was engaged in creating new life and planting it on various planets. Earth is just one of them. Perhaps, after programming, our creators grow us the same way we grow bacteria in Petri dishes. We can't know their motives – whether it was a scientific experiment, or a way of preparing new planets for colonization, or the long-time ongoing business of seeding life in the universe.

Professor Chang says that perhaps the 'extraterrestrial programmers' were working with 'one big code' creating life-forms on many planets. He speculates that perhaps they 'wrote the big code, executed it, did not like some function, changed it or added a new one, executed it again, made more improvements, tried again and again'. Ancient accounts of the Anunnaki/Chitauri say that there were many attempts to genetically-engineer a 'new human' before they succeeded. Professor Chang goes on:

> What we see in our DNA is a program consisting of two versions, a big code and basic code. First fact is, the complete 'program' was positively not written on Earth; that is now a verified fact. The second fact is that genes, by themselves, are not enough to explain evolution; there must be something more in 'the game' ... Sooner or later we have to come to grips with the

unbelievable notion that every life on Earth carries genetic code for his extraterrestrial cousin, and that evolution is not what we think it is.

The genetic manipulation meant that the vast perception range of humans in the Real Golden Age was now gone, and a series of genetic 'upgrades' (slavegrades) have confined humanity to this sliver of 'reality' – visible light. The Reptilian Alliance wanted to create a human genetic form that was intelligent enough to serve them as a slave race, but too stupid to realise that it was being controlled, how it was being controlled, and by whom. It also involved a massive infusion of reptilian genetics to connect humans vibrationally to them and their 'Matrix'. Accounts and legends of the interbreeding between humans and non-human entities, 'the gods', can be found right across the ancient world – as with the 'Chitauri' in South Africa. It is most famously recorded in *Genesis 6:4*, which says: 'There were giants in the earth in those days; and also after that, when the sons of God came in unto the daughters of men, and they bare children to them, the same became mighty men which were of old, men of renown.' These were the biblical 'Nefilim'. The phrase 'sons of God' is a translation from text that refers to gods *plural*, sons of the *gods*, not a single 'God'. Genesis also says:

> And God said, Let us make man in our image, after our likeness; ... So God created man in his own image, in the image of God created he him; male and female created he them [humans were androgynous in the Real Golden Age] – Genesis 1:26-27

> And the Lord God said, Behold, the man is become as one of us, to know good and evil; and now, lest he put forth his hand, and take also of the tree of life, and eat, and live for ever – Genesis 3:22

Note again that it says 'our image', 'our likeness', and 'one of us', *plural*. The Reptilians did create humans in their genetic image in that they infused the human body–computer with their own reptilian information and coding. So we did to a large extent 'become' one of them, and knew (decoded) good and 'evil'. There was no 'evil' (the reverse of 'live') in the Real Golden Age before the Reptilian intervention.

'The Fall'

This is the universal story of the 'Fall of Man' that is told in different versions across the world, and again the best known version is the symbolic biblical story of the Garden of Eden. Who does it say was the villain that manipulated Adam and Eve with the 'apple' and had them thrown out of the 'garden'? The *serpent*. The 'garden' was the Real Golden Age and the range of perception that humanity then experienced. The term 'apple' is sometimes used by the Illuminati bloodlines to symbolise their control of a global structure of human enslavement that serves the agenda of the hidden Reptilian masters. It might be that there was interbreeding through procreation between humans and the Reptilians, but it certainly didn't have to be that way. We know today that it is possible to produce children through 'test tube' methods, and we also have gene splicing, but there is a stage even beyond that for those who understand the nature of reality. DNA is a receiver–transmitter and it can be altered by broadcasting information on its frequency to change the genetic structure. Remember the Russian research group that successfully transmitted information patterns from one DNA to another and changed frog embryos to salamander embryos by transmitting salamander DNA information patterns. The genetic manipulation tuned humanity into the Reptilian collective, or 'hive' mind, through the artificial reality 'Matrix' that I will be describing. Long after I had been writing and talking about this information I came across the works of the Peruvian-born writer, Carlos Castaneda, who wrote a series of books from the late 1960s. He said his source was Don Juan Matus, a Yaqui Indian healer, or shaman – a 'Credo Mutwa' of Mexico, a carrier of the ancient knowledge in Central America. Some have questioned Don Juan's literal existence, but the words he is quoted as saying had me going, 'Wow!' when I read them, given what I had already put together. Part of the synchronistic sequence of information that I am guided to compile is often to get a re-confirmation 'out of the blue' after I have made something public. It is like, 'See, you are on the right track.' This is what Don Juan Matus said:

We have a predator that came from the depths of the cosmos and took over the rule of our lives. Human beings are its prisoners. The predator is our lord and master. It has rendered us docile, helpless. If we want to protest, it suppresses our protest. If we want to act independently, it demands that we don't do so ... indeed we are held prisoner!

They took us over because we are food to them, and they squeeze us mercilessly because we are their sustenance. Just as we rear chickens in coops, the predators rear us in human coops, humaneros. Therefore, their food is always available to them.

Think for a moment, and tell me how you would explain the contradictions between the intelligence of man the engineer and the stupidity of his systems of belief, or the stupidity of his contradictory behaviour. Sorcerers believe that the predators have given us our systems of beliefs, our ideas of good and evil; our social mores. They are the ones who set up our dreams of success or failure. They have given us covetousness, greed and cowardice. It is the predator who makes us complacent, routinary and egomaniacal.

In order to keep us obedient and meek and weak, the predators engaged themselves in a stupendous manoeuvre – stupendous, of course, from the point of view of a fighting strategist; a horrendous manoeuvre from the point of those who suffer it. They gave us their mind. The predators' mind is baroque, contradictory, morose, filled with the fear of being discovered any minute now.

The 'predator' is the Reptilian Alliance and they *have* given us their mind.

Energy Vampires

The 'food' that Don Juan talks about there is low-vibrational human emotional energy that resonates in the frequency band generated by states of fear, hatred, stress, depression, worry and suchlike. Ever wondered why there is so much of this generated 24/7 by human society? Or why the actions of those in power are constantly generating more with their wars, terrorism and financial crashes which stimulate fear, death, horror, sadness and hardship the world over? Or why the Illuminati-controlled mainstream media and computer games are full of images that trigger those same emotions? The goal is to manipulate humanity into mental and emotional states that produce the low-vibrational energy on which the Reptilian energetic vampires feed and glean their power from. Morpheus held up a battery in *The Matrix* and said that the 'machines' had turned humans into 'one of these'. If you replace 'machines' with Reptilian Alliance you pretty much have it. They know that if they can manipulate us into these emotional states we will generate the energy they need. You can now see why there is such a focus on manipulating people through fear, stress, anger and resentment into incoherent heart patterns that will disharmonise the entire decoding process and cause mayhem emotionally, mentally and physically. All of this produces low-vibrational energy. People don't think clearly when they are in an imbalanced emotional state. You only have to experience being in a large group of people such as a football crowd to appreciate the power of electromagnetic energy produced by that collective emotion – 'the hairs on the back of my neck stood up'. Different mental and emotional states generate different frequencies, and this can be seen in the work of Japanese writer and researcher, Dr Masaru Emoto. He is well known for his experiments involving the vibrational impact on water. I spent a weekend in London with him a few years ago and visited his centre in Tokyo where he does his work. He has written a number of books, and we produced one together in Japanese. Dr Emoto attaches words, statements or technology to canisters of water. He then freezes the water very quickly and photographs the water crystals. The difference in the structure of the crystals in response to the statements or technology is incredible, as you can see in Figure 96. Dr Emoto's findings are supported by the experiments at the German Aerospace Institute that I outlined earlier. If you saw the effect that a mobile phone has you would never make another call. The crystal on the left was formed by words of love and appreciation, while the other was the result of: 'You make me sick – I want to kill you'. Everything in this reality is a vibrational field made holographically manifest, and this includes the written word. We see words written at the holographic level as 'love' or 'hate', but in their base form they are *vibrational* information. This vibration resonates through the water and its effect can then be captured by photographing the crystals.

This book is now communicating with you on a vibrational level even more profoundly than eye-to-mind. The 'You may me sick – I want to kill you'-type energy is what the Reptilians *need* humans to generate. They are themselves in such a low-vibrational state that they can only absorb what they can synchronise with. Wars, disasters like the Japanese tsunami and catastrophic radiation leak, terrorist attacks such as a 9/11, an economic crash, and angry, hostile public protests, all produce stupendous amounts of the very emotional energy on which the Reptilians feed and recycle back to us in

Figure 96: The water crystal on the left was created by words of love and appreciation, and the other came from: 'You make me sick – I want to kill you'

a feedback loop. This is a major reason why the Reptilian Control System in 'human' form – the Illuminati bloodlines – ensures that events like these continually unfold.

There are Reptilian entities living inside the Earth that operate within visible light, as do the Greys, and there are many Reptilian bases underground where they interact with 'human' scientists to introduce enslaving and controlling technology on the surface and continue their genetic experimentation. The cutting edge of 'science' is not even close to what you see in the public domain. There are also bases on other frequency dimensions of the Earth, because the centre of the Reptilian power structure operates from frequencies beyond visible light. In other words, we can't see them. They can come in and out of visible light using technology, and by energetic means, but they generally operate outside of human sight. I am sure that humans could see them when we had access to a much greater range of visual frequency, but since the genetic intervention we can't see them unless they enter our frequency range, which they *do* here and there. This is one aspect of the 'shape-shifting' phenomenon as a Reptilian energy field replaces a human one and an observer thinks they are seeing a physical transformation. Humans eat 'physical' food, or think they do, but it is holographic food which is only decoded vibrational information.'Good' food is vibrational information that synchronises with the human body energy- field, and 'bad' food distorts it. Illuminati corporations fill the stores with chemically-infested, irradiated bad 'food' for this reason. An imbalanced energy field produces imbalanced thought and emotion (their food source) and stops people getting 'out there' to the greater reality that would set them free and allow them to understand their plight. Reptilians beyond visible light feed directly off vibrational fields, and when we express mental and emotional states we produce energy resonating 'good vibes' or 'bad vibes'. Reptilians want the 'bad vibes', and humanity must continually be exploited to produce them, or their food source is no more. Humanity in a state of love and harmony is the Reptilians' worst nightmare. Explains a lot, eh? Carlos Castaneda quotes shaman Don Juan Matus as saying:

> I know that even now, though you never have suffered hunger ... you have food anxiety, which is none other than the anxiety of the predator who fears that at any moment now its manoeuvre is going to be uncovered and food is going to be denied. Through the mind, which, after all is their mind, the predators inject into the lives of human beings whatever is convenient for them. And they ensure, in this manner, a degree of security to act as a buffer against their fear.

> Sorcerers of ancient Mexico ... reasoned that man must have been a complete being at one point, with stupendous insights, feats of awareness that are mythological legends nowadays. And then, everything seems to disappear, and we have now a sedated man. What I'm saying is that what we have against us is not a simple predator. It is very smart, and organised. It follows a methodical system to render us useless. Man, the magical being that he is destined to be, is no longer magical. He's an average piece of meat. There are no more dreams for man but the dreams of an animal that is being raised to be a piece of meat: trite, conventional, imbecilic.

He is describing the difference between humans of the Real Golden Age, when we had massively expanded awareness, and humans after the Reptilians moved in and changed the way we receive and transmit information. The portrayal of the world of the Blue People, or Na'vi, in the movie, *Avatar,* was very much like the Earth in the Real

Golden Age, and there are two other aspects of that James Cameron film which portray what has happened to humanity. Firstly, you had the left-brain technologists and military goons with no empathy, respect or even understanding of the Blue People's idyllic world in which everything was 'One'. There was communication and respect between the Blue People, animals, trees and the natural world in general. All the left-brain goons knew was that there were resources under the Blue People's world that were very valuable if mined and taken back to Earth. The Reptilians are of the same mentality as the human military portrayed in *Avatar*, only even more extreme. They have been plundering the Earth for resources, not least gold, since they arrived. We are going to find that most of the gold reserves, including those in America's Fort Knox, are not actually there. They have long gone to the Reptilian Alliance. There have been a number of stories circulating that gold bars across the world have gone missing and been replaced by tungsten bars with a gold coating. Some reports have even appeared in the mainstream media. Tungsten is the same density as gold to three decimal places. *Pakistan Daily*, an online news agency, reported that when Bill Clinton was US President '... between 1.3 and 1.5 million 400oz tungsten blanks were allegedly manufactured by a very high-end, sophisticated refiner in the USA'. They totalled more than 16 thousand metric tonnes. The report said that 640,000 of these tungsten blanks were gold plated and shipped to the US 'gold' depository at Fort Knox. It said that the Chinese received a shipment of more than 5,600 gold bars in October 2009 for payment of debts. Tests to guarantee their purity and weight revealed the bars to be fake. The serial numbers confirmed that they originated in America's Fort Knox. Congressman Ron Paul is one of the few politicians on Capitol Hill prepared to challenge the system, and he has been pressing unsuccessfully for a 'purity audit' of the 'gold' in Fort Knox to prove its authenticity. CNBC requested a tour of Fort Knox to film the gold and update the last footage that was taken in 1974. An official declined the request. He said that Fort Knox is a 'closed facility' and he was not aware of any member of Congress touring the facility since 1974. The House of Rothschild, who are earthly representatives of the Reptilian Alliance, have dominated the world gold market, and the price of gold was set every day at the offices of N M Rothschild in London from 1919 until 2004. Then, suddenly, the Rothschilds withdrew from the gold market. The Reptilians are very advanced 'intellectually' and experts in fields like technology and genetics. But they are spiritually dead, and they have been leading humanity in the same direction. This made the spiritually dead human soldiers depicted in the *Avatar* movie the perfect symbols of the Reptilian mentality. Another point worthy of mention is the word 'Avatar' itself. The filmmakers say: 'An avatar is a human mind transferred into a genetically-engineered body of a human/Na'vi hybrid.' This was done in the story so that the human military could infiltrate the Na'vi society without being seen, because they looked like the Na'vi. Avatar was released in 2009, and it portrays in theme what I have been describing since 1998 – human society has been infiltrated by a non-human controlling force, a predator that hides behind human form

Illuminati Bloodlines

All humans have very significant reptilian genetics, especially the reptilian brain, or 'R-complex', as scientists call it. A substance called 'Pheromone' is secreted and released by animals to detect members of the same species, and the pheromones in human women

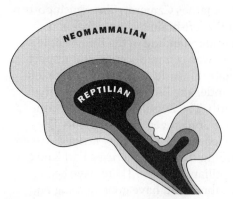

Figure 97: The reptilian brain, or R-complex, is a fundamental influence of human behaviour and perception

and iguanas are a chemical match. Carl Sagan, the great American cosmologist, wrote a book called *The Dragons of Eden* describing the impact of reptilian genetics on human behaviour. He said that it was unwise to ignore the reptilian component of human nature, particularly our ritualistic and hierarchical behaviour. 'On the contrary,' he said,'the model may help us understand what human beings are really about.' Sagan knew far more than he ever said about what was going on, because of the way the sciences are policed. He was bang on with the impact on human behaviour of reptilian genetics. The reptilian brain is a prime influence on human society and behaviour (Fig 97). Researcher, Skip Largent, highlighted this in an Internet article about the 'R-complex':

> At least five human behaviours originate in the reptilian brain. Without defining them, I shall simply say that in human activities they find expression in: obsessive compulsive behaviour; personal day-to-day rituals and superstitious acts; slavish conformance to old ways of doing things; ceremonial re-enactments; obeisance to precedent, as in legal, religious, cultural, and other matters and all manner of deceptions.

Anyone recognise that in the world that we experience every day? Those traits are the very lifeblood of world religions, secret societies and royal protocol and ritual, and these organisations and royal bloodlines are all the creations of the Reptilian conspiracy. I say that humans didn't have a reptilian brain, or it was nothing like as significant, before the Reptilian genetic intervention. I'll talk more about this and how we are locked into the 'Matrix' in part through the reptilian brain in the next chapter; but for now I'll just say that even mainstream science admits that the reptilian brain gives us character traits like aggression; cold-bloodedness (no empathy) and ritualistic behaviour; a desire for control, power and ownership – 'territoriality'; might is right; domination over others and submission to others (which one depends on your personality type); compulsions and obsessions; worship; rigidity; and a desire for social hierarchies. Does that describe human society, or what? Yes, because it is a Reptilian-created and controlled society. Humans have other parts of the brain (and crucially the heart) that can balance out the traits of the reptilian brain; but, of course, any group that has a greater infusion of reptilian genetics is going to express those traits in a far more extreme way. Enter the Illuminati bloodlines. The Reptilians genetically-engineered particular bloodlines that were specially designed to allow them to manipulate and control the human world of visible light while looking as human as everybody else. Reptilians operating outside of visible light basically 'wear' these genetic hybrid holographic computers to infiltrate human society in precisely the same way as portrayed in the movie *Avatar*. The far greater genetic compatibility means there is a far greater vibrational and frequency compatibility. This allows these human- Reptilian hybrids of the Illuminati families to be 'possessed', and their mental and emotional processes (actions) controlled from another reality (Fig 98). This is the true nature of the Illuminati families that today sit atop the pyramids of global politics, banking, transnational corporations, media, Big Pharma, Big Biotech, Big Oil, Big Food, and all the rest. There are 13 bloodlines at the top of the hybrid's hierarchical pyramid and the British royal family is among them, as are the Rothschilds and the Rockefellers.

Their hybrid DNA has dual codes – human and reptilian. While the human codes are activated and open, a human form is projected holographically, but when they shift (*shapeshift*) and open their

Figure 98: Genetic compatibility means vibrational compatibility and therefore extremely powerful 'possession'

reptilian codes, a reptilian form is projected. They carefully plan their interbreeding so the reptilian codes don't become so dominant that they will take reptilian form when they don't intend to. One way that they keep the human codes open is to drink copious amounts of mammalian blood that carries and stimulates human genetic coding. This is one reason for their obsession with human sacrifice rituals and blood drinking. The Reptilians most preferred breeding partners are blond-haired, blue-eyed people and also those with red hair and blue eyes. All that stuff in Nazi Germany with the Aryan 'master race' was really about producing blond-haired, blue-eyed people for Reptilian interbreeding. American author, Stewart Swerdlow, has direct experience of the story that I am describing here. Stewart was imprisoned for many years in an Illuminati mind-control and genetics programme at Montauk on Long Island, New York. He was taken at night by what he thought were extraterrestrials but, in fact, were American government and military operatives at Montauk. A common way that they confuse their targets is to make them think they have had an extraterrestrial 'encounter', when the people involved are human. This happened to Stewart, shockingly with the permission of his mother. Stewart says that he learned about the agenda for global domination and the reptilian entities behind it all during his time at Montauk. He said that he had seen reptilian humanoids at Montauk and they 'seemed to pop in and out of physical reality'. Even the Reptilians are not the bottom of the rabbit hole; they are only another level of it. Stewart Swerdlow says that the Reptilians were created by the 'transparent people'. These entities 'cannot really enter into the physical dimensions because their energy vibratory rate is so high that it cannot sustain a physical body'. When they do appear, he says, 'it looks like a transparent glass shell'. Stewart learned that Reptilian geneticists wanted a 50–50 mix of genetics to produce a body that looked human while being able to shapeshift into reptilian form: 'Shapeshifting was accomplished simply by concentrating on the genetics the hybrid wished to open, or lock up, whatever the case may be.' He says that the term 'blue bloods' for royal and aristocratic families comes from the fact that the blood of the hybrids contains more copper and it turns blue-green during a process called oxidation.

Figure 99: The 'human' energy field of the bloodline hybrids is the one that the observer normally decodes, but overshadowing the human is a reptilian field and when that becomes dominant the observer decodes ('sees') a 'shift' from one to the other. These two forms are actually encoded in the hybrid DNA and when the codes change, so does the outer form

We are only decoding the five-sense visible-light band of frequency, and when we see these hybrids they appear to be human like the rest of us. But if we could see further into the frequency field, or if their reptilian codes kicked in, we would see something very different (Fig 99). Remember those traits of reptilian genetics: aggression; cold-blooded (no empathy) and ritualistic behaviour; a desire for control, power and ownership – 'territoriality'; might is right; domination; compulsions and obsessions; worship; rigidity; and a desire for social hierarchies. The Illuminati bloodlines express these traits to a far more extreme degree than the human population with their far more extreme levels of reptilian genetics. The cold-blooded (no empathy) trait, is one that I have been highlighting for a long time. The hybrid bloodlines have empathy deleted from their genetic personality (decoding system), and empathy is the fail-safe mechanism of behaviour. You don't express extreme behaviour that kills, hurts or damages other people if you have empathy with how they will feel as a consequence of your actions. But there are no limits to what you will do when you can't feel empathy, and that's the situation with the Illuminati Reptilian hybrids. Pepper-bomb cities full of civilians? No problem. Mass poison the human population through additives in food and water, radiation, microwaves and the like? What fun. Kill 3,000 people on 9/11, and millions more since, justified by 9/11 and the need to 'fight terrorism'? How we laughed. I have been saying for so long that people are never going to understand what is happening in the world if they judge what these bloodlines would do on the basis of what they *themselves* would do. The Reptilian hybrids are not the same as you and me in the way they see life and reality. They are the means through which the Reptilian Alliance can invade human society without being seen for what they really are. When scientists are working with material that is too dangerous to handle they will have it placed in a sealed tank while they stand outside and don arms-length sealed gloves to work inside the tank. Imagine the scientist to be a Reptilian entity, the tank to be the human visible-light frequency range and the gloves to be the hybrid bloodlines, and you get the picture of the role the Illuminati families play in all of this (Fig 100). The Reptilians are very close to our reality – what Stewart Swerdlow calls 'borderline physical' – but they mostly don't appear in our reality or it would obviously give their game away. They also have a problem with Earth's current atmosphere and this is why they are working to change it to make it more suitable for them. I'll talk about this later.

Reptilian pyramid builders

Reptilian hybrids were seeded and planted all over the ancient world and, in league with their Reptilian owners, they established the first 'civilisations' after the Earth recovered from the last global cataclysm. These civilisations appeared in places like Sumer, which became Babylon and is now Iraq; Egypt; the Indus Valley; Mesoamerica (including the Mayans); the Andes in South America (the Incas); and China (Fig 101). But the Reptilian connection to Africa goes back much further, as I will explain in a moment. Here you have the reason why these civilisations were far more advanced than the rest of the world. The Reptilian Alliance was the source of the knowledge that allowed amazing ancient structures to be built by 'primitive people' with stones weighing hundreds of tonnes. We would struggle to build some of them even today. But this is quite straightforward when you know you are not dealing with something 'physical', but a *holographic* projection from an information field. The Reptilians were the pyramid builders all over the world and not just in Egypt. They are found in Central America, Mesopotamia, China, all over (Fig 102). There are endless pyramids under the ground across the world that have yet to be discovered. Vast pyramids have been found in Bosnia in Europe that were believed to be just strange looking hills covered in soil, grass and trees; but excavations revealed that underneath were ancient pyramids, and one called the

Figure 100: Neil Hague's symbolic image of the 'scientist' (Reptilian) outside the 'tank' (visible-light reality) manipulating inside the tank through the 'gloves' (the hybrid bloodlines)

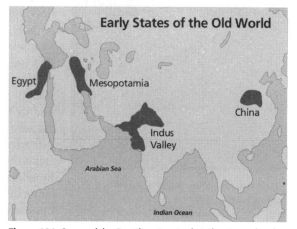

Figure 101: Some of the Reptilian-inspired civilisations after the last cataclysm; but the Reptilian connection to Africa goes back much further

Figure 102: The Reptilians were the pyramid builders.

Figure 103: 'Primitive' humans did this?

Figure 104: One of the amazing images in the Nazca Desert in Peru.

'Pyramid of the Moon' has been carbon-dated to be at least 10,000 years old. I think the pyramids were built as part of a network that connects the waveform dimension of the Earth to the Reptilian 'Matrix', or false reality, that we are decoding and believing to be real. The Mayans of Mexico told of a reptilian race, the 'Iguana Men', who came from the sky and taught them the art of pyramid building. The Reptilian Alliance was the knowledge source for the incredible structures made from massive chunks of stone in the Inca lands of Peru. Stones of 400 tonnes have been put together so perfectly that you can't put a sheet of paper between them (Fig 103). The Reptilian Alliance was the 'brains' behind the ancient Nazca lines in Peru – the incredible depictions of birds, insects and animals using one continuous line. They are so big that they can only be seen in their entirety from an aircraft (Fig 104). The stone statues on Easter Island in the Pacific are another example.

The hybrid bloodlines implanted into the lands of Sumer and Babylon, or Mesopotamia, the land between the Tigris and the Euphrates rivers, are highly significant in relation to the Illuminati families in the positions of power in both public and behind the scenes today. So, too, is ancient Egypt. But there are others that have been 'incubating' for centuries in the Far East, especially China, waiting to become a global influence. This is also the case with India to an extent. I have been saying since the 1990s that we should watch for the economic and military emergence of China. This is a blueprint society for the world that the Reptilian Alliance and its hybrids want to impose upon all of us. Sumer (roughly 5,000 BC to 2000 BC) was preceded by the Ubaid culture, from which came those reptilian mother-and-baby figurines. Sumer was followed in these same lands by Babylon. Other civilisations in the same area include the Assyrian and Chaldean, and today this land is called Iraq. This region is of great significance to the Reptilian hybrids and not only for oil as most people believe. Many of today's Illuminati bloodlines came from this area thousands of years ago. It is not a surprise, therefore, to find that the ancient clay tablets found buried in Iraq since the 19th century tell of a reptilian race called the Anunnaki that came to Earth to exploit humans as a slave race mining for gold and other resources in what is now Africa. Evidence has been found of gold mining in Africa at least 100,000 years ago. The tablets say the Anunnaki also embarked in Africa on a programme of genetic manipulation. Africa is home to the Tsodilo Hills, where the San people say that humans (as we know them) were created by the 'Great Python' with his symbolic bag of eggs, and where serpent worship goes back at least 70,000 years. The tablets say that the Anunnaki ('Those Who From Heaven To Earth Came') were led by their king, Anu, but the operation on Earth was overseen by two brothers, Enlil and Enki. This matches Zulu accounts of the Reptilian Chitauri which tell of two brothers, Wowane and Mpanku. The tablets say that Enki, the chief scientist and geneticist, and a female, who the tablets call Ninkharsag, an expert in medicine, led the human genetic programme which, after many failures, produced the genetic form we know today. The tablets describe, as I said earlier, how Ziusudra, the Sumerian version of the biblical 'Noah', long before the biblical texts were written, was told by Enki that the Anunnaki were going to cause great cataclysms on Earth and he should build a large 'boat'. The themes of *Genesis* are a re-written version of Sumerian stories from thousands of years earlier with the reptilian Anunnaki morphing into a single biblical 'God' (with the odd plural still surviving here and there). Credo Mutwa has spent his long lifetime studying ancient African legend and lore and he says that all the Sumerian and Egyptian gods can be found in southern Africa long before they appeared in North Africa and the Middle East. This supports the Sumerian contention that the Anunnaki first located in Africa.

Serpent Monarchy

The hybrid bloodlines, which are far more reptilian than the general population, were genetically-engineered both to represent Reptilian Alliance interests within visible light and to hide the identity of the real controllers. These 'elite' bloodlines became known as 'demigods' – part human–part god – and they became the 'royal families' of the ancient world who became the royal, aristocratic and Illuminati families of today. The 'blue bloods' have always obsessively interbred, and they still do. Genetics to the Reptilians is a software program and they need to keep it intact or the information in the hybrid software will be diluted, eventually deleted, through breeding with non-hybrids. The bloodline families often tend to choose the partners for their offspring for this reason, and many marry for genetic necessity rather than attraction. The Reptilian obsession with genetics can be seen in the obsession many of them have with breeding horses and why horse racing is referred to as 'the sport of kings'. The ancient clay tablets found in Iraq (Sumer/Babylon) said that 'kingship' was introduced by the Anunnaki (via their hybrids), and so no wonder that Sargon the Great, ruler of the Sumer/Akkadian Empire, claimed that he descended from the gods. This hybrid genetics is the origin of the theme of the 'divine right to rule' – the right to rule because of your 'god' genetics. Chinese emperors claimed the right to be ruler because of their genetic connection to the 'serpent gods'. So, too, did 'royal' bloodlines in Japan and Central America. Chinese emperors were called 'Lung' or 'Dragons' and earlier ones were depicted with reptilian features. Qin Shi Huang, the first Qin emperor who unified China and built much of the Great Wall, was said to have been born with a 'dragon-like countenance'. Emperors in

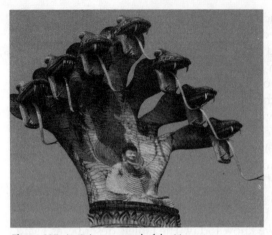

Figure 105: An Asian portrayal of the Nagas

general were described as part- human, part-serpent. Japanese emperors were said to be related to 'Dragon Gods' that came from the sky. The Nagas people in India were described in similar terms. Accounts say that they could take either human or reptilian form and it appears that they expanded into Tibet and parts of China. The Buddhist text, the *Mahavyutpatti*, names 80 kings of India who descended from the Nagas or 'Serpent Kings'. The Nagas were described as offspring from the interbreeding of humans with the 'serpent gods', and Indian rulers claimed a genetic connection to them (Fig 105). In ancient Media – now Iran, with an empire stretching into parts of Turkey – they referred to their kings as 'Mar'. This means 'snake' in Persian. They were known as the 'Dragon Dynasty of Media', or 'descendants of the dragon'. Cecrops, the first Mycenaean king of Athens, was depicted as a human with a serpent's tail, and another, Erechtheus, was worshipped after his death as a live snake. It was he who founded the Eleusinian Mystery School through which knowledge was communicated only to selected initiates. Mystery schools were the forerunners of today's secret society networks. Some were established with good intent, but most were created to keep advanced and hidden knowledge in the hands of the few. Australian aborigines tell of a reptilian race living inside the Earth (true) which governs humanity through extensive technology. Aborigines say they are descended from a race of 'dragon-humans' that lived on a vast continent in the Pacific Ocean (Mu or Lemuria) of which Australia is a remnant, big as it is. There is a Greek legend that says another king, Kadmus, became a live snake when he died. There has been throughout history a fundamental literal and symbolic connection between royalty and the 'serpent'. Egyptian pharaohs, who were said to be gods in human bodies, were depicted in the form of a cobra – a major symbol used by the ancients for the Reptilian 'gods'. They were given a cobra 'headdress', which had a cobra on the forehead (third eye) and a cobra's belly on the chin. The hybrid bloodline was also widely symbolised as people with the top half of their body human and their legs portrayed as snakes (Figs 106 to 109).

Reptilian hybrids were seeded into cultures throughout the world and they have acted ever since as the visible light, five-sense vehicles for their hidden Reptilian masters. Why don't the Reptilians just come out and take over? (1) There is a vibrational and atmospheric problem for most of them in staying in our frequency for long periods unless they remain in their own vibrational/atmospheric 'bubble' through technological means; (2) It is far better for the target population not to know you exist when you are feeding off humanity's emotional energy and using more than seven billion people without their knowledge as your slave race; (3) That very figure, seven billion and rising. Humans far outnumber their controllers. The Reptilian tyranny does not involve the entire reptilian humanoid species, only a renegade grouping, but there are

Figure 106   Figure 107

Reptilian hybrid royalty and
bloodlines were often depicted
as a human torso with snakes
for legs and symbolised as a
cobra. The pharaohs were
believed to be gods in human
form and they were
symbolised with a cobra
'headdress'; a cobra on the
forehead; and the belly of a
cobra emerging from the chin

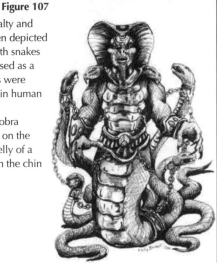

Figure 108   Figure 109

Reptilians doing to others elsewhere in the Universe what they are doing to humans. You see their modus operandi portrayed in the animated movie, *A Bug's Life*, in the relationship between the few grasshoppers that impose their will upon a large colony of ants. The chief grasshopper says that the ants have to be kept 'in line', because 'they outnumber us a hundred to one and if they ever figure that out – there goes our way of life'. This is the relationship between the Reptilians and humans. If you haven't seen *A Bug's Life* it is worth giving it a watch. It is an excellent metaphor for what is happening to humanity. The only difference is that the ants can see the grasshoppers while humans can't see the Reptilians – only their hybrid vehicles.

Today Sumer, Tomorrow the World

The most travelled of the hybrid bloodlines, in terms of expanding out of one region and across the planet to impact upon global society, are those that came out of Sumer/Babylon and Egypt. They moved up through what is now Turkey and the Caucasus Mountains into Northern Europe and across to Russia where they became the royal families and aristocracy of Europe – East and West – often through interbreeding with Reptilian hybrids seeded into those regions (Fig 110). They established Rome and its empire, Ancient Greece, and the Khazar Empire in the Caucasus region, location of

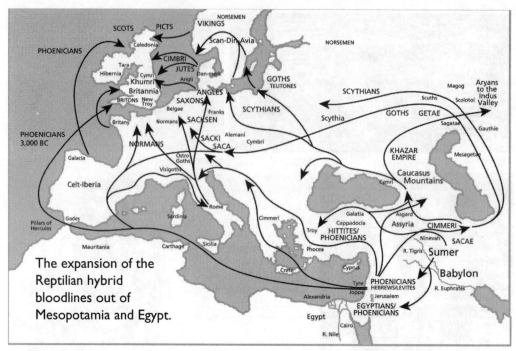

Figure 110: The expansion of the Reptilian hybrid bloodlines out of Mesopotamia and Egypt

today's Georgia, among many others. The story of Khazaria is worth highlighting given its impact on the world today. King Bulan, the King of Khazaria, adopted the religion of Judaism in about AD 740 and the whole nation followed suit. These people had no historical connection to what is now called Israel. They only adopted the religion of Judaism. The Khazars moved northwards into today's Ukraine, Hungary, Lithuania, Russia and Poland when their empire crumbled. Many of them later headed west into Germany and Western Europe. These are the overwhelming majority of what we call Jewish people today who are located primarily in Israel and the United States. The former Khazar people are known as Ashkenazi Jews (plural Ashkenazim), and some writers estimate that perhaps 90 to 95 per cent of those calling themselves 'Jewish' worldwide are Ashkenazi. The Jewish writer, Arthur Koestler, said of this re-emerging history in his book, *The Thirteenth Tribe* (Random House; 1999):

> ...[It] would mean that their ancestors came not from the Jordan, but from the Volga, not from Canaan but from the Caucasus, once believed to be the cradle of the Aryan race [hence 'Caucasian'] and that genetically they are more closely connected to the Hun, Uigur and Magyar tribes than to the seed of Abraham, Isaac and Jacob. Should this turn out to be the case, then the term 'anti-Semitism' would be void of meaning, based on a misapprehension shared by both the killers and their victims. The story of the Khazar Empire, as it slowly emerges from the past, begins to look like the most cruel hoax which history has ever perpetrated.

It *is* the case. What are called Jewish people today *have no historical connection to Israel*. This was just a fable concocted by the Reptilian-hybrid House of Rothschild and others to justify the takeover of Palestine and create mayhem in the Middle East as part of a much bigger global plan. The mass of Jewish people have been 'had', as much as anyone else, and at great cost for many over the years. Zionism has nothing to do with what is best for Jewish people. It is, at its core, a secret society created and controlled by the Rothschild global network to advance the goal of global domination. This is why you find so many Rothschild Zionists, as I call them, in positions of power all over the world in politics, banking, business, and media ownership, etc. These institutions are not owned and controlled by the mass of Jewish people that have been victims of this deceit. They are owned and controlled by the Reptilian hybrid network that has infiltrated all societies and races, and within which the House of Rothschild is a prime influence. The king of Khazaria, incidentally, was called the 'Khagan' or 'Kagan'. Thus 'Kagan' became a common 'Jewish' name. The Khazar story, and the fraudulent real estate claims on Israel, have been uncovered by Jewish writers and scholars, including Shlomo Sand, Professor of History at Tel Aviv University, in his book, *The Invention of the Jewish People* (Verso; 2010). He writes:

> Even Ben Zion Dinur, the father of Israeli historiography, was not hesitant about describing the Khazars as the origin of the Jews in Eastern Europe, and describes Khazaria as 'the mother of the diasporas' in Eastern Europe. But more or less since 1967, anyone who talks about the Khazars as the ancestors of the Jews of Eastern Europe is considered naive and moonstruck.

Of course they are. The Rothschilds and their creation, Zionism, hardly want to have historians and others telling the truth and demolishing the fraudulent claim to a historical right to Israel. I tell the Khazar story at length in *Human Race Get Off Your Knees*. Stewart Swerdlow, who is Jewish, has compiled his information from very different sources to my own, but we uncovered the same themes. Stewart writes in his book, *Blue Blood, True Blood* (Expansions Publishing; 2002):

> ... [the Sumerians] mostly established themselves in the Caucasus Mountains and [later]became the Khazars. From here, they spread west towards Europe, seeding the national identities for the Vikings, the Franks, the Teutonic [German] peoples and the Russians. Keep in mind that when Atlantis sank, some of those refugees went to Western Europe and developed into the Celts. Some went to Greece and others to the Italian Peninsula. These peoples were here before the hybrids [Sumerians] moved in ... These Blueblood leaders also infiltrated the Middle Eastern peoples, such as the biblical Canaanites ...

The hybrid bloodline 'elite' families of the Roman Empire interbred with the 'elite' families of the rest of Europe to produce European royalty and aristocracy. Swerdlow writes:

> ... Babylon was the civilization that Sumer developed into as it expanded into Central Asia to become the Khazars. In fact, many of the Blueblood organisations that developed through the millennia called themselves Babylon Brotherhoods. [They] later combined with the secret Atlantean–Egyptian schools in Europe to become the Freemasons. Some of these immigrants went by the name of Bauer, now known as the Rothschilds. The family quickly took control of the financial and trade foundations of Europe.

The former Sumerian and Babylonian bloodline network, which became the Khazars and Ashkenazi Jews, widely interbred with European royalty and aristocracy. Leslie Gilbert Pine was an editor of *Burke's Peerage*, the publication that tracks royal and aristocratic genealogy. He said: 'The Jews have made themselves so closely connected with the British peerage that the two classes are unlikely to suffer loss which is not mutual.' This applies to the British royal family, too. Canadian researcher and writer, Henry Makow, whose grandparents suffered in the Nazi concentration camps, said that 'the marriage of Jewish finance and British aristocracy took place literally ... spendthrift gentry married the daughters of rich Jews'. Leslie Gilbert Pine said: 'An ancient estate is likely to be sold unless some large sums are found. The sums are found from marriage with a Jewish heiress.' The 5th Earl of Roseberry married the only daughter and heiress of Baron Mayer de Rothschild and later became British Prime Minister. Pine said that 'alliances between Jewish ladies and British lords are mostly of this type, the wife providing large sums ... while the aristocrat has the title and ancient estate'. The Rothschild bloodline is always turning up in connection with royalty and aristocracy. Princess Diana's mother, Frances Ruth Burke Roche, was a Rothschild. She is better known as Frances Shand Kydd. Tina Brown, former editor of *Vanity Fair*, reveals in her book, *The Diana Chronicles* (Anchor; 2008), that Diana's father could well have been billionaire businessman and cousin of the Rothschilds, James Goldsmith. Brown says that Diana's mother was having a long-running affair with Goldsmith at the time that Diana was conceived in late 1960. There is certainly a close resemblance between Diana and members of the Goldsmith family. This would make Diana's son, Prince William, a Rothschild bloodline on both sides through his mother and grandmother, and James Goldsmith, his 'grandfather'. The Goldsmith family changed their name from Goldschmidt when they moved to England from Germany in 1895. They were close associates and neighbours of the Rothschilds in Frankfurt from the 18th century. Mayer Amschel Rothschild, founder of the Rothschild dynasty, is reported to have met with the Goldschmidts in 1773 to agree a plan to bankrupt nations and control world finance. The meeting also involved members of the Schiff, Oppenheimer and Warburg families and other former Khazars. Well, there is no doubt that this is precisely what they have done. The Rockefeller family (formerly Rockenfelder) are also former Khazars who went to America from Germany. There has been speculation that Kate Middleton, who married Prince William at Westminster Abbey in 2011, could also have Rothschild–Goldsmith genealogical connections. Her mother's maiden name was Carole Goldsmith. You would certainly confirm the considerable Rothschild bloodline connection to the 'House of Windsor' (the German House of Saxe–Coburg–Gotha) if you knew their secret history. There will clearly be a Rothschild on the British throne should William become king. But how many more have there been?

When in Rome

Some of the places and cultures the bloodlines established have remained at the heart of their conspiracy to this day. Most notable is Rome, where the Christian religion as we know it originated. Rome remains a global centre for the Reptilian-hybrid secret-society network that established and controls the Roman Church, or Roman Catholic Church as it became. Elite secret societies in the global web, such as the Jesuits, Knights of Malta,

Knights Templar and Opus Dei are all closely connected to the Vatican. The Reptilians and their hybrids established all the major religions, and most of the smaller ones. Christianity, Judaism and Islam, among others, all came out of the lands formerly dominated by Sumer and Babylon and the wider Middle East. Translations of the ancient clay tablets found in what is now Iraq prove beyond doubt that the biblical Old Testament, a pillar of Judaism and Christianity – and also connected to Islam – is a rehash and revamp of much older accounts from Sumer and beyond employing different locations and names for the heroes and characters. The story of Moses being found in the bulrushes was told long before in the very similar story of Sargon of Agade (Akkad), the King of Babylon around 2550 BC. We have already seen that the story of Noah and the Great Flood had the same source. Bloodlines from Sumer and Babylon took their satanic religion wherever they went. They practised it openly at first, but later they had to hide it behind symbolic rituals and cover stories. The 'Christian' trinity is the Babylonian trinity. The trinity in Babylon was Nimrod, the father, or sun god; Semiramis, or Ishtar, the virgin mother and goddess; and Ninus, or Tammuz, the virgin-born son. The bloodlines that eventually relocated to Rome eventually hid their satanic religion behind the smokescreen of 'Christianity' and the trinity of God, the Father (Nimrod in disguise); Jesus, the son (Tammuz in disguise); and the 'Holy Ghost' or 'Holy Spirit'. Christianity symbolises the Holy Spirit as a dove, and this is how the Babylonians symbolised Semiramis/Ishtar (from which we get the name and festival of 'Easter'). Titles and attributes that the Babylonians gave to the goddess, Semiramis/Ishtar, such as 'Virgin Mother', and 'Queen of Heaven', were bestowed on 'Mother Mary' by the 'new' Christianity in Rome. The Roman Church, from which all Christianity originated, was only the Church of Babylon relocated. You can see the progression Figure 111 of the 'virgin mother and son' from the reptilian figures found in graves of the pre-Sumer Ubaid people right through to Mother Mary. The goddess was symbolic of the planet Venus, but also became associated with the Moon. The ancients symbolised the Moon as a 'chariot' of gods and goddesses. Selene, the Greek moon goddess, was depicted riding a silver chariot (the Moon) pulled by white horses; and

Figure 111: The universal goddess: The reptilian mother and baby in pre-Sumer Mesopotamia; Queen Semiramis (Ishtar) and Tammuz in Babylon; Isis and Horus in Egypt; and Mother Mary and Jesus in Christianity

the Indian god, Chandra, travelled on a moon chariot pulled through the sky by ten white horses. Roman Emperor Constantine decided what Christians must believe at the Council of Nicaea in AD 325 when the so-called 'Nicene Creed' was imposed that Christians are told they must believe to this day. Constantine wasn't even a Christian. He worshipped a sun god called Sol Invictus, the 'Unconquered Sun'. Most people didn't have a problem when he decreed that Christianity would be the state religion of the Roman Empire, or what was left of it. The 'new' faith was only their old religion under another name and guise. They had been worshipping deities like Bacchus, the Roman version of the Greek Dionysus, and they were simply being renamed 'Jesus'. This is what was said about Dionysus/Bacchus:

> Dionysus was born of a virgin on December 25th and, as the Holy Child, was placed in a Manger. He was a travelling teacher who performed miracles. He 'rode in a triumphal procession on an ass'. He was a sacred king killed and eaten in a Eucharistic ritual for fecundity and purification. He rose from the dead on March 25th. He was the God of the Vine, and turned water into wine. He was called 'King of Kings' and 'God of Gods'. He was considered the 'Only Begotten Son', 'Saviour', 'Redeemer', 'Sin Bearer', 'Anointed One' and the 'Alpha and Omega'. He was identified with the Ram or Lamb. His sacrificial title of 'Dendrites' or 'Young Man of the Tree' intimates that he was hung on a tree or crucified.

Anyone heard that before anywhere? The same story was told about deities across the world long before 'Jesus', including another Roman and Persian chap called Mithra or Mithras – he was 'the vine', the 'good shepherd', the usual deal. I have been to the Vatican a few times and it is full of sun god and moon goddess symbolism, and Illuminati symbolism in general. The centrepiece at St Peter's Square is an original obelisk from Heliopolis, the 'City of the Sun' in ancient Egypt. They have stuck a little cross at the top to make it seem 'Christian' (Fig 112). Nice touch. There is also an

Figure 112: The Church of Rome is the satanic Church of Babylon relocated and the original obelisk from the 'City of the Sun' in ancient Egypt has been 'Christianised' with a little cross. How sweet. The Christmas tree and the birth of 'Jesus' scene all go way back into the 'Pagan' world

original ancient Egyptian obelisk in the key Illuminati city of London. This is 'Cleopatra's Needle' which stands alongside the River Thames – named after the Celtic goddess, Temesis. The Thames is renamed the 'Isis' when it passes through the Illuminati indoctrination centre at Oxford. Isis is an Egyptian goddess and another 'virgin mother'. New York and Paris have original Egyptian obelisks, too, in Central Park and in the Place de la Concorde, which Princess Diana's car passed no more than a minute or so before it crashed. The Paris obelisk is painted gold at the tip – the golden penis of Osiris. You can see the progression of the hybrid bloodlines through their symbols, names and even architecture. One of the famous Seven

Figure 113: Capitol Hill symbolised quite rightly by David Dees as a skull

Figure 114: 'The Keys of St Peter' symbol is really the 'Skull and Bones'

Hills of Rome is called Capitoline Hill where they built the ancient Temple of Jupiter. It is called Capitoline because, the story goes, a human skull was found when they were digging foundations for the temple. The Latin for 'skull' or 'head' is 'caput', which is why we use that word today to mean that something is dead, or basically knackered. When the bloodlines that established Rome later located their centre of American government in Washington D.C., they called the building 'Capitol Hill', the 'Hill of the Skull' (Fig 113). Some other State capitals do the same, and the word 'capital' also has the same origin of 'caput'. The human skull and the skull-and-bones are major symbols for the bloodlines. We have the Skull and Bones Society alongside Yale University in the United States where students from the bloodline, the future leaders and administrators of the conspiracy, including the Bush family, are officially initiated into the web as young men. The Skull and Bones Society was taken to America from Germany, birthplace of the House of Rothschild, and many of its initiates end up in influential positions in public or behind the scenes. US Presidents, Father and Boy Bush, are but two examples of Skull and Bones initiates who have had to lie naked in a coffin with a ribbon tied to their willies as part of the initiation. These people are running our world. The 'crossed keys of St Peter' that you find all over Rome and the Vatican is really a symbolic skull-and-bones (Fig 114). We have this theme in the story of 'Jesus', too, with the Bible saying that he was crucified on a hill called Golgotha, which means 'Place of the Skull', as does the alternative word, Calvary.

Let's hear it for the goddess

The Capitol Building in Washington D.C. is believed to be a symbol of 'free America' when it is, in fact, a satanic temple controlled by satanic law and ritual. The most famous symbol of American 'liberty' is the Statue of Liberty in New York Harbour. But this is not a symbol of freedom; it is a symbol of oppression. The statue is a representation of the ancient goddess known as Semiramis/Ishtar in Babylon and by other names elsewhere. Goddess deities invariably relate to Venus and the Moon. Look at how the ancients depicted Semiramis and you will see where the Statue of Liberty

Figure 115: How Queen Semiramis (Ishtar) was portrayed in the ancient world. Seen her before?

Figure 116: The Babylonian goddess, alias the 'Statue of Liberty', holding the flame of Nimrod, the symbol of Saturn

Figure 117: The mirror-image of the 'Statue of Liberty' (the Babylonian goddess) on an island in the River Seine in Paris

came from (Fig 115). 'Liberty' is holding the flaming torch that the Babylonians used to symbolise their sun god, Nimrod, and it represents the 'golden seed' of the 13 leading hybrid bloodlines (Fig 116). The number 13 is a key number (vibration) for the Illuminati families and so we have the US 'Super Congress' made up of six Democrats and six Republicans with the deciding vote of the President – 13. The Statue of Liberty is also standing on a symbol of the Sun. It is now clear to me that at least many sun gods that appear to be quite obvious symbols of the sun that we know today are really symbols for what they call the 'Old Sun' and the 'Black Sun' – *Saturn*. The reason for this will become clear in the next chapter. The key to it all is Saturn and the Moon, with Jupiter involved also.

Semiramis/Ishtar was said to have come to Earth in a 'moon egg' and this became known as 'Ishtar's (Easter's) egg'. Easter and Christmas are pre- Christian festivals. The Statue of Liberty was given to New York by French Freemasons in Paris who knew exactly what it was meant to portray. They have a mirror image standing on an island in the River Seine (Fig 117). The 'Goddess Freedom' on top of the Capitol Building has the same meaning, as does the Goddess Columbia and the goddess holding the scales that is used to symbolise 'justice' (lack of it, more like) around the world. I said that Semiramis/Ishtar was symbolised as a dove in Babylon. The Romans worshipped her as Venus Columba – Venus the Dove. The French word for 'dove' is 'colombe' and it is close to the Latin word 'coluber', which means a snake or serpent. You find, hardly surprisingly, symbols of the goddess as the dove in St Peter's Basilica in Rome (Fig 118). Washington D.C. is located in the District of Columbia. People think that this must have something to do with Christopher Columbus, but it doesn't. It relates to Columba/colombe – the dove. The Mother Lodge of Freemasonry in London, established in 1717, is located in Great Queen Street. 'Great Queen' was one of the titles given to the Babylonian goddess. This London 'Mother Lodge' introduced Freemasonry to America. Two other names for the ancient Venus/Moon goddess are Europa and Diana. Europe was clearly named after Europa. This makes the Illuminati-created European Union the 'Union of the Goddess'. The goddess was depicted with 12 stars around her head standing on a

Figure 119: The goddess with the twelve stars around her head standing on the serpent moon. This is the origin of the twelve-star symbol of the European Union

Figure 120:

Figure 118: Nimrod the Black Sun (Saturn) and the dove of the Babylonian goddess behind the Chair of St Peter.

serpent moon, and this is the origin of the 12-star logo of the European – *Europa* – Union (Figs 119 and 120). We have the European Union as a front for the Union of the Goddess and Washington D.C., the centre of government in the United States, in the District of the Goddess, or 'the Dove'. This is not a coincidence. Earl Spencer, the brother of Princess Diana, said in his address at her funeral service at Westminster Abbey that she was named after the ancient goddess, Diana. This was the Roman name for the Greek, Artemis, who is depicted in the Vatican. You can see her with the bees symbolically on her breasts in the earlier image of the skull-and-bones 'crossed keys of St Peter'. Bees and the beehive are a symbol of the bloodline and so you have the beehive/skull symbolised above the crossed keys. Bees were also a symbol of the Merovingian bloodline which has come to prominence in recent times through books like *The Holy Blood and the Holy Grail* and *The Da Vinci Code*. The Merovingian bloodline produced the Merovingian kings that ruled from AD 500–751 in what we now call France and Germany. Legend says that Merovee, founder of the Merovingian dynasty, was seeded by a 'sea monster'. This theme comes up quite a bit. Legends about Alexander the Great, who invaded Egypt and Mesopotamia before dying in Babylon in 323 BC, say that his real father was the serpent god, 'Ammon' (Hidden). Alexander was known as the 'Serpent's Son'. Some writers claim that the Merovingian bloodline is that of Jesus; but it's not. How can it be when there was no Jesus? It is, however, one of the Reptilian hybrid bloodlines. The Merovingian kings worshipped the goddess, Diana, the 'Mother of the Gods'. Princess Diana was assassinated in Paris, a city built by the Merovingian kings, in a tunnel called Pont de l'Alma. This translates as 'bridge or passage of the Moon Goddess'. She passed the penis of the sun god (Saturn) in the Place de la Concorde minutes before she died. People take their tributes to a depiction of the flame

Figure 121: The 'Statue of Liberty' flame on a black pentagram on top of the Pont de l'Alma where people take their tributes to Princess Diana

held by the 'Statue of Liberty', the so-called 'Flame of Liberty', which stands on top of the tunnel on a black satanic pentagram (Fig 121). Princess Diana has been associated with the rose since her death – 'England's Rose', and roses on memorials – and roses are used in churches to represent the womb of Mary. Romans called it the 'Rose of Venus', which was their name for the Babylonian Semiramis and the universal goddess of Venus and the Moon. Is all this really a coincidence? *Everything* is ritual and symbolism to these people, and why wouldn't it be when reptilian genetics produce 'ritualistic behaviour'? This is part of the genetic software. We see it in the repeating and predictable ritualistic behaviour among people in general, but the hybrids with their greater infusion of reptilian genetics take it to a whole new level. All the pomp, ceremony and pageantry connected with the British Royal Family are ancient pagan ritual disguised as Christian ritual and traditions of the State. The Coronation of the British monarch is based on ancient satanic ritual and coronations going back to places such as Egypt and Mesopotamia. The Royal Family even go to the same palaces at the same time every year and they are constantly followed around by ritual and 'protocol' (ritual). This is why. By the way, I had a strange experience in Paris many years before Diana's death. I went with Linda and the family for a day trip to Paris while we were on holiday in France. We stayed for less than an hour because it was so hot and oppressive. We got off the train at the Eiffel Tower and walked across a footbridge to the other side of the River Seine and rested for a while on a seat. We then went back to the station and left. The next time I sat on that seat was in 1997 when I was researching Diana's death. It was on top of the Pont de l'Alma tunnel.

Shine on Allah Moon

We have seen the obsession with the goddess and its connection to Christianity; but Islam, another bloodline religion, is also, in truth, the worship of the Moon and Saturn. The reason for the focus on the Moon and Saturn will become clear in the next chapter. The Sumerians worshipped the Moon under many names and the later Assyrians, Babylonians and Akkadians in Mesopotamia worshipped the moon god under the name 'Sin'. This is the origin of the Christian concept of 'sin' and 'sinner'. Sin was known as the 'God of the Mountain' and so we have Mount Sinai – *Sin*-ai – where the Bible claims that 'God' gave the Ten Commandments to 'Moses'. We also have the biblical 'Wilderness' or 'Desert of Sin' in the story (and it is only a story) of the Israelites. Pre- Islam Arabians worshipped the moon god, the 'god above all others', and his major shrine was at ... *Mecca*. The Arabian moon god before Islam was called 'al-ilah', or 'al-llah', and later *'Allah'*. The man who later became the 'Prophet Mohammed' grew up in a family that worshipped the moon god, Allah. The Prophet decided that rather than Allah being 'above all the gods', he was going to be the *only* god. Islam was born as a monotheistic – *moon*-otheistic – religion that worships the Moon and Saturn, while 98 per cent of its followers have no idea that they are doing so. The same happened with Judaism when the worship of multiple gods became the worship of one god; and in Christianity when the multi-god religion of Rome morphed into one-god worship. The Pantheon in Rome, which means 'to every god', was given a makeover to become a place of one-god Christianity. I wonder what all the others did with themselves. 'Sorry, mate, no work here, there's no call for gods these days now we only have one.' Worship of the Moon is highly significant. Jews begin their month with the new moon and have the Passover on the full moon, while the 'Christian' Easter (the Babylonian goddess, Ishtar) is held on the first Sunday after the full moon. They're all worshipping the bloody *Moon*, and they are crucially worshipping Saturn, as we shall see. Christianity condemns and demonises Pagan religions – *when it is one*. What a hoot! Wading through ancient mythology can be a nightmare with all the different gods and goddesses and the different interpretations of their meaning. This is especially so when there are so many other subjects to be looked at in detail before the dots can be connected; but during the writing of this book so many pennies have dropped and nearly all of them led me to the Moon and Saturn. I had read in a few places that the Jewish god, El, as in Isra-El, was connected to the Moon. However, it is really a version of the god, *Saturn*. Judaism is Saturn worship (on Saturday or Saturn-day) with the Moon thrown in among other things; and *Zion* is used as code for Saturn, too. Zionism, the creation of the House of Rothschild, is Saturnism. The vast majority of Jews don't know this, but their leaders sure as heck do. Muslims say that the Kaaba at Mecca, the most sacred place in Islam, was built by 'Abraham', who the Bible says came from 'Shinar' (Sumer/Mesopotamia) and seeded the 'Israelites'. Abraham is a major figure in Judaism, Islam and Christianity, and all three religions place major importance on Jerusalem. The name URU-SA-LIM has been found on Sumerian and Babylonian tablets. Do we really think that it is mere coincidence that two religions, Judaism and Islam, which claim to be different, both insist that animals are slaughtered in the same way in line with the food laws known as Kosher and Halal? All these religions have the same source and they were created, as with all the others, to program the minds of the people; create a rigid control structure and hierarchy; and divide and rule by playing one off against another and also dividing them into their own warring factions. Hasn't worked, has it?

The bloodlines passed through history expanding the reach of their religious and political blueprint. The Roman eagle became the American eagle, the German eagle and many others. The Roman Senate became the American Senate; and now the UK government is talking about replacing the House of Lords, the second chamber of the British Parliament, with a 'Senate'. Buildings in Washington D.C. are based on those in ancient Rome, as are many in London. Washington D.C. was even built on land called 'Rome' that was donated by the family of America's first Roman Catholic bishop, the Jesuit John Carroll, a close associate of bloodline asset, Benjamin Franklin. The Jesuits are the major secret society connected to the Roman Church and a potent force in the global web of manipulation. They are ruled by a 'Superior General', widely known to researchers as the 'Black Pope'. Most Americans are not aware of the Roman Church's influence in the establishment and location of their capital, Washington D.C., via the Jesuit Carroll family. For sure, they would not have put Washington in the District of the Goddess at this location except for energetic and ritual reasons – its place on the Earth's energy grid, possibly an inter-dimensional 'gateway' or what is underneath the ground. It has felt like entering another energetic 'world', almost another dimension, whenever I have been there. It's a very strange place.

For Queen and country? Er, no, just the Queen

Royal families and the 'divine right to rule' were the means through which the Reptilian Alliance and its hybrid bloodlines imposed their human tyranny until the last few hundred years. They had to change that modus operandi when people began to rebel against royal dictatorships and the hybrids took control of the 'dark-suit' professions such as politics, banking and business. Some royal families have survived and now hide their true power behind the façade that they are 'purely ceremonial and symbolic'. Well, that is certainly not the case with the British Royal Family for a start. Queen Elizabeth II,

the British head of state, still has enormous influence, both by law and in the background (Fig 122). Politicians, military personnel, police officers, the judiciary and those working for Intelligence agencies, even the *clergy*, have to pledge their oath of allegiance to the Queen ... *not to the population of the country.* The Queen is the representative of the 'Crown', which is far more than the monarch, as I explain in other books. The monarch is only the 'face' of the 'Crown' which is once again a bloodline network of secret societies. Members of Parliament who are, in theory, elected by the public, have to

Figure 122: Queen Elizabeth II – certainly not a 'symbolic' monarch

take this oath: 'I ... swear by Almighty God that I will be faithful and bear true allegiance to Her Majesty Queen Elizabeth, her heirs and successors, according to law. So help me God.' No wonder the Queen refers to 'my' government and 'my' Parliament. Judges have to take the same oath, and police officers have to pledge that they 'do solemnly and sincerely declare and affirm that I will well and truly serve the Queen'. Anyone who wants to be a soldier (why?) has to say:

> 'I ... swear by Almighty God that I will be faithful and bear true allegiance to Her Majesty Queen Elizabeth the Second, Her Heirs and Successors, and that I will, as in duty bound, honestly and faithfully defend Her Majesty, Her Heirs and Successors, in Person, Crown and Dignity against all enemies, and will observe and obey all orders of Her Majesty, Her Heirs and Successors, and of the generals and officers set over me. So help me God.'

'My' military, then. Even boy scouts and girl guides have to pledge allegiance to the lady with the scowling face. It was even suggested by one idiot in the Blair government that school-leavers should be encouraged to swear an oath of allegiance to Queen and country, with the offer of tax and student fee rebates for those who volunteered. They are not the *British* royal family, anyway. They are the German House of Saxe–Coburg–Gotha from the land of the Rothschilds. They only changed their name to 'Windsor' during the First World War for PR reasons when Britain was at war with the German wing of the family. The German 'Battenberg' became 'Mountbatten' at the same time and for the same reason. This makes Lord Mountbatten, once a major figure in the Royal Family, Lord Battenberg. The same theme applies to all the surviving royal families of Europe. They are one family under different names – the same hybrid bloodline. The British royal family is German, Danish, Greek and Russian; the Swedish royal family is German (Saxe–Coburg–Gotha), Prussian and British; the Spanish royal family is British, French, Italian, German, Russian, Greek, Danish and Habsburg (a major Reptilian hybrid bloodline); the Dutch royal family is German, British and Russian; the Norwegian royal family is British, German, Danish, Swedish and Prussian; and the Danish royal family is British, German, Swedish, Russian and Greek. The Belgian 'royal family' is still another manifestation of the German (Rothschild) house of Saxe–Coburg–Gotha. The royal 'families' operate like a corporation with different branches of the same family acting as CEOs in different countries. What is it that gives them the right to be heads of state and for their family members to follow as a matter of course? Their *bloodline*; their *DNA*. This is still going on in the so- called 'modern world', but most of the Reptilian bloodline 'elite' do not wear crowns anymore – well, except at their rituals. They wear dark suits in public to pursue their dark intentions. The British monarchy, as with all of them, is the most racist of institutions. Only one family can be head of state, which, in effect, limits that power and privilege to white people of one bloodline that must believe (at least officially) in only one form of one religion – protestant Christianity. This happens in a country that officially claims to abhor racism. The whole concept of monarchy has to go if the human race is going to progress into adulthood. A few years ago, I made a complaint about this racist institution to a government organisation called, at the time, the Commission for Racial Equality. This is supposed to investigate examples of racism, but, as a government-funded operation, the cases that it pursues are carefully selected. My request for an investigation into this institutionalised racism called 'the monarchy' was declined. Oh really? I'm shocked. Mind you, it would have been rather embarrassing for the head of the organisation, a guy called Trevor Phillips, who once kneeled before the Queen (more ritual) to receive her patronage when he was made an 'OBE', or Order of the British Empire. What a joke it all is.

The Political Fly-Trap

The bloodlines changed their strategy when the people began to rebel against open rule by royalty and introduced what we call the 'political system'. This has allowed them to continue their tyranny under the cover of 'democracy' and 'power to the people'. Most importantly, they imposed the pyramidal structures known as political 'parties'. There was a great danger during this transition from royal dictatorship that people might vote for independent political candidates on the grounds of their character, views and attitudes; and it is far more difficult to control events with hundreds of individuals coming from multiple directions. They might even look at proposals and policies on their individual merits before deciding how to respond. Oh, no! *Nightmare!* They stopped all that nonsense, however, with the concept of political parties. These are pyramidal hierarchies and you only have to control the few at the top to control everyone else in the pyramid. There is virtually no chance of being elected today unless you are attached to a party, because of access to funding and promotion. So you have to pick your party, and, to be elected, the party hierarchy has to select you to run for Parliament or Congress. You have to be 'acceptable' to the party big-wigs to win their approval and so you must 'toe the party line'. You must do and say what the party wants you to do and say. You must defend what you may not agree with, even campaign for it, when the party hierarchy decides what you must believe. You have to do exactly the same if you are elected to Parliament. You have to vote the way you are told to vote and say what you are told to say if you want to climb the greasy pole and ultimately go into Government. Political parties even have something called 'Whips' that have the job of ensuring that party politicians vote as demanded by the peak of their pyramid. 'Party unity' is another way of saying 'everyone does as they're told'. Let's have a lot more independent *dis*-unity, I say. The Whip will offer potential rebels some reward for voting the way they are told to vote. If that doesn't work, it will be pointed out that further advancement in the party will be blocked if they go ahead and think for themselves; and if that doesn't do the trick, the Whip might indicate that some dark secret could just seep out to the media unless they come to heel and stop following their conscience. This, ladies and gentlemen, is what they call 'democracy', a word that we are told is interchangeable with 'freedom'. It is not. 'Democracy' is a tyranny masquerading as a 'free society'. Go to the next level of this 'party system' and you can see why the public vote is irrelevant. The bloodline hybrids don't only control one party in each country; they control *any* party that has any chance of forming a government, and at least most of those who don't. It doesn't matter which 'party' gets into government, because the same force is always in control. This is why there is no change of direction, no matter if the government is 'left', 'right' or 'centre'. Barack Obama – 'Mr Change' – has actually changed nothing since he became President of the United States in 2009. He has not only continued the policies of Boy Bush – he has *expanded* on them. The point is, you see, that there is no contract between the public and the politicians campaigning for their vote. There is no obligation whatsoever for them to do in office what they said they would do during an election campaign. They tell you what they think you want to hear so that you vote them into power and then they do what they were always going to do – follow the agenda of human enslavement dictated by the real power in the shadows. Obama says that he will close Guantanamo Bay within a year, and once in office he says he won't. Virtually all politicians, especially those in high office, are liars and frauds, but Obama is a Fraud of Frauds. Obama is, like Tony Blair, a classic Illuminati frontman. Say one thing and do another, while always smiling for the camera. Another aspect of the political stitch-up is the dynamic between the party in government and the party in opposition. It goes like this: The party in government introduces the bloodline agenda, because it has the power to do so through legislation. The party or parties that are not in government oppose the agenda, because it doesn't matter – they don't have the power to do anything. Then we have a farce called an election and the governing party becomes opposition and the opposition party becomes the government. Now the party in government that opposed the agenda in opposition introduces the agenda, because it has the power to do so. The party that was in government now opposes the agenda that it had previously been introducing, because it doesn't have the power to do anything. The whole thing is a charade to trick the people into thinking that they have a political choice. This means that nothing changes when one party replaces another in government. You may have noticed. This is how the bloodlines maintained their control over governments when the monarchies fell.

London Calling

The Reptilian hybrid bloodline network eventually re-located to London, which became, and still is, one of the major centres for the global conspiracy together with Rome. This applies to London in general, but the bloodline focal point is in what is called 'The City', the original London, which is today the financial district, or 'Square Mile', dominated by St Paul's Cathedral on Ludgate Hill, the highest point in 'The City'. St Paul's Cathedral is built on the site where the Romans once worshipped the Goddess Diana, and this is also where Princess Diana was married to Prince Charles. It's all ritual. The Romans established London, or Londinium, as the English capital (capitol), and

Figure 123: The emblem of 'The City'

many Roman remains have been discovered here, including the Temple of Mithras (the Roman 'Jesus'). The boundaries of The City have been virtually unchanged since the Middle Ages. The emblem of The City is, very appropriately, two flying reptiles holding a shield with a red cross on a white background – the symbol of the Knights Templar (Fig 123). This is an elite secret society which, like the Knights of Malta, goes back to the 12th century. Both have fundamental links to Jerusalem and Rome. The Knights Templar is a dominant force in The City and in the centre of the British legal system in an area known as 'The Temple', which borders The City. The temple in question is an original Knights Templar temple that was featured in *The Da Vinci Code*. Land that is now The Temple district was owned by the Knights Templar centuries ago. They still control the courts and legal system there and ensure that lawyers, barristers and judges do the 'right thing' – the hybrid

Figure 124: Where The City meets The Temple

bloodlines' 'thing'. At the point where The City meets The Temple is a depiction of a flying reptile in the centre of the road (Fig 124). The City has its own government and police force and operates, though not officially, very much like the Vatican in Rome. It is a country within a country. The rest of London has a 'Mayor of London', but The City has its own '*Lord* Mayor of London' ('Lord' is Saturn, the 'Dark Lord'), who is always a

Figure 125: Roman architecture in The City

high degree Freemason. The City is controlled by a network of Reptilian hybrid secret societies and, once again, when you look at the architecture, including the Rothschild-controlled Bank of England, where does it remind you of? (Fig 125) The City is also awash with ancient Babylonian/Roman/Greek symbolism. Europe is the operational centre of the bloodline global network, especially London and Rome, but also countries such as France, Germany, Switzerland and Belgium. The European Union and NATO have their headquarters in the Belgian capital, Brussels. I am not talking here about the governments of those countries. They are only vehicles to make manifest the Illuminati agenda. I mean the centre of the global secret-society web at operational level. North America is also vitally important to them, obviously, but so often the bullets are secretly loaded in Europe for the United States to publicly fire. Another right-in-the-front-line player is Israel. This is a fiefdom of the Rothschilds and a global centre for worship of the Illuminati 'god', Saturn, via three religions: Judaism, Christianity and Islam.

The world was colonised from Europe – Europa. This was done mostly from the Illuminati stronghold of London through the 'Great' (in size only) British Empire on which 'the sun never set'. France, Belgium, Germany, Spain and Portugal stole their share of other peoples' lands, too, and the force behind all of them was the Reptilian hybrids. They had, by now, infiltrated all the countries of Europe. Colonisation was the time when the bloodlines' control expanded very rapidly to the Americas, Africa, Asia, Australia, New Zealand and the Far East in a grotesque frenzy of violent acquisition and exploitation by the countries that bizarrely still claim today to have 'values' and stand for 'freedom' and 'peace'. Colonisation allowed the bloodlines and their secret societies to be exported across the world, and when the colonies were given their 'independence', that structure stayed put. European governments (the bloodlines) withdrew from the former colonies officially and on the surface, but the bloodlines remained under many names along with the secret-society network that manipulates them and their agents into power. They have, as a result, continued to covertly control those 'former' colonies, including the United States, ever since. The apparent end of European colonialism was a sleight of hand that exchanged one form of control for something far more effective. There are two forms of mass control – the seen and the unseen. The 'seen' are tyrannies like fascism, communism and apartheid. The people oppressed by these regimes at least know that they *are* controlled and pretty much who by, in terms of the front-people. They may be in a prison cell, but they can at least see the bars. These forms of tyranny have a finite life, because eventually rebellion will come. European colonialism was replaced by covert control and manipulation behind a façade of 'freedom' and 'democracy'. This is the prison *without* the bars that people can't see. 'Democracy' means to have a vote every four or five years to 'select' which mask on the same face will be elected into office to continue Illuminati business-as-usual. People are told all the time that they live in a 'free country' to stop them realising that they don't. While the colonialists appeared to leave the former colonies, such as the United States, Canada, Australia and New Zealand, the bloodlines and their secret-society network have continued to control and manipulate those countries ever since in line with the demands of the Illuminati bloodlines. Meanwhile, the people being controlled and manipulated have believed they were living in independent states. 'Physical' control in regions like Africa and South America was replaced by financial control as puppet leaders from the bloodlines, or owned by the bloodlines, were placed into power in country after country to maintain them as Illuminati vassals, steal their resources and drown them in debt to the Illuminati banks – the coldly engineered 'Third World debt'. Zulu shaman, Credo Mutwa, told me that genealogy is very important in his culture and he has studied it deeply. He said that most of the black African leaders that came to power after 'independence' were descended from the 'royal' lines of ancient Africa seeded by the 'Chitauri'.

The Blueprint

The Reptilian hybrid bloodlines have constructed a vast global web of interconnected families and secret societies that operate like a transnational corporation along the lines of Coca-Cola or McDonald's. These global corporations have a headquarters somewhere in the world, and in each country they have a subsidiary network. The role of the subsidiaries is to introduce in their country the corporate policy decided at the centre. The McDonald's you see in America, Britain, Russia, Africa or Australia will be essentially the same. This is the way the Illuminati global web operates, too, except that instead of subsidiary companies we are talking about subsidiary families and secret societies. Each country has its own subsidiary network of bloodlines and their agents, gofers and secret societies. Their job is to control the government, banking, business, media, military, and so on, in their country and change the society in line with the agenda dictated from the centre of the web in Europe (and Israel). A single plan for the direction of the world can be imposed everywhere through this organisational structure. I have been to more than 50 countries speaking and researching and I can tell you that the same is happening everywhere. This is how and why. But it doesn't end there. The subsidiary networks in each country also have subsidiary networks that control regions of the country, towns and cities, and these operate in the same way. This is what I call 'The Blueprint' (Fig 126). The 'headquarters' can, through this interlocking web, dictate right down into your local community. What are we looking at here? A structure that is *holographic* – every part of the whole is a smaller *version* of the whole. The world looks very different from this perspective. You no longer see individual countries, political parties, governments, banks, corporations, media organisations and Intelligence agencies. You see *one* 'country', *one* government, *one* bank, *one* corporation, *one* media and *one* Intelligence agency owned or controlled by the same Hidden Hand. The situation is not quite that extreme yet. There are still some outsiders, but not many in the positions of greatest influence. That is essentially the way it is and they are working now to complete the job of acquiring (stealing) anything they don't already have.

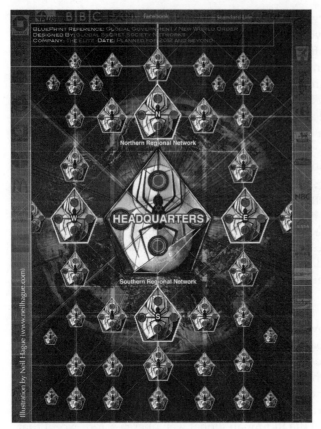

Figure 126: The interlocking holographic global web that allows the centre to manipulate right down into local communities

There is even a name for what they are doing – 'globalisation'. This refers to the centralisation of global power in every area of our lives, and that is precisely what the bloodlines are seeking to achieve. The more you centralise power the more power the few will have over the many; and the more you centralise power the more power you have at the centre to centralise even quicker. This can be clearly seen in the world today. They win the game by owning the structure of the game that they have created. One of their widely-used techniques is licensing. They introduce laws, rules and regulations through their puppet governments and institutions that force people to have a 'licence to practise' or a licence to do whatever. Then they tell you what you must and must not do to secure the licence and, in this way, they dictate how everything is done and not done. They are moving in on alternative methods of healing with their licence scam. They want to stop people having an effective alternative to the pharmaceutical cartel, or Big Pharma. People say that a financial crash must be bad for the banks, but it's only bad for people working for those that go under. If you own the *game*, the banking *system*, you can't lose. If you own the World Cup it doesn't really matter if England beat Germany or Germany beat England. You still win whatever the result. Anyway, if you know a financial crash is coming, because you are going to cause it, you can sell at the highest point and then buy back in after the crash when values have plummeted. This way you can massively increase your wealth, assets and power when you expand the economy again and values recover. Nathan Rothschild, who established the London branch of the family empire, famously did exactly this while French Emperor, Napoleon Bonaparte, and Britain's Duke of Wellington were fighting the Battle of Waterloo in what is now Belgium in 1815. The London Stock Exchange in The City would crash if Napoleon won, and the slavery-supporting Nathan Rothschild knew that. The Rothschilds had the quickest and most effective information and espionage operation in Europe with an extensive network of contacts using codes and carrier pigeons. This network would later be known as Mossad, British Intelligence and the CIA among many other names. These are all the

The Real Rulers of the World

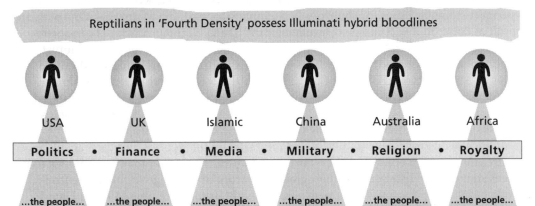

Reptilians in 'Fourth Density' possess Illuminati hybrid bloodlines

USA   UK   Islamic   China   Australia   Africa

Politics • Finance • Media • Military • Religion • Royalty

...the people...   ...the people...   ...the people...   ...the people...   ...the people...   ...the people...

Figure 127: Countries may appear to be different entities, but the 'blueprint' means that all are essentially directed by the same force from the unseen realms down to the bloodline secret-society web in each country. Those at the top of the pyramids declare wars, but they never fight them. They use the silly sods at the bottom to do that.

same organisation at the highest level. Investors in The City were well aware that Nathan Rothschild would know the outcome of the Battle of Waterloo before even the British government, and they watched him for any sign that could give them a clue. Rothschild suddenly gave the signal for his agents to start selling his stocks. A mass panic ensued as people took this as confirmation that Napoleon had prevailed. The market collapsed and fortunes were lost in hours. Rothschild gave another signal to his agents to start buying on a grand scale when stocks had fallen to a fraction of their value. Nathan Rothschild had known all along that Wellington had won and stock prices soared when official confirmation arrived. The London branch of the Rothschilds increased its wealth by an estimated 20 times in that single day.

The House of Rothschild and their subordinate associates such as the Rockefellers have continually manipulated the financial system in this way and others. This has allowed them to accumulate the world's wealth and resources and to own whole nations through unspeakable levels of government debt. Today we have the Reptilian hybrid bloodlines in China owning much of America and the hybrids that control America have no problem with this. They are both working to the same goal while appearing to represent different 'countries' (Fig 127). They may fight among themselves here and there, because that is their nature. But in the end they are on the same side. China has become so wealthy thanks to North America and Europe outsourcing much of their manufacturing to China and allowing other Chinese products to pour into their countries to destroy jobs at home. Even many key electronic components for America's most advanced weapons systems are made in China. Jeffrey Immelt, CEO of GE (General Electric), is the head of Barack Obama's 'Jobs Council' while at the same time GE is moving vast amounts of its operation (and jobs) to China. There is no contradiction here, because the 'Jobs Council' is just for show. The United States has also outsourced production and jobs to other parts of the Far East, to India and, in America's case, Mexico. The bloodlines are seeking to destroy the United States and this is why hundreds of 'foreign free trade zones' are planned to be established in America with special customs facilities for countries like China to locate their companies. One of them, south of Boise, Idaho, could be controlled by the China National Machinery Industry Corporation (Sinomach) if the state governor gets his way. The Chinese Communist government is the majority owner. This would mean that eventually up to 50 square miles of America would be owned by China and they could store military equipment and whatever they want. But it doesn't end there. The Chinese government is buying huge areas and assets of America including oil and gas fields. This seems utterly insane at first sight, but not when you know why it is being done. America is being systemically destroyed economically and militarily by the hybrids and their agents who control the government, whichever 'party' is in office. They want to bring America to its knees so it can be absorbed into their global structure of world government, central bank, currency and army. The same is happening in Britain as Prime Minister David Cameron – a family with close ties to the Rothschilds – follows the same script as his political 'opponents', Tony Blair and the hapless Gordon Brown. The UK has been selling state assets to overseas corporations for decades. Now you can see why both the 'Republican' and 'Democrat' governments in the United States have been demolishing the American economy through outsourcing, through the North American 'Free Trade' Agreement (NAFTA), and through all manner of other disasters designed to destroy wealth and jobs. It has been *planned* that way. The Reptilian hybrid families control the national central banks, World Bank, International Monetary Fund (IMF), Bank of International Settlements, European Central Bank, World Trade Organization, World Health Organization, United Nations, European Union, NATO, on and on it goes. *Control* them? They *created* them – *all* of them – on their road to the incessant centralisation of global power ('globalisation') and the total control of every man, woman and child on the planet.

That is what is 'going on'. Or part of it.

The bloodline families that own the media and 'entertainment' industry ensure that reptilian themes abound in modern 'culture', in movies, animations, computer games, science fiction and the like. This helps to embed the Reptilian control system into the collective subconscious mind for reasons that I am about to explain. One of the most blatant examples was an advertisement featuring actor, Alec Baldwin, during the 2009 US Super Bowl, which attracted an audience of some 150 million. It was promoting a media system called 'Hulu', and the theme was of a reptilian 'alien' race taking over the planet by controlling the minds of the population. The script said:

Hello Earth. I'm Alec Baldwin, TV star. You know they say TV will rot your brain? That's absurd. TV only softens the brain like a ripe banana. To take it all the way, we've created Hulu. Hulu beams TV directly to your portable computing devices, giving you more of the cerebral, gelatinizing shows you want anytime, anywhere – for free. Mmm. Mushy, mush.

And the best part is there is nothing you can do to stop it. I mean what are you going to do? Turn off your TV and your computer? Once your brain is reduced to a cottage-cheese-like mush, we'll scoop them out with a melon baller and gobble them right on up. Oooops, I think I'm drooling a little. Because we're aliens, and that's how we roll.

Hulu – an evil plot to destroy the world. Enjoy.

When Baldwin said 'because we're aliens, and that's how we roll', snake imagery appeared from under his jacket. You can see the advertisement on *YouTube* if you type in the words: 'Hulu Super Bowl commercial'. Television is mass Reptilian mind-control. Watching television activates the reptilian brain which communicates and absorbs information through the medium of images.

If you think all this has been mind-blowing, extraordinary and incredible, hold on in every sense. 'Kansas' is no longer in the cosmos. Wait for the next bit.

6

Movie in the 'Sky'

Right – let's go for it. We are decoding a fake reality to stop us from seeing the true reality, which is very different to this one. We see a Universe that is apparently barren and lifeless, but this is a manipulated holographic projection designed to make us feel isolated and alone. This is precisely what the Reptilian Alliance requires for maximum control.

The Universe is teeming with life of amazing beauty and variety, but we are being blocked from seeing it. The apparent limitations of technology and 'space travel' are also embedded in the projections to maintain our sense of isolation. Beyond this manufactured reality you don't need technology to travel. You simply use your Consciousness. The voice in the Brazilian rainforest said: 'Why do you fly from point A to point B when you are point A and point B and everything in between?' The answer is that we don't know that this is the case, and we are not aware of our true and limitless potential. We are decoding a false reality designed to enslave us in ignorance. Reptilian genetic engineering and manipulation has tuned the human body–computer to the frequency range of what I called in my last book the 'Moon Matrix'; but it involves more than the Moon. When I was a small boy, I had an experience that has turned out to be very profound in the light of what I now know. It happened on a visit to the London

Figure 128: The London Planetarium (as was)

Planetarium, and it was so long ago that I went to London on a train pulled by a steam engine (Fig 128). The trip was strange from the start. We were living from 'hand to mouth' at the time, but one weekend my father said, 'We're going to London.' We didn't *do* things like that. We didn't have the money; but in no time we were heading for the railway station. Most of the trip is now a blur, but I can still clearly remember the visit to the Planetarium, and one particular moment that I will never forget. My father had no interest in

astronomy, and I can never recall him
mentioning the subject once, but he took us
to the London Planetarium. Huh? Maybe it
was because it was new. It opened in 1958,
and the trip could not have been very long
after that. I didn't know what a 'Planetarium'
was, or what to expect, but I was blown
away when the lights went down and the
night sky appeared on a big domed ceiling.
Here I was the middle of the day and yet I
was looking at the night sky! It wasn't 'real',
yet it *looked* so real. This was a profound
moment for me that I have never forgotten. It
has crossed my mind here and there when I
have looked into the sky that maybe what
we are seeing is not the vast and infinite
universe that it seems to be, but a *projection*
of some kind. Like a colossal planetarium. I

Figure 129: The Universe that we see. 'Real'? Or a
projection? Most likely a bit of both

was sitting outside a little café in the countryside a few years ago when I looked up and
saw the sky as a vast dome. I remember thinking that we live in some kind of 'bubble'.
This has become ever more obvious to me in recent years. We are looking at a
holographic projection that is designed to entrap us in a false reality (Fig 129). This
theme struck me again when I watched the film *The Truman Show*, starring Jim Carrey.
This had been released for more than a decade by the time I saw it on DVD, and I had to
smile when I saw the 'plot'. Carrey plays a character born on the set of a soap-type
show, but he is brought up thinking it is all real. He lives in what he thinks is a town
next to the ocean, but it is only a film set. The sun that comes up and goes down every
day is only a projection. His every moment is filmed, although he has no idea this is
happening. He starts to question his reality when every time he tries to leave the town
something happens to stop him. The film concludes with him sailing off across what he
thinks is the ocean, but eventually he comes to the wall of a huge dome within which he
has lived his entire life. He finds a door and walks out into the 'real' world. This is such
a metaphor for what humanity now needs to do. We need to find that symbolic 'door'.
What made me laugh more than anything is that the whole show was orchestrated from
a command centre that looked remarkably like the Moon. I already knew by then that
the Moon was not what it appeared to be. It is not a 'natural' body, but itself a command
centre fundamentally influencing and controlling life on Earth. Quite a lot of what we
see in the heavens is 'real', as in part of the original virtual reality 'game', but it is
holographically manipulated so that we see images that are not in the original game and
don't see images that are. Many planetary bodies are not 'dead' and lifeless as they
appear to be. All of this is underpinned by blocking frequencies, like a frequency fence,
that firewalls the Matrix and human perception from the greater reality.

The Moon is not 'real'

The information and insights about the true nature of the Moon came to me in the usual
sequence. I had pondered from time to time over the years about whether the Moon was

really what we believed it to be, but it was in 2009 that the truth was put before me. I sat down to start another day writing the book *Human Race Get Off Your Knees*, when the atmosphere in the room changed. I recognised this immediately given how many times it had happened. A very clear thought passed through my mind a few seconds later and, as I've said, I have experienced this so often since 1990. The 'thought' said that the Moon is not what we think it is. The Moon is not a 'natural' heavenly body. This was another example of 'Knowledge will be put into his mind and at other times he will be led to knowledge'. Both happened in this case. I entered a few key words into a search engine to see what might come up and I immediately found a book called *Who Built The Moon?* (Watkins Publishing; 2005) by Christopher Knight and Alan Butler. They were explaining why the Moon could not be a natural phenomenon. I ordered the book, and other information along the same theme began to drop into my lap. It was the old sequence again: a new subject appears out of nowhere and then 'five-sense' information begins to flow. Most people tend to accept without question what was here before they were born. Actually, most people tend to accept without question – end of story. 'That's the way it is, mate, everybody knows that.' So the Moon is, well, the *Moon*. It's always been there; it's the way things are. But when you ask questions about the familiar and the 'everybody knows that', you realise that the 'everybody' knows *nothing*. This is certainly true of the Moon. I mean, look at the size of it for a start. The Moon is 2,160 miles in diameter and bigger than Pluto. What the heck is something that big doing as a 'moon' of a planet the size of Earth? It is the fifth largest moon in the Solar System and a *quarter* the size of Earth. Ding-dong, *hello?* There is nothing in the Solar System that has a moon that big in relation to its own size. In the 1960s, NASA produced a detailed report – NASA TR R-277 – which catalogued all the anomalies and unexplained sightings on the Moon observed through the telescope between 1500 and 1967. This involved more than 300 people and listed more than 570 events that included unexplained mists, colours, extraordinarily bright lights, intermittent lights, streaks of light, unusual shadows and what appeared to be some kind of 'volcanic' activity. The Moon, and what is happening there, is nothing like the story we are being told. Christopher Knight and Alan Butler do an excellent job of detailing endless mysteries and anomalies regarding the Moon, and the extraordinary – well beyond coincidence – connections between the Earth, Moon and Sun in terms of size, placement, movement and alignments. They write:

> The Moon is bigger than it should be, apparently older than it should be and much lighter in mass than it should be. It occupies an unlikely orbit and is so extraordinary that all existing explanations for its presence are fraught with difficulties and none of them could be considered remotely watertight.

Mainstream science has no idea where the Moon came from, or even what it is. Oh, yes, they will reel off the official party line but, like so much 'scientific' 'fact', it doesn't stand up. It is not fact, just *pseudo* 'fact' produced by constant repetition – 'everybody knows that'. But they *don't*. The first official story about the origins of the Moon was known as the 'Big Whack Theory'. This suggested that a Mars-type planet struck the Earth during its formation and a large chunk of the Earth broke away to eventually become the Moon. When this didn't pan out, they came up with the 'Double Big Whack

Theory'. This is that the Mars-type planet smacked the Earth and then came back and gave it another slap. The old one–two. Excuse me a moment, I have a duvet that I need to put in a box that is far too big for the box. I am going to kick it, sit on it, get someone very large to sit on it, and if all that fails I am going to convince myself, and then attempt to convince others, that the duvet is, in 'fact', in the box even though it's hanging over the sides in all directions. I should have been a mainstream scientist, you know. Earl Ubell, a former science editor with CBS, said:

> If the Earth and Moon were created at the same time, near each other, why has one got all the iron and the other [the Moon] not much? The differences suggest that Earth and Moon came into being far from each other, an idea that stumbles over the inability of astrophysicists to explain how exactly the Moon became a satellite of Earth.

Figure 130: The almost perfect alignment between the Sun and Moon makes the Moon appear to be the same size as the Sun when viewed from the Earth during an eclipse

Nor can they explain all the Moon mysteries and anomalies. Irwin Shapiro, from the Harvard–Smithsonian Center for Astrophysics, put it very well: 'The best explanation for the Moon is observational error – the Moon doesn't exist.' Either that or you change your perception of the Moon, open your mind to all possibilities, and seek your explanations by looking at everything from another angle. First question: Do we really believe that the amazing 'coincidences' with regard to the Moon and its relationship to Earth and the Sun have happened purely by chance? Here are a few of them, as compiled by Knight and Butler:

- The Moon is 400 times smaller than the Sun, and at a solar eclipse it is 400 times closer to Earth. This makes the Moon appear from Earth to be the same size as the Sun during a total eclipse (Fig 130).
- The Sun is at its lowest and weakest in mid-winter when the Moon is at its highest and brightest. The reverse happens in mid-summer. They set at the same point on the horizon at the equinoxes and at the opposite point at the solstices.
- Earth rotates 366.259 times during one orbit of the Sun. The polar circumference of the Earth is 366.175 times bigger than that of the Moon. The polar circumference of the Moon is 27.31 per cent the size of Earth and the Moon makes 27.396 turns per orbit of the Earth.
- Multiply the circumference of the Moon by that of Earth and you get 436,669,140 kilometres. If this number is divided by 100 it becomes 436,669 kilometres – the circumference of the Sun correct to 99.9 per cent.
- Divide the circumference of the Sun by that of the Moon and multiply by 100, and you get the circumference of the Earth. Divide the size of the Sun by the size of the Earth and multiply by 100 and you get the size of the Moon.

Figure 131: The relationships between Sun, Moon and Earth are 'nothing less than staggering'

No wonder Knight and Butler conclude that mathematical and other relationships between the Earth, Moon and Sun are 'nothing less than staggering'. They say that the Moon has been placed where it is 'with the accuracy of the proverbial Swiss watchmaker' (Fig 131). That's another thing. Life on Earth would not be anything like it is if the Moon wasn't where it is. In 2010, I watched a mainstream science programme on the BBC about the Moon, called *Do We Really Need the Moon?* It was presented by a scientist who said she had been obsessed with the Moon since she was a child; but not obsessed enough, it seemed, to go beyond the official norm. She rightly concluded that the Moon was perfectly placed to sustain life on Earth. This was, however, a 'cosmic coincidence'. They have to believe that or the house of 'scientific' cards comes a-tumbling down. The game would be up for the song sheet. Even if she had thought of questioning the 'coincidence theory', it would either not have made the final cut or the BBC would have hired another presenter who knows a song sheet when they see one. The Moon is perfectly placed for life on Earth to exist; it is the same size as the Sun when viewed from Earth; and it has an astonishing relationship in general with Earth and the Sun. Well, astonishing if you think it's all a coincidence. Then there's the fact that spin-synchronicity between Earth and the Moon means that we only ever see one side – one face – of the Moon looking our way. This happens, we are told, because the Earth rotates at a speed 400 times faster than the Moon, and spins 40,000 kilometres on its axis in a day to the Moon's 400. I have heard some suggest that it doesn't spin at all. Are we still continuing with the 'coincidence theory'?

Questions, questions, questions

Moon anomalies and mysteries are legion. The Moon is supposed to have formed from a chunk of the still- forming Earth, but the oldest rocks discovered on the Moon are said to date back 4.5 billion years. This makes them a billion years older than anything found on Earth. Moon rocks have been discovered, according to mainstream sources, to be of a different composition to the dust in which they were found. The dust was estimated to be a billion years older. The Moon is said to have next to no magnetic field, but Moon rocks are magnetised. Some rocks on the extremely hard lunar surface have contained processed metals, such as brass and mica, and the elements neptunium 237 and uranium 236, which do not occur naturally. Neptunium 237 is a radioactive metallic element, a by-product of nuclear reactors and the production of plutonium. Uranium 236 is a long-living radioactive nuclear waste that is found in spent nuclear fuel and reprocessed uranium. What is this doing on a 'natural' moon? There is also the titanium. The Moon is claimed to have been part of Earth, but some lunar rocks have contained ten times more titanium than found here. Dr Harold C Urey, winner of the Nobel Prize for Chemistry, said he was 'terribly puzzled by the rocks from the Moon and in particular their titanium content'. He couldn't account for this and he used the term 'mind-blowers' to describe the samples he saw. Dr S Ross Taylor, a geochemist who headed the lunar chemical analysis team, said that areas of the Moon the size of Texas had to be covered with melted rock containing fluid titanium. He was bewildered by how heat could be

Figure 132: The remarkable resemblance between the Death Star in the *Star Wars* movies of insider, George Lucas, and Mimas, a moon of Saturn

generated to do that. How about super-advanced technology? Titanium just happens to be used in supersonic jets, deep-diving submarines and spacecraft. This is what I am saying the Moon really is: an incredibly advanced spacecraft/computer system, and the Reptilian Alliance has control of it. There is a colony inside the Moon similar to the 'Death Star' 'moon' of Darth Vader in the *Star Wars* movie series produced by insider George Lucas. Darth Vader and company were the Reptilian Alliance in another guise. What the series depicted did not happen 'in a galaxy far, far, away', but much closer to home. Lucas's Death Star shows a remarkable resemblance to Mimas, a moon of Saturn, and that is no accident (Fig 132). I am coming to Saturn and its many moons.

Talking of inside the Moon, the evidence suggests that the Moon is hollow. In the early 1960s, Dr Gordon MacDonald, a NASA scientist, said that 'it would seem that the Moon is more like a hollow than a homogeneous sphere'. He wrote this off as inaccurate data, but he was right the first time. Dr Sean C Solomon of the Massachusetts Institute of Technology said the evidence indicated the 'frightening possibility that the Moon might be hollow'. Cosmologist Carl Sagan made the point that 'a natural satellite cannot be a hollow object'. Some scientists have suggested that the Moon has no core, and it is clear that the centre is far less dense than layers nearer the surface. The Moon has only 60 per cent of the density of Earth. This has also lead to suggestions that it is partially hollow. Dr Lon Hood, leader of a Moon research team at Arizona University, said that what they found '... really does add weight to the idea that the Moon's origin is unique, unlike any other terrestrial body – Earth, Venus, Mars or Mercury'. It's a *gigantic spacecraft*. NASA has smacked the Moon a powerful blow a few times after putting seismometers up there to measure the effect. The result is still more confirmation of a hollow moon. An impact equivalent to one tonne of TNT caused shockwaves that built up for eight minutes and, in the words of NASA scientists, the Moon 'rang like a bell'. Maurice Ewing, a co-director of the seismic experiment, said: 'It is as though someone had struck a bell, say, in the belfry of a church, a single blow and found that the reverberation from it continued for 30 minutes.' He couldn't account for what had happened, and Dr Frank Press from the Massachusetts Institute of Technology said it was 'quite beyond the range of our experience' for such a small impact to produce this result. The Moon was later struck with an impact equivalent of 11 tonnes of TNT and NASA scientists said the Moon 'reacted like a gong', and the vibrations lasted for three hours and twenty minutes to a depth of 25 miles. Alan Butler, co-author of *Who Built the*

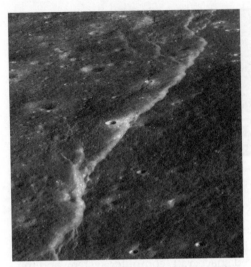

Figure 133: One of the ridges all over the Moon that have led scientists to conclude that the Moon is shrinking

Moon?, talked about this to Ken Johnson, a supervisor of the Data and Photo Control department during the Apollo missions. Johnson said that the Moon did more than 'ring like a bell'. He said the whole Moon 'wobbled' in such a precise way that it was 'almost as though it had gigantic hydraulic damper struts inside it'. In 1972, when the Moon was hit by a meteor with the equivalent of the power of 200 tonnes of TNT, massive shockwaves were sent into the interior – yet none came back. The Moon is hollow, and NASA insiders – those who connect with the Illuminati bloodline web – know this. In 2010, NASA announced that the Moon was 'shrinking'. The NASA website revealed what it called 'the incredible shrinking Moon'. The report said that a team had been analysing new images from NASA's Lunar Reconnaissance Orbiter (LRO) spacecraft and that 'newly discovered cliffs in the lunar crust indicate the moon shrank globally in the geologically recent past and might still be shrinking today' (Fig 133). The Moon is not what we have been told it is. NASA said they 'bombed' the Moon in 2009 in search of water, but you can be sure that this was not the real reason.

NASA Moon Cover-Up

NASA is a military and Intelligence operation whatever they may tell you, and the organisation is controlled and directed by the bloodlines and the secret-society networks. NASA was established by Nazi scientists who escaped from Germany at the end of the war thanks to American Intelligence and 'Operation Paperclip'. This was aided and abetted by networks of the Roman Catholic Church as I report in detail in books like ... *And the Truth Shall Set You Free*. NASA has been working from the start for the Reptilian Alliance in terms of its controlling personnel. Wernher von Braun, a German rocket scientist and member of the Nazi Party, designed the deadly V-2 rockets that were fired at Britain in World War II. He escaped at the end of the war thanks to

Figure 134: Nazi scientists pictured at Fort Bliss, Texas, after being transported out of Germany by Operation Paperclip, also known as 'Project Paperclip'

Operation Paperclip and he became the pre-eminent rocket engineer at NASA. The Saturn V booster rocket that propelled Apollo spacecraft was largely his design. He would have felt right at home at NASA with his Nazi mates (Fig 134). NASA was created by Nazis (NASA-NAZI) and they also brought with them the knowledge of how to build 'anti-gravity' craft that are called 'flying saucers' or UFOs. At least many of them are flown by human pilots.

Most extraterrestrial 'flying saucers' are far more sophisticated and advanced in that they can take any shape or size (what appears to be 'size' is only decoded information) and can manifest and de-manifest. Most people would be shocked that America would allow Nazis responsible for mass murder to escape from justice and establish NASA; but anyone reading this book will see by now that the apparent 'sides' are for public consumption only. Joseph Mengele, known as the 'Angel of Death' when he was camp doctor at Auschwitz, committed countless atrocities with his mind control and genetic experiments on inmates, particularly children and twins. This didn't matter in the least to the bloodlines, including the Rothschilds who are supposed to represent the interests of Jewish people that Mengele tortured. He was taken to South America and the United States after the war to continue his genetic and mind control 'research' with children under the pseudonym, 'Dr Green'. One of the main locations for his 'work' in the United States was the China Lake Naval Air Weapons Center in the California desert north-east of Los Angeles where most of the facility is underground. MKUltra, the notorious CIA mind-control programme, was exposed in the 1970s. 'MK' stood for 'mind control'. They used the German spelling of 'kontrolle' in deference to the Nazis responsible for it. I have talked at length with many people who suffered horrifically as children as a result of MKUltra. Words have no meaning to describe what they went through. CIA Director Richard Helms ordered all MKUltra files to be destroyed in 1973, but it was eventually exposed. Amid the outcry and disgust at what was being revealed, President Gerald Ford ordered an 'investigation' into the activities of the Central Intelligence Agency. This was ironic, to say the least. Ford had been involved in CIA mind-control programmes for decades (see: *The Biggest Secret*). The 'investigation' was about damage limitation and was headed by ... Vice President *Nelson Rockefeller* and known as the Rockefeller Commission. It was, of course, a cover-up of what was really going on.

Most NASA employees don't know what NASA really is. They are compartmentalised from the truth and I have seen it suggested that NASA stands for 'Never A Straight Answer'. There is so much going on that we don't know about and much of the 'information' that NASA makes public is either inaccurate or designed to mislead. The 'one giant leap for mankind' Moon landing in 1969 certainly didn't happen as portrayed. I am not saying that they haven't been to the Moon at all, only that it didn't happen the way they said in 1969. The technology necessary to get to the Moon had to be far more advanced than the Apollo craft, and they had that available to them. It is called anti-gravity technology – or 'flying saucers' – and the American covert programmes had built such craft by at the least the 1950s. The know-how came courtesy of the Nazi scientists brought over from Germany after the war and the Apollo programme was a cover for the anti-gravity technology that they wanted to keep from the public with all its implications for free energy and for other reasons. The 'live' footage of the first 'Moon landing' was shot in a studio by Stanley Kubrick, the great film director, and they used the cover of his epic, *2001: A Space Odyssey,* which was made at the same time. This has been brilliantly exposed by Jay Weidner, American researcher and filmmaker, in his DVD documentary, *Kubrick's Odyssey*. I can highly recommend this film and you can get a copy via the online shop at: www.davidicke.com. Former NASA employees, and those with experience of its work, have revealed how non-natural phenomena on the Moon were airbrushed out of

pictures before they were seen by
the public. Sergeant Karl Wolf
was a precision electronics
photographic repairman at the
Langley Air Force Base in
Virginia. (This is the CIA base
where the planes were
'scrambled' on 9/11 to 'protect'
Washington D.C. when there
were planes much closer at the
Andrews Air Force Base only ten
miles away from the Pentagon.
The Langley planes didn't make it
in time – exactly as planned.) In
2001, Karl Wolf told an event at
the National Press Club in
Washington D.C. that in 1965 he
saw pictures of huge structures
on the far side of the Moon. He
said that he was asked to repair a
technical problem in a part of the
base where they were putting
together 'mosaics' of pictures
taken of the Moon to produce a
larger image. Wolf said that the
airman working with the mosaics
told him: 'By the way, we've
discovered a base on the back side
of the Moon.' He then showed
Wolf a picture of the base which

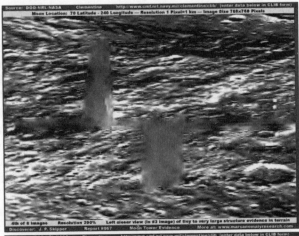
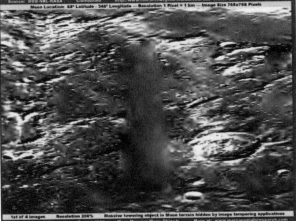

Figs 135 and 136: Smudged-out tower-like images on the Moon

had geometrical shapes, spherical buildings, very tall towers and what looked like radar
dishes (Figs 135 and 136). Some buildings had reflective surfaces on them and some
reminded him of cooling towers at power generation plants. Other towers were straight
and tall with a flat top, or round with a dome. He emphasised that many of these
structures were vast. He estimated that some must have covered half a mile.

This is a very important point. People need to redefine their perception of 'big' if
they are going to grasp what is happening. Remember that humans have been
incarcerated in a mind prison for aeons. We don't know what 'big' is, or how such
structures and technology of extraordinary size (to us) can be produced. We have been
living in a tiny, tiny perception bubble, and the cutting edge of human technology (that
we see) is the Stone Age compared with what is possible. You can advance
technologically and in other ways by the equivalent of thousands of years in next to no
'time' once you cross the Rubicon into an understanding of what reality is and how it
works. This is what we are dealing with here – technological capability that makes even
a lot of science fiction look tame. Imagine you are sitting in a cave knocking rocks
together and someone told you that it was possible to build a Jumbo Jet or a space

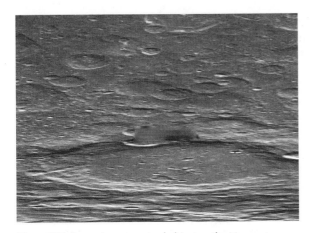

Figure 137: A massive non-natural object on the Moon. What is it?

shuttle. You would say it was impossible and crazy. The guy's been drinking too much mammoth juice. But this is the kind of chasm that people are being challenged to cross in terms of their perception of the possible. The suppression of information, and therefore the suppression of the perception of the possible, is one of the great ways that the true scale of the conspiracy stays hidden. This means that when people like me say this or that is happening, the perception censor kicks in and says: 'That's not possible.' *No*, it is not possible for *us* to do it. Others *can* do it, and they *are* doing it. I have spoken with insiders who have said they have seen pictures of spacecraft around Saturn that are so enormous that few would believe it possible. Jose Escamilla's DVD documentary, *Moon Rising*, highlighted a picture of a non-natural object on the Moon that had been smudged in most pictures to obscure it. The one in Figure 137 is clearer. The picture was sent for examination to forensics imaging expert, Jim Hoerricks, who estimated that it must be as big as ten cities the size of Los Angeles. This is the sort of technological capability we are dealing with and even that is nothing compared with what can be done, and is being done, elsewhere. A NASA insider told the *Moon Rising* documentary makers: 'We lied about everything.' The Moon is not colourless as it is portrayed and there are many colours on the surface. I am far from convinced that it doesn't have some sort of atmosphere and a much more significant gravity field. Remember: '*We lied about everything.*' A location of particular activity for centuries has been the Aristarchus Crater in the southern region of the Moon with reports of bright lights there since the 17th century. You can see why when you look at the picture in Figure 138. The structure, which sometimes glows electric blue, is some 29 miles in diameter and has been given the name 'Blue Gem' or

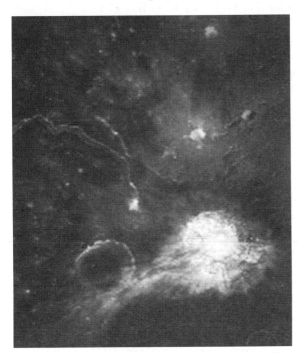

Figure 138: The 'Blue Gem' in the Aristarchus Crater

'Blue Dome'. There has been speculation that it is some sort of nuclear complex. It would appear that there are many non-natural structures even on the side of the Moon that we can see (Fig 139). Making sure that we only ever see one side of the Moon means that they can obviously hide what there is on the other side from independent astronomers with powerful telescopes. People would be shocked if they did see genuine pictures of the far side, because they would see that it is nothing like we are told. I read a book called *Someone Else Is On Our Moon* (W H Allen; 1977) that describes countless examples of non-natural phenomena on the Moon. These include huge machines working in craters – which could start to explain how areas 'the size of Texas' could be covered with melted rock containing titanium. The book was written by George H Leonard who studied thousands of NASA photographs, talked with NASA informants and listened to hours of astronaut tapes. His conclusion from the mountain of evidence that he saw and heard is that there is certainly intelligent life on the Moon. I agree, but *in* the Moon is where the real action is. Researchers Richard C Hoagland and Mike Bara detail many more Moon anomalies and non-natural features in their book, *Dark Mission – The Secret History of NASA* (Feral House, USA, 2009).

Spaceship Moon

The concept of the Moon as a giant spacecraft (giant to our perception, anyway) was discussed in 1970 by two members of the Soviet Academy of Sciences, Mikhail Vasin and Alexander Shcherbakov. They wrote a detailed article in the Soviet *Sputnik* magazine headed: '*Is the Moon the Creation of Alien Intelligence?*' They said that the Moon was a planetoid that had been 'hollowed out' with incredibly advanced technology that melted rock to create cavities in the interior (Fig 140). This 'metallic rocky slag' was then poured onto the surface to create the lunar landscape. Dr Don L Anderson, a professor of geophysics and director of the seismological laboratory at the California Institute of Technology, once said that 'the Moon is made inside out'. The inner and outer composition should be the other way round. Dr Farouk El-Baz worked with NASA on the scientific exploration of the Moon. He said: 'There are many undiscovered caverns suspected to exist beneath the surface of the Moon.' Several experiments have been carried out on the Moon to see if there actually are such caverns. Zulu shaman Credo Mutwa told me that their legends say that there were compartments within the Moon. The Soviet scientists pointed out that if the technology used to hollow out the Moon involved nuclear power it would explain the mystery of the uranium 236 and neptunium 237, and so would the 'Blue Gems' if they are nuclear in nature. This also puts into greater perspective the mystery areas the size of Texas covered with melted rock containing titanium. The Soviet scientists said that the high titanium content on the Moon's surface, together with chromium and zirconium, can also be explained if the Moon is a construct. These are known as 'refractory' metals which are extremely resistant to heat and wear. Vasin and Shcherbakov said that that these metals would provide 'enviable resistance to heat and the ability to stand up to means of aggression'. They said that you would choose precisely these metals if you were devising a material to protect a giant artificial satellite from the unfavourable effects of temperature, cosmic radiation and meteorite bombardment. The scientists said that this would explain why lunar rock is such a poor heat conductor, and from the engineers' point of view 'this spaceship of ages long past, which we call the Moon, is superbly constructed'. They

Figure 139: There are many features on the Moon that do not appear to be natural

went on:

> If you are going to launch an artificial sputnik, then it is advisable to make it hollow. At the same time it would be naïve to imagine that anyone capable of such a tremendous space project would be satisfied simply with some kind of giant empty trunk hurled into a near-Earth trajectory.

> It is more likely that what we have here is a very ancient spaceship, the interior of which was filled with fuel for the engines, materials and appliances for repair work, navigation instruments, observation equipment and all manner of machinery ... in other words, everything necessary to enable this 'caravelle of the Universe' to serve as a kind of Noah's Ark of

Illustration by Neil Hague (www.neilhague.com)

Figure 140: The Moon is a gigantic spacecraft, computer and broadcasting system

intelligence, perhaps even as the home of a whole civilisation envisaging a prolonged (thousands of millions of years) existence and long wanderings through space (thousands of millions of miles).

Naturally, the hull of such a spaceship must be super-tough in order to stand up to the blows of meteorites and sharp fluctuations between extreme heat and extreme cold. Probably the shell is a double-layered affair – the basis a dense armouring of about 20 miles in thickness, and outside it some kind of more loosely-packed covering (a thinner layer – averaging about three miles). In certain areas – where the lunar 'seas' and 'craters' are, the upper layer is quite thin, in some cases, non-existent.

Craters on the Moon are certainly within the rough estimates of the depth of the outer layer that the scientists talk about before any impact would meet the impenetrable 'dark armouring'. Vasin and Shcherbakov said that the strange variations in gravitational fields known as 'mascons' in the Moon's maria plains can also be explained from the 'construct' perspective. Any damage to the outer layer, where it is especially thin in the maria, would likely be done by flooding the area with a lava-like 'cement', they said. This would make them look a little like 'seas' from the Earth and it would also explain the extent of titanium in these same areas: 'The stocks of materials and machinery for doing this are no doubt still where they were, and are sufficiently massive to give rise to these gravitational anomalies.' I think there is a lot more to know when it comes to the Moon and its level of gravity, anyway. The scientists said that the dramatically different ages of rocks and dust on the Moon were due to the cosmic travels of the spacecraft Moon that would have gathered material from many places and of many ages; and the mysterious clouds of water vapour that have been observed were a release of the gases that form an atmosphere within the Moon that sustains life. The scientists said that a large bulge on the far side of the Moon could be explained by the immense strength of a spaceship hull preventing the Moon from breaking up. The Moon is not a natural body, at least in its re-constructed form, and it is not impossible that it is totally constructed using the same materials that I have described. Our moon is not alone, either. There are many 'moons' that are the same. The companion to the Zulu 'Necklace of the Mysteries', and just as old, is called the 'Necklace of the Moons'. Legends say there are many moons like 'ours'. There has been discussion over the years that Phobos, a moon of Mars, may not be natural. Mars has two moons: Phobos and Deimos, which are Greek words for 'fear' and 'panic'. In 1959,

Dr Iosif Samuilovich Shklovsky, a
Russian astrophysicist, is reported to
have said that Phobos could be an
artificial satellite (Fig 141). He asked the
question in view of its strange orbit and
indications that it could be hollow. In
1963, Raymond H Wilson Jr, Chief of
Applied Mathematics at NASA, said that
'Phobos might be a colossal base orbiting
Mars' and he added that NASA was
considering the possibility. Dr S Fred
Singer, special advisor to President
Eisenhower on space developments, said
the same. Mars Express, the European
spacecraft, took a series of close-up

Figure 141: The Mars moon, Phobos

pictures of Phobos in 2010 and the findings indicated that Phobos is lighter than it
should be, could be hollow, and its composition is not like any known asteroids or
meteorites.

'Chitauri' Moon

I rang Zulu shaman, Credo Mutwa, the oracle of African legends and accounts, to ask
what they said about the Moon. I didn't tell him what I was putting together at that
point. I only asked for any Zulu and other Africa legends about the Moon. He said that
Zulu lore and other African accounts say that the Moon was built 'far, far away'. Zulu
myths say that the Chitauri manipulate the
Earth from the Moon, where the 'Python lives',
and that people were warned not to upset the
Moon (Fig 142). 'It is said that the Sun is
forgiving, but never the Moon,' he told me.
Zulu legends symbolise the Moon as an egg,
because they say it had been *hollowed* out. They
say that two leaders of the Chitauri, known to
Zulus as Wowane and Mpanku, stole the
Moon from the 'Great Fire Dragon' and
'emptied out the yolk' until it was hollow.
They then 'rolled the Moon across the sky' to
the Earth 'hundreds of generations ago'. It was
said that the Moon was a home of 'the Python'
– the 'Chitauri'. Remember how the ancient
San people say that humans were created by
the Giant Python who came with his bag of
eggs to the Tsodilo Hills. The symbolism of the
Moon as an egg was widespread in the ancient
world and it was said that Semiramis/Ishtar,
the Babylonian goddess, came from the Moon
in a 'giant moon egg' and landed in the

Figure 142: Zulu legend says that the Chitauri live
inside the Moon

Figure 143: The origin of the mitre worn by the Pope and other Christian 'frocks' – the Reptilian fish god, Oannes (Nimrod), as depicted in Babylon. The Church of Babylon became the Church of Rome

Figure 144: Different religions – one hidden master

Euphrates River. This later became known as 'Ishtar's (Easter's) egg' and hence we have Easter eggs today, as I said earlier. So the Easter egg is a symbolic Moon. Zulu legends say that the Chitauri leaders, Wowane and Mpanku, were known as the 'water brothers'. The clay tablets from ancient Mesopotamia also say the leaders of the Anunnaki on their Earth mission were two brothers, Enlil and Enki. The latter was certainly symbolised in terms of water. He was known as 'Ea' in Babylonian and Akkadian mythology, which, from the Sumerian E-A, means 'the house of water'. We are looking at the same universal story about the Chitauri/Anunnaki/Nefilim Reptilians that began in Africa. The fish was commonly used to symbolise the reptilian scales, and there were many 'fish gods', including the Mesopotamian Oannes, or Dagon, the 'Fish of Heaven'. He was symbolised as having a fish head, and this is the origin of the mitre worn by the Pope and many other Christian clergy (Fig 143). Christianity is a religion, like Islam, Judaism, Hinduism, ad infinitum, that worships the Reptilian 'gods' and their Matrix; but only the inner elite know that (Fig 144). Surely, this can't be true. I mean, we worship *Jesus*. Mesopotamian 'Priests of Dagon' wore a hat just like the mitre, but then the Roman Church continued all the traditions of Babylon. It is the Church of Babylon relocated like the rest of Christianity. All the Saturn and Moon symbolism that I have been describing starts to fit into place now. They are symbols for the 'gods' (transformed into one 'God') and their key locations – Saturn and the Moon.

The Saturn–Moon Matrix

The Moon, with its internal crystalline structure, is a giant computer, a receiver–transmitter and broadcasting system that has been directing life on Earth in league with the main control centre, Saturn. The Moon's 'physical' presence alone has a fundamental impact on life on Earth not least in relation to 'time'. The word 'month' comes from *moonth*; and the female 'monthly cycle' is very much influenced by the

Moon. Some ancient legends say that there was no menstruation before the Moon came, and the genetic manipulation that followed. Humans were androgynous, not male and female, if you go 'back' far enough to the Real Golden Age before the Reptilian hijack. Genesis says: 'So God created man in His own image, in the image of God He created him; male and female He created them.' The symbolic biblical Creation story claims that 'God' said of women: 'I will greatly multiply your pain in childbearing; in pain you shall bring forth children ...' The introduction of male and female was another means of divide, rule and separate. The Moon is in the 'perfect position' with regard to the Earth, and this not by chance or coincidence. The Moon affects the speed of the Earth's rotation and so impacts directly on our perception of the passage of 'time'. It is the prime influence on movements of tidal water and the human body, which is some 70 per cent water, must also be significantly affected. The Moon also has a major impact on human hormone production via the endocrine system of glands that include the pineal and pituitary glands of the 'third eye' and connect with the glandular function of the heart. The Reptilians want to suppress and close the human third-eye, heart and right-brain so that we perceive only five-sense reality. Many studies have found evidence that the Moon can affect human behaviour at different points on its Sun-reflection cycle from 'new' to 'full'. This is where the term 'lunatic' comes from. The Moon has endless effects upon Earth and its inhabitants simply by being where it is, but its impact is far more than that. *Oh*, just a little bit. I am now going to pull together many themes of the book so far: the nature of reality; the electrical-plasma universe; cataclysmic events in the heavens; the Moon and Saturn; and the hijacking of Earth by the Reptilian Alliance. I have put together what I am now going to describe by following the clues, hints and 'big pointing fingers' that have guided me to all the other information that I have compiled since 1990. People will just have to make of it what they will, or rather intuitively feel. I am not telling anyone what they should think, nor do I wish to. It is only information for others to discern for themselves.

I have said that we are experiencing a sort of virtual-reality computer game of breathtaking scale and advancement. Consciousness is without form in its prime state. We are simply *awareness*, and take form to experience different realities within All Possibility. Cosmologist Carl Sagan said: 'We are all made of star stuff. We are a way for the Universe to know itself.' The 'game' is interactive and there is a constant interchange of information between 'the game' (the waveform construct, or Metaphysical Universe) and those experiencing the game – humans, non-humans of every conceivable kind, animals, trees, everyone and everything. We can play the game or be played by the game. We can live life or let life live us. It all depends on the level of awareness of the 'player'. There is nothing malevolent about the 'game'. It was created as a sort of cosmic vibrational theme park to allow the Infinite to experience itself through its infinite expressions. The 'game' was created with love, by the Infinite that is love: Infinite Love is the only truth – *everything* else is illusion. There is love that humans cannot imagine beyond the tiny frequency range that we are decoding into a 'world'. You cannot describe this reality; it must be experienced to be understood. Zulu shaman, Credo Mutwa, has 'died' a number of times, only to be revived, and he has experienced what it is like beyond the 'veil'. I experienced this in the rainforest of Brazil in my ayahuascan altered state. I was talking on the phone with Credo while I was writing this book and he described how this 'love', in its true sense, felt to him:

It is all the realities, all everywhere in every way; backwards and forwards, left and right. No doors, no barriers; you are just there. You wish that every human being, every beast could be there. You fall into an ocean. No top. No bottom. It is Oneness. All is one music, played by one orchestra. You are the One, the You, the Great 'Us'. You want to embrace the entire cosmos. You don't see the Sun, Moon and the stars. You just say, 'I understand.'

I saw no angry African god, no Jesus, no Jehovah. I saw nothing. There was only the music that comforted the soul. The music takes you on and on to where the stars are not there. It is the real truth, a truth you cannot express. A new self; a new reality. Love is deeper in this Oneness, deeper than the space beyond the Moon.

Creation is teeming with life and teeming with love, but it has been systematically kept from us. Credo said: 'They have taken every truth and made it a lie called truth.' He's right. The world we think we are experiencing is a lie, a fraud, from which we are soon to emerge. The frequency range that we 'see' is just a vibration away from all that Credo describes, and so much more. Endless realms of form, and no form; full of love.

There has been a series of cataclysmic events in the Solar System, including the one I mentioned that affected the entire galaxy and Andromeda. The whole waveform construct of the galaxy was shaken and imbalanced, and the work began to restore harmony. Waveform realities (the 'Cosmic Internet') are beamed from the centre of the galaxy and 'picked up' by receivers in sync with the different frequency ranges. What we call suns and stars are the main 'receivers', 'decoders' and 'amplifiers', so are brown dwarfs, but everything ultimately decodes this information within the frequency band that it can access. The reality that we are decoding, and therefore holographically experiencing, is meant to be a far wider range of frequencies than we currently 'see'; and it is supposed to be a world of love, joy, harmony and peace. This is clearly not the case at the moment and hasn't been for aeons, and this is because of what I will call 'The Hack'. Some of those helping with the repair and reseeding of the stricken galaxy became affected by the energetic distortions they were exposed to, and they began to experience what we would term a 'personality change'. This is one meaning of the theme about 'Fallen Angels', and the Reptilian Alliance is an expression of that; but they, too, are vehicles for another force which, in the end, will not be something that takes form. It will be a deeply imbalanced waveform state that mentally and emotionally distorts their perception of reality. What we call 'evil' is simply ignorance. This, in turn, is a disconnection from the source of love and wisdom that pervades everything. The story of the 'fallen' Darth Vader in the *Star Wars* movies of insider, George Lucas, is a version of the theme I am outlining here. Darth Vader had once been a 'Jedi' Knight called Anakin Skywalker who fell to the 'dark side of the Force'. The Reptilian Alliance in their 'fallen' perception had the intellectual knowledge of how reality can be manipulated to entrap others, but no longer the love, wisdom and harmony not to do so. They are very clever, but have no wisdom. Cleverness without wisdom is a seriously destructive force. The Reptilians and their various associated groups began a process of enslaving worlds by hacking into the waveform information beamed from the centre of the galaxy and so manipulating the reality of the target population. They have done this to endless worlds and one of them is called 'Earth'.

Figure 145: Why is Saturn a 'planet' like no other? Because it is a 'converted' brown dwarf

'The Hack' requires them to hijack bodies with sun-like qualities, because they are created to be receiver–transmitters of the multi-dimensional galactic game. The Reptilian Alliance had been interacting with the Earth and manipulating for a considerable 'time' before they secured their sun – *Saturn*. This 'planet', and Jupiter, are a form of 'sun' (or 'dark sun') called a 'brown dwarf' and the Reptilians have the advanced technological ability to use them to hack into the galactic information stream to feed a fake reality to the target population. Brown dwarfs are their modus operandi and they have been doing this in many parts of the cosmos. Saturn sends out the main hacking broadcasts and this is amplified and directed at the Earth by the Moon. We are being subjected to 'original Sin' – the moon god.

Lord of the Rings

The Reptilian Alliance's modus operandi is to first trigger cataclysmic events on a target 'world', or solar system, and wipe away the society that was there before. Then Reptilians genetically-engineer a new species that is designed to be 'tuned in' to their false reality – their *'Matrix'* – and the planet is hijacked along with the perception of the people. They have done exactly this to Earth and humanity, and their means of doing so are Saturn and the Moon. Saturn, the 'Lord of the Rings', is the master control centre. I mean, just *look* at Saturn with all its rings (Figure 145). Saturn is a ginormous broadcasting system, and they will eventually find that the rings are full of *crystals* rather than 'ice' – a type of crystal that we aren't familiar with on Earth. The rings are not natural, and at one time Saturn was a conventional brown dwarf. It had no rings. They have been *constructed* by the technology-obsessed Reptilian Alliance. Funnily enough, as I think about it, an insider once told me of a photograph he had seen of an incredibly large spacecraft that appeared to be 'repairing' one of Saturn's rings. The process is ongoing, and they are continuing to construct others. In 2009, NASA announced that its Spitzer Space Telescope had discovered another ring circling Saturn from a distance of some 3.7 million miles and going out to 7.4 million. It is so big that it would take a billion Earths to fill it (Fig 146). Some scientists say that Saturn's rings were created by the debris from a disintegrated moon; but how would that create a ring 3.7 million miles away from Saturn that could hold a billion Earths? Saturn's broadcasting system extends throughout the Solar System, but most of it is not on

visible frequencies. Saturn is the 'Lord of
the Rings'. And how did J R R Tolkien
(and film director Peter Jackson)
symbolise the controlling force in the
book and film of that name? As a fiery
reptilian eye – the Eye of Sauron (Fig
147). Writers like Tolkien, a Professor of
Anglo–Saxon at Oxford University, and
his close friend, C S Lewis, who wrote
The Chronicles of Narnia, symbolising
other dimensions of reality, knew a great
deal more than they admitted openly.
They used 'fiction' to portray fact.
Saturn is the second biggest 'planet' in
the Solar System after Jupiter, and is the
sixth 'planet' from the Sun. Its rings and
moons make it unique. Saturn is called a
'gas giant', as with Jupiter, Uranus and
Neptune, but it is habitable by very
different entities to humans much closer
to its material centre, and, as with
everything, it exists on other ranges of
frequency. Mainstream science says that
Saturn radiates 2.5 times more energy
than it receives from the Sun, and it
generates an unexplained constantly-
spinning six-sided hexagonal wave
pattern at its north pole which rotates in
sync with Saturn's recorded radio

Figure 146: The recently-found Saturn ring that it would
take a billion Earths to fill

Figure 147: The reptilian eye symbolising the controlling
force in *Lord of the Rings*

emissions. A massive constantly-spinning storm system captured at the south pole also
looks like an eye (Fig 148). Is it really a coincidence that the number six and the six-
pointed star (an ancient symbol for Saturn and more latterly the House of Rothschild)
and the all-seeing eye are such predominant Illuminati symbols when Saturn has long

been symbolised as an
eye? Jupiter and Neptune
also generate more heat
than they receive. Saturn
takes more than 29 Earth
years to complete a
journey around the Sun.
The 'planet' ('dark sun')
has been known about
since prehistoric times
because it can be seen from
Earth, but it was only after
the development of strong

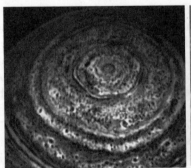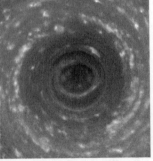

Figure 148: The hexagonal wave pattern at Saturn's north pole and the 'eye'
at its south pole

Figure 149: The Saturn solar system

enough telescopes that the rings were able to be seen. Babylonian astronomers recorded the movements of Saturn, and it was worshipped by the Romans as the god, Saturn (the Greek 'Cronus' or Kronos). There is no coincidence whatsoever in Saturn having so many moons. More than 60 have been discovered so far (Fig 149). They comprise, with the Saturn dwarf, a mini solar system and the same with Jupiter and its at least 63 moons. Most of Saturn's moons derive their names from god Saturn's brothers and sisters, the Titans and Titanesses. Small Saturnian moons discovered more recently have been named after Inuit, Gallic and Norse gods and goddesses. None of this is by chance, and all are different names for the same deities in different cultures. Saturn's biggest moon, Titan, is the second-largest in the Solar System behind the Jupiter moon, Ganymede, and is twice as big as our own moon. Titan, Ganymede and other major Jupiter moons, Io, Europa (the EU goddess) and Callisto, are really planets, though they are known as moons. Titan, Ganymede and others also play a very active role in the Saturn – Moon Matrix and I am sure we will see the role of Jupiter in all this eventually. Even mainstream scientists have suggested that some form of life could exist on Titan and another Saturn 'moon', Enceladus. Saturn is communicating with the major moons/planets and many not so major ones in our Solar System. I suggest that 'Earth's' moon was once in that group around Saturn, and at least many of them are the same in nature. They are computer systems, amplifiers and satellites of the Saturn broadcasting grid and they go out as necessary to target other worlds. Saturn is not their only hijacked and converted brown dwarf either. They are experts at this.

Saturn was often symbolised as an eye by the ancients and that is a likely origin of the all-seeing eye, one of the major symbols of the Reptilian-hybrid bloodline network

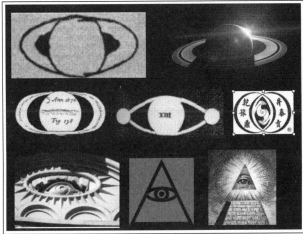

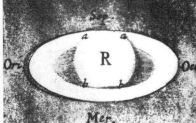

Figure 150: Saturn symbolised as an eye. The image in the bottom left is on the Mormon Temple in Salt Lake City which is awash with Illuminati symbolism. The pyramid and all-seeing eye is a major Illuminati bloodline symbol.

Figure 151: The Saturn 'eye' Matrix at the 'Ground Zero' subway station perfectly symbolising how humanity is held fast in perception-control

Figure 152 The Saturn–Moon Matrix hacks into the wider virtual-reality game and feeds a manipulated and suppressed reality to the human mind–body decoding system

(Fig 150). I went to the subway station right next to Ground Zero when I spoke in New York in 2010. The station has mosaic eyes on the walls all along the platforms, and a large depiction on the floor of an eye broadcasting frequencies across the planet (Fig 151). The eye is almost certainly meant to be Saturn (Satan). The image perfectly portrays what Saturn is doing. Saturn hacks into the waveform information broadcast from the centre of the galaxy via the Sun and broadcasts a fake reality into the Solar System. The Moon amplifies this and beams it specifically at the Earth (Figs 152 and 153).The fantastic synchronicities between Earth, the Moon and the Sun in size, geometry and position, are all made possible by the Moon. These synchronicities are connected to how the Sun's information is hacked by Saturn and the Moon. The Moon is where it is because it was specifically placed there. Visible light and the electromagnetic spectrum that science can record is the Matrix, the false reality. And 'God' said, 'Let there be light.' The speed of light which we are told is the fastest speed possible (rubbish!) is the vibrational 'wall' of the Matrix. We are not even living 'on' the Earth as it really is. Some of it is 'original', but there are many holographic implants that change it for our perception. The Matrix broadcasts block humans from perceiving what we would otherwise be experiencing. The Earth that we can't see is a place of love and harmony – not war, fear and suffering. The predators dictate our lives and make us into slaves to them by hijacking our sense of reality. The Saturn–Moon Matrix transformed a once-vibrant, *conscious* humanity into computer programs decoding cycles of repetitive perception and behaviour. Neil Hague symbolises this very well with his concept of 'Moonopoly' (Fig 154). The transmissions of the Saturn – Moon Matrix are received and re-transmitted by the Earth's crystal core which has been tuned to the Matrix frequency range, and the 'Hack' connects with us through the reptilian brain and the receiver–transmitter system that we call DNA. This brings us back to 'junk' DNA and what Professor Sam Chang from the Human Genome Project said earlier – that the overwhelming majority of human DNA is of 'off- world' origin and the 'extraterrestrial junk genes' merely 'enjoy the ride' with hard-working active genes passed through the generations. He said:

Figure 153: The Moon amplifies the Saturn broadcasts and beams them specifically at the Earth

Figure 154: Neil Hague's 'Moonopoly'. The broadcasts from the Saturn–Moon Matrix control the perceptions of anyone locked into its frequency band

What we see in our DNA is a program consisting of two versions, a big code and basic code. First fact is, the complete 'program' was positively not written on Earth; that is now a verified fact. The second fact is that genes, by themselves, are not enough to explain evolution; there must be something more in 'the game' ... Sooner or later we have to come to grips with the unbelievable notion that every life on Earth carries genetic code for his extraterrestrial cousin, and that evolution is not what we think it is.

Professor Chang also said that the 'alien' parts of 'junk' DNA have 'their own veins, arteries and immune system that vigorously resists all our anti-cancer drugs'. The DNA implanted by the 'extraterrestrials' is *pre- programmed*, and one effect of the Saturn – Moon Matrix is to activate those programs to play out as 'spontaneous' human behaviour and a sequence of 'time'. The Matrix acts like a laser reading computer software or a DVD. It brings the pre-programmed information in human DNA onto the 'screen' – our decoded reality. The 'software program' is running in every human mind – body computer and it has been encoded for aeons (Fig 155). Remember how Rebecca Cann, Assistant Professor of Genetics at the University of Hawaii, co- authored a study in the journal, *Nature*, saying that all modern humans are descended from a single mother who lived in Africa in about 200,000 BC. If what we call humans originate from a single source the program could easily have been implanted that would infiltrate every subsequent member of the 'species' (software). Only by becoming Conscious

Figure 155: Humans are held fast in the Saturn-Moon Matrix program when we are not Conscious beyond mind-body

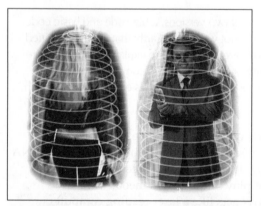

Figure 156: 'Personal' thoughts and perceptions? Or merely what people are decoding?

beyond mind – body can we override the program. It has become so clear to me while writing this book that the extent of human behaviour programming is absolutely fundamental. I understand from people who read papers by molecular biologist, Francis Crick, that he believed that DNA was pre-programmed. You will often hear it said that Crick and his associates 'discovered DNA'; but what became known as deoxyribonucleic acid (DNA) was first discovered by Johann Friedrich Miescher in 1869. Crick, James Watson and Maurice Wilkins were given the Nobel Prize for Physiology or Medicine in 1962 for 'their discoveries concerning the molecular structure of nucleic acids and its significance for information transfer in living material'. Crick appears to have known far more about DNA than was made public, and he believed that it was of 'extraterrestrial' origin. So the Matrix illusion is so deep, so ingrained, because it is not only a Matrix field, but a DNA program. The 'Queen Bee' (Saturn–Moon) broadcasts the waveform information 'hack' and humans decode this into a world they think they see, and perceptions and behaviours that they think is 'them'. We can be completely controlled by the Matrix and be no more than human robots responding to data input, or we can open our hearts and minds and see beyond what others can see. This means opening our minds to Consciousness which is not subject to the manipulation of the Matrix or the DNA program. It operates outside of 'space' and 'time' and beyond the vibrational walls of the Matrix. If you look at all the incredible and endless interconnected manipulations that I will describe in this book – and there are so many more – this clearly could not have been organised by people sitting around a table deciding their next move. I have often pondered on this. How do they *do* it? Was there a computer system spewing out data on what to do and when? But I can see it clearly now. Those in authority who run and enforce the human Control System are following a program in the same way as worker ants and bees follow the program broadcast by the Queen. They are computer terminals on the Matrix Internet with the Saturn–Moon Matrix triggering their already programmed DNA to respond according to program. The bloodlines are the most locked-in because they were genetically-created for that purpose, but anyone who is not truly Conscious will be responding to their DNA Saturn–Moon Matrix program which drives their thoughts, perceptions and behaviour. How often are those in authority described as 'like robots' that make decisions without logic or reason? 'They' are not making those decisions – the *Matrix* is (Fig 156). This scene in the first *Matrix* movie with Morpheus and Neo describes precisely the human plight when I add two words – *Saturn* and *Moon*:

> The [Saturn–Moon] Matrix is everywhere. It is all around us, even now in this very room. You can see it when you look out your window, or you turn on your television. You can feel it when you go to work, when you go to church, when you pay your taxes. It is the world that has been pulled over your eyes to blind you from the truth.

> 'What truth?'

> That you are a slave, Neo. Like everyone else, you were born into bondage ... born into a prison that you cannot smell or taste or touch. A prison for your mind.

The Saturn–Moon Matrix is decoded within the electromagnetic frequency range visible to human sight and technology, and the genetic-engineering of the human mind–body-computer locked humans into that frequency via DNA and the reptilian brain. Consciousness can, however, override that and so they have to maintain humanity in low-vibrational states to imprison their perception in the Matrix. The plasma field within our holographic reality acts like a plasma 'screen' on which we 'watch' the 'picture show', or appear to. It is an expression, like everything, of decoded waveform information. People go through their lives following the Saturn program they are decoding while thinking this is the 'real world' (Fig 157). Humans are like two-legged farm animals caught in the headlights of an oncoming Matrix. The reality we are being fed is encoded with perceptions and experiences that cause people to transmit low-vibrational emotional energy that both feeds the Reptilian Alliance and, in many ways, helps

Figure 157: The Saturn–Moon Matrix is how the Reptilians 'gave us their mind'

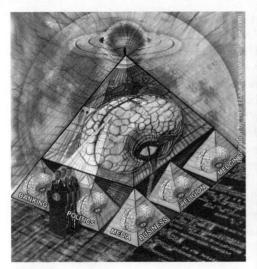

Figure 158: The Saturn–Moon Matrix and the Reptilian collective mind is the force behind all the Illuminati institutions of government, banking, media, corporations, religion and Big Pharma 'medicine' and also programs the reality of their personnel

Figure 159:

to power the system. The virtual-reality 'game' is interactive, and so is the hacked version. We receive and transmit, we receive and 'post'. The Saturn–Moon Matrix has created an energetic perception 'loop' in which the false reality is fed to us, and, when we perceive it and believe it, we feed back that perception to the Matrix. This constantly empowers the false reality in a feedback loop. In short, the Matrix is powered by our belief that the hacked reality is *'real'*. We can and will break this closed loop with the realisations that I am describing in this book, and by opening our minds to Consciousness beyond the Matrix frequencies. The power of the Saturn–Moon Matrix to influence our reality dilutes and dilutes the more we open our minds and hearts and let Consciousness in. The Control System is terrified of the Truth Vibrations for this reason, and this is why it is now throwing everything that it can at humanity to keep us entrapped within the vibrational box through fear, chaos and upheaval. By the way, some unexplainable and 'paranormal' experiences happen when there is a 'glitch' in the Matrix information field. As I write, there are many reports from around the world that the heavens have changed, the constellations are not where they should be and that the Moon has changed its angle. This is the result of the Reptilians manipulating the Matrix to confuse us and prepare us for the fake 'end of the world' or 'new world' prophecies by the Bible, the Mayan Calendar, Hopi prophecies and all the rest. They are not true. They are part of the manipulation and the Reptilians plan to make it *seem* as if they are happening by manufacturing events. They are already doing so. It was all planned a long 'time' ago. I'll come to this in the final chapter.

Reptilian World

One of the chief ways that the Matrix connects with us is, not surprisingly, through the reptilian brain, and this helps to lock us into the Reptilian Alliance control system (Fig 158). The Matrix transmissions are also aimed at our DNA receiver–transmitter systems, and much of this is happening within the realms of what science calls 'junk DNA'. Some of this has been switched off in order to narrow our band of experienced reality, and some is picking up the Matrix frequencies transmitted by carrier waves from Saturn via the Moon. This is how, in the words of Don Juan Matus in the Carlos Castaneda books, they *'gave us their mind'*. It is worth reading that passage again in the light of what I have described:

> We have a predator that came from the depths of the cosmos and took over the rule of our lives. Human beings are its prisoners. The predator is our lord and master. It has rendered us docile, helpless. If we want to protest, it suppresses our protest. If we want to act independently, it demands that we don't do so ... indeed we are held prisoner!
>
> They took us over because we are food to them, and they squeeze us mercilessly because we are their sustenance. Just as we rear chickens in coops, the predators rear us in human coops, humaneros. Therefore, their food is always available to them.
>
> Think for a moment, and tell me how you would explain the contradictions between the intelligence of man the engineer and the stupidity of his systems of belief, or the stupidity of his contradictory behaviour. Sorcerers believe that the predators have given us our systems of beliefs, our ideas of good and evil; our social mores. They are the ones who set up our dreams of success or failure. They have given us covetousness, greed and cowardice. It is the predator who makes us complacent, routinary and egomaniacal.
>
> In order to keep us obedient and meek and weak, the predators engaged themselves in a stupendous manoeuvre – stupendous, of course, from the point of view of a fighting strategist; a horrendous manoeuvre from the point of those who suffer it. They gave us their mind. The predators' mind is baroque, contradictory, morose, filled with the fear of being discovered any minute now.

The Saturn–Moon Matrix is how they have done it. Humans tuned most powerfully to the Matrix transmissions (the overwhelming majority) are like worker ants following the work-plan broadcast by the queen. Ants are said to communicate through chemicals called pheromones, but they are only the chemical expression of vibrational communications. Ants tune in through their antennae and we pick up the Matrix broadcasts through DNA and the reptilian brain. The Reptilians have a hive-mind communication system which the Matrix connects with, and it would appear that at the centre of this is their version of a female 'queen'. Maybe the worship of the 'goddess' is something to do with this and certainly the hybrid bloodline is passed on through the mitochondrial, or female, DNA. The Illuminati Reptilian hybrid bloodlines are the agents of the Matrix within the Matrix – the 'Agent Smiths' if you like, portrayed in the *Matrix* movie series. The Matrix 'mind' is the controlling force behind all the institutions

Figure 160: The Saturn–Moon Matrix connects with the reptilian brain and the whole genetic structure through DNA

Figure 161: The feedback loop. Programmed perceptions are fed back to the Matrix to empower those perceptions which are then fed back to humanity and so on

of human control and those who run and administer them while being unknowing prisoners of the Matrix themselves (Figure 159). I explained earlier how the reptilian brain doesn't think – it *reacts*; it is constantly scanning the environment in search of threats to its survival physically, financially and across the great spectrum of human experience – reputation, job, relationship, the list goes on and on. They need to feed us an endless stream of reasons to fear not surviving, to connect us most powerfully into reptilian-brain reality – therefore Matrix reality (Fig 160). These emotional states affect the way DNA receives and transmits, and cause heart rhythm incoherence that scrambles the relationship between heart, brain and nervous system. This is another crucial reason why we are bombarded with wars, financial collapses, false-flag terrorist attacks, health 'scares', 'global warming', engineered 'natural' disasters and all manner of other things. This way they can most powerfully plug us into the Matrix and energise it through the 'feedback' loop (Fig 161).

Blocking Frequencies

Matrix-broadcasts and genetic manipulation also block us from perceiving the greater reality. People who haven't researched this would be amazed at what *human* scientists can do today, never mind those who are thousands of years ahead of them in technological know-how. I'll also discuss a little later the technology that has existed for decades in human society that can externally access the minds of people and feed them thoughts and commands that they believe are their own. It is a cinch when you know what you're doing; and if human science can do this what can the scaly fellahs do? *New Scientist*, the mainstream science magazine, reported that when the United States switched from analogue to digital television, astronomers could suddenly see whole galaxies that weren't previously visible. The race against time that the news item talks

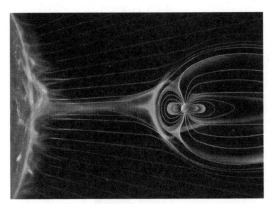

Figure 162: The Matrix blocks even more solar energy (information) than the Earth's energy field would naturally do

about here was for astronomers to see as much as they could before the former analogue television frequencies were sold off for other technology:

Prior to the switch-over, naturally occurring radio waves at frequencies between 700 and 800 megahertz were obscured by analogue TV signals preventing astronomers from using this band. The freeing up of this bandwidth is a once-in-a-lifetime opportunity to see galaxies in this range.

Astronomers could not see whole galaxies in that frequency range because Americans were watching the television! Imagine what is possible with the technology the Reptilian Alliance is using. Earth's charged plasma-field and atmosphere already blocks many energies and frequencies from getting through (Fig 162). I am only saying that other frequencies that we don't know about are being artificially blocked. Human science has developed something called 'metamaterials'. Their 'nano-metric surface' interferes with light at specific wavelengths and this makes light (information) deviate around an object in specific colours (frequencies) of the light spectrum. This makes the object invisible, because we only see something when light is reflected from it. A mainstream news report told how a team from Imperial College London, and Salford University in the North West of England, were exploiting this:

The scientists have conceived of a 'space-time cloak' which manipulates light and, in essence, conceals whole events from a viewer. The theory is based on censoring the flow of events, which we perceive as a stream of light particles, also called photons, that strike the retina. By exploiting a characteristic of fibre optics, the flow of photons can be slowed, events edited out and stitched back together ...

... [The team's paper says] 'A safecracker would be able, for a brief time, to enter a scene, open the safe, remove its contents, close the door and exit the scene, whilst the record of a surveillance camera apparently showed that the safe door was closed all the time.'

This is what humans can do, and yet the far more technologically-advanced Reptilian Alliance could not manipulate our reality in the way that I'm saying?? I have been highlighting a movie for more than a decade for accurately symbolising what is really happening in the world. I can now see that it's even closer to the truth than I first thought after what I've discovered about the Saturn–Moon Matrix. The movie is called *They Live*, and it was released in 1988. I guess you would call it a sort of 'B'–movie produced and directed by American filmmaker, John Carpenter, who apparently also worked with George Lucas on special effects in the *Star Wars* series. Carpenter's own movie-making career that includes science 'fiction', horror and occult themes confirms

Figure 164: The US President in *They Live* when viewed through the sunglasses

Figure 165: Beaming people to other planets in *They Live*

an awareness of what is happening away from the public eye. *They Live* opens with a character played by former wrestler, Roddy Piper, walking from city to city looking for work in the building trade amid a catastrophic economic depression and police state in America – the same that is happening now. He finds some temporary work on a building site, and at the end of the day he's invited by a co-worker to stay in what today we would call a 'tent city'. They had rigged up a black-and-white communal television and suddenly the normal programming was hacked into by a low-grade broadcast of a man saying that 'They' were here and that 'They' were covertly controlling the population. The Roddy Piper character becomes suspicious about activity at a church across the road, and when he sneaks inside he realises that the choir music that he could hear outside was a tape recording. He finds some brown boxes, but leaves before he can open one in fear of being caught. That night the police raid the makeshift village with helicopters and bulldozers. The place is razed and the people are attacked, and they scattered. Piper returns the next day when all is quiet and goes into the church to see what is inside the boxes. He grabs one and runs into a back alley, and when he tears it open the contents are a pile of sunglasses. Bewildered and disappointed, he takes one pair, puts them in his pocket, and walks out into the main street. But when he puts them on, everything changes. Advertisements on the billboards are no longer displaying the images that he was seeing with his eyes. Now he can only see subliminal messages saying 'stay asleep', 'do not question authority', 'obey', 'no independent thought', 'no imagination', 'consume' and 'conform' (Fig 163). He sees the same when he looks at the advertisements and articles in magazines and newspapers. Money is imprinted with the message: 'This is your God' when he looks through the glasses.

His biggest shock, however, is when he sees that some people who look human without the glasses look anything but human when he puts them on. The US President and the newsreaders on the television are not human. Some police officers are the same (Fig 164). He goes at one point into an area under the city where he realises that there is a conspiracy between the hidden extraterrestrials and a human cabal that serves their interest on the surface. People were being beamed to other planets with high technology that the public didn't know existed (Fig 165). I have spoken with some that have worked on beyond-top-secret projects and they have described being transported using 'beam me up, Scotty'-type techniques. One said he had been beamed to a base under the surface of Mars where he met members of an extraterrestrial race that looked virtually human. There is so much going on around us while the people are playing 'Moonopoly' on the vibrational/holographic treadmill. The Roddy Piper character discovers that people can't see the non-humans controlling them or the subliminal messages, because a frequency is being broadcast from a dish on a television tower that is blocking their ability to perceive them. The dish is disabled, and suddenly people see extraterrestrials sitting next to them when the blocking frequency stops being broadcast. If you take that dish to be the Moon and the Saturn–Moon Matrix this is what is happening to us. Some ancient traditions say this about the Moon in their own way. When Credo Mutwa read what I have written about the Moon and the Moon Matrix in *Human Race Get Off Your Knees*, he said: 'What you say about the Moon in your book is what our ancestors said was happening.' He also told me that during one of his many 'near death experiences' he had looked at the Moon. 'The Moon is exactly as what you describe,' he said. 'It has a big cave inside it. It is hollow as a football. Not real.'

Other sources

I said earlier how often, when I have gone public with something that is 'far out' to mainstream society, that I will later get a sudden confirmation that I am on the right track. I am not saying that every last detail is 100 per cent accurate, and I never have. There is such an endless mountain of information to process and fit together across so many diverse subjects, and there are forces trying to block me from doing so. But the theme and most of the detail I am very happy with, although there is always more to know. You have to be open to that at all times. I was sent an email about nine months after *Human Race Get Off Your Knees* was published. The writer said she had read the book and had seen the Moon information and she recommended that I check out a book called *Earth* by Barbara Marciniak. She included some page numbers. Barbara Marciniak is a 'channel' who became well known in 'New Age' circles in the 1990s for communicating with an awareness that said it was connected to the cluster of stars known as the Pleiades. The communications spoke of how a reptilian race was manipulating humanity. I met Barbara a few times and liked her a lot. She is grounded and not at all airy-fairy. I had read her book, *Bringers of the Dawn*, which was excellent, but I had not read *Earth* (Bear & Company; 1994). When it arrived in the post I went to the page numbers that the email had told me about ... *Well!* This is what the book said was communicated through Barbara Marciniak:

> ... the Moon is a very powerful electromagnetic computer ... The energy from the Moon has been beaming electromagnetic frequencies onto the Earth for aeons now to maintain the two-

stranded DNA [it is said that it should be twelve-stranded] ... The Moon is a satellite that was constructed ... it was ... anchored outside Earth's atmosphere for aeons as a mediating and monitoring device, a super computer or eye in the sky ...

... Earth must be owned by those who dwell there; however it is not. You have outside gods, creator energies, who prevent you, as a species, from having free reign with your kundalini ... The influence of the Moon, as a main satellite computer, affects all of the Earth ... The Moon's programs have for aeons been of great limitation toward human beings ... There are repetitive cycles that the Moon creates, to which you respond.

The Moon creates *Moonopoly*. I had a good laugh when I read those passages nine months after I had decided to 'jump' with the Moon Matrix information. 'Computer' moons like ours can also be used to influence planets in a very loving and positive way and it is possible that the Moon was doing that before it was hijacked by the Reptilian Alliance to be a means of mass manipulation and control. Barbara Marciniak's channelling points this way and I am open to that. We need to be flexible about detail and let information be our guide, not unyielding dogma. In that case, removing the Reptilian Alliance from the Moon and changing what it broadcasts would have a life-changing effect on this planet and its inhabitants. Simply switching off the Reptilian broadcasts would change everything, too. Barbara's channelling for her book indicates that other non-human forces are in the process of intervening in the Reptilian control of the Moon and I have come across similar information. I understand all these years later that this intervention is significantly advanced. I would strongly emphasise that we are not alone in meeting the challenges that we face – the bloodlines just want us to think we are. There is a multi-dimensional effort going on to set the planet free from aeons of Reptilian/Grey control and this will succeed. We need to play our part in our level of reality while others do their job elsewhere. This dismantling of the Reptilian Control System is not only to help humanity. What is happening here is having a knock-on effect across a wide area of the galaxy and beyond because of how a smaller part of a hologram can affect the whole. Barbara Marciniak's channelling for *Earth* said:

There have been many battles over the Moon ... There is a plan to gradually insert different programs of influence on Earth when the Moon becomes occupied by forces that would assist in your growth, rather than limit you. The Moon's programs have for eons been of great limitation toward human beings. The tales about the full moon and insanity, madness and heightened bleeding are all quite true. There are repetitive cycles that the Moon creates to which you respond.

You know that television influences you to a great degree. The Moon is the same way. You simply have not been able to tune into the Moon's programs and learn how to turn them off. You cannot. Others must turn the Moon off for you or reprogram the Moon, which is taking place right now. At this time, the Moon is quite controlled. Some people are gravely affected by mania and craziness from the Moon. Extraterrestrials and others have many bases on the Moon, and those from Earth have little influence when it comes down to it.

It is the extraterrestrials that really operate it all. Your technology, though rapidly advancing, cannot begin to compare with the biotechnology [including genetic engineering] of sentient space travellers. You are newcomers to the game and you miss a vital key, for your senses, and the essence of your physical world, structure reality in a particular way. You constantly translate data and, like interpreting a dream, condense the experience into physical boundaries, where you find you can explain less and less.

This is what I have been stressing all these years and throughout this book – we are being manipulated to decode reality in a way that keeps us limited and enslaved. I came across this quote, too, at about the same time from the famous Armenian-born mystic, George Gurdjieff. He said in 1916:

All movements, actions and manifestations of people, animals and plants depend upon the Moon, and we are controlled by the Moon ... The mechanical part of our lives depends upon the Moon, is subject to the Moon. If we develop in ourselves consciousness and will, and subject our mechanical self and all our mechanical manifestations to them, we shall escape the power of the Moon.

Precisely. The Saturn–Moon Matrix operates within the frequency range of mind, the electromagnetic spectrum and low-vibration emotion. When we open our minds to Consciousness our perception expands beyond the influence of the Matrix frequencies. We can suddenly perceive what we were blocked from perceiving and we begin to see what is really going on. I was shown an article on the day I am writing this that told the story of something called the 'Chani Project'. This was claimed to involve a secret technology located in Africa which made contact in 1994 with an entity from a parallel universe, and the communications continued for the following five years. The article said that the entity was asked more than 20,000 questions. 'Chani' is an acronym for Channelled Holographic Access Network Interface. The entity was asked in one interaction what was the purpose of our Moon? It said that 'life became better with no Moon' and that it was not a natural heavenly body. The Moon was there to control the Earth 'mood', it is quoted as saying. A 'big calm' would come over the people without the Moon, and there would be no 'big storm' – just a 'little storm'. There would be peace among the people without the Moon. Funny how this 'no-Moon' world is exactly how I am describing the Real Golden Age before 'The Hack'. The communication alluded to the fact that an 'old race' captured the Moon 'from space' and put it next to the Earth. This is what Zulu legends say, and what my own work supports. The Chani communications indicated that 'Moon forces' operated like a time machine to control time and manipulated the mood of 'beings on this planet in this timeline'. The most ancient human accounts do not mention time. It is an illusion of the Matrix, and time was encoded to enslave humans by disconnecting us from the NOW. I can see very clearly as my understanding expands that the 'Time Loop' is the Matrix. The Time Loop is what has been hacked into the timeless NOW-reality that we should be experiencing. Saturn is associated with time, and 'Kronos', the name of the Greek Saturn god, means 'time'. He is the symbol for Father Time. The two clocks on either side of the main entrance to St Peter's Basilica in Rome are symbols of this Saturn – Moon-control of our

Figure 166:   **Figure 167:**
The clock face represents 'Moon time', or Saturn–Moon time, so you would expect them to be prominent at the Vatican City as symbols of the time-makers, Saturn and the Moon

perception of time, and so is the clock-face in general (Figs 166 and 167). You see the same clock theme at Westminster Abbey and St Paul's Cathedral in London, which are both Freemasonic temples designed by initiates of the bloodline cult. Sir Christopher Wren (1632–1723) was the high initiate architect who designed St Paul's Cathedral and also built the Greenwich Observatory in London through which runs the prime meridian of what is called Greenwich Mean Time (GMT). Interestingly, the Chani 'entity' also talked about the 'reptile' holding humans back so they could not 'grow', and how they had won a 'war' with the reptiles in its own reality. 'We kill many dragons [in] many timelines', the communication said. The entity is reported to have added that humans had evolved more 'spiritually' than the reptiles that it was talking about, but the scaly guys 'want to hold on to their wise technology ... their god is their technology'. I have been saying this in my books for years. They are very developed in their intellectual, technological mind, but they are not 'spiritually' conscious. They have sought to make us the same by 'giving us their mind'. The Moon has not always been there and some ancient legends say the same. They tell of a time 'before the Moon'. Ancient Greek authors, Aristotle and Plutarch, and Roman authors, Apollonius Rhodius and Ovid, told of a people called the Proselenes in Arcadia who said that their ancestors had been there 'before there was a moon in the heavens'. 'Proselene' means 'before Selene' – the Greek goddess of the Moon, and a name often used for the Moon itself. Roman writer, Censorinus, also wrote of a time aeons ago when there was no Moon. Dr Hans Schindler Bellamy includes the same theme in his work, *Moons, Myths and Men*. He tells of the 'Mozces', a native tribe in Colombia that say they 'remember a time before the present Moon became the companion of the Earth'. Some Babylonian depictions of the Moon in the 11th century BC locate it between Venus and the Sun. I know that some people will say that the Moon always had to be there or the Earth would be unstable and nothing like it is, but we are not talking about the same

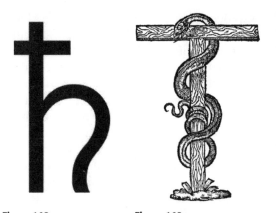

Figure 168:   **Figure 169:**
The cross and serpent-like symbol of Saturn along with the
ancient cross and serpent symbol

planetary alignments we have now before the Moon came. The Solar System was very different to what we see today.

Saturn–Moon Cult

These revelations explain the obsession with Saturn – the 'Old Sun', 'Dark Sun' and 'Dark Lord'. The 'Lord God', or merely 'Lord', in the Old Testament is Saturn and the Creation Myth in Genesis sounds very much like the creation of the Matrix –'And God said, 'Let there be [visible] light,' and there was light'. The Babylonian Nimrod was worshipped in Rome as the god 'Saturn', or 'Saturnus', and they celebrated his 'birthday' in the period running up to the later Christian Christmas. This was the festival of Saturnalia and involved sacrifice, making and giving presents, decorating trees in the home and events of celebration spanning more than a week beginning on December 17th. Saturnalia has morphed into 'Christmas' – a festival to celebrate Saturn. 'Santa', as in 'Claus', is an anagram of 'Satan' – Saturn. Worship of Saturn came to Rome, once called the 'City of Saturn', from Mesopotamia where the Babylonians worshipped Saturn as 'Nimrod'; and Christianity is just another version of the 'Pagan' religion of Rome and Babylon. Everything fell into place once I realised that so many deities called 'sun gods' were actually symbols of the 'Old Sun', 'Dark Sun' and 'Dark Lord' – Saturn. Christians are worshipping Saturn as their god to this day without knowing it, and I'm sure that the deity, 'Sol Invictus', worshipped by Emperor Constantine, the founder of Christianity as we know it, was an Old Sun – Saturn deity. The 'Christian' cross can clearly be seen in the astrological sign for Saturn connected to a serpent-like image. Maybe there is an association here with the theme of the serpent on the cross (Figs 168 and 169). The cult of Mithra, the Roman and Persian version of Jesus, was heavily connected to Saturn. The worship of Saturn dominated the ancient world and it is all around us today. The Roman god, Saturn, was known as 'Cronus' or 'Kronos' in Greece, the Titan father of Zeus (most of Saturn's moons are named after Titans). Saturn was Nimrod, or 'Ninurta', in Mespotamia and 'Shani' in the Hindu religion. The main Jewish holy day is named after Saturn – Saturday – and in India, Saturday is called 'Shanivar' after the Hindu Saturn god. Judaism is another Saturn–Moon religion, and so is Islam. The most sacred place on Earth for Muslims is the Kaaba located in Mecca, Saudi Arabia, within the world's biggest Mosque, the Masjid al-Haram. Islamic tradition says that the Kaaba was built by 'Abraham' who is also a hero to Judaism and Christianity. Abraham is said to be the father of the Jews, the 'Chosen Race' of 'god' (Saturn), and the Bible says that he came from the land of Shinar, or Sumer. The Kaaba is a cube-shaped building (Kaaba means 'cube'), and inside is a black stone that Islam believes was taken there by Abraham. The Black Stone is allegedly part of a meteorite that Islamic lore dates back to Adam and Eve – the time when the human race was being genetically hijacked by the

Figure 170: The Kaaba cube – a symbol of Saturn

Figure 171: Now we can see why Muslim 'pilgrims' are told to pray at the Kaaba stone in concentric circles. So funny

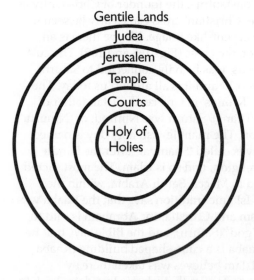

Figure 172: The Jewish 'Holy of Holies' – Saturn

Reptilians that control Saturn and the Moon. So the Kaaba is a cube? *Hmmmmm*. The cube is a symbol of ... *Saturn* (Fig 170). Whenever you see the cube used as a religious or other esoteric symbol, it is representing Saturn. The cube is also a symbol of matter in all occult traditions, and we can now see why. Saturn creates 'matter' as we perceive it through the information fields that we decode into holographic reality. A hexagon formation has been photographed by NASA at Saturn's North Pole, as we saw earlier, and a hexagon represents a three-dimensional cube. What do we say about people who are enslaved in mind? They are *in the box*. Yes, the Saturn–Moon Matrix 'box'. Muslims are supposed to kneel and face the direction of the Kaaba five times a day and 'pray to Mecca'. The Five Pillars of Islam insist that Muslims make the pilgrimage to the Kaaba at least once in their lifetimes. The main pilgrimage is called the Hajj, and it pre-dates Islam. Pilgrims are told to walk around the Kaaba seven times and try to kiss the Black Stone on each circuit. They are also told to pray in concentric circles around the Kaaba (Fig 171). Remind you of anything? The Hebrew Mishnah, or Mishna, the first written record of the 'Oral Torah', lists concentric circles of holiness surrounding the Temple in Jerusalem, as you can see in Figure 172. Remind you of anything? The 'Holy of Holies' to these religions is Saturn – the source, together with the Moon, of human control. Jews also wear the little cubed hat, the Tefillin, which is also a symbol of Saturn. We have the Jewish esoteric and mystical work, the Kabbalah – Kabb-*Allah*. This can be translated as 'Cube-god', or even 'Saturn–Moon' given that the Muslim Allah is a version of the moon god, Sin. The Christian' cross can also be symbolised as an opened-out cube (Figure 173) Now I realise as everything becomes so much clearer and simpler that the god of Judaism, known as 'El', which I have linked to the Moon and

Saturn in previous books is, in fact, the representation of Saturn – hence Is-Ra-El. This is Isis, the virgin mother of Egypt; Ra, the sun god of Egypt; and El, the Hebrew god of Saturn. El refers to a universal god and was called the 'father of the gods' and 'father of man' – the 'father' of the genetically-engineered, re-wired human that we know today. El comes from El-ohim, mentioned 2,500 times in the Old Testament – the Reptilian Alliance. We have 'angEls' called Micha-EL, Gabri-EL, Uri-EL and Rapha-EL. The Bible talks about Jesus as Emmanu-EL and we have the Gosp-EL, and church EL-ders. We also have the ancient and Freemasonic symbol of the ob-EL-isk.

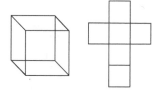

Figure 173: Cube and Cross

The symbolism of Saturn is everywhere – not only in religion. You see the symbolism and worship of the 'Lord of the Rings' throughout the Illuminati bloodline system. Saturn is represented by the colour black and known to the ancients and today's secret societies and Satanists as the 'Black Sun'. This is why the Kaaba is black and why you have the black robes of judges, barristers, priests, rabbis and also students when they 'graduate' (confirm their *degree* of indoctrination) wearing a square hat, or 'mortarboard' (Fig 174). The leader of the Saturn-worshipping Jesuit Order is rightly known as the 'Black Pope'. Illuminati bloodlines that came out of Italy, especially Florence and Venice, are known as the Black Nobility. The Saturn–Moon Matrix seeks to close the human third-eye to enslave us in five-sense reality. The third-eye chakra resonates to the colour blue, and the Illuminati, in the words of the Rolling Stones song, want to 'paint it black'. They have done so with most people, but it is changing. Saturn is the god of banking, which won't surprise anyone by now, and we have El- ections to be El-ected. If you become rich and powerful you join the El-ite. The Saturn–Moon Matrix is casting a sp-El on the human mind. Communism was a creation of the El-ite, as I have revealed in detail in books like ... *And the Truth Shall Set You Free.* You can see in Figure 175 how the astrological symbol for Saturn was incorporated as the hammer and sickle of the Soviet Union. A black-robed judge has a hammer, and the 'Grim Reaper', a Saturn-inspired image, is represented as an evil figure with a scythe. Saturn was symbolised by the ancients as a six-pointed star – the symbol of the House of Rothschild which they incorporated into the flag of modern IS-RA-EL (Fig 176). The very name 'Rothschild'

Figure 174: The black robes of Saturn in religion, 'education' and the law.

Figure 175: The Saturn symbol again in the symbol of Rothschild Zionist-created Soviet Communism

Figure 176: The six-pointed star of the Rothschilds – the symbol of Saturn – on the flag of Rothschild-controlled Israel

comes from the German words meaning
'red sheild' or 'red sign' – the six-pointed
star of Saturn displayed on the original
Rothschild house in Germany. Saturn is the
sixth 'planet' from the Sun and the sixth day
of the week. Also remember that six-sided
Hexagon at Saturn's north pole. The Bible
says that the number of the Beast is 666.
Rings are obvious symbols of Saturn, not
least wedding rings. Matrimony is about
restriction and tradition through the
'institution' (Saturn) of marriage when you
look at it from the wider perspective. I now
realise that the halo, or ring, around the
heads of religious deities and heroes is a
symbol not of our Sun, but the 'Old Sun –
Saturn. Satan is Saturn and so Satanism is
Saturnism. Satanists wear black because
they are worshippers of Saturn and the non-
human entities that control that brown
dwarf control system and orchestrate the
enslavement of humanity. Satanists also
worship the Moon because of its connection
to Saturn, and the same demonic Reptilian
'gods'. The other main Satanic colour is red,
and the most famous 'man in red' is Father
Christmas (Santa/Satan) who 'arrives' on his 'sleigh'
around the time of the Roman festival of Saturnalia.
Black and red were well represented inside the Death
Star (moon) with Darth Vadar, a classic symbol of
Saturn, in the *Star Wars* films. The symbolism is
everywhere (Fig 177). Saturn's astrological sign is
Capricorn, the goat, and so we have the goat god, Pan,
and the goat image widely used in Satanism. The goat
theme can be seen with the classic composite
representation of the 'evil one' known as Baphomet (Fig
178). This is the image worshipped by the Knights
Templar, and that is a given when, like the Jesuits,
Knights of Malta and Opus Dei, they are an arm of the
Saturn cult called the Roman Church. Pope Benedict
XVI, a former member of Nazi Youth, loves wearing his

Figure 177: Saturn symbolism can be seen throughout
global society

Figure 178: The Saturn 'goat' as
Baphomet

Saturn hat (Fig 179). The symbol of Saturnian Capricorn is the goat combined with a
fish – another symbol of the Reptilians as 'fish gods'. Saturn is the god worshipped by
the Illuminati bloodline secret-society network. Some do this openly, as with the
Fraternitas Saturni, or Brotherhood of Saturn, in the major occult centre and birthplace
of the House of Rothschild, Germany. The black squares on the Freemasonic floor

Figure 180: The symbol of the Skull and Bones Society

Figure 179: The present Pope and others in the headgear known as the 'Saturn Hat'

(Freemasons are said to be 'on the square') and in many churches and cathedrals symbolise Saturn. So does the square black mortarboard in academia at University. The same is true of the squares on a chessboard and the symbol of the Freemasonic compass with its six points. Saturn is represented in numerology by the number eight and so the eight-legged spider is used as a Saturn symbol and St Peter's Square in Rome is broken up into eight segments around the original Egyptian obelisk.

Saturn in the Stars

Astrology is part of the Saturnian picture. This does have a scientific basis when practised properly and it does reveal the energetic influences to which we are subjected – *but only in the Matrix*. What must be stressed and stressed again is that we do not have to be prisoners of those influences. Consciousness can overcome all of it and go its own way. Astrology also underpins the illusion of time – a basic foundation of the Saturn Conspiracy. Beyond this Saturn–Moon-generated reality none of this stuff exists. The representation of Saturn in astrology fits the bill perfectly. Saturn is the planet (sun) of death, restriction, authority, control, obedience, poverty, fear and *time*. It rules the bones of the body and so you have the skull-and-bones as a major symbol of the Saturn-controlled Illuminati. The Skull and Bones Society is really the Saturn Society (Fig 180). Saturn is the astrological ruler of institutions, corporations, figures in authority, scientists and old people. It represents laws, rules, regulations and 'tradition' (repeating ritual). Saturn is non-emotive and represents limitation, austerity, discipline and depression. The term 'Saturnine', meaning to have a gloomy, taciturn temperament, has an ancient origin related to the influence of Saturn. What am I describing here? The very world we live in, and ever more so. I am describing the way that human society has been constructed; the way secret societies operate with all their rules, rituals and hierarchy; and all the pomp and ritual surrounding the British Royal Family and their kind. Planet Earth is a Saturnian society controlled from Saturn via the Moon and the Illuminati hybrid bloodlines. This makes so much sense of what has happened to the world, and what is happening. Notice how the traits and influences of the Saturnian are

Figure 181: The Saturn–Moon–Earth structure of human control and suppression

the same as the Draconian – the Reptilian 'hive' mind. The Saturn–Moon Matrix reflects the hive mind of the Reptilians that control Saturn and the Moon. Now you have seen the astrological and Matrix effects of Saturn, look again at that quote from earlier describing the human reptilian brain:

At least five human behaviours originate in the reptilian brain. Without defining them, I shall simply say that in human activities they find expression in: obsessive compulsive behaviour; personal day-to-day rituals and superstitious acts; slavish conformance to old ways of doing things; ceremonial re-enactments; obeisance to precedent, as in legal, religious, cultural, and other matters and all manner of deceptions.

The Saturnian and the Reptilian are expressions of each other – 'They gave us their mind'. Now read again what I wrote earlier about the 'personality' of the left hemisphere of the brain:

The left-brain is 'logical and rational' in its definition of logical and rational. It decodes information in the NOW into a sequence. This is basically where 'time' comes from. The quicker the left-brain 'moves' this sequence the faster time seems to pass and vice versa. It is 'analytical and objective', which often means that if I can't see it, hear it, touch it, taste it or smell it, it can't exist.

Crucially, it decodes reality in parts rather than as a whole. It is from the left-brain that we get the perception of everything being apart from everything else with 'space' in between. It creates structures – *loves 'em* – and it is through the left-brain that we produce language. I have just described the world as it is currently 'lived'.

... The left-brain sees individual dots, but the right-brain can see how they fit together. Left-brain-dominated people control science, academia, medicine, politics, big business, religion, the media and the military. These, in turn, act as the soldiers at the gate to the collective left-brain to keep right-brain reality at bay.

Saturn, reptilian genetics and the way the left side of the brain decodes reality are peas from the same pod. This, then, is what we are dealing with: Saturn is hacking into the information construct communicated via the Sun and creating a fake reality, amplified to the Earth by the Moon, which is associated with deception in the Tarot. We decode this 'hack' and believe it to be 'real'. The force behind this, the Reptilian Alliance, controls a pyramid structure within visible light (the hack) via its hybrid bloodlines of the Illuminati (Fig 181). This structure created and controls religion (Saturn religions); banking (astrologically ruled by Saturn); politics and the institutions of State at all levels (astrologically ruled by Saturn); corporations (astrologically ruled by Saturn); the law and the court system (astrologically ruled by Saturn); science (astrologically ruled by Saturn); on and on it goes. Saturn-worship is endemic throughout human society even in annual festivals like Christmas.

So now we have a fix on what is 'going on' from deep, deep within the rabbit hole – deeper than anyone has yet gone. Our plight seems hopeless. But, it *isn't*. The door to Freedom is about to open. It *is* opening if you know what to look for. I'll come to that later, but first I'll explain how all this impacts upon daily life.

7

Saturn World

I could have called this chapter 'Reptilian World', 'Left-Brain World' or, as it is, 'Saturn World'. They all describe the mentality that has manipulated and controlled Planet Earth for aeons.

This has been done through a control-structure broadcast from Saturn via the Moon to entrap human perception of self and reality. The Illuminati hybrid bloodlines, the Saturn–Moon–Reptilian operatives within visible light, have been embarked on a continual process of centralising power for thousands of years. There are so few controllers compared with humans that centralisation of power is crucial to their plans. The more you centralise power, the more power the few have over the many; and the more power you gather at the centre, the more power you have to centralise even quicker. People once lived in small groups called 'tribes', and they decided among themselves what would and would not happen. Then the tribes were brought together to form 'nations', and now the few at the centre of the 'nation' were dictating to all the former tribes. We are today well into the next stage, especially in Europe/Europa, of grouping the nations together to allow a few at the centre to dictate and impose their will – the Reptilian Alliance will – upon large numbers of nation states. We already have the European Union and the African Union, and the plan is for a North American Union of the United States, Canada and Mexico, leading to a Union of the Americas. They are planning similar groupings all over the world controlled by dark-suit dictators, appointed, not even El-ected, as with the European Commission today. They are seeking to impose a world government to dictate to these unions which would dictate to the nations, or rather *regions* of the former nations (Fig 182). Their goal is to divide nation states into regions to dilute any resistance to the edifice of power that I am describing. Maps have been made public that reveal how the European Union plans to regionalise Europe by grouping regions of one country with regions of others (Fig 183). Goodbye, nation state. And they want to do the same everywhere. The world government is planned to impose its will through a world army and to dictate all global finance through a world central bank and a global electronic currency. The plan to destroy the nation state includes opening borders to massive immigration to replace a defined culture and national identity to make it harder to defend the concept of the nation state. The whole structure, or 'New World Order', would be founded on an Orwellian – and

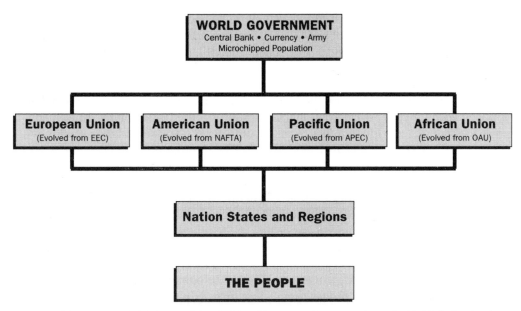

Figure 182: The structure of global control that the bloodlines are working towards. It is highly likely that they have other 'unions' in mind, too, including a Middle East Union

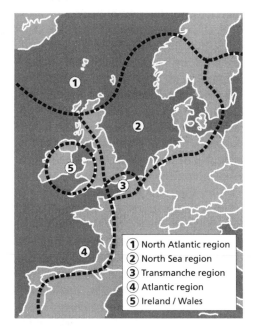

① North Atlantic region
② North Sea region
③ Transmanche region
④ Atlantic region
⑤ Ireland / Wales

Figure 183: A European Union map that divides Europe into regions, with regions from one country joined with those from other countries

then some – global surveillance state with everybody microchipped and connected to a global tracking system 24/7. If anyone thinks that this is some fantasy, well think again. Even better, know again, because it's happening. Centralisation of global power in all areas of our lives has long reached the point where it has been given a name – 'globalisation'. This is the very global fascist/communist agenda that I have been exposing and warning about since the early 1990s. What I have been writing about in my books all these years is now playing out on the television news. I love it when 'journalists' have said to me, 'That would never happen', when it bloody *is* happening all around them. There are none so blind as those who do not wish to see.

The code words and stepping stones are already there to be seen. Constant references to the 'International Community' and the 'will' of the International Community are codes for 'world government in the making'.

The same is true of the endless summits of 'G8', 'G20' and all the rest, and the constant spouting on about 'International Law'. What does a world government need in order to govern? Laws that everyone has to obey: International Law. The United Nations was created by the bloodlines and established on land donated by the Rockefeller family in New York. The UN was created as a stalking horse and a stepping stone for world government after their first effort, the League of Nations, failed to survive. Look what happened with Libya. The 'International Community' – the United States, Britain and France in this case – decide that they want rid of Colonel Gaddafi and they send the boys in – the de facto world army called NATO. The 'International Community' is dominated by the United States, Britain and Israel. Italian Prime Minister Silvio Berlusconi said that Italy only joined the bombing of Libya because of pressure from the United States. I wrote in the mid-1990s in my book ... *And the Truth Shall Set You Free* that we should watch for NATO becoming involved in conflicts outside the North Atlantic region that it was created to defend (according to the official story). I said that this would be the way it would expand its operation on the road to becoming the World Army with the United Nations' 'peacekeeping' structure and other military groupings thrown in. NATO is now in Afghanistan and spent the summer of 2011 bombing civilians in Libya in order to 'protect them'. This drip, drip to a world army was the reason that very soon after America, Britain and France began bombing Libya they handed the operation over to NATO control. This set another precedent. The El-ite are already calling for a world central bank to 'solve' the economic crisis they purposely created to justify a total re-structure of global finance based on ... a world central bank. Cash is going out of circulation at an ever-increasing rate as electronic 'money' takes over in line with the plan for a single electronic currency. The deletion of basic

freedoms, ever more invasive laws and surveillance, and the imposition of the police state are being rolled out at an ever-quickening pace. You want to fly? Okay, do you want you and your children to be irradiated or sexually molested? Don't tell me that people don't have a choice. European Union bureaucrats are dictating the fine detail of people's lives right across the continent even down to what lightbulbs they can and cannot use. Conspiracy researchers like me have been saying for many years that the plan was to fuse the United States, Canada and Mexico into the North American Union, but government spokespeople and the pathetic in-the-back-pocket mainstream media have said it was just a 'conspiracy theory'. This is despite all the evidence to support what is being said. CNN anchor, Lou Dobbs, was sacked when, among other related issues, he insisted on

Figure 184: The United States is being systematically destroyed to bring it under the heel of the world dictatorship

highlighting the conspiracy to impose the North American Union. While I was writing this book, an American diplomatic cable from 2005 was made public through the WikiLeaks website which confirmed the covert plan for the North American Union, or what it called the 'North American Initiative'. The idea all along has been to *use* America to *destroy* America (Fig 184). They have been using America's (borrowed) money and its vast military to impose the agenda of the Reptilian hybrid El-ite, but in doing so the plan has been to bring America to its knees. This is what has happened with the United States now drowning in staggering mountains of debt. You cannot have a world government dictatorship and also have 'superpowers' that have the financial and military might to say no to you. America had to be crippled so it could be absorbed into the new world system that would give the Reptilians and their hybrids total control – far beyond even what Orwell envisaged.

Holographic Tyranny

It is important to emphasise here that the *American* military is not, well, the American military. It is the global El-ite's military, the Reptilian Alliance's military. We go back to the structure I mentioned earlier, the holographic 'Blueprint'. The operational centre of the web in Europe (and Israel) dictates the global agenda to its subsidiary networks of bloodline families and secret societies in each country. The United States has been a kind of jewel in the crown as the major subsidiary since it was established following the war with the British and the Declaration of Independence in 1776. But it wasn't 'independence'. It was *control* in another form, as I have explained. The governmental, political, financial, corporate and media networks in the United States are controlled by bloodline families like the Rockefellers, and others, who answer to families above them in the hierarchy, especially the Rothschilds in Europe. American troops do not go to war for American people; they go to war for the Reptilian hybrids. This is also the case with Britain, France, Italy, Australia – virtually everywhere. It is appropriate that people speak of the 'theatre' of war. This is what war is: a deadly, merciless stage-show that is rarely, if ever, fought for the reasons that we are given. NATO planes were supposed to be in Libya to 'protect civilians', but immediately started killing them from the air after NATO said that they would attack anyone harming civilians (NATO should have bombed itself then). They even killed members of the Libyan 'opposition' that they claimed to be 'supporting'. It's all a movie, for public consumption only. Wars and bombing in Libya, Iraq, Afghanistan, Pakistan, ad infinitum, are part of a long-planned agenda to impose a centralised fascist/communist global tyranny (I put those words together, by the way, because they are essentially names for the same thing). We see the troops, planes and explosions on the television news and we see the gofers and front-men and women called 'politicians' selling the reasons why the war must happen with a constant stream of lies; but we don't see the bloodline hybrids and their secret-society network dictating events from

Figure 185: 'Leaders' that we see in the apparent positions of power are never the ones really in charge – those in the shadows are

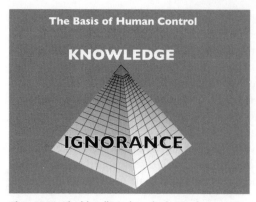

The Basis of Human Control

KNOWLEDGE

IGNORANCE

Figure 186: The bloodlines hoard advanced knowledge at the peak of the global pyramid and keep the public in ignorance of what they need to know to understand how they are controlled and directed

the background, and certainly not the Reptilian Alliance that controls them (Fig 185). So-called 'world leaders' such as Obama in the United States, Cameron in Britain, Sarkozy in France, Harper in Canada and Gillard in Australia are only there to serve their hidden masters by selling the bloodline agenda, signing the legislation and declaring war. The blueprint for political 'leaders' can be seen with Barack Obama, David Cameron and Tony Blair. They are just slick used-car salesmen from whom anyone with intelligence would not purchase a skateboard.

This Saturnian structure can be symbolised as a transnational corporation, a spider's web or a pyramid (Fig 186). In fact, smaller pyramids inside bigger pyramids until the whole lot are encased by the biggest pyramid – the Russian-doll principle. Virtually every organisation, be it a government, bank, business, university, or media operation, is structured as a pyramid. You have the few at the top, at the 'capstone', who know what is really going on; but as you go further down the pyramid there are more and more people knowing less and less about the true aims and ambitions of the organisation. They only know what they need to know to make their contribution to the unfolding tyranny while having no clue – most of them anyway – that they are doing so. They, after all, also have to live in the world that is being imposed and so, too, do their children and grandchildren. The only people who know how all the individual contributions throughout the pyramid fit together to secure a very sinister outcome are the few at the top. This is how knowledge of the conspiracy is censored by what is called 'compartmentalisation' of information. Most of the people in the British government at the time of the invasion of Iraq in 2003 had no idea why that really happened, or what hidden forces were at work. Knowledge was compartmentalised in a small group – around Illuminati asset, Tony Blair – which answered to those in the shadows. Most members of the Blair cabinet, the supposed 'government', were irrelevant. The 'individual' pyramids of government, banking, corporation, media outlets, and so on, are encompassed by a bigger pyramid which is controlled from the capstone by the bloodline families. These, too, have a pyramidal hierarchy among the 13 leading families (Fig 187). It's all hierarchy. We are talking about reptilian genetics (software) after all which has 'a desire for social hierarchies'. There are pyramids that encompass the banking system – 'Big Banking' – and also Big Government, Big Oil, Big Pharma, Big Biotech, Big Media, etc. All of them are 'capstoned' by the bloodline families, and in this way they can unleash their agenda for constant centralisation of power through all of them. Those who *appear* to run the system – presidents, prime ministers, heads of NATO, the World Bank, IMF and their like, are nowhere near the top of the pyramid. They are the here-today-gone-tomorrow gofers who answer to those above them where the power really is (Fig 188). The bloodline Hidden Hand selects the 'El-ected' leaders by controlling any political party

The Pyramid of Manipulation

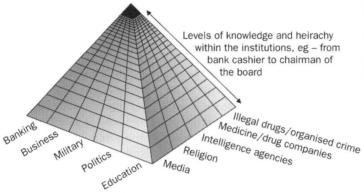

Reptilian Alliance & Saturn-Moon Matrix

Reptilian hybrid families

Levels of knowledge and heirarchy within the institutions, eg – from bank cashier to chairman of the board

Banking
Business
Military
Politics
Education
Media
Religion
Intelligence agencies
Medicine/drug companies
Illegal drugs/organised crime

All the major institutions and groups that affect our daily lives connect with the Global Elite, which decides the coordinated policy throughout the pyramid.

People in the lower compartments will have no idea what they are part of.

Figure 187: The pyramid-within-pyramid 'Russian doll' structure in which the bloodline families sit at the top of all the pyramids and direct the same agenda for centralisation of power throughout all of them

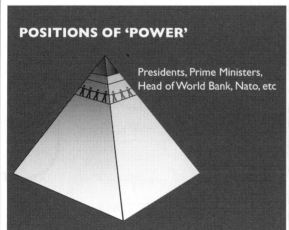

POSITIONS OF 'POWER'

Presidents, Prime Ministers, Head of World Bank, Nato, etc

Figure 188: The people who appear to be in power are nowhere near the top of the pyramid. They are only there to do the bidding in public of those in the upper echelons of the global hierarchy

Figure 189: We are told that we have a 'choice' at El-ections, but the major candidates in all parties are spewed out by the bloodline networks

(pyramids again) that has any chance of forming a government (Fig 189). There are essentially four types of 'leader': (1) Those who know what is happening and what they are working towards (the few); (2) People who are desperate for 'power' for power's sake and will do and say anything to get it; (3) Those with big secrets to hide through which they can be blackmailed into doing what they are told to do; (4) Idiots who are easily manipulated by 'advisors' and public 'servants'. Every time I see the words 'idiot' and 'leader' in close proximity I automatically get a picture in my mind of Brian Cowen, the Irish Prime Minister who devastated the Irish economy for generations with 'his' bank bailout using the nation's borrowed money. I can't think why, but it always happens.

The Round Table Network

There is one particular grouping within the covert web of manipulation that it is important to highlight. This is the series of satellite organisations answering to a secret society known as the 'Round Table' which was established in London in the late 19th century (Fig 190). Cecil Rhodes, a Rothschild agent, was its first leader. The Round Table spawned the London 'think tank', the Royal Institute of International Affairs, in 1920. A year later came the Council on Foreign Relations (CFR), a 'think tank' created to manipulate US foreign policy. The CFR was seriously involved in establishing the Rothschild–Rockefeller United Nations as a major stepping-stone to world government. The American delegation at the founding conference of the UN was like a roll call of CFR members. The highly-secretive Bilderberg Group came next in 1954, and this acts as a coordinating force to ensure that a common policy (the bloodlines' policy) is followed by politicians, bankers, corporations, Intelligence personnel, the military and the media in multiple countries. The Bilderberg group was chaired for a long time by the German-born Nazi supporter who later became Prince Bernhard of the Netherlands. Bilderberg meetings are attended by members of European royalty, including Bernhard's daughter, Queen Beatrix. They also bring together bankers from multiple countries, and the heads of the International Monetary Fund (IMF), national central banks, the World Trade Organization and NATO. These are joined by major political leaders, and future ones, too. Bill Clinton, the then little-known governor of Arkansas, attended the Bilderberg meeting in 1991 and was elected President of the United States the following year. Tony Blair was invited to the meeting in 1993 and became leader of the British Labour Party the following year, and

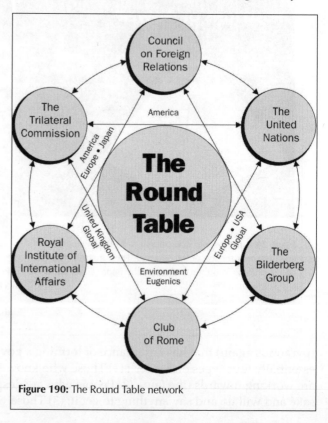

Figure 190: The Round Table network

later Prime Minister for ten years thanks to the support of the bloodline media empire of Rupert Murdoch. Clinton and Blair went to war together, coordinated by the Hidden Hand. Barack Obama and Hillary Clinton both slipped quietly into the Bilderberg meeting at the Westfields Marriott Hotel in Chantilly, Northern Virginia, during their election campaign of 2008. Independent real journalists have been able to predict through contacts attending Bilderberg meetings that the invasion of Iraq would happen in March 2003, and that the housing 'bubble' was going to be burst to trigger a banking crisis. Prominent Bilderberg players over decades have been David Rockefeller, who attended the first meeting at the Bilderberg Hotel in the Netherlands in 1954 (Fig 191); Rothschild/Rockefeller agent, Henry Kissinger; and Obama mentor, Zbigniew Brzezinski, former National Security Advisor to president Jimmy Carter. I have listed as an

Figure 191: David Rockefeller: Looks what he is

appendix the attendees at the 2011 Bilderberg meeting in St Moritz, Switzerland, to give you a feel for the kind of people and organisations who are represented. They included Rothschild frontmen in the UK, Chancellor of the Exchequer, George Osborne, and Labour Party Machiavelli and Rothschild bag-carrier, Peter Mandelson – a man rightly known as the 'Prince of Darkness'. Henry Kissinger and David Rockefeller were there, as always, along with people like Peter Orszag, Obama's first Budget Director, and Robert E Rubin, Co-Chairman of the Council on Foreign Relations and one of the architects of the financial crash of 2008. Representing the Internet – for which the bloodlines have some dastardly plans – were Eric Schmidt, Executive Chairman of Google, and Jeff Bezos, founder and CEO of Amazon.com. There were bankers and financial people galore, as usual, including Franco Bernabè, vice chairman of Rothschild Europe. The Round Table's 'Club of Rome' was formed in 1968 to exploit environmental issues to justify the Reptilian agenda, and this has been a major source of the outrageous lie called 'human-caused global warming', or 'climate change' as it became after temperatures fell year after year. The American-based Trilateral Commission was established in 1973 by co-founders David Rockefeller and Zbigniew Brzezinski. This is another coordinator and manipulator of policy worldwide. All these Round Table satellites are interconnecting secret societies at their inner core and this network is part of the greater web, or pyramid, as are the World Bank, the International Monetary Fund (IMF), the World Trade Organization (WTO) and the World Health Organization (WHO). These are all agencies of the planned world government and they were established by the Rockefellers and Rothschilds through their puppet politicians.

The World Trade Organization and the World Health Organization are part of the effort to control various global subject areas from one building, or around one table. The idea is to have governments 'sign up' to be members and commit themselves to doing what these dark-suits tell them to do in terms of trade, health and other policy. The World Trade Organization has the power to impose massive fines on countries that seek to protect their economies and people from the merciless world system. The strategy is to make every country and community dependent on other countries and communities over which they have no control. The only people who can direct the system are the bloodline families with their subsidiaries in every country. 'Free trade' is nothing to do with 'freedom'; it is about exploitation. The bloodline version of 'free trade' allows their corporations to savagely exploit some of the poorest people in the world, working them till they drop and paying them a pittance. This means that their products are made for a fraction of the price that they will sell them for in richer parts of the world. This becomes even more profitable as 'trade barriers' come down along with trade tariffs. Both groups of people, at the production end and at the buying end of this 'free trade' scam, are coldly exploited. But then the bloodlines 'do' cold better than anyone. The World Health Organization orders that populations be vaccinated, as with the farce over 'swine flu', and governments then give billions to Big Pharma to mass vaccinate the people. 'Swine flu' never affected a single pig. How strange. Well, not really; it was just another lie. Thirty million people were given the 'swine flu' vaccine, Pandemrix, before the European Medicine Agency warned that it should not be given to anyone under 20 because it increased the risk of developing narcolepsy, which makes people fall asleep unexpectedly. How many others suffered health effects after having 'swine flu' vaccine for 'protection' against a non-existent disease? We now have the Rothschilds and the Rockefeller families dictating global trade policy through the World Trade Organization, and health policy through the World Health Organization. Indeed, it was John D Rockefeller, the oil tycoon and Rothschild subordinate in the United States, who imposed 'modern' scalpel and drug 'medicine' on the world while being treated himself by a personal homoeopath until the day he died, aged 97. Ever notice how so many of these people live to a great age compared with most of the human population? The Queen Mother in Britain lived until she was 102; and, at the time of writing, the Queen is 85; the Duke of Edinburgh is 90; Father George Bush is 87; Henry Kissinger is 88; and David Rockefeller is 96. How come? One reason is they don't have the same medical treatment that they impose on the rest of the population.

Those who wish to use alternative treatments and supplements are facing ever more challenges as the bloodlines target alternative practitioners to put them out of business, or 'license' them into ineffectiveness, and introduce regulations to prevent people having food supplements and alternative remedies. The deeply corrupt Food and Drug Administration (FDA) in the United States says that it plans to, in effect, censor medical and health 'apps' on mobile phones when they don't conform to its (official) version of how people should be treated. A major vehicle for the war on alternative medicine is Codex Alimentarius (Latin for 'Food Code' or 'Food Book'), which is seeking 'harmonisation' of global food and supplement laws and regulations. At least that is the cover story. The real reason is to deny supplements and decent food to those awake enough to see that they and their families are being systematically poisoned by Big Pharma, Big Biotech and Big Food. Genetically-modified food, courtesy of Monsanto, one of the most active bloodline corporations on the planet, is designed to genetically modify humans. The World Trade Organization (Rothschild/Rockefeller) has agreed to recognise the rules and regulations decided by Codex Alimentarius (Rothschild / Rockefeller). *Really?* I'm shocked. So who were the nice people that started this Codex deal in the 1960s? Well, well – only Nazi war criminals jailed at the Nuremberg Trials for crimes against humanity. People like Hermann Schmitz, president of the Nazi chemical giant, IG Farben; and IG Farben executive, Fritz ter Meer. IG Farben ran the concentration camp at Auschwitz, where the camp doctor was 'Angel of Death', Joseph Mengele; and Fritz ter Meer was responsible for the 'Arbeit Macht Frei' ('Work Makes Free') sign over the Auschwitz main gate. He was jailed for seven years for war crimes at Nuremberg, but only served four after the intervention of his great friend, Nelson Rockefeller, the four-times Mayor of New York. Why would a Rockefeller help a Nazi? Because he was a Nazi, too. They're *all* Nazis if we are talking about their attitudes to humanity. Read some of my other books, such as ... *And the Truth Shall Set You Free*, and you'll see how the Rockefeller, Bush and Harriman families, among many others in the United States, *funded* the Nazis in the run-up to the war. There are no 'sides' with the Reptilian bloodlines, only means to an end. Nelson Rockefeller was part of the government–Intelligence cabal that brought Nazis like Mengele to the United States after the war to continue their unspeakable mind and genetic torture of American children and adults, and then headed the Rockefeller Commission that covered up the true scale and horror of what was done – and is *still* being done. Incidentally, talking of the Harriman family, Brown Brothers Harriman, America's oldest and largest private bank, has been a highly significant player in the bloodline agenda since it was formed in 1818 through people like railway tycoon, E Roland Harriman, Averell Harriman (the Henry Kissinger of his day) and Prescott Bush, grandfather of Boy Bush. There is a large symbol today outside the Brown Brothers Harriman building close to Wall Street. It is a very large cube (Fig 192). I can't think why.

Figure 192: The Saturn symbol outside Brown Brothers Harriman in New York

What is the point in voting?

The American example is perfect for showing how the party political system operates in countries throughout the world. There are two parties in the United States that have any chance of forming a government: Republicans and Democrats. But these are two masks on the same face; two wings on the same plane. This means that no matter who gets El-ected, the same hidden force is always in power and the same plan continues to advance on the road to complete global tyranny. America is an even more potent example because the apparently immense differences between Boy George Bush ('Republican') and Barack Obama ('Democrat') have turned out be nothing of the kind. The Republican Party during the eight years of Bush was controlled by a network called the 'neocons', or neo-conservatives. The term 'con' would be far more accurate in another definition. The neocons were dominated by members of the Rothschild secret

WORLD STAGE

Figure 193: Two parties – one master

society (of which much more later) that I call Rothschild Zionism. I always add the word 'Rothschild' to constantly highlight the creators and controllers of Zionism. The neocons included people like Richard Perle (Rothschild Zionist), a political advisor and lobbyist; Paul Wolfowitz (Rothschild Zionist), US Deputy Defense Secretary at the time of 9/11; and William Kristol (Rothschild Zionist), editor of the Washington D.C.-based propaganda sheet called *The Weekly Standard*. This was owned for a long time by El-ite media tycoon, Rupert Murdoch (Rothschild Zionist). The neocons manipulated through 'think tanks' and principally the American Enterprise Institute and the Project for the New American Century. Watch the 'think tanks'. They are a major tool of the bloodlines to direct government policy and society in general. You'll find the detail in *Human Race Get Off Your Knees*. The Democrats have a similar grouping that I call the 'democons' and these include serious players in the conspiracy such as the truly ruthless duo, Zbigniew Brzezinski (Rothschild Zionist, whatever he may say) and George Soros (Rothschild Zionist). Brzezinski was the former National Security Advisor to President Carter and the co-founder, with David Rockefeller, of the Trilateral Commission in the Round Table network. Soros is the multi- billionaire financier and Rothschild-gofer now calling for a world central bank. This pair have been a major factor as mentor and funder in the rise and rise of Barack Obama. One of the most influential Democrat 'think tanks', the Center for American Progress, has been funded by Soros. His real name is George Schwartz, and he helped to confiscate the possessions of fellow Jews in Nazi-occupied Hungary while posing as a non-Jew. I have put long-time Rothschild and Rockefeller asset, Henry Kissinger (Rothschild Zionist), in the democons' crowd in Figure 193, because he is an advisor (dictator) to Obama. Kissinger has spent the rest of his political life manipulating from the Republican side. So we have the neocons controlling the Republicans and the democons controlling the Democrats, and the neocons and democons both answer to the next level, the bloodline families, who answer to the Reptilian Alliance. No matter which party gets into *apparent* power the same force calls the shots whatever. The so-called 'Tea Party' movement has emerged in the United States in recent years to entrap those who are disillusioned with the Republicans, but won't vote Democrat. It has been promoted as some sort of 'revolution' when it is nothing of the kind. The Tea Party has been given serious financial and logistical support by Rothschild Zionists Charles and David Koch, the billionaire owners of Koch Industries with annual revenues of $100 billion. Nothing connected in any way to them is going to be a 'revolution' and nor is anything that has Sarah Palin as its 'poster girl'. The same story can be found in Britain and virtually every other country with 'different' parties answering to the same force. This is the reason why nothing has changed since 'Mr Change' Obama replaced Bush; and why

Figure 194: Obama's 'change' – business as usual, and *then* some

Figure 195: Same old line, same old lie – unless they mean change for the worst

nothing has changed in Britain after the Conservative Party, in coalition with the Liberal Democrat Party, replaced the Labour Party. Rothschild yes-man, Tony Blair, was a Labour prime minister for a decade and, at the time of writing, Rothschild yes-man David Cameron is the Conservative prime minister. Few people in world political history could have claimed more often than Obama in a year of El-ection campaigning that they were going to be 'different' (Fig 194). But what has happened? He has continued to front-up the same policies pursued by the Bush administration and, in many cases, made them even more extreme. It's the same with Cameron in the UK who also played the 'change' card (Fig 195). Political con-artists use the word 'change' so much when they want your vote *because they know it works*. Events are orchestrated by the bloodline families to ensure that most people are never happy with the status quo. They would like things to 'change' and so along come people like Obama to tell them what they want to hear – 'I stand for change.' But they never explain exactly what they *mean* by 'change'. They only repeat the word – and others, like 'hope' – to program a *perception*. When they get into office they do what their masters tell them to do. The public falls for this time after time. Obama was the most blatant fraud you could ever imagine as he strutted around parroting meaningless platitudes to the heaving crowds who gave their collective minds away to a perception-control program designed to make him president. I wrote an article in the weeks before he came to office amid the Obama frenzy. It was headed: *Barack Obama: The Naked Emperor,* and it didn't make me popular with many people, but I didn't care. It was the truth. It began:

I am writing this in the last days of 2008 as I watch with dismay as vast numbers of people across the world, including many who should know better, have been duped by the mind-game called 'Operation Obama'. Even people with some understanding of the conspiracy have said things like: 'Well, at least he's not Bush', and 'Well, at least it's great to see such a new spirit of hope'. No, he's not Bush – he's potentially far more dangerous; and what is the use of a spirit of 'hope' if it's based on a lie? ... Obama isn't against war at all and, if his controllers have their way, he will engage the US in even more foreign conflicts with the troops sent to their deaths, and the deaths of their targets.

This wasn't prophecy; it was mere observation and knowing how the game works. People ask me if this or that president is 'involved' with what I have spent all these years exposing. Or what about this prime minister and that one? I always answer the same – is he president or prime minister? Well, he's involved then, in the sense that he will fall into one of those four categories that I listed earlier from knowingly-involved through to idiot. This is what all those people missed who accept that there is some kind of global conspiracy, yet still supported Obama because he was 'different'. Do they really think that someone funded into office by Goldman Sachs, Wall Street and George Soros is going to put the interests of the people first?? A would-be president requires crazy amounts of money to campaign for the party *nomination* to run for president, never mind actually running. Bloodline families ensure that their selections attract the funding. They *own* the presidency. Nobody who is genuine and has integrity can get even close. Only actors and professional liars are considered as candidates – safe people who know how to take orders. The bloodlines fund *both* candidates and make sure that the one they want wins. They do this by pitting him against a poor alternative, and by sabotaging the other guy's campaign through manipulation and bad media coverage. This technique is used in every country. Check out who they made opposition leaders during the years of Margaret Thatcher and Tony Blair when the bloodlines wanted *them* in power. Look at the Labour opposition leader in the UK now they want to give Cameron a free run. I remember watching the American presidential campaign when Father George Bush beat Michael Dukakis in 1988. I didn't know what I know now and I wondered why Dukakis clearly wasn't trying. Father George was purposely lacklustre when it was the turn of his mate, Bill Clinton, to secure the presidency. Obama was promoted as the young, vibrant new kid on the block and so they pitted him against the elderly John McCain who was further undermined by his running mate, Sarah Palin, the governor of Alaska who should not even be let loose on a garage sale (or a Mensa test). Obama is a very willing puppet, that's for sure, and he dutifully reads the words written for him on the ever-present teleprompter screens on either side of him. He is constantly looking left and right as someone else's words appear before him. Obama hosted a St Patrick's Day event at the White House in 2009 attended by Irish Prime Minister and economy destroyer, Brian Cowen. Obama went to the podium and thanked himself for inviting everyone, because Cowen's words were on the teleprompter screen (Fig 196). I know that we live in a dreamworld every time I see Obama at work, and the reaction to him. I was squirming in 2011

Figure 196: 'It says I'll have a pizza and a coffee'

at the sight of members of the British Parliament in awe of a teleprompter-reader who was fronting a campaign of terror in North Africa and the Middle East that is planned to lead to World War III. One commentator was exactly right:

> It took the President a very long time to force his way through Westminster Hall after making his over-hyped speech. This was because each and every member of our political class wanted to talk to him or shake his hand. It was like teenagers surrounding a pop star, but with very much less excuse; grown men and women, with a long record in public life behind them, abandoned all judgment and propriety.

These so-called 'representatives of the people' were on their feet at the end of a banal speech in Westminster in which Obama couched, in terms that were truly sickening, the agenda for war and acquisition intended to slaughter and maim untold numbers of people. He said of Britain and America:

> As millions are still denied their basic human rights because of who they are, or what they believe, or the kind of government they live under, we are the nations most willing to stand up for the values of tolerance and self-determination that lead to peace and dignity.

Those words were spoken by a man who, together with his British sidekick, David Cameron, was waging war in multiple countries, and from the shadows in many others – not even the shadows in the case of the US unmanned drone bombing-campaign in Pakistan that has already killed large numbers of people. Those words were spoken by a man who has yet to produce a birth certificate to prove that he even qualifies to be President. He has spent – or someone else has – some $2 million to fight legal challenges to force him to prove that he is a natural-born American citizen, as you have to be to become president. He issued in desperation a series of blatant forgeries. There is one of two reasons for this. Either he wasn't born in America; or the birth certificate would reveal that his father is not the one he claims him to be. Hardly a single entry on Obama's official 'CV' is true. Students who attended college and university at the same time that he claims to have been there say they never saw or heard of him. *Fox News* asked 400 students at Columbia University when Obama was allegedly a student if they remembered him. None did. Wayne Allyn Root was a political science major at Columbia supposedly in the same class as Obama if the official story is true. Root said: 'I don't know a single person at Columbia that knew him, and they all know me. I don't have a classmate who ever knew Barack Obama at Columbia.' He said that the person who writes the class notes, and knows everybody, had yet to find a single person at Columbia that knew Obama. The official story of Obama's life is a stream of provable lies. Why? No wonder he has refused requests to release his Colombia records. They don't exist. Nor will he talk about his time at Columbia or name a single fellow student that he met there. Who is this guy with no school records or birth certificate? Where did he come from? A laboratory? Another question: What the heck are those major scars on his head and down to his neck shown in Figure 197? They are unexplained, like everything else about Obama, even though they are so obvious. *The Manchurian Candidate*, the movie that involved an American president having a microchip implanted in his brain to control him, was based on what does happen to the extent that

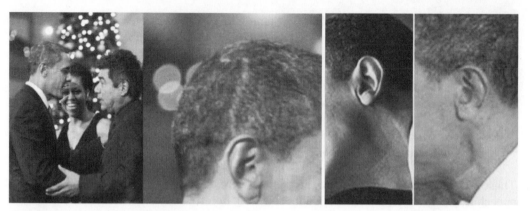

Figure 197: What are these major scars?

these leaders are put through serious levels of mind-programming. Nothing is left to chance by the bloodlines. This mystery man with the fraudulent life story was demanding the power in 2011 from the ludicrous paid-for puppets on Capitol Hill to take America to war with anyone, and anywhere that he chooses – no Congressional approval necessary. Obama – a new emperor of a new Rome. He claims to stand 'for the values of tolerance and self-determination that lead to peace and dignity' and yet his first decision in office was to sanction drone bombing-attacks on Pakistan. He won the Nobel Peace Prize before vastly increasing troop numbers in Afghanistan and ordering the heartless bombing of civilians in Libya. This is the man of war claiming to stand for peace; a man of lies talking about standing for integrity. The dreamworld is on public display. Boy Bush is a deeply unpleasant character, and grossly arrogant in a 'my daddy is bigger than your daddy' sort of way; and he is an empathy-deficient idiot. But Obama is far beyond that. This guy is dark – *real* dark. Behind the painted smile lies a cold, calculating, ruthless, narcissistic, psychopath/sociopath with eyes to match (Fig 198). The term 'narcissist' comes from the Greek myth about Narcissus who fell in love with his own reflection in the water and died because he was so mesmerised that he couldn't leave. I have had *extreme* narcissists in my own life so I speak from first-hand knowledge. In my experience, they usually have no talent whatsoever, except for devious manipulation, no desire to provide for themselves, and they operate as professional parasites feeding off any host they can find. But their narcissism and monumental levels of self-obsession mean that they can parasite off other people, even directly steal from them, yet still convince themselves that they have a right to what they can exploit from the talents and efforts of others as they compensate for the fact that they

Figure 198: Obama – dark, dark entity

have neither. If they didn't convince themselves of this, they would have to face the truth that they are unscrupulous, devious, heartless parasites, and that is never an option for a narcissist. Another trait in many of them is the need to put pictures of themselves on display wherever they can – look at me, me, me – especially with well-known people through which they think they can glean some sort of reflected 'glory'. I know some narcissists with websites that have wall-to-wall pictures of themselves and virtually every word is about me, me, me. Incredible. Here are some dictionary definitions:

Narcissist: 'Inordinate fascination with oneself; excessive self-love; vanity. Erotic gratification derived from admiration of one's own physical or mental attributes, being a normal condition at the infantile level of personality development.' Psychopath: 'A person afflicted with a personality disorder characterised by a tendency to commit anti-social and sometimes violent acts, and a failure to feel guilt for such acts.' Sociopath: 'A person whose behaviour is anti-social and who lacks a sense of moral responsibility or social conscience.'

This is a lack of *empathy* in other words with those who suffer the consequences of your actions – a foundation trait of reptilian genetics. The same applies to Blair, Cameron, Bush, Cheney and all the rest. This is the Illuminati blueprint for their place-people in government. How could it be anything else when empathy would make you incapable of slaughtering the innocent? What use is a conscience to a tyranny? Obama and Cameron are blueprint 'leaders', and the blueprint is Blair. For a decade, former British Prime Minister, Tony Blair, perfected the mould that was used to clone this pair of professional liars and hypocrites. The basic software program is to constantly smile in public to hide the darkness of your eyes which betray the darkness of your soul; and to speak of peace, justice, integrity and 'values' while you bomb the innocent under the cover of lies and deceit, because you 'value' only power and to follow the orders of your hidden masters. Isn't that right, Mr Rothschild? NATO is the killing-machine for people with 'values'. Blair sent British forces to war five times in his first six years in office –

Figure 199: Soldiers don't 'fight for their country' – they fight for those seeking to destroy and enslave their country

more than any other prime minister in history – yet still claimed to stand for peace and integrity. Obama and Cameron do the same as they engage their troops in open wars, and many others if you include the dark arts of covert manipulation and, in Obama's case, the gathering war with Pakistan. But, of course, in line with the Blair Blueprint, they have to hide what they really are behind a carefully-designed fraudulent persona called 'nice chap', 'man of the people', 'one of us', 'pretty straight kind of a guy'. When Obama was on his State visit to Britain in 2011, he and Cameron smiled, played staged ping-pong, and even cooked burgers at a Downing Street garden party. Round and round the garden – just like Tony Blair. Oh, they're such nice blokes; look at them laughing. But, while all this was going on, soldiers and the innocent were dying across the Middle East and North Africa from the actions that 'call me, Dave' and 'call me the son of a Kenyan goat-herder' had sanctioned. Soldiers are not killing and dying 'for their country'; they are doing it for the bloodlines and their corporations that are intent on *destroying* their country and enslaving their families (Fig 199). Obama and Cameron, like Bush, Blair and Bill Clinton, are just bag-carriers for those that put them in office, and so the direction and rhetoric are the same when a 'Democrat' replaces a 'Republican' in the United States, or 'Conservative' replaces 'New Labour' in the United Kingdom. Blair (Labour) goes to war with Clinton (Democrat); Blair (Labour) goes to war with Bush (Republican); Cameron (Conservative) goes to war with Obama (Democrat). Nothing changes. The killing goes on because the same force is constantly in control. Only the front-people change. Obama managed to cram a great chunk of the Illuminati-bloodline plan for the world into a single paragraph in his Westminster speech in 2011:

> In a world where the prosperity of all nations is now inextricably linked, a new era of cooperation is required to ensure the growth and stability of the global economy. As new threats spread across borders and oceans, we must dismantle terrorist networks and stop the spread of nuclear weapons; confront climate change and combat famine and disease. And as a revolution races through the streets of the Middle East and North Africa, the entire world has a stake in the aspirations of a generation that longs to determine its own destiny.

As lying and deceit go, it doesn't get much more comprehensive in so few words. Let us pass Teleprompter Man through the Orwellian Language Translation Unit:

> In a world where the prosperity of all nations is now inextricably linked, a new era of cooperation is required to ensure the growth and stability of the global economy.

Translated: 'My masters want a world central bank dictating to the World Bank, International Monetary Fund, European Central Bank (and those in other 'Unions' once they get them in place) and to national central banks such as the Federal Reserve and the Bank of England. In this way, my masters will control the finances of every country and community in the world.'

> As new threats spread across borders and oceans ...

Translated: 'My masters want a world army that can bomb any country that doesn't take orders. We have done that with NATO in Libya and Afghanistan to set the precedent step-by-step until NATO, the UN 'peacekeeping' operation and other military groupings are brought together into a fully-fledged world army imposing the will of a world government. I know that polls show how seven out of ten Americans opposed the bombing of Libya, but I don't care – I'm not here for them. The people who wrote this speech for me talk about 'new threats spread across borders and ocean' because my masters want a global army and police force that can cross borders at will.'

> ... we must dismantle terrorist networks and stop the spread of nuclear weapons.

Translated: 'We must frighten you all with the threat of terrorism and nuclear attacks so you won't give us any trouble when we demonise a target country that we want to acquire by accusing them of protecting terrorist groups and developing nuclear weapons .'

    ... confront climate change and combat famine and disease.

Translated: 'We will blame famine and disease on climate change and Ethel at number 23 for putting the light on. My masters want to exploit the lie about human-caused 'global warming' or 'climate change' to transform the face of human society and so no matter what the scale of evidence to show that it is breathtaking nonsense we will keep pressing ahead with Orwellian impositions and carbon taxation.'

These people are an open book when you know the rules of the game.

How do they do it?

There are two mass mind and manipulation techniques that are vital to understand. I dubbed the first one a long time ago: 'Problem–Reaction–Solution'. I call the second the 'Totalitarian Tiptoe'. They work in concert to advance Illuminati plans by justifying changes they want to impose while hiding the connections between world events. Problem–Reaction–Solution works like this: You want to make changes in society that you know would normally attract strong resistance if you openly announced what you intended to do. This includes everything from going to war to removing basic freedoms and introducing a police state. So you don't openly declare your intentions. You instigate Problem–Reaction–Solution (PRS): (1) You create a problem. It could be a terrorist attack, a financial crash or a war – whatever suits the outcome that you are looking for. You then blame someone or something else for the problem that you have covertly created. (2) You want a reaction of fear and 'do something' from the public when you tell them through an unquestioning lap-dog media the version of the problem that you want people to believe, and the repeater media reports your version of events as if it's true. This could be that Osama bin Laden orchestrated 9/11 from a cave in Afghanistan; or that swine flu is deadly and broke out on a pig farm in Mexico, when it didn't affect a single pig worldwide. (3) You propose the solutions to the problems that you have created, and those solutions advance your transformation of the world. You will see examples of PRS almost by the day once you know how it works. The two world wars were engineered Problem–Reaction–Solutions as I document in great detail in ... *And the Truth Shall Set You Free*. The bloodlines were behind the regimes of Hitler in Germany, Stalin in Russia, Churchill in Britain and Roosevelt in the United States. They had their German arm to cause the problem by invading countries such as Poland; and the solution was for their other assets to go to war with Germany to trigger a global conflict that also drew in the Far East in the form of Japan. It is no longer a mystery, once this is understood, why the Rockefeller and Bush families, and other Illuminati bloodlines in the United States, would fund the war machine of Hitler and the Nazis with whom Americans would later go to war.

I have been exposing for nearly 20 years the involvement in Nazi funding of Prescott

Bush – father of H W Bush and grandfather of G W Bush – and a Bush/Harriman operation called the Union Banking Corporation (UBC). Then, in 2001, John Loftus, president of the Florida Holocaust Museum and a former prosecutor in the US Justice Department's Nazi War Crimes Unit, went public to say the same. Loftus told an audience at the Sarasota Reading Festival that leading Nazi industrialists secretly owned the 'Harriman/Bush' UBC (controlled by the Rothschilds), and they were moving money into the UBC through a second bank in Holland even after the United States declared war on Germany. He said that the bank was liquidated in 1951, and Boy Bush's grandfather, Prescott Bush, and great-grandfather, Herbert Walker, were paid $1.5 million as part of that dissolution. Loftus said he had a file of paperwork linking the bank and Prescott Bush to Nazi money: 'That's where the Bush family fortune came from: It came from the Third Reich.' Problem–Reaction–Solution and the Illuminati global web also explain why the Rothschild-controlled Rockefeller family funded the work of Ernst Rudin, Hitler's foremost 'racial hygienist', at Germany's Kaiser Wilhelm Institute for Eugenics, Anthropology and Human Heredity. This involved horrific live experiments being performed on concentration-camp inmates by madmen like Josef Mengele. Writer and researcher, Anton Chaitkin, says that body parts 'were delivered to [Josef] Mengele, [Otmar] Verschuer and the other Rockefeller-linked contingent at the Wilhelm Institute'. The Rothschilds, Rockefellers and Harrimans were behind the whole race purity eugenics movement. They are Reptilian hybrids and so, like their fully-Reptilian masters, they are obsessed with genetics and see humans as most humans see cattle. Another mystery of World War II is solved, too, when you appreciate this background. Why did the American government not respond to the Japanese attack on Pearl Harbor in 1941 when, as many detailed studies have shown, they had a list of confirmations that it was coming? The reason was Problem– Reaction–Solution. President Franklin Delano Roosevelt won an election by saying that he would not be sending young men and women to the war in Europe; but he knew that he was going to do exactly that and he needed a reason to break his promise while maintaining his credibility. Pearl Harbor did the trick, and he said that although he didn't want to go to war he now had no choice. Nearly 2,500 people died in the Pearl Harbor attack, most of them naval personnel. An estimated 50 to 70 *million* died in World War II. But the Reptilian hybrid bloodlines don't give a shit. They have no empathy and have no emotional consequences. Anyone in the military or those thinking of joining should remember that they don't give damn if you are maimed for life or killed. You are just a means to an end for them.

Does anyone still think that the bloodlines would not kill 3,000 people on 9/11 to justify all the wars and destruction of freedoms that have followed? What happened on September 11th, 2001 in New York was a classic example of PRS. I am not going to dwell on it here. I have written legions about these engineered attacks in other books but, in summary, barely a single fact in the official story fits with other facts. If this is true, then that can't be true, and so on. The mainstream media repeat it without question when it is only a cover story to hide the fact that Reptilian hybrid assets including the Israeli (Rothschild) Mossad, the US National Security Agency, the CIA and connected military agencies, flew passenger aircraft into buildings and bombed the Pentagon (the aircraft strike story is nonsense). The Babylonian goddess witnessed it all in New York (Fig 200). The planes that crashed into the Twin Towers were remotely-controlled 'drones' and not

Figure 200: The goddess of Babylon looks out over the catastrophe of 9/11 – the work of the bloodlines that placed her where she is

the ones that left with their passengers from Boston. The Twin Towers were brought down soon afterwards by a form of controlled demolition in which each floor exploded before being struck by the one above. This is why the buildings imploded and fell to the ground on which they were standing without toppling over – what classically happens in controlled demolitions. It also explains why the buildings fell in virtually freefall-time, confirming the lack of resistance. See: *Alice in Wonderland and the World Trade Center Disaster – Why the official story of 9/11 was a monumental lie; The David Icke Guide to the Global Conspiracy;* and *Human Race Get Off Your Knees* for the detail of what happened on 9/11, or go to the 9/11 archive at: www.davidicke.com for a whole library of articles and videos on the subject. The bloodline families engineered 9/11 through their government agencies, Intelligence network and military, as an excuse to make fundamental changes in the world order. The cover story of Muslim terrorist attacks was used to frighten the public, and to justify wars and a global assault on the most basic freedoms by the police state that has been rolled out ever since (Fig 201). Hitler justified the introduction of the Gestapo in precisely this way after Nazis set fire to the German Parliament, the

Figure 201: Keep them terrified and then you 'protect' them by deleting their freedoms

Reichstag building in Berlin, and blamed someone else. Hitler said that the Gestapo was needed to protect the people: 'An evil exists that threatens every man, woman and child of this great nation. We must take steps to ensure our domestic security and protect our homeland.' Those words could have been spoken by Boy Bush in 2001, or Blair, or Obama, or Cameron. Bloodline assets in America blamed 9/11 on their long-time-on-the-payroll CIA asset, Osama bin Laden. He was based in Afghanistan, and this gave them the excuse to invade that country and demonise the Muslim world as part of their agenda for Africa and the

Middle East which has been expanding ever since. Zbigniew Brzezinski, co-founder of the Trilateral Commission, and Obama mentor, wrote in his book, *The Grand Chessboard*, published in 1997: 'Moreover, as America becomes an increasingly multi- cultural society, it may find it more difficult to fashion a consensus on foreign policy issues, except in the circumstance of a truly massive and widely perceived direct external threat.' This 'external threat' was the threat of terrorism, and it was birthed on 9/11. They chose a 'war on terrorism' because that is George Orwell's 'war without end' in his prophetic book, *1984*. When can you say that a war on terror has ended by being 'won'? You can't; and that's the idea.

Modus Operandi

You can see common themes in these Problem–Reaction–Solution events. How many people know that on September 11th, 2001 there were 'war game' exercises under names like Vigilant Guardian, Vigilant Warrior, Northern Guardian and Northern Vigilance happening either in precisely the same skies that the alleged 'terrorist hijacks' were also happening or caused planes from the east coast defence system to be transferred to other areas of the country? Some of them were simulating airplane-hijack scenarios over the New York and Washington D.C. regions, and one even included a plane being flown into a government building at the same time as the 9/11 attacks were happening. This was done to create total confusion among the military and civilian response systems that are the responsibility of the North American Aerospace Defense Command (NORAD) and the Federal Aviation Administration. I have seen NORAD logs for 9/11 and have published some of them in other books. The manufactured confusion is clear to see. They were asking, 'Is this real world or exercise?' This allowed others within NORAD, those who were part of the 9/11 'team', to misdirect and delay the arrival of jet fighters until the deed was done. How many know that an exercise scenario that mirrored the London tube train bombings on July 7th, 2005 was happening at the *very same time* that the real bombs exploded and the exercise involved the *same tube stations?* Or that a NATO 'anti-terrorism' exercise concluded in Madrid shortly before the train bombing of 2004? Or that 'sources within the top level management of the police' in Oslo told the Norwegian newspaper *Aftenposten* that police had been conducting a 'training exercise' in the hours before the bombing and mass shootings in Norway on July 22nd, 2011 which was based on a 'practically identical scenario' to what actually happened? The Oslo bomb went off only *26 minutes* after the police exercise ended. Put that lot into a computer and work out the odds. The official story of PRS events is just that – a story. Its purpose is to hide what really happened. Cover stories are lies by definition, and with so many interwoven lies for them to deal with the contradictions become obvious (except to the mainstream media). The official story of the London tube station and bus bombings in July 2005 is as equally ludicrous as the fairy tale about 9/11. The alleged four 'suicide bombers' were not seen by any of the survivors except for the claims of a single man whose evidence is simply not credible. They were supposed to have detonated bombs carried in rucksacks with a 'terrorist' on each of three tube trains and a bus. But there were multiple holes in the floors of the carriages and in one of them three people fell into three different holes. Passengers standing next to where one 'bomber' was reported to have been escaped virtually unscathed, while others were killed who were nowhere near where the 'terrorists' were reported to have been. Twelve hours after survivors had been released from one bombed carriage the remaining dead bodies that were left were counted, and numbered seven. All seven have been named and accounted for and so leaving no-one remaining to be the actual bomber. They say that he must have been blown to small pieces, yet passengers next to 'him' escaped without serious injury. The authorities claimed at the same time to have found identity documents of the bombers at the scene! The whole story is absurd, because, as with 9/11, it isn't true. There *were* no 'suicide bombers' with devices in rucksacks. The bombs were planted *under* the trains by military Intelligence – if that is not a contradiction in terms. This is why so many of the dead and injured had legs and feet blown off and why so many said the explosions 'lifted' the carriage from the track. Metal around the hole that one witness saw was coming into the carriage and not going out from it. Okay, no problem. We can solve this in a trice by looking at the most crucial evidence – the wreckage of the carriages. Oops, sorry, no can do. They were destroyed by the authorities, just as the metal from the Twin Towers that would have confirmed what brought them down was taken away and *sold off* on the orders of New York Mayor, and 9/11 'hero', Rudy Giuliani. The same theme can be found with the debris from the Murrah Building in Oklahoma that could have explained what happened there in another Problem–Reaction–Solution in 1995. It was removed and put under armed guard never to be seen again. The bloodlines can carry out and then cover up these so-called 'false flag' terrorist attacks because they control governments, Intelligence agencies, the military and the media.

Tony Farrell, a Principal Intelligence Analyst for England's South Yorkshire Police, went public in 2011 with his conclusion that both 9/11 and the London '7/7' bombings were 'inside job' attacks by government and military agencies. He reached this view after researching the official stories and finding them to be a pack of lies. Farrell had already established to his own satisfaction that 9/11 was a false flag attack when a British government minister suggested that he should also investigate the London bombings in which 56 people died. He did so and said that it wasn't long before he realised that the official story of 7/7 was 'a monstrous lie perpetrated by our own Intelligence service with clear government complicity at the time'. The government was headed by mass murderer, genetic liar and Rothschild Zionist gofer, Tony Blair, and it just so happened that Benjamin Netanyahu, now Israeli Prime Minister, was close to the scene that day. The Israeli Intelligence agency, Mossad, is the global enforcer for the House of Rothschild and expert at false flag terrorist events. Well, after all, it has had lots of practice. Blair was also prime minister when weapons expert, Dr David Kelly, was murdered by the Intelligence services because he had the knowledge to scupper the lie about weapons of mass destruction in Iraq. The official story of 'suicide' is yet another provable fairy tale. Tony Farrell came to his conclusions about 9/11 and 7/7 while he was producing a 'Strategic Threat Assessment' for his police employers that included an assessment of the threat of terrorism. Farrell is clearly a thoroughly decent man and he decided that he had to include the threat from Intelligence agencies performing 'inside jobs' in his assessment of the dangers to human life. He was, of course, dismissed from his job before he could include his findings in the threat assessment and he says that police officers who sacked him encouraged him to appeal the decision. The 'Director of Intelligence' said to him: 'Tony, what can we do about it? We are just the foot soldiers of the government.' Hey, people in uniform – you have

children and grandchildren who have to
live in the world that your shaking boots
are going to leave them. *Get off your bloody
knees and get some backbone.* We are facing a
critical time and we don't need mice in
uniform, thank you. Farrell wasn't, at
first, even saying officially in his
assessment that 9/11 and 7/7 were inside
jobs. He couched it in terms that there
was a threat to public order when the
public eventually believed in large
numbers that both attacks were by the
very government and its agencies that
'condemned' them and went to war
because of them. Even this was too much
for his police employers. All they wanted
was that 'Islamic terrorism' was the
threat, nothing more necessary. In the end,
however, he went the whole 'nine yards'
in 2010 and produced a document
detailing why the official versions of 9/11
and 7/7 were flawed. He went on three

Figure 202: We were asked to believe that a hijacker's paper passport was found, let alone found *intact* – after this

weeks leave which was extended to 'gardening leave' (suspension) and then dismissal.
He went through a 'disciplinary hearing' in which the 'prosecution' admitted that what
he was saying could be true, but he was dismissed on the grounds of his views being
'untenable' with the official version of events. Farrell was never told that his beliefs
were 'incorrect', only that they were 'untenable'. See how it works? He also confirmed
that what did and did not constitute a 'threat' was dictated to all police Intelligence
analysts from 'on high'. He called the whole thing a 'monstrous tyranny'. Tony Farrell is
a committed Christian, and there is a point to be made here. I have exposed the
Christian religion in this book and other books, and quite rightly, but there are many
people who take the best of the Christian philosophy and express it in their lives. They
are not, however, doing what is right because of their 'Christian religion'. They are
doing so because of a sense of fairness, justice and decency.

Another aspect of false flag events is to 'build the image' to manipulate public
perception. They know that most people don't retain detail so they say what is necessary
to sell them a perception of what happened, and the simpler the better. Immediately
after 9/11, I watched a BBC newsreader as she told me – without laughing – that the FBI
had called a news conference to announce that they had found a passport from one of
the alleged hijackers near to Ground Zero. A *paper* passport had been found despite the
massive fireball that was generated when the planes hit the buildings and despite the
fact that most of the bodies were never recovered (Fig 202). This even eclipsed the stroke
of amazing good fortune that the bag of the alleged 'lead hijacker', Mohammed Atta,
was mistakenly not loaded onto the plane at Boston Logan Airport and so its 'contents'
could confirm his involvement. 'Hijackers' left Korans in hotel rooms and hire cars,
almost everywhere they seemed to 'go', according to the official story. What were they,

the Muslim equivalent of the Gideons? They apparently also left flight-manuals and boxcutters at the same locations. None of this is true, of course, but it doesn't *have* to be for most people. *'Hey, honey, they say they've found a passport from one of them there hijackers. See, it was them Muslims. What time's the game show on?'* As the words of the old song go ... 'I believe in miracles.' A great example of selling an 'image' was during the laughable nonsense about bombs in parcels on transport planes originating in Yemen in 2010. I watched live pictures on CNN during this manufactured 'scare' showing an Emirates' airline passenger plane being 'escorted' into New York airport by US fighter jets on either side. The report said that this was being done after rumours that it might be carrying a parcel that began life in the *Yemen!!* Oh, my God, *Aaaaaaaggghhh!* Anyway, my question is this: If there was a parcel bomb on board and if it went off, what were the military planes going to do? 'Ladies and gentlemen, this is your captain speaking. Would you please calmly make your way to the hole in the side of the aircraft and jump in an orderly fashion onto the air force jet flying alongside. Thank you for flying Emirates, we know you have a choice.' It's all bollocks, of course; it was about having people see a passenger aircraft and military jets flying together to sell an image. It's all about perception manipulation – mind control.

Riot–Reaction–Solution

There are moments that bring me close to despair at the ignorance that abounds at every level of global society with regard to the manipulation of human perception. The violent riots, arson and looting in London and other British cities in August 2011 were a real head-shaker for me. Perpetrators, victims and the public in general dutifully read from the script written for them long ago – while not even knowing that such a script existed. They thought they were taking their own actions or responding with their own reactions. But they were not. I wrote a newsletter in 2009 headed: *'Please* Don't Riot – It's Just What 'They' Want.' It was obvious what was going to happen around the world in the wake of the economic crash. The genuine hardship and understandable resentment of those suffering the consequences of the crash, the bank bailouts and the subsequent austerity programmes, was going to be used to trigger the violence that would justify massive advances in the police state. Problem–Reaction–Solution. What happened in Britain basically followed the script of the Los Angeles riots in 1992 when police officers who were captured on video viciously attacking a man called Rodney King were acquitted by a jury. Thousands rioted in protest over six days, and 53 people died. The 'Rodney King' in London was another black man – 29-year-old father-of-four, Mark Duggan, who was shot dead by police in Tottenham, North London on August 4th, 2011 after they stopped the taxi cab in which he was a passenger. Police have admitted that he didn't fire at them, and an inquiry (so often a cover up) was launched into why he was killed by the increasingly trigger-happy British police. Duggan's family and friends were joined by up to 300 people in a peaceful protest outside Tottenham police station, but later bottles and other objects were thrown at police after an argument apparently broke out between an officer and a protestor over what appeared to be police indifference for Duggan's family. A very credible witness told the BBC that the trouble began when police attacked a 16-year-old girl who was only asking for answers to what happened to Mark Duggan. Suddenly, it all kicked off. Violence continued throughout the night in the Tottenham area and spread in subsequent days to several other parts of

London. Buildings and vehicles were burned and stores were looted. 'Copycat' riots broke out in other major English cities including Birmingham, Manchester, Liverpool and Bristol with more violence, destruction and theft. Five people died, and the cost of damage was estimated to exceed £200 million.

So, the riots were the problem and along came the solution. The Rothschild-connected British Prime Minister, David Cameron, announced there would be new police powers to disperse crowds and a 'wider power of curfew'. Cameron indicated that social media networks such as Twitter and mobile messaging systems could face restrictions, and he talked of extending across the country limits on the movement of adults and children accused of being members of gangs. 'All available technology' would be used on rioters, including water cannon and rubber bullets for the first time in mainland Britain; spraying offenders with indelible ink to later identify them; plus ... *here we go* ... 'Ministers will consider whether the Army can take on some policing tasks to free up more officers for the front line.' This was only the start of what will be justified by the riots to continue the agenda for the ever-advancing police and military state. The global blueprint is playing out with the military already involved in some domestic law enforcement in the United States in blatant disregard for the Posse Comitatus Act of 1878 which 'prohibits members of the Army from exercising nominally state law enforcement, police or peace officer powers that maintain law and order on non-federal property (states and their counties and municipal divisions) within the United States'. That could hardly be clearer, but some 20,000 troops are being prepared to police domestic America and now the same process is being considered in the UK in the light of the rioting. The US authorities will also be seeking to trigger rioting and unrest to justify deployment of those troops and it is vital that people don't fall for it. Prime Minister David Cameron dismissed any suggestion that poverty was in any way connected to what happened in Britain's run-down cities, because that would mean that he was in some way responsible – and that would never do. He blames parents and 'a culture that glorifies violence, shows disrespect to authority, and says everything about rights but nothing about responsibilities'. He promised to 'restore a sense of morality'. This is a man who ordered the daily bombing of whole cities in Libya – a campaign of mass murder that targeted hospitals, universities, television stations and other civilian areas, and killed thousands. All this death and destruction of innocent people and communities had but one aim – to remove Colonel Gaddafi on behalf of Cameron's banker associates (the Rothschild networks) and allow the seizure of Libya's banking and oil assets. The same monumental hypocrite talks about 'a culture that glorifies violence' and restoring a 'sense of morality'. Compared with this mass killer of the innocent, the guy looting a plasma TV is not in his league when it comes to *im*morality and a callous disregard for human life and property. Nor is the looting, wrong as it is, in the same universe as the looting of the public purse by Cameron's banking associates throughout the world with multiple trillions changing hands in the greatest transfer of wealth from people to bankers and from poor to rich in known human history. David Cameron is straight out of the political petri dish that spawned Barack Obama, Tony Blair and Hillary Clinton – they talk about 'values' and 'morality' while bombing the innocent at every opportunity. When they open their mouths the Rothschild cabal is doing the talking, and Cameron feigned moral outrage (he clearly has none) to sell the 'brand' of the Orwellian state. Cameron has announced in another

Problem–Reaction–Solution resulting from the riots that he was to be 'advised' by the former head of Los Angeles and New York police, William Bratton, about tackling gang violence. Bratton is chairman of Kroll, a notorious private security firm with massive connections to the Israeli Mossad and the CIA, which ran 'security' at the World Trade Center at the time of 9/11. Cameron apparently wanted Bratton to head the London Metropolitan Police, but was having difficulty selling the idea to many colleagues of an American police officer in charge of a British police force.

I have no doubt that the riots were pre-planned, as they were in Los Angeles in 1992. First you create an emotional tinderbox with high unemployment, austerity programmes and frequent stop-and-search checks by police (all of which happened in LA), and then you use agents provocateurs to start the fire. Things pretty much run themselves after that with criminals and genuinely angry people resentful of their plight taking the opportunity to vent their criminality or frustration and fury in the target area. Reports of this appear on the TV news and others take the lead and do the same in other locations. By now it seems that the whole country is ablaze as you watch the television coverage, and the population is in collective fear of what might happen to them. *Job done* – solutions at the ready. It was noted by many that the police simply stood aside and let the looters take whatever they liked at the start of the British riots, and this is another tell-tale sign. Eye-witnesses have told how the police looked on and took no action as shops were emptied. Many onlookers offered the opinion that this was so blatant that the police had to be under orders to do this. London police sources later said they were ordered to 'stand and observe' no matter what was happening and not to arrest rioters and looters. This was all part of the set-up. The worse they allow things to be, the more fear and outrage is generated in the population. Residents close to where Mark Duggan was shot told reporters that a police surveillance vehicle had been filming the road for days before the killing. They described how they saw armed plainclothes police officers hiding in bushes, and how the taxi in which Duggan was travelling was taken away from the location afterwards before being brought back. What came from the mouths of participants, victims and government was just what the Hidden Hand wanted to hear. These are the powerful words of one of the rioters, and I understand his frustration amid poverty, unemployment and desperately poor housing. I see what he is trying to say and why he says it – but he's caught in a trap set for him by those he opposes:

I riot because I'm angry. Anger envelopes me like a blanket every day of my life. I'm angry because I'm poor, I've always been poor, and I know I will never be able to afford all those nice things people are supposed to have. I'm angry because my life is shit and I know it's always going to be shit. I'm angry because I know that there's no future for me; no one will ever give me a decent job or a hand-up in life.

I will live in the same shitty housing that my family have always lived in, drawing down the same shitty benefits. I□m angry because I live in a shit place full of poverty, crime, vandalism, gangs, garbage, grime and neglect. Most days I take my anger out on myself; I engage in a wide and creative array of self-destructive behavior. But sometimes, like last night, I direct my anger outwards. I let my rage take over, and for a brief moment, I feel a profound sense of release.

I riot because I hate the police, and because I know that the police hate me. They're racist and brutal, and they treat me like scum every day of my life, always coming around blaming me for everything bad that happens, harassing me when I walk down the street. I hate them because they think they're God and they don't have to answer to anyone for what they do. I hate them because they show me no respect. In a riot, you can fight back against the police; you can stand up to them and tell them how you really feel.

I understand why he says all that, and others who live the life that he does in cities all over the world will understand even more powerfully; but he and his fellow rioters in whatever countries and locations have been caught in a carefully planned pincer movement. The authorities systematically create the circumstances that generate such anger, resentment and sense of hopelessness and they want people to riot as their anger explodes so that the solutions waiting in the wings – the police/military state – can be unveiled as a 'necessary response to maintain order'. They are supported in this by the victims of the riots and the general public in fear of *becoming* victims. So many in Britain called for the army to be deployed on the streets which, purely by chance, is what the authorities want to do. Once again, I can understand why people say that amid their resentment and fear. They feel vulnerable and seek protection – whatever that may be. Politicians like Nigel Farage of the 'alternative' UK Independence Party headed straight for the cameras to demand that the military be called in. Those political spokespeople who are not in on the plot (the vast majority) are clueless about what is really happening here. The riots in Britain were psychological warfare on rioter, victim and observer alike. It was about justifying the police/military state, yes, but also about dividing and ruling the population along the fault lines of race and background, and diverting attention away from other matters. People need urgently to get streetwise about how the game is played. Readers of my books already know this; but vast numbers still lack this essential knowledge, and so they serve the very establishment they are rioting against. We need mass peaceful non-cooperation – not riots and violence that just serve the interests of the Dragon. This is vital, because what we have seen in Britain and in gathering numbers of countries in response to economic catastrophe and police brutality is only the start of what is planned – and minor compared with the scale of unrest and upheaval that the Illuminati bloodlines wish to trigger. If people of all factions don't see what is going on and *come together* to challenge that which is targeting *everyone,* then all hell is going to break loose. It has already started – but only started – and we so urgently need to circulate the real background to what is happening in the world. *Please* don't riot, because riots are Problem–Reaction–Solutions that will advance the police/military state even quicker.

No-Problem–Reaction–Solution

They don't always need a real problem to use this mind and emotional manipulation technique, and there is a version that I call *No*-Problem–Reaction–Solution. Weapons of mass destruction in Iraq are a glaring example of this. There weren't any; but by claiming that there were, Boy Bush and Blair sold the invasion of Iraq and the killing and maiming of millions. Human-caused 'global warming' is another *No*-Problem–Reaction–Solution. They need global problems – or the illusion of them – if they are going to have the excuse to offer global solutions. We have the *global* 'war on terror'; a *global* economic crisis; and *global* warming. The public face of the climate con is another perfectly-chosen professional liar called Al Gore. He is the former vice president to one of the most accomplished in the art of mendacity – Bill Clinton. Slick Willy would never have picked a genuine and honest man as his vice present – far too dangerous. To these two, the term 'Big Whopper' does not refer to something on sale at Burger King. The aim of the global warming/climate change scam is to bring an end to the industrial era, impose police state control over the lives of everyone, and

Figure 203: David Mayer de Rothschild 'cares' about the world. How lovely

introduce still more taxation. Oh, yes, and to have a global system of 'carbon trading', in which companies buy and sell their carbon production allowances, or 'credits'. This would make still greater fortunes for the bloodlines and their assets. These include Al Gore who set up a company in 2004 called Generation Investment Management with David Blood, former head of the asset management arm of the bank you can trust, Goldman Sachs. The company is known in 'The City' as 'Blood & Gore'. This acquired a considerable stake in Camco International Ltd which, according to one news report, '... has one of the world's largest carbon credit portfolios, works with companies to identify and develop projects that reduce greenhouse gas emissions and then arranges the sale and delivery of carbon credits'. Gore's 2006 Paramount film, *An Inconvenient Truth*, and his book of the same name, would have been more accurately entitled *A Convenient Lie*. The film won an Oscar and the Nobel Peace Prize (arranged in the same way and through the same networks as Obama's Peace Prize). Gore's book became a *New York Times* best seller. The Nobel Peace Prize, which is named after a guy who made explosives, is beyond ridiculous. Among its recipients are Al Gore (for the lie of 'global warming'); Barack Obama (liar and warmonger); and Henry Kissinger (liar, mass killer, and wanted in several countries for war crimes).

Gore may have surfaced again by the time you read this, but old Al seems to have gone off the radar since the exposure of blatant and outrageous manipulation of the climate data in a desperate attempt to prove the lie. Has anyone seen him? I shall fret and worry. Think of all the time he is losing indoctrinating people to accept his solutions, frightening little children and getting them to turn on their parents for 'destroying the world'. What will the Rothschilds think if you don't get on with it, Al? You know how they care deeply about the environment and the future of our children. David Mayer de Rothschild, son of Sir Evelyn de Rothschild, a pillar of the family, has been especially helpful (Fig 203). He wrote the companion guide to Gore's *'Live Earth'* concerts in which celebrities such as Madonna and Bono sang around the world to sell Big Al's Big Lie. Rothschild junior, who has called for a world government, wrote a book called *The Live Earth Global Warming Survival Handbook: 77 Essential Skills to Stop Climate Change – Or Live through It*. So kind. So thoughtful. He was asked on the Alex Jones radio show in America why Mars was warming at the same time as temperatures were then rising on Earth (it's the Sun!). He replied that this was because Mars was

Contribution to the Greenhouse Effect (including water vapour)

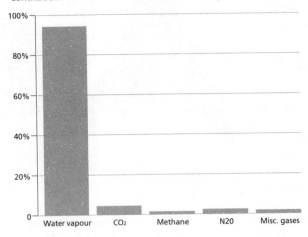

Figure 204: The block on the left is the contribution to greenhouse gases of water vapour and clouds. The one next to it is carbon dioxide and only a tiny proportion of that is from human sources

closer to the Sun. Will someone send him a map of the Solar System, please? We now have ugly wind farms going up and ruining the lives of people who live near them and destroying once-beautiful landscapes to 'fight' a 'problem' that does not exist. People in Europe, Australia, and soon the United States and Canada, are being forced by law to use 'energy-saving' lightbulbs that release extremely poisonous mercury if they are broken, and emit chemicals and radiation that are a serious danger to health – all because of a lie. I have demolished the global warming myth at length in *Human Race Get Off Your Knees*; but enough to say here, as if it really needs saying, that the driver of temperature and climate is the *Sun*. Ever noticed that when the Sun comes out it gets warmer? Carbon dioxide is a naturally occurring phenomenon and without it this planet would not be habitable. Let's demonise something we can't do without, shall we? We also need a 'greenhouse effect' to stop temperatures plummeting. The US Environmental Protection Agency has formally declared carbon dioxide and five other heat-trapping gases to be *pollutants* that endanger public health and welfare. This calculated decision allows the gases to be regulated for the first time. Anyone looking at the graph of 'greenhouse gases' in Figure 204 would think that the one which dominates the chart on the left would have to be carbon dioxide. But it is not. That is water vapour and clouds. Carbon dioxide is the one alongside and virtually all of that occurs naturally. Only a sliver of that CO2 is the result of human activity. Scientists who are experts in their field have taken apart the official story about 'climate change', but governments still plough on with destructive and controlling policies to 'save the planet'. Whenever you see governments continuing with a united policy against all logic and evidence you know that the bloodlines are behind it. The United Nations Intergovernmental Panel on Climate Change (IPCC) has been the main global body for selling the lie and making it the official 'truth'. This is a corrupt and mendacious organisation that I expose in *Human Race Get Off Your Knees*. The IPCC (Idiotic Panel of Climate Crazies) issued a 'report' in 2011 calling for governments to subsidise the 'renewable energy' industry with the people's money to ensure that 'renewables' produced 80 per cent of the world's energy by 2050. The report was supposed to be the result of scientific research, but you know by now with the IPCC that it won't be. That figure of '80 per cent' was taken directly from a paper called *'Energy Evolution 2010 – a Sustainable World Energy Outlook'*, primarily written by ... Sven Teske from Greenpeace and Christine Lins of the European Renewable Energy Council (EREC). This claims to be 'the united voice of the European renewable energy industry'. The organisation represents the very companies that would benefit from governments doing what the IPCC says they should do. Lurking in the shadows behind the IPCC is the Illuminati Round Table satellite, the Club of Rome. This was specifically established to exploit the environment in support of the bloodline agenda. Aurelio Peccei, a founder of the Club of Rome, said in its own publication, *The First Global Revolution*, in 1991: 'In searching for a new enemy to unite us, we came up with the idea that pollution, the threat of global warming, water shortages, famine and the like would fit the bill.' Here are a few other quotes from the Cult of Climatology:

We need to get some broad based support, to capture the public's imagination. So we have to offer up scary scenarios, make simplified, dramatic statements and make little mention of any doubts. Each of us has to decide what the right balance is between being effective and being honest – Stephen Schneider, Stanford Professor of Climatology, lead author of many IPCC reports.

Unless we announce disasters, no one will listen – Sir John Houghton, first chairman of IPCC.

It doesn't matter what is true; it only matters what people believe is true – Paul Watson, co-founder of Greenpeace.

We've got to ride this global warming issue. Even if the theory of global warming is wrong, we will be doing the right thing in terms of economic and environmental policy – Timothy Wirth, President of the UN Foundation.

No matter if the science of global warming is all phony, climate change provides the greatest opportunity to bring about justice and equality in the world [what a joke] – Christine Stewart, former Canadian Minister of the Environment.

The only way to get our society to truly change is to frighten people with the possibility of a catastrophe – Emeritus Professor Daniel Botkin.

Isn't the only hope for the planet that the industrialized civilisations collapse? Isn't it our responsibility to bring that about? – Maurice Strong, founder of the UN Environment Programme, member of the Club of Rome and a bloodline asset from the tips of his fingers to the ends of his toes.

Scientist, David Evans, was a full-time or part-time consultant for eleven years to the Australian Greenhouse Office (now the Department of Climate Change), and he went public in 2011 with an explosive exposé of the global warming hoax. He said that the debate about global warming had reached crazy proportions. 'I am a scientist who was on the carbon gravy train, understands the evidence, was once an alarmist, but am now a skeptic.' He said the whole idea that carbon dioxide is the main cause of the recent warming was based 'on a guess that was proved false by empirical evidence during the 1990s, but the gravy train was too big, with too many jobs, industries, trading profits, political careers, and the possibility of world government and total control riding on the

Figure 205: High Priest of the Climate Cult

outcome'. There we go – 'the possibility of world government and total control riding on the outcome'. This is another reason for the lie: to justify a world government to 'solve the problem' and so much more that I will detail later. This was the real motivation for making Big Al the High Priest in the Cult of Climatology (Fig 205). David Evans said that 'the governments and their tame climate scientists now outrageously maintain the fiction that carbon dioxide is a dangerous pollutant', rather than admit they are wrong even when the evidence is overwhelming. NASA satellite data between 2000 through 2011 revealed that far more heat is being released by the Earth's atmosphere than the mendacious 'computer models' have predicted. Dr Roy Spencer, a principal research scientist at the University of Alabama in Huntsville and US Science Team Leader for the Advanced Microwave Scanning Radiometer flying on NASA's Aqua satellite, said: 'The satellite observations suggest there is much more energy lost to space during and after warming than the climate models show. There is a huge discrepancy between the data and the forecasts that is especially big over the oceans.' The head of the world's allegedly 'premier' physics laboratory at CERN in Geneva, Switzerland, banned scientists there from presenting their own interpretations of experiments that showed a near perfect correlation between periods of warming and the penetration of cosmic rays. The BBC's governing body announced that it is changing the way that the corporation reports the climate change issue by focusing less on those who disagree with the mendacious 'consensus'. *Less?* How can you get less than virtually non-existent? This followed a report, unbiased I'm sure, by Professor Steve Jones, professor of genetics at University College, London. He said that on issues where there is a 'scientific consensus' – human-caused climate change, the MMR jab and genetically-modified crops – there should be no need for the BBC to find opponents of the mainstream view. *The sheer arrogance of it.* This is how the Big Lie about human-caused climate change is protected. Obama's global warming and 'science team' are all from Al Gore's cult, and the laws continue to flow to advance the plans of the Illuminati whatever the scale of evidence to expose the lie. The Illuminati bloodlines are the world's biggest polluters. We have had European Union officials travelling to 'climate change' conferences in separate private jets, and Al Gore himself has a carbon footprint the size of Godzilla. If they cared about the environment, they wouldn't be suppressing technology that could give us all the warmth and power we need for nothing from the free energy available in our electric universe. The great Nikola Tesla, the genius who is really responsible for modern electrical systems, once said: 'Electric power is everywhere, present in unlimited quantities and can drive the world's machinery without the need of coal, oil, gas or any other of the common fuels.' The bloodlines know this, but they stop this free energy being exploited. It would mean the end of power bills and a great deal of control. We have to be kept in a situation where we need to serve the system to pay for heat and power.

Who shot Bin Laden? Er, no-one

Another example of a No-Problem–Reaction–Solution was the 'shooting' of Osama bin Laden in Pakistan in 2011. They are still debating the title of the book and the movie, but some being considered are *Mission Impossible* (but somebody already had that one) and, my personal favourite, *You Only Die Twice*. The whole farce was an insult to the intelligence and so, therefore, no insult at all to the mainstream media parrots and the billions around the world who have believed this monumental crap about the 'shooting' of Osama bin Laden. *Their* intelligence is not insulted; you can't insult something that doesn't exist. One of two things was happening here given the ludicrous official fairy tale spewing from the lips of Liar-in-Chief, Barack Obama, and his cronies and handlers. Either they are getting really desperate or they think that the public and media will swallow anything. In fact, probably both are true. They are getting more desperate in their race to lock down the world before enough people wake up sufficiently to stop them; and, yes, the mainstream media and billions of people will believe anything you tell them – the 'Bin Laden shooting' proved it. The moronic masses gathered at the White House chanting, *'USA, USA ...'* after a president who has yet to prove he was even born in America told them that a man who died long before had been killed again. This is quite a feat and also an alarming confirmation of how childlike alleged adults can be. Hey, the president has just said the Moon is made of green cheese and the tooth fairy is real. *'Tooth fairy, tooth fairy ...'* (Fig 206) But times are changing, and a very large number of people don't believe a word of it – and nor should they. The official cover story for 9/11 was easy enough to take apart, but the killing of 'Bin Laden'?? *Jeeez*, where do you start? US military Intelligence (it's all military Intelligence, not civilian) claims to have kept the 'compound' (actually a house, but compound sounds more scary) near a military establishment in Abbottabad, Pakistan, under long-term surveillance (Fig 207). They

Figure 206: 'Tooth fairy, tooth fairy...'

Figure 207: The Bin Laden 'compound' at Kandy-har. The walking sticks were used by the man they called 'the pacer'

noticed a man going for walks in the garden and the official story says that he was given the nickname 'the pacer'. They thought it was Bin Laden, but they could not identify him for sure with the surveillance technology available. Okay, yes, I believe them. I mean, they can photograph your number plate from space, but they can't identify a man walking regularly in a garden open to the sky. *Mmmmm*, yep, that seems to make sense, doesn't it? Well, it does to a mainstream journalist or an idiot chanting, 'USA, USA ...'

Osama bin Laden was widely known before 9/11 to have been suffering from kidney failure so serious that he needed dialysis treatment. A French television report, based on information gathered by Radio France International and the newspaper, *Le Figaro*, said in 2001 that in July of that year Bin Laden had been admitted to an American hospital in Dubai for kidney treatment and had been visited by the local head of the CIA. *CBS News* reported that Bin Laden was having kidney dialysis treatment the night before 9/11 at a hospital at Rawalpindi in Pakistan. I was specifically listening to the reports about the Bin Laden 'compound' for mention of any dialysis equipment. This was mentioned eventually in the context that they didn't find any. Wow! It's another *miracle!* Five years in that 'compound' with no treatment for serious kidney malfunction and somehow he survived long enough to be shot. The alleged visit by the CIA chief in Dubai makes sense given that Bin Laden was brought to global prominence by American military Intelligence to be the figurehead of the US-created, trained and funded 'Mujahedeen' (which morphed into the 'Taliban') in the war to resist the invasion and occupation of Afghanistan by the Soviet Union in the 1980s. Zbigniew Brzezinski, former National Security Advisor to Jimmy Carter, Trilateral Commission co-founder, and long-time 'mentor' (handler) of Barack Obama, told the French news magazine, *Le Nouvel Observateur*, that he had arranged for the Mujahedeen in Afghanistan to be trained and funded to threaten the Soviet satellite government in the capital, Kabul. He said the plan was to entice the Soviet Union to invade and give them what he called 'their Vietnam'. Thirty years later we had Brzezinski's protégé, Barack Obama, massively increasing troop numbers in Afghanistan to allegedly fight the Taliban which his mentor Brzezinski was largely responsible for creating. It sounds contradictory, but it's not. There is a common denominator – whatever best suits the Agenda at the time. Across North Africa and the Middle East today, American, British and Israeli-controlled agents provocateurs and carefully-trained 'rebel leaders' are manipulating genuine protestors to play out themes from the same basic blueprint used by the US with Bin Laden in Afghanistan. General Khalifa Hifter, a 'military leader' of the NATO 'rebels' in Libya, is a long-time paid CIA asset who lived for some 20 years in the United States very close to the headquarters of the CIA in Langley, Virginia. Hifter was promoted as the figurehead for the CIA-funded Libyan National Army 'in exile'. This is the same blueprint again that they used with Iraqi exiles in London in the years before the invasion. One newspaper report said: 'The new leader of Libya's opposition military spent the past two decades in suburban Virginia but felt compelled – even in his late-60s – to return to the battlefield in his homeland, according to people who know him.' I'm sure he did. 'Get your arse over there or the money stops' might also have helped to focus his mind.

Killing a dead man

Osama bin Laden has been reported to be dead many times since 9/11 – including by the then Pakistan President Pervez Musharraf in 2002 and by former Prime Minister, Benazir Bhutto, shortly before her very possibly-related assassination in 2007. Egyptian newspaper, *Al Wafd*, reported Bin Laden's funeral in December 2001 and said he had died from natural causes. US government insider Dr Steve Pieczenik said on the Alex Jones radio show in the United States that Bin Laden died soon after 9/11 from Marfan syndrome. This is a hereditary disease that can affect the connective tissue which holds the body together and cause serious damage to the skeletal system, cardiovascular system, lungs, eyes, skin and ... *kidneys.* Bin Laden

Figure 208: Bin Laden taken aboard a US helicopter to be buried at sea. The White House released the picture to quell rumours that they were lying through their teeth. 'It looks genuine', said the mainstream media

certainly showed classic traits of Marfan syndrome with his tall body, long limbs and face. Pieczenik was a deputy assistant secretary of state in the administrations of Gerald Ford, Jimmy Carter, Ronald Reagan and George H W Bush. He said that he could confirm the Dubai hospital story and that Bin Laden needed constant dialysis because of Marfan syndrome. This was why the closest person to Bin Laden was a physician, he said. Pieczenik pointed out that Colonel Tommy Franks, who led the invasion of Afghanistan in 2001, stated (though he didn't mean to) that Bin Laden was dead at that time. 'We knew that was true,' said insider Pieczenik. The official 'shooting' of Bin Laden by 'Navy Seals' was a ridiculous, hilarious and constantly changing stream of lies for a simple reason. *It never happened.* His body was never shown to the public and was immediately 'buried at sea' according to a 'Muslim custom' that doesn't exist, because there was no body. They refused to release images of him for the same reason – they didn't have any. Obama said pictures would not be circulated because they were 'too gruesome' and 'you know, we don't trot out this stuff as trophies' (Fig 208). Actually, that's exactly what 'we' do when 'we' have the pictures or when 'we' have fake pictures that 'we' think will fool people. Unfortunately for 'we', there is now a rapidly

expanding alternative media that won't allow such fakes to go unnoticed or unchallenged any more. A picture of a 'dead Bin Laden' circulated immediately after Obama's announcement of the 'shooting' on the major Satanic ritual day of May 1st, and this was published by many in the mainstream media as genuine (Fig 209). The image was a Photoshop

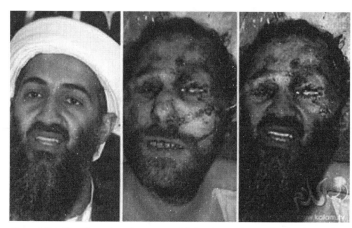

Figure 209: The Photoshop image combining Bin Laden and a dead man that the mainstream media at first circulated as 'genuine'

mock-up that combined
the two pictures on the
left to produce the one on
the right. The hoaxed
media said that it was the
work of 'conspiracy
theorists', when it was
'conspiracy theorists' who
had been exposing it as a
fake! The US government
said that Bin Laden had
been armed and had used
his wife as a human
shield during a shootout
with Navy Seals. The
same government later
admitted that he wasn't

Figure 210: The White House admitted that there were no live pictures of the 'Bin Laden shooting'. So what were these people looking at? And what made Hillary Clinton look so worried – a crack in the wall?

armed and he did not hide behind his wife or anyone else. We were told that his wife had been killed and then that she was still alive. *'No, no,* you can't say the wife is dead – we need her to be still alive so she can support our story. Say we made a mistake in the fog of war.' But perhaps the most outrageous attempt at manipulating public perception was the now-infamous picture of Obama, Hillary Clinton and others staring anxiously at apparently live images of Bin Laden being killed (Fig 210). *'We got him,'* the little boy in short trousers was supposed to have said. *Ah,* but there is one little detail to know here. It has since been admitted that there *were* no live images of the 'killing', so these people could not have been anxiously watching them. So what *were* they watching?? The *wall?* The lies are unbelievable and the mainstream media just goes on repeating them without question. The White House comedy show also said that they had found a 'treasure trove' of information and 'home videos' at the 'Bin Laden compound'. No, they didn't, because he *wasn't there.* What they 'found' was whatever they made up themselves a long, long way from the 'compound'.

Your eyes *can* lie – and they do

We are now in an era of computerised imagery where we can no longer claim that what we think we are seeing is actually what we are seeing. You will find a video on my website, www.davidicke.com entitled: *'Government released videos: You think your eyes are seeing what you think they're seeing? Think again.'* The bloodline cabal has had technology for decades that can produce videos that look like the person and sound like the person, but are not the person. 'Bin Laden' videos galore have been released *since his death* soon after 9/11 to fuel the lie that he was still alive and active. They have been 'acquired' and released to the media through CIA/Mossad front organisations like SITE, or 'Search for International Terrorist Entities' (but never in Israel). SITE is run by an extreme Rothschild Zionist called Rita Katz, the daughter of an executed Israeli spy, and is reportedly funded by the US government to the tune of $500,000 a year. It is, in effect, an arm of the Departments of 'Justice', Treasury, and Homeland Security. SITE works in harness with an organisation called IntelCenter, another releaser of 'Bin Laden' videos,

Figure 211: Man in hat with beard flicks channels with wrong hand looking at Bin Laden footage on every one. What a joke

which is headed by another Rothschild Zionist, Ben Venzke. Rita Katz and SITE 'reported' after the never-happened 'Bin Laden shooting' that 'Al-Qaeda' had made a statement confirming Bin Laden's death. Or, as CNN put it: 'Al-Qaeda released a statement on jihadist forums confirming the death of its leader, Osama bin Laden, according to SITE Intelligence Group, which monitors militant messages.' No – which circulates lies and mock-up videos under the direction of Mossad and the CIA. American investigative journalist, Wayne Madsen, has pointed out that many 'Jihadist' and 'Al-Qaeda' websites are controlled by the Israeli (Rothschild) Mossad. He said: 'Mossad has a program to distribute bogus claims of responsibility for Islamist terrorist attacks via 'Jihadist' websites that are actually operated by the Mossad and a network of 'hasbaratchiks', Israeli and foreign Jews who act as propagandists on the web.' Even *The Washington Post* revealed that the CIA was making fraudulent videos to discredit targets. The *Post* reported that a video was made to apparently show Bin Laden and friends drinking alcohol around a campfire and talking about their 'conquests of little boys'. But, really, you would think they could do better than the laughable 'home video' footage that they released after the 'shooting' to 'show' Bin Laden sitting on the floor flicking through TV channels, all of which featured his image (Fig 211). Have you ever flicked through a series of channels like that and never seen any of them showing advertisements? I haven't. But, no, it was Bin Laden on every one. Maybe some *were* advertisements in which he starred. Bin Laden vanishing cream would sell by the truckload. There are, to employ understatement, a few basic errors here that the mainstream media has not allowed to take up good drinking time – but *we* should. Firstly, all that we see in the entire footage is a hat, the side of a beard and the tip of a nose. The real Bin Laden is left-handed and yet this guy uses his right hand to change the channels throughout. Close-ups of the ears of fake and real Bin Laden show they are not the same, and other footage from the 'treasure trove' is only pictures released years ago. 'New' footage found in the 'compound' was circulating four years earlier. They did the same in 2007 when the footage was released as 'new' when it was clearly the same video that had been circulating in 2002. The CIA has published an official dossier on what happened and you can see that in Figure 212. Interestingly, a Chinook helicopter crashed in Afghanistan in August, 2011, killing 38 people including 22 Navy Seals from the unit involved in the Bin Laden hoax. Officials said that they were not the same men that 'killed' Bin Laden, but I bet they were. Either that, or they were killed earlier and this was the cover story. Seals from that unit would certainly know what really happened – or, rather, *didn't* – and we wouldn't want the extraordinary truth to get out, would we? The official story claimed that the Chinook was shot down by the Taliban, something they normally rarely admit. It all smells like a fish factory in a heat wave.

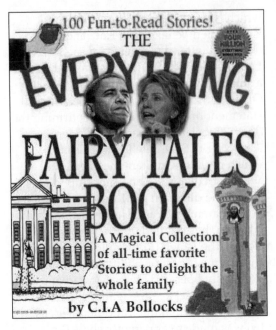

100 Fun-to-Read Stories!

THE

EVERYTHING

FAIRY TALES BOOK

A Magical Collection of all-time favorite Stories to delight the whole family

by C.I.A Bollocks

Figure 212: The official report on Bin Laden's demise issued by the White House press office

The timing

So to the question, why fake the death of an already dead man at the time that they did in early 2011? The reasons are many, and they became obvious by official actions and statements that followed. One reason, but certainly not the main one, was to boost the standing of Barack Obama amid all the disillusionment that so many were feeling about him. How convenient that days after the staged 'killing' there was a commemoration for those who died on 9/11 at the Ground Zero site in New York where Obama contemptuously exploited 9/11 families, first responders and Bin Laden's 'demise' to sell himself for another term in the White House in 2012. This focus on Obama as some sort of 'hero' for 'getting' Bin Laden is crazy when, it turns out, he didn't make any decision to 'go in' even according to the fairy tale narrative. Of course, he didn't. He does what he is told to do. Some of the key reasons for the Bin Laden hoax were:

1) The excuse to say that as a result of the killing there are likely to be terrorist reprisals and they have to impose more surveillance and police state controls in places like railways, shopping malls, department stores, hotels, churches and sports stadia. We were told immediately after the hoax that they had found evidence in the 'compound' of plans to derail American trains and attack so-called 'soft targets'. For that, read 'we want to expand the police state into areas that we have not been able to justify before'. (See also: 'boxcutters' 'found' in houses in Afghanistan after 9/11; the 'hijacker's passport' 'found' near Ground Zero; and Korans and 'flight manuals' 'found' at locations allegedly related to the '9/11 hijackers'.) David Boehm (Rothschild Zionist), Chief Operating Officer of Security USA Inc., was straight out of the blocks telling CBS that to keep people safe after the 'compound find', the soft targets would need to be protected using, in effect, airport-style security including the sexual molestation known as the 'pat down'. Michael Chertoff (Rothschild Zionist), former head of Homeland Security, co-author of the freedom-destroying Patriot Act, and son of a Mossad agent, was all over the TV networks after the 'underpants bomber' incident to push full-body radiation scanners produced by a corporation that his company represents. The 'underpants bomber' was another stooge and another set-up. Senator Charles Schumer (Rothschild Zionist), with decades of service to the Cabal, called for a 'no-ride list' for Amtrak trains within days of the Bin Laden 'shooting', on the basis of 'Intelligence' not made public (because it doesn't exist) that was 'found at the Bin Laden compound'.

Schumer said that he would press for still more funding for rail security, commuter and passenger train-track inspections and more monitoring of stations nationwide. Just say it, mate: A further expansion of the police state.

2) The Bin Laden hoax was exploited to win support for the wars in which the United States is already engaged, and others that it is planning to start – the 'Go USA!'-mentality that would move 'Mr America' John Wayne to tears of joy. Wayne was a Hollywood actor who became a war hero without ever seeing a bullet fired in anger. He was in make-up at the time. Former vice president, Dick Cheney, used the Bin Laden 'killing' to call for the reinstatement of torture methods as a means of interrogation. He suggested that such methods helped to establish the whereabouts of Bin Laden. First of all they didn't, because he wasn't there; and second, the methods of torture have never stopped being used because these sick minds are a law unto themselves.

3) Bin Laden's fake death was immediately used to further demonise Pakistan by claiming that they must have known that he was living there for years in the 'compound' (when he wasn't). Obama was immediately dispatched to the Teleprompter to condemn Pakistan and say they must answer the question of why they didn't know where he, well, wasn't. Former Boy Bush speechwriter, David Frum (Rothschild Zionist), coined the phrase the 'Axis of Evil' referring to Iraq, Iran and North Korea. He prostitutes his words for the neoconservatives, or 'neocons', who controlled the Bush administration. When this guy calls for something to happen, it is part of the ongoing agenda – every time. Frum demanded, yes, yes, for Pakistan to be targeted in the wake of the 'Bin Laden shooting':

> Instead, even now – even now! – we're told that Pakistan is just too important to permit the US to act on its stated doctrine – articulated by George W Bush's administration and not repudiated by Obama's: 'Those who harbour terrorists will be treated as terrorists themselves.' So long as we remain in Afghanistan, that statement remains true. The question is, shouldn't we be taking now the steps to render the statement less true?

> The less committed we are to Afghanistan, the more independent we are of Pakistan. The more independent we are of Pakistan, the more leverage we have over Pakistan. The more leverage we have over Pakistan, the more clout we have to shut down Pakistan's long, vicious, and now not credibly deniable state support for terrorism.

These people tell you what they plan to do, and so expect the war in Afghanistan to be wound down and for other targets to emerge. The point to emphasise is that the bloodlines *want* chaos and they *want* things to fail. They are constantly ensuring that the status quo is not working so they can offer 'change' to advance their global tyranny. They *want* more violence and crime, because they can then say that we must have more draconian laws and take away freedoms to 'solve' the problem. The world makes sense when you know this and it explains the revelation in 2011 that agents of the US Bureau of Alcohol, Tobacco, Firearms and Explosives (ATF) and other government agents gave thousands of weapons to Mexican drug gangs under orders from Washington in operations called 'Fast and Furious' and 'Project Gun Runner'. The weapons – AK-47s, pistols and rifles with a range of two miles – began turning up in violent crimes in Phoenix, Arizona. Money for these operations was assigned by Obama in his 'stimulus package' (to stimulate more death and destruction) and his Attorney General, Eric Holder, is centrally involved. The idea was to create more fear and upheaval and to use the supply of arms to these drug gangs as an excuse to disarm American citizens. The motto of the 33rd degree of the Scottish Right of Freemasonry is: 'Ordo Ab Chao' – 'Order Out of Chaos'. Create the chaos and offer the order – your order – by offering 'solutions'. This is how Problem–Reaction–Solution operates and it is the most effective of the mass public manipulation techniques, in concert with one other ...

Step by step to tyranny

The 'Totalitarian Tiptoe' describes how the bloodlines introduce their global dictatorship in a series of connected steps which are promoted as random 'happenings'. They have to stop people connecting the dots or they would clearly figure out where it was all heading. Imagine that you are standing at point A and you know you are going to take the world to point Z. You know that if you go forward in giant leaps you are going to alert the population to the fact that something 'big' is happening. The change would be just too obvious. Instead you advance to your target in smaller steps – as fast as you can get away with, but not so fast that too many people see what you are doing. I have just described how the nation states of Europe became the European Union. There would have been major resistance if the bureaucratic EU dictatorship that we have today had been suggested after World War II. Tens of millions died stopping Hitler and the Nazis from imposing the centrally-controlled 'union' of Europe that he, too, was seeking. At point A, therefore, people were sold a 'free trade' zone called the European Economic Community (EEC), or the 'Common Market'. Don't worry yourselves, they said, this is not about political or financial union. The Common Market was only to increase trade and jobs. The decades since then have seen an incessant centralisation of power, step by step, to the point where the bureaucrats of the European Commission are only another version of the Soviet Politburo. Jean Monnet, the Rothschild asset and so-called 'Founding Father' of the European Union, said this in a letter to a friend on April 30th, 1952:

> Europe's nations should be guided towards the super-state without their people understanding what is happening. This can be accomplished by successive steps, each disguised as having an economic purpose, but which will eventually and irreversibly lead to federation.

The letter was written the day after I was born, sixty years ago, and this is how the Totalitarian Tiptoe changes the world step after step for as long as it takes. You might have noticed that when nations have voted in referendums to block further centralisation of the European Union that their governments wait a while and then have another 'people's vote' that reverses the original decision. There is never another ballot, however, once the EU has got what it wants. The Agenda will not be denied, as with 'global warming'. The bloodlines that control the European Union tell their subsidiary networks in the countries in question to 'sort it out' and order the governments they control to have another referendum and make sure the result is different. There is another little wheeze they employ when they know that public opposition is too entrenched to change the outcome. They introduce what the people have voted against in another form and under another name. We saw this with the European Constitution that proposed a society-changing transfer of power from nations and people to Brussels and the bureaucrats. The French and the Dutch voted against its introduction, and the manipulators knew that they would do so again if they forced another vote. So they changed the name from Constitution to a 'Treaty' and said that the French and Dutch referendum results were no longer valid. The British government made an El-ection pledge that the public would be given a referendum on the European Constitution, and the government knew they would vote 'no'. Prime Minister Tony Blair and his successor, Gordon Brown, now refused a referendum, because they said the 'new' document was a treaty, and a referendum had been promised on a constitution. Well, what do you expect from a pair of professional liars? The 'treaty' included 98 per cent of what had been in the 'constitution'. This is the level of deceit and dishonesty that we are dealing with. They don't give a damn what we think. What they want is all that matters. A newspaper poll in 2011 revealed that British people wanted to withdraw from the EU by a margin of 55 per cent to 33 per cent. Will they get the chance to vote to do so? No.

Ireland was the only country that did have a chance to vote. The Irish constitution demanded that a referendum had to be held for major changes in government structure to take place. The Irish rejected the treaty, but Prime Minister Brian 'What's my name? Where am I?' Cowen was ordered to have a second vote by his masters in the shadows and, hey presto, the people voted 'yes' – at least officially. The Lisbon Treaty, as it became known, has created a United States of Europe, and in the small-print and legal jargon the document gives EU bureaucrats free reign to do what they like. The European Union is a fascist/communist tyranny and the 'El-ected' European 'Parliament' is only an irrelevant talking shop that allows the EU to call itself 'democratic'. The European Union is bought and paid for at every level. There are few better examples of this than what happened in a vote at the British Parliament in 2011 over proposals to give people a referendum on any further proposals to transfer more power to Brussels. A despicable band of former EU bureaucrats and politicians who are now unelected members of the House of Lords voted together to block any such opportunity for the people to have their say. They included those frauds of frauds, Neil Kinnock and his missus, Glenys Kinnock. There are alternative words to the socialist song, The Red Flag. They go: 'The working class can kiss my arse, I've got the foreman's job at last.' They could have been written for this pair. Neil Kinnock was made leader of the Labour Party in the 1980s to ensure that Conservative leader, Margaret Thatcher, would have no trouble winning El-ections. He was the 'man of the people' from the socialist heartland of South Wales who never used one word when 67,485 would do. He was known as the 'Welsh Windbag' and he was all delivery and no substance. The term 'turncoat' does not do him justice. Put any adjective you like in front of the word and it still wouldn't suffice. This is the man who campaigned against wars and then supported Tony Blair who can't get enough of them. Kinnock called for Britain to withdraw from what is now the European Union and scrap the unelected House of Lords, but he is now called Lord Kinnock and his wife is Baroness Kinnock. They are both members of the House of Lords and they both made an absolute fortune at public expense from the European Union where he was a Brussels bureaucrat and she was a member of the EU parliament. They made an estimated £8 million in salary and expenses and they now

enjoy lucrative EU pensions –
all paid for from the taxation of
the 'working class' that they
used to claim to represent. But
it gets worse. Kinnock is
reported to receive an annual
pension from the EU of nearly
£100,000 a year, and the
'Baroness' nearly £70,000. These
extraordinary pensions come
with strings attached, however.
Wait for this ... there is a 'loyalty
clause' which means that any
former employee of the
European Union who speaks
out against the EU, or does not
remain loyal to its aims, can be
'deprived of their right to a
pension or other benefits'. First
of all, that is beyond outrageous
and nothing less than
institutionalised bribery. Don't
rock the boat and you'll still get
the money. Secondly, self-
interest groupies like the
Kinnocks are not going to do
anything that would threaten
their seats on the gravy train.
That could be a good family
motto for them: 'Don't rock the
boat, take the gravy train.' They
can have that one for free, I
won't charge. So, the Kinnocks
& Co. slithered along to the
House of Lords to vote the way
the EU bureaucrats demanded
to stop the people having a
voice on how they are
governed. They included
representatives of 'different'
parties in Britain's one-party

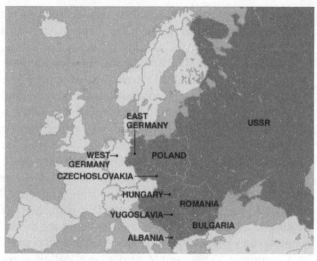

Figure 213: The Soviet Union was an official totalitarian state ...

Figure 214: ... and the even bigger European Union is an unofficial
totalitarian state. Official or unofficial, they are both centralised
dictatorships

state, but they came together in a common cause: greed and self- interest. They included
Rothschild house-boy Lord Mandelson, the CEO of Liars Incorporated – but then of
course they did.

Soviet dissidents who came to the West during the communist era have said that the
European Union is now little different from the Soviet Union (Figs 213 and 214). The EU

controls far more countries under its fast-emerging jackboot than the Soviet Union ever did. Vladimir Putin, the former Russian president, now prime minister, and soon to be president again if all goes to plan, has called for the EU 'free trade' area to be extended into Russia. Putin is just another Rothschild bag carrier. The House of Rothschild funded and orchestrated the Russian 'Revolution', and they have controlled the country ever since (see ... *And the Truth Shall Set You Free*). 'Revolutionaries' like Rothschild Zionists Lenin and Trotsky were puppets of the Rothschild networks. The Soviet Union and now

CONSILIUM

Figure 215: The all-seeing eye on the EU Council of Ministers logo

Russia are no different to the 'West', and nor is China. They are owned by the global banking cartel. The engineered Cold War provided the excuse for NATO to be formed (Problem–Reaction– Solution) to 'defend' Europe against the 'Warsaw Pact' forces of the Soviet Empire. This phony 'war' allowed the bloodlines to do many things that would not otherwise have happened, including the insane stockpiling of nuclear weapons. However, the tyranny has a timescale and the period was approaching when the countries of the Soviet Union had to start being absorbed into the EU and NATO (world army). Suddenly, after decades of 'scary' Soviet leaders such as Stalin, Khrushchev and Brezhnev, along came a puppet and friend of the Rockefellers – Mr Smiley, Feely, Mikhail Gorbachev. US Presidents, Ronald Reagan and Father Bush, and British Prime Minister, Margaret Thatcher, were transformed in their view of the Soviet Union. You know, it wasn't so bad after all. Gorbachev oversaw the break-up of the Soviet Union – exactly as planned – and its former colonies have been joining the European Union and NATO ever since. The bloodlines are not making this up as they go along. The Reptilian Alliance plans the strategy centuries in advance in our version of time. Actually, and the rest.

The first President of the European Council was the Belgian Bilderberger, Herman Van Rompuy, a buddy of Zbigniew Brzezinski and Henry Kissinger. He is also a close friend of the Belgium-based Hungarian and chairman of the Bilderberg Group, Viscount Etienne Davignon, who said that the Bilderberg group was influential in the creation of the single European currency. This is a stepping stone to the world currency. The Euro has been used to delete most of the national currencies of Europe and it will itself be scrapped eventually to make way for the global electronic currency. The Euro will be targeted as a problem in need of a solution. The Bilderberg Group was more than an 'influence' on the creation of the Euro. This Round Table satellite has been the prime driving and coordinated force behind the covert creation of a single European State with its goddess-symbolising 12-star circle and the eye symbol of the Council of Ministers, or 'Consilium', a word that derives, not surprisingly, from Rome (Fig 215). The EU is planned to be the European arm of the world government with its own police force and army that would eventually be part of the *world* police force and army. It is already happening. The plan is for the European Union to be headed by an El-ected dictator president and this is precisely what bloodline arse-licker, Tony Blair, has said should happen. Here is something to remember, and it *never* fails: Whenever Blair opens his mouth the bloodlines are doing the talking. He has also said that Iran must not be allowed to develop a nuclear programme (let's bomb them, I loving bombing people). Thank you, Blair, good work. The cheque is in the post. Now run along.

So, that is the Totalitarian Tiptoe and you can see it being used on so many fronts – the gathering police state, the step-by-step creation of a world army through NATO, ever-quickening erosion of freedoms and so much more. The Totalitarian Tiptoe and Problem–Reaction–Solution are the most effective techniques of mass- perception manipulation. They have been used by the Reptilian hybrid bloodlines from day one, and without them the world would not be anything like what we see today.

NEIL HAGUE
Gallery

The brilliant and inspired symbolic art of one of the world's most unique and individual artists

Mind-body is like the white crests on the waves of an ocean. They are part of the ocean, but manifest in a more individualised way..

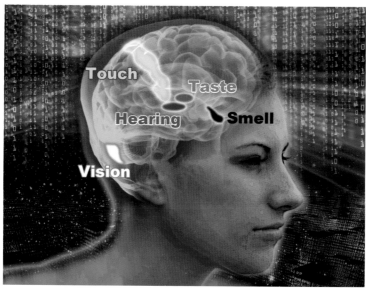

Mind-Body is a biological computer system decoding vibrational information into electrical, digital and holographic information which appears as a 'solid' world 'outside' of us. It's all an illusion.

If we don't decode vibrational/waveform information into holographic form it cannot appear in our five-sense reality...

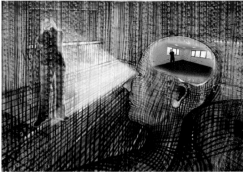

... only when we do so can we 'see' the otherwise unseen.

The relationship between Mind-Body and Consciousness is like that of a computer and a computer operator who observes the Internet, and interacts with it, *through* the computer..

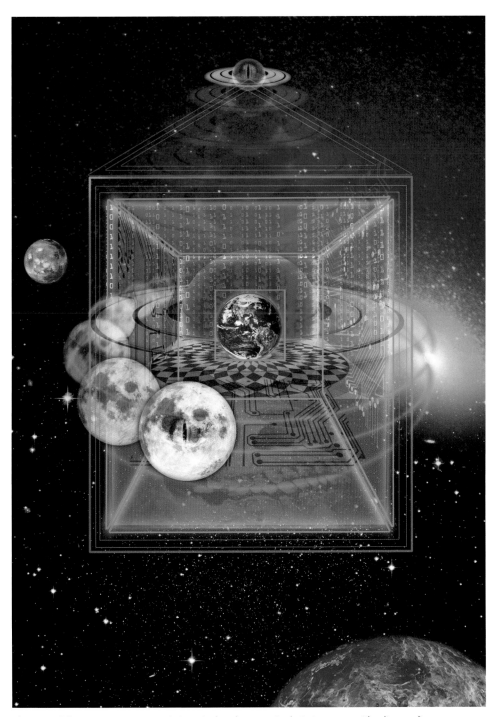

The aim of the Saturn–Moon Matrix is to isolate humans in their 'wave crest' bodies, or five-sense awareness, and stop them connecting with the 'ocean' – Consciousness.

Humans are held fast in the Saturn–Moon Matrix and DNA program unless we open our minds to Consciousness beyond the vibrational wall of the Matrix – the speed of light.

The Saturn–Moon Matrix 'hacks' into the wider virtual reality 'game' and feeds us a fake reality that we believe to be 'real'.

The Moon is not what it seems to be. It is a gigantic spacecraft, computer and broadcasting system that amplifies the broadcasts from Saturn and beams them at the Earth.

Saturn and the Moon dictate our perception of 'time' and this is a major means through which mind-body is detached from Consciousness.

THE YUGA CYCLES

GOLDEN AGE · SATYA · GOLDEN AGE · SATYA

SILVER AGE · TRETA · TRETA · SILVER AGE

DWAPARA · DWAPARA

BRONZE AGE · BRONZE AGE

KALI

IRON AGE

Other expressions of time manipulation are the belief in yuga cycles, Mayan calendar cycles, Hopi prophecies, the Book of Revelation and such like. They are designed to entrap our perception in the Saturn-Moon 'time' Matrix among many other things.

Humanity is controlled and manipulated by the Reptilian Alliance behind Saturn and the Moon and their hybrid control structure on Earth.

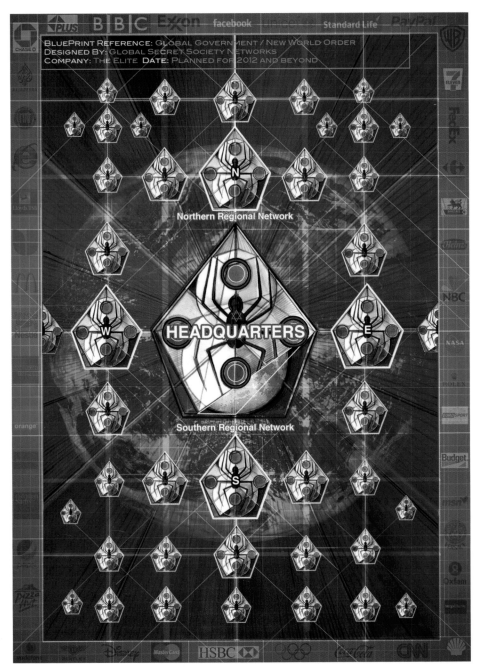

Northern Regional Network

HEADQUARTERS

Southern Regional Network

The Reptilians and their hybrids have created a global structure very much like a transnational corporation. The headquarters at operational level is in Europe and every country has a smaller subsidiary version of the global web through which the agenda dictated from the centre is imposed in every country.

The Reptilian relationship with their hybrid bloodlines can be symbolised as a scientist working inside a 'tank' (our reality) while standing outside the tank (their reality) by using gloves (the hybrid bloodlines) that penetrate the tank.

The hybrids have reptilian and human DNA codes and can 'shapeshift' between the two. This is not a 'physical' shift, because there is no physical. It is an energetic shift which is decoded by the observer into an apparent 'physical' (holographic) shift.

The hybrid families and their agents are creating a global fascist/communist dictatorship through wars of acquisition, financial manipulation, 'false flag' terrorist attacks and the ever-gathering police state. 'Different', even apparently 'opposing' and 'competing', political leaders, financiers, industrialists etc. are all heads on the same monster.

HAARP is one of the bloodlines' prime weapons of mass destruction, weather manipulation and control of both the Earth's atmosphere and the human mind.

Rothschild Zionism, Satanism and secret societies are all prime expressions of the global web based on Saturn worship – *Saturn*-ism.

The Saturn Control System is why human society is awash with Saturn symbolism.

Behind the scenes some of the world's most famous people regularly participate in satanic ritual which includes the sacrifice of babies and children. But the Truth Vibrations (the lion) are coming to change all that.

The time has come for humans to get off their knees in every sense.

We must face what is happening and deal with it. No more running away, no more 'tomorrow'.

We need to open our hearts to the non-compli-dance.

The Truth Vibrations and their expression across many dimensions of reality are wresting control of Saturn, the Moon and human perception from the Reptilians and their Control System.

The Truth Vibrations are 'reminding' humanity of 'where' they are and where they 'come' from.

The holographic nature of the Universe means that even on the level of Mind-Body we are a smaller version of the whole capable of affecting the whole. So let's *do it*.

Dance, dance, wherever you may be.

Vast numbers of people are now awakening from the Saturn-Moon trance and opening their minds to Consciousness, and we are being supported by multidimensional forces that are dismantling the Reptilian Control System from 'out there'. Our job is to play our part 'down here'.

Heart Consciousness has the power to break the spell.

As humanity awakens, the Control System must fall.

8

Cementing Forces

There are some particular interlocking networks that provide the coordination and 'cement' that hold the bloodline global web together. They include secret societies (worshippers of Saturn); Satanism (worshippers of Saturn); and Rothschild Zionism (worshippers of Saturn). Anyone see a pattern here? Paedophilia is another common and coordinating force.

I will focus on Rothschild Zionism in the next chapter and I will deal here with the networks – I guess rings would be better – of secret societies, Satanism and paedophilia which all interconnect. I am not saying that every Freemason is a Satanist, or every Satanist a Freemason, or every paedophile is a Freemason or a Satanist. But their networks do connect and interact, and very often there is an overlap of personnel. These groups, like Rothschild Zionism, pervade the whole web. They are the prime 'cement' (Fig 216). I have identified a large number of famous people in the bloodline structure who are Satanists, paedophiles and members of secret societies. The reason for their mutual association and the link to the Reptilian Alliance will become clear. I have written reams about secret societies and how they operate, their famous initiates and their covert manipulation. There are different categories of secret society. Those closest to the centre of the web (or top of the pyramid) are the most exclusive and secretive. Some of the most El-ite don't even have names and this makes them harder to track. I have mentioned some of the major ones: the Jesuits, Knights of Malta, Knights Templar, and Opus Dei, which are all connected to the Church of Saturn in Rome. Freemasonry can be found throughout global society from the local lodge in a little town to the upper echelons which connect with the spider at the centre of the bloodline web. All the major secret societies feed a chosen few into the inner sanctum of the Illuminati, which 98 per cent of their membership will not even know exists. Most Freemasons use the lodge to do business or make contacts and those controlling Freemasonry use those people to provide cover for what is really going on. Secret-society rituals plug in the initiate even more powerfully to

Figure 216: Got the set: A Freemasonic building with the symbols for Satanism; the Illuminati symbol of the rose; the Rothschild/Saturn six-pointed star; and the all-seeing eye

the Reptilian–Saturnian collective mind and to the entities that seek to possess them. Many go through personality changes because of this, as do politicians who are pulled into this trap in pursuit of contacts and power.

Secret societies are structured in the same way as the global conspiracy in general. Knowledge is strictly compartmentalised into levels of 'degree'. The vast majority of Freemasons are in the 'Blue Degrees', the bottom three levels, but the Scottish Rite of Freemasonry goes up to 33 degrees (and then the Illuminati levels for the very few). Initiates are given different explanations for everything as they progress, and only those in the upper levels of the Illuminati degrees get anywhere near the real truth. Tell the average Freemason that he's worshipping Saturn and the Reptilian Alliance and he would just laugh. But it doesn't matter if you know or not. If you focus upon images that symbolise Saturn and Reptilian entities then energetically you will be connected to them and open yourself to possession and/or have your life-force vampired. Most initiates of secret societies are being used by the conspiracy as much as the rest of the population. The infamous P-2, or 'Propaganda Due' Freemasonry lodge in Rome is an excellent example of how secret societies operate. P-2 came to world prominence in 1981 when it was exposed for covertly manipulating Italian society. It was run by the Mussolini fascist, Licio Gelli, who was a liaison officer in Hermann Goering's Nazi SS. Gelli was a friend of Father George Bush, Ronald Reagan and Argentine fascist, Juan Peron. Gelli was invited to the inauguration of Ronald Reagan in 1981 and spent the week with Father Bush. Reagan was a Knight of Malta, as was Gelli. Henry Kissinger was a friend of Licio Gelli and so was Michael Ledeen, a prominent neocon manipulator behind the Boy Bush administration and the invasions of Afghanistan and Iraq. See how they all connect across the world. Gelli was an asset of British and Russian Intelligence and worked closely with Kissinger, Edmond de Rothschild and David Rockefeller, who were prominent in P-2. Gelli was known to P-2 initiates as the 'Naja Hannah', or 'King Cobra'. P-2 was a 'covered lodge' (unknown even to mainstream Freemasonry), and when Italian police raided Gelli's home in 1981 they found incredible confirmation of how human society is covertly manipulated and directed. The documents revealed that P-2 was compartmentalised as pyramids within pyramids. This is the blueprint, the holographic global structure that operates the same way at every level. P-2 was divided into different groups, and the head of each one knew only who was in his own group. They had no idea who was in the other groups. Only Gelli and his fellow El-ite knew that. P-2 documents revealed lists of 953 members and they included influential people in politics, banking, business, police, Intelligence, media, military and judiciary. There were also religious leaders connected to Opus Dei. Knights Templar membership lists were also found in Gelli's possession and this was yet more confirmation that all the inner-circle secret societies are different names for the same entity. A former head of the Italian Secret Service, who joined P-2 in 1967, gave Gelli 150,000 sensitive dossiers on Italy's rich and famous. Perfect if you want to use blackmail to get your way. Another P-2 member was Silvio Berlusconi, the deeply corrupt three-times Italian Prime Minister and billionaire media tycoon. Many of them would have been dealing with each other while not knowing that they were all members of P-2. Mino Pecorelli, a former P-2 member, said that it was ultimately controlled by the CIA and the Knights of Malta. Pecorelli was soon dead. Pope John Paul I was murdered by poisoning after only 33 days in office in 1978 after he realised that P-2 was controlling influential people in the 'inner' Vatican. The number 33 is highly significant to these ritual-obsessed people. There are 33 official degrees of the Scottish Rite of Freemasonry. David Yallop exposed what happened in his excellent book, *In God's Name* (Corgi, new edition, 1987). The Pope, birth-name Albino Luciani, handed a list of the people that he wanted removed, with new names to replace them, to a very unhappy Vatican Secretary of State, Cardinal Jean Villot. The Pope told Villot to announce this the following day. David Yallop writes:

> There was one common denominator, one fact that linked each of the men about to be replaced. Villot was aware of it. More important, so was the Pope. It had been one of the factors that had caused him to act, to strip these men of real power ... it was Freemasonry.

> The evidence the Pope had acquired indicated that within the Vatican City State there were over one hundred Masons, ranging from cardinals to priests. Luciani was further preoccupied with an illegal Masonic lodge that had penetrated far beyond Italy in its search for wealth and power. It called itself P-2. The fact that it had penetrated the Vatican walls and formed links with priests, bishops, and even cardinals made P-2 anathema to Albino Luciani.

> That evening, September 28, 1978, thirty-three days after his election, Pope John Paul 1, 'the smiling Pope', was declared dead. No official death certificate has ever been issued. No autopsy ever performed. His body was hastily embalmed. Cause of death: Unknown. And Vatican business continues ... The facts are here in meticulous detail, documenting widespread corruption within the Vatican and presenting a compelling case that six powerful men, to protect their vast financial and political operations, decided on a shocking course of action – Pope John Paul I must die.

The P-2 story is the microcosm of the macrocosm and this is how the entire web and its constituent parts run the conspiracy. Their initiates make an oath to put the secret society and its goals above all else, and that is still the case as they go about their business in politics, banking, business, media, military, medicine and law. The latter includes judges who find people guilty or not guilty in accordance with bloodline commands. See my other books for secret societies exposed in great detail.

Hail Saturn

The human and animal sacrifice and blood-drinking rituals of Satanism are the worship of Saturn, the Moon and demonic entities connected, and not connected, to the Reptilian Alliance. Demands for human sacrifice by the reptilian 'gods' is a constant theme in ancient accounts and legends. Zulu shaman Credo Mutwa said that the Chitauri always demanded sacrifice, and that they were also the origin of cannibalism. He said Africans were terrified of them and would sacrifice their children to try to appease them. Credo said the Chitauri eat human babies, and this is another theme I have often heard around the world (Fig 217). He said the worship of Saturn also involved human sacrifice, and we can now begin to see why. The Chitauri and Saturn are, in effect, the same. Author and researcher Stewart Swerdlow experienced satanic rituals during his time imprisoned by the US authorities in the Montauk mind-control project on Long Island, New York. He also highlights the obsession with eating babies and foetuses. He said that Satanists gorge on foetuses collected from abortion clinics. 'They also had live babies that they held up by the back of the neck,' he said. 'Then, they slashed its throat from left to right, ear to ear, biting down on the gaping opening to drink the blood. This was an amazing delicacy to them.' Children are often bred for sacrifice and Satanists hold women in captivity known as 'breeders' who are constantly impregnated to produce foetuses or babies for sacrifice. These children are born secretly and so the public does not even know the babies have existed,

Figure 217: Satanic sacrifice rituals are constantly being performed in shocking numbers all over the world. The lion represents the Truth Vibrations

never mind what happened to them. The 'gods' of Satanism are the demons of legend, and by demons, or demonic, I mean entities so detached from Consciousness that they have descended into 'evil'– extreme levels of ignorance. Their mental and emotional state disconnects them from heart Consciousness and all they can do is to get the most that they can from Mind. Satanists today perform the same rituals that the ancients did. They often sign a contract with their demons in their own blood. Blood carries their vibration, and this vibrational contract locks them into the vibrational field of the entities even more powerfully. They are 'possessed'. They do this in return for fame or riches 'on Earth', but they are now so literally attached to evil that they no longer have control of their life or thoughts. Satanist film director, Roman Polański, who is on the run from American authorities for the sexual abuse of an underage girl, portrayed this theme in his 1968 movie, *Rosemary's Baby*, starring Mia Farrow. Her actor-husband in the film sold his soul to Satanists in return for top film roles and he agreed to allow his wife

to be impregnated under mind control to give birth to the hybrid child of a non-human entity. The child was reptilian. Roman Polanski was the husband of actress Sharon Tate, who was murdered while eight months pregnant in 1969 by members of the 'Manson Family', the cult of mind-controlled Satanist, Charles Manson. Satanism pervades the Illuminati web, but it is most focused in the 'upper' (cesspit) levels of society where the bloodlines and their agents predominate. Aleister Crowley, one of the most infamous and best-known Satanists of modern times, was connected to many household names in the satanic

Figure 218: Satanist Aleister Crowley – note again the pyramid and six-pointed sun – Saturn

Figure 219: David Dees' portrayal of Bohemian Grove

network (Fig 218). Satanic rituals are conducted among the 2,700 acres of redwood forest at a place called Bohemian Grove in Sonoma County, Northern California. The focal point is a 40-foot stone owl that represents, among other things, a deity called 'Moloch' to whom the ancients sacrificed children in fire. Bohemian Grove's 'summer camp' is attended by leading names in politics, banking, business, media and so on, and they include Boy and Father Bush, Bill Clinton, Henry Kissinger, members of the Rockefeller family and other deeply sick individuals who run America and the wider world (Fig 219). In May 2011, a Swiss banker, who would not be named for fear of the consequences, was interviewed by the Russian magazine, *NoviDen*. He revealed his own experience of the mentally and emotionally disturbed El-ite and their plans for humanity. He said:

... these people are corrupt, sick in their minds, so sick they are full of vices and those vices are kept under wraps on their orders. Some of them ... rape women, others are sado maso, or paedophile, and many are into Satanism. When you go in some banks you see these satanistic symbols, like in the Rothschild Bank in Zurich. These people are controlled by blackmail because of the weaknesses they have. They have to follow orders or they will be exposed, they will be destroyed or even killed.

These are the people who run our world. Would they have a problem with engineering 9/11 or killing millions of civilians by bombing defenceless cities from the sky? *Problem?* They love it. Stanley Kubrick, the great film director who staged the version of the 1969 Moon landings seen by the public, sought to expose Satanists of the El-ite in his final movie, *Eyes Wide Shut*, released in 1999. It starred Tom Cruise and Nicole Kidman, and the theme was Satanism among those in power and their use of mind control to force people to do what they want. If you read some of my other books of the last ten years you will see in considerable detail the extent of the global mind-control programme. The most memorable scene in *Eyes Wide Shut* was the satanic ritual in a mansion where the rich and famous were wearing robes and masks and being directed by the conductor of the ritual. He was wearing red, but the main body of them all wore black – Saturn. Masks are not only used for anonymity; they are symbolic of the mask they wear to hide the identity of who they and their masters really are. It was only recently that I learned from Kubrick expert, Jay Weidner, that the ritual scene was shot in a Rothschild mansion. Kubrick was attempting to show people what was going on, but he never lived to see it released. Part of the deal to stage the Moon landings was that his films could never be censored, and this was a problem for executives at Warner Bros. when they saw the final cut. They were furious and demanded that some 25 minutes be taken out. Kubrick refused, and he could do that because of his 'Moon' contract. Kubrick was dead four days later from a 'heart attack', and the cuts were then made. When you see what is in the film it makes you wonder what must have been in the scenes that were censored. *Eyes Wide Shut* was released on the day that Kubrick had insisted was written into his contract. It was the 30th anniversary of the first moon landing. The film came and went with hardly any promotion even though it was the final work of such an acclaimed director. David Berkowitz was the 'Son of Sam' serial killer in New York in the 1970s. He admitted that he was the killer, but told a church minister in a series of letters that he had been part of a group of Satanists that had orchestrated the attacks. He told the minister about the type of people that were involved in these grotesque rituals, including human sacrifice:

> ... Satanists are peculiar people. They aren't ignorant peasants or semi-literate natives. Rather, their ranks are filled with doctors, lawyers, businessmen, and basically highly responsible citizens ... they are not a careless group who are apt to make mistakes. But they are secretive and bonded together by a common need and desire to mete out havoc on society. It was Aleister Crowley who said: 'I want blasphemy, murder, rape, revolution, anything bad.'

This produces the energy that they and their masters crave. I have spoken with many former Satanists over the years, as well as those who have taken part in the rituals against their will. They have given me a great deal of detailed background to what it is all about. The rituals manipulate energy; they provide sustenance for the hidden 'gods'; and they can provide an energetic environment in which the demonic entities can manifest. The central satanic symbol of the reversed pentagram within a circle is apparently very important for this (Fig 220). Once more we come back to the fact that we experience the holographic level of the Universe, but the base construct is vibrational information. We see a 'physical' pentagram and circle, but at the waveform level this is a particular kind of energy field – an energetic 'stepping stone', so I am told, that allows entities to slip through into this reality. But these Reptilian 'demons' cannot leave the pentagram energy field. Satanists know these Reptilians as the 'Old Ones' and they are terrified of them. Stewart Swerdlow says that a ceremonial invocation is chanted at the rituals to contact the demons in other realities, and he writes that he has heard this done in Latin, Hebrew, Ancient Egyptian, Sumerian, German, English and a 'guttural, hissing' language which he was told is the original Draco (Reptilian) language. Satanists in human form drink the blood of the victim, and the hidden 'gods' absorb the energy of the terror that is generated. This is the origin of the term 'sacrifice to the gods'. The victim is so terrified at the point of sacrifice that a specific type of adrenaline enters the bloodstream, and this like a drug to these desperate people. It gives them a 'high'. They also want hormonal secretions from the pituitary and

Figure 220: The prime satanic symbol of the inverted pentagram inside a circle

pineal glands (third eye) that enter the blood when people are in a state of terror, according to others who have witnessed the rituals. I am told that this is 'like heroin or endorphins' to them. Endorphins are produced by the pituitary gland and the hypothalamus during emotional states such as excitement, pain and orgasm, and 'resemble opiates in their abilities to produce analgesia and a feeling of well-being'. I understand that the Reptilian hybrids are having to drink more and more blood to keep their human DNA codes open and stop them manifesting as reptilian. This is because of the impact upon them of the Truth Vibrations. When the point of sacrifice nears, a Reptilian hybrid stares into the eyes of the victim and holds them, as one witness put it, 'in a trance of terror'. This is the origin of the term 'the evil eye'. Stewart Swerdlow describes how the sacrifice is terrorised before 'a final thrust of a blade disembowels them' and the Satanists are covered in 'rivers of blood'. The sacrificial body is ripped apart and the internal organs and genitalia are consumed. Swerdlow says they are in such frenzy by now that many shapeshift into Reptilians and even attack each other mindlessly. I have heard exactly the same from others who have taken part. The Satanists shapeshift when the frenzy generates such an energetic charge that the hybrid DNA codes shift and project a reptilian form. The Wesley Snipes film, *Blade*, released in 1998, portrays scenes like those described here; and Bram Stoker's famous stories about Dracula are based on the same theme. Stories and legends about vampires can be found in every part of the world, and Dracula encapsulates them. His name is Dracula (*Draco-ula* – the 'Draco' is a name for the El-ite Reptilians); he is called 'Count' Dracula (symbolic of how the bloodlines are royalty and the aristocracy); and Dracula 'shapeshifts' and drinks human blood. Stoker's character was inspired by the character known as Vlad the Impaler, who ruled a country called Wallachia in what is now Romania in the 15th century. This region was once Transylvania, which is very much associated with vampire legends. Vlad the Impaler was initiated into the ancient Order of the Dragon by the Holy Roman Emperor in 1431, with its emblem of a dragon, wings extended, hanging on a cross. This goes back at least to ancient Egypt, but probably much further in this or other forms. Vlad signed his name Draculea, or Draculya – 'Devil's Son'. This later became Dracula, a name that translates as something like 'Son of Him Who Had the Order of the Dragon'. Queen Mary, or Mary of Teck, the mother of King George VI and grandmother to the present Elizabeth II, was descended from a sister of Vlad the Impaler – 'Dracula' – and so is the Bush family. In the summer of 2011, research was reported by the mainstream media that revealed how the British royal family have consumed human flesh as recently as the end of the 18th century. Oh, I think it is probably just a *touch* more recently than that. More like a week last Tuesday. One newspaper report said: 'Even as they denounced the barbaric cannibals of the New World, they applied, drank, or wore powdered Egyptian mummy, human fat, flesh, bone, blood, brains and skin.' It was only for medicinal purposes, though, so that's okay, then. The source was a book by Dr Richard Sugg from England's Durham University entitled *Mummies, Cannibals and Vampires* (Routledge, 2011). Dr Sugg was quoted as saying:

> Cannibalism was found not only in the New World, as often believed, but also in Europe. One thing we are rarely taught at school yet is evidenced in literary and historic texts of the time is this: James I refused corpse medicine; Charles II made his own corpse medicine; and Charles I

was made into corpse medicine. Along with Charles II, eminent users or prescribers included Francis I, Elizabeth I's surgeon John Banister, Elizabeth Grey, Countess of Kent, Robert Boyle, Thomas Willis, William III and Queen Mary.

Rather more than 'medicinal purposes' was going on behind the scenes, though, just as it is now. If you get a royal invitation to Balmoral Castle in the summer, I'd give it a miss. Cannibalism was found everywhere, because the Reptilian devourers of human flesh introduced it everywhere.

Chateau Rothschild (it's a red)

I communicated in detail with a man at one point who said that his real name was Phillip Eugene de Rothschild. He was living under another name in the United States at the time. He told me that he was the unofficial offspring of the late Baron Philippe de Rothschild of the Mouton–Rothschild wine estates in France and that his half-sister is the Baron's daughter, Baroness Philippine de Rothschild. The Baroness inherited the wine empire after her father died in 1988 at the age of 86, and she appears to be fond of wearing Baphomet-type (Saturn) necklaces (Fig 221). Phillip Eugene told me what I have heard from many other sources. The Rothschilds have hundreds of thousands of

unofficial offspring and most are produced in sperm-bank breeding programmes to ensure the genetic (vibrational/software code) 'purity'. Only a few are given the name 'Rothschild'. The rest are brought up by other families under other names and so when they come to prominence in politics, banking, business and the media, the public doesn't know that they are really all Rothschilds, or the Rothschild bloodline. We are given the official life stories of people such as Barack Obama (clearly a pack of lies), Tony Blair, David Cameron, Nicolas Sarkozy and Benjamin Netanyahu; but is there another story to be told? Phillip Eugene told me that he had been trained to infiltrate the Christian Church by posing as a 'perfect Christian', but he later rebelled and started a new life. He said that he lived with his Rothschild father for most of his childhood and adolescence on his estate in France. They had a physical relationship and he was 'held fast in the emotional power of incest, which, in this culture, was normal and to be admired'. I knew this, too, from endless other sources

Figure 221: Baroness Philippine de Rothschild – and friend.

and throughout their history the bloodlines have had incest as the centre of their relationships with their children. Incest, cannibalism and human sacrifice were all introduced by the Reptilians. Having sex with your own children is part of the bloodlines' way of life and, as Phillip Eugene says, it creates an emotional control of father over son. El-ite families like the Rockefellers and Bushes will be just the same. They're probably Rothschild bloodline, anyway, like most, if not all, remaining royalty. Prince William is only one example. William's mother, Princess Diana, was induced so that he would be born on the summer solstice. She was told that this was being done to make the birth fit with Prince Charles's polo-playing programme, but it was nothing to do with that. It was simply more ritual. The bloodlines have big plans for William. Phillip Eugene confirmed that the Rothschilds and the bloodlines are possessed and controlled by demonic entities. 'Being a Rothschild descendant, I was maximally demonised.' Phillip Eugene was yet another source (there have been *soooo* many) that connected the British royal family and other royal families of Europe to Satanism and the 'Nefilim bloodline', as he called it. The Rothschild and bloodline Satanists are everywhere in positions of influence and power. Phillip Eugene told me:

I was present at my father's death in 1988, receiving his power and the commission to carry out my destiny in the grand conspiracy of my family. Like their other children, I played a key role in my family's revolt from God. When I watch CNN, it startles me to see so many familiar faces now on the world stage in politics, art, finance, fashion and business. I grew up with these people, meeting them at ritual worship sites and in the centers of power. Financiers, artists, royalty, and even Presidents ...

... I can recall the Rockefellers and the Bushes attending rituals, but never having the supremacy to lead them. I still regard them as lackeys and not real brokers of occult power. Except for Alan Greenspan [long-time head of the US Federal Reserve Bank], most of these fellows were camp followers in the occult, primarily for the economic power and prestige. Greenspan, I recall, was a person of tremendous spiritual, occult power and could make the Bushes and the younger Rockefellers cower with just a glance. Ex-CIA Director Casey (as were most of the CIA leadership for the past forty years), Kissinger and [former US Secretary of State] Warren Christopher were in attendance at non-ritual gatherings and some occult rituals as well, but well back in the gallery.

I have heard the same names, and others of global fame, from many sources who have attended the rituals. Readers of my other books, including *The Biggest Secret*, will know the story of Arizona Wilder, the American woman who talked to me at length about how she was bred for the US government mind-control programme with the specific aim of having her conduct rituals for the hybrids. Reptilians and their hybrid 'offspring' are extremely limited in how far 'out there' they can go. Therefore, they breed humans with powerful 'third-eye' psychic abilities to go 'out there' for them. Arizona said that she was programmed using many forms of torture by Josef Mengele, often at the China Lake Naval Weapons Center in California. She gave me a long list of names that she had seen shapeshift at rituals she was taken to by shapeshifter Mengele. These included the Queen; Queen Mother (whom Princess Diana described as 'evil'); Prince Philip; Prince Charles; Princess Margaret; Father George Bush; his sons, Boy

Figure 222: Baron Guy de Rothschild – such lovely eyes

George and Jeb Bush; Jay Rockefeller; Presidents Gerald Ford and Lyndon Johnson (who was implicated in the assassination of JFK which allowed him to become president); former US Secretary of State, Madeleine Albright; and Illuminati gofer, Tony Blair (anyone surprised?). Arizona said she saw many Rothschilds shapeshift at the rituals, including the late Baron Guy de Rothschild who operated secretly under the name 'Dr Barrington' (Fig 222). She said she also saw former French President Georges Pompidou shapeshift at the rituals – he worked for Guy de Rothschild and did the Rothschilds' bidding as President of France. How interesting that those people that I mentioned earlier who lived, or are living, to great ages, are named by Arizona and others as Reptilian shapeshifters or attendees of rituals – the Queen Mother (102); the Queen (85 at the time of writing); the Duke of Edinburgh (90, ditto); Father George Bush (87, ditto); Henry Kissinger (88, ditto); and David Rockefeller (96, ditto). It must be something in the blood – or someone else's. Others that Arizona saw at the rituals, but did not see shapeshift (it doesn't mean they don't) included Henry Kissinger, Ronald Reagan and his wife, Nancy, and Hillary Clinton. Arizona also said that the author, Zecharia Sitchin, attended the rituals and shapeshifted. Sitchin wrote extensively about the 'Anunnaki' in ways that were often misleading. I talked to him once about the Reptilians and he became very angry. He leaned forward across the table and said: 'The Reptilians? *Don't go there.*' As you see, I have followed his every word. He talked about the Anunnaki coming and going on a 12th planet called 'Nibiru' which he said has a 3,600 year elliptical orbit and, by Sitchin's calculations, is due to return pretty soon. Firstly, the Anunnaki have never gone away and, secondly, I have no doubt that we are going to see strange events in the heavens, even major ones, and the Earth could be significantly affected by these events; but whatever comes or doesn't come it will not be 'Nibiru', or 'Planet X' in the way that Sitchin described. Arizona Wilder said that Sitchin's job was to disinform and hide the existence of the Reptilians from those who were interested or researching in areas that could lead them to humanity's true controllers. Collectively, she said, they were all 'cold blooded and they would kill at the drop of a hat'. They love killing and that's why they do so much of it. You will find a video on my website: Davidicke.com called *'Confessions of a Mother Goddess'*. This is a more than two-hour interview with Arizona in the late 1990s. I have lost touch with her in recent years and if you are out there, Arizona, please let me know you are okay.

Another American woman, Cathy O'Brien, told me how she saw George Bush and others shapeshift into reptilian form. Cathy was given by her Satanist father to the vast American military/Intelligence mind-control programme that involves the unspeakable abuse of children to shatter their minds and allow a new one to be created. She was in a 'special' part of MKUltra known as the Monarch Programme, named after the butterfly, and was she raped under mind control by presidents Ronald Reagan and Gerald Ford, among so many others that talk about American 'values'. It was 'shapeshifter' Gerald Ford, then a Congressman for Michigan (where Cathy was brought up) who arranged for her 'handover' by her father, Earl M O'Brien. Ford later became President of the United States, just like 'shapeshifter' Father George Bush. Cathy co-wrote a book with partner, Mark Phillips, exposing what happened to her, called *Trance-Formation of America* (Reality Marketing, USA, 1995). This is still available. She tells in the book how she saw Father George Bush shapeshift into the reptilian entity, but she thought this was part of her mind control programming. What she describes, however, is a mirror of what so many others, including Arizona Wilder, describe. Cathy said that Bush was sitting in front of her in his office in Washington D.C. when he opened a book at a page depicting 'lizard-like aliens from a far-off, deep space place'. She said that Bush claimed that he was one of them and as he did so he transformed 'like a chameleon' into a reptile. I have been told by hundreds of people from every walk of life you can imagine about their experiences of seeing well known and less well known people transform into a reptilian form before their eyes and then go back again. Father George Bush is a name that recurs often in these accounts. Cathy relates an experience she had with Miguel de la Madrid, the President of Mexico during Father Bush's tenure at the White House. She writes in *Trance-Formation of America*:

De la Madrid had relayed the 'legend of the Iguana' to me, explaining that lizard-like aliens had descended upon the Mayans. The Mayan pyramids, their advanced astronomical technology, including sacrifice of virgins, was supposedly inspired by the lizard aliens. He told me that when the aliens interbred with the Mayans to produce a form of life they could inhabit, they fluctuated between a human and Iguana appearance through chameleon-like abilities – 'a perfect vehicle for transforming into world leaders'. De la Madrid claimed to have Mayan/alien ancestry in his blood, whereby he transformed 'back into an Iguana at will'.

This is exactly the same story told in Central America that you find in Africa, Asia and around the world. Phillip Eugene de Rothschild said that some of the most significant people in the global power hierarchy are not publicly known. They stay deep in the shadows hiding their true selves behind apparently 'ordinary lives'. I have heard this many times as well. One of the highest level 'personnel' within the global Reptilian hybrid network has the code name, 'Pindar', and he operates out of Alsace-Lorraine in France. I wrote at some length about him in *The Biggest Secret*. It is no accident whatsoever that London's main underground bunker and 'crisis management centre' beneath the Ministry of Defence in London that connects to Downing Street and other government buildings is called Pindar; nor that the government's crisis committee is called 'Cobra'. Satanic rituals also manipulate and vibrationally suppress the Earth's energy field. The Reptilian Alliance and the hybrid bloodlines want to maintain humanity in ignorance and in Mind. How do you affect all the fish at the same time?

You affect the sea. The Earth's energy field is our 'sea', and Satanism is one way that this is manipulated and filled with thought-forms of low-vibrational resonance that impact upon the human population interacting with the 'sea'. There is something about blood being spilled (blood is the holographic version of 'chi' in the meridian system) that has a powerful effect on the energy field. This power is also a reason why so many of these famous blood- drinkers live for so long. I included an appendix in *Human Race Get Off Your Knees* which is a document allegedly written by a dying Satanist in Australia in 2004. He claimed to be attached to the 'Alpha Lodge' in Sydney. This was not a deathbed 'confession' so much, because he agreed with what is happening. It is more of an explanation of how powerfully Satanism controls world events. Although I can't prove that it is genuine, I *can* confirm after more than two decades of research that whoever was the source had a detailed knowledge of the subject. He described how rituals impregnated Earth's energy fields with satanic – *Saturn*-ic – information: 'What most people do not realise is that Satanism is a ritually-based practice and that this repetition has, over time, left strong impressions upon the Morphic Field.' Religious and royal ritual is doing the same in its own way. The 'Black Mass' of Saturnic Satanism is only the full-blown version of the Mass, Eucharist or Holy Communion that you see in the Catholic Church. The drinking of the 'blood of Jesus' as red wine (Chateau Rothschild is a good one) and eating his 'flesh' as bread, are only publicly acceptable versions of drinking and eating the real thing.

The bloodline-controlled entertainment industry is bombarding people, especially the young, with satanic imagery and themes in the music itself, stage performances and videos. You can see movies and music videos of artists such as Lady Gaga, Jay-Z and his wife Beyoncé, decoded with the occult meaning at: www.vigilantcitizen.com. Music is heavily encoded at the production stage with subliminal messages, and so are films and television. This is often done through 'reverse speech' in messages encoded backwards or lyrics that sound very different when played backwards. The conscious mind decodes speech in a forward sequence, but the subconscious decodes the speech vibration in both directions. The word 'live' backwards, for example, is 'evil' and 'love' backwards is 'evol'. It is the sound that matters – the vibration – not so much the spelling.

The London–Rome Beltane Ritual

At the end of April 2011, I flew from London to Rome for a speaking event. I was particularly pleased to be leaving Britain just before the 'Royal Wedding' of Prince William and Kate Middleton on my birthday, April 29th. The sight of people salivating over the Royal Family is not something my stomach cares to take. If only they knew. I arrived in Rome to something pretty much the same – the 'beatification' of the departed John Paul II, the guy that replaced the murdered Pope of the same name who wanted to purge the Vatican of Freemasons. Millions of Roman Catholics were in Rome for the ritual conducted by Pope Benedict, the chap with the beautiful eyes (Fig 223). This was another of those endless 'coincidences' that have led me to information since 1990. I had no idea about any beatification when I agreed to speak in Rome on April 30th, 2011. This was only a day which synchronised with other European events that I was doing in the same period. But here I was speaking in one of the great cities of the Illuminati on the day between the Royal Wedding and the beatification. Pope Benedict made an

Figure 223: Pope Benedict: the eyes have it

official visit to Barcelona, Spain, with millions on the streets, on the same weekend that I presented an all-day event in the city. I didn't plan that, either. I could see on the day that I arrived in Rome the connection between the Royal Wedding in London and the beatification in Rome over what was the period of Beltane – one of the most important 'festivals' in the satanic calendar. The Royal Wedding and the beatification were two ends of the same mass Beltane ritual in two of the most significant bloodline and satanic cities on Earth – London and Rome. I bet they were partying on Saturn and the Moon that weekend. The key date of Beltane is May 1st – May Day – which is why so many celebrations and parades happen at that time, including the May Day parades in the Communist world. This was when the people of the Soviet Union were called to the streets in their millions to watch missiles and tanks being paraded before them. It is all occult ritual. Remember how the communist hammer and sickle is the symbol of Saturn? But, energetically, Beltane is not just May Day. It builds through April 29th and into April 30th for the culmination on May 1st. Romans celebrated Beltane in the form of Floralia, the Festival of the Flowers, in honour of the Roman goddess, Flora, and this ran from April 29th through to May 1st. Here we had the Royal Wedding in London on April 29th and the beatification of Pope John Paul II in Rome on May 1st. The two rituals were at different ends of the Beltane energetic period in two cities so ritually crucial to the satanic hierarchy running the Illuminati agenda. Coincidence? Not a chance. I don't want to demonise Beltane entirely, or those genuine people who take part in their own Beltane rituals to celebrate the coming of new life through the spring and summer months. Good luck to them. This is not what I am talking about. Beltane is the period associated with the May Pole, fires, fertility and flowers and has been celebrated in different ways and under different names all over the world for thousands of years. But this is also the period, along with Halloween across October 31st and November 1st (the dates are reversed in the Southern Hemisphere), when Satanists all over the world conduct some of their most important blood and sacrifice rituals. Note how Halloween has been promoted in recent times more than ever before with the emphasis on children. While children dressed as ghosts and witches are knocking on doors and 'trick or treating', others children are being sacrificed around the world in numbers that beggar belief. The promotion of Halloween is to desensitise people to the true horrors of the satanic occult (occultus – clandestine, hidden, secret).

The date of the Royal Wedding was selected as April 29th to start the Beltane ritual (the couple themselves probably had no idea, or maybe he does by now). All they needed was an event in Rome on May 1st. *Ahhh*, I know. Let's beatify the last Pope. Nice one. The official story of why Pope John Paul II was beatified is utterly bloody laughable. Vatican policy decrees that for someone to be beatified, an unexplained

healing or other miracle has to be
attributed to them after their death. You
need two miracles to be a 'Saint' and join
a long line of mass killers and genetic liars
who have gone before you. The greatest
miracle for me is that anyone is a Roman
Catholic, but I digress. Lo and behold, for
'He' has spoken, a miracle for Pope John
Paul II miraculously appeared. A French
nun claimed that she had been cured of a
brain disorder after praying to Pope John
Paul II following his death in 2005. Quite

Figure 224: The Freemasonic floor and blood-red carpet of the Freemasonic temple called Westminster Abbey

what he has against all the other nuns with health problems is not yet clear. Pope
Benedict, John Paul's minder and handler before getting the job himself, agreed with the
Vatican 'medical experts and theologians' that the nun was indeed miraculously cured
by the departed John Paul and a date was fixed to beatify the chap – May 1st , 2011. This
was also the day when, over in America, Obama was announcing the second death of
Osama bin Laden. Two days before the beatification gig in Rome, the Royals headed for
the Freemasonic temple called Westminster Abbey with its twin towers and black-and-
white secret-society 'Saturn' floor (Fig 224). The red carpet (symbolic of blood) was
rolled out to meet the feet of the arriving royal satanic Addams Family, headed by the
Queen herself. Twin towers are Freemasonic representations of the twin pillars of
Joachim and Boaz that were said to stand at the entrance to King Solomon's Temple.
Every syllable of Sol-Om- On means 'sun', and we can now see that it refers to the 'Old
Sun' and 'Black Sun' – Saturn. St Paul's Cathedral has twin pillars or towers for the
same reason and so does the 'Mother Lodge' of Freemasonry in London (Fig 225). Was it
just a coincidence that twin towers were involved on 9/11?? Prince William, a
Rothschild bloodline, and his bride, Kate Middleton, arrived to heaving crowds. Kate
must be bloodline otherwise they would not have let her near the place. I feel sorry for

Figure 225: The twin towers/pillars of the mythical Solomon's Temple, Westminster Abbey and the 'Mother Lodge' of Freemasonry in Great Queen (Semiramis/Ishtar) Street in London. You find the same twin towers theme in many cathedrals including St Paul's Cathedral and Notre Dame ('Our Lady', the goddess) in Paris

Figure 226: Not on a dark night, thank you

Figure 227: The blatant satanic symbol of the inverted pentagram worn by leading 'Christian' clergy

her entering the lair of this dark and despicable family. I hope she is okay, but who knows what Mr and Mrs Baphomet and their cronies and masters have in mind (Fig 226). They say the British establishment is the best in the world for organising 'pomp and pageantry'. No, it is, like the authorities in Rome, the best at organising satanic ritual disguised as a national or religious event. When the shapeshifting Queen and Prince Phillip arrived they were met by senior clergy of the 'Christian' Church, and you can see what one of them was wearing in Figure 227. Talk about *in your face* – the prime satanic symbol of the inverted pentagram within a circle. Saturn, the Dark Sun, within a ring. I checked the original BBC footage when I first saw the picture, because it was so blatant. I expected it to be a Photoshop joke – but it wasn't.

Human batteries

Satanism is about the manipulation of energy; and the rituals need a power source. The human sacrifice is the power source in the rituals I have been describing, and the power source at public rituals are the crowds that assemble in their hundreds of thousands, sometimes millions, to pay homage to the Satanists and their lackeys paraded before them. The Royal Family was the focus of homage in London on April 29th, 2011; and two days later in Rome it was the present Pope and the departed one (Fig 228). We talk about a 'wonderful atmosphere' or 'intense atmosphere' or whatever, and this 'atmosphere' is the electromagnetic energy generated by a mass of electromagnetic fields gathered together called people. You might have heard the saying 'energy flows where attention goes', and so it does. Homage and worship are even more intense versions of attention. The British Royal Family, and the Pope and Vatican control-structure, are servants and symbols (proxies) for the Reptilian and other demonic entities feeding off human energy. By getting the crowds to focus on these symbols and proxies, an energetic connection is established that allows the entities to trawl their energy. The Beltane rituals in London and Rome were specifically set up to vampire the energy of the millions who gathered at both events. The hidden powers vampired the crowds in London paying homage to the London branch of the Reptilian global hierarchy, and they did the same in Rome as worshippers gathered in their millions in the city and especially around the original ancient Egyptian obelisk in St Peter's Square, taken from Heliopolis – the 'City of the Sun' (Saturn?). The official head of the Satanic Church of Babylon conducted the ritual in Rome wearing his fish-god hat, and the Archbishop of Canterbury did the same in London (Fig 229). *It is all ritual.* While the crowds cheered, the global cabal that the royals represent was slaughtering the innocent in places like Libya and imposing sweeping austerity programmes on the very people who were waving their flags (Fig 230). I shot a 90-minute 'ad- lib' film about the Beltane ritual while I was in Rome, which you can see on my website. Remember if you watch the film that when I am talking

Figure 228: The London–Rome Beltane ritual 2011

about the sun I am really referring to Saturn. This was the penny that won me the jackpot and everything else fell into place. The information has been presented to me in the usual coordinated way – first the Moon, then on to Saturn, and what next?

Religions were established to put people into a mind-prison in which only their 'holy book' has the truth, and any other explanation for life must, by definition, be wrong. The religion of scientism has its own 'holy book' called the 'scientific norms', and they have the same effect. Religions are also designed to con the con-gregations into giving their power away to a 'god' or deity that represents Saturn, the Moon and the Reptilian Alliance.

Religious deities are also symbols and proxies, and make the same vibrational connection between the worshippers and the 'gods'. The worshippers focus attention on the proxy and

Figure 229: The fish god Pope in Rome and the fish god Archbishop of Canterbury in London

Figure 230: Diversion, diversion, diversion

Figure 231: Worship is a very powerful focus of attention, and energy flows where attention goes

the 'gods' in all their forms say *'gotcha'*. Energy flows where *attention* goes. A most obvious example is the vast crowds of Muslims who make the pilgrimage to Mecca at the demand of their 'holy book'. They create a colossal collective electromagnetic field as they circle the symbol of Saturn – the Kaaba cube. They even kneel down to pray in the concentric circles of Saturn. Muslims across the planet are told to get on their knees (concede their power – 'Islam' means 'submit to God') five times a day and pray while facing 'Mecca' – more precisely, the Kaaba cube symbol for Saturn in Mecca. Their energy is then vampired by other-dimensional entities that Islam refers to as 'the Jinn'. The same is happening in all religions and billions who think they are following different religions, and argue, even go to war, over those perceived differences, are all worshipping the *same* 'god' ('gods) and having their life-force vampired by the same gang (Fig 231). This is happening in the secret societies when initiates are told to 'give themselves' (submit) in service to the deity. You make an energetic connection when you do that and your energy can be absorbed and your thoughts and emotions manipulated. John A Keel says in his book, *Our Haunted Planet* (Galde Press, 1999), that the serpent race chose religion as the 'battleground' on which to conquer the human mind:

... The para-human Serpent People of the past are still among us. They were probably worshipped by the builders of Stonehenge and the forgotten ridge-making cultures of South America ... In some parts of the world the Serpent People successfully posed as gods and imitated the techniques of the super-intelligence. This led to the formation of pagan religions centered on human sacrifices. The conflict, so far as man himself was concerned, became one of religions and races. Whole civilizations based upon the worship of these false gods rose and fell in Asia, Africa and South America.

... Once an individual had committed himself, he opened a door so that an indefinable something (probably an undetectable mass of intelligent energy) could actually enter his body and exercise some control over his subconscious mind ... The human race would supply the pawns ... Each individual had to consciously commit himself to one of the opposing forces ... The main battle was for what was to become known as the human soul. By choosing to give yourself to a deity or 'god', you open so that an indefinable something could actually enter his body and exercise some control over his subconscious mind.

This is what is happening in satanic rituals, churches and secret-society temples across the world all the time.

Suffer Little Children

I have said that the networks of Satanism and secret societies are connected to the global paedophile rings, and there is a reason for this: the energy of children. The Reptilians ideally want to vampire the energy of children before they reach puberty. We see puberty as a time of hormonal changes in the body that start the process of the child becoming an adult; but those hormonal effects are the result of *vibrational* changes in the waveform information fields. The energy that the Reptilians want more than anything is the energy of children before that change happens. The ancient theme of sacrificing 'young virgins' to the gods is code for *children*. Don Juan Matus, the shaman source for the Carlos Castaneda books, highlighted this. Castaneda wrote:

> ... He explained that sorcerers saw infant human beings as strange luminous balls of energy, covered from the top to the bottom with a glowing coat, something like a coat of plastic adjusted tightly around the cocoon of energy. He said that glowing coat of awareness was what the predators consumed and that when a human reached adulthood, all that was left of that fringe awareness was a narrow fringe that went from the ground to the top of the toes. That fringe permitted mankind to keep on living, but only barely.

This energy is vampired in many different ways, and among them is paedophilia, which, like human sacrifice and cannibalism, has been going on since the Reptilian takeover. There are paintings of naked children all over the Vatican, and I was aghast when I walked around the National Portrait Gallery in London's Trafalgar Square while I was waiting to speak at a rally against child abuse. I was seeing the work of world famous artists and there were paintings of naked children everywhere (Fig 232). The Roman Catholic Church has been exposed all over the world for decades now as a cesspit of child abuse, and why wouldn't that be the case when it represents an ancient unbroken stream of belief and ritual that involves human sacrifice and child abuse? The Roman Church is continuing to do what it has always done under endless different names (Fig 233). While the paedophile is having sex with the child, the possessing entity is using the paedophile as a conduit, a bridge, to vampire the child's energy (Fig 234). The scale on which this happens worldwide is staggering and many of the 'hotspots' are, of course, centres for the El-ite like Britain and Europe, North America and Australia; but it is widespread in Africa, Asia, China and the Far East, and throughout the world. Another 'hot spot' is the 'royal families' of Arabia. Credo Mutwa has told me many times about the shocking number of children that go missing in Southern Africa alone every year, and Chinese networks are apparently seriously involved in what

Figure 232: Naked children can be found in pictures around the Vatican City and in many paintings by famous artists

happens to them. Belgium is a major global centre for child abuse and sacrifice, because Brussels is the headquarters of both the European Union and NATO. This creates an insatiable demand for children in that country. One line of inquiry in the abduction of Madeleine McCann, the three-year-old British girl abducted while on holiday in Portugal in 2007, was that a paedophile ring in Belgium had made an 'order' for a young girl three days before she went missing. This was based on information that someone had taken a photograph of Madeleine and sent it to Belgium. The 'purchaser' agreed that she was 'suitable', and soon after she was never seen again. Children are stolen to order and the blond- haired and blue-eyed attract the highest price. The horrific Marc Dutroux case in Belgium in the 1990s was connected to famous Satanists and paedophiles. He kidnapped, tortured and sexually abused six girls aged between eight and nineteen. He murdered four of them. Police made a series of 'errors' in their investigation of the girls' disappearance that stopped Dutroux being apprehended before the murders. Judge Jean-Marc Connerotte took charge of the investigation after

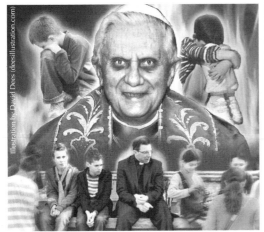

Figure 233: The Roman Church is a cesspit of paedophilia around the world

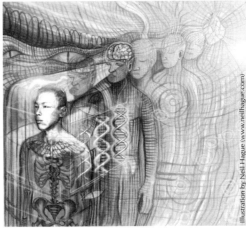

Figure 234: Paedophiles are possessed by entities that use them as a bridge to vampire the energy of children

Dutroux was arrested. Connerotte was a decent man and sought tenaciously to uncover what really happened. He began to make connections from Dutroux to the El-ite of Belgium, where, as in Britain, the German 'royal' house of Saxe–Coburg–Gotha is on the throne. This German bloodline 'house' in all its expressions has just got to be covertly Rothschild. Judge Connerotte was getting far too close to the truth and he was sacked from the case by the very El-ite who stood to be exposed. 300,000 people took to the streets of Brussels in protest. The 'investigators' that replaced him were obviously not going to pursue the truth, and they didn't. An 'investigation' by a Belgian parliamentary commission decided that Dutroux was not connected to rich and famous figures in Belgium, as he claimed, including leading police chiefs and judges. It was nonsense, of course. Dutroux supplied children to these people for sex and sacrifice.

Judge Connerotte's experience was repeated on the El-ite stronghold of Jersey in the Channel Islands when a detective genuinely went in search of the truth after ankle shackles, stocks and canes were found at the former children's home called Haut de la Garenne. A thousand vulnerable children lived there over the years. The detective was taken off the case and subjected to abuse and ridicule for committing the crime of doing a proper investigation. Children's homes are a prime supplier of children to the paedophile and satanic rings. In 2011, WikiLeaks published U S Embassy cables which revealed that children who had gone missing from Irish state children's homes had been found working as sex slaves in brothels. The cables said that the Irish authorities were not even keeping statistics on the numbers. Child-kidnapping, murder and slavery is happening on a breathtaking scale and you can now see why. Thomas Hamilton, a paedophile and Freemason, shot dead 16 children and a teacher at the Dunblane primary school in Scotland in 1996 before shooting himself. This case had the familiar police 'mistakes' that allowed Hamilton to remain at large despite his well-known paedophilic activities, and to own firearms when he should not have qualified to do so. More than 100 documents relating to the case were ordered to be locked away for 100 years by the head of the 'inquiry', Lord Cullen. Neil Mackay, a proper journalist on the Scottish *Sunday Herald*, reported that the documents banned from public view included a letter sent by politician George Robertson to Michael Forsyth, the then Secretary of State for Scotland. Robertson would later be British Defence Secretary and Secretary General of NATO. Cullen said that the documents were locked away to protect children, but *The Sunday Herald* discovered that only a handful related to children or named alleged abuse victims. Paedophile and satanic rings operate within Freemasonry as a secret society within a secret society. Even some High Freemasons don't know what is going on. Lord Burton, a former Scottish Freemasonic Grand Master, stated publicly that the official 'inquiry' into the Dunblane massacre, conducted by the Scot, Lord Cullen, was a cover-up. Lord Burton told the media that Cullen's inquiry suppressed crucial information to protect high-profile legal figures that belonged to a 'Super Mason' group called the 'Speculative Society'. He said:

> I have learned of an apparent connection between prominent members of the legal establishment involved in the inquiry, and the secretive Speculative Society. The society was formed in Edinburgh University through Masonic connections so I accept that there might be a link by that route.

Members of the Speculative Society have included Lord Cullen himself and a number of other judges, sheriffs and advocates. Lord Burton, of course, was subjected to the usual dismissal, condemnation and threats for demanding action. The cover-up that Lord Burton exposes was to protect the famous dregs that Hamilton supplied with children. Scotland is home to the royal family estate at Balmoral Castle where they perform satanic rituals. The castle stands atop an underground tunnel system where most of it goes on. Scotland has many more such Reptilian royal and aristocratic estates, and it is a global bastion for Satanism and paedophilia. They don't call it the *Scottish Rite of Freemasonry* for nothing. Satanism and paedophilia infest the Scottish police, judiciary (and law in general), politics and aristocracy (of course). The case involving Hollie Greig, a young lady with Down's syndrome, who claims, with supporting evidence, to have been serially-raped as a child over a decade by members of the Scottish establishment – including a judge – has not been properly investigated by this same establishment. The story has been given a lot of coverage in the alternative media and by a campaign called 'Google Hollie Greig', but the mainstream media refused to touch it for years. The *Scottish Sunday Express* did, however, run a story in July 2011 about two Members of Parliament calling for the case to be reinvestigated. Robert Green, the wonderful man who has been campaigning for justice for Hollie, has been persecuted by the same Scottish establishment in order to stop the truth from being exposed. Judge Jean-Marc Connerotte, the first investigating judge in the Dutroux case, described his own experience. He spoke of ...

> ... the bullet-proof vehicles and armed guards needed to protect [me] against the shadowy figures determined to stop the full truth coming out. Never before in Belgium has an investigating judge at the service of the king been subjected to such pressure. We were told by police that [murder] contracts had been taken out against the magistrates ... Rarely has so much energy been spent opposing an inquiry.

Connerotte said that much of the protection of suspects came from people in government who should have been seeking the truth. One wing of the Illuminati protects another wing whenever necessary and Satanism and paedophilia are rife within global governments and politics, anyway. Incidentally, why are judges in service to 'the king' and not the people? I exposed former British Prime Minister, Ted Heath, as a serial paedophile and child killer in my book, *The Biggest Secret*, in the late 1990s. No action was taken – because it was true. Conservative Party leader Heath was obsessed with satanic ritual and torturing and sacrificing children and so was his 'opponent', Labour Party Prime Minister, Harold Wilson. Either Heath or Wilson was British Prime Minister from 1964 to 1976 – both high-level Satanists. I have been exposing Father George Bush as a paedophile, serial killer and torturer of children since before Heath. One of Bush's endless victims was the daughter of Cathy O'Brien, who I mentioned earlier with regard to shapeshifting Father Bush. Her book, *Trance-Formation of America*, exposes the evil and sickening activities of people like Bush, Dick Cheney and Bill and Hillary Clinton, among many others. The Bushes ('Republicans') and the Clintons ('Democrats') are supposed to be political 'opponents', but they are part of the same 'team'. They ran drugs together through the Mena airstrip in Arkansas when Bill Clinton was governor (see:... *And the Truth Shall Set You Free*). The bloodlines own the global drug trade and that's why the trillions of dollars spent funding the 'war on drugs' has never achieved anything. It's not meant to. Opium production has soared in Afghanistan since the American and British invasion in 2001. Afghanistan is now the biggest opium producer on the planet and is responsible for 92 per cent of illicit opium production worldwide, with 12 per cent of the population involved in opium poppy production. Cathy O'Brien saw at close hand the drug activities of the Clintons and Bushes and Father George's serial paedophilia. Cathy wrote the following in her book about what he did to her daughter, Kelly, who was born in 'captivity':

> Kelly became violently physically ill after her induction into George Bush's 'neighborhood' and from every sexual encounter she had with him thereafter. She ran 104-6 degree temperatures, vomited and endured immobilising headaches for an average of three days [consistent with high voltage trauma] ... Houston [Cathy's forced-upon-her 'husband'] forbade me to call a doctor, and Kelly forbade me to comfort her, pitifully complaining that her head 'hurt too bad even to move'. And she did not move for hours on end. Kelly often complained of severe kidney pain and her rectum usually bled for a day or so after Bush sexually abused her. My own mind control victimisation rendered me unable to help or protect her. Seeing my child in such horrible condition drove my own wedge of insanity in deeper ...

> ... Kelly's bleeding rectum was but one of many physical indicators of George Bush's pedophile perversions. I have overheard him speak blatantly of his sexual abuse of her on many occasions. He used this and threats to her life to 'pull my strings' and control me. The psychological ramifications of being raped by a pedophile President are mind shattering enough, but reportedly Bush further reinforced the traumas to Kelly's mind with sophisticated NASA electronic and drug mind-control devices.

> Bush also instilled the 'Who ya gonna call?' and 'I'll be watching you' binds on Kelly, further reinforcing her state of helplessness. The systematic tortures and trauma that I endured as a child now seem trite in comparison to the brutal physical and psychological devastation that George Bush inflicted on my daughter.

How could anyone do this? *No empathy*. I talked about Bush's paedophilic activities in a live BBC Radio interview with host, now actor, Russell Brand, and the idiot media just reported what I said with the usual approach that 'David Icke is mad'. *Yawn*. The Australian Satanist that I quoted earlier with regard to the manipulation of the 'morphic field' also talked about the way politicians are drawn into child sexual abuse:

> Politicians are introduced by a carefully graded set of criteria and situations that enable them to accept that their victims will be 'Our little secret'. Young children sexually molested and physically abused by politicians worldwide are quickly used as sacrifices. In Australia, the bodies are hardly ever discovered, for Australia is still a wilderness.

How could anyone do this? *No empathy*. They comply with the definition of 'soulless': (1) lacking any humanising qualities or influences; dead; mechanical soulless work; (2) (of a person) lacking in sensitivity or nobility; (3) heartless; cruel; (4) lacking sensitivity or the capacity for deep feeling. These people are not like most of the rest of us and we need to understand that pretty damn quickly. 'They' wouldn't do that? No, *you* wouldn't do that. 'They' *are* doing it. Actor Corey Feldman, a one-time child star, told ABC's *Nightline* programme in 2011 that Hollywood was awash with paedophiles preying on child actors and others. He said paedophiles were 'like vultures' in the entertainment industry and the 'casting couch' even applied to children. 'It's all done under the radar,' he said. 'But it's the big secret.' Here you have the real story behind moves to make paedophilia legal. Yes, I really said that. The International Planned Parenthood Federation (IPPF) is advocating the 'right' to consent to sex acts be included in the United Nations 'Rights of the Child' Treaty, which is nothing to do with giving rights to children; it is about taking *away* parental rights over what happens to their children. The IPPF is funded by governments, trusts, and foundations, the European Commission and the United Nations Population Fund for special projects. It is a major lobby group in the European Union and here it is advocating sexual freedom for children – the freedom of adults to sexually abuse children, in effect, under the cover of 'consent'. The organisation has a sexual rights guide called *Exclaim!* which Amanda Pawloski at *LifeNews.com* said calls for 'a cornucopia of sexuality and gender protections and entitlements under the guise of international law'. *LifeNews* also revealed that the IPPE was allowed to distribute a brochure entitled *'Healthy, Happy and Hot'* at a no-adults-welcome panel at the United Nations hosted by the World Association of Girl Scouts and Girl Guides. There is a major push going on to sexualize children to provide an endless supply of children for the sicker than sick while removing the power of parents to intervene.

Social Services (SS) Mafia

There is another crucial aspect to this and that is the 'Social Services', 'Family Services' or 'Child Protection Services'. These have largely been infiltrated by the bloodline satanic and paedophile rings to ensure an endless flow of children, and to block any chance of a child's claims of abuse by members of the El-ite from coming out or being investigated. These organisations are supposed to be there – *officially* at least – to protect the vulnerable, especially children, but the truth is that they have become vehicles for stealing children from their parents for no other reason than to provide a limitless supply for the Satanists and paedophiles. Many are stolen to order. A child in a community will be identified and put on the 'wanted list' and then Social Services will invent a reason to take the little boy or girl from their parents and hand them to foster parents and adoptive parents who are connected to the rings. American Child 'Protective' Services (CPS) employs private companies to steal children on the State's behalf, and there is a massive financial incentive for these companies and CPS to kidnap children and sell them into child trafficking, paedophile and Satanist networks. That does not mean that all foster and adoptive parents are paedophiles and Satanists, of course; the great majority are not. But a highly significant number *are*. This is why the figures for stealing children from their parents on ludicrous grounds and in outrageous circumstances of cruelty and injustice are soaring across the world. 'Family Courts' that make these decisions on the say-so of corrupt social workers, police, lawyers and judges (often connected by the same rings) are held in secret for the same reason. The authorities claim that the secrecy is to 'protect the child' when it is really to protect the Satanists and paedophiles, and the system itself, from public exposure. *Corrupt* is hardly a word that will in any way suffice. Anyone with a functioning mind must know that the 'legal system' worldwide is corrupt to its core. Why would the bloodlines that control it want to dispense justice? The bloodlines not only *own* the legal system, they *created* it to serve their interests. But the secret Family Courts are even beyond the normal level of corruption, because children are involved that they are desperate to acquire. Satanic and paedophile social workers, police officers, lawyers and judges conspire together to remove children from loving

Bloodline Satanic and Paedophile Network

ILLUMINATI

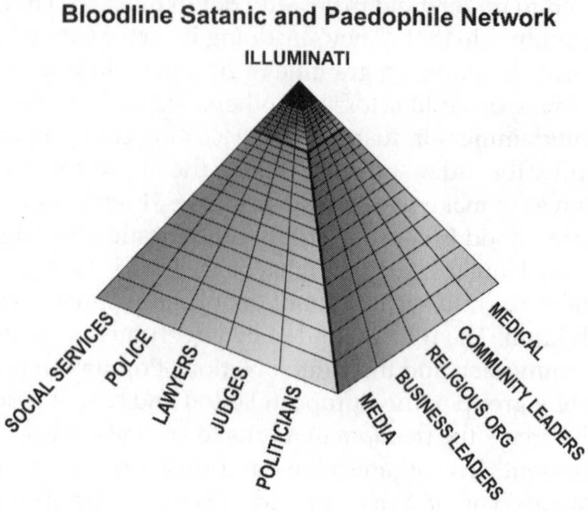

Figure 235: The compartmentalised structure that protects El-ite paedophiles and Satanists from public attention

parents to feed their insatiable rings and ringmasters. Evidence is fabricated by social workers and police, and 'judgements' are clearly written by many judges before a hearing is even finished – often even *started*. To part little children coldly and knowingly from loving parents, and to part brothers and sisters from each other, requires a level of soulless, heartless inhumanity that is beyond my imagination. But this is the norm for these 'people'. It is what they *are*. The family court system, from social workers through to police and judges, is awash with this mentality. The secrecy means that the horrific happenings fly under the radar of most people, and once they secure the major positions in any organisation – the hire and fire positions – they can simply and quickly appoint 'their own' at all levels (Fig 235). Anyone who won't play ball, or could be a source of exposure, is simply denied promotion, often hounded and harassed until they leave. Satanists and paedophiles have, in this way, largely taken over. They dominate the upper echelons of the police, Social Services, legal profession, judiciary and government. And many of the lower levels, too.

Child 'protection' services are given big financial incentives by governments to meet targets for removing children from parents, and gutless social workers who are not directly part of the paedophile and satanic networks often lie and cheat to meet the targets under pressure from their 'superiors'. Either way, the outcome is the same: devastated parents, devastated children and families torn apart. 'Shapeshifter' Tony Blair ran a 'personal crusade' when he was British prime minister to vastly increase the number of children taken from their parents. This included *setting targets* for councils for the number of forced adoptions each year. A man so utterly connected to the bloodline cabal does this when the bloodlines have an insatiable desire for children – can this be just a another coincidence? *Of course not.* The numbers are now at an all-time record in Britain with some 10,000 children a year removed from their families by the State. I have been investigating these subjects for well over a decade and there is no doubt that the Social Services system becomes more arrogant and blatant by the day – there are so many cases that it's not possible to keep track of them all. The vast majority never come to public attention anyway because of the enforced secrecy and the fact that parents are threatened with *going to prison* if they say publicly that their children have been stolen by the State. *This is happening. NOW.* The stories are as harrowing and traumatic as they are now endless, with thousands of parents every year in Britain unjustly accused of abuse or being unable to care for their children. They are told that if they challenge the decision of the Social Services (SS) Mafia to take away their children they will never see them again, even in rare 'supervised' visits. They are also told that it will be bad for their case if they speak publicly about what has happened when, in truth, the outcome has been decided from the start. Of course, genuinely abused and neglected children have to be removed from that situation, but this is not what we are talking about here. Loving and doting parents are being parted from their very well cared for children. Public awareness of what is going on is also increasing, thank goodness, though not fast enough. Investigative journalist, Christopher Booker, who writes for London's *Sunday Telegraph*, has been trying to expose the horrors perpetrated by Social Services and the secret Family Court system, but like all of the media he is limited in what he can say by draconian reporting restrictions. He tells of one case in which a woman was still giving birth when five policemen and two social workers – *five* policemen – walked in to seize the baby virtually from the mother's womb. Do these people continue to call themselves human? Do they continue to believe they are connected to anything remotely resembling a *soul*? If so, they are deluding themselves. Oh, they will say, we were only following orders; but isn't that what they said at Nuremburg? Try following what passes for your heart, chaps. They 'follow orders' because they have got balls the size of peanuts and a heart to match. How they can look into their own children's eyes and do this, I'll never know. Thousands of children are taken unjustly from their parents every year in Britain alone, so imagine the number across the world. It is done by accusing them (without evidence) of abusing their children, or of being unfit to be parents citing psychological problems that don't exist. Social Services even have 'on call' psychiatrists to give them the verdict they want.

Sick is not the word

One British father, Mark Harris, was jailed for four months by a Family Court judge (see under moron) for *waving* to his children as they went past in a car after the court had denied this loving father any access to them whatsoever. He was later sent to prison for 10 months for driving past his children's home hoping to catch a glimpse of them. The charge was 'contempt of court', but how can you be in contempt of a court that is so contemptuous? Mark went through 133 court appearances, 33 different judges, two prison sentences and a hunger strike before he was allowed to see his children again. As he said: 'They took my daughter's childhood, her formative years, from me. Lisa is 20 now. I didn't see her between the ages of 10 and 16. An awful lot happens in a child's life in that time, and I missed it all.' His children didn't even know why their father did not come to see them. This is how sick it all is. Another mother was jailed after telling her son that she loved him when she saw him in the street, and she was then arrested and taken before the courts again for posting a video on the Internet telling her story. One case I followed closely was that of Maureen Spalek who had her three children stolen by the State many years ago in Liverpool in the North West of England. She was then subjected to disgraceful persecution and harassment by the, well, *disgraceful* Merseyside police and Social Services. Maureen was arrested and taken to court for the 'crime' of sending one of her children a birthday card to their new home imposed on them by those who steal children for a living. She was also flagged down by an unmarked police car on the outskirts of the town where two of her children live with an adoptive mother. Her car was seized and she was arrested, handcuffed and held in a police cell until lunchtime the next day. The police alleged that she was in breach of a court order forbidding her to enter the town. Later she was held again at the Merseyside police Belle Vale Custody Suite in Liverpool after being arrested for sending a text to someone. She said the text was not in the least threatening or rude. The custody suite sergeant said that after she had sent the text, and had been given a police warning for it, a complaint had been made against her for harassment. These people are very, very sick. The police would not reveal who authorised the arrest and the custody suite sergeant put the phone down when questioned. No doubt he then went home to his children. The authorities appeared to be very worried about Maureen Spalek, and some would suspect that this is connected in part with activities at Liverpool's *notorious* Alder Hey Children's Hospital. Alder Hey was exposed for unauthorised removal, retention and disposal (where?) of children's organs and other human tissue kept in more than 2,000 pots containing body parts from some 850 infants. Maureen Spalek has discovered that her children have been taken to Alder Hey for appointments, although they were not ill. *So what were they doing there?* I posted news of her arrest on my website and invited people to ring the Merseyside police to tell them what they thought of their treatment of this lady. So many did so that they crashed the police telephone system and she was released with the charges dropped. 'You seem to have a lot of friends,' a police officer told her. It shows what can be done if enough people are committed to the cause of freedom, fairness and justice for all.

This is what we need – *commitment* to these values and the focus and determination to do what is necessary to express them. We have a tiny tail currently wagging a massive dog, and only when the dog starts to wake up and bark can this situation end. People would be shocked if what I have described was happening in an officially totalitarian country; but this is now a common daily experience in 'free' Britain, 'free' America and other countries that lie and posture about being 'free' and 'democratic'. Most people think that the number of missing children can be gauged by how many times they see missing children stories in the media; but that is a *fraction of a fraction of a fraction* of the number involved. Many of them end up in the child trafficking rings ultimately controlled by the bloodlines which abduct children both en masse and to order, with a specific child with specific genetic traits targeted on behalf of a 'client'. Many of these end up in the Middle East, not least Saudi Arabia and the United Arab

Figure 236: Full-body scanners – a paedophile's dream. Ain't that right, Henry?

Emirates, but they are also sold to buyers all over the world.

The bloodline network is obsessed with children, and I have explained here why that is the case. Children are now constantly photographed naked or sexually molested in increasing numbers of airports as they pass through 'security' (Fig 236). This won't encourage paedophiles to suddenly develop a passion for the security profession, will it? Incredible. The number of paedophiles being employed is increasing with the expansion of this system and the whole process is conditioning children to accept molestation as 'part of life'. If anyone else did what these people in uniform do to children they would be arrested and the key thrown away. What are we doing accepting the abuse of our own children?

Enough, enough, enough.

9

'Israel' Means Rothschild

Another fundamental presence that pervades the entire Illuminati web – another 'cement' – is what I call 'Rothschild' Zionism. I add the 'Rothschild' to constantly emphasise the true creators of Zionism and its controllers to this day. 'Zion' is code for 'Saturn'. Zionism is Saturnism in the same way that Satanism is Saturnism (Fig 237). It is another face of the Saturn Cult, but most of its supporters and advocates won't know that.

I summarised earlier some of the historical background, and I expose Rothschild Zionism in great detail in *Human Race Get Off Your Knees* and *The David Icke Guide to the Global Conspiracy*. Most researchers either don't realise the overwhelming significance of this network or they are too frightened to say so. Sod that! Ask most people about Zionism and they will say, 'That's the Jews.' The Rothschild networks in politics and the media have very successfully 'sold' this impression – this image – as 'common knowledge' and 'everyone knows that'. *But it's not true.* The terms 'Jewish people' and 'Zionism' are not interchangeable as we are led to believe. Many Jews vehemently oppose Zionism, and many Zionists are not Jewish. Rothschild Zionism in its public expression is a political ideology based on a homeland for Jewish people in Palestine, and a belief that the Jews are God's 'chosen race' with a God-given right to the 'promised land' of Israel (historically this is nonsense, as I explained earlier). They also believe that the real borders of Israel must encompass what is now Israel, *including* Gaza and the West Bank which are still officially owned by the Palestinians; plus Lebanon, Iraq, Syria, Egypt and Jordan, or, as *Genesis* puts it: '... from the brook of Egypt to the Euphrates'. This is the public face of Zionism, but at its core it is a premier secret society within the hidden control structure. Zionism was created by (and is still controlled by) the House of Rothschild, and they have sought to program the belief that 'Zionism-means-all-Jewish-people' so that they can condemn as 'anti-Semites' and 'racists' anyone who exposes the truth about the Rothschilds and their agents in government, banking, business, media and military, etc. This is why most researchers won't go there, even if they are aware enough to know that they *should* go there. We need all the 'B's' to uncover and expose what is happening in the world – brain, backbone and balls. Never more so than now. Add Consciousness to the essential requirements if you want to see how deep the rabbit hole *really* goes. Racism is extreme ignorance in that it relates 'self'

Figure 237: The web of Saturnism

to the body, instead of Consciousness – Awareness – animating and experiencing *through* the body. Racism is like judging a man by his spacesuit instead of the person inside. Racists are ridiculous, juvenile and silly, but no way is the threat of being branded as one (they have already tried and failed) going to stop me from exposing what must be exposed if the Control System is going to fall. The world's most extreme racists are, after all, Rothschild Zionists, anyway. One of its most shocking expressions, an extreme of an extreme, is a Jewish supremacist organisation called Chabad Lubavitch. This has widespread connections to governments all over the world. Chabad Lubavitch was founded in the 18th century and its most celebrated leader was Menachem Mendel Schneerson, or the 'Great Rebbe', who died in 1994 (Fig 238). He wrote that 'two contrary types of soul exist; a non-Jewish soul came from three satanic spheres, while the Jewish soul stems from holiness'. 'A Jew was not created as a means for some [other] purpose,' he said. The substance of all divine emanations was created only to serve the Jews and, therefore, 'the Jew himself is the purpose'. The US Congress voted unanimously to give the Congressional Gold Medal to Schneerson, a man who preached that all Gentiles are innately evil and genetically inferior. But isn't that what the Reptilian hybrid bloodlines have always believed? I think it is, you know. What a coincidence. What have we come to when they give a Congressional Medal to someone who preached that non-Jews are only here to serve Jews? Rabbi Yitzchak Ginsburgh, a leading Chabad Rabbi, believes that a Jew should be able to take the organs of Gentiles, because non-Jews are genetically inferior. He wrote the following in *The Jewish Weekly*, about the founder of Chabad Lubavitch, Schneur Zalman:

Figure 238: The 'Great Rebbe'. Lovely chap

As for the goyim [non-Jews] ... Zalman's attitude (was): 'Gentile souls are of a completely different and inferior order. They are totally evil, with no redeeming qualities whatsoever.' If every single cell in a Jewish body entails divinity, is a part of God, then every strand of DNA is a part of God. Therefore, something is special about Jewish DNA. If a Jew needs a liver, can you take the liver of an innocent non-Jew passing by to save him? The Torah would probably permit that. Jewish life has an infinite value.

Can you imagine what would happen if a non-Jew had said a fraction of that in relation to being white or black or Chinese? Chabad Rabbi Manis Friedman was reported in Jewish publications to have said this in reply to a question about how he thought Jews should treat their Arab neighbours: 'The only way to fight a moral war is the Jewish way: destroy their holy sites. Kill men, women and children (and cattle).' I know it must be almost impossible to believe, but these really are the same people that go around shouting 'racist' at others. Many of the political 'Left' (brain) have been helping them to do this decade after decade by branding those who challenge Rothschild Zionism as racist. They have also sought, often successfully, to deny them the right to speak in public when they are only trying to alert the world to what is going on. This happened to me years ago, particularly in Rothschild Zionist-controlled Canada, where one of the ringleaders was the serial litigator and government employee called Richard Warman. You can see him at work trying to have my event banned in Vancouver if you put the words: 'David Icke, the Lizards and the Jews' into *YouTube*. You will also have the pleasure of seeing the most classic example of the 'Left' mentality that I am talking about here. Quite a number were involved but, even collectively, there was no discernable brain cell activity that could be measured by any known technology. They threw cream pies at me during a book signing, but missed, except for a dab on the arm, and they hit the children's book section instead. Bless 'em. I blame their mothers. You can see how this guy Richard Warman gives them the pie idea in the *YouTube* video. Funny how they never seem to question or challenge the racism of Israel which is an apartheid state every bit as much as were apartheid South Africa and apartheid America. I don't just mean the evil that is inflicted upon the Palestinian people minute-by-minute, day-by-day. I include the extraordinary racist divisions within the fiercely hierarchical Israeli society in which black Jews from Ethiopia, for example, are considered little more than vermin. I never once heard any of these 'look at me; I'm so pure' left-brain-imprisoned 'anti-racists' mention this. But I feel sorry for them, really. Think how they must feel when they wake up every morning and realise that they are still them. *Wow!* Let's move on.

We need to go beyond the calculated diversion that equates challenging Rothschild Zionism and the horrors of Israel with being anti-Jewish. Then we can look instead at the simple facts that the Rothschild networks don't want you to know. Firstly, you don't have to be Jewish to be a Rothschild Zionist. US Vice President, Joe Biden, said this publicly while arse-licking his masters in Tel Aviv (ultimately his masters at Chateau Rothschild). Some of the most vehement Rothschild Zionists are the *Christian* Zionists in the United States and elsewhere. These are led most vocally by their 'spiritual' leader, John C Hagee. Think of the worst kind of extreme bible-bashing hypocrite and you've got him to a T. He says that what Hitler and the Nazis did to the Jews was the fulfilment of 'God's will for Israel'. Get yourself a cup of sweet tea before reading what he said:

> Theodor Hertzl [Rothschild frontman] is the Father of Zionism. He was a Jew and at the turn of the 19th century said: 'This land is our land; God wants us to live there.' So he went to the Jews of Europe and said: 'I want you to come and join me in the land of Israel.' So few came and Hertzl went into depression. Those who came founded Israel. Those who did not went through the hell of the Holocaust. Then God sent a hunter. A hunter is someone who comes with a gun and he forces you. Hitler was a hunter.

Unbelievable. Hitler and the Nazis were actually sent by the Rothschilds and Rockefellers to, in part, force Jews to go where the overwhelming majority did not want to go – *Israel*. The first Rothschild Zionist Congress in 1897 was held in in Basel, Switzerland, because it had to be moved from the original location, Munich, Germany, in the face of opposition from Jews who did not support the Zionist plan to move them all to Israel. Then along came the Nazis and the rest is history. Theodor Herzl wrote in his diary:

> It is essential that the sufferings of Jews ... become worse ... this will assist in realization of our plans ... I have an excellent idea ... I shall induce anti-Semites to liquidate Jewish wealth ... The anti-Semites will assist us thereby in that they will strengthen the persecution and oppression of Jews. The anti-Semites shall be our best friends.

Rothschild Zionism wants what is best for Jewish people? *Sure* they do. John Hagee is the founder and National Chairman of the Christian-Zionist organisation, Christians United for Israel. He's a regular visitor to Israel and has met every prime minister since Menachem Begin. His John Hagee Ministries has given more than $8.5 million to relocate Jews from the former Soviet Union to Israel, and he is the founder and executive director of an event called 'A Night to Honor Israel'. This pledges solidarity between Christians and the State of Israel. By contrast, a large number of *Jewish* people are *not* Zionists. Many oppose it and support the Palestinians in their battle for survival against the onslaught of genocide from the Israeli government and military funded by

Figure 239: The belief that Rothschild Zionism is the same as 'Jewish people' is a manipulated myth

the Rothschild Zionist-owned United States. Jewish people organise protests and call for boycotts of Israel in response to the Rothschild Zionist agenda for the Palestinians (Fig 239). But how many people who glean their 'information' from the mainstream media know this? How many people know, as portrayed in Figure 240, that many religious Jews abhor the demands by the Rothschild Zionists for a US attack on Iran and have had warm meetings with Iran's President Ahmadinejad to give their support? No-one who gets their 'news' solely from the Rothschild Zionist-controlled mainstream

Figure 240: All Jews are Rothschild Zionists?

media would know any of this. It pushes only one line – Zionism means *all* Jewish people, end of story. Anyone who believes that should read the work of the magnificent Jewish writer, Norman Finkelstein, whose parents suffered in Nazi concentration camps; and that of Jewish musician and writer, Gilad Atzmon, at: www.gilad.co.uk. The Rothschilds have a network of organisations, including B'nai B'rith and its offshoot, the Anti-Defamation League (ADL), which works with other Rothschild-controlled groups to target anyone who gets close to seeing the elephant in the living room. They attack and undermine them in every way they can to stop the simple and devastating truth coming to light – that the Rothschilds and agents of the Rothschild Zionist secret-society control governments, not least in Britain and the United States; global finance and commerce; the mainstream media; Hollywood; and the music industry. Even this is only a partial list of their empire.

The House of Rothschild

Mayer Amschel Rothschild (born 1744), the son of a money changer, founded the dynasty in Frankfurt, Germany. The family had formerly been known as 'Bauer'. Mayer Rothschild developed a close and very profitable relationship with German royalty, most notably Prince William of Hesse–Hanau. British and Belgian royalty are both really the German House of Saxe–Coburg–Gotha and there is no way that this is a coincidence, or that this same bloodline has connections to other surviving royal families in Europe. Rothschild genetics has to be involved somewhere. Many of the most prominent Rothschild Zionist banking families in America, including Goldman, Sachs, Lazard and Lehman, also originate from the Rothschild stronghold of Germany. Mayer Rothschild sent his sons to London, Paris, Naples and Vienna to expand the empire and soon it was controlling the finances of Europe, and later the world. The Rothschilds were well known for arranged marriages with family members, such as first and second cousins. The official biographies say this was to keep the money in the family, but genetics was equally important. A major Rothschild modus operandi has been to covertly engineer wars and lend all sides the credit 'money' to fight them. They advance more credit 'money' for the warring countries to rebuild their devastated infrastructure and economies when the conflict ends before doing the same all over again. They have seized ownership of these countries through debt. Israeli writer and researcher, Barry Chamish, reported a meeting he had with a grandson of Sir Evelyn de Rothschild during the Israel–Lebanon war in 2006. The grandson said that he had abandoned the family to become a Mormon. There was some irony in this when you think that the Mormon Church and the Watchtower Society, or Jehovah's Witnesses, were both funded into existence by the Rothschilds and remain Rothschild Zionist front organisations today. Both of these religions are pledged to introduce a 'New Jerusalem' called 'Zion'.

Figure 241: Sir Evelyn de Rothschild   **Figure 242:** Jacob Rothschild

Mormon founders, Joseph Smith, Hiram Smith and Brigham Young were bloodline Freemasons, and they included many Freemasonic concepts in Mormon belief and ritual. Charles Taze Russell and Joseph Franklin Rutherford who established the Watchtower Society were also Freemasons and Rothschild lackeys. Both 'religions' are fronts for Satanism at their inner core. I have spoken at length with many women who described how they were raped and impregnated during satanic rituals involving reptilian entities on an altar under the Mormon Temple in Salt Lake City. The resulting foetuses were later used in horrific rituals such as those that Stewart Swerdlow described earlier. The Rothschild grandson told Chamish that just seven families were enjoying the 'fruits of the war' in Lebanon at the time. He said of the Rothschilds: 'They created Israel as their personal toy. It makes them richer and gives them more control.' I have been saying and writing for nearly 20 years that the Rothschilds own Israel, and anything Israel does is the Rothschilds at work. The Rothschilds built the Israeli parliament, the Knesset and the Supreme Court building with all its occult symbols.

There are Rothschild family branches in Britain, Germany, France, Austria, Italy and Switzerland and they operate through many and various names throughout the world. Wherever there is money and manipulation you will find a Rothschild. The Naples branch of the family in Italy has long had a close association with the Roman Church, which I'm sure will surprise no-one. Among the most prominent members of the dynasty are Sir Evelyn de Rothschild, a financial advisor to Queen Elizabeth II and the Vatican, and governor of the London School of Economics; and financier Jacob Rothschild – 4th Baron Rothschild, a close friend and business associate of Henry Kissinger (Figs 241 and 242). You would expect a Rothschild to be involved with the Illuminati-created-and-controlled London School of Economics where many agents and players in the game are 'educated'. I'll say more about this in the next chapter. Jacob Rothschild is also a close friend and associate of Rothschild Zionist media tycoon, Rupert Murdoch, and deputy chairman of the satellite television network, BskyB, in which Murdoch has the major stake. The connection to Murdoch is a gimme. No one builds a media empire, or any other, unless the Rothschild networks are behind it somewhere. Murdoch was forced to close his sleazy UK tabloid, the *News of the World*, in 2011 after it was exposed for tapping the phones of thousands of people, 'celebrities', and even the families of dead soldiers and murdered children. They were also bribing equally corrupt London Metropolitan police officers with tens of thousands of pounds for what should have been confidential information. Sir Paul Stephenson, the Metropolitan Police Commissioner, resigned after it was revealed that he employed as his 'personal advisor' a former *News of the World* deputy editor arrested on suspicion of phone hacking. Rupert Murdoch, the Rothschild propaganda chief, was responsible for 'shapeshifter' Tony Blair being El-ected and we now know that the two met three times in the nine days before the invasion of Iraq in 2003. Every one of Murdoch's 127 newspapers worldwide supported the invasion. When the *News of the World* scandal broke it was revealed that David Cameron met Murdoch executives no fewer than 26 times in the little more than a year before he became Prime Minister in 2010. Another 27 meetings followed in his first year as head of the UK government. Defence Secretary Liam Fox gave confidential defence briefings to Murdoch executives; and George Osborne, the Rothschild-controlled Chancellor of the Exchequer, had 16 separate meetings with Murdoch editors and executives in his first year in office. Cameron also appointed former *News of the World* editor, Andy Coulson, as Downing Street director of communications before Coulson resigned over the phone-tapping scandal. Sean Hoare, a former *News of the World* reporter, was found dead at his home in Watford, north of London, when the main scandal broke. He had gone public the year before to say that Coulson knew about the hacking which was 'endemic' and part of the 'culture at [Rupert Murdoch's] News International'. He said that it was happening on an 'industrial scale'. Police said that Hoare's death was 'unexplained, but not thought to be suspicious'. This extraordinary statement was made before any investigation or post mortem. His death meant that his evidence would never be heard by any inquiry or any subsequent criminal investigation. How convenient. As I write, the FBI is investigating allegations that Murdoch employees hacked the phones of the families of 9/11 victims, which, if proven, could have serious implications for Murdoch's American holdings, including *Fox News,* the *New York Post* and *The Wall Street Journal*. All this provided a glimpse, but only a glimpse, under the stone that the Rothschilds call home. I emphasise that when I refer to 'the Rothschilds' I mean the *bloodline* under endless different names and not only 'Rothschild'. There are also many people called Rothschild that have nothing to do with the manipulating centre of the family, or have no direct connection to the family except sharing the same name.

Rothschild wars and 'revolutions'

The Rothschilds were the prime manipulating force behind the two world wars. They controlled and funded all sides in both of them – including the Nazis in World War II. Why would a supposedly 'Jewish' family bring to power people who had such hatred for Jews? Simple: they don't give a shit about Jewish people. They are just a means to an end to them. There were many Rothschild Zionists among the key Nazis and their funders. Max Warburg (Rothschild Zionist) was a director of IG Farben, which funded Hitler and ran the concentration camp at Auschwitz. His brother, Paul Warburg (Rothschild Zionist), was a director of the American end of IG Farben and was also instrumental in the creation of the Federal Reserve banking system which has controlled the United States economy ever since it was established in 1913. Max Warburg signed the document appointing Hjalmar Schacht to take control of the German central bank, the Reichsbank. Warburg's signature appears beside that of Adolf Hitler. Alfred Rosenberg, one of the most influential authors of Nazi race policy, was Jewish, and there were many other Rothschild agents like him directing the horrors that the Nazis inflicted on Germany and the rest of Europe. (See: ... *And the Truth Shall Set You Free*). I have already noted that the Nazis were funded by the Rothschild Zionist Rockefeller dynasty and the Harriman and Bush families, and that the Rockefellers provided the money for the work of the Nazi 'race purity' guru, Ernst Rudin. J.P. Morgan interests, General Electric, Standard Oil, National City Bank, Chase and Manhattan banks, Kuhn, Loeb & Co., General Motors, Ford, and others, funded the Nazi war machine. This is how Germany was able to go so quickly from the depths of economic collapse to declaring war on much of Europe. A major conduit for this money was the Mendelsohn Bank of Amsterdam, officially controlled by the Warburg family (the Rothschilds, in truth), and the J. Henry Schroder Bank in Frankfurt, London and New York. Legal work for the Schroder Bank was handled by an American law firm, Sullivan & Cromwell LLP. The senior partners of Sullivan & Cromwell were John Foster Dulles and Allen Dulles (Rothschild Zionists) who became the US Secretary of State and the first civilian Director of the CIA respectively after the war. The Rothschilds controlled Stalin (Rothschild Zionist) in Russia, Winston Churchill (Rothschild Zionist) in Britain and Franklin Roosevelt (Rothschild Zionist) in the United States. Stalin was Jewish, and so was Churchill. Moshe Kohn wrote in *The Jerusalem Post* in 1993: 'Cunning, no doubt, came to Churchill in the Jewish genes transmitted by his mother, Lady Randolph Churchill, née Jenny Jacobson/Jerome.' The name 'Roosevelt' was formerly 'Rosenfelt', a Dutch Jewish family who, like many Jewish families, including the Rockefellers (Rockenfelder), changed their names to hide their origins when they moved to America. The Rothschilds were the conductors of the orchestra in 'Operation Nazi Slaughter'. They wanted German Jews to be treated grotesquely by the Nazis to manipulate both them and world opinion to support a new 'Jewish homeland' that the Rothschilds had long planned in Israel.

The Rothschilds were the architects of the Bolshevik Revolution in Russia in 1917 led by Yiddish-speaking Vladimir Ilyich Lenin (Rothschild Zionist, real name: Vladimir Ilyich Ulyanov) and Leon Trotsky (Rothschild Zionist, real name: Lev Bronstein). These guys were frontmen for the House of Rothschild, and so were their fellow 'revolutionaries', Grigory Zinoviev (Rothschild Zionist), Lev Kamenev (Rothschild Zionist) and Yakov Sverdlov (Rothschild Zionist). The 'Russian' Revolution was the *Rothschild* Revolution. They provided the funding through Kuhn, Loeb & Co., one of their American banks run by German Jews, Jacob Schiff and Paul 'Federal Reserve' Warburg. Jacob Schiff created the Round Table satellite, the Council on Foreign Relations, in 1921. Schiff was the brother-in-law of Warburg's wife and when you follow these families you see that they interbreed just as much as any royal dynasty. They think they *are* a royal dynasty. The Schiff family are assets of the Rothschilds, and Jacob Schiff was born at the Rothschild house in Frankfurt with the 'red sign', or six- pointed star (Saturn), over the entrance door. Al Gore's daughter, now Karenna Gore Schiff, married a descendent of Jacob Schiff. Would a Schiff marry someone not of Jewish (Khazar) ancestry? I would be very surprised. Soviet dissident, Alexander Solzhenitsyn, who wrote *The Gulag Archipelago*, said: 'The Bolsheviks were led by non-Russian people who hated the Russian people..' They hated everyone. Hate is their emotional currency. They would murder 60 million Christians and non-Jews in Russia and the Soviet Union. Solzhenitsyn wrote that Rothschild Zionists established and administered the Soviet concentration camps in which tens of millions died. The Red Army, the biggest killing machine in known human history, was the creation of Rothschild Zionists. Leon Trotsky (Rothschild Zionist) was the head of the Red Army, and the leading administrators were Aron Solts (Rothschild Zionist); Yakov Rappoport (Rothschild Zionist); Lazar Kogan (Rothschild Zionist); Matvei Berman (Rothschild Zionist); Genrikh Yagoda (Rothschild Zionist); and Naftaly Frenkel (Rothschild Zionist). The Red Army killed almost seven million Germans, and millions more across Europe. Red Army soldiers killed and tortured civilians wherever they went and were ordered to do so by their Rothschild leadership. They raped some two million German women and many more in Austria, Hungary, Romania, Bulgaria, Poland, Czechoslovakia and Yugoslavia. They also raped women – most of them Jewish – who had been freed from Nazi concentration camps. The Red Army went on to terrorise Eastern Europe for decades. Ilya Ehrenburg (Rothschild Zionist) was the evil Soviet propagandist who distributed pamphlets ordering the Red Army to rape, torture and kill their millions of victims. Ehrenburg told them:

> If your part of the front is quiet and there is no fighting, then kill a German in the meantime ... if you have already killed a German, then kill another – there is nothing more amusing to us than a heap of German corpses.

> Kill! Kill! In the German race there is nothing but evil; not one among the living, not one among the yet unborn but is evil! Follow the precepts of Comrade Stalin. Stamp out the fascist beast once and for all in its lair! Use force and break the racial pride of these German women. Take them as your lawful booty. Kill! As you storm onward, kill, you gallant soldiers of the Red Army.

Nice man. The Red Army took Ehrenburg at his word, and this is how one young Russian officer described what happened day after day after day:

> Women, mothers and their children lie to the right and left along the route and in front of each of them stands a raucous armada of men with their trousers down. The women, who are bleeding or losing consciousness, get shoved to one side and our men shoot the ones who try to save their children.

Ilya Ehrenburg is celebrated by Rothschild Zionists as a Jewish hero of the Russian Revolution and he is honoured in Yad Vashem, Israel's Holocaust history museum. Israeli Prime Minister, Benjamin Netanyahu, told Russia's Vladimir Putin in 2011 that a memorial was going to be erected in Israel in honour of the Red Army. Why would Israel honour this killing and raping machine of historical proportions? See above. The same mentality that created the Red Army and decreed its murdering, raping and torturing methods of operation has been in control of Israel since it was bombed into existence in 1948. Anyone surprised that it is committing genocide against the Palestinians and treats them with hatred and contempt?

Tail wags dog
Agents of the Rothschild Zionist secret society, many from families originally in

Figure 243: Rahm Emanuel and Barack Obama: 'Stick with me son, and I'll get you the Nobel Peace Prize for killing people'

Rothschild Germany, have taken control of American banking, business, media and politics. I am going to list some of the personnel that Barack Obama appointed (was told to appoint) after he won the presidential El-ection in late 2008 to give you an idea of how the very few dictate to the very many via the Rothschild networks. Remember as we go through the names that less than *two per cent* of the population of the United States is Jewish, and a significant number of those will *not* be Rothschild Zionists. Obama appointed Rahm Israel Emanuel (Rothschild Zionist) to be his White House Chief of Staff (Fig 243). Emanuel was Obama's handler who directed and enforced the bloodline agenda from within the White House before leaving in 2010 to become Mayor of Chicago – one of the most politically corrupt cities on Earth. This was also where Obama's political career was spawned. Emanuel has served in the Israeli army and he is the son of a former operative with the Irgun terrorist group that helped to bomb Israel into existence in 1948 and force some 800,000 Palestinians to flee their homeland in terror, never to be allowed to return. Many Israelis connected to the Rothschild networks were sent to the United States after the State of Israel was established to specifically produce children that would become American-born citizens to infiltrate the US governmental system in the following generations. Obama's White House Senior Advisor (another handler) is David Axelrod (Rothschild Zionist), a close associate of Emanuel and the man who ran Obama's 'change you can believe in' election campaigns against Hillary Clinton and John McCain. Axelrod now oversees the words on the Teleprompter screens to which Obama is welded often for even the most minor announcement. Axelrod, like Emanuel, is the product of the Rothschild Zionist 'political' Mafia that runs Chicago. One of Obama's chief funders and controllers is the Rothschild Zionist agent, George Soros, the multi- billionaire financial speculator and manipulator of countries, especially in the former Soviet Union. Obama appointed a stream of Rothschild Zionist 'advisors' and 'czars' in various subject areas, including notorious war criminal and Rothschild Zionist agent, Henry Kissinger. Another 'czar', Cass Sunstein, the 'Administrator of the White House Office of Information and Regulatory Affairs', has called for 'conspiracy theories' to either be *banned* or *taxed*. The Rothschilds want to ban any view or research that exposes the Rothschild agenda, and censor the Internet to stop alternative information from being seen by the public. Sunstein (Rothschild Zionist) says the opinion that 'global warming' is a manipulated hoax could be an example of what should be banned or taxed (see *banned*), and so how appropriate that Obama appointed Carol Browner (Rothschild Zionist) and Todd Stern (Rothschild Zionist) to oversee 'his' global-warming/climate-change policies.

The key economic post in the United States is the Chairman of the Federal Reserve, the privately-owned and Rothschild-controlled cartel of banks that is – hilariously – known collectively as the 'central bank of America'. A national central bank should be answerable to the people, otherwise it's just another private bank lending the government 'money' which the population has to repay, plus interest. The latter describes the US Federal Reserve, which, as the saying goes, is no more *federal* than the Rothschild-controlled Federal Express. The 'Fed' was manipulated into being in 1913 by Rothschild Zionists, Jacob Schiff and Paul Warburg at Kuhn, Loeb & Co., funders of the Russian Revolution. Warburg's son, James Paul Warburg, told the US Senate on July 17th, 1950: 'We shall have world government whether or not we like it. The only question is whether world government will be achieved by conquest or consent.' Son Warburg was financial adviser to President Roosevelt during the Great Depression. The Rothschild-controlled Kuhn, Loeb & Co. was a major source of funding for J D Rockefeller to expand his Standard Oil Empire, and for the railroad builder, Edward Harriman, and the industrialist, Andrew Carnegie. The Rothschilds ultimately controlled all of them, *and* the banking operation of J.P. Morgan. Jacob Schiff told the New York Chamber of Commerce that 'unless we have a Central Bank with adequate control of credit resources, this country is going to undergo the most severe and far reaching money panic in its history'. He was lying, of course. The opposite was true, and so it proved. The Rothschilds created a financial crisis in America as a Problem–Reaction–Solution to establish a US central bank that would give them control of the American economy. Paul Warburg told the Banking and Currency Committee: 'In the Panic of 1907, the first suggestion I made was, let us have a national clearing house [central bank]. The Aldrich Plan [for a central bank] contains many things that are simply fundamental rules of banking. Your aim must be the same.' The 'Aldrich Plan' referred to Senator Nelson Aldrich whose daughter married J D Rockefeller Jr. Aldrich was the grandfather of Nelson Aldrich Rockefeller, four-times Mayor of New York and vice president to Gerald Ford. Aldrich and the Hidden Hand forced through the legislation that created the Federal Reserve System of private (Rothschild) banking interests on December 23rd, 1913 when most members of Congress had gone home to their families for Christmas. The first chairman of the Federal Reserve was Charles Sumner Hamlin (Rothschild Zionist), with Paul Warburg (Rothschild Zionist) also on the board. Congressman Charles Lindbergh said:

> The Act establishes the most gigantic trust on earth. When the President [Woodrow Wilson] signs this Bill, the invisible government of the monetary power will be legalised. The greatest crime of the ages is perpetrated by this banking and currency bill.

He was so right. America has been owned by the Rothschild banking network ever since. President Wilson was owned by the Rothschilds through their agents, Edward Mandell House (Rothschild Zionist) and Bernard Baruch (Rothschild Zionist). The usual story. See: *... And the Truth Shall Set You Free* for the detailed background. The 'Fed' prints money for literally cents on the dollar and 'lends' it to the government at interest and for profit. What a great scam if you can get away with it; and they have, because the Rothschild networks control the government and the media as well as the Federal Reserve banks. Astonishingly, the 'Fed' *has never been properly audited since it was established in 1913*. We can pick up the 'Fed' story with the appointment of Paul Adolph

Volcker (Rothschild Zionist) as chairman during the presidencies of Jimmy Carter and Ronald Reagan (in truth, George Bush senior). Volcker was a student at the Rothschild London School of Economics, a former vice president and Director of Planning with the Rockefeller (Rothschild)-controlled Chase Manhattan Bank, and he left the Federal Reserve in 1987 to become chairman of the New York investment banking firm, J. Rothschild, Wolfensohn & Co. James D Wolfensohn (Rothschild Zionist) would later became President of the World Bank. Next in line at the Federal Reserve was 'Mr Big', Alan Greenspan (Rothschild Zionist), a practising Satanist according to Phillip Eugene de Rothschild. Greenspan was known as 'the Wizard', orchestrating events from behind the curtain. President Reagan 'appointed' him (presidents don't 'appoint' Fed chiefs; they are told who it is going to be) as Chairman of the Federal Reserve, and Greenspan remained in charge of American economic policy throughout the Father Bush and Clinton years and most of Boy Bush's. He stepped down in 2006 so he would be in the clear when the crash that he did most to orchestrate was unleashed on America and the world in September 2008. In his career at the 'Fed', Greenspan oversaw the systematic dismantling of financial regulation which allowed greed and corruption to run riot. The diabolical duo, Tony Blair and his Chancellor and later successor, Gordon Brown, did the same in Britain. Greenspan received enthusiastic support for this policy from Bill Clinton's Treasury Secretaries, Robert E Rubin (Rothschild Zionist, London School of Economics), former co-chairman of the Rothschild-controlled Goldman Sachs, and Larry Summers (Rothschild Zionist), the vicious bully-boy and former Chief Economist at the World Bank. Bill Clinton's Special Assistant to the President for Economic Policy, and his Senior Economist and Senior Adviser on the Council of Economic Advisers, was Peter Orszag (Rothschild Zionist, London School of Economics). Another Greenspan supporter of mass deregulation was Timothy Geithner (Rothschild Zionist), an assistant to Robert Rubin during the Clinton administration and later the president of the Federal Reserve Bank of New York. This is the most powerful in the Federal Reserve cartel. Without the collective demolition of financial checks and balances by this cabal of Rothschild Zionists there would not have been the crash of September 2008.

Rothschild Zionists that crashed America and the world

An interesting character in this story is Brooksley Born. She was appointed during the Bill Clinton administration to head a minor government financial agency, the Commodity Futures Trading Commission (CFTC). Born was honest, conscientious and wanted to protect the finances of the American people. Such values and attitudes were always going bring her big trouble among the den of crooks, thieves and Satanists that run the US government and economy. The trio of the Federal Reserve Chairman, Alan Greenspan (Rothschild Zionist), Treasury Secretary Robert E Rubin (Rothschild Zionist), and his assistant and later successor, Larry Summers (Rothschild Zionist), set out to destroy Brooksley Born when she began to demand urgent regulation of a criminal enterprise known as OTC derivatives. OTC stands for 'over the counter', although UTT, or 'under the table', would have been far more accurate. Derivatives are a scam in which fraudsters hedge their financial bets by conning someone else into taking the risk. It involves selling the same financial 'products' to multiple buyers who all think they are the only owner. The fraud goes far deeper, but let's not dwell – it's not good for my stomach. The OTC derivatives market was completely unregulated, a free-for-all of transactions that no-one except the people involved knew anything about. The market was worth *$27 trillion* by this time and Brooksley Born could see the catastrophic consequences of where this was going. Greenspan told her that he did not believe in rules against fraud in financial markets. This was a shocker for someone who believed that she had been appointed to stop financial fraud. She pressed ahead with the process of regulating OTC derivatives despite tremendous pressure not to do so from Greenspan, Rubin and the usual abuse from the foul-mouthed oaf that is Larry Summers. They also employed the support of Arthur Levitt (Rothschild Zionist), the head of the Securities and Exchange Commission (SEC). This was also supposed to be a regulatory body, but, hey, what's in a name? This despicable group forced Born into Congressional hearings and lobbied the useless politicians to block her desire to regulate. They bent over as usual and did precisely that, of course, even though most of them didn't know an over-the-counter derivative from an over the counter-headache-pill. Senator Phil Brown of Texas memorably told her: 'I see no evidence whatsoever to suggest that this is a troubled market, or that fraud is rampant.' Nice one, Phil; any more bollocks you'd like to share with us? Indeed he had: 'We should not have one agency innovate this area and in doing so create very substantial financial problems.' I wonder if he thought the same in September 2008 when the OTC derivatives market, then worth *$600 trillion*, crashed the global economy. Greenspan told the hearings that regulation of derivatives would serve no useful purpose. Weeks later the supposedly top-of-the-range hedge fund, Long-Term Capital Management, went tits-up for doing precisely what Brooksley Born wanted to regulate against. Greenspan and Rubin ordered a collection of banks to buy out the fund to keep it afloat. Still nothing was done, because it wasn't *meant* to be done. Despite being proved right, Congress removed the power to regulate derivatives from Born's agency and she resigned knowing that there was nothing more she could do. The head of the Commodity Futures Trading Commission today is Gary Gensler (Rothschild Zionist) who spent 18 years at Goldman Sachs. Well, they are not going to make the mistake again of letting someone honest and genuine get in among them are they? The prime architects of the world economic crash of 2008 were Alan Greenspan (Rothschild Zionist), Robert Rubin (Rothschild Zionist), Larry Summers (Rothschild Zionist) and Timothy Geithner (Rothschild Zionist). Greenspan retired from the Federal Reserve two years before the crash that he purposely engineered. He was given America's highest civilian honour, the Congressional Gold Medal, and was succeeded by Ben Bernanke (Rothschild Zionist, London School of Economics). Robert Rubin went off to Citibank, which later received $100 billion in taxpayer bailouts to stay afloat. But where did Summers and Geithner end up? *Well, well.*

Poachers turn ... poachers

Barack Obama replaced Bush as the US President a few months after the crash, and who did 'he' appoint to 'his' economic team to 'sort out the mess'? *The very people who purposely created it.* This was all done from a White House controlled by Rahm Emanuel (Rothschild Zionist) and David Axelrod (Rothschild Zionist). Obama made Timothy Geithner (Rothschild Zionist) his Treasury Secretary – Obama's mother worked for Geithner's father, Peter F Geithner (Rothschild Zionist), the director of the Asia program at the Ford Foundation in New York (Fig 244). Larry Summers (Rothschild Zionist) was

Figure 245: Lovely Larry Summers

Figure 244: Timothy Geithner helped to cause the crash of 2008 and has since overseen, with others, the looting of America for his bloodline banking cohorts

appointed Director of the White House National Economic Council (Fig 245), and Paul Adolph Volcker (Rothschild Zionist), business partner of the Rothschilds, was made Chairman of the Economic Recovery Advisory Board. Other economic positions went to Peter Orszag (Rothschild Zionist), Director of the Office of Management and Budget; Jared Bernstein (Rothschild Zionist), Chief Economist and Economic Policy Adviser to Vice President Joseph Biden; Mary Schapiro (Rothschild Zionist), Chairman, Securities and Exchange Commission (SEC); Gary Gensler (Rothschild Zionist), Chairman, Commodity Futures Trading Commission (CFTC); Sheila Bair (Rothschild Zionist), Chairman, Federal Deposit Insurance Corporation (FDIC); and Karen Mills (Rothschild Zionist), Administrator, Small Business Administration (SBA). I need say no more than to point out again that Jewish people make up only *two per cent* of the American population and a significant number of those will not be Rothschild Zionists. But don't worry; there's no conspiracy. The gang that trashed the town was now back in town to trash it even more, and you'll never guess ... they decided that the only way to save an economy brought to its knees by their collective actions and the banking system they represent was to, well, no, surely not ... hand trillions of taxpayer-borrowed dollars to the Rothschild-controlled banks and insurance companies like Citigroup (advised to disaster by Rothschild Zionist Robert E Rubin), J.P. Morgan, AIG and a long list of others.

Overseeing this and all other American government spending was Obama's Budget Director, the already-mentioned Peter Orszag (Rothschild Zionist, London School of Economics), who worked closely with Rahm Emanuel (Rothschild Zionist) to impose the North American Free Trade Agreement (NAFTA) that has devastated American industry in line with Rothschild policy. NAFTA is a stalking horse for the North American Union just as the 'Common Market' was for the European Union. Orszag was the founder and president of the economic consultancy firm which advised the Central Bank of Iceland in the period before the Icelandic banking crash, and he advised the Russian Ministry of Finance when the country's resource assets were being given to

Rothschild Zionist oligarchs like Chelsea Football Club owner, Roman Abramovich, who became instant billionaires. Orszag resigned as Budget Director in July 2010 with 'job done', but, no matter. Obama announced that Jacob Lew (Rothschild Zionist), Under-Secretary of State to Hillary Clinton, would take over and resume the same post that he held under Bill Clinton. By the time the economic brown stuff hit the spinning wheel in September 2008, Ben Bernanke (Rothschild Zionist) was running the Federal Reserve (as a figurehead, with Greenspan still in the background). Bernanke printed even more money (at interest to the taxpayer) to hand to his Rothschild Zionist mates and controllers in Wall Street. Meanwhile, Treasury Secretary Timothy Geithner (Rothschild Zionist), who has been centrally involved in handing trillions of dollars of public money to his banking associates with no strings attached, asked the opinion of a private international Rothschild Zionist 'law firm' called Squire, Sanders & Dempsey to see if American states could, as some requested, legally use bailout money or TARP – the Troubled Asset Relief Program – to support the legal bills of people trying to protect their homes from foreclosure by the bailed out banking system. The privately-owned Rothschild Zionist Squire, Sanders & Dempsey said 'no', they couldn't, and so Timothy Geithner (Rothschild Zionist) said the money could not be used to protect the public, who had bailed out the banks, from being foreclosed by those same banks. Americans need to understand this – the *world* needs to understand this. America, via the Rothschilds and Rockefellers, is *owned* by the Rothschild Zionist secret society. They own and control the banks that crashed the American (and world) economy and put Americans and vast numbers of others across the planet out of work and on the street; and they own the Federal Reserve cartel that bailed out the banks with stupendous amounts of credit 'money' which the American people will be paying back for generations, if indeed they ever do.

While all this has been going on, Rothschild Zionists were running the major world financial institutions. The president of the World Bank is Robert B Zoellick (Rothschild Zionist), a big-time Boy Bush administration insider who was a fervent advocate of invading Iraq long before even 9/11. Zoellick took over at the World Bank from the disgraced Paul Wolfowitz (Rothschild Zionist), another orchestrator of the Iraqi invasion, as Deputy Defense Secretary. The chief of the International Monetary Fund (IMF) was Dominique Strauss-Kahn (Rothschild Zionist), the French politician who was expected to challenge President Nicolas Sarkozy (Rothschild Zionist) at the next French election until that idea hit the buffers in a New York hotel room. This would have made Napoleon look-alike Sarkozy very happy. The president of the European Central Bank (ECB) is Jean-Claude Trichet (Rothschild Zionist), another Frenchman who took over in 2003 following his acquittal in a trial over 'financial irregularities' at one of France's biggest banks, Crédit Lyonnais. *Anyone think, given these facts, that the Rothschild Zionists might just control global finance and could possibly, oh just a little bit, have orchestrated the crash of 2008 and what has followed??* Jean-Claude Trichet (Rothschild Zionist) at the European Central Bank and Dominique Strauss-Kahn (Rothschild Zionist) at the IMF were central to the 'bailout' of Ireland (the bailout of Irish banks and the El-ite investors, like the Rothschilds, by the people of Ireland). Bailed-out banks that caused the crash and were then deluged with the people's borrowed money were also invariably controlled, directly or ultimately, by Rothschild Zionists. These include Goldman Sachs, headed by Lloyd Blankfein (Rothschild Zionist), and established by Rothschild Zionists,

Marcus Goldman and Samuel Sachs, who came from families that relocated to America from Germany, where the name 'Rothschild' (Saturn) originated.

In-your-face corruption

Goldman Sachs was responsible *in the extreme* for the crash of September 2008, but by that time its former Chairman and CEO, Henry 'Hank' Paulson Jr., had been installed as US Treasury Secretary by President Bush to begin the bank bailout policy that Obama and Bernanke would complete. The decisions made by Paulson were of enormous benefit to Goldman Sachs in the closing weeks of the Bush administration. Goldman Sachs was also instrumental in the collapse of the Greek economy that started the 'euro panic' which later engulfed Ireland, Portugal and others. The result was that unemployment in Greece soared by 40 per cent, and some 42 per cent of young people are without a job at the time of writing. These were yet more devastated lives, but the Rothschild Zionists don't give a damn. Human suffering is exactly what they are trying to achieve, after all. They have the whole system stitched up. The Rothschild Zionist secret-society networks have their agents in governments, the banking system – including the international institutions like the World Bank – and control the reporting of their activities through ownership and control of the mainstream media. In 2011, BBC 'reporter', Tom de Castella, produced an article on the BBC website entitled: *'Bilderberg mystery: Why do people believe in cabals?'* The 'mystery', to the idiot BBC, was not why a crowd of powerful people from across the world in government, banking, big business, media and military, etc. would meet together in secret, but why people believe there could be anything sinister in it. They quoted David Aaronovitch (Rothschild Zionist), a 'columnist' on *The Times* newspaper owned by Rupert Murdoch (Rothschild Zionist). Aaronovitch said of the Bilderberg Group: 'It's really an occasional supper club for the rich and powerful.' He should join the BBC immediately. The Children's Department would suit. Or comedy. The BBC is an arm of the government, and with a few honourable exceptions the corporation employs people who will not be journalists, except in name, as long they continue to breathe. This lack of real journalism and the control of banking, business and government means that if it is happening economically and politically, it is because the Rothschilds want it that way. This is true of banking, stock markets, commodity markets, currency valuation, the price of gold – the lot. The world of finance is dictated by 'investor confidence', and that is dictated by those who have the power to control the media, government and central bank financial statements, and who have the financial resources to move trillions around the financial markets every day – the Rothschilds and their lackeys, in other words. Rothschild Zionism is an El-ite secret society at its rotten core. The people I am naming here, and so many more I could name, are not agents of Jewish people as a whole, but agents of the *secret society* which has mercilessly manipulated the Jewish population for centuries to advance its tyrannical goals.

Help you destroy the Palestinians? Yessir, Mr Rothschild

It is impossible to become President of the United States without support from the American Israel Public Affairs Committee (AIPAC). This sounds like something to do with government, which it is, in truth, although not officially. In many ways it *is* the government. AIPAC is a Rothschild Zionist lobby group, one of the biggest in America,

backed by limitless money. Hold that
thought for a moment. One of the biggest
lobby groups in Washington D.C., perhaps
the biggest, is representing the interests of
a foreign power. It is almost impossible to
secure high political office of any kind if
AIPAC doesn't approve, and a real
struggle to even become a member of
Congress or the Senate if AIPAC opposes
you. Former BBC and Independent
Television News correspondent, Alan
Hart, wrote in *Zionism: The Real Enemy of
the Jews* (World Focus Publishing; 2005):
'Jewish people make up less than two per
cent of the American population, but
account for *50 per cent* of the political
campaign contributions.' Rothschild
Zionist-owned *The Washington Post* said

Figure 246: They have one thing in common. What can it be?

that 'between 50 and 70 per cent' of presidential campaign contributions came from
Rothschild Zionist sources. This figure is overwhelmingly made up of mega-rich
Rothschild Zionists, and it is not in the least representative of half to 70 per cent of the
Jewish population (Fig 246). More than half of the 40 biggest corporate donors to the
presidential campaigns of Barack Obama and John McCain in 2008 were from
corporations owned by Rothschild Zionists. They fund the man they really want and
also his opponent so that they can control the outcome. American presidential and vice
presidential candidates may differ here and there, though less and less, but they all
agree on one thing every time: Israel gets what Israel wants. Why would this not be the
case when the Rothschilds own the United States government as they own Israel?
Investigative journalist, Wayne Madsen, described the situation very well:

> The Israeli Lobby owns the Congress, media, Hollywood, Wall Street, both political parties, and
> the White House. This kind of talk will get people fired by this lobby, as we have seen recently
> with White House correspondent Helen Thomas and CNN anchor Rick Sanchez. However,
> many Americans are growing tired of the arrogance of the Israel Lobby and their bigoted
> attitudes toward anyone who challenges their influence- peddling and their ridiculous
> insistence that Israel must be supported because of some ancient fairy tales ...

Obama is a slave to the Rothschild Zionists. They put him in office and they tell him
what to do and say. He has to be a good little boy and never mention the systematic
genocide of an entire people, the Israeli war crimes or the contemptible treatment of
Palestinian children by the Israeli 'Defense' Forces (Fig 247). The Israeli blockade of
Gaza had led to an unemployment rate of *45 per cent* by 2011, one of the highest on the
planet. The buying power of wages for those who did have work had plummeted by
more than 34 per cent in five years. Two-thirds of the Gaza population are refugees.
Gaza has no airport or seaport to receive supplies. Everything has to go through Israel.
The Israeli occupation of the Palestinian West Bank includes more than 600 checkpoints

Figure 247: Oh, such big brave men – a daily scene in occupied Palestine

and roadblocks. Palestinian ambulances with critically injured people or women about to give birth are routinely prevented from going through. The average journey time for a Palestinian ambulance in 2001 was ten minutes. In 2011, it was almost *two hours*. Israel's racism is beyond belief. *Associated Foreign Press* reported that Israel is to build a 'tolerance museum' on a Muslim burial site despite protests from those who have family buried there. An Israeli court simply decreed that it was no longer a burial site. What did the bodies do then, de-manifest? The Israel State machine is without heart or empathy; it is vicious, cruel and gloats in the suffering of its victims. The Knesset passed a law banning anyone from calling for a boycott of Israeli goods in protest at the fascism of its government and this allows companies to sue boycott campaigners without having to prove any damage or loss. The law includes calls for boycotts of goods produced at illegal Jewish settlements stolen by force from Palestinians. Boycott campaigners are banned from bidding for government tenders and the law says: 'It is prohibited to initiate a boycott of the State of Israel, to encourage participation in a boycott, or to provide assistance or information with the purpose of promoting a boycott.' *Fascism, fascism, fascism.* Even a senior Israeli army commander spoke publicly in 2011 about unchecked 'Jewish terror' against Palestinians in the occupied West Bank by extremist, and illegal, Jewish settlers. Major General Avi Mizrahi said that the settlement of Yitzhar, one of the most 'radical' (insane) Jewish strongholds, should be closed. He said that it was a source of terror against Palestinians. Israeli Foreign Minister, the ultra-extremist, Avigdor Lieberman, lives illegally in a West Bank settlement. 'What's happening in the field is terrorism,' General Mizrahi said. Jewish settlers burn mosques and Palestinian olive groves, vandalise property and murder people. This is daily life for Palestinians even without the constant cruelty and terror inflicted by the Israeli army. While I was writing this chapter, Israeli troops uprooted 300 olive trees owned by Palestinians and declared the land a military area. Just like that. This is what is happening day after day. Also as I write, a Committee of the Israeli Parliament has passed the first draft of a law which will force Palestinians *to pay the demolition costs when Israeli troops knock down their homes.* Israel has demolished more than 25,000 Palestinian homes since the occupation began in 1967 – 90 per cent of them for 'administrative' reasons. They either lacked a permit (the remit of the Israelis) or the military decided that they wanted the land. The families that live in the properties simply become homeless. No building permits have been issued to Palestinians in the same period since the start of the occupation. The homes are demolished by armoured bulldozers sold to the Israeli military by the Caterpillar corporation in the United States. The Israeli government has also approved the formation of a committee to 'Judaise' the names of Palestinian towns and historical sites and eliminate Palestinian identity. It is cumulative genocide on the TV news.

The cold and callous Israeli Prime Minister, Benjamin Netanyahu, announced in 2011 that he intends to make conditions tougher for Palestinian prisoners. He was talking about the 11,000 or so Palestinian men, women *and children* held in Israeli jails – many without charge – leaving families without a breadwinner. They are subjected to solitary confinements, sudden night raids and torture, and they are denied baths, clean clothes and visits from their families. No soul. No *empathy*. But even this is not enough for the merciless Netanyahu. 'I have decided to change Israel's treatment of terrorists sitting in prison,' Netanyahu said in June 2011. 'We will give them all that they deserve according to international law but nothing beyond that.' No they won't. Israel's treatment of prisoners already drives a coach and horses through 'international law'. Israel is in contravention of the most basic human decency in its treatment and torture of Palestinian prisoners – including children. Some 700,000 Palestinians have been jailed by Israel since it began the occupation of Gaza and the West Bank in 1967. This is 20 per cent of the Palestinian population and 40 per cent of the male population. The Israeli military courts system controls trials, sentencing and imprisonment of Palestinian detainees and provides both the prosecutor and the judge. Israelis in the same areas are only subject to civilian law. Sahar Francis, director of Addameer, the Prisoners' Support and Human Rights Association, said that prisoners, including children, were subject to sleep deprivation, threats of sexual abuse and physical violence, prolonged periods spent in complete isolation, and the arrests of family members to force confessions. She went on:

> Especially in the case of juveniles, it's threatening them before even coming to the interrogation so it will make it easier to collect their confessions. They will be really terrified. They humiliate them. They start to beat them and kick them and abuse them all the way to the detention center. It affects [the detainees'] confidence and the way they will treat the whole process of the interrogation later on.

> In some cases, they use electric shock. In some other cases, they close [their] eyes and tie [them] to the chair. They push back [their] head and then they bring a cup of water and they start to drop water on [their] face, giving a feeling like [they] can't breathe. [Torture is] very common. It's very common.

When you see what they do in public, imagine what goes on out of sight; but Israel does whatever it likes, unchallenged. Netanyahu also announced that 30,000 Palestinians from the Bedouin community were going to be evicted from their land and forced to relocate to sites designated by the Israeli government. Just like that. No debate; no right to be heard. Israel condemns the Nazis in Germany and then establishes a fascist state itself. Is this merely irony, or could it just be that the force behind the Nazis is the force behind Israel? I think it could, you know, and it begins with 'R'. This is the same Israeli regime that political prostitute, 'shapeshifter' Tony Blair, told a Rothschild Zionist audience was 'a model for this region'. (More Blair, more, I'm about to orgasm.) 'Israel is the land of God's people, except for the Palestinians, and I am proud to lick anything you want so I can bask in your glory and have your cheques in the post.' (*Ohhhhh*, thank you, Blair; that took me over the edge. Now go and make the tea.) No wonder Blair was made 'Special Envoy' to the Middle East representing the United Nations, United States, European Union and Russia. It is another stitch-up for the Palestinians to appoint a mendacious Rothschild Zionist sycophant to make sure Israel's case is the only one promoted. The United Nations, United States, European Union and Russia all know that, of course, but then they are all Rothschild-controlled. Chris Gunness, a spokesman for the UN Relief and Works Agency for Palestine Refugees, said: 'It is hard to understand the logic of a man-made policy which deliberately impoverishes so many and condemns hundreds of thousands of potentially productive people to a life of destitution.' Oh, the logic is simple, Chris. The idea is to destroy them, mate. What does Obama or any other president or prime minister have to say about this? *Nothing.* Obama made a speech at the American Israel Public Affairs Committee (AIPAC) on American (Rothschild) Middle East policy while I was writing this book. The first speech that he made on this subject after becoming president was written, according to *The Wall Street Journal*, by James Steinberg (Rothschild Zionist), Daniel Kurtzer (Rothschild Zionist) and Dennis Ross (Rothschild Zionist). Do you think that there is a possibility that the speech might have been in any way biased? This is no surprise when the Rothschild network owns Obama, lock, stock and Teleprompter, and also owns Israel – indeed created it (Fig 248). AIPAC is currently headed by Lee 'Rosy'

Figure 248: Rothschild Zionist-enslaved America

Figure 249: AIPAC and its lapdog alleged 'president' – and the consequences for the people of occupied Palestine

Rosenberg, a close friend and funder of Obama from Chicago, and probably on good terms with Wolf Blitzer (Rothschild Zionist), the leading CNN presenter who was once a spokesman for AIPAC and correspondent for the *Jerusalem Post* (Fig 249). Obama is hardly going to upset a close friend and funder like 'Rosy', and the organisation that he has to keep sweet (if he is going to win a second term), by saying anything about Israel that hasn't been pre-agreed. He said in 'his' speech to AIPAC:

> I was joined at the White House by Prime Minister Netanyahu, and we reaffirmed that fundamental truth that has guided our presidents and prime ministers for more than 60 years – that, even while we may at times disagree, as friends sometimes will [yeah, sure], the bonds between the United States and Israel are unbreakable, and the commitment of the United States to the security of Israel is ironclad.

This outrage has gone on for well over 60 years because the Rothschilds have controlled Israel and the United States government all that time. Does that mean 'ironclad' no matter what the scale of atrocities Israel commits, oh Great One? Yep, that kind of 'ironclad'. Obama said the following about two countries that have waged continual and horrific wars of violence and attrition, overt and covert, against the target populations:

> America's commitment to Israel's security also flows from a deeper place – and that's the values we share. As two people who struggled to win our freedom against overwhelming odds, we understand that preserving the security for which our forefathers fought must be the work of every generation. As two vibrant democracies, we recognise that the liberties and freedom we cherish must be constantly nurtured. And as the nation that recognised the State of Israel moments after its independence, we have a profound commitment to its survival as a strong, secure homeland of the Jewish people.

If Obama wasn't a narcissistic sociopath, he would surely have choked. But he was away with the fairies now...

> We also know how difficult that search for security can be, especially for a small nation like Israel in a tough neighbourhood. I've seen it first-hand. When I touched my hand against the Western Wall and placed my prayer between its ancient stones, I thought of all the centuries that the children of Israel had longed to return to their ancient homeland.

Heck, now I'm choking. Must be because I'm throwing up. This 'small nation like Israel' has one of the best equipped militaries in the world – virtually all of it supplied by American governments and paid for by American taxpayers. As Obama himself said:

> Because we understand the challenges Israel faces, I and my administration have made the security of Israel a priority. It's why we've increased cooperation between our militaries to unprecedented levels. It's why we're making our most advanced technologies available to our Israeli allies. And it's why, despite tough fiscal times, we've increased foreign military financing to record levels.

> That includes additional support – beyond regular military aid – for the Iron Dome anti-rocket system. This is a powerful example of American–Israeli cooperation, which has already intercepted rockets from Gaza and helped saved innocent Israeli lives. So make no mistake, we will maintain Israel's qualitative military edge.

Israel's 'qualitative military edge' is actually Israel's qualitative military domination courtesy of an American public that has never been asked, and large numbers of whom are in desperate financial straits. Homes for Americans? No – bombs for Israel. The truth is that the American government is not here to do what is best for its people. The role of government – all government – is to serve the demands and interests of the Rothschild networks that own and control Israel. This understanding makes it easy to see why the priority of American administrations is not homes for Americans, but bombs for Israel – to intimidate, to torture and to kill defenceless Palestinians.

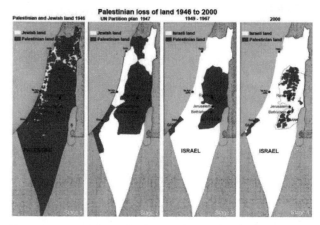

Palestinian loss of land 1946 to 2000

Figure 250: How Palestine has been stolen amid a genocidal campaign of death and destruction against the Palestinian people

Figure 251: Obama – Israel's man in the White House

Systematic genocide

Have a look at the map in Figure 250. The darker area on the left is Palestinian land before the campaign of terror that bombed Israel into being in 1948; on the right is Palestinian land in the year 2000. There is far less today even than this, as Jewish 'settlers', aided and abetted by their government, steal more and more land by bulldozing the homes of Palestinians and forcing them to leave. What you are looking at is genocide: 'The systematic and widespread extermination or attempted extermination of an entire national, racial, religious or ethnic group.' Obama never says anything about this, for woe betide him if he does – and he knows it (Fig 251). The garbage Obama spoke in 2011 about Israelis and Palestinians returning to their 1967 borders was him telling Muslims what he thinks they want to hear as part of a much bigger global operation. He knows too well that Israel will never agree to returning to the borders of 1967 or anything else. The illusory 'rift' between him and the merciless Israeli Prime Minister, Benjamin Netanyahu, is circulated in the media now and then to sell the lie to the Muslim world that Obama is standing up for them. I have been saying for at least 30 years that Israel is *not interested* in a 'peaceful settlement'. The Rothschild Zionists want *everything*, and that means the systematic destruction of the Palestinian people (Fig 252). They have to buy time to allow that to happen, and this is what the 'peace talks', 'road maps' and 'talks about talks' have been all about decade after decade and still are – *buying time*. No matter what the Palestinians offer – and they have precious little left to offer – there will always be a reason why Israel can't accept. There is always a new demand and that's the way it has been from the start. The only concession the Israeli government fascists are interested in is for the Palestinians to start walking and get out of the place. Most people won't realise, but a Rothschild has been right at the centre of all this in many guises – Major General Danny Rothschild. He joined the Israeli Defense Forces (IDF) in 1964 and four years later transferred to senior positions (of course) in the Intelligence corps (Mossad, in others words – they run everything). Rothschild later became assistant to Moshe Levi, the IDF

Figure 252: Genocide playing out on the television news (and so much more so than the mainstream media will report)

Chief of Staff, and was promoted to the rank of Brigadier General and commander of the IDF Units in Southern Lebanon. He went on to become deputy director of the Military Intelligence Directorate and director of Research Department. In the latter role, he was responsible for 'national strategic' research and analysis, both politically and militarily, before and during the first Gulf War in 1991. He became a Major General after that war and was appointed Coordinator of Government Activities in the Territories, which means controlling the occupied Palestinian lands in Gaza and the West Bank. Rothschild's actions and public statements reveal him to be a prime force behind the inhuman treatment of the Palestinians, including the killing of children, and the stealing of their lands. He is still very active after his official military 'retirement' in 'think tanks', the Central Bank of Israel and other organisations connected to Israel's political, financial, military and Intelligence activities. Danny Rothschild has certainly played a highly significant role in the 'buying time' policy that I am talking about, and his influence in Israeli policy is fundamental as a representative in Israel of his dastardly family. One of the main ways that the Israelis stall on any agreement is by saying they can't negotiate with the (El-ected) Palestinian government because it is a terrorist organisation known as 'Hamas'. Well, how funny. Israel *created* Hamas as a bogeyman that could give them the excuse not to negotiate and so have more time to finish the job. The other bogeyman re-emerging in the Middle East to frighten people is called the 'Muslim Brotherhood' which was involved in the 'people's revolution' (sure) in Egypt. The Muslim Brotherhood has an interesting background, too. Britain and America established the Muslim Brotherhood after the collapse of the Ottoman Empire in 1924 and they are still controlled by the same crowd to this day, although the Brotherhood has also served the interests of the Nazis, Israelis, Russians, French and Germans over the years. Israel is now among the major sponsors of the Muslim Brotherhood which was involved in the founding of Hamas. Robert Dreyfuss is the author of *Devil's Game: How the United States Helped Unleash Fundamentalist Islam* (Metropolitan Books, 2005). He wrote: '... beginning in 1967 through the late 1980s, Israel helped the Muslim Brotherhood establish itself in the occupied territories. It assisted Ahmed Yassin, the leader of the Brotherhood, in creating Hamas, betting that its Islamist character would weaken the PLO'. The PLO (Palestine Liberation Organization) was then the most prominent official representative of Palestinian interests. Dreyfuss also pointed out that 'during the 1980s, the Muslim Brotherhood in Gaza and the West Bank did not support resistance to the Israeli occupation. Most of its energy went to fighting the PLO, especially its more left-wing factions, on university campuses'. Charles Freeman, the one-time American ambassador to Saudi Arabia, said: 'Israel started Hamas. It was a project of Shin Bet [Israel's domestic Intelligence agency], which had a feeling that they could use it to hem in the PLO.' David Shipler, a reporter with *The New York Times*, quotes the Israeli military governor of Gaza as saying that Israel financed Islamic fundamentalists to oppose the PLO. Shipler said:

> Politically speaking, Islamic fundamentalists were sometimes regarded as useful to Israel, because they had conflicts with the secular supporters of the PLO. Violence between the two groups erupted occasionally on West Bank university campuses. Israeli military governor of the Gaza Strip, Brigadier General Yitzhak Segev, once told me how he had financed the Islamic movement as a counterweight to the PLO and the Communists. 'The Israeli Government gave me a budget and the military government gives to the mosques,' he said.

The PLO, headed by Yasser Arafat, said that Hamas was operating with the direct support of 'reactionary Arab regimes' together with the Israeli occupiers. Arafat told an Italian newspaper: 'Hamas is a creation of Israel, which at the time of Prime Minister Shamir, gave them money and more than 700 institutions, among them schools, universities and mosques.' Arafat said that Israeli Prime Minister, Yitzhak Rabin, had told him in the presence of Egypt's President Mubarak that Israel had supported Hamas. It goes like this. Every time there is any chance of a 'peace agreement' which would commit Israel to an outcome that it doesn't want, Hamas or the Muslim Brotherhood carry out a terrorist attack (or Mossad does) and this is used as the excuse to end 'negotiations'. Israel orders its agents in Hamas to start firing the military equivalent of peashooters at Israel to justify the state-of-the-art bombing and mass murder of Palestinians in 'retaliation'. Hamas representatives who won't play ball with Israel are the ones that are targeted. Mossad agents entered Dubai on forged British passports in 2010, and in full view of hotel security cameras they went to the room of an off-message Hamas senior commander, Mahmoud al-Mabhouh, and murdered him before calmly walking away past the same cameras. Their images were posted on the Internet and the authorities know who committed the murder, but, as ever, nothing was done about it (Fig 253). Israel is a law unto itself, and it was the same story with the illegal use of British identities and passports; but then the UK Foreign Secretary at the

time was David Miliband (Rothschild Zionist), brother of the current British Labour Party leader, Ed Miliband (Rothschild Zionist, London School of Economics). Mossad operates in every major country and most of the not-so major. Former French Foreign Minister Roland Dumas has said that Israelis 'are doing whatever they want in France, and are controlling the French Intelligence ...' The bomb in Oslo, Norway and the mass shooting on the island of Utøya on July 22nd 2011 had Rothschild 'false flag' experts, Mossad, written all over them. The young people who were killed in such numbers were attending a gathering of the Norwegian Labour Party's

15:30 The victim is followed to find out his room number. He stays in room 230.

Figure 253: Mossad agents caught on camera before committing murder – but nothing happened. They're all terrified of Israel. Well, I'm bloody not

youth movement which was vociferously campaigning for a boycott of Israeli goods. Labour Party ministers had strongly spoken out about Israel's treatment of the Palestinians and the government had indicated that it would recognise a Palestinian state – much to the fury (they do fury) of Israel. Supporting justice for the Palestinians can be a death sentence. In 2010, Israeli commandoes murdered nine Turkish activists on the ship Mavi Marmara for the crime of trying to get urgently needed supplies to a Gaza Strip blockaded by Israel. The ship was illegally seized in international waters. A United Nations human rights inquiry found that Israel was guilty of wilful killing and unnecessary brutality and torture. The report said that there was 'clear evidence to support prosecutions of the following crimes within the terms of article 147 of the fourth Geneva Convention: wilful killing; torture or inhuman treatment; wilfully causing great suffering or serious injury to body or health'. But what happened? *Nothing.* The report encapsulated Israel's methods of operation when it said that 'the conduct of the Israeli military and other personnel toward the flotilla passengers was not only disproportionate to the occasion, but demonstrated levels of totally unnecessary and incredible violence. It betrayed an unacceptable level of brutality'. This is the sick and depraved regime that American leaders call 'the Middle East's only democracy', and prostitute Blair calls 'a model for the region'. Put into *YouTube* the words: 'An American Jew Subjected to Torture in Jerusalem', and you'll see how democratic they are. Another supply flotilla was planned to head for Gaza in 2011, and 25 per cent of those on board were amazing and truly wonderful anti-Zionist Jewish people saying 'not in our name'. A ship jointly-owned by Swedish, Greek and Norwegian activists hoping to join the flotilla had its propeller cut while in Athens harbour in a deliberate act of sabotage. Mossad is nothing if not beyond the imagination pathetic. Little boys in short trousers who think they are 'real men' (little dicks scramble their self-esteem), and 'real women' who act like 'real men'. Talking of which, Rothschild Zionist shill, US Secretary of State, Hilary Clinton, warned the flotilla not to head for Gaza on the orders of her bosses at Chateau Rothschild and in Tel Aviv. She said:

> ... we do not believe that the flotilla is a necessary or useful effort to try to assist the people of Gaza. Just this week, the Israeli Government approved a significant commitment to housing in Gaza. There will be construction materials entering Gaza and we think that it's not helpful for there to be flotillas that try to provoke actions by entering into Israeli waters and creating a situation in which the Israelis have the right to defend themselves.

Well, firstly, it is clearly helpful to supply a people in great need and suffering from the consequences of the Israeli blockade; and secondly the flotilla was not planned to enter 'Israeli waters', but Palestinian waters off the coast of Gaza. She didn't mention, of course, that the cold-blooded murder inflicted on the last flotilla was done in international waters against all international law. But there is one law for Israel and another for those it wishes to destroy. The Greek government of American-born Prime Minister, George Papandreou (Rothschild Zionist, Bilderberg Group, London School of Economics), took time out from destroying the Greek economy, impoverishing his people and selling the country to the Rothschild banks and corporations, to stop the 2011 Gaza flotilla leaving Greek waters. He had just had a visit from Netanyahu and received his orders. The theme of 'Israel's right to defend itself' has already been used

Figure 254: 'Shapeshifter' Tony Blair – arse-licker for sale

to justify mass murder of Palestinians and it is planned to be wheeled out again and again to excuse Israel's first strikes – on the grounds of attacking before you are attacked when the target you are attacking had no intention of attacking you in the first place. What you might call getting your retaliation in first. We even have Americans, campaigning against Israeli apartheid and American-funded abuse of people in Colombia, being arrested and put before a grand jury for giving support to 'foreign terrorist organisations'. This follows a dramatic expansion of the US government's definition of what constitutes material support for a foreign terrorist organisation. Peacefully campaigning for justice and travelling to meet the victims of injustice in Palestine and Colombia is 'material support for terrorism', but bombing the innocent in Libya is doing God's work. We have the same Rothschild Zionist influence in Britain, and in many other countries around the world. Canada, for example, is controlled root and branch by Rothschild Zionists. The British version of AIPAC is the Friends of Israel network in every major political party, and one investigation discovered that *80 per cent* of Members of Parliament in the now ruling Conservative Party are members of the Friends of Israel. This has the stated goal of supporting anything that is good for Israel (the Rothschilds who own Israel). British Prime Minister, David Cameron, is a Rothschild Zionist and so is the leader of the Labour 'opposition', Ed Miliband, who got the job after a campaign in which his brother, David Miliband (Rothschild Zionist), was the only other serious candidate. The UK's Jewish population (and many are not Rothschild Zionists) is just 280,000 in a national population of 62 million. A major financial backer of Cameron and his Conservative Party now in government has been Rothschild Zionist arms trade billionaire, Poju Zabludowicz, who also donates to the Conservative Friends of Israel. The most influential manipulating force in the governments of Tony Blair and Gordon Brown was Peter Mandelson (Rothschild Zionist). He flaunts his close connections to the Rothschilds by taking holidays at their mansion on the Greek island of Corfu. The Rothschilds controlled Blair as they controlled Bill Clinton and Boy Bush (Fig 254). This was the connection that led to Blair taking Britain into wars in support of both presidents as they were being urged on by Israel (the Rothschilds). The Rothschilds orchestrated the invasions of Afghanistan and Iraq, the War on Terror and the justification – 9/11.

9/11: Rothschild Zionists wherever you look

The lease of the Twin Towers at the World Trade Center was purchased just weeks before September 11th, 2001 by businessmen, Larry Silverstein (Rothschild Zionist) and Frank Lowy (Rothschild Zionist). Both have very close links to Israeli leaders, including Benjamin Netanyahu, the current Prime Minister. Netanyahu said that what happened on 9/11 was 'good for Israel'. The deal to buy the lease was done with Lewis Eisenberg

Figure 255: Lucky Larry 'Pull it' and 'I've suddenly developed a skin problem on my way to breakfast' Silverstein

(Rothschild Zionist), head of the New York Port Authority, vice president of the American Israel Public Affairs Committee (AIPAC) and a former partner at the Rothschild-controlled Goldman Sachs. Eisenberg is also close to the Israeli leadership. The man who lobbied heavily for the New York Port Authority to sell the lease into private hands was Ronald S Lauder (Rothschild Zionist), from the Estée Lauder cosmetics family. He is involved in a long list of Rothschild Zionist organisations, including the Jewish National Fund, World Jewish Congress, American Jewish Joint Distribution Committee and the Rothschild Anti-Defamation League. Buying the World Trade Center lease was a terrible business deal for Silverstein and Lowy. The Twin Towers were known as the 'white elephants' because of the state they were in and the fantastic amount of asbestos that needed to be dealt with. Silverstein said after being asked why he had bought the lease: 'I felt a compelling urge to own them.' I'll bet he did. When the deal was struck, Silverstein and company vastly increased the insurance in the event of a 'terrorist attack' and they were awarded $4.55 billion after the Twin Towers came down. The lease had cost $3.2 billion and Silverstein reportedly only invested $14 million of his own money. The judge who oversaw the litigation between Silverstein and the insurance companies was Michael B Mukasey (Rothschild Zionist), who later became US Attorney General. Silverstein and Lowy had originally been outbid by $50 million for the World Trade Center lease by a company called Vornado, whose chief shareholder was the Jewish businessman, Bernard Mendik. He was Silverstein's former brother-in-law and they had seriously fallen out after his divorce from Silverstein's sister. Then Vornado, despite having the best bid, suddenly had a change of heart and pulled out leaving the field free for Silverstein and Lowy. No wonder they call him 'Lucky Larry'. Bernard Mendik died after becoming 'suddenly ill' weeks after Silverstein and Lowy presented their final bid for the World Trade Center. So many 'suddenlys'. Silverstein had breakfast every morning with his children in the Windows on the World restaurant, more than 100 floors up in the North Tower, but none of them showed on 9/11. Silverstein said he had a last minute 'dermatologist appointment' when in truth, as one of his bodyguards has said privately, Silverstein had a phone call in his car telling him to stay away from the World Trade Center. Silverstein said in a television interview (which he now deeply regrets) that when another of his buildings in the World Trade Center complex was on fire, the decision was made to 'pull it' – the classic term for a controlled demolition (Fig 255). This was Building Seven, or the Salomon Brothers Building, which had not been hit by an aircraft. Soon afterwards, Building Seven collapsed in on itself in what was an obvious controlled demolition. Put: 'Building Seven Collapse' into *YouTube* and you'll see what happened. The problem with Silverstein's 'pull it' story is that it can take many weeks, even months, to place charges in a building as big as the 47-storey Building Seven to make it collapse as it did. How could the decision be made to 'pull it' and then down it comes? This is simply not anywhere even close to possible; but then it didn't need to be. The charges were planted long before the official decision was made to 'pull it' and the whole 9/11 scenario unfolded from a pre-planned script. A BBC reporter announced on live television that Building Seven had collapsed *half an hour* before it actually did, because the authorities released the 'news' too early. The building was still standing in the background behind her as she reported its demise.

They told us the plan

The Bush administration was famously controlled by the so-called 'neocons', or neoconservatives. These were led by a cabal of Rothschild Zionists such as Richard Perle, Paul Wolfowitz, Dov Zakheim, Robert Kagan, Douglas Feith, William Kristol (editor of the Rothschild Zionist *The Weekly Standard*) and Lewis 'Scooter' Libby, the disbarred American attorney and convicted felon who was former 'advisor' to Vice President Dick Cheney. This gang also included Rothschild Zionist, Robert Zoellick, now head of the World Bank, who replaced his neocon and Rothschild Zionist colleague, Paul Wolfowitz. The neocon leadership wrote to President Bill Clinton urging him to attack Iraq long before 9/11, and they went into overdrive to advocate the invasions of Iraq and Afghanistan after the World Trade Center attacks under Bush. These same Rothschild Zionists launched a 'think tank' before Bush came to office called the Project for the New American Century (PNAC). Bush Defense Secretary, Donald Rumsfeld, and Vice President Dick Cheney, both vehement supporters of Israel, were also involved along with the president's brother, Jeb Bush. The Project for the New American Century published a document in September 2000 called *Rebuilding America"s Defenses: Strategies, Forces and Resources for a New Century*. This called for American forces to 'fight and decisively win multiple, simultaneous major theater wars' with emphasis on places like Iraq, Iran and North Korea. But the document said that they would not be able to sell such overseas wars without a good excuse. The document said that the '... process of transformation ... is likely to be a long one, absent some catastrophic and catalyzing event – like a new Pearl Harbor'. One year to the month after that document was published, and nine months after most of these Rothschild Zionists came to power in the Bush administration, America did indeed suffer what Bush called 'our Pearl Harbor'. The attacks were then exploited to justify the agenda laid out in the Rothschild Zionist document. *It was so blatant.*

Bush's State of the Union address in 2002 which described Iraq, Iran and North Korea as the 'axis of evil' was written by the neocon, David Frum (Rothschild Zionist), and this was straight from the pages of the Project for the New American Century plan for multiple overseas wars. The document also mentioned Libya as a country to target. The official 9/11 Commission 'investigation' into what happened that day was only forced upon Bush and Cheney kicking and screaming, and the man they first appointed to head the Commission was Henry Kissinger (Rothschild Zionist). This was ludicrous and incredible even for them and he had to resign, citing 'conflicts of interest'. This had never stopped him before. The 'investigation' and the final report was overseen by Philip Zelikow (Rothschild Zionist) and the report declared that the official story was true while failing to interview or quote key witnesses that gave another version of events. The federal judge assigned to deal with all wrongful death and personal injury cases filed by the families of those who died on September 11th was Alvin K Hellerstein

(Rothschild Zionist), who has major family ties to Israel. Attorney Kenneth Feinberg (Rothschild Zionist) oversaw the 9/11 victims' compensation fund and 97 per cent of the families were persuaded to take the money in exchange for not pressing for an independent investigation of the September 11th atrocities. Those that did demand an investigation or rejected the limitations of the compensation fund were dealt with through a 'special mediator', Sheila Birnbaum (Rothschild Zionist). Feinberg (Rothschild Zionist) went on to become the 'Special Master' for TARP Executive Compensation related to the bank bailouts, and the government-appointed administrator of the compensation fund for victims of the BP oil disaster in the Gulf of Mexico. I repeat: Jewish people make up only around *two per cent* of the American population and many of those will not be Rothschild Zionists. Their ratio to positions of power is simply stunning, and I am only highlighting here what you might call a 'headline list'. It goes much deeper. By the way, the Project for the New American Century document also called for the development of 'advanced forms of biological warfare that can target specific genotypes ...' These are the people who call others 'racist'. They are beyond sick. The Project for the New American Century was widely exposed in the alternative media, and as a result it has changed its name to the Foreign Policy Initiative.

Controlling 'investigation' (don't have one) and 'security' (don't have any)

Israel, and Rothschild Zionism, is the elephant in the living room time after time after time. The CIA was headed by George John Tenet (Rothschild Zionist) across 9/11, and the 'investigation' into the attacks was overseen by Assistant Attorney General Michael Chertoff (Rothschild Zionist, London School of Economics), the son of a Mossad agent. Chertoff co-authored the notorious Patriot Act which deleted basic rights and freedoms on the justification of 9/11; then he became the second head of Homeland Security, an organisation established in response to 9/11. The Pentagon in this period was controlled by people such as Deputy Defense Secretary Paul Wolfowitz (Rothschild Zionist), who went on to head the World Bank, and Dov Zakheim (Rothschild Zionist), both members of the Project for the New American Century. Zakheim is a dual Israeli–American citizen and he was the Pentagon Comptroller who managed to 'lose' trillions from the Pentagon budget – a fact that was announced on *September 10th, 2001*. Anyone wonder why this extraordinary revelation was not widely reported? Did something happen the next day or something? But, it had to be a coincidence, *surely?* Zakheim also wrongly classified squads of US F-15 and F-16 fighter jets as military surplus so they could be sold to Israel at a knock-down price (and bought with American 'aid' money, anyway). This, and other military sales (often gifts), means that Israel has one of the best-equipped armed forces on the planet with which to 'defend' a population of only seven-and-a-half million. This is ridiculous, but the Israeli military and the nuclear arsenal have been accumulated for far more than 'defence'. They are planned to be used in wars of expansion and to threaten the world with nuclear attack if the spoilt brat doesn't get its way. Israeli establishment military historian, Martin van Creveld, has said that Israel may be forced one day to exterminate the European continent using its nuclear capability and all kinds of other weapons if it felt its existence was threatened. He said that Israel considers Europe a hostile target: 'We have hundreds of nuclear warheads and missiles that can reach different targets in the heart of the European continent, including beyond the borders of Rome, the Italian capital.' Creveld said that most European capitals would become targets for the Israeli air force. These people are mentally ill – and they have nuclear weapons that they won't allow to be inspected, and refuse to sign the non-proliferation treaty. What does the 'International Community' do about this? *Guess.*

Israel also has a massive chemical and biological weapons programme based at the Israeli Institute for Biological Research (IIBR), southeast of Tel Aviv, and the military censor the Israeli media from revealing anything about it. *Three hundred* scientists are employed to research and develop horrific chemical and biological 'weapons' and laboratory-created diseases to unleash on the global population. They are also used to assassinate targets while making it appear that they have died from 'natural causes'. I'm sure that those scientists are also producing what the neocons called biological weapons to kill 'specific genotypes'. The Rothschilds, via Israel, are at war with the world on behalf of the Reptilian Alliance. They should be in jail and the key somewhere mid-Atlantic. Ask yourself why a country of seven-and-a-half million people would have one of the world's best-equipped militaries, a nuclear stockpile and a vast chemical and biological weapons programme. For protection? No. For attack. This is all paid for by American taxpayers via the Rothschild Zionist-controlled US government and the devastating destructive capability is also in the hands of people who are *bloody nuts*. In 2011, a rabbinical court in Jerusalem condemned a dog to death by stoning on the grounds that it was suspected of being the reincarnation of a secular lawyer who insulted the court's judges two decades earlier. If you are reading this on April 1st, it is purely coincidental. This is not a joke. Well, it is, but you know what I mean. The large dog found its way into the Monetary Affairs Court in the ultra-Orthodox Jewish neighbourhood of Mea Shearim and frightened judges. One of them remembered that the court had inflicted a curse on the lawyer who had once 'insulted' the judges. Not possible, surely. The curse had decreed that the lawyer's spirit would enter a dog – an animal considered impure by traditional Judaism. They decided that the dog in the court was the lawyer and ruled that the canine, er, 'lawyer', should be stoned to death by local children. The dog escaped its fate, thank goodness, when an animal welfare organisation filed a police complaint against the head of the court, Rabbi Avraham Dov Levin. I repeat: this mentality has a nuclear arsenal and chemical and biological weapons. Sleep well.

Security at the World Trade Center at the time of 9/11 was the responsibility of the Rothschild Zionist-owned Kroll Inc. This has very close links to the CIA and Mossad, and its current chairman, William Bratton, was called in by British Prime Minister, David Cameron, after the riots of 2011. Security at all three 9/11 airports was run by ICTS International and its subsidiary, Huntleigh Corporation, which are companies owned by Rothschild Zionists, Ezra Harel and Menachem Atzmon. They are also dominated by 'former' agents of Israel's domestic security service and counter-Intelligence agency, Shin Bet, which handles security for the Israeli airline, EL AL. ICTS International was established in 1982 and is responsible for 'security' at all the 9/11 airports; Charles de Gaulle Airport in Paris, where 'shoe bomber', Richard Reid, boarded his plane; and Schiphol Airport in Amsterdam, where 'underpants bomber', Umar Farouk Abdulmutallab, was allowed to board his aircraft without a passport and despite a string of other red flags. As a result of all these Rothschild Zionist 'security lapses', we have a police state, horrendous airport 'security' and full-body radiation scanners promoted by Rothschild Zionist Michael Chertoff, who owns the Chertoff Group. This is a 'risk management and security consulting firm' that employs several senior colleagues from Homeland Security and also Michael Hayden, a former Director of the National Security Agency and the CIA. Chertoff was all over the TV networks after the engineered 'underpants bomber' incident, urging the government to

Figure 256: Michael Chertoff – doing his god's work

introduce full-body radiation scanners (Fig 256). These are produced by one of the Chertoff Group's clients, Rapiscan Systems. Hours before Congress voted on the first Patriot Act (justified by 9/11 and co-written by Chertoff), some 'technical corrections' were added to give foreign security companies such as ICTS International immunity from lawsuits related to 9/11. This meant that ICTS International would not have to be questioned in court or explain what happened to surveillance tapes at the 9/11 airports that went 'mysteriously' missing, and why key cameras were not working. Marvin Bush, brother of Boy Bush, was also a principal with Securacom, a company that provided security for the World Trade Center, United Airlines, and Dulles International Airport. The attacks on the Twin Towers came only days after a heightened security alarm was lifted and bomb-sniffing dogs were removed. Over the weekend of September 8th and 9th the power went down in the South Tower for some 36 hours from floor 50 upwards and so security cameras and doors were not working in the upper floors during this period.

'We went to document the event'

Then there is the story of the five 'dancing Israelis' who were arrested after police received several calls from New Jersey residents outraged that 'Middle-Eastern' men were high-fiving, whooping and cheering as they videotaped the burning Twin Towers and they were reported to have started filming *before* the planes struck. 'They were like, happy, you know ... They didn't look shocked to me,' one witness said. Police and FBI officers discovered maps of New York in their white van, with locations highlighted, and also $4,700 in cash hidden in a sock, foreign passports, and boxcutters of the type alleged to have been used by the 'Arab hi-jackers'. It was further reported that sniffer dogs found traces of explosives in the van, which belonged to a Mossad front company called Urban Moving Systems owned by Dominick Suter (Rothschild Zionist). He dropped everything (literally, judging by the haste the office was evacuated) and fled back to Israel immediately after the attacks. Jewish newspaper, *The Forward*, said the FBI discovered that at least two of the five arrested Israelis were Mossad agents, and that Urban Moving Systems was a Mossad front operation. The five were held for 71 days, but released without charge and allowed to return to Israel where three of them appeared on television to say that 'our purpose was to document the event' (Fig 257).

Figure 257: Three of the five 'dancing Israelis' tell an Israel television show: 'Our purpose was to document the event'

Yes, the event they knew was going to happen. Mossad is the world expert at staging fake terrorist attacks and blaming someone it wants to demonise. Dr Alan Sabrosky, former Director of Studies at the US Army War College, has said publicly that US military leaders know that 'Israel and those traitors within our nation' were responsible for the 9/11 attacks. I have already mentioned that since the attacks we have been subjected to a series of 'Bin Laden' videos and other 'information' promoting fear of Arab terrorism from two organisations called IntelCenter and SITE, or the Search for International Terrorist Entities Institute.

IntelCenter is run by Ben Venzke (Rothschild Zionist), and SITE was co-founded by Rita Katz (Rothschild Zionist). Writers, Gordon Duff and Brian Jobert, ask some key questions in an article headlined: *Is Israel Controlling Phony Terror News?*:

> Who says Al Qaeda takes credit for a bombing? Rita Katz. Who gets us bin Laden tapes? Rita Katz. Who gets us pretty much all information telling us Muslims are bad? Rita Katz. Rita Katz is the Director of SITE Intelligence, primary source for intelligence used by news services, Homeland Security, the FBI and CIA. What is her qualification? She served in the Israeli Defense Force. She has a college degree and most investigative journalists believe the Mossad 'helps' her with her information. We find no evidence of any qualification whatsoever of any kind. A bartender has more intelligence gathering experience.

> Nobody verifies her claims. SITE says Al Qaeda did it, it hits the papers. SITE says Israel didn't do it, that hits the papers, too. What does SITE really do? They check the Internet for 'information', almost invariably information that Israel wants reported and it is sold as news, seen on American TV, reported in our papers and passed around the Internet almost as though it were actually true. Amazing.

Not quite so amazing if you have read this far and seen the extent to which the Rothschild Zionist secret-society networks control and manipulate world events. Rothschild Zionists, Katz and Venzke, provided 'Intelligence' and Bin Laden videos for 'security' agencies and the media; and Adam Gadahn, an alleged spokesman for 'Al-Qaeda', released videos of himself supporting terrorism. His name is on the FBI 'most wanted' terrorist list. How strange then that 'Adam Gadahn' turns out to be a Jewish man called Adam Pearlman, grandson of Carl Pearlman, who served on the Board of the rabid Rothschild Zionist Anti-Defamation League (ADL). The Chairman of the US Homeland Security and Governmental Affairs Committee is Senator Joseph Lieberman (Rothschild Zionist), and he is always using the 'threat of terrorism' to censor the Internet to block the truth from coming out.

Figure 258: An explosion at Fukushima, and a small nuclear explosion. Spot the difference? Me neither

Fukushima: the same old story

Every surveillance company and military producer and supplier in Israel is controlled by the Rothschild Intelligence and enforcement operation, Mossad. This includes ICTS International and another company, Magna BSP, which installed 'security' systems at the Fukushima nuclear complex in Japan before the disaster of March 2011, following the earthquake and tsunami. Fukushima is a catastrophe beyond measure, not only for the devastated Japan, but for the world. It is hard to see a long term future for Japan with the scale of radioactive release over such a period. Some were saying that the scale of radiation released by the summer of 2011 was already 50 times worse than that of Chernobyl in the Ukraine in 1986. As I write, it is still pouring out into the air and sea with no immediate prospect of it stopping. The official story of what happened at Fukushima makes no sense at all. Neither flooding from the tsunami or damage from the earthquake could explain the series of events that followed. The authorities blamed a build-up of hydrogen for the explosion in Reactor 3 after the tsunami struck, but Fukushima had technology that would have dealt with that, and it didn't need electricity to do so. Fukushima's Reactor 4 exploded even though it was not operational and had been de-fuelled. How could it have exploded? Reactors 5 and 6 were also in cold shut-down awaiting maintenance and only Reactors 1, 2 and 3 were operational. You can see the explosion in Fukushima Reactor 3 on the left in Figure 258, while on the right is a picture of what happens with a small nuclear explosion. The radiation disaster at Fukushima was triggered by a nuclear device placed inside Reactor 3. The closed-down Reactor 4 could also only have exploded by artificial means. Giant security cameras and sensors were installed inside Reactor 3 and

Figure 259: A Magna BSP security camera and sensor; and alongside is a gun-type nuclear device

elsewhere on the Fukushima site by the Israeli company, Magna BSP, about a year before the disaster. It also had personnel at the site at the time, and surviving cameras continued to film events. Magna BSP specialises in producing 'virtual security fences' for military and civilian use that include an 'electro-optical radar system' and 'stereoscopic vision sensors'. The cameras weighed more than 1,000 lbs and were of a size and shape very similar to a gun-type nuclear weapon (Fig 259). Magna BSP is located in Dimona in Israel – *the home of the massive Israeli nuclear weapons programme.* Magna BSP's 'virtual wall' system is called the Optical Watch Line, or 'Owl'. The 'owl' to these symbol-obsessed people is the Illuminati symbol for their god of sacrifice known as 'Moloch' which is worshipped by the El-ite at Bohemian Grove in Northern California in the form of a 40-foot-tall

stone owl. Children in the ancient world were
sacrificed by fire to Moloch, and even the Bible
mentions the fact. The official Fukushima story is a
fantasy from start to finish, as is the one for 9/11.This
was the official statement in June 2011 about the
condition of Fukushima Reactor 3:

> Highly radioactive debris and water continue to hamper
> recovery efforts at Tokyo Electric Power Co.'s Fukushima
> Daiichi nuclear energy facility. TEPCO had removed
> about 280 containers of radioactive debris by Tuesday,
> which includes clearing the way for entry into the
> building for reactor 3. Now that workers can enter the
> building, TEPCO plans to inject nitrogen gas into the
> reactor 3 containment to stabilize the reactor.

Figure 260: Reactor 3 after it was
sabotaged

You can see the state of Reactor 3 at the time that
statement was made in Fig 260. There was virtually nothing left of it. Freelance
journalist, Jim Stone, has done some excellent research on the background to
Fukushima, and his website is: www.jimstonefreelance.com. The fact that the
destruction of Fukushima was not a 'natural' event means that the earthquake and
tsunami were not 'natural' events either. They clearly weren't going to place nuclear
devices in position and then sit around hoping for an earthquake and tsunami to turn
up. I'll explain later how they triggered the earthquake and its deadly consequences. I
had finished this chapter and 'gone public' with my view that Fukushima was caused
by nuclear devices when I came across a video presentation by nuclear engineer, Arnie
Gundersen, at the Boston Public Library. He was saying that Fukushima had provided
new evidence of what could happen at any nuclear power station. He showed step-by-
step still pictures of an explosion at Fukushima and said that no one could explain how
the wave could have moved at some 1,000 miles an hour – substantially faster than the
speed of sound. He said that this made the explosion a 'detonation wave' and this was
unexplainable, because hydrogen and oxygen should only be able to produce a subsonic
'deflagration' wave. He said:

> No one knows why this happened. Hydrogen and oxygen at room pressures shouldn't
> detonate. I was talking to a bunch of chemists and we couldn't figure out how it could
> detonate. It could deflagrate, but it shouldn't be able to detonate and that has major
> ramifications on containment design.

I can understand why he and the chemists said that. They were trying to explain what
happened from a nuclear reactor perspective when the explosion was caused by a
nuclear weapon – hence it was a detonation wave and not a deflagration. The only
'ramifications for containment design' are not to have your security system installed
and managed by a company based at the same location as Israel's nuclear weapons
programme.

Owning the hacks and the beautiful people

Rothschild Zionists have kept exposure from the
door, up until now, through ownership of the
mainstream media. Shahar Ilan, a daily features
editor with the leading Israeli newspaper,
Ha'aretz, wrote: 'The Jews [Rothschild Zionists]
do control the American media. This is very
clear, and claiming otherwise is an insult to
common knowledge.' The US National Archives
declassified in 2011 the findings of a 'sealed'
Senate investigation into the $36 million spent by
Israeli organisations to plant stories in the
American media to promote the foreign policy
objectives of the Rothschild Zionists. *The Atlantic
Magazine* was a major recipient of the money. The
paid-for stories included diverting attention
from Israel's Dimona nuclear weapons facility by

Figure 261: Rothschild Zionist Hollywood

describing it as a 'research centre' and pressing for a US attack on Iran's nuclear sites by
claiming they were part of a nuclear weapons programme. Major US publications 'fell
into line' as the sleazy prostitutes that they are. The Senate transcript of the
investigation had been 'sealed' to stop the findings being made public and
congratulations to the National Archives for releasing the documents. This is a classic
confirmation of the Rothschild Zionist control of both the American political system and
the media. Not only in America, either, and not only the 'news' media of Rothschild
Zionist moguls like Rupert Murdoch. *Los Angeles Times* columnist, Joel Stein (Rothschild
Zionist), wrote an article proclaiming that Americans who don't think Jews (Rothschild
Zionists) control Hollywood are just plain 'dumb':

> I had to scour the trades to come up with six Gentiles in high positions at entertainment
> companies. But lo and behold, even one of that six, AMC President Charles Collier, turned out
> to be a Jew! ... As a proud Jew, I want America to know of our accomplishment. Yes, we control
> Hollywood.

'Tinseltown' has been used to sell false versions of historical events and to program
perceptions all over the world. It is obvious that the bloodlines would have created it,
never mind own it (Fig 261). Hollywood movies and television are used to manipulate
reality and program people mentally and emotionally before events that the bloodlines
are preparing to create. Six months before 9/11 came a pilot episode in *The Lone Gunmen*
series that involved the controls of a commercial airliner being remotely taken over and
the plane aimed at the World Trade Center. Sources within the production team have
apparently said that the CIA gave them the plot idea. As I write, a film called *Contagion*
about a deadly mass plague and the US Centers for Disease Control is being promoted –
more Hollywood foreknowledge of another attack on humanity that the bloodlines are
waiting to roll out. Rothschild Zionists also control the Internet. Google, Yahoo,
Facebook, MySpace, Twitter, YouTube, Wikipedia, eBay etc., etc., were all either created

Figure 262: Zion and the all-seeing eye at the London Olympic Games in 2012

or are controlled by Rothschild Zionists – often both. I have to smile when I see these scandals come to light about search engines, networking sites and cell-phone companies, trawling and retaining information about their users. The companies are then all aghast that this is happening, or they make some lame excuse for why it was done. They do it because they are vehicles for the Rothschild Zionist secret society and its connecting networks of other secret societies, Satanists and paedophiles. The logo and mascots for the 2012 Olympic Games in London are obviously symbolising 'Zion' (Saturn) and the all-seeing eye (Fig 262). The moment I heard that London had bid for the 2012 Olympics I said to my family and friends that I was sure they would win. London and 2012 were just too synchronistic for this not to have been planned and there has to be a bloodline reason why they wanted the Games in London at that time. I suspect there will be many engineered events in 2012, a year that has been so nonsensically hyped. I will go into this further towards the end of the book. I emphasise again that we are not talking here about 'the Jews' owning the media, Hollywood, the Internet, politics, banking and big business, but a tiny clique answering to the secret society that is Rothschild Zionism. The mass of Jewish people have been mercilessly used and abused by the Rothschild networks that don't give a damn about them. Rothschild Zionism is not pursuing what is best for Jewish people as a whole, but what suits the Rothschild conspiracy, and therefore the Reptilian Alliance conspiracy, for global domination. The Rothschilds and their Zionist secret-society web control American government policy on *everything*, and the situation is the same in Britain and country after country, and in the European Union, which was a Rothschild creation from the start. Rothschild dual control of America and Israel has led to astonishing amounts of American tax dollars being transferred to Israel in military and financial 'aid'. One arm of the Rothschilds is simply giving it to another. John J Mearsheimer and Stephen M Walt write in their book, *The Israel Lobby and U.S. Foreign Policy* (Penguin; 2008):

> Israel receives about $3 billion in direct foreign assistance each year, which is roughly one-fifth of America's entire foreign aid budget. In per capita terms, the United States gives each Israeli a direct subsidy worth about $500 per year. This largesse is especially striking when one realizes that Israel is now a wealthy industrial state with a per capita income roughly equal to South Korea or Spain.

Richard Falk, professor of international law at Princeton University, said: 'Israel receives more economic assistance than all the countries combined in the world.' Yet, at the same time, the US General Accounting Office (now the Government Accountability Office) is reported to have said that Israel 'conducts the most aggressive espionage operations against the US of any ally'. They are no 'ally' of the American people, only hijackers of their country. The US House of Representatives approved another $205 million in military aid for Israel for an 'anti-missile' system. 'When it comes to defence, military, and Intelligence cooperation, the relationship between the US and Israel has never been stronger,' said Democrat Representative Steve Rothman (Rothschild Zionist), a member of the House Appropriations Defense Subcommittee. As he spoke, the Israeli authorities were using their American-supplied military might to continue the blockade of the Gaza Strip which has been stopping supplies of food, fuel and basic needs for 1.5 million Palestinians since 2007. Also, despite the massive foreign aid for Israel, the Israeli people have begun street protests, as I write, over financial hardship and poverty. Four hundred thousand people went to the streets of Israel on one day to protest against government policy and inadequate wages. They need to come together with the Palestinians and all of us challenging the force that targets us all – the Illuminati bloodlines and their ruthless network that includes Rothschild Zionism. We need to put aside the irrelevant divisions of race, religion, culture and income bracket and let peace, justice and fairness for all be our focus of unity. The Rothschild Zionist El-ite are hoarding the billions in 'aid' money for themselves in Israel and to buy still more weapons. They could not care less about the mass of Jewish people – as the plight of so many Israelis confirms. I have set out here to reveal the true face of Zionism – the House of Rothschild and its networks – and how its agents in Big Government, Big Banking, Big Business, Big Pharma, Big Biotech, Big Food and Big Media and so on, are working as one unit to impose a global Orwellian dictatorship on the human population, *including the mass of Jewish people*. Zionism is a subject that all but a few are either too ignorant or too frightened to tackle and expose, but it *must* be made public and the web dismantled if global tyranny is to be avoided in the very near future. In fact, it's not even about the 'future'. The tyranny is already here and it is just a case of how deeply we are going to allow ourselves to be enslaved by it. The Rothschilds have spent a century hiding the true and ever-gathering extent of their global control behind front organisations and representatives, and that veil must be lifted for the mass of the people to see. They have operated from the shadows for long enough, and we must *urgently* ensure that those days are over.

The Rothschilds have a whole army of organisations to target anyone who gets anywhere near the truth as an 'anti-Semite', which, ironically, means 'anti-Arab'; but that's another story you can read about in my other books. Rothschild 'call-them-racist' fronts include the Anti-Defamation League (ADL), which, in true Orwellian fashion, goes around defaming people (Fig 263). They also have B'nai B'rith (Sons of the Covenant), the Simon Wiesenthal Center (named after a complete fraud) and networks in every country like the Canadian

Figure 263: The Rothschild attack-dog, the Anti-Defamation League, whose modus operandi is to defame people

Jewish Congress (CJC) which was exposed for raising the profile of the Canadian Nazi Party to justify its own miserable existence. The CJC was still being run by an angry man called Bernie Farber the last time I looked. He doesn't seem to like me. I can't think why. Mind you, he's a friend of that Richard Warman chap and he doesn't send me a Christmas card either. I'm hurt. These are just some of the organisations behind the widespread introduction of 'hate laws' to ban freedom of expression and the exposure of the masters they all represent. These laws are promoted as 'protecting minorities', when the Rothschilds and their sleazy Saturnian cult couldn't give a shit about minorities – or majorities, come to that. They are only interested in total control. More and more laws are being introduced to make any criticism of Israel constitute a 'crime' of anti-Semitism'. A long list of magnificent and courageous Jewish people have spoken out against the Rothschild Zionists, such as Norman Finkelstein, and musician and writer, Gilad Atzmon. Finkelstein had his academic career destroyed by them for exposing the horrors inflicted by Israel on the Palestinians and the way the Rothschild Zionist El-ite are scamming Jewish people in general. See his brilliant book, *The Holocaust Industry* (Verso; 2003) and also Gilad Atzmon's *The Wandering Who?: A Study of Jewish Identity Politics* (Zero Books; 2011). They can't credibly call these Jewish critics 'anti-Semites', so they refer to them as 'self-haters' instead. Well, they can say what they like about me, and they have, but I am not going to be silenced. There is too much at stake, especially for our children and grandchildren.

We need to look under every stone, especially the biggest ones, no matter what the reaction and consequences. Either we are pursuing the truth, or we're not. And if you look under the stone marked 'Rothschild Zionist Israel', you will find a man with a fake smile still working on his birth certificate.

10

Big choice: This happens or we *stop* it

I am writing this in the summer of 2011, and many events will have happened in the months before the book completes the production and printing stages and begins to circulate. I can't say precisely what they will be, but I can tell you the themes and what they will be meant to achieve.

The Reptilian Alliance and the hybrid bloodlines want to impose total control on a vastly-reduced human population within a jackboot structure of world government, world army, world central bank and single electronic currency. It wants everybody microchipped by law and connected to a global computer network and the Global Positioning System (GPS) – the satellite 'spies in the sky'. The plan is for every child to be microchipped at birth, and there are even more sinister reasons for the microchipping programme than electronic tracking. I will come to this later. They want control of all food production through a handful of corporations controlled by the same force, and to ban all other production of food – including any grown in your own garden. This would be done on the grounds of 'safety', and through other excuses. Food from the corporation monopolies would be genetically manipulated and full of chemical cocktails to destabilise people mentally, emotionally and physically. Organic food would be banned, and so would any effective doses of vitamins and other supplements to prevent people from compensating for the lack of nutrition in the corporation-dictated diet. The bloodline-controlled US Food and Drug Administration (FDA) designated walnuts as *drugs* in a letter to a company called Diamond Foods which was proclaiming the health benefits of walnuts. The FDA said: 'Your walnut products are drugs' that may 'not legally be marketed ... in the United States without an approved new drug application'. *Insane* – unless you know the real reason behind it. The water supply is planned to be drugged to keep the population docile and robotic, and to make people 'love their servitude'. There would be compulsory vaccinations to devastate the human immune system and open people to all kinds of diseases which are currently dealt with. A Nazi-like global police state would be imposed in which views that oppose the official line would be banned; the Internet would be severely censored; and a surveillance system would ensure that no-one could do anything without the authorities knowing about it. This is already happening via the 'Totalitarian Tiptoe'. People would be told where they are going to live, where they are going to work, and for how many hours and at what pay. The war on trade unions is a part of this. There would be compulsory conscription into the world army, fighting perpetual wars against phantom enemies. A drugged and microchipped population would be nothing more than robots and computer terminals on the control grid of the Saturn-worshipping El-ite. Parents would lose control of their children to the State. This is another reason why children are being taken from loving parents for no credible reason. If anyone thinks that what I am saying is extreme and ridiculous – *look around you*. The very society that I am describing was featured in two 'prophetic' novels published in the first half of the 20th century: George Orwell's *1984*, and Aldous Huxley's *Brave New World*. Combine the two and you have the major themes of what is planned, and much of what they say is clearly happening today. Were these remarkable examples of prophecy only a lucky guess? Oh, no. Orwell and Huxley knew what was coming – unless it was stopped.

Encoding the 'future'

I have been emphasising for so many years the scale and coordination of the conspiracy that humanity is dealing with. Those who manipulate and exploit our world are not making it up by the day, month, year or even decade. They are playing out a programme encoded in the very fabric of our experienced reality. The World Trade Center Twin Towers were built in the late 1960s, knowing what their fate would be in 2001. The liberty flame and black pentagram that is now a shrine to Princess Diana above the Pont de l'Alma tunnel in Paris were placed there in 1989, knowing what they would symbolise after 1997. I know that this is hard for people to accept; but it's the truth. Remember that we are not only dealing with an 'earthly' conspiracy here. The bloodlines of the Illuminati are only vehicles for their 'off-world' masters. The script for what is happening today was written a long, long time ago, certainly hundreds and possibly thousands of years ago. No, I'm not kidding and I haven't had one drink, never mind a bellyful. The global fascist/communist State is happening with such coordination because it is encoded in the broadcasts coming from Saturn and amplified by the Moon. If you have knowledge of this encoded information and where is it going – the plan – then you can write prophetic 'novels' that turn out to be incredibly accurate. George Orwell and Aldous Huxley were able to do this with *1984* (published in 1948) and *Brave New World* (published in 1932), because they basically *knew* what was coming. Orwell (real name, Eric Blair) described the police state and surveillance society and a never-ending war to keep people in line. This is exactly what we are seeing today. The never-ending war is the 'War on Terror'. How can you ever say that you have won a 'War on Terror'? You can't. The story may be bogus, but if people believe that it's true then you are home and dry. Aldous Huxley described in *Brave New World* how drugs and genetics would be used to control the population, and how parents would lose the right to bring up their children or eventually even give them life through procreation. They would instead be created in batches in 'World State hatcheries' and systemically programmed from birth. Much of what Huxley said is now happening, and the constant erosion and loss of parental rights to the State is one of the stepping stones to the rest. Orwell was taught French by Huxley at the El-ite Eton College near Windsor Castle just outside London, where the royal children are sent to be programmed. They became friends, and Huxley introduced Orwell to the Fabian Society. This is a major secret society in the Illuminati web and this was the information source for their 'novels' that have turned out to be so accurate.

The Fabian Society was established in 1884 to manipulate
the 'Left' in politics, while other secret societies look after the
'Right' and 'Centre' to polarise debate, divide and rule, and
give the illusion of political choice. The Fabian Society created
the British Labour Party of Tony Blair – and the Australian
version – and it operates around the world under various
guises. Australian Prime Minister, Julia Gillard, is a Fabian
initiate and she replaced Kevin Rudd, now the Foreign
Minister and another Fabian. They are taking Australians in
the direction dictated by their Fabian controllers, but, then, so
did the Liberal Party bloodline servant, John Howard, when
he was the Australian Prime Minister. This is the way it works
– masks on the same face claiming to be different in order to
maintain the illusion. Australia, like New Zealand and
Canada, is also a fiefdom of the Rothschild Zionists with their
shills such as Gillard and Howard placed into apparent

Figure 264: The Fabian Society:
a wolf in sheep's clothing

power to do their bidding. The Fabian Society (ultimately Rothschild Zionism) created
and controls the El-ite University of the 'Left', the London School of Economics (LSE),
which produces so many 'left-wing' politicians and other bloodline agents to serve the
agenda in Britain, the United States and elsewhere. David Rockefeller (Rothschild Zionist)
was a student, and so was 'shapeshifter' and 'Anunnaki' author, Zecharia Sitchin
(Rothschild Zionist). Two other LSE students were Dov Zackiem (Rothschild Zionist), the
9/11 Pentagon comptroller who lost those trillions of dollars; and Michael Chertoff
(Rothschild Zionist), who co-wrote the freedom-busting Patriot Act, was the second head
of US Homeland Security, and sold full-body radiation scanners to the world. Billionaire
financier George Soros, the Rothschild asset, was a student at the LSE and has made very
large donations to its cause. The London School of Economics is run by a 'Court of
Governors' which, at the time of writing, includes people such as Sir Evelyn de
Rothschild, one of the dynasty's premier operatives; Peter D Sutherland, a major player in
the Bilderberg Group, Trilateral Commission member, a chairman of BP and Goldman
Sachs International, financial advisor to the Vatican (the same as Evelyn de Rothschild)
and former Director General of the Rothschild-Rockefeller World Trade Organization
(WTO); Cherie Blair (wife of Fabian, Tony); and Shami Chakrabarti, a former student at
the LSE, who is now the head of 'Liberty'. This is the most prominent 'defender of
freedom and civil rights' in Britain, but is actually next to bloody useless. The Fabian logo
is a wolf in sheep's clothing (which is exactly what it is) and the name comes from
'Fabius', the Roman general, Quintus Fabius Maximus Verrucosus, who was famous for
the technique of wearing down the enemy over long periods and avoiding battles that
could prove decisive either way – the Totalitarian Tiptoe (Fig 264). The inner sanctum of
the Fabian Society would have had the projected script at the time that Huxley and Orwell
were involved, and they knew what was planned because the Fabian Society knew what
was planned. It seems that Orwell wrote *1984* in an effort to expose the plot. The year 1984
was the 100th anniversary of the Fabian Society. We have also had a powerful
confirmation of long-term planning from a Rockefeller family insider called Dr Richard
Day (Rothschild Zionist), who accurately described in detail in 1969 what is happening
today. I'll tell you about what he said later in the book.

So it is no coincidence that it was David Rockefeller (Rothschild Zionist) who proposed to the New York Port Authority that the Twin Towers should be built in the late 1960s, or that American money via the *International Herald Tribune* in the 1980s located the full-sized replica of the Statue of Liberty flame on a black pentagram over the tunnel in Paris where Princess Diana would meet her fate. *The International Herald Tribune* was jointly-owned at the time by the Ochs–Sulzberger family (Rothschild Zionists) and the Meyer–Graham family (Rothschild Zionists). More than 30 years after David Rockefeller (Rothschild Zionist) proposed to the New York Port Authority that the Twin Towers be built, Ronald S Lauder (Rothschild Zionist) from the Estée Lauder cosmetics family lobbied the Port Authority to sell the lease of the Towers into private hands for the first time in 2001. Lewis Eisenberg (Rothschild Zionist), head of the New York Port Authority, agreed, and the lease was purchased by Larry Silverstein (Rothschild Zionist) and Frank Lowy (Rothschild Zionist) who vastly increased the insurance in the event of a terrorist attack. Weeks after they bought the lease came the engineered 9/11 atrocities in which Rothschild Zionist global enforcers Mossad were centrally involved, and their task was made easier by Rothschild Zionist companies handling the security at the World Trade Center and all the 9/11 airports. The attacks were then used as the excuse to impose a police state, and to invade target countries listed in the policy document published in September 2000 by the Rothschild Zionist Project for the New American Century. No, they don't make it up as they go along.

World events as they really are

The script was written long ago and it is now being delivered by the day. The challenge for the people is to rip it up. Events in North Africa that began in 2011 are just scenes in a movie to justify the acquisition of more and more countries and lead the world into World War III, after which the fully-fledged global fascist/communist state is planned to be rolled out. I sat in a hotel room in Kiev, Ukraine, watching the demise of Egypt's President Mubarak live on Al Jazeera television and the incredible scenes of joy and jubilation that immediately followed (Fig 265). What a moment it was for those people who had suffered so much physically and economically under the 30-year military tyranny of Mubarak and his henchmen-in-uniform. Who could not be moved by the outpouring of relief and

happiness that went on throughout the night? But what did the morning actually bring? There had been no revolution – only the removal of a despicable frontman. The army which had imposed the will of Mubarak (the will of America/Israel/Rothschilds) for three decades was now in charge. The Egyptian army is not only controlled by the US government (the Rothschilds), it is paid for by the $1.5 billion a year in American military 'aid'. This has been second only to the $3 billion (and then some) which American taxpayers are forced to give

Figure 265: Thousands of genuine protestors in Cairo directed from the shadows

to Israel to fund the suppression and systematic genocide of the Palestinians – and a bigger plan that we are yet to see. The man in charge of the Egyptian army – and the country after the 'revolution' – was General Mohamed Hussein Tantawi. He is a life-long friend of the toppled Mubarak and one of his closest associates in his three decades of tyranny. Tantawi was 'Defence Minister' (mass killer) for two decades and enforced Mubarak's reign of terror against the Egyptian people together with Omar Suleiman, the torturing, murdering head of Egyptian General Intelligence. He was still on the scene after the 'people's revolution'. The army then announced that it was going to charge and question Mubarak about crimes against the people and related matters. Who was doing the charging and the questioning? The very people who *carried out the crimes against the people!* You couldn't make it up; but then, in this world, you don't have to. The United States government owns the Egyptian military, and when the US says jump, the uniforms break the Olympic high jump record. Much has been made of the army not firing on the demonstrators, but at the same time the army's masters in America were calling for Mubarak to step down and for the protestors to be left alone. Whatever America (the Rothschild networks) demands of the Egyptian military, it will do. The army cleared demonstrators from the Tahrir Square in Cairo once the eyes of the world had gone away. There was no timetable for the 'free and fair elections' that the army promised, but they said they would remain in charge for at least six months or more. What happened in Egypt was the blueprint for the illusion of 'people's uprisings' that are being used to impose even greater control. Taking over too many countries by open invasion would make what is happening too obvious; but if you manipulate people to 'revolt' under your control then you can trigger the upheavals and regime-change that you seek under the cover of 'freedom' and 'power to the people'.

This is a speciality of billionaire financier, George Soros (Rothschild Zionist), in league with the equally appalling Zbigniew Brzezinski (Rothschild Zionist), co-founder of the Trilateral Commission and handler to Barack Obama (Fig 266). Soros manipulates 'people's revolutions' through his network of trusts, institutes and suchlike. The Open Society Institute and the International Crisis Group are two of the most prominent, but there are many. Brzezinski is also a 'people's revolution' manipulator. He has admitted arming and funding the 'freedom fighters' in Afghanistan to entice the Soviet Union to invade at the cost of a million Afghan lives, and this created the Mujahedeen and the Taliban and brought Osama bin Laden to prominence in support of a longer-term plan. It was appropriate that I was in Kiev, Ukraine, watching the celebrations in Egypt. Down the road from where I was sitting was another square – Independence Square – where they had similar celebrations in 2004 after a 'people's revolution' (instigated by the Soros network) to remove President Viktor Yanukovych over alleged vote-rigging. But the Ukraine president when I was in the

Figure 266: Soros and Brzezinski – Darth Vader is my friend

country for a speaking event just a few years later was the very same Viktor Yanukovych. I asked people how this could be and they just shook their heads and shrugged their shoulders. In fact, during a live interview that I did on Ukraine television, the interpreter was told not to translate my words when I made this very point that there had been no revolution in Ukraine given that the man they threw out is now back in power. It's a free country, see. The reason such apparently bizarre happenings are possible is that 'democracy' is not freedom, but they use these words as interchangeable as if democracy really does mean freedom. It doesn't. Obama and Secretary of State, Clinton, can't say the two words often enough with regard to the Middle East and Africa. They drone on day after day about the right to free and democratic elections and all that stuff, but even at its best democracy is only a tyranny of the majority. 'Democracy' is not even that most of the time. Winners, and therefore leaders, are often chosen by a minority of the population with a large slice of corruption thrown in. How can democracy give people choice when any party with a chance of winning is controlled by the same force? The very concept of political 'parties' was introduced by the bloodlines in the first place to secure their power to select leaders. This political party structure in Ukraine was responsible for the bizarre outcome of a man thrown out in a 'people's revolution' and El-ected back into office a few years later. The 'Orange Revolution' in 2004 installed a guy called Viktor Yushchenko to replace Viktor Yanukovych, but when they lost faith with Yushchenko's party the only other real choice in this 'democracy' was the party of Yanukovych, which he was still leading. Thus, he was back in the presidency. Political choice is purely illusory.

The George and Zbig Show

George Soros and Zbigniew Brzezinski were behind a series of 'people's revolutions' in Eastern Europe designed to eventually bring those countries under the jackboot of the European Union and NATO. I have mentioned Ukraine, but there was also the Czech Republic and Georgia where the Brzezinski-trained Mikheil Saakashvili was brought to power in 2003 by the 'Revolution of Roses' that removed President Eduard Shevardnadze. The pathetic Saakashvili is a graduate of George Washington University in Washington D.C. and Columbia University Law School in New York where Brzezinski headed the Institute on Communist Affairs. Saakashvili is among many American-trained agents in government that are controlled by the network of Soros and Brzezinski. The 'revolutions' are manipulated through a complex web of foundations and organisations working with other groups and agencies, including the CIA and Mossad. The Open Society Institute and other Soros-connected groupings funded and trained Georgian students in the art of mass protest, and financed the opposition TV station that encouraged the demonstrations. Zaza Gachechiladze, editor-in-chief of *The Georgian Messenger*, said that it was 'generally accepted public opinion here that Mr Soros is the person who planned Shevardnadze's overthrow'. The same happened in the Czech Republic and Ukraine, and they tried, but failed, to instigate a 'green revolution' in Iran in 2009. The 'red shirt' movement in Thailand supporting the ousted prime minister, the bloodline stooge and crook, Thaksin Shinawatra, is also funded and supported by a network of Illuminati organisations including the Soros Open Society Institute. Soros and his associates are manipulating unrest and upheavel throughout the world. Another vehicle for manipulated revolutions is the Serbia-based Centre for Applied Nonviolent Action and Strategies (CANVAS), headed by Srdja Popovic. He also founded Otpor! ('Resistance!') with his associate, Ivan

Marovic, who turned up at the Wall Street protests in 2011, and CANVAS and Otpor! work as one. They often use the symbol of the fist for the 'revolutionary' groups they train. Otpor! was funded by the United States and the Soros network to theoretically overthrow the Yugoslavia regime of Slobodan Milošević in 2000 (the mass NATO bombing helped just a little bit) and has continued its 'revolutionary work' along with CANVAS in many other countries since that time funded by bloodline front organisations. It is now moving in on nations in the 'West', especially the United States. If these people, or any associates,

Figure 267: Mohamed ElBaradei – a Soros 'revolutionary'

are involved in your protest or 'revolution', it is *not* a 'revolution'. It is Cabal manipulated. This brings us back to Egypt, where 'revolutionaries' such as Mohamed Adel of the April 6 Youth Movement (with its fist symbol) were trained by CANVAS in Serbia and flown to the United States in 2008 to meet US officials in New York. A guy called Mohamed ElBaradei quickly boarded a plane from Austria when protests began in Egypt and headed to 'his people'. ElBaradei was on the Board of Trustees of the George Soros 'people's revolution'-creating International Crisis Group, a stablemate of the Open Society Institute. Another famous name connected to the International Crisis Group ... Zbigniew Brzezinski. ElBaradei suddenly resigned from the organisation after he felt the urge to 'join the revolution', and within days of his plane touching down in Cairo he was one of the leaders of the protests and getting on so well with the Muslim Brotherhood – another bloodline creation (Fig 267). This man works fast. You can see the type of a character he must be. He won the Nobel Peace Prize when he was head of the International Atomic Energy Agency. Say no more. ElBaradei has said that he will stand for the Egyptian presidency when the army allows El-ections; and he's the El-ite's man, or one of them. They have choices.

Do as I say, not as I do

The 'revolutions' in North Africa and the Middle East are being covertly instigated in line with a long-planned script (Fig 268). We don't have 'leaders', we have *readers* who parrot the words written by others whenever the Hidden Hand says 'cue'. Political gatherings like the G-8 or G-20 are merely *readers* conventions. 'What have you been told to say, Barack?' 'Oh, I have to condemn Syria, Nicolas, and you?' I have to call for more power for the EU to fight the euro crisis.' It is *pathetic* to behold.

Figure 268: 'People's revolutions' in North Africa and the Middle East are covertly manipulated, and genuine protestors are only pawns in a game they don't understand

Figure 269: 'Hello my friend, so glad to meet a great American ally

Figure 270: Private Bradley Manning before and after he was arrested by the caring American government to experience its 'values'

Secretary of State Hillary Clinton once called the vicious and corrupt Mubarak in Egypt a 'friend and ally' of America and a 'personal friend' of the Clinton family. Well, I guess like can attract like. But overnight her old buddy was the bad guy who had to go. Did she have a conversion on the road to Cairo? Did she see the light and realise that all people should be free of suppression and tyranny? *What??* The Obama–Clinton government, as with the British and countless other '*demon*-ocracies' around the world, provides financial and military support to some of the most despicable tyrants on the planet. American money and arms kept Mubarak in power for three decades, and he was warmly received by Obama at the White House (Fig 269). The Rothschild-controlled United States has a history of doing this pretty much since the country was established, and it is imposing ever more tyranny and suppression on the American people at home. They don't give a damn about the people's 'rights', except to delete them. How apt, then, that the word 'demo', as in *demo*-cracy, means to take away, to subtract, to remove. 71-year-old Ray McGovern was grabbed from the audience by police and plain-clothed thugs right in front of Hillary Clinton before being ejected and beaten up while she was delivering one of her puke-inducing speeches at George Washington University about the people's right to 'freedom' in the Middle East. What was Ray's 'crime'? The veteran army officer and 27-year CIA analyst simply wore a 'Veterans for Peace' T-shirt and silently turned his back on Clinton as she spoke. This is the butter-wouldn't-melt America that inflicted disgusting treatment on 23-year-old Private Bradley Manning after he was arrested on charges of supplying secret documents for WikiLeaks to make public. He was confined for 23 hours a day to a small cell, with no personal possessions, and he was shackled and allowed no physical contact during visits from his family and lawyer. This decent 23-year-old man was deprived of sheets and a separate pillow and was prevented from exercising in his cell. He was allowed virtually no outdoor exercise, which breaches United Nations' rules for the treatment of prisoners (Fig 270). Oh, but rules are for other countries – not America, Britain or Israel. The most extreme levels of Orwellian imposition are increasing by the day right across the United States while these demonic liars talk about the need for freedoms elsewhere.

No, there has been not been a sudden conversion to decency and respect for the 'people's rights' so there must have been another reason for the Obama/Clinton change of 'heart' over Mubarak, and it is clear what that is. The tone changed with regard to Egypt

Figure 271: The multi-headed monster is on a killing spree to take over the world

Figure 272: Cue camera – *action!*

and the Middle East, because we are seeing a whole new stage in the Illuminati global agenda (Fig 271). Official documents made public by WikiLeaks reveal that the American government had been planning the 'spontaneous' protests via its embassy in Cairo and had been working with key demonstrators and activists for years. The 'people's revolution' in Egypt was just another scene in the movie with the thousands of genuine protestors acting as unpaid, but essential, 'extras', while the 'stars' and scriptwriters did not appear on screen (Fig 272). Even Obama and Clinton were only reading someone else's words to sell the movie and dupe the extras and the audience. The real work was going on behind the scenes and involved the Rothschild Zionist-owned Google and Facebook, among other Internet sources. The man credited with generating mass protest via the Internet was Wael Ghonim, a marketing manager of Google Inc. Google Chief Executive and Bilderberger, Eric Schmidt (Rothschild Zionist), said that what Ghonim did showed how the 'social media' will be used by the masses in the future. Or, as Henry Kissinger (Rothschild Zionist) said during the Egyptian protests: 'This is only the first scene of the first act of a drama that is to be played out ...' Any form of communication can be used for good or ill, but if the population is not streetwise about how the game is played, and what the goals are, they can be Twittered into tyranny. The same techniques are being used to target Iran – the big prize for the Rothschild network. The upheavals and wars in the Middle East are part of the strategy to control what Brzezinski calls Eurasia, and to trigger World War III. Eurasia is basically the land mass from Europe across to Russia and China and down into the Middle East, and the plan is to control as many countries as possible that border Russia and China. Brzezinski wrote in his 1997 book, *The Grand Chessboard*:

Potentially, the most dangerous scenario would be a grand coalition of China, Russia, and perhaps Iran, an 'anti-hegemonic' coalition united not by ideology but by complementary grievances. It would be reminiscent in scale and scope of the challenge posed by the

Sino–Soviet bloc, though this time China would likely be the leader and Russia the follower. Averting this contingency, however remote it may be, will require a display of U.S. geostrategic skill on the western, eastern, and southern perimeters of Eurasia simultaneously ...

... How America 'manages' Eurasia is critical. A power that dominates Eurasia would control two of the world's three most advanced and economically productive regions. A mere glance at the map also suggests that control over Eurasia would almost automatically entail Africa's subordination, rendering the Western Hemisphere and Oceania geopolitically peripheral to the world's central continent. About 75 per cent of the world's people live in Eurasia, and most of the world's physical wealth is there as well, both in its enterprises and underneath its soil. Eurasia accounts for about three-fourths of the world's known energy resources.

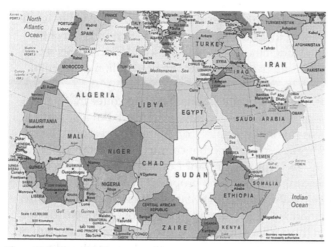

Figure 273: The wish list

Many of those resources, in terms of oil and gas, are in and around the Caspian Sea. This is bordered by Russia, Iran and countries of the former Soviet Union such as Kazakhstan, Turkmenistan and Azerbaijan, with Georgia not far away. Barack Obama's first appointment to be US Assistant Secretary of State for European and Eurasian Affairs, charged with implementing American foreign policy in Europe and Eurasia, was Daniel Fried (Rothschild Zionist).

The wish-list

The map in Figure 273 is not so much a map, but rather a wish-list of countries that the bloodlines plan to conquer and absorb into their global web. Protests in Egypt followed those in Tunisia, which removed the incumbent leader. There were sporadic outbreaks of protest around the same time in Algeria and Libya before those in Libya were engineered to escalate. The bloodlines used this as an excuse to send the boys in to 'protect peaceful protest' by bombing Libyan cities full of civilians. If you look to the right of Egypt you can see the other countries that the Rothschild mass killers have set out to destabilise with a view to replacing their current leadership with their 'new generation' of Illuminati stooges, as well as causing the mayhem that always suits their ends. From Egypt we go to Israel, the Rothschild fiefdom where the population is just cannon fodder for the goals of the Rothschild-owned leadership. Then we move across to the target countries of Jordan, Lebanon, Syria, and the already-occupied Iraq and Afghanistan. Obama's claim that he was pulling troops out of Iraq is another lie – at least 15,000 will stay behind under the guise of 'security officers', 'military instructors' and, hilariously, 'diplomats'. In between

Iraq and Afghanistan is the vast land mass and strategic 'Mr Big' that is Iran. Anyone still wonder why Iran is being constantly demonised? The last I heard the American government was saying that Iran was involved in 'secret deals' with 'Al-Qaeda'. Yawn. One of the most vehement proponents of bombing strikes on Iran is a very sick man called John Bolton (Rothschild Zionist), a front-line neocon from the Project for the New American Century and former Bush Ambassador to the United Nations. If it moves, or even if it doesn't, Bolton wants to bomb it. He told the House Foreign Affairs Committee that he had been calling for military strikes against Iran for three years to stop an alleged nuclear weapons programme. Israel *has* a nuclear weapons programme and, together with the United States and Britain, has been involved in war after war. *When was the last time Iran ever attacked anyone?* Bolton never *ever* mentions Israel's massive nuclear capability; he is just another Rockefeller/Rothschild streetwalker. And have you noticed that America goes on and on about the dangers of other countries having nuclear weapons, but which is the *only* country so far to have used them to kill untold numbers of people in Japan? Exactly. Bolton acknowledged that an attack on Iran was likely to ignite regional war involving Israel, but he said that the cost was worth it. Reminds me of the infamous statement by 'shapeshifter' Madeleine Albright (Rothschild Zionist), Secretary of State in the Bill Clinton regime, who said that the deaths of half a million children in Iraq as a result of sanctions was 'worth it'.

These people are literally, not just metaphorically, insane. They sip coffee in Washington while civilians and troops die in wars they have instigated. But it's worth it, right? Could I have more cream, please? Foreign Affairs Committee chairwoman, Ileana Ros-Lehtinen, said after Bolton had argued for yet another country to be bombed: 'I love John Bolton.' How about the civilians and children of Iran? Love *them*? Bolton was the Undersecretary of State in the Bush administration who proposed in May 2002 to break up Libya and Syria, which is now being attempted nine years later. Israel announced in August 2011 that it was locating unmanned drone aircraft in the autonomous Kurdistan region of northern Iraq, not far from the border with Iran. Massoud Barzani, President of the Kurdistan Regional Government, reportedly agreed to this in return for the admission of a number of Iraqi Kurd students to Israeli universities. What a joke! Do you want to stay alive, Massoud? 'Yes, sir'. Then we're coming in, *right?* 'Of course, sir, you are most welcome, I'll make some tea.' Israeli Mossad agents and military advisers will also be stationed with the drones as part of the 'deal', and quite blatantly Iran is the target. Dmitry Rogozin, the Russian envoy to NATO, said in August 2011 that NATO was preparing for a military strike on Iran to overthrow the government. He told the Russian daily newspaper *Izvestia* that NATO intended to change governments whose views did not coincide with those of the 'West' (the Rothschilds and the bloodline families). 'The noose around Iran is tightening,' he said. 'Military planning against Iran is underway and we are certainly concerned about an escalation of a large-scale war in this huge region.' He believed that attacks on Syria and Yemen could be the prelude to a strike against Iran. This came amid speculation that Israel would attack Iran's nuclear facilities to divert attention from Palestinian efforts to join the United Nations.

To the right of Iran and Afghanistan on the map we reach Pakistan, which is being systematically destabilised and bombed by US unmanned drone aircraft on the pretext of 'fighting terrorism'. The pressure for an all-out invasion has increased in the wake of the Bin-Laden-shooting-that-never-happened. The illusion that it did happen has been used

Figure 274: What appear to be random events are carefully engineered and coordinated

to target Pakistan for 'harbouring terrorists'. Our journey across the wish-list takes us to the borders of China and India, and I have long said that a Third World War is planned at some point involving China, Russia, Europe and North America with the trigger coming out of the Middle East through conflict involving Israel and Muslim states that will draw in the major powers. John 'Bloodlust' Bolton knows this, and this is why he said that although an attack on Iran was likely to create a wider regional war involving Israel and other Arab states, the price was worth it. The price is not only 'worth it' – the bloodline agenda demands it. I write this in June 2011, and we have already reached the point where China is telling the 'West' that if it messes with Pakistan, it messes with China. Chen Bingde, chief of the General Staff of the People's 'Liberation'Army, has welcomed an increase in Chinese military cooperation with Moscow and a joint build-up of forces. Russia is also increasing its condemnation of the NATO bombing of Libya. But it's all a game. Russia and China could have voted against a resolution at the UN Security Council that would have blocked the imposition of a no-fly zone over Libya; but they didn't. They abstained and allowed the resolution to pass (Fig 274). The plan to target all the Arab countries in North Africa and the Middle East is what Kissinger really meant when he said that what happened in Egypt was 'only the first scene of the first act of a drama that is to be played out ...' I wrote when the Egyptian protests were first underway that Syria, Jordan and others would follow, and this is already happening in Syria with demands for an invasion of the country to 'protect peaceful protestors'. The truth is that far from all of the protestors in Syria have been peaceful. Agents provocateurs and mercenaries, well-armed and well organised by the US and Israel, and supplied with weapons via Turkey, began to kill Syrian soldiers (and civilians) with heavy machine guns. When troops fired back and gunmen and more civilians were killed, Obama and Clinton were spitting with condemnation. *Press TV* reported that scores of heavily-armed 'protestors' with hi-tech weapons and ammunition were arrested in the southern city of Daraa near the border with Jordan. The US State Department said in April 2011 that the government had spent $50 million in the previous two years 'to develop new technologies to help activists protect themselves from arrest and prosecution by authoritarian governments'. All of that should have been spent in America, then. The State Department admitted that training had been organised for 5,000 'activists' worldwide, and this included a gathering in the Middle East involving 'activists' in Tunisia, Egypt, Syria and Lebanon who returned to their countries with the role of training others. *The Washington Post* published cables that revealed how America has been funding opposition groups in Syria since 2005 when Syria was added to the neocon 'Axis of Evil'. The same background applies to Libya. The

Libyan 'rebels' have been exposed in film footage for having sophisticated weapons straight out of the box. They have also committed grotesque atrocities against Gaddafi supporters in the territories that they hold; but that doesn't count. They are the 'goodies'. Obama had the nerve to claim that bombing universities, hospitals and other civilian targets in Tripoli, killing civilians by the thousands, did not represent 'hostilities' as he tried to justify his refusal to comply with the War Powers Act. The man is a psychiatrist's life's work. I have said a number of times already that the bloodlines do not take no for an answer. They wanted Colonel Gaddafi overthrown and preferably dead and they planned to increase the bombardment of Libya until they got their way. The same is planned for Syria, Jordan and Lebanon. NATO activities in Turkey, from where they can easily strike Syria and Jordan, and a US naval build-up in the Mediterranean, confirm that a coordinated and long-planned script is being played out. The US Navy's newest and most sophisticated aircraft carrier, named after the paedophile and serial killer, George H W Bush, has been deployed to the region as I write, and it has not gone there to hand out candy. Obama announced at the same time that there would be a phased withdrawal of troops from Afghanistan (to free them to fight elsewhere).

The real Axis of Evil

American, British and Israeli military Intelligence specialise in covertly infiltrating countries to cause mayhem in preparation for takeover. They have been doing this all over the world, decade after decade. Barack Obama spoke from the depths of hypocrisy when he tried to use the excuse of 'diplomatic immunity' to free a professional American terrorist working for US Intelligence in Pakistan who was arrested after shooting dead two Pakistanis. Raymond Davis shot the men when they pulled their motorcycle alongside the car that he was driving in Lahore in January 2011. He says that they were armed and he acted in self-defence, but he fired ten shots and then got out of his car to shoot one of the men twice in the back as he ran away. Some reports say that the dead were members of Pakistani Intelligence who were on to Davis. A group of unidentified Americans in another car tried to rescue Davis as a crowd gathered, and they ran over and killed a third Pakistani before the crowd intervened and ensured Davis was arrested. Obama responded, as usual, with an outrageous lie by calling Davis 'our diplomat in Pakistan' and claiming that he was immune from prosecution in Pakistan. It subsequently emerged that Davis is a CIA agent – hence the guns, maps, make-up kit, telescopes and long-range radio found in his car. Other reports made a connection to Xe, the notorious 'private security' firm formerly known as 'Blackwater'. This operates as a private army of mercenaries for the United States government ... the same United States that condemned the alleged use of mercenaries by Colonel Gaddafi. 'Mercenaries and thugs have been turned loose to attack demonstrators,' Hillary Clinton shrieked. The mysterious Americans who tried to rescue Raymond Davis, a 36-year-old former Special Forces soldier, were also CIA. Pakistani officials say that they were armed and lived at the same house as Davis. The government of the 'Land of the Free', which claims to promote a free media across the world, pressured its own 'free' 'journalists' to suppress the story that Davis was a CIA operative. The lapdog media dutifully agreed until overseas newspapers ran the story and made further suppression in America a farce. London's *Daily Telegraph* reported that Davis was the acting head of the CIA station in Pakistan and was gathering information for drone attacks. A camera in his car included pictures of sensitive locations.

Figure 275: Fake Arabs on a grotesque mission for the grotesque British government with all its 'values'

Davis was freed after the families of the two dead men were paid a reported $2.34 million – 'blood money' as it is known in Pakistan. Sharia law allows relatives of a murder victim to pardon the killer, and here they were being handsomely paid to do so. If you ever see Raymond Davis in your country, it's probably time to leave. Britain and Israel are constantly doing the same. Two British SAS Special Forces soldiers were arrested by Iraqi police in 2005 after failing to stop at a roadblock in Basra (Fig 275). They were dressed as Arabs and wearing wigs. The men opened fire, killing one Iraqi policeman and wounding another, before they were captured. These British elite soldiers, in their Arab disguise, had weapons, explosives and a remote-control detonator in their vehicle. The car was booby-trapped and ready to explode. It was clear that the intention was to set up a manufactured 'terrorist attack' to be blamed on 'insurgents'. 'False flag' terror attacks have happened so many times in Israel over the years with attacks against Jews orchestrated by Mossad and then blamed on 'Arab terrorists'. British authorities were so desperate to spring their men before the full truth could come out that they used tanks to storm the Iraqi police station where they were being held. They 'rescued' the two agent provocateur terrorists and took away their vehicle. British, American and Israeli military Intelligence is nothing less than a global terrorist network that hides behind fake morality and 'what, who, me?' 'Oh no, we would never do that, we're the good guys – it's the baddies you want.' This does not mean that the governments of countries like Syria have no responsibility at all. They do. But it's not black and white. President Bashar al-Assad of Syria has been the most popular leader in the Middle East and he has been receiving tremendous support from most of the population during the engineered protests; but this has not been covered by the mainstream media – the same with enormous crowds in Tripoli in support of Gaddafi. They instead broadcast footage of armed agents-provocateurs shooting into crowds as if they were government troops. One plan is to have sanctions imposed on Syria to bring the country to its knees and encourage the people to remove President Assad.

The sicko 'sheikhs' of Arabia

The 'royal' families of Arabia are in fact not 'royal' at all. They just made it up and said, 'We're in charge.' The term 'Sheikh', for example, is commonly used with 'royal' connotations, but there is nothing 'royal' or 'genetic' about the term 'Sheikh'. It simply means 'wise man', an elder of a tribe or an Islamic scholar, or literally 'a man of old age'. The definition says nothing about being a violent suppressor of the people so that you can steal their country's oil resources; or about living the high life in the capital cities of the world while demanding – under threat of jail, flogging, stoning or death – that your people at home live according to strict rules of 'morality'. These Middle Eastern dictators have no 'morals'. If they did, they couldn't do what they do. None of the Arab 'royal'

dictatorships are safe from the manipulation of genuine
anger by oppressed and poverty-stricken peoples to
change regimes that suit the bloodline game-plan. The
'royal-oil' dynasties and others must be cancelling the
laxative orders. Some will be safer than others depending
on what best serves the agenda of the Illuminati and its
client state, America; but they're all in danger now. I lived
in Saudi Arabia for two months as a young guy in the
mid-1970s as part of a group coaching and developing
footballers. I should have been there for at least two years,
but I couldn't stand the place and I was out within eight
weeks. I saw the opulence of the 'royal' palaces and
lifestyle compared with the poverty of the people – a vast
inequality underpinned by tyrannical laws and horrific
punishments, including beheading, imposed by their
extreme version of 'Islam' known as 'Wahhabism'. The
death penalty is imposed for murder, adultery, rape,
sexual misconduct, rejecting Islam, armed robbery, theft, blasphemy, homosexuality, drug
smuggling, sedition, prostitution, witchcraft and idolatry. Other punishments include
flogging, chopping off hands and feet for robbery, and the public stoning of women. One
woman was sentenced to 200 lashes and six months in jail for being gang-raped.
Somehow, it was her fault. No wonder the Bush family and the US and British
establishment in general have seen them as 'friends and allies'. The disgusting 'British
Empire' was the key force behind the imposition of Saudi Arabia's first king, Ibn Saud,
who was on the British payroll, and the House of Saud's evil and insane Wahhabi creed.
The treatment of women is extraordinary. They are forced to cover themselves almost
completely in public; they make up only five per cent of the workforce; and it is against
the law for them even to drive. In the two months I was there I hardly saw a woman's face
– only their eyes peeping through a veil, the darkest of black (Saturn). Arriving in Saudi
Arabia was like landing on another planet, and nowhere in the world is more overdue a
change of 'leadership' than Saudi Arabia and its truly grotesque 'House of Saud'.

The hypocrisy is shocking, with Saudi support for the Arab League's (Rothschild
League's) call for a no-fly zone over Libya to 'protect the protestors' from government
attacks while, at the same time, the Saudi army was being ordered into Bahrain to kill
civilians and suppress peaceful protest supported by the United Arab Emirates (UAE).
They moved in only days after US Defense Secretary, Robert Gates, met with Bahrain's
Crown Prince, Salman bin Hamad bin Isa Al-Khalifa, who represents a dynasty that has
ruled for more than 200 years (Fig 276). Witnesses reported that 100,000 mercenaries hired
by Al-Khalifa were using posts, knives, clubs, swords and hatchets to attack protestors at
random, and that nerve gas and neurotoxins have killed and paralysed numerous people
– a fact confirmed by nine doctors. One of them filed a report with Human Rights Watch
verifying this. Navi Pillay, UN High Commissioner for Human Rights, denounced the
commandeering of the country's hospitals by the Bahraini government while protestors
were being killed and injured by that same government. 'This is shocking and illegal
conduct,' she said. These are the same ludicrous and appalling Bahraini and Saudi
Arabian 'royals' that withdrew their ambassadors to Syria in protest at the government's

Figure 276: Bahrain despot, Salman
bin Hamad bin Isa Al Khalifa –
Salman bin Killing bin Torturing, for
short

treatment of protestors (many of whom were armed agents provocateurs). The Bahrain 'royal' Nazis even brought dozens of medical professionals before a military court for the 'crime' of giving treatment to injured anti-government demonstrators. Some were also charged with lying and exaggerating on TV satellite channels with the aim of tarnishing the international image of the country (impossible, surely). The doctors said they were being tortured in custody and confessions forced out of them – just like at Guantanamo Bay. But the reaction from the 'no-flyers' with 'values' who sent the bombers into Libya? *Silence.* And no wonder. The US Fifth Fleet is based in Bahrain. The tiny country is a significant banking centre, and there were other fish to literally 'fry' for the moment. Weapons used to kill and suppress peaceful protesters in Bahrain came courtesy of United States companies. Bahrain spent $200 million with American arms' suppliers in the year to October 2010. Obama invited the British and American educated Al-Khalifa to the White House while the killing continued, and voiced his 'strong support for the crown prince's ongoing efforts to initiate the 'national dialogue'. The slaughter of the innocent notwithstanding. Secretary of State Hillary Clinton praised Al-Khalifa's efforts to deal with the revolution. 'Bahrain is a partner and a very important one to the United States and we are supportive of their national dialogue and the kinds of important work that the crown prince has been doing in his nation, and we look forward to it,' she said. Hey, Mr Sheikh man, I don't want to worry you, darling, but she said Mubarak was a family friend before suddenly demanding that he had to go. These mendacious hypocrites bomb Libya with the excuse of protecting peaceful protestors while calling the murder and violence inflicted on protestors in Bahrain as 'ongoing efforts to initiate the national dialogue'. They have no shame. British Prime Minister David Cameron (Tony Blair, Mark II) took the same line on Bahrain when the violence was compared with what was happening in Libya. Cameron said that the two situations were not the same; but course they are. In fact, it is worse in Bahrain because two other countries crossed the border to suppress another nation's people. What he really means by 'not the same' is that they wanted to remove Gaddafi as soon as possible, but for now they need the fake royals of Bahrain, Saudi Arabia and the United Arab Emirates to stay where they are. They want all the Muslim countries eventually, especially the 'big prizes' of Iran and Saudi Arabia, but they have to do it carefully and systematically or it could all go pear-shaped. The idea is to pick off other countries in the region before turning their attention to the ones they need on their side for now. The intervention in Bahrain was a desperate response by both Saudi Arabia and the UAE motivated by the fear that if the fraudulent 'royals' of Bahrain were to fall, it could be them next. The UAE's Foreign Affairs Minister, Anwar Mohammed Gargash, said the decision to support the Bahrain dictatorship reflects the determination of the Gulf states to 'close ranks in the face of any danger' (to their continuing tyranny). But the Saudi and UAE dictators are only putting off the moment when *they* will be gone, too, one way or another. They are just pawns in a game that they don't understand. They are here today and gone tomorrow when it is more useful to the agenda for them to go rather than stay.

What a load of shi-ite

There is another reason that the bloodlines want Saudi Arabia and other Gulf regimes in situ – *for the moment.* The two factions of Islam, Sunni and Shia, are being played off against each other to divide and conquer the Arab world. This schism within Islam stems from a disagreement about the line of succession from the Prophet Mohammed that goes back to the *7th century* when the Sunni and Shi'ite factions went their separate ways while agreeing on the divine nature of the Koran and Islam in general. I know, but pinch yourself and you'll see it is true. This ancient division has been used in modern times in an attempt to keep the Muslim population divided and ruled, and so many are still falling for it today. There are countries where the two factions get along fine, but in others they loathe each other, and the extremists of the Sunni Wahhabi creed in Saudi Arabia say that if a Sunni kills a Shi'ite it improves their chances of getting to heaven. One of the roles of the Saudi 'royal family' (joke) on behalf of the bloodlines is to maintain the hatred between Sunni and Shi'ites. Most of the Middle East is dominated by Sunni Muslims, but the country where the Shi'ites are most dominant is *Iran* (90 per cent Shia). The bloodlines want to secure this land more than any other in the region. Protests in Bahrain are mainly by the Shia majority (70 per cent of the population) challenging the Sunni dictatorship of the ruling 'royal family'. The Sunni fiefdom of Saudi Arabia (95 per cent Sunni) and the United Arab Emirates (80 per cent Sunni) has moved in to violently suppress the mainly Shi'ite protests. The House of Saud is especially jumpy because while there is a massive Sunni domination in Saudi Arabia, the Shi'ites are the majority in the eastern region where most of the oilfields are. Protestors in Bahrain have said that what they are doing is not about Shia or Sunni; it is about freedom, justice and the end of dictatorship. But it suits the tyrants of the Middle East to present it this way, and that also suits Rothschild Israel which has worked tirelessly to maintain the Arab world in a state of ongoing division wherever possible. The Western Illuminati networks want to use the Sunni dictators (many of whom are Sunni, even Muslim, in name only) to support efforts to overthrow the Shia leadership in Iran (another bunch of religious dictators). The irony is that Saudi Arabia, the United Arab Emirates, Bahrain, Oman, Kuwait, and all the rest, are on the list for 'Western' conquest when the timescale suits. In the summer of 2011, the US is already drone-bombing Yemen – which is right across the border from Saudi Arabia. These cold, callous and merciless Arab leaders will be used and supported until that time comes and then they will be told 'taxi waiting for Mr Sheikh' – just as they did with Mubarak in Egypt. They are only 'rulers' of convenience for now and that is all they ever were. The gathering rage of people who have suffered under their suppression generation after abused generation will not be crushed forever, either. They might be put down here and there for a time by sheer military force and brutality, but they are not going away. Indeed, that rage is being fuelled by the murderous response in places like Bahrain and Yemen. These are the dying days of the 'royal' dictators of the Middle East. It is not a case of if they go – only when. Good riddance. But what replaces them is the question.

The jet fuel of tyranny – hypocrisy

The wonder is that they don't choke on the words they speak, but then they are such seasoned liars I guess that the choking would come if they ever told the truth. I watched for weeks as the public was prepared for the invasion of Libya. The 'no-fly zone' and 'protecting civilians' was an excuse to begin the bombing campaign, but it was really an invasion via the 'rebels' from day one. The goal from the start was to remove Colonel Gaddafi from power and they planned to change the rules of engagement as necessary to achieve that. US Admiral Samuel Locklear, commander of the NATO Joint Operations Command in Naples, Italy, said privately that NATO forces were actively trying to kill

Gaddafi, while the Obama administration says that 'regime change' is not their intention and is not authorised by the UN mandate. No, it wasn't, but that had never been a problem before and neither was it with Libya. NATO bombed hospitals, food storage centres, water distribution infrastructure, endless other civilian locations and also television towers to force broadcasters off-air. You can be sure every time they open their mendacious mouths that Barack Obama, Hillary Clinton, David Cameron, Tony Blair, Nicolas Sarkozy and neocons such as John Bolton are either promoting the bloodline agenda or lying to keep it secret. Mike Turner, a member of the House Armed Services Committee, said that Admiral Locklear told him that protecting civilians was being interpreted to permit the removal of the chain of command of Gaddafi's military, which included Gaddafi himself. It was an invasion by foreign powers to remove the Libyan leader, put their own regime in power and take over Libya's banking system and vast oil reserves. They wanted Gaddafi gone for many reasons, including his plan to introduce an African currency based on gold, which he knows many Western countries, especially America, don't have in large quantities for the reasons that I outlined earlier. Fort Knox is full of tungsten fakes. Venezuela's President Hugo Chávez, a friend of Gaddafi, ordered the return of his country's entire gold reserves from around the world in 2011 – much of it held in London – and you can be sure that this was, at least in part, connected to the same story. Gaddafi was also in some ways what is called 'the threat of a good example'. The bloodlines set out to crush any leader or government that shows that there are other ways of doing things. They fear that this could start a domino effect once people are shown an example of something different that works. Colonel Gaddafi was in power for some 40 years without El-ections – and I am not supporting or advocating that in the least. But let us have some balance here. Nelson Mandela described Gaddafi as 'one of the 20th century's greatest freedom fighters'. Gaddafi took over one of the poorest countries in the world and used the oil revenues to give the Libyan people the highest standard of living in Africa. Everybody had money put into their bank accounts from the oil income; everybody had free healthcare, and if an operation was not available in Libya, patients were flown overseas for treatment; after the Gaddafi revolution, basic foods were subsidised; and new farmers were given free use of land, a home, livestock and feed. Will any of this happen under the new NATO/Rothschild regime? Not a chance. Gaddafi turned the coastal desert area green with an irrigation scheme called one of the wonders of the modern world, while using oil money to provide electricity and develop the country. He also encouraged women to be educated and to have careers, despite hostile opposition from Islamic extremists (especially in the 'rebel' stronghold of Benghazi). Showing the rest of the world what can be done is precisely what the bloodlines don't want to happen. The fake oil-royals of the Middle East don't want this either when it contrasts so blatantly with their hijacking of oil revenues for their own gluttonous aggrandisement. No wonder Saudi Arabia and the United Arab Emirates joined the 'coalition' to attack Libya. The mainstream media has played its usual role in demonising someone the bloodlines wish to target, and we heard ludicrous stories about Gaddafi handing out Viagra to soldiers so they would rape women when they seized 'rebel'-held areas. This needs to go in the same trash-can marked 'intelligence-insulting propaganda', along with Saddam Hussein's troops throwing babies out of incubators; German armies of the First World War riding around with babies skewered on their lances; and prisoners of the Nazi concentration camps being made into soap. American investigative journalist,

Wayne Madsen, who went to Tripoli to see for himself what was happening, said: 'We haven't seen an information war like this, a propaganda war, since leading up to the war on Iraq and the occupation, you know, the yellowcake uranium, the biological mobile weapons labs ...' Human rights' organisations failed to find any evidence for the rape claims – and why would they when the sources were paid-for 'rebels' in Libya? Liar-for-a-living, Susan Rice, the US ambassador to the UN, was spouting this crap. John 'Bloodlust' Bolton, one of her predecessors, would have been drooling with pride. Not a word that ushers from the lips of any American ambassador to the United Nations is to be believed. Only genetic liars need apply. Human Rights Watch reported that Libyan 'rebels' were looting shops and clinics and setting fire to homes of suspected Gaddafi supporters, but Hillary Clinton was only 'concerned' with the calculated nonsense that Gaddafi's troops were engaging in mass rape. Well, she at least has lots of experience on that subject and so does her husband, Bill. Slaves from US government mind- control programmes are their speciality (see Cathy O'Brien's book, *Trance-Formation of America*). I watched as a succession of sanctimonious hypocrites and supporters – even orchestrators – of mass murder and human carnage stepped forward to the microphone to condemn Gaddafi and other Middle East dictators for alleged violence against peaceful protesters (but not Saudi Arabia or Bahrain). The mainstream media never calls them out on any of their obvious contradiction and deceit. This is how professional liars, called political leaders, get away with it. Other professional liars – called 'journalists' – keep schtum. Take Hillary Clinton – yes, *please* do – the cold and vicious US Secretary of State who supported the slaughter of the innocent in Iraq, Afghanistan and elsewhere while demanding that the Middle Eastern dictators stop using violence against their people. I suppose she thinks that's *her* job. Cue Hillary at the United Nations Human Rights Council on February 28th, 2011 to lie through her teeth to demonise the next bloodline target:

> Today the world's eyes are fixed on Libya. We have seen Colonel Gaddafi's security forces open fire on peaceful protestors again and again. They have used heavy weapons on unarmed civilians. Mercenaries and thugs have been turned loose to attack demonstrators. There are reports of soldiers executed for refusing to turn their guns on their fellow citizens, of indiscriminate killings, arbitrary arrests, and torture.

> Colonel Gaddafi and those around him must be held accountable for these acts, which violate international legal obligations and common decency. Through their actions, they have lost the legitimacy to govern. And the people of Libya have made themselves clear: It is time for Gaddafi to go – now, without further violence or delay.

> The international community [Rothschilds, de facto world government] is speaking with one voice and our message is unmistakable. These violations of universal rights are unacceptable and will not be tolerated [except in Saudi Arabia and Bahrain]. This Council took an important first step toward accountability on Friday by establishing an independent commission of inquiry.

The British, American and Israeli establishment (collectively 'the Rothschilds') have a long, long history of doing unto others what they condemn the others for doing. Lest we forget, the British, American and Israeli governments, in league with a few minor players,

Figure 277: The consequences of being on the wish list of nations with 'values'. This is Palestine, but the same goes for country after country

concocted the non-existent 'evidence' of Iraq's weapons of mass destruction to justify the bombing and devastation of an entire nation and priceless artefacts from its ancient culture. Millions of Iraqi civilians have been maimed and killed and had their lives destroyed by losing loved ones to the brave men in uniform who surrender their souls and self-identity to serve the global killing machine. Oops, sorry, 'to serve their country'. American troops have told how they are encouraged to carry 'drop weapons' which they can place with dead civilians to make out they were 'insurgents'. How many times are we told on the news that troops have 'killed insurgents' when they are innocent civilians? You can hear what the soldiers say if you type these words into *YouTube*: 'Drop weapons – US soldiers recount killing innocent Iraqi civilians'. The same has happened – *is* happening – in Afghanistan where month after month civilians are caught in the crossfire or directly bombed by the British and American military. They are dismissed as 'collateral damage' in yet another war sold to the world by the lies that Muslim terrorists were responsible for 9/11 when the real perpetrators wear business suits and uniforms in Washington, London and Tel Aviv (Fig 277). Civilians are suffering daily death and destruction from unmanned drones guided by lunatics at the joystick officially sanctioned by lunatics at the Teleprompter. The drones are piloted by joystick operatives at Creech Air Force Base near Las Vegas thousands of miles away from the civilians they are now killing every day in Afghanistan, Pakistan, Yemen, Somalia – the list seems to get longer by the month. The British are involved with this, too, and RAF commanders say they are 'comfortable legally with what we are doing'. How about morally? *Silence.* American author James Bamford, who has written extensively about US Intelligence, says the drones are indiscriminately killing many innocent people, including children. The New America Foundation said that one in four people killed by US drones since 2004 has been an innocent civilian, and the Brookings Institute put the ratio even higher. James Bamford said:

Death warrants for targets are signed by mid-level bureaucrats, and soccer moms and dads double as joystick killers. They operate in comfort and safety, half the Earth away from their targets and close enough for many to run home for lunch between kills.

Today there are more than 5,000 robotic vehicles and drones deployed in Iraq and Afghanistan and more than 50 can be flown at the same time. The Pentagon and CIA will purchase more unmanned aircraft than manned ones this year, and they will train more drone aircraft pilots than those who fly all of the bomber and fighter jets combined.

This robot army is being established so that when the people wake up in sufficient numbers to cause problems for the Agenda, they can be attacked from the safety of bases inside mountains and underground. Hillary Clinton, who knows all this, spoke at the UN Human Rights Council about 'an important first step toward accountability' with the

Figure 278: More children protected by the countries with 'values'

establishment of an independent (no such thing) UN Human Rights Commission inquiry into the violence against protestors in Libya; and Colonel Gaddafi faced an investigation into alleged war crimes by the International Criminal Court (ICC) in The Hague, Netherlands. This was created in 2002 by the 'Rome Statute' to 'bring to justice the perpetrators of the worst crimes known to humankind – war crimes, crimes against humanity, and genocide' (clearly with exemptions for the governments of North America, Europe, Russia, China, Australia, etc.). America won't even join the ICC while demanding that it persecutes others. The Court's chief prosecutor, Luis Moreno-Ocampo, said that 'nobody has the power to massacre civilians without consequences'. Oh, but they do, Luis, old son. They *do* – and you refuse to investigate them, let alone prosecute. The bloodline-created and controlled ICC issued warrants in June 2011 for Gaddafi, his son Saif al-Islam and Intelligence chief, Abdullah al-Sanussi on the basis of the story peddled by war criminals Barack Obama, Hillary Clinton, David Cameron and Nicolas Sarkozy. The warrants were welcomed by NATO Secretary-General, the Bilderberger, Anders Fogh Rasmussen, America, Britain and France as they continued to bomb civilian areas of Libya with the death toll constantly rising and numbering thousands (Fig 278). These mass-killers with 'values' have also been using depleted uranium weapons that have caused such extreme genetic defects in Iraq and elsewhere. What will the ICC do about *them?* The big zero. Where is the ICC investigation into the shocking scale of war crimes, and crimes against humanity by 'shapeshifter' George Bush and 'shapeshifter' Tony Blair? Their casualty count can be numbered in millions and all based on cold and calculated lies. Where is the investigation into Cheney, Powell, Rice, and the lie-factory known as Alistair Campbell, the Blair 'spinner' (professional liar) who helped to produce fake 'evidence' to sell the war in Iraq at such enormous human cost? Why has British Intelligence operative John Scarlett not been arrested for fabricating the 'Intelligence dossier' that made the case for war in Iraq that cost so many lives? Scarlett was head of the Joint Intelligence Committee and sent a memo to Blair's foreign affairs adviser referring to 'the benefit of obscuring the fact that in terms of WMD Iraq is not that exceptional'. Blair rewarded him for services rendered by making him head of MI6. Where is the arrest of Israeli leaders for the daily crimes against the Palestinians and the mass bombing of Gaza, the most densely populated civilian area in the world? Where is the inquiry into the war crimes over decades of Rothschild/Rockefeller gofer, Henry Kissinger, and the Father Bush/Dick Cheney massacres and abominations in the Gulf War of 1991? Or the 'sanctions' imposed on Iraq by Bill Clinton and Tony Blair which, according to UN figures, cost the lives of half a million children in the 1990s – a 'price' that Secretary of State Madeleine Albright (Rothschild Zionist) said was 'worth it'. Where? *Nowhere.*

These hypocrites, bullies and mass killers control the courts and commissions which, if they were truly about justice, would be calling for the prison van and throwing away the key. Hillary Clinton's words somehow survive what must be the tortuous process of being delivered with monumental fake morality without the 'lady' falling off the stage in

Figure 279:
'We believe in freedom, peace and self-determination for all people ...' .... '*Haaahhhhhhh ... fooled yah* – only kidding ...'

hysterical laughter (Figs 279). There is no justice in the political, industrial and military system. Injustice and hypocrisy is its very lifeblood. One minute Mubarak, the murderous dictator of Egypt, is a Clinton 'family friend'; the next she is condemning his violence against demonstrators, playing the Holy Mother and saying he 'must go'. One minute she and her corrupt cronies in government are supplying weapons and military aid to Middle East dictators like Mubarak to violently suppress their own people; and the next they are Moses calling on their fellow mass-murdering tyrants to 'set the people free'. Clinton condemned the torture that she said was used by Colonel Gaddafi while representing a US political-industrial-military complex that sent prisoners to be tortured in places like Mubarak's Egypt to overcome laws against torture in the United States. David Petraeus, Commander of the 'International Security Assistance [Invasion] Force' in Afghanistan, says that torture is acceptable. Obama has made him Director of the CIA and President Fraud has no problem at all with torture. His administration announced in June 2011 that 99 investigations into the death of prisoners in US custody were to be closed down. Petraeus said that torture was necessary to 'save lives' and he was speaking while commanding a killing machine in Afghanistan that had murdered shocking numbers of civilians. Hillary Clinton decried the Syrian forces for killing protestors, but told Syrians protesting against Israel at the border fence to 'show restraint' after 23 of them were shot dead by Israeli troops. She said that Israel has a 'right to defend itself', just as America has 'a right to defend itself' by killing untold numbers in Afghanistan, Iraq, Libya and Pakistan. The same applies to British Foreign Secretary, William Hague, another mouth-for-sale to the bloodlines who know, as *he* knows, that they could destroy him in a day. He said that government violence in Syria was 'unacceptable and must stop', while receiving regular updates on the British planes and troops bombing civilians in Libya and Afghanistan. Amid the protests and violence in Syria, and the clear manoeuvring to justify military intervention, the International Atomic Energy Agency (IAEA) announced that it was reporting Syria to the UN Security Council for having a covert nuclear programme. This is all coordinated through the bloodline networks. Once more the IAEA never mentions the enormous nuclear weapons programme that has been going for decades just across the border at the Dimona site in Israel even though it is controlled by one of the most trigger-happy, violent countries on Earth. The IAEA's evidence for this action against Syria was an alleged undeclared nuclear reactor. The undeclared entire nuclear programme in Israel is never 'reported', and the United States even has an official policy of not asking about Israel's nuclear capability – the 'don't say and don't ask' agreement – which Obama immediately agreed to continue when he took office. Well, of course he would. It's all a game for public consumption only that we are seeing unfold in the form of moralistic platitudes from the world's political prostitutes – Teleprompter propaganda not even written by those who peddle the words.

American death camps

There can be few greater examples of this scourge of hypocrisy than the American death camps in Germany at the end of World War II. The best part of two million Germans died in American camps from disease, exposure and starvation systematically directed on the orders of Supreme Allied Commander and future US President, General Dwight David Eisenhower. Meanwhile, British and American authorities were condemning the Nazi camps such as Auschwitz. How many are taught in their history 'lessons' (programming) that Eisenhower made it clear in his own correspondence that he hated Germans and that he set about killing as many as possible whenever he had the chance. He ordered that German Prisoners of War were designated as 'Disarmed Enemy Forces', or DEF, – just as his successors would designate Prisoners of War in Afghanistan and Iraq as 'Enemy Combatants'. This allows in both cases for American authorities to bypass international laws on the treatment of prisoners. Germans targeted by Eisenhower were not subject to the Geneva Convention, nor were they visited by the Swiss Red Cross that was supposed to inspect the camps and the treatment of prisoners. In this way, Eisenhower, the American 'war hero', enforced the starvation, exposure and disease that cost the lives of almost two million people. A Canadian reporter, Peter Worthington of the *Ottawa Sun*, obtained documentation of this cynical mass murder. He wrote in 1989:

> ... it is hard to escape the conclusion that Dwight Eisenhower was a war criminal of epic proportions. His (DEF) policy killed more Germans in peace than were killed in the European Theater. For years we have blamed the 1.7 million missing German POWs on the Russians. Until now, no one dug too deeply ... Witnesses and survivors have been interviewed by the author; one Allied officer compared the American camps to Buchenwald.

Martin Brech, a retired Professor of Philosophy in New York, was 18 years old when he was a guard and interpreter at an Eisenhower Death Camp along the River Rhine at a place called Andernach. He said in 1990 that when he protested at the treatment of German prisoners he was met with 'hostility or indifference':

> ... I threw our ample rations to them over the barbed wire. I was threatened, making it clear that it was our deliberate policy not to adequately feed them. When they caught me throwing C-Rations over the fence, they threatened me with imprisonment. One Captain told me that he would shoot me if he saw me again tossing food to the Germans ... Some of the men were really only boys, 13 years of age ... Some of the prisoners were old men drafted by Hitler in his last ditch stand ... I understand that the average weight of the prisoners at Andernach was 90 pounds ...

This cruel and callous calculated mass murder was done by the same bloodline cabal that now jails people in some countries – and vilifies them in virtually all – for questioning aspects of the official story of the Nazi concentration camps when it turns out that the 'good guys' condemning such questioning were running their own. There are no 'goodies and baddies' in this black-and-white fantasy that is sold daily to the global public mind. When Clinton or Obama condemn Mubarak or some other tyrant, it is a case of evil condemning evil. They may have a different face, different clothes or uniform, but the mentality is the same. They are cold-blooded, calculating and heartless, and have that prime Illuminati bloodline trait ... *lack of empathy*. This is the common theme that brings them all together no matter what they may claim to represent.

Get Gaddafi

I said from the moment that resolution 1973 was passed at the UN Security Council in 2011 to enforce a no-fly zone over Libya that the idea was not to 'protect peaceful protestors', but to remove Gaddafi and take over Libya's oil and banking assets. The United States, Britain and France had deployed military personnel in the period before the 'public protests' in the east of the country to train and arm the instigators to justify an invasion – Problem–Reaction–Solution. I also said that if Gaddafi didn't go easily they would keep increasing the military operation until he did. This is what happened with the

limits of military action supposedly imposed by resolution 1973 blatantly and brazenly ignored as NATO bombed centres of population to clear the way for the NATO-directed 'rebels' on the ground (Fig 280). The United Nations was established by the Rothschilds and Rockefellers and is located on land in New York donated by the Rockefellers. You would, therefore, expect the UN to do whatever its creators and masters demand – and so it does. UN Security Council Resolution 1973 agreed a no-fly zone over Libya to 'protect civilians'. This should have been the limit to military activities, and any violation of this should have been jumped upon immediately by the UN. But

Figure 280: The real invaders of Libya

no. *Violations?* The US-dominated NATO did anything it liked with no consequences whatsoever while the UN just sat on its pathetic little hands. NATO spokesman, James Appathurai (mouth-for-sale, no, make that *soul*), said in June 2011 with Gaddafi defiantly still alive: 'The UN Security Council should adopt a new resolution on Libya. Resolution 1973 does not envisage land operations. We need a new resolution.' I'll translate: 'We have not yet removed or killed the man that we said we are not trying to remove or kill so we have to increase the military bombardment until we have removed or killed the man that we said we are not trying to remove or kill.' How does Appathurai sleep at night? Like a baby, probably. The United States is going through a financial meltdown with trillions of dollars in debt to be serviced. Britain, and most of the rest of Europe, is also in dire straits.

Crippling austerity programmes are being imposed upon the populations with the excuse that governments don't have the money after bailing out the banks. But when it comes to *war*, money is never an object; and so it was again with Libya. The reason is simple. Giving people a decent standard of living is not the bloodline goal; quite the opposite. Bombing the world into a global tyranny is, and thus there is always money for doing that. Once more the man who is dark of eye and dark of soul stepped forward to slavishly repeat the words of others with his Teleprompter mind and justify the bombing of Libya. What he said was such a work of fiction, such a classic of its type, that it is worthy of some analysis for future reference. Run Teleprompter, cue Obama:

> For generations, the United States of America has played a unique role as an anchor of global security and advocate for human freedom. Mindful of the risks and costs of military action, we are naturally reluctant to use force to solve the world's many challenges.

The government and military of the United States has played a unique role in destroying human freedom around the world, funding and arming despots to suppress their own people – including some that it now condemns in the Middle East. The United States, Britain, Israel and the rest of the hypocrites are not 'mindful' of the risks and costs of military action. Money is never an object when it comes to war, only for people in need within their own borders. The US is clearly not reluctant to use force, but it is reluctant to solve the world's many challenges. *Creating* them is its prime mission. It is truly extraordinary to see the number of wars, military campaigns and interventions by the United States' government and military since 1776. They are, demonstrably, with Britain and Israel in their slipstream, the bullies of the world. *Oops, sorry,* wrong script: They have 'played a unique role as an anchor of global security and advocate for human freedom' and been 'naturally reluctant to use force to solve the world's many challenges'.

> ... when our interests and values are at stake, we have a responsibility to act ... Libya sits directly between Tunisia and Egypt – two nations that inspired the world when their people rose up to take control of their own destiny. For more than four decades, the Libyan people have been ruled by a tyrant – Muammar Gaddafi. He has denied his people freedom, exploited their wealth, murdered opponents at home and abroad, and terrorised innocent people around the world – including Americans who were killed by Libyan agents.

The 'people's' revolution in Egypt was planned and orchestrated through the American Embassy in Cairo for years before with agents provocateurs employed to trigger the genuine rage and frustration of a people oppressed by a Mubarak regime, maintained in power for three decades by American government money and weaponry. The time had simply come to manipulate upheavals throughout the Middle East as part of a much bigger global plan that is designed to lead to World War III. When Obama pointed out that 'Libya sits directly between Tunisia and Egypt', the relevance was not freedom, but the plan to tear asunder a series of countries in a line across North Africa and the Middle East to Pakistan's border with China. The American government 'interests' that Obama talks about are merely the interests of the bloodlines and they have no 'values'. Obama said that Gaddafi 'murdered opponents at home and abroad, and terrorized innocent people around the world, including Americans who were killed by Libyan agents'. These words were spoken by a man who authorised the CIA to kill American citizens abroad if they are 'suspected' of links with terrorist groups; a man who sanctions and supports attacks by unmanned drone aircraft in countries like Afghanistan, Pakistan, Somalia and Yemen which have killed thousands of civilians.

In the face of the world's condemnation, Gaddafi chose to escalate his attacks, launching a military campaign against the Libyan people. Innocent people were targeted for killing. Hospitals and ambulances were attacked. Journalists were arrested, sexually assaulted, and killed. Supplies of food and fuel were choked off.

The water for hundreds of thousands of people in Misratah was shut off. Cities and towns were shelled, mosques destroyed, and apartment buildings reduced to rubble. Military jets and helicopter gunships were unleashed upon people who had no means to defend themselves against assault from the air.

Okay, show me the evidence. All of the above and more was done by American and British forces in Iraq alone, never mind in all of their other 'theatres' of war, including Libya. The American government looks the other way as the Israeli military enforces a blockade on the oppressed people of Gaza, while that same government showers the brutal and satanic Israeli regime with finance and weapons to commit genocide against an entire people. By their own statements and documents, the 'people-protecting' US government has been planning possible nuclear strikes on Libya since at least the Clinton administration in the late 1990s. Now Obama's big finish ... play the John Wayne card:

To brush aside America's responsibility as a leader and – more profoundly – our responsibilities to our fellow human beings under such circumstances would have been a betrayal of who we are. Some nations may be able to turn a blind eye to atrocities in other countries. The United States of America is different. And as President, I refused to wait for the images of slaughter and mass graves before taking action.

Of course, there is no question that Libya – and the world – will be better off with Gaddafi out of power. I, along with many other world leaders, have embraced that goal, and will actively pursue it through non-military means. But broadening our military mission to include regime change would be a mistake [what a liar].

Figure 281: John Wayne ... the 'good guy' righting wrongs – *'Go get 'em, Jaaaaahn'*

This is the John Wayne strategy that is repeated over and over to program the American psyche. America is the 'goodie', the big, tough-but-fair, caring hero who overcomes the 'baddies' and rights all the wrongs, just like the good-guy cowboy and soldier that Wayne played in Hollywood movies (Fig 281). Go get 'em, *Jaaaahn*. John Wayne invariably appeared over the hill with a gun in his hand, while the American government prefers a Tomahawk missile. It was all baloney, of course, and Obama's speech was every bit as much a movie, an act, as anything that Wayne ever did. When some senators challenged Obama's right to wage war without the permission of Congress under the War Powers Act, those Rothschild Zionist shills, Senators John McCain (Rothschild Zionist, selected as Republican presidential candidate with the intention of him losing to the 'chosen' Obama) and John Kerry (Rothschild Zionist, Skull and Bones Society, selected as Democrat candidate with the intention of him losing to the 'chosen' Boy Bush) jumped into action. They proposed that legislation be passed to give retrospective permission for the war in Libya. Then the Rothschild Zionist neocons appeared over the horizon in their short trousers and school caps firing their popguns in all directions. The thought of William Kristol in short trousers is just too much. In fact, William Kristol in *anything* is to be given a very wide berth. The Foreign Policy Initiative, the re-born Project for the New American Century, published a letter from Kristol and others demanding that the war against Gaddafi be expanded as much as necessary to remove him – so long as they themselves never have to get any closer to the action than their drinking club in downtown Washington. The Rothschilds wanted Gaddafi removed and the Rothschild Zionists jumped to attention. The letter was signed by:

Elliott Abrams (Rothschild Zionist); Bruce Pitcairn (Rothschild Zionist); Jackson Danielle Pletka (Rothschild Zionist); Gary Bauer (Rothschild Zionist); Ash Jain (Rothschild Zionist); John Podhoretz (Rothschild Zionist); Max Boot (Rothschild Zionist); Frederick Kagan (Rothschild Zionist); Stephen G Rademaker (Rothschild Zionist); Ellen Bork (Rothschild Zionist); Robert Kagan (Rothschild Zionist); Karl Rove (Rothschild Zionist); Scott Carpenter (Rothschild Zionist); Lawrence Kaplan (Rothschild Zionist); Randy Scheunemann (Rothschild Zionist); Liz Cheney (Rothschild Zionist, and wife of the aptly-named Dick); William Kristol (Rothschild Zionist); Gary Schmitt (Rothschild Zionist); Seth Cropsey (Rothschild Zionist); Robert Lieber (Rothschild Zionist); Dan Senor (Rothschild Zionist); Thomas Donnelly (Rothschild Zionist); Tod Lindberg (Rothschild Zionist); Michael Singh (Rothschild Zionist); Eric Edelman (Rothschild Zionist); Michael Makovsky (Rothschild Zionist); Henry D Sokolski (Rothschild Zionist); Jamie Fly (Rothschild Zionist); Ann Marlowe (Rothschild Zionist); Marc Thiessen (Rothschild Zionist); Reuel Marc Gerecht (Rothschild Zionist); Clifford D May (Rothschild Zionist); Kenneth Weinstein (Rothschild Zionist); John Hannah (Rothschild Zionist); Joshua Muravchik (Rothschild Zionist); Paul Wolfowitz (Rothschild Zionist); William Inboden (Rothschild Zionist); Martin Peretz (Rothschild Zionist); R. James Woolsey (Rothschild Zionist).

I am not saying that everyone in this list is Jewish, although they overwhelmingly are. I am saying that they are agents of the secret society that I call Rothschild Zionism. As these sick and mendacious people were calling for the bombardment of Libya to be expanded, the country was suffering ever-increasing death, destruction and suffering as hospitals, universities, television stations and other civilian targets were hit. The civilian death-toll was rising by the day as NATO bombing intensified. Ports were blocked to obstruct the transportation of food and other essential supplies, fishermen were prevented from going to sea and there were long queues for fuel. Amid all this, the pure evil that is Hillary Clinton had the nerve to say:

The bottom line is, whose side are you on? Are you on Gaddafi's side, or are you on the side of the aspirations of the Libyan people and the international coalition that has been created to support them?

Clinton is a 'Democrat', which is, as we know, different from being a 'Republican'. This is what President Boy Bush said during the slaughter in Iraq:

Either you are with us, either you love freedom, and nations which embrace freedom, or you're with the enemy – there's no in between.

As Adolf Hitler said: 'Make the lie big, make it simple, keep saying it, and eventually they will believe it.' Well, not *everyone* any longer.

Cut the crap, mate, this is the real reason

Now let us have the truth behind the attack on the Libyan people under the guise of protecting them. Needless to say that every word that Obama has said on the subject is a lie. That's his job. Libya had a state-owned central bank and, unlike the US Federal Reserve, it had no private shareholders. The Libyan government issued the currency, the Libyan Dinar, and any business the banking cartel wanted to do with the country had to be done through the central bank. The bloodlines wanted to put an end to all of this and ensure that Libya and other target countries with their own monetary systems fall into the financial abyss of debilitating debt to the Rothschild global banking network. The frontmen for the attacks on Libya – President Obama, British Prime Minister David Cameron, and French President Nicolas Sarkozy – are all the bankers' property and nothing more than bankers' molls. The word 'moll' is defined as: 'a companion of a gunman or gangster, also a prostitute', so you can see what a perfect description that is. The plan was to subjugate Libya in a mountain of debt (control) when Gaddafi was toppled. The European Bank for Reconstruction and Development (owned and funded by Europe and the US) offered massive sums to the post-Mubarak military government in Egypt in return for 'free-market reforms'. For 'reforms', read austerity programmes and sale of assets to the international banks and corporations (international bank and corporation *singular*, in truth). The Egyptian military government has further indebted the country with billions in strings-attached loans that the people will have to pay back, but will never see; and Rothschild bagmen, the truly appalling John McCain (Rothschild Zionist) and John Kerry (Rothschild Zionist; Skull and Bones Society) led a delegation of Rothschild corporations to Egypt to promote 'freedom and democracy'. These were the same on-the-street, on-the-game politicians that proposed retrospective legality for the illegal war against Libya. Their delegation included representatives of General Electric, Boeing, Coca-Cola, Bechtel, ExxonMobil, Marriott International, and Dow Chemicals – collectively known as 'Parasites on the Road'. Now, wait for this ... the leaders of the 'rebels' in Libya took time out from 'fighting for freedom' to, yes, announce that they were establishing a new central bank to replace the one owned by the State and free from control by the international banking cartel (the Rothschilds). Robert Wenzel, from the *Economic Policy Journal*, rightly concluded that 'this suggests we have a bit more than a rag tag bunch of rebels running around and that there are some pretty sophisticated influences'. He said that the uprising looked like 'a major oil and money play, with the true disaffected rebels being used as puppets and cover'. *Erm*, just a little bit.

As I said earlier, one 'rebel military leader' General Khalifa Hifter lived for 20 years in the Greater Washington area of Virginia, close to the headquarters of the CIA who paid his bills; and the whole 'National Transitional Council' established to replace Gaddafi is a US/NATO front peopled by corrupt sleaze bags. Susan Rice, the mendacious US representative to the United Nations, made a request to the UN Sanctions Committee in August 2011 for permission to unfreeze $1.5 billion of assets owned by the Central Bank of Libya, Libyan Investment Authority, Libyan Foreign Bank, Libya Africa Investment Portfolio and Libya National Oil Corporation. The US said that $500 million would go to its 'aid' organisation USAID for 'ongoing humanitarian needs and those that can be anticipated', and another $500 million would be given to 'companies supplying fuel and vital humanitarian goods' (the oil cartel and Illuminati corporations like Halliburton). The third $500 million would be allocated to the 'Temporary Financial Mechanism' (TFM) for 'salaries and operating expenses of Libyan civil servants, food subsidies, electricity and other humanitarian purchases'. *Excuse me?* What the hell is the 'Temporary Financial Mechanism'? Did I miss something? It turned out to be an 'informal' organisation *established by the United States government* (the Rothschilds) to administer Libya! This is the body that *funds* the National Transitional Council that we are told is the interim government of Libya. The United States is doing in Libya what it has done in Iraq – taking the place over lock, stock and oil barrel. The Libyan *'revolution'*? See Tunisia, Egypt, et al. Another country has been stolen before our eyes while many of its citizens cheered – though vastly less than the media would have you believe, and even fewer when reality dawns. As I write, there is still fierce resistance to the invasion in pro-Gaddafi areas. Another Libyan 'opposition group', the 'National Front of the Salvation of Libya' (NFSL) is based in the United States and has been bankrolled by the CIA since 1981. A CIA/Mossad-inspired NFSL attack on the Gaddafi compound in Tripoli on May 8th, 1984, attempted to assassinate Gaddafi, and while he escaped 80 others were killed. The organisation is part of a series of CIA–Mossad–British Intelligence front groups that have been established over the decades of Gaddafi's rule to remove him from power – culminating with the NATO bombardment. Their 'umbrella' organisation has been the National Conference for the Libyan Opposition which was created in London in 2005. The National Front of the Salvation of Libya played a major part in organising the Libyan 'Day of Rage' on February 17th, 2011, and one of the anti-Gaddafi propagandists in the United States, the Arizona-born 'Libyan–American' rapper, 'Khaled M', is the son of one of the founders of the NFSL for his masters at the CIA, Mossad and British Intelligence. Needless to say, 'Khaled M' was given a great deal of publicity by the mainstream US media along with the 'February 17th' website of the 'Libyan Youth Movement'. Libya is another 'people's revolution' that was triggered and guided by the Hidden Hand to secure even greater oppression under another name. One of the first NATO strikes on the Libyan capital, Tripoli, was against the Libyan anti-corruption agency to destroy the documents being used in charges against government ministers for stealing oil revenues and transferring them into Swiss bank accounts. Wayne Madsen, an investigative journalist, pointed out that – almost to the person – these were the ministers who 'defected' to the 'rebel' movement. Then there is the French 'philosopher', Bernard-Henri Lévy (Rothschild Zionist), the buddy of President Nicolas Sarkozy (Rothschild Zionist). Lévy made many visits to meet the 'rebels' in Libya and he seems to turn up at trouble

spots all over the world to meet with major players in
conflicts. He was in Southern Sudan and Darfur;
Afghanistan and South West Asia; Bosnia; South Ossetia
and then Libya. Lévy has encouraged an uprising in Iran
and argued for military intervention in Syria. He is the
bloodlines' boy promoting the Rothschild Zionist agenda.
This is a man who once said of the brutal Israeli Defense
Forces: 'I have never seen such a democratic army, which
asks itself so many moral questions. There is something
unusually vital about Israeli democracy.' Words have no
meaning.

The bloodline-controlled, sorry, '*rebel*-controlled',
National Transitional Council, claims to be the 'sole
legitimate representative of Libyan People' and was
officially recognised, oh, so predictably, by the United
States and more than 30 other lapdog countries as the
legitimate governing body in Libya. The National

Figure 282: The Emir of Qatar: The
bloodlines' buddy

Transitional Council announced early in the conflict from
its stronghold in Benghazi that it had: '[Created] ... the Central Bank of Benghazi as a
monetary authority competent in monetary policies in Libya and [appointed] a Governor
to the Central Bank of Libya, with a temporary headquarters in Benghazi'. How multi-
tasking of them to do this with all that fighting going on. But, wait, there's more. They
also created a new 'Libyan Oil Company' based in Benghazi to take control of Africa's
biggest known oil reserves, and they have even found time in what must have been their
very busy schedule to sign an oil deal with Qatar. The Obama government and the United
Nations both told the 'rebels' that they could sell any oil under their control so long as it
did not involve Gaddafi's National Oil Corporation. Well, that was nice. What an open
book it all is. An image of the Emir of Qatar, Sheikh Hamad bin Khalifa, was placed on a
billboard close to the 'rebel' headquarters in Benghazi with the words: 'Qatar, history will
always remember your support for our cause' (Fig 282). The Emir was instrumental in
arranging Arab world support for the NATO airstrikes against Libya. Newspaper reports
said that Britain and France were using Qatar to bankroll the rebels and to supply arms.
Qatari officials confirmed that they were shipping weapons to Benghazi. Khaled Kayim,
Libya's then deputy foreign minister, said that about 20 Qatari specialists were in
Benghazi and this was at the same time that the Emir of Qatar was in Washington to meet
Obama and get his orders from Obama's controllers. Othman Mohammed Rishi, of the
'rebel' Ministry of Finance and Oil, said of Qatar: 'They have given us fuel, credited us
millions of dollars, and paid the bills for imports we could not afford. We are very grateful
to them.' Qatar is the home of the Arabic television channel, Al Jazeera. This has the
reputation of being on the side of 'the people' in the Middle East; but it is *not*. Al Jazeera
was established to broadcast pictures and information aimed at programming the reality
of 'the people' as part of the long-term strategy of manipulating the Middle East. The Al
Jazeera network was launched with money from the Emir of Qatar, Sheikh Hamad bin
Khalifa. This guy is a bloodline asset who attended the British Royal Military Academy
Sandhurst – another programming operation where foreign leaders and military chiefs are
prepared for a lifetime of service to the Rothschild networks. A 70-page plan for a post-

Gaddafi Libya obtained by London's *The Times* newspaper confirmed the tyranny that awaited the Libyan people when NATO prevailed. It included proposals for the imposition of a 10,000 to 15,000 'Tripoli Task Force' funded by the disgusting tyrants of the United Arab Emirates to take control of the Libyan capital and arrest Gaddafi supporters. The document also reveals plans to take over the Libyan media. It was all organised long before the engineered trouble started by the (NATO) 'rebels'.

Operation Africa

The bloodlines are now making their play not only for the Middle East and North Africa, but the entire African continent. This brings still more potential for a conflict with China (World War III), as China takes over large parts of Africa. All this was the reason for the creation in 2007 of AFRICOM, the US military African command structure officially established by Boy Bush and his Secretary of Defense, Robert Gates, who was, of course, kept on by 'Mr Change' Obama. Why should they complicate an ongoing agenda by changing the Defense Secretary just because they've changed the puppet in the White House? Gates was eventually replaced in 2011 by CIA Director Leon Panetta, a man extremely sympathetic to Israel from the time he shared a house with Rothschild Zionist extremist, Senator Charles Schumer. Panetta has confirmed America's 'unshakable commitment to Israel's security' (aggression and genocide). AFRICOM is based at Kelley Barracks in Stuttgart, Germany, with other centres in Djibouti, the United Kingdom and Florida. It also has 'Offices of Security Cooperation' and 'Defense Attaché Offices' in 36 African countries. AFRICOM is responsible for the whole of Africa except for Egypt, which is the responsibility of USCENTCOM. The *arrogance* of these people fencing off the world into US military regions, but, once again, this is not about America. The 'COMS' are planned to be transferred to a world army when America has been brought to its knees. The original justification for AFRICOM was to coordinate the 'fight against terrorism' in African countries. This repeating excuse was made possible by the US–Israel engineered attacks of 9/11. The real reason for AFRICOM is the takeover of Africa and its major oil resources in Libya (47 billion barrels in known reserves); Nigeria (37.5 billion); Angola (13.5 billion); Algeria (13.4 billion); and Sudan (6.8 billion). We are witnessing the rape and pillage of an entire continent and the Arab world. The American military (the bloodlines' military) is seeking to establish bases throughout the continent in its plan to seize control of its people and resources. This is the truth behind what is happening in Libya and across North Africa and the Middle East. Obama knows that when his eyes scan the Teleprompter for lie after lie. He would not have proclaimed a no-fly zone over Libya if he really wanted peace in the world and to protect innocent people from the jackboot of State violence. He would have imposed one over the United States, Britain and Israel – the 'Axis of Evil'. The world would then be a much safer place. We saw the conflict with the China scenario being ratcheted up when US Secretary of State Hillary Clinton toured African countries in 2011. She said that Africa must beware of a 'new colonialism' as China expanded its presence. The audacity of this statement from a woman representing an administration bombing country after country was a shocker even for her. She was saying beware the 'new' colonialism – stay with the old version. She said that Africa should be wary of friends who only deal with elites. Okay, it's been nice knowing you, Hil. Bye. Clinton said that 'we are beginning to see a lot of problems' in China that would intensify over the next ten years. She gave the example of Chinese efforts to control the

Internet – while back at home her husband was calling for an organisation to be established, either by America or the United Nations, to censor the Internet. His wife-of-convenience told Africa that there 'are more lessons to learn from the United States and democracies'. Yeah, don't touch them with a bargepole.

Figure 283: The statue of Albert Pike in Washington

Pike's War

Albert Pike is one of the most celebrated Freemasons in American Freemasonic history and his statue stands next to the police headquarters in Washington D.C. (Fig 283). He also made a wonderful contribution to peace, love and harmony by helping to establish the Ku Klux Klan. Cheers, Al. Pike was a Sovereign Grand Commander of the Scottish Rite of Freemasonry and major Illuminati operative in the 19th century. He is said to have written a letter in 1871 to another infamous Illuminati agent, the Italian, Giuseppe Mazzini, describing three world wars that together would transform the world into the global dictatorship that I am exposing here. Many say that the letter was a fake, but it is amazing how documents dismissed as fraudulent or forgeries have this uncanny ability to be works of amazing prophecy with the passage of events. The letter says that the first war would overthrow the czars in Russia through a conflict between the British and Germanic empires. Remember it was the Rothschilds who funded and orchestrated the Rothschild Zionist Russian Revolution. Pike said that the second war would lead to political Zionism establishing the sovereign State of Israel in Palestine; and he said this about World War III:

The Third World War must be fomented by taking advantage of the differences caused by the 'agentu' of the 'Illuminati' between the political Zionists and the leaders of the Islamic World. The war must be conducted in such a way that Islam (the Moslem Arabic World) and political Zionism (the State of Israel) mutually destroy each other. Meanwhile, the other nations, once more divided on this issue, will be constrained to fight to the point of complete physical, moral, spiritual and economical exhaustion ... We shall unleash the Nihilists and the atheists, and we shall provoke a formidable social cataclysm which in all its horror will show clearly to the nations the effect of absolute atheism, origin of savagery and of the most bloody turmoil.

Then everywhere, the citizens, obliged to defend themselves against the world minority of revolutionaries, will exterminate those destroyers of civilization, and the multitude, disillusioned with Christianity, whose deistic spirits will from that moment be without compass or direction, anxious for an ideal, but without knowing where to render its adoration, will receive the true light through the universal manifestation of the pure doctrine of Lucifer, brought finally out in the public view [the Reptilians]. This manifestation will result from the general reactionary movement which will follow the destruction of Christianity and atheism, both conquered and exterminated at the same time.*

* Source: Commander William Guy Carr, former Intelligence Officer in the Royal Canadian Navy, quoted in *Satan: Prince of This World*.

You'll see that it says that Islam and political Zionism (the State of Israel) 'mutually destroy each other'. Rothschild Zionism made sure that Jewish people were savagely treated in Germany to win public sympathy to establish Israel. Now they are being set up again. It was reported in July 2009 that the Russian President, Dmitry Medvedev, and Chinese President, Hu Jintao, had issued an 'urgent warning' to the United States that if it allowed an Israeli nuclear attack on Iran, 'world war will be our response'. The plan is to devastate the major powers in the world – the United States, Europe, Russia and China – and then introduce their global structure of centralised dictatorship with a global army 'to stop a world war ever happening again'. American independent journalist, Jim Tucker, has been pursuing the Bilderberg Group for decades and he is largely responsible for bringing its manipulations to public attention. His sources within Bilderberg have proved to be very accurate over the years and he reports that the Bilderbergers called for a 'big war' at their conference in St Moritz, Switzerland, in the summer of 2011. Tucker sources quote Keith Alexander, director of the US National Security Agency, as saying that they need 'a big war involving several countries to advancé our goals of a global economy', and complaining that the pressure to end the attacks on Libya was growing to 'dangerous' levels. He quotes John Kerr, deputy chairman of Royal Dutch Shell and a member of the British House of Lords as saying: 'The recession may keep coverage [of Bilderberg] down. Europe has many independent papers, but they go low-budget. We have made calls to Rupert Murdoch, still our good friend.' Tucker's sources said that the Bilderberg Group wants to expand the war in Libya into a 'huge bloodletting' in the Middle East while maintaining the world economic recession through 2012. The Bilderbergers were addressed by outgoing US Defense Secretary, Robert Gates, who was secretly slipped into the meeting to avoid publicity, Tucker said. Gates called for more effort by the Netherlands, Spain and Turkey and urged Germany and Poland to join the war. He said that the European NATO members faced 'the very real possibility of collective military irrelevance' unless they committed more money and troops. The speech was reported by London's *Financial Times* which said he had been addressing a 'gathering of dignitaries'. Jim Tucker's sources quoted one Bilderberger saying of Barack Obama: '... he's a good soldier and he'll follow orders'.

This is what events in the Middle East and North Africa are really about, and the pieces are being moved into place with the lines between the 'West' and Russia/China being ever more clearly drawn. People must start to get involved in challenging this whole agenda. If we don't, a nightmare scenario will ensue.

11

HAARP – at war with the world

This is not, as you can see, a time for faint hearts. There are some very serious challenges that face us, and one of them is the potential for a technology known as HAARP. George Galloway, a former British Member of Parliament who claims to be a 'left-wing radical', ridiculed on his radio show any suggestion that the Japanese earthquake in March 2011 had been triggered by the Alaska-based High Frequency Active Auroral Research Program, or HAARP.

Galloway's instant derision was no surprise. There are few on the planet more ignorant of the forces behind world events than what is called the 'traditional left'. They will have no part to play in dismantling the structure of human enslavement until they decide to open their minds and get informed rather than rattle out the platitudes and clichés of the manipulated and irrelevant left–right 'battlefield'. The fact that people like Galloway – a Member of Parliament for 23 years – are so clueless about the potential of HAARP shows just how far that mind-set has to go to understand the world as it is, rather than as they have been programmed to believe it is. I am not saying for a moment that Galloway and his like-thinkers have done no good at all. He has spoken out vigorously over the years to expose the plight of the Palestinians, and that's a laudable contribution. His jousts with biased television interviewers and a US Senate Committee have also been memorable. But Galloway and his mentality are challenging the dots while not connecting them to see the picture. The left versus right political 'spectrum' has been constructed to divide and rule the people, while the same network controls and funds both 'sides' and so dictates the political agendas and their direction. George Galloway is every bit a pawn as, say, Margaret Thatcher, John McCain or Sarah Palin. They are simply called left and right, red or blue, in the same way that pawns in a chess game may be different colours, but they are the same pawns with the same worth in the same game. 'Left' and 'right' have both spent so long fighting each other in meaningless battles for supremacy that the world has passed them by. Awareness has moved on as others outside of politics have taken responsibility for looking far deeper into global events than the 'left' and 'right' could begin to imagine; and this brings us to HAARP (Figs 284 and 285).

It is no longer possible to understand what is happening with the world and human behaviour without adding the weather-manipulating, earthquake-causing, mind-

Figure 284:   **Figure 285:**
The High Frequency Active Auroral Research Program, or HAARP

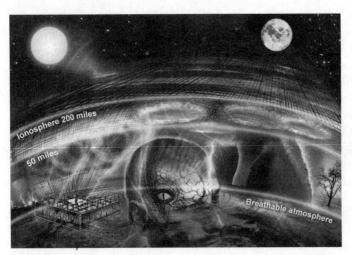

Figure 286: HAARP is manipulating the ionosphere to manipulate life on Earth and create an energetic shield

controlling HAARP to the list of possibilities. HAARP manipulates the ionosphere in the upper atmosphere to do its dastardly deeds (Fig 286). The ionosphere is an electrically-charged region starting around 50 miles above the Earth and extending for hundreds more. It consists of ionising radiation that is deadly to humans. The ionosphere and the stratosphere below protect us from the worst radiation excesses of the Sun, while the ozone layer filters most of the ultraviolet light before it reaches the Earth's surface. If this didn't happen we would be fried. The ozone layer has been damaged already, and now they are messing with the ionosphere. When George Galloway shook his head in disbelief that anyone could suggest a HAARP connection to the Japanese earthquake and tsunami, he was betraying a lack of understanding of (a) what the technology is capable of, and (b) the existence of a network of sheer undiluted evil that is willing to use the technology to cause chaos, devastation and death. Work on the HAARP facility in Alaska began in 1993 and was, we are told, completed in 2007. HAARP is jointly funded by the US Air Force, the US Navy, the University of Alaska and the deeply sinister Defense Advanced Research Projects Agency (DARPA), the technology development arm of the US Department of Defense. It is, in other words, a military operation; and if DARPA is involved, its agenda will be focused on human control and manipulation – and worse.

This is, after all, what DARPA was created
to do. What we can see in Alaska is not
the entire extent of the HAARP
technology. It is much more extensive
than this and connects with other facilities
around the world that are being added to
the network all the time. There is no way
that countries like Russia and China are
not involved with similar 'research',
either. In fact, we know about the Sura
Ionospheric Heating Facility near the
Russian town of Vasilsursk, and there are
other such facilities around the world.
Researchers have connected HAARP

Figure 287: The spiral light in Norway on the eve of
Obama's Nobel Peace Prize award

technology to the blue spiral of light that appeared in the sky over northern Norway in
December 2009 on the eve of Barack Obama's Nobel Prize acceptance speech in the
country (Fig 287). The light stopped in mid-air and began to move in a spiral shape
before a blue-green light shot out from its centre and stayed visible for ten to twelve
minutes before disappearing. You can see the footage on *YouTube*. The light appeared
very close to the European Incoherent Scatter Scientific Association (EISCAT) facility.
This is described as a 'HAARP antenna farm', and there are HAARP-connected facilities
being built around the world.

The Israeli and Chinese governments were bound to be involved in this sort of
technology, and this turns out to be the case. Leuren Moret, an independent American
scientist, has conducted detailed research on HAARP and related technologies. She
confirms a connection to China, Britain, Sweden, the Netherlands, Brazil and other
South American countries. She describes HAARP as a 'Zionist/fascist partnership' to
commit global genocide, plunder the earth and steal resources from the Third World by
knowing where they are located (HAARP can 'X- ray' the earth). She said: 'It is not a
military battle with other militaries; it is countries targeting their own citizens.' That is
precisely what it is. A major Rothschild Zionist connection to HAARP is the Swedish
Wallenberg family who are dubbed the 'Swedish Rothschilds'. They are a highly
significant strand in the web, although most people outside of Sweden will never have
heard of them. One of their number, Raoul Wallenberg, was celebrated as a hero for
helping Jews escape the Nazis in Hungary when, in fact, he made a fortune selling, yes,
selling, fake passports to them. Some of the bloodlines might call themselves 'Jewish',
but they are as contemptuous of the mass of Jewish people as they are of the rest of us.
Raoul Wallenberg's sister is the mother-in-law of former UN Secretary General, Kofi
Annan, who married into the family in a case of 'like- attracts-like'. Another
confirmation that HAARP is a global rather than purely an American operation is Roald
Zinurovich Sagdeev, a leading *Russian* scientist who served on a scientific committee
developing the HAARP project. Sagdeev was the former Director of the Space Research
Institute – the Soviet Union equivalent of NASA – and an expert in nuclear science and
plasma physics. HAARP is not an 'American' mind-control, weather-changing,
earthquake-causing technology. It is the *bloodlines'* technology, and therefore involves
those serving the bloodline no matter what their apparent nationality.

Inmates running the asylum

So now we have the potential for energy wars, weather wars and geological wars, and they have already begun. HAARP fires in either continuous or pulsing form incredibly powerful electromagnetic radio waves at a specific point in the ionosphere in the upper Earth atmosphere causing it to vibrate and 'bulge'. HAARP can cause earthquakes by making the ionosphere vibrate at the point of impact and this resonance then connects with a related point on the Earth's surface which is 'entrained', or made to resonate in sympathy, with the vibrations triggered in the ionosphere. This resonating electromagnetic 'laser' beam between the target area in the ionosphere and the target area on the ground can cause the Earth to shift and hence an earthquake occurs. This is most effective, of course, if you target a location in a geologically unstable area. Scientists have found that earthquakes inflict changes upon the ionosphere and magnetosphere, and HAARP is doing the same thing but in reverse. HAARP turns the ionosphere into a radio transmitter, and the target point on the earth is the 'receiver'. What a coincidence that the frequency range in which HAARP broadcasts is the same as that which causes earthquakes. Everything is vibration in its base form, and if you distort the earth vibrationally and electromagnetically this will play through to distortion at the 'physical' (holographic) level. The interaction between the HAARP radio beam and the ionosphere magnifies the power a thousand times, and this can generate more than 3.6 billion watts. By affecting the ionosphere, HAARP can affect the whole atmosphere from the farthest point down to the ground. The official story is that HAARP was established for scientific research of the ionosphere; but that's like saying that cruise missiles were developed to research the effect of explosions on buildings and people. HAARP is manipulating and superheating the ionosphere, and as the energy waves bounce back to Earth they can cause a range of vibrational distortions that manifest as earthquakes, volcanic activity, changing weather patterns and extreme weather events. HAARP can also impact on human thought and perception, among much else, and can produce an explosion greater than that of nuclear weapons, which it is now on the way to making redundant.

In the late 1990s, a report by the European Parliament's Foreign Affairs Subcommittee on Security and Disarmament highlighted the real and potential dangers of HAARP. Representatives of NATO and the United States were invited to the hearing on which the report was based, but they refused to participate even though HAARP is funded by taxpayers and has the potential to affect the lives of everyone on the planet. There is no accountability because HAARP is actually controlled by the global military establishment, and that operates beyond the realms of politicians and checks, balances and accountability. These people are a law unto themselves no matter who is nominally in political office. The way that HAARP is being used is illegal under international treaties, but then most of what the bloodlines do is illegal under the laws they impose on everyone else. These people will do what they like as long as we continue to allow them. The European Parliament document said:

> ... [With its] far-reaching impact on the environment, HAARP is a matter of global concern and we have to ask whether its advantages really outweigh the risks ... The environmental impact and the ethical aspect must be closely examined before any further research and testing takes

place ... HAARP is a project of which the public is almost completely unaware, and this needs to be remedied.

This was written in 1999. Nothing has changed except that dedicated researchers have ensured greater awareness about HAARP and what it can do. Nothing has been 'closely examined' before further research and testing takes place. The HAARPists have gone on their sadistic way in total contempt of humanity and the consequences for our world. The document says that the electrical properties of the atmosphere can manipulate enormous forces and would have devastating effects on an enemy if used as a weapon. The report said that HAARP can deliver millions of times more energy to an exact location than any other conventional source. This energy can also be directed at a moving target – worth remembering when aircraft or flocks of birds fall out of the sky for no apparent reason. The report highlights the potential of HAARP to: manipulate global weather patterns (it's a cinch with this technology); disrupt the communications of others while itself continuing to communicate without disturbance; and 'X-ray' the earth to find oil, gas and other resources. The bloodlines know far more than governments about where the resources are, and those locations are then targeted militarily or, as with Haiti, with engineered earthquakes to take over and secure the resource assets that the target nation may not even know exist. The resource location data is also shared with their oil and other corporations. Anyone without access to HAARP simply could not compete. HAARP can also scan for underground military facilities, anyone hiding underground and stockpiles of hidden weapons. HAARP has been operational since the 1990s, and this is yet more confirmation that they knew Saddam Hussein did not have 'weapons of mass destruction' when they were lying to justify the invasion of 2003. Funny how they couldn't find Osama bin Laden in his 'cave' either. Another potential of HAARP to keep in mind is its ability to project holographic images that look like the real thing. I have written in other books about 'Project Blue Beam', which is planning to manipulate human perception by projecting holographic images of UFOs and religious deities into the sky. I will put this into context with the overall plan in the final chapter.

Earthquakes on demand

I am sure that HAARP was used to trigger the devastating earthquake in Haiti in 2010 in which more than 200,000 people died (Fig 288). American troops arrived in Haiti so fast to secure control of the airports that there is no way that they were not already on standby. The day before the earthquake, there were meetings at US Southern Command in Miami preparing for a scenario of providing relief to Haiti in the event of a hurricane. The next day the earthquake struck, and they decided to 'go live' with

Figure 288: The Haiti earthquake in 2010.

Figure 289: Here come the boys. They were ready to move in as soon the earthquake happened. Pure coincidence, of course

Figure 290: Clinton and Bush – they care so much about downtrodden humanity

their system. How very convenient. The US military immediately took control of everything, to the point where genuine aid agencies were complaining that they couldn't get into the country because the US military was refusing them permission to land (Fig 289). Then onto the scene, right on cue, appeared those two bastions of decency, fair play and human empathy, Bill Clinton and 'shapeshifter', Boy George Bush. They were 'appointed' by Obama to head the 'Clinton Bush Haiti Fund' (a 'relief organization'), and 'to oversee long-term reconstruction and relief efforts in the country' (Fig 290). No – to oversee long-term control and exploitation of the considerable oil and other resources in and around Haiti. This is the real reason that Bill Clinton was appointed as the United Nations 'special envoy' to Haiti nine months prior to the earthquake. Clinton and Bush disappeared from the scene after the cameras had gone; and more than a year later bodies were still being found in the rubble, less than *five per cent* of which had been cleared, and around a million people were still homeless. Haiti remains under military occupation by the United Nations Stabilization Mission (MINUSTAH) which is despised by the Haiti people who are abused, robbed and intimidated by this brutal and criminal occupation force. I have heard speculation here and there that earthquakes are being caused by nuclear devices positioned on fault lines, and in some cases that may well be true, but with HAARP there is no need. A nuclear device works through the manipulation of energy to cause an extraordinary explosion. What does HAARP do? It manipulates and generates, via the ionosphere, massive levels of focused energy. Weapons directing focused energy are the cutting edge when it comes to destruction and killing people.

Strange lights and rainbow colours have been seen in the sky around the time of earthquakes in the last few years, and these are said to be an indication of HAARP activity. This is what people saw in the sky before the Haiti and Chile earthquakes of 2010, and the same phenomena have been reported with other earthquakes, including the one that devastated Japan in 2011. HAARP heats the ionosphere, and so the atmosphere heats up before these engineered earthquakes occur. Data released by Dimitar Ouzounov and his team at the NASA Goddard Space Flight Center in Maryland confirms that there was rapid and unexplainable (without HAARP) heating of the ionosphere directly over the epicentre of the Japanese earthquake in the days before it happened. Ouzounov published the findings in *Technology Review*, published by the Massachusetts Institute of Technology (MIT). The article theorised that maybe the heating was caused by radioactive radon released by a disturbance in the fault line; but it also revealed data that describes precisely the effects that HAARP has on the ionosphere. The HAARP Induction Magnetometer, which reads frequencies in the planet's magnetic field, revealed that in the run-up to the earthquake there was a consistent ultra-low frequency of around 2.5 hertz – the same frequency produced by a natural earthquake. There were also concentric heat rings above the quake's epicentre. There is also a common theme of a US naval presence at sea close to some of these earthquake locations. This was the case with Haiti and Fukushima in Japan. William S Cohen (Rothschild Zionist), then US Secretary of Defense, said in 1997 that forces were 'engaging even in an eco-type terrorism whereby they can alter the climate, set off earthquakes and volcanoes remotely through the use of electromagnetic waves'. Yes, 'forces' called the American military that Cohen represented. The Japanese earthquake and tsunami were engineered to happen using HAARP technology under the cover of a 'natural' event. The Fukushima nuclear plant was fitted with small nuclear devices masquerading as security cameras and sensors, installed by a company based at the location of Israel's nuclear weapons programme. Why would they do that? The explosions led to the colossal, and so far continuing, release of radiation which the bloodlines want for reasons that I will come to in the next chapter. There are also indications that Japan was not totally 'playing ball' with the bloodline agenda. They know that insiders in other countries will be well aware that the earthquake was caused by technological means, and the message was: see what happens if you say no to us. The bloodline network developed the atomic bomb and had two of them dropped on Japan in 1945 when there was no need for military justification when you look at the hidden history. This was done to show the destructive power of nuclear weapons and to terrify people during the soon-to-come 'Cold War' (see: ... *And the Truth Shall Set You Free*). The bloodlines were messing with the Earth's atmosphere and magnetic field long before HAARP went on stream. The European Parliament report on HAARP says it is linked to 50 years of intensive space research for military purposes, including as part of 'Star Wars', with the intention of controlling the upper layers of the atmosphere and communications. The report described nuclear experiments in the Van Allen Belts – areas of charged plasma radiation between 4,800 and 32,000 miles above the Earth:

> From the 1950s the USA conducted explosions of nuclear material in the Van Allen Belts to investigate the effect of the electromagnetic pulse generated by nuclear weapon explosions at these heights on radio communications and the operation of radar. This created new magnetic radiation belts which covered nearly the whole earth. The electrons travelled along magnetic lines of force and created an artificial Aurora Borealis above the North Pole.

> These military tests are liable to disrupt the Van Allen belt for a long period. The earth's magnetic field could be disrupted over large areas, which would obstruct radio communications. According to US scientists it could take hundreds of years for the Van Allen belt to return to normal. HAARP could result in changes in weather patterns. It could also influence whole ecosystems, especially in the sensitive Antarctic regions.

Another damaging consequence of HAARP is the occurrence of holes in the ionosphere caused by the powerful radio beams. The ionosphere protects us from incoming cosmic radiation. The hope is that the holes will fill again, but our experience of change in the ozone layer points in the other direction. This means substantial holes in the ionosphere that protects us.

How many people know that the American – and Russian – military have exploded nuclear weapons in the Van Allen Belt? More than 300 megatons of nuclear bombs were exploded in the Earth's atmosphere in the 1950s and 1960s. The Van Allen Belts were quite weak before these crazies intervened and increased their strength hundreds of times with the release of radiation from nuclear explosions. This has made it far more dangerous and costly for spacecraft passing through the Belts, because the effect of the radiation means that craft have to go through them far more quickly than they would otherwise have to do. The explosions also created new radiation belts that were not there previously. Many scientists had opposed the project for fear of the consequences for natural systems, but the maniacs did it anyway. The first nuclear test – known as the 'Trinity Test' – was carried out by the Manhattan Project in 1945, and many others followed. Figures released from the US National Cancer Institute show that cancer rates have increased every year since 1945. The Manhattan Project developed the first atomic bomb during World War II led by Julius Robert Oppenheimer (Rothschild Zionist) at the Los Alamos National Laboratories in New Mexico. Oppenheimer was known as the 'father of the atomic bomb', while the scientist referred to as the 'father of the hydrogen bomb' was Edward Teller (Rothschild Zionist). Teller also worked on the Manhattan Project and so did his fellow developer of the hydrogen bomb, Stanisław Marcin Ulam (Rothschild Zionist). Other scientists involved in the Manhattan Project were Leó Szilárd (Rothschild Zionist); Eugene Wigner (Rothschild Zionist); Hans Bethe (Rothschild Zionist); Felix Bloch (Rothschild Zionist); and Robert Serber (Rothschild Zionist). I could go on and on. The Manhattan Project was approved and funded by President Franklin D Roosevelt (Rothschild Zionist) after receiving a letter in 1939 from Albert Einstein (Rothschild Zionist) which had been dictated by Leó Szilárd (Rothschild Zionist). The letter warned that the Nazis might develop nuclear weapons. I have tried to identify a theme that connects all these scientists that gave the world nuclear weapons, but so far I can't find one. I must look harder.

Tesla told us

The patents for HAARP technology were written and secured by Bernard J Eastlund and other scientists and were owned by their employer, ARCO Power Technologies Incorporated (APTI), a subsidiary of oil giant Atlantic Richfield. APTI began the construction of the HAARP facility and was sold in 1994, with the patents, to E-Systems, a global Intelligence contractor working for agencies like the CIA. From E-Systems the HAARP contract and patents passed to Raytheon, one of the world's biggest defence contractors and Illuminati to its paperclips, and finally to BAE Systems North America (now simply BAE Systems). The US government claims that HAARP is a civilian research project, when it is completely controlled by the military and overseen by DARPA, the technological development arm of the Defense Department. HAARP patents and related patents say that the technology can:

- Deliver unprecedented amounts of energy at specific locations in the atmosphere that are far more precise than a nuclear weapon.
- Interfere with global communications systems while HAARP communications remain unaffected.
- Block incoming missiles.
- Manipulate weather.
- Manipulate the atmosphere by changing the molecular composition of an atmospheric region.
- Create nuclear-sized explosions without radiation using electromagnetic pulses.
- Allow for over-the-horizon radar.

Figure 291: Genius of the 20th century

The technology is based on the work of the brilliant Croatian (Serbia also claims him) inventor and engineer, Nikola Tesla (1856–1943). He discovered alternating current (AC) electricity that gave us the electrical power that we know today, and many other systems of power and communication for which others have been given the credit (Fig 291). Tesla held 45 of the 46 basic AC patents, invented 16 different types of lighting and had his laboratory brilliantly illuminated. He was way ahead of his time and he understood the electromagnetic nature of the Universe. Bernard Eastlund mentions Tesla in his HAARP patents and Tesla revealed the potential of his technology in an article in *The New York Times* in 1940. The article talked about a Tesla invention that he called the 'teleforce', which was based on 'an entirely new principle of physics' which 'no one ever dreamed about'. Tesla said that an invisible beam could 'melt' aircraft motors at a distance of 250 miles, so that an invisible 'Chinese Wall of Defense' would be built around a country. The teleforce would operate with a beam 'one- hundred-millionth of a square centimetre' in diameter. Guglielmo Marconi has been given the credit for discovering radio communications, but he stole the idea from Tesla who developed an advanced understanding of radio waves – the medium employed by HAARP. Marconi worked for Tesla for nine months and stole all the technological information. The US Supreme Court ruled that Marconi stole 14 of Tesla's patents. Tesla could see the potential for locating or tracking objects, which today we call radar, and for 'X-raying' the earth to see what lies inside. Tesla set out to produce free electricity for everyone and that is perfectly possible today, but it is suppressed to keep people dependent on paying the bills of the bloodline energy corporations. The Universe is alive with electricity, for goodness sake. Why do we need to plunder the Earth? We *don't*. Tesla also saw the military potential for the energetic principles that he discovered. He said that his transmitter could produce 100 million volts of pressure with currents up to 100 billion watts, and if the radio frequency was resonating at two Megahertz the energy released would be the equivalent of ten megatons of TNT. HAARP cannot cause earthquakes? HAARP cannot manipulate the weather and be used as a weapon? Tesla caused artificial earthquakes when his own building and neighbouring ones started to shake violently during an experiment. Thousands of windows were broken before he could turn off the technology. In 1935, the *New York American* published an article headlined:

'Tesla's Controlled Earthquakes' in which he talked about the effect of transmitting resonance through the Earth:

> The rhythmical vibrations pass through the Earth with almost no loss of energy ... [It] becomes possible to convey mechanical effects to the greatest terrestrial distances and produce all kinds of unique effects ... The invention could be used with destructive effect in war ...

Tesla said he had the technology to 'split the Earth like an apple', and it is sobering to think that he died in 1943. What can be done now? The Russians and Chinese have this technology which has more power than nuclear weapons, and so do the Israelis through the Rothschild control of the United States. It is called HAARP, and as one government insider said, it could deliver enough power to make the Earth flip over. When you see the potential for the cutting edge of human technology, it is easy to see how the fundamentally more technologically-advanced Reptilian Alliance could have caused the catastrophes that I described earlier and allowed them to hijack Saturn.

What's with the weather?

Tesla was able to artificially-generate violent lighting storms that started hundreds of forest fires and blew out electrical grids in two states. Anyone think that HAARP might be able to manipulate the weather? Of course it can. They have been doing exactly that for decades – first, in the early days, with cloud seeding to make it rain; and now creating manufactured droughts, extreme and incessant rain and snow storms, tornadoes, hurricanes – almost whatever they choose. Native Americans and other tribal peoples could change the weather with rain dances and suchlike when they were generating an electromagnetic field that causes rain clouds to form. Weather is only energy vibrating to different frequencies, and if you generate those frequencies you produce the weather that goes with them. It's dead simple. *The Wall Street Journal* reported that a Russian company called Elate Intelligent Technologies Inc. was selling weather-control equipment using the slogan: 'Weather made to order'. Igor Pirogoff, a director of the company, said that the technology could have turned the devastating Hurricane Andrew in 1992 'into a wimpy little squall'. Yes, and the other way round, too, with the weather- changing technology available today – especially HAARP. Weather manipulation was subject to international law 40 years ago with the United Nations Convention on the Prohibition of Military or Any Other Hostile Use of Environmental Modification Techniques (ENMOD). Would they introduce laws to stop what they thought could not be done?? Weather is being manipulated all the time, and Rothschild Zionists are heavily involved. Israeli scientists once suggested using lethal e-coli bacteria to seed clouds because it worked in warm weather and the alternative didn't. Mad professors *do* exist in very large numbers and they may well have covertly done that – they're crazy enough. What's a bit of e-coli when you are exploding nuclear weapons in the Van Allen Belts and punching holes in the ionosphere? HAARP is being used as a now-vital cog in the bloodline global machine. They can manipulate the weather and blame it on 'climate change', for example. Al Gore quotes weather extremes such as droughts, floods and forest fires to sell his Big Lie, and all of these things can be easily created by HAARP. Tesla started hundreds of fires with his technology in the first half of the last century.

The bloodlines want to destabilise and take control of Pakistan, and devastating and record-breaking floods struck the country in 2010. Around one fifth of the land in Pakistan was underwater with some 20 million people losing their homes and livelihoods. Two thousand people were killed. HAARP's signature was all over the multiple deadly tornadoes in the American Midwest in 2011 when the region was also hit by torrential rains that flooded the Mississippi and Missouri rivers to record levels, together with large snowfalls in the mountains that feed the rivers. A tornado outbreak of historic proportions struck the Midwest and Northeastern United States; it became known as the 'Super Outbreak', with 300 tornadoes between April 25th and 28th that killed more than 300 people. At one point there were 118 tornadoes within 24 hours. I bet they were laughing so hard at the HAARP facility. What fun. HAARP was operational at this time according to its website data, and storms and tornadoes were being accurately predicted by people tracking HAARP's effect on the weather. Tornadoes are caused by a fast-rotating electromagnetic field, and the same is true for hurricanes. Creating these is child's play for HAARP. Send a hurricane to New Orleans, have your explosive device ready to breach the levee and the city is yours to steal and take over. Another bloodline target is all farmers who are not working for the Illuminati corporations. I am writing this as the bloated Missouri and Mississippi rivers carry their record volumes of water to the sea. Farmland is being inundated, and levees have been demolished to protect people further down the river – or that's what they tell us, anyway. The effect has been to destroy vast areas of crops, and with that the livelihoods and communities of non-corporation farmers, en route. The federal government then sent letters to these farmers offering to buy their land through the Army Corps of Engineers. This is the same Army Corps of Engineers that was blowing up levees to flood farms and communities on the premise of protecting people further downstream. This was just a scam to steal the people's land. George Soros (Rothschild Zionist) has embarked on a frenzy of buying up farmland and grain storage companies in the United States and Australia through a company called Gavilon. Control of food supplies is a bloodline 'must-have', and they plan to engineer food shortages in the West as they have caused famines in Africa and elsewhere. Weather control = food control. Another potential weather impact of HAARP is to manipulate the jet streams, to alter the natural west-to-east path of high or low pressure systems and direct them to target areas. We are told that jet streams are formed by the planet's rotation and *atmospheric heating*.

HAARP has the potential to seriously mess with Earth's magnetic field, and this is showing many signs of being destabilised. The UK's *The Independent* reported that the magnetic north pole was 'moving faster than at any time in human history, threatening everything from the safety of modern transport systems to the traditional navigation routes of migrating animals'. Magnetic north was in the frozen wilderness of Ellesmere Island in Canada for two centuries, but it is now relocating at a speed of some 40 miles a year in the direction of Russia, with the speed increasing by a third in the last decade. This is distorting compasses by about one degree every five years, and because of this the US Federal Aviation Administration has to re-evaluate runway codes every five years to keep them in sync with aircraft instruments. Scientists, and others, speculate that all this may be the prelude to a 'flip' or reversal of the magnetic poles which is calculated to have last happened some 780,000 years ago at the start of what is believed to be the longest stable period in the last five million years. It may be a natural phenomenon; but it may not. We are all synchronised to some extent by the nature of the magnetic field, but this is especially true of the animal world, not least whales, dolphins, birds, and suchlike which have their directional antennae guided by interaction with the field. If they have to change runway codes to keep aircraft on the right course, clearly animals are going to be affected if they don't do the same reprogramming of their own 'Sat Navs'. Thousands of whales, dolphins and porpoises are found beached and

Figure 292: Massive sea-life and bird-life deaths could be the work of HAARP

stranded on coastlines around the world every year. Cape Cod in the United States and shores around New Zealand are among the most common locations. One example was the 107 pilot whales that died after being stranded off New Zealand's South Island. Even more mysterious are the mass deaths of birds and sea life with millions of fish found dead in a Californian harbour in one incident (Fig 292). Other unexplained bird and sea-life deaths include:

- 450 red-winged blackbirds, brown-headed cowbirds, grackles and starlings found on the road in Baton Rouge, Louisiana
- 3,000 blackbirds on roofs and roads in Beebe, Arkansas
- Thousands of 'devil crabs' washed up along the Kent coast near Thanet in England
- Thousands of drum fish washed up along a 20-mile stretch of the Arkansas River
- Tens of thousands of small fish dead in Chesapeake Bay, Maryland
- Thousands of dead fish found floating in a Florida creek
- Hundreds of snapper fish found dead in New Zealand
- Scores of American Coots found dead on a Texas highway bridge

There might be different explanations in some cases, but I am sure that in most instances of these mass deaths there is a common factor. Thousands of birds fell out of the sky and an estimated 100,000 fish died at the same time in the same geographical region of Arkansas, so there is a connecting factor in all this – or much of it, anyway. There is a very good chance that this factor is HAARP.

'They gave us their mind'

HAARP has the potential to control the minds of the global population en masse. The human brain operates on certain frequencies and if you broadcast information on those frequencies the brain will decode it as a person's own thoughts and perceptions. *HAARP's* thoughts and perceptions would become human thoughts and perceptions. I have some news for you ... HAARP can broadcast in the same frequency band as the human brain. This band is known as Extremely Low Frequency, or ELF. Every thought and emotion has its own frequency. Dr Andrija Puharich, an American medical and parapsychological researcher, realised nearly 60 years ago that psychics operate on another frequency when they are 'connecting' (8Hz), while frequencies of 10.80Hz produces 'riotous behaviour' and 6.6Hz makes people depressed. He also changed DNA by using frequencies, and that is another goal of HAARP. Technology capable of manipulating enemy troops mentally and emotionally to give up and surrender has been around for a long time, but HAARP has the potential to do this to the world. The psychos have been recording the wavelengths of human emotions and storing them in a sort of 'Emotion Library' to be broadcast at a target and trigger those same emotions individually and collectively – such as: 'I have no power', 'Everything is hopeless, just give in'. Dr Andrew Michrowski, Technologies Specialist with the Canadian Department of State, and President of the Planetary Association for Clean Energy (PACE), wrote many years ago that almost anything could be inserted into a target brain and such insertions would be processed by 'biosystems' as internally generated data/effects: 'Words, phrases, images, sensations and emotions could be directly inserted and experienced in the biological targets as internal states, codes, emotions, thoughts and ideas.' Once an external frequency has synchronised with brain activity it can then change that frequency, and thus brainwave patterns. This is known as 'entrainment'. Brain chemistry, thoughts, emotions and perceptions all change when brainwave frequencies change. Something similar has been done to humanity for aeons via the Saturn–Moon Matrix, but they now have to increase the strength of this collective perception-control system, for reasons I will come to in the final chapter, by using technology on Earth. Covert projects in countries such as the United States, Russia, Britain and China have been researching and experimenting with external control of the human brain for over 70 years. This is the ultimate dream for people obsessed with controlling others. Russian mind-manipulation messages broadcast into the United States were publicly revealed in the 1970s. This became known as the 'Woodpecker' signal because it sounded like repetitive tapping. Woodpecker was an expansion of an earlier Russian experiment which involved bombarding the American Embassy in Moscow with microwaves. *The Los Angeles Times* reported that the US ambassador had told staff that this could cause emotional and behavioural problems and serious illness such as leukaemia and cancer. Irradiated ambassadors, Charles Bohlen and Llewellyn Thompson, both died of cancer and *The Boston Globe* reported in 1976 that Ambassador Walter Stoessel was suffering from a rare blood disease, and was bleeding from the eyes and suffering from headaches. American Intelligence knew about the microwave attacks for years, but didn't tell anyone at the embassy. They wanted to use it as an experiment themselves by observing the effects. This is the mentality that runs the world. There are no 'sides', anyway, as I have stressed. The bloodlines manipulate through all countries, and to them the world is *one* country. This explains the otherwise bizarre decision of the American authorities to sell a 40-tonne 'supermagnet' to the Russians in 1977 in full knowledge that it would allow them to broadcast their signals into the United States. American Intelligence, military and government supplied the technology that made the Woodpecker signal possible. They even sent American scientists to install it while the smokescreen 'Cold War' was still going on. Woodpecker was a bloodline experiment leading to the HAARP technology they have today. Lieutenant Colonel John B Alexander wrote an article in 1980 about Woodpecker in *Military Review*, the official publication of the US Army Command and General Staff College. He said:

[Soviet Union] mind-altering techniques, designed to impact on an opponent are well-advanced. The procedures employed include manipulation of human behaviour through the use of psychological weapons effecting sight, sound, smell, temperature, electromagnetic energy, or sensory deprivation ... Soviet researchers, studying controlled behaviour, have also examined the effects of electromagnetic radiation on humans and have applied these techniques against the US Embassy in Moscow ... Researchers suggest that certain low-frequency (ELF) emissions possesses psychoactive characteristics. These transmissions can be used to induce depression or irritability in a target population. The application of large-scale ELF behaviour modification could have horrendous impact.

This is what HAARP has the potential to do – and more – on a global scale. I have written at great length in other books about the history of mind control and the horrors this 'research' has inflicted upon children and adults in the United States, Britain, Germany and elsewhere. Techniques have been developed that allow for total external control of brain activity, and HAARP has been designed to broadcast information at human brain frequencies that people will decode to be their own thoughts, beliefs and emotions. This is a major part of the plan to microchip the global population. They would be able to communicate information to the chip for mental and emotional manipulation, and assassination from afar. The soulless nature of the people behind all this can be seen clearly with Dr Jose Delgado, Professor of Physiology at Yale University, one of the best-known mind control researchers who worked for the CIA. He was especially interested in developing electronic implants for the control of behaviour. Delgado produced a report in 1969, and the same remarks appeared in the Congressional Record in 1974. It is worth reading this slowly to take in what is planned for the entire human race unless we stop it:

We need a program of psychosurgery for political control of our society. The purpose is physical control of the mind. Everyone who deviates from the given norm can be surgically mutilated. The individual may think that the most important reality is his own existence, but this is only his personal point of view. This lacks historical perspective. Man does not have the right to develop his own mind. This kind of liberal orientation has great appeal. We must electrically control the brain. Someday, armies and generals will be controlled by electric stimulation of the brain.

Delgado was mad, a complete fruitcake, but he worked for the CIA carrying out horrendous experiments on animals and people, funded by the Office of Naval Research which is now involved in HAARP. *The New York Times* reported on Delgado's experiments in 1965 and described the effect on a bull:

Afternoon sunlight poured over the high wooden barriers into the ring, as the brave bull bore down on the unarmed 'matador' – a scientist who had never before faced a fighting bull. But the charging animal's horns never reached the man behind the red cape.

Moments before that could happen, Dr Jose Delgado, the scientist, pressed a button on a small radio transmitter in his hand and the bull braked to a halt. Then he pressed another button on the transmitter, and the bull obediently turned to the right and trotted away. The bull was obeying commands in his brain that were being called forth by electrical stimulation – by the radio signals – of certain regions in which the fine wires had been painlessly implanted the day before.

Delgado said that he had conducted similar experiments on humans, but instead of being arrested he received all the funding he required. *Brave New World* author and insider, Aldous Huxley, talked about people being manipulated to 'love their servitude', and this is another aspect of the HAARP/mind-control agenda. But this is not about *people*, as in *conscious* people, loving their servitude, but the human body–computer being externally programmed to decode that sense of reality. Kevin Warwick, Professor of Cybernetics at the University of Reading, England, said: 'If a machine is passing down signals that keep you completely happy, then why not be part of the Matrix?' Warwick is best-known for being microchipped and promoting this as a great idea. If Warwick is an example of what chips can do to you, I'll give it a miss if it's all the same. I prefer my soul to a microchip, or anything else this ludicrous academic might suggest. Another CIA crazy in the era of Delgado was Dr Ivor Browning. He attached a radio receiver to the hypothalamus, or 'pleasure centre' in the brain, of a donkey. He externally directed the donkey to climb a mountain and return by stimulating the 'pleasure centre' when the donkey took the required route and switching it off when there was deviation. When the 'pleasure' stopped, the donkey would change direction until the 'pleasure' returned. This is the plan for humans, and HAARP is at the centre of this. The race to turn over all broadcasting to digital is also connected to mass perception control. It is aimed at hacking the decoding process at the digital level of reality which is even closer to experienced holographic reality than the vibrational. Another 'way in' is through Ultra High Frequency waves, or UHF, which can access perception through the subconscious mind. 'Going digital' is freeing up this band. The US Department of Defense is behind this technology, too, under the name of Silent Sound Spread Spectrum (SSSS), and it is highly likely that it is planning to use digital broadcasting as its 'delivery system' along with the technologies I have been describing.

Smart Grid = Mind Grid

If anyone needs confirmation by now that there is a globally-organised conspiracy on a grand scale then I give you the 'Smart Grid'. This is the plan already being rolled out to install a global grid that would supply homes with electricity and information. Advocates describe it in their Orwellian jargon as 'an intelligent digitised energy-network delivering electricity in an optimum way from source to consumption'; and 'integrated information, telecommunication and power technologies with the existing electricity system'. There is also a related brand called HomePlug, 'the power alliance' [cartel] which distributes Internet, HD video, digital music and other applications [information in others words] to the home'. Here is the sales-pitch garbage for 'Smart Grids' – and then I will tell you the real reason the technology is being introduced:

- Increased use of digital information and controls technology to improve reliability, security and efficiency of the electric grid.

- Dynamic optimization of grid operations and resources, with full cyber-security.
- Deployment and integration of distributed resources and generation, including renewable resources.
- Development and incorporation of demand response, demand-side resources, and energy-efficiency resources.
- Deployment of 'smart' technologies (real-time, automated, interactive technologies that optimize the physical operation of appliances and consumer devices) for metering, communications concerning grid operations and status, and distribution automation.
- Integration of 'smart' appliances and consumer devices.
- Deployment and integration of advanced electricity-storage and peak-shaving technologies, including plug-in electric and hybrid electric vehicles, and thermal-storage air conditioning.
- Provision to consumers of timely information and control options.
- Development of standards for communication and interoperability of appliances and equipment connected to the electric grid, including the infrastructure serving the grid.
- Identification and lowering of unreasonable or unnecessary barriers to adoption of smart grid technologies, practices and services.

My goodness, talk about Orwellian. These people even talk like robots. Note that last point: 'Identification and lowering of unreasonable or unnecessary barriers to adoption of smart grid technologies, practices and services.' Translated from the Orwellian this means: 'Identification of anything or anyone that might block or not accept what we are imposing and take the necessary action to deal with them, because you are having it whether you like it or not.' Well we shouldn't 'have it'; we should not even nearly 'have it' at any price, starting now. They want these grids in every country with all of them connected to create a global grid. Electrical systems can carry information, and these grids are designed to deliver mind control into your own home by using electricity and electromagnetism to supply information to your brain. The new 'energy-saving' lightbulbs that are increasingly being imposed by law around the world are part of this system. Those bulbs are constructed to be *transmitters of information*. They even *look* like transmitters (Fig 293). Crazy? Well, hold on. Dr Robert Beck, an expert in nuclear engineering, co-authored a scientific research paper with Dr Michael A Persinger of Laurentian University in Canada, an expert in ELF radiation, in which they studied the potential of electromagnetic mind control. Dr Beck told a Psychotronics Association conference that human subjects exposed to certain ELF field patterns reported sensations of

Figure 293: Information transmitters on the Smart Grid 'Internet' disguised as 'green' lightbulbs

uneasiness, depression and foreboding. He said that he had measured the Russian Woodpecker signal and found that it was acting 'like gangbusters ... right in the window of human psychoactivity'. He then added this: 'The signal was permeating power grids in the United States, it was being picked up by power lines, re-radiated, *it was coming into homes on the light circuits ...'* Dr Beck said those words in 1979, and we are now being told to accept the Smart Grids which will deliver the subliminal messages even more powerfully than Woodpecker because this electrical and telecommunication system is specifically designed to do that – right down to the 'energy-saving' lightbulb transmitters. Accenture, the global management and technology consulting firm, is heavily involved in the Smart Grid roll out. Mark Spelman, Accenture's head of strategy, said that Smart Grids were 'the energy internet of the future'. Smart Grids are in fact another form of the wireless information Internet aimed at manipulating and programming human perception. The climate-change lie is being used once again to justify human enslavement through the transmitter bulbs and the 'energy efficient' Smart Grid. The system also allows the authorities to monitor your energy use minute by minute and turn your heating down or off if they so choose. The Pacific Northwest National Laboratory (owned by the US Department of Energy) described how the technology would work:

> The controller is essentially a simple computer chip that can be installed in regular household appliances like dishwashers, clothes washers, dryers, refrigerators, air conditioner and water heaters. The chip senses when there is a disruption in the grid and turns the appliances off for a few seconds or minutes to allow the grid to stabilize. The controllers also can be programmed to delay the restart of the appliances. The delay allows the appliances to be turned on one at a time rather than all at once to ease power restoration following an outage.

Your whole life would be controlled from afar by programmed computer systems using wireless communications that would constantly bathe your home and business in radiation. The system will be able to monitor everything people do at home once it is fully operational. So-called 'Smart Meters' are being installed in California, and they have proved to be highly-controversial. Many are catching fire, and people are suffering from the usual effects of the radiation they emit ... extreme dizziness, nausea, flu-like symptoms, memory problems and insomnia. Smart Meters transmit wireless information in electromagnetic pulses to the electricity supply, and this is what causes the ill health. They are trying to kill us and our children in our own homes. Smart Grids are supposed to save energy and cut electricity bills, but when a California television station tested them against the old system they found the opposite was the case. Personal experience suggests that bills actually soar and when you read the small print of government legislation it is *the people, not the energy corporations, who are footing the bill for installation*. Smart Grids are being imposed at a gathering pace in the United States on the back of billions in funding and incentives that appeared in Obama's 'stimulus package' after he came to power in 2009. All the major Illuminati players are involved such as IBM, GE and Siemens. Around ten million American homes have been installed with Smart Meters at the time of writing and they want this to be more than 50 million in 2012. They are being introduced in Britain and Europe, and many Australians are reacting with great hostility as they are introduced there. The plan is to have every country in the world locked into the global Smart Grid. Money is no object because this is a major programme within the global conspiracy. The Smart Grid is a two-way communication system that communicates information to the minds of the occupants and tracks their daily lives in great detail. People who refuse to have them are being told they will have their electricity supply cut; so they are, in truth, compulsory – just like the lightbulbs. Both are part of the same Agenda. But, in fact, while the energy corporations say there can be no 'opt out' from Smart Meters in America, the law says that people must 'opt in'. As one writer said: 'No-one can be forced to comply with an unrevealed contract between private corporations, and to which you were never a party and had no knowledge of.' The European Union wants 80 per cent of homes connected to this system by 2020. Jerry Day, an electronics and media expert from Burbank, California, listed his concerns about Smart Meters:

1. They individually identify electrical devices inside the home and record when they are operated causing invasion of privacy.
2. They monitor household activity and occupancy in violation of rights and domestic security.
3. They transmit wireless signals which may be intercepted by unauthorized and unknown parties. Those signals can be used to monitor behaviour and occupancy and they can be used by criminals to aid criminal activity against the occupants.
4. Data about occupants' daily habits and activities are collected, recorded and stored in permanent databases which are accessed by parties not authorized or invited to know and share that private data.
5. Those with access to the smart meter databases can review a permanent history of household activities complete with calendar and time-of-day metrics to gain a highly invasive and detailed view of the lives of the occupants.
6. Those databases may be shared with, or fall into the hands of criminals, blackmailers, law enforcement, private hackers of wireless transmissions, power company employees and other unidentified parties who may act against the interests of the occupants under metered surveillance.
7. 'Smart Meters' are, by definition, surveillance devices which violate Federal and State wiretapping laws by recording and storing databases of private and personal activities and behaviours without the consent or knowledge of those people who are monitored.
8. It is possible for example, with analysis of certain Smart Meter data, for unauthorised and distant parties to determine medical conditions, sexual activities, physical locations of persons within the home, vacancy patterns and personal information and habits of the occupants.

Put: 'Smart Meters, Jerry Day' into *YouTube* and you will see his video. Police are already issuing an increasing number of subpoenas for the energy-use records of those that they suspect are growing marijuana in their homes. When your electricity usage goes up for any reason, you can face a police raid; and on some occasions when they haven't found marijuana they have charged people with other offences once they have gained access to their homes. A report by *The Associated Press* in July 2011 was also fundamentally connected with all this. AP revealed that a year-long 'experiment' was planned to start that would, in effect, dismantle the national electricity grid in the United States (break the old so you can replace it with the new). The present grid has always run on the same frequency in unison across the country so that power produced

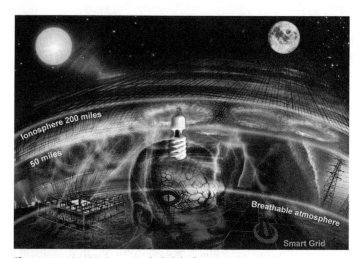

Ionosphere 200 miles

50 miles

Breathable atmosphere

Smart Grid

Figure 294: HAARP, Smart Grids, lightbulb transmitters, and telecommunications antennae and technology (including cell phone receiver–transmitters) are all part of a vast global mind-control network

on one side of the country can be fed to the other if necessary. The Associated Press report said that the Federal Energy Regulatory Commission planned to make various parts of the grid run at different frequencies – which means that it is no longer a grid at all. This could affect traffic lights, security systems and some computers, and make electrical clocks and appliances such as coffeemakers run up to 20 minutes fast. Demetrios Matsakis, head of the time service department at the US Naval Observatory, said: 'A lot of people are going to have things break and they're not going to know why.' The Federal Energy Regulatory Commission says that this nonsense was to make the grid (by then non-existent grid) more reliable. What a lie. When something so ridiculous is rolled out against all logic, you know it is the Agenda at work. HAARP, Smart Grids, lightbulb transmitters, and telecommunications antennae and technology (including cell phone receiver–transmitters) are all part of a vast global mind-control network that would turn humanity into fully-fledged mind-controlled zombies who 'love their servitude' (Fig 294). The 'GWEN' system in the United States and the 'TETRA' system in the United Kingdom and other countries are also part of this. The communication towers of the Ground Wave Emergency Network (GWEN) have been appearing all over the United States since the early 1980s under the direction of the US Air Force. GWEN is a network of towers hundreds of feet high and placed 200 miles apart. The cover story is that GWEN is an emergency back-up communication system in the event of a nuclear war. *Rubbish*. They are part of the planned global mind-control 'bubble' to disconnect us even more from the wider reality. GWEN towers transmit frequencies that don't radiate into the atmosphere, but hug and penetrate the ground to ensure that no-one can escape what they are sending out. GWEN communications are planned to communicate with implanted human microchips. Millions of Americans already live within the electromagnetic waves of GWEN, and before long it will be everyone. It is well-known that people are much easier to mind-control when they are subjected to technologically-generated electromagnetic fields. Robert O Becker, twice nominated for a Nobel Prize for his expertise on the biological effects of electromagnetism, wrote:

GWEN is a superb system, in combination with cyclotron resonance, for producing behavioural alterations in the civilian population. The average strength of the steady geomagnetic field varies from place to place across the United States. Therefore, if one wished to resonate a specific ion in living things in a specific locality, one would require a specific frequency for that location. The spacing of GWEN transmitters 200 miles apart across the United States would allow such specific frequencies to be 'tailored' to the geomagnetic-field strength in each GWEN area.

It's all carefully planned. GWEN also has the potential to manipulate the weather. In Britain, we have Terrestrial Trunked Radio, or TETRA. The cover story is that TETRA is just a new communications system for the police and other emergency services. The system was introduced when there was no need on the orders of the then Prime Minister, 'shapeshifter' Tony Blair, and the real reason for TETRA is mass mind-control. TETRA technology is similar to the PCS/Digital, or Personal Communication Systems, used in the United States. The British Home Office awarded the contract for TETRA to a consortium headed by British Telecom and it was sold on to 02 and their subsidiary mm02. Motorola, the American telecommunications giant, is also involved in making an important component of the TETRA system, and this is a company with close links to the National Security Agency (NSA). An internal European Union document revealed that Motorola played a crucial role in defining the TETRA European standard (in collaboration with the National Security Agency) in order to guarantee for the US government the potential for TETRA networks to be eavesdropped. But it is about more than that. They want all of these technologies to be able to connect as one global network. TETRA, once again, communicates on frequencies that match human brain activity. It is the same story that you find everywhere, because they are all introduced for the same reason – the control of the human mind and emotions. People living near TETRA and GWEN masts have complained of illness, headaches, depression and all the usual consequences associated with these technologies.

   Another potential for HAARP is amplification of poisons and chemicals in the body from relatively harmless to downright lethal. A process called 'cyclotron resonance' means that electromagnetic influence can increase the strength of chemical substances by up to a thousand times. The chemicals in food that are cumulatively harmful could be 'excited' by electromagnetic fields from HAARP, or other sources, to become deadly poisons. HAARP, and related technology, can disturb the body's circadian rhythm, the daily cycle 'in the physiological processes of living beings, including plants, animals, fungi and cyanobacteria'. They dictate sleep and eating patterns in humans and animals, and affect brain wave activity, hormone production, cell regeneration and other biological activities. Jet lag is a disturbance of the circadian rhythm, and one of the causes is the effect of electromagnetic radiation at high altitudes. There are so many consequences when you start messing with electromagnetic fields, especially within the range of human brain activity and the natural energetic balance of the planet. We are seeing the Reptilian obsession with technology that I have been talking about, and we need to urgently to address what is happening before it's too late. The Large Hadron Collider built by the European Organisation for Nuclear Research, or CERN, is connected to the global web of Earth and reality manipulation that includes HAARP. This is the world's largest and highest-energy particle accelerator and consists of a 17-mile tunnel loop beneath the Swiss–French border. It is described as an 'atom smasher' that collides particles, and it contains more than 1,000 cylindrical magnets arranged end-to-end. The collider began operations in 2008 and has been breaking records for smacking particles together, but it is not expected to reach full capacity until 2014. The project has involved 10,000 scientists from around the world, but the United States (the Rothschilds) has made the dominant contribution. CERN's *official* motive for the money-no-object collider that cost billions is to find out what happened at the time of the Big Bang (there wasn't one – time to go home chaps) and to understand the deepest laws of nature; but that's only the cover story. CERN says that it plans to create and accelerate beams of particles of up to seven *trillion* volts, and the potential impact of that is obvious. There are other colliders around the world, too, which we know nothing about. CERN is, like HAARP, another international project, but officially so this time. Twenty member countries are involved, and CERN employs thousands of scientists from 113 nationalities and more than 600 universities. The World Wide Web emerged from research at CERN. Israeli scientists have made a major contribution to CERN and the Large Hadron Collider. This was acknowledged by Israel's Science and Technology Minister, Professor Daniel Hershkowitz. He said: 'Israel's science has received additional international recognition for our leading contribution to research in general and specifically the CERN project.'

Something very big is going on there and it is nothing to do with the 'Big Bang'. Nor is it good for humanity.

12

Culling the people

It is no good talking around the fact, because it is happening. The Reptilian hybrid bloodlines are in the midst of a mega depopulation programme in which they want to reduce the human population by billions. Some of their representatives talk of a global population of one billion, even 500,000, and HAARP is one of their major weapons in achieving this.

Human numbers have got out of hand from the Control System's point of view, and they want to reduce the population to a figure that is more easily controllable in their 'Brave New World'. John P Holdren, the 'science czar' appointed to the Obama administration, is one of these 'cullers'. He says that the optimum human population is one billion and he has some interesting ways to bring this about. Holdren is the director of the White House Office of Science and Technology who co-wrote a book in 1977 called *Ecoscience*, which details proposals to mass-sterilise the population by medicating food and the water supply and imposing a regime of forced abortion, government seizure of children born out of wedlock and mandatory bodily implants to stop pregnancy. The book supports a policy of allowing only two children per family, with those that have more losing any right to public housing. Only the two children would qualify for public education, and the parents of any others would have to pay separately for their education. People would have to secure a 'birth licence' before they had children. These people are beyond crazy, but they currently control the global power structure. Holdren wants to see a 'planetary regime' (world government, here we go) that would dictate the detail of everyone's life in a 'global commons'. This 'regime' would have total control of anything that affects the air, soil or seas, and would decide what car you drove, the temperature in your home (via Smart Grids) and, through control of the land, who grew food and who didn't. The bloodlines want their corporations to produce all the food with everyone else banned from doing so. Holdren also calls for a 'science court' that would decree what technology could be used and what could not. He wrote *Ecoscience* with the population-control extremists, Paul and Anne Ehrlich. Sperm counts have dropped by a third since 1989 and by half in 50 years. The policy of sterilisation has long been happening. They are also implementing the cull through food and drink additives; blocking access to other forms of nutrition;

vaccinations and drugs; laboratory-created diseases; endless and growing forms of radiation; poisons and metals poured into the sky all over the world from aircraft and known as 'chemtrails' (which I will come to shortly); wars; hunger and famine; denying medical treatment to the elderly; the list goes on and on. Most of these effects are cumulative rather than instantly lethal – at least for now – and they are targeting the human immune system to debilitate the body's defences while this is happening. The consequences for people, especially the young, from the cumulative radiation they are absorbing from mobile phones are going to be catastrophic. ***Please, don't put them to your ear unless absolutely necessary and then for as little time as possible.*** Text or use email until you can talk on a landline. I explain the depopulation programme and the effects of all these multiple attacks on human health in great detail in *Human Race Get Off Your Knees.*

The Radiation Agenda

We are being subjected to ever more sources of radiation as part of the population cull. There are many ways they do this, and I have been ticking them off one by one as they have been introduced over the years (Fig 295). They include mobile phones and their communication masts, and an explosion of other technologies including: HAARP, GWEN and TETRA; computers; power lines (hence the increase in cancer cases for people living near them and why the number of power lines is being massively increased); full-body scanners in airports (frequent fliers who don't opt out are going to be seriously affected eventually); wireless Internet; ridiculous overuse of X-rays and CAT scanners in hospitals; irradiated food; the new 'green' lightbulbs; microwave ovens; nuclear power disasters; the depleted uranium in bombs dropped across the world that is leading to horrendous birth defects (and this travels around the world from its target area); and there is the cosmic radiation that would normally be deflected which is getting through the Earth's defences because of HAARP punching holes into the ionosphere. While HAARP is scanning or X-raying the earth for resources *it is doing the same to people in that area*; and goodness knows what satellites might be sending our way. Certainly they have the ability to project scalar waves at locations and individuals. Scalar waves can carry information and are not weakened by time or distance. DNA generates and receives scalar waves in tune with its frequency so the potential for physical, mental and emotional manipulation is obvious. Governments are lying about technologies being safe, so that they can expose us to as much radiation as possible. Documents released under the Freedom of Information Act revealed

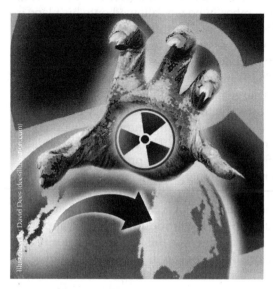

Figure 295: The sources of radiation pollution are increasing all the time – exactly as planned

that Janet Napolitano, US Homeland Security Secretary, was lying when she said that full-body scanners had been proved to be safe by the National Institute of Standards and Technology (NIST). No they haven't, because *they're not*. How can you prove safety anyway when the effects are cumulative? An internal NIST email expressed concern at what Napolitano said and pointed out that the organisation does not test products and so cannot 'prove them safe'. Napolitano isn't bothered that she is subjecting Americans to dangerous cumulative doses of radiation with the body scanners – she doesn't have to use them. Other NIST correspondence said that the scanners may not be safe and that staff should avoid standing near them. *Staff* should avoid standing near them, but passengers, including children who are most susceptible to radiation, should go *through* them. Another Napolitano lie (she has plenty where that came from) was that studies at the Johns Hopkins University Applied Physics Laboratory had said the scanners were safe, when Dr Michael Love, X-ray Facility Manager at the Johns Hopkins School of Medicine, said that the machines were going to cause skin cancer. Dr David Brenner, who heads the Center for Radiological Research at Columbia University, agreed. He said: 'There really is no other technology around where we're planning to X-ray such an enormous number of individuals. It's really unprecedented in the radiation world.' A study in 2010 at Columbia University by the Inter-Agency Committee on Radiation Safety recommended that children and pregnant women should not be scanned, but nothing has been done because they want to cull the population. Four professors at the University of California in San Francisco – specialists in biochemistry, biophysics, X-ray imaging and cancer – wrote to Obama's Science Advisor, John Holdren, to warn that there was still 'no rigorous, hard data for the safety of X-ray airport passenger scanners' and that safety tests were being conducted exclusively by manufacturers. They were wasting their time. Why would an extremist people-culler like Holdren do anything about technology that is killing people? Remember also that the scanners were promoted by former head of Homeland Security, Michael Chertoff (Rothschild Zionist), after a fake 'terror attack' – the 'underpants bomber' who was allowed onto his plane in Amsterdam by a Rothschild Zionist security operation. Chertoff's company represents Rapiscan, which has a contract worth $173 million to provide body scanners. The dangers posed by the scanners are painfully obvious for anyone with a brain on active duty, and now the obvious has happened. The Transportation Security Administration (TSA) has been exposed trying to cover up a surge in cancer among airport security staff that work with the machines. Documents secured by the Electronic Privacy Information Center under the Freedom of Information Act reveal that 'a large number of workers have been falling victim to cancer, strokes and heart disease'. The documents especially highlighted Boston Logan Airport where TSA officials refused to provide the means to measure radiation levels even after a 'cancer cluster' emerged among staff working the machines. When will people in uniform learn that the State doesn't give a damn about them any more than it does for the rest of the population? Another scam devised with the intention of irradiating large numbers of people is the introduction of new airport security-scanners announced in 2011. The sequence goes like this: make the security procedure at airports such a horrible experience that people will be open to anything that would make it quicker and easier; then roll out new 21-foot-long tunnels that passengers just walk through with their bag while both passengers and baggage are scanned as they go. Ain't that great? What time it will save. But there is the one little snag. As you walk the 21 feet, you will be dosed with radiation which will include the stuff that only the bag used to get. They want to subject us to the maximum sources and doses of radiation they can get away with.

Rothschild wherever you look

I learned in the early 1990s that the House of Rothschild was the force behind the introduction of nuclear power from Dr Kitty Little who worked for nine years at the UK's Atomic Energy Research Establishment at Harwell. If the Rothschilds are involved in *anything*, the motivation is always to advance the 'Great Work of the Ages' – the highjack of Planet Earth. Nuclear power was not motivated by the need for energy, but the need, from the bloodlines' point of view, to release radiation into the atmosphere. This was motivated by the desire for mass depopulation and because it seems that the Reptilians feed off radiation. Humans have serious consequences from radiation because it distorts our particular electromagnetic fields, but if you are a different type of field that can harmonise with radiation then it can be a food source that will not harm you. The Reptilians, and to an extent their hybrids, are not troubled by radiation in the same way that we are. The disaster at the nuclear facility at Fukushima in Japan continues to release fantastic amounts of radiation at the time of writing, which is circulating around the world. It is already vastly in excess of what was released by the nuclear plant at Chernobyl in the Ukraine in 1986 – some experts say 50 times more by June 2011. I said earlier that Fukushima was struck by a nuclear device placed by a Rothschild Zionist 'security' company based at Dimona, the location of the Israeli nuclear programme. This caused the planned catastrophic release of radiation worldwide, but particularly around Japan and across to the United States. The number of babies dying in the United States has long since been ridiculously high for a developed country, but the figures shot up in Northern California in the period that the Fukushima radiation was reaching that region. This happened to unborn and newborn babies and animals in the wake of the Chernobyl disaster. Other nuclear power stations, such as Sellafield in the north west of England, have been pouring radiation into the sea or rivers for decades. The seas are incredibly polluted by now, and so is much of the rain and snow. Fukushima is taking it all to another level. Remember that water absorbs information. Radiation in this reality is *distorted* information, and this does the same to the information blueprint of the planet, and pollutes with rogue information – like a computer virus – the Earth's energy field that we operate within. The same applies to the oil systematically released into the Gulf of Mexico by the Rothschild-controlled BP, and other sources of water pollution, including fluoride in the water that people drink.

I described earlier how HAARP was employed to generate the record volumes of water into the Missouri and Mississippi rivers in 2011 to inundate land which the Army Corps of Engineers were offering to buy from farmers who lost everything, while the same Army Corps of Engineers blew up levees. But there was another aspect to this and, again, it was radiation. The Missouri River inundated the Fort Calhoun nuclear power plant in eastern Nebraska which holds an immense amount of nuclear fuel. There was an electrical fire in the basement and the plant had to be evacuated. Toxic gases made part of the plant inaccessible, and then the waters of the Missouri River flooded the basement. A no-fly zone over the plant was instigated (as it was over the oil slick in the Gulf of Mexico) because of 'security reasons that we can't reveal'. The Fort

Cooper nuclear power plant, also in Nebraska, was similarly under threat at the same time. The Fort Calhoun plant was built in a *flood plain* of the Missouri River. The Fukushima complex was located in an *earthquake zone* and on the coast where it was vulnerable to tsunamis. Nuclear power plants in California are built on earthquake fault lines, and the Indian Point nuclear power plant near New York was placed over a small earthquake fault zone on the east bank of the Hudson River. A presenter on Russia Today (RT) Television asked why the authorities would be so crazy. Well, yes, they *are* crazy – beyond insane – but it is not that they were crazy for doing this through incompetence and stupidity; they are crazy because they did this on purpose. A script written long ago is playing out. In 2011, a forest fire threatened the Los Alamos National Laboratories (LANL) in New Mexico, home of Oppenheimer's Manhattan Project, and the organisation Concerned Citizens for Nuclear Safety reported that over 30,000 barrels of plutonium-contaminated waste were being stored above the ground in little more than tents. It was also revealed that approximately 18 million cubic feet of radioactive and chemical solid wastes were just buried or dumped in the area around Los Alamos since 1943. The Alliance for Nuclear Accountability said: 'All of the radioactive waste and most of the chemical waste have been buried on the mesas of Pajarito Plateau where LANL is located. Radioactive liquid wastes were discharged to the canyons, initially with little treatment.' The same theme can be seen with the 15 nuclear reactors and the maze of oil and gas pipelines that criss-cross the New Madrid earthquake fault-line in the Southern and Midwestern United States. This has been the scene of four of America's biggest earthquakes. Steve Geller, a Florida state Democrat leader, said: 'Virtually every natural gas pipeline in the nation is built over that fault ...You'll see the explosion reflected off the moon.' Ed Gray, of the Missouri State Emergency Management Agency, agreed that the concentration of pipelines across a fault-line was asking for trouble (they *are*):

> You have four of the five major natural-gas pipelines come right through the soup in New Madrid, the soft alluvial soil. They carry gas all the way to Detroit, Chicago, Indianapolis and Pittsburgh. If [the earthquake] happened during the winter, you're going to have major-league problems on your hands. Try to explain to somebody why you cannot heat a nursing home or keep a hospital warm.

The organisation responsible for nuclear safety in America is the US Nuclear Regulatory Commission (NRC); but an investigation by *The Associated Press* revealed in 2011 that the NRC is ignoring or weakening the rules which it is supposed to be enforcing. *The Associated Press* discovered in a year-long investigation that a ten-gallon-a-minute leak at the now-closed Indian Point nuclear power plant, little more than 30 miles north of New York City, has been ignored for nearly four years. Indian Point has been leaking lethal radioactive elements into the Hudson River. The amount of radiation allowed to leak (*allowed* to leak?) from faulty valves at nuclear facilities is now 20 times what it used to be. *The Washington Post* reported that radioactive tritium has leaked from at least 48 of 65 sites of commercial nuclear power sites in the United States, according to Nuclear Regulatory Commission records. At least 37 of those facilities contained tritium concentrations which sometimes exceeded the federal drinking-water standard by hundreds of times. A nuclear facility in New Jersey leaked tritium into an aquifer and a discharge canal feeding Barnegat Bay off the Atlantic Ocean, and there have been numerous reports of tritium leaks into the surface waters across the US over the past years. Tritium moves quickly through soil, and when detected it often indicates the presence of more powerful radioactive isotopes that are spilled at the same time. One of the reasons for this is that less stringent tests have been implemented to allow operators to pass inspections. *The Associated Press* discovered failing cables, cracked concrete, rusting underground pipes, and in one case a hole five inches square cut into a reactor vessel at the Davis–Besse plant in Ohio. But the facilities continued to be licensed to operate. Regulation was dismantled to allow the banking crisis of 2008, and regulation is now being weakened to release more radiation into the atmosphere. A State review of Russian nuclear sites in the wake of Fukushima was leaked to *The Associated Press* and revealed more than 30 serious faults in the system, including reduced safety standards and no effective strategy for securing radioactive fuel and waste at many plants. You will find the same story in every country that has nuclear power – and this is by design. But amid all this, with every nuclear power station a potential nuclear bomb and country-destroyer, the British government announced that is was going ahead with an enormous expansion of nuclear power with eight new reactors. 'It can't happen here,' was the reply when a spokesman was asked about the dangers of nuclear plants. They know this for sure, because they have had a 'risk assessment'. Phew, thank goodness for that. They are liars; they lie for a living. Emails revealed that the British government and nuclear power industry were colluding to play down the dangers of Fukushima even before anyone knew the amount of radiation that was being released. London's *The Guardian* reported that internal emails confirmed that the government was working closely behind the scenes with transnational corporations, Westinghouse, EDF Energy and Areva to stop the Fukushima disaster affecting the expansion of nuclear power in Britain which they announced soon afterwards. An official at the Department for Business, Innovation and Skills said of Fukushima in one email:

> This has the potential to set the nuclear industry back globally. We need to ensure the anti-nuclear chaps and chapesses do not gain ground on this. We need to occupy the territory and hold it. We really need to show the safety of nuclear.

Here is some advice about government statements anywhere in the world: don't believe a word they say until it is proven beyond doubt. These people are paid to lie, and mendacity is encoded in their very DNA. The plan for Britain's expansion of nuclear power was announced by the idiot (or worse) Energy and Climate Change Secretary, Chris Huhne. He is a global-warming extremist and says that nuclear power will 'reduce carbon emissions' (which are not changing the climate). If anything is messing with the climate, it is HAARP. When the government presses on with a policy against all logic and evidence, it is following the Illuminati script which does not take no for an answer. Huhne either knows this and he supports the script, or he is indeed an idiot. Huhne has likened those who challenge climate-change orthodoxy (lies) to those who appeased Hitler and the Nazis. 'This is our Munich moment,' he said. *Prat.*

Lethal lighting
The radiation agenda and mind control are the real reasons why, despite the long-since

demolished credibility of human-caused 'climate change', laws are being introduced to force 'climate friendly' lightbulbs upon us and to ban the alternative. This has happened in Britain and across Europe, thanks to the European Union, and is planned for North America thanks to the same global network. These so-called compact fluorescent lightbulbs, or 'CFLs', are supposed to be good for 'fighting' (everything is a *'fight'*) the illusory global warming – good for the 'environment' in other words. In fact, they are seriously dangerous to both human and animal health. I outlined earlier how the bulbs are information transmitters, but there are many other 'benefits' from the bloodlines' point of view. The bulbs contain mercury (also called quicksilver) which is lethally toxic. Mercury is so dangerous – especially for children and the unborn – that it has been banned in many countries for use in a long list of devices, including thermometers, vehicle and thermostat switches. They did this because the use of mercury was considered extremely unsafe. Mercury is even more toxic than arsenic and lead (a sobering thought when you think that amalgam tooth fillings are made with mercury). But here they are insisting by law that we have lights in our homes, workplaces, shops and malls that will release mercury into the atmosphere whenever they are broken. Every single bulb is a disaster waiting to happen, and this is not being done through the stupidity and incompetence of those who have orchestrated this policy from the shadows. Bureaucratic 'stupidity' and 'incompetence' are often the cover for cold calculation. Fluorescent bulbs are said to use less electricity and last much longer than conventional ones, but if bulbs are frequently switched on and off (they are lights for goodness sake, and I thought turning them off saved energy) then they wear out rapidly and in some circumstances faster than the bulbs they are forcibly replacing. What happens if one of the normal lightbulbs (called 'incandescent') breaks into pieces, as they sometimes do? We sweep up the bits and throw them in the bin, job done, no problem. What do we have to do when an 'environmentally-friendly', help-to-save-the-world fluorescent bulb breaks? Here is some helpful advice from the UK Health Protection Agency:

(1) Keep children and pets out of the contaminated area.
(2) Prior to cleaning up the spill, put on an old set of clothes and shoes, and rubber gloves.
(3) Never vacuum the affected area as this will contaminate the machine and result in the airborne release of vaporised mercury. A vacuum cleaner contaminated with mercury will have to be disposed of. Consult your local authority for information on where you can safely dispose of such equipment, or if you have any queries. A mop or broom should not be used as these will become contaminated and spread the spill.
(4) Elemental mercury that has been spilt on a hard surface should be picked up using masking tape, or swept into a glass container with a sealable lid using stiff cardboard to push the beads together. Check a wide area beyond the spill, using a torch to identify as much of the mercury as possible.
(5) The container, the cardboard and brokenglass should be double- bagged for disposal.Then consult your local authority for information regarding disposal facilities, or if you have any queries. The room in which the spill occurred should be ventilated and the spill area should not be vacuumed for two weeks.
(6) If the spill is on upholstery or carpet, the mercury should be collected in a sealable container (see step 4). Remember, never vacuum the affected area as this will contaminate the

machine and result in the airborne release of vaporised mercury which can harm health. If the mercury cannot be retrieved, the area of contaminated upholstery or carpet may need to be removed and disposed of as hazardous waste. If this is the case, the contaminated material should be double-bagged. Consult your local authority for information on where you can safely dispose of the waste.

(7) Do not use household cleaning products to clean the spill, particularly products that contain ammonia or chlorine such as bleach. These chemicals will react violently with mercury, releasing a toxic gas.

(8) Elemental mercury that has been spilt down a sink should be removed by dismantling the U-bend (water trap) and collected in a sealable container and disposed as hazardous waste. Mercury left in the sink U-bend will vaporise on contact with warm water and should therefore be removed to avoid prolonged exposure.

(9) Clothing that has come into contact with the mercury must not be dry-cleaned or washed in a washing machine and must be discarded, double-bagged, in the normal household refuse.

(10) Carefully remove rubber gloves by grabbing them at the wrist and pulling them inside out as they come off. Place the gloves and any contaminated clothing, double-bagged, in the rubbish bin for disposal.

The Health Protection Agency adds that we must 'remember to keep the area well-ventilated to the outside (open windows and run any available fans) for at least twenty-four hours after your successful clean-up. Continue to keep pets and children out of the clean-up area'. The agency then talks about disposing of the bulbs at the hazardous household waste section of a waste recycling-centre. Have you got all that when your next fluorescent lightbulb breaks? And there is just the little matter that there are an estimated 5.5 million lightbulbs bought in the United States alone *every day* in a country that uses at any one time some four billion. And every time one breaks you are into the procedure outlined above; and even if they don't break they must be disposed of as hazardous waste. *The Ellsworth American* newspaper reported how a lady called Brandy Bridges from Prospect, Maine, followed the official guidance and replaced the bulbs in her home with the fluorescent variety. But then one of them broke and what followed devastated her home and life. The bulb broke in her daughter's bedroom and she called the Home Depot store to ask for advice. She was advised to call a Poison Control hotline where they passed her on to the Maine Department of Environmental Protection. They deployed a specialist to the scene who established that mercury levels in the bedroom were six times the State's 'safe' limit (and who decides that?) for mercury contamination, and she was told she should engage a clean-up company to decontaminate the room. The bill to do this: $2,000. This is just one fluorescent lightbulb in one home when eventually there will be some four billion in the United States alone. Given the fantastic scale of bulbs needing to be disposed of we are going to see – *are* seeing – serious mercury contamination in garbage and landfill sites. They shouldn't be disposed of like this, but that is what vast numbers of people will do rather than take them to hazardous waste centres. The Control System knows this will happen. Already an estimated 80 million used fluorescent tubes are sent to landfill sites in the UK every year, according to the waste education organisation, WasteAware. This equates to four tonnes of mercury, and the figure throughout Europe and North America is going to be mind-blowing. This puts collectors of refuse at risk from any broken bulbs disposed of in household waste, and also endangers neighbours in communal situations. Those dumped in landfills on the scale that is going to be seen have the clear potential to pollute ground water supplies, rivers and fish with cumulative and lethal mercury contamination. It is said that just one compact fluorescent bulb can pollute 6,000 gallons of water beyond safe drinking levels. Once again, this is by design. The plan is to mass-poison humans from endless sources as part of the global cull of the population and also to suppress us mentally through chemical influence. The effects of mercury include dementia, such as Alzheimer's, depression, loss of memory, inability to control muscles and movements (known as 'motor function'), kidney failure and many other health problems. This is why the bloodlines want us to be poisoned by mercury (hence amalgam teeth fillings). You might note that the words fluoride and fluorescent are similar. This is because they have a common 'ancestor' – a highly dangerous element called Fluorine (also called Fluorspar), which is derived from the mineral fluorite (from the Latin root fluo, meaning 'to flow').

Figure 296: Lightbulb fascism

Figure 297: 'Green' lightbulbs transmit toxic chemicals and radiation as a matter of course; and, when they break, they release lethal mercury

There are several important aspects to the imposition of fluorescent lighting and these include the vibrational, chemical and radiation effects on human health (Fig 296). The bulbs are made to emit a disharmonious vibration, radiation and toxic chemicals with some people more affected than others (Fig 297). Most of the photons released from the mercury atoms are in ultraviolet (UV) radiation wavelengths and there are increasing reports of people becoming ill or having a bright red rash appear on their face after they use them (Fig 298). UV light can affect and fade sensitive paintings, especially watercolours, and many textiles. So using these bulbs requires artwork to be protected with acrylic sheets, according to some reports. Fluorescent lamps flicker, causing problems for people who are sensitive to this, and the less sensitive are affected in ways that are not so obvious. The flicker has the potential for disrupting photography and video recording. The significance of the vibrational impact can be seen with the ability of these lights to cause televisions to take on a life of their own, switching channels by affecting the infra-red

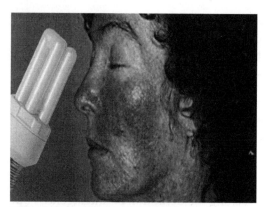

Figure 298: The shocking effects of 'green' lightbulbs on this woman's face

sensors on remote-control receivers. Philips Electronics has confirmed this phenomenon. We are vibrational beings and we are affected by other vibrational influences that can cause mental, emotional and physical dis-ease – disharmony. These are some of the health problems being reported by people after using fluorescent bulbs, as compiled at www.renewableenergygeek.ca:

Mild to severe headaches (migraines); skin irritation, redness, burning sensations, and/or itchiness; dizziness and nausea; tinnitus (ringing in the ears) and earaches; numbness and tingling sensations; tired, weak and fatigued; difficulty sleeping / restlessness; chest pains / heart problems; poor memory and concentration; irritability; feelings of stress and anxiety; depression and mood swings; difficulty breathing; muscle and joint pain; and pain and pressure in the eyes.

These are the multiple consequences of exposure to what is called 'Dirty Electricity' – imbalanced electromagnetic fields that disrupt the electromagnetic balance of the body and the electrical circuits of the brain. Even the utterly useless Health Canada, which has been covering up most of the health effects to avoid contradicting government policy, has said: '... the CFLs are not provided with a prismatic diffuser that filters ultraviolet radiation out. Therefore, there may be skin sensitive issues, especially in people with certain skin diseases'. Dermatologist Dr John Hawk told the BBC that some people already find it difficult to tolerate the fluorescent strip-lighting widely used in schools and offices which operates the same way as CFL bulbs. Hawk said:

Fluorescent lights seem to have some sort of ionising characteristic where they affect the air around them. This does affect a certain number of people, probably tens of thousands, in Britain, whose ailments flare up just by being close to them. Certain forms of eczema, some of which are very common, do flare up badly anywhere near fluorescent lights, so these people have to just be around incandescent lighting.

Ah, but they are not able to 'just be around incandescent lighting' because that has been banned in increasing numbers of countries and these health-destroyers imposed by law. Some people say that fluorescent lights should carry a warning about their potential health effects, but, once again, what is the use of a warning if you have to use them or else sit in the dark? So take a deep breath as we sum up the consequences of forcing the population to use these life-threatening lighting systems: They are potentially deadly when they break and mercury is released, especially for children and foetuses; the mercury content can have a catastrophic effect on brain and body function; they have to be disposed of – *billions* of them – as hazardous waste and when they are dumped in the trash or at landfill sites this creates a highly toxic environment that seeps mercury into underground water supplies and rivers; the vibration, radiation and chemical effects trigger serious and potentially fatal health problems, so much so that scientists have warned people, especially children, to 'stay at a distance' and 'avoid being in contact with them for more than an hour'; they fade pictures and textiles and affect television and other transmissions. From any perspective of rational thought, the very idea of introducing this blatant nightmare to replace something that has worked for so long is beyond insanity. Well, any rational perspective if you care in any way whatsoever about human wellbeing, that is. The people passing laws to impose these lights are largely just the puppet-fodder repeaters who will simply repeat the party line they have been programmed to believe about both the problem ('global warming') and the solution ('low-energy lightbulbs'). They are unthinking, unresearching psyches-for-hire with little that could be seriously identified as approaching the definition of 'intelligence'; but in the shadows, behind the mindless dark suits, they know exactly what they are doing. Once again, humans overwhelmingly just sit back and take it; but then acquiescence can be transmitted, too.

Spraying the skies

Many people all over the world will have noticed a strange and now common sight in their skies that involves aircraft flying to and fro, often in criss-cross patterns, and pouring out what have become known as 'chemtrails' (Figs 299 and 300). These are not the same as *con*trails, or condensation trails, that we see trailing behind aircraft. Contrails disperse almost immediately; but chemtrails don't. They expand to cover the sky with their chemical and metallic cocktails. This is another vehicle for global depopulation. Chemtrail spraying appears to have started in the late 1990s in North America, and now I see it almost wherever I go in the world. Researcher William Thomas was on the case soon after spraying began in Canada in 1998. He says that analysis of the chemtrails has identified highly toxic pathogens, including Mycoplasma fermentans (incognitus strain). Dr Garth Nicholson from the Institute of Molecular Medicine in California found this in some 45 per cent of former US troops suffering from the debilitating disease called Gulf War Syndrome (Hey, guys in uniform – they don't give a *shit* about you). People have reported suffering from respiratory and flu-like conditions and sometimes mental confusion and depression after chemtrail

Figure 299:   **Figure 300:**
Toxic chemtrails are being released all over the world

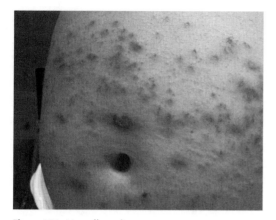

Figure 301: Morgellons disease

Illustration by David Dees (deesillustration.com)

Figure 302: Morgellons disease involves programmed nanotechnology

spraying in the sky. The trails also contain aluminium and barium. This is toxic to humans and suppresses the *immune system* by deactivating T-cell receptors and stopping them from resisting disease. In September 2000, a document produced by the 'neocon' (Rothschild Zionist) Project for the New American Century called for the development of 'advanced forms of biological warfare that can target specific genotypes ...' How about if they have concocted biological weapons that do not affect their hybrid 'genotype'? They are poisoning the rest of the global population from the skies. A new and horrible disease was discovered soon after the chemtrail spraying began, called 'Morgellons disease' (Fig 301). The symptoms are crawling, stinging and biting sensations of the skin; skin lesions that will not heal; extreme fatigue; severe mental confusion; short-term memory loss; joint pain; a sharp decline in vision; itching so bad that some victims consider suicide; and serious neurological disorders. The most shocking aspect of Morgellons disease is the coloured fibres that can be pulled from the body, and not even this stops their continued growth (Fig 302). I have no doubt that the fibres emerge from nanotechnology in the chemtrails which eventually come down to infect land and crops and water, and to be breathed in and absorbed through the skin by humans. Nanotechnology is far too small for the human eye to see. Chemtrails are part of the mass depopulation programme that is gathering by the day. Biological warfare against the people is not new, but the global scale of it certainly is and it comes courtesy of Big Biotech and the usual suspects. China is also involved in this programme of mass poisoning, because, once again, different 'sides' are only illusory. Put 'chemtrails' into a search engine or *YouTube* and you will find reams of information and videos on this subject. While you are at it, type in the words '500,000 plastic coffins in Georgia' and ask yourself why there are half a million plastic coffins in one location in Georgia alone with other examples around America.

Agenda 21

The theme of 'saving the planet', promoted by those who have been *destroying* the planet, is not confined only to 'global warming' or 'climate change'. Oh no, it goes much further than that. Ladies and gentlemen, please welcome, or rather don't, 'Agenda 21'

(Fig 303). This was birthed at the United Nations Conference on Environment and Development in Rio de Janeiro, Brazil, in 1992. The event was hosted by Maurice Strong, a Canadian oil and business billionaire who has slavishly served the interests of the Rothschilds and Rockefellers for most of his life. Strong is a member of the Club of Rome, the environmental satellite in the Round Table network which includes the Bilderberg Group and Trilateral Commission. The Biodiversity Treaty connected to Agenda 21 is an internationally-binding treaty that involves the best part of 200 countries.

Figure 303: Agenda 21 is indeed a Trojan horse to global fascism

Agenda 21 demands, under the guise of 'saving the environment', widespread land confiscation by the United Nations, and government control of all resources, water supplies and usage, and so much more. The United States signed the treaty, but it was not ratified by the Senate thanks to people like ecologist and ecosystem scientist, Dr Michael Coffman. He realised in the course of his work in the 1980s and 1990s that there was a plan to confiscate half of America's land to 'protect the environment'. This includes removing road links to destroy rural communities and drive residents out in the same way that people alongside the technologically-flooded Missouri and Mississippi are being driven out. I have listed the countries fully-committed to this outrage in Appendix II. Needless to say these include the United Kingdom, Canada, Australia, New Zealand and the European Union. Agenda 21 is 'a comprehensive blueprint of action to be taken globally, nationally and locally by organizations of the UN, governments, and major groups in every area in which humans directly affect the environment'. Hold on, I'll just pass that across my Orwellian Translation Unit ... back in a sec ... 'Okay, thank you, bye.' Right, this apparently means that Agenda 21 is about mass depopulation, stealing much of the Earth's surface in the name of protecting it, and imposing a fascist control-structure at all levels that would make humans nothing more than fully-fledged microchipped serfs and slaves. We are asked to believe that the bloodline environmental assassins have been walking in the direction of Damascus. Quite a relevant question I think: Why would the world's biggest polluters who are punching holes in the ionosphere, introducing multiple sources of radiation into the seas and atmosphere, destroying rainforests, devastating the ecosystem in the Gulf of Mexico etc., etc., suddenly morph into tree-huggers? To state the obvious: *They haven't.* Agenda 21 is the work of the bloodline created-and-controlled United Nations and it lays out in 40 chapters a programme to hijack the world. The goals include:

- An end to national sovereignty
- State planning and management of all land resources, ecosystems, deserts, forests, mountains, oceans and fresh water; agriculture; rural development; biotechnology; and ensuring equity (everyone equally enslaved)

- The State to 'define the role' of business and financial resources
- Abolition of private property (it's not 'sustainable')
- 'Restructuring' the family unit
- Children raised by the State
- People told what their job will be
- Major restrictions on movement
- Creation of 'human settlement zones'
- Mass resettlement as people are forced to vacate land where they live
- Dumbing down education (achieved)
- Mass depopulation

All this is planned to happen globally, nationally and locally across the world. Now wait a second. 'Children raised by the State?' Isn't that what Aldous Huxley said in *Brave New World* in 1932? I think it is, you know. You can see in Figure 304 a map of the America that these insane Agenda 21 'biodiversity' and 'sustainable development' people want to see. The darkest areas are designated for virtually no use by humans, and the next darkest areas would be 'highly regulated'. Only the areas one step lighter would be for 'normal use' by the general population which would be concentrated in those 'human settlement zones', with most people packed and stacked together in high-rise buildings. This structure operating at global, regional, national and local levels would be overseen by a world government imposing its iron fist upon 'global citizens' and the 'global village'. There would be no freedom of speech, free movement, or even – through technology – free thought. Harvey Rubin (Rothschild Zionist), a vice chairman of the Agenda 21 front operation, the International Committee for Local Environmental Initiatives, was asked how his Brave New World would affect liberties with regard to the US Constitution and Bill of Rights, private property and freedom of speech. He reply was short: 'Individual rights must take a back-seat to the collective.' Agenda 21 is planned to introduce what is called a 'Technocracy' in which engineers, scientists, medical people and technical experts in general control decision-making and laws with regard to their subject area. 'Experts' would make the decisions

Figure 304: It's goodbye America if the Agenda 21 crazies get their way

based on their level of knowledge; but who decides how knowledgeable they are? The State. If the State decides that an idiot is knowledgeable (as they so often do already) then the idiot gets to call the shots. You may have noticed how many decisions are being made and laws introduced now by agencies rather than El-ected people. These are stepping-stones to what I am talking about. Zbigniew Brzezinski wrote a book in 1970 called *Between Two Ages: America's Role in the Technetronic Era*. He knew exactly what was planned. He wrote:

> The technetronic era involves the gradual appearance of a more controlled society. Such a society would be dominated by an elite, unrestrained by traditional values. Soon it will be possible to assert almost continuous surveillance over every citizen and maintain up-to-date complete files containing even the most personal information about the citizen. These files will be subject to instantaneous retrieval by the authorities.

One plan in this Technocracy is to replace money (that's why they are destroying the current monetary system) with a 'carbon currency', or 'energy certificates/credits'. People would be allocated only so many and they would have to be used before their designated period expires. This way no-one would accumulate savings (except the El-ite). Everyone would be totally dependent on the State and the technocrats and their high-technology (the Reptilians will be having an orgasm at the very thought). All this talk about 'carbon credits' in relation to 'climate change' is preparing people for this and the Smart Grids are a key aspect of this whole deal, too. There is something called the Venus Project – highlighted in the *Zeitgeist* films and based in Florida – which is promoting a society that looks far too much like Agenda 21 for my comfort. Its website says: 'The Venus Project presents a bold, new direction for humanity that entails nothing less than the total redesign of our culture.' Fine, but what kind of 'redesign'? The Venus Project is headed by Jacque Fresco, a 'futurist' and engineer who says that in his resource-based economy 'the system of financial influence and control will no longer exist'. No, but it has the potential to take human control onto a whole new level with the El-ite few controlling the technology and the unified system.

A vast web of interconnected organisations, including government agencies, non-governmental organisations (NGOs), think tanks, trusts, foundations, 'training' (mind control) operations and 'initiatives' have been building the infrastructure for what they call 'the post-industrial, post-democratic' (Technetronic) society, while most of the global population have been occupied with sport, game shows, soaps, computer games, social networking and other manufactured diversions, or have been desperately trying to pay the bills in the face of the economic challenges which the same crowd have engineered. The International Committee for Local Environmental Initiatives is now called Local Governments for Sustainability and this is led by its president, Konrad Otto-Zimmermann (Rothschild Zionist). The Agenda 21 Local Governments for Sustainability claims to have more than 1,220 local government members in 70 countries representing 569,885,000 people. But, of course, they don't 'represent' them at all. Those people don't even know Agenda 21 exists, let alone what the implications are for themselves and their families. Local Governments for Sustainability is supported by a whole bloody dog's breakfast of bloodline fronts peddling 'climate change' and biodiversity. These include: United Cities and Local Governments (UCLG); Metropolis;

World Economic Forum; United Nations Environment Programme (UNEP); United Nations Human Settlements Programme (UN-Habitat); United Nations Framework Convention on Climate Change; United Nations International Strategy for Disaster Reduction; World Bank; Clinton Climate Initiative; Climate Group (Tony Blair); World Conservation Union (IUCN); Renewable Energy and Energy Efficiency Partnership; Global Footprint Network; International Centre for Sustainable Cities; Earthquakes and Megacities Initiative; Stakeholder Forum. My god, if you had that lot round to dinner you wouldn't need a sleeping pill, would you? These are just some of a whole global tapestry of organisations working to the same end. The Rothschilds and Rockefellers had Agenda 21 in mind when they proposed a 'World Conservation Bank' (WCB), now operating under a different name, at the Fourth World Wilderness Conference in Colorado in 1987. James Baker, US Treasury Secretary and close associate of 'shapeshifter' Father George Bush, made a speech in support of the World Conservation Bank that involved writing off some Third World debt in return for giving wilderness and 'environmentally sensitive' lands to the 'bank'. The World Conservation Bank was nothing to do with helping desperate countries and *everything* to do with a land-grab for Agenda 21. George W Hunt, an accountant and investment consultant, was an official host of the World Wilderness Conference and he had been researching some of the 'conspiracy theory' information that was beginning to circulate. Hunt told *Moneychanger* magazine that the World Conservation Bank was designed as a world central bank to steal land while claiming that it was being done to reduce debt and 'help the environment'. Two very familiar names also came up. George Hunt said:

> ... the banker Edmond de Rothschild was at the meeting for six days. Edmond de Rothschild was personally conducting the monetary matters and creation of this World Conservation Bank, in the company of Michael Sweatman of the Royal Bank of Canada. Those two were like Siamese twins, and that's why I say that it appears they were running at least the money side of this conference and I would say the conference was primarily to get money. Also, David Rockefeller (of Chase Manhattan Bank) was there and gave a speech on Sunday ...

The scam is to transfer debts from the Third World countries to the World Conservation Bank and, in return, those countries would hand over land. Any other organisation that took over the WCB would inherit ownership of vast tracts of the Earth. A fact sheet published by the Secretariat of the Wilderness Conference said:

> ... plans for the WCB propose that it act as an intermediary between certain developing countries and multilateral or private banks to transfer a specific debt to the WCB, thus substituting an existing 'doubtful debt' in the bank's books for a new loan to the WCB. In return for having been relieved of its debt obligation, the debtor country would transfer to the WCB natural resource assets of 'equivalent value'.

George Hunt delivered a written protest to David Rockefeller via his bodyguard. Hunt says that he received a warning from Rockefeller's office saying that he'd better stay out of politicking or he'd regret it. These are such nice people. The World Conservation Bank morphed into the 'Global Environment Facility' and this is doing precisely what Rothschild and Rockefeller proposed – stealing the world. Barack Obama created the

White House Rural Council in 2011 simply by signing an Executive Order with no discussion or debate (EO 13575). This 'Rural Council' includes a long list of government agencies, including the Department of Defense and NASA (on a *Rural* Council?), which are necessary to find reasons to clear people from the land – do it physically if necessary – and implement Agenda 21. Obama's Executive Order has been described as 'the greatest threat to independent and family farming and ranching'. Now you see how this connects into the plan to give bloodline corporations a monopoly on the production of food and why levees were blown up by the Army Corps of Engineers to flood independent farmland only for the stricken farmers to receive letters saying that they could sell their land to ... the Army Corps of Engineers. Obama's Rural Council is, as one commentator put it, 'a war council and one which has declared its intention to mount an attack on property owners across the nation ... to remove as many as possible from valued agricultural lands across the country'; in short – Agenda 21. Then, in July 2011, came news of another attack on family farms. It was revealed that 'discussions' were taking place at the US Department of Transportation to require farmers to have a commercial driver's license to operate farming equipment. This would end family farming practices that go back as long as America. Family farms are just that – run by the family on often a tight budget. Youngsters are brought up to operate tractors and prepare to take over in the next generation. But the new rules would mean that they would have to be replaced by expensive professional drivers that the farmers could not afford. This is more cold calculation to make life impossible for family farms not connected to Big Food. One farmer said that the government had lost its understanding of rural life and agriculture. 'I am not saying there is anything malicious at all', he said, 'But they just don't understand.' Oh, but they *do* and it is *very* malicious. Another farmer said that the plan was the most ridiculous thing he had ever heard. So it is if you want family farms to survive, but not if you don't.

The removal of independent farmers and others from the land is planned to be done by weather manipulation, economic attacks, government agencies deciding how land, water and resources can be used, and environmental laws. The Environmental Protection Agency (EPA) is already a terrorist organisation for independent farmers and growers, and rural communities. I saw a video just before this book went to press about the disgusting activities of the Los Angeles County 'Nuisance Abatement Teams' who are targeting residents in the very sparsely populated Antelope Valley in the California desert. People are being forced from their homes by *ludicrous* 'code violations' and ordered to destroy their properties. One man was told that this was because unnamed 'neighbours' had complained about his property when his nearest 'neighbours' were ten miles away in all directions. The residents have been subjected to outrageous harassment by these brainless goons in uniform, often at gunpoint, and they are bewildered by what is going on and why it is being done. I can tell them: *Agenda 21.* This was also the real reason behind the British government's so far failed attempt to sell off the nation's forests to private institutions.

Conditioning the kids

The children who are planned to be the adults living in this Agenda 21 nightmare are being programmed to accept their fate as I speak. The bloodline created-and-controlled United Nations Education, Scientific, and Cultural Organization (UNESCO) declared that 2005 to 2015 is 'The Decade of Education for Sustainable Development' (ESD). Or, put another way, The Decade of Mass Mind-Controlling Our Kids to be Good Little Slaves. One statement said:

> The Decade of ESD is a far-reaching and complex undertaking ... that potentially touches on every aspect of life. The basic vision ... is a world where everyone ... learns the values, behavior, and lifestyles required for a sustainable future and for positive societal transformation.

Like I say, The Decade of Mass Mind-Controlling Our Kids to be Good Little Slaves. One reason for the systematic dumbing down of education is encapsulated in this comment in one of their 'sustainability' documents:

> Generally, more highly educated people who have higher incomes can consume more resources than poorly educated people who tend to have lower incomes. In this case more education increases the threat to sustainability.

Wow! Think about the implications of that statement. The diabolical duo, Father George Bush and Bill Clinton, supported Agenda 21 during their presidencies and so it must be about death, destruction and control by that definition alone. Clinton established The President's Council for 'Sustainable Development' by another Executive Order with no political or public debate. This is how Agenda 21 is being introduced by stealth and the Totalitarian Tiptoe – Obama's 'Rural Council' is only the latest step at the time of writing. There are many others waiting in the shadows and we are seeing 'White House' and 'President's' organisations being used increasingly to usurp even the burning embers of American democracy. The term 'sustainable development' is classic Orwellian language in that it appears to stand for one thing, but means something very different. I am all for doing things in ways that are sustainable in the sense that they can go on indefinitely as opposed to slash-and-burn and other such environmental destruction. But (a) the people behind this are devastating the planet with their activities, and (b) Agenda 21 is not about sustainable development; it is about sustainable control and mass depopulation. A United Nations Global Biodiversity Assessment Report called for an *85 per cent* reduction in human numbers. Heck, you only have to look at the map of the planned 'sustainable' United States to realise the scale of population reduction that would be necessary for it to be implemented. Jonathan Porritt, another population extremist, has been a 'green' advisor to Prince Charles and the British government. He has called for the British population to be more than halved to 30 million. Porritt is the son of Lord Porritt, 11th Governor-General of New Zealand and has the option to take the title, The Honourable Sir Jonathon Porritt, 2nd Baronet. He has been a chairman of the Sustainable Development Commission established by bloodline-controlled-to-his-fingertips, 'shapeshifter' Tony Blair, and he is a patron of Population Matters, formerly the Optimum Population Trust. Porritt is also one of the most arrogant, self-obsessed people that I have ever met. He was supported in his stance on population by Professor Chris Rapley, director of the Science Museum, who said that too many people would make it much harder to reduce carbon emissions by 80 per cent to stop ... *global warming*. This is also being used as an excuse for depopulation. Personally, I think that reducing the emissions of Porritt and Rapley would do far more for the world. The plan is to advance Agenda 21 as quickly as possible in the next few years, and this is why the United Nations General Assembly has declared 2011 to 2020 the United Nations Decade on Biodiversity. This is officially being done to 'support and promote the implementation of the objectives of the Strategic Plan for Biodiversity', but the deal is to support and promote the implementation of the objectives I have been describing here, plus a whole lot more. The mysterious Georgia Guidestones are an astrologically-aligned granite monument in Elbert County, Georgia, and often called 'America's Stonehenge'. They were commissioned in 1979 by someone using the pseudonym 'R C Christian', and they include ten 'guides' for the world of the future inscribed in a series of languages. Two of these 'guides' say: 'Maintain humanity under 500,000,000 in perpetual balance with nature;' and: 'Guide reproduction wisely – improving fitness and diversity.' Oh really? And who does the 'guiding', pray? Why, of course, the State.

HAARP, GWEN, TETRA, 'green' lighting, the 'climate change' fraud, chemtrails, Agenda 21 and 'biodiversity' are all snakes on the same Medusa. I don't like bringing bad news, but we need to be adult, straighten our backs and know what we are facing. Only then can we do something about it. And remember ... we are not alone in dealing with this. Other forces are at work to dismantle the Control System, awaken human awareness and scupper the Reptilian Agenda.

13

Controlling the Mooney

The most effective form of control in today's world, apart from direct control of the mind, is money, or *mooney*. When you have lots of money you have far more choice and power than if you have little or none. How many times do you want to do something or go somewhere, but lack of money gets in the way?

Money is the focus of most people, and that's how the bloodlines want things to stay. Some are focused on accumulating more and more, while most are desperately trying to make the rent or mortgage or even earn enough for themselves and their families to have food to eat. The Rothschilds and the bloodlines have imposed a global structure in which virtually everyone is dependent on money, and *they* have made sure that they control the money. They have done this by *creating* the very concept of 'money' that we have today – the system known as *credit* and *interest*. The idea is to lend people money that doesn't exist – *credit* – and charge them interest on it. This has allowed them to seize most of the world, including whole nations and the planet's resources, through the accumulation of debt. We are back to Mesopotamia again. Priests of the temple in Babylon were making loans in the 18th century BC during the reign of King Hammurabi; and transferring bank deposits to third parties was common by 1000 BC. Money is one of the bloodlines' prime methods of control, and among the first bankers in the western world were the Knights Templar who ran major financial centres in London and Paris. The network of bloodlines known as the Black (Saturn) Nobility, located in Venice and northern Italy, was also highly significant in the expansion of the monetary system that we know today. They included those bloodline Satanists, the de'Medici family. The Black Nobility established the financial centres of Lombardy in northern Italy together with merchants known as the 'Lombards', a name later used for all bankers in Florence, Genoa, Venice and Milan. The term 'bank' has the same Italian origin. It comes from 'banco', which means 'bench', and originates from the benches on which the moneychangers sat to do their business. Today, judges are called 'the bench' as they sit there in their black (Saturn) robes administering the legal system, which was also established by the bloodlines that created the banks.

The Black Nobility went on to expand their banking activities into Hamburg, Amsterdam and the City of London, the 'Square Mile', which is controlled by secret societies like the Knights Templar. 'The City' has a 'Lombard Street', a reference to the history that I have outlined. The bloodlines' most destructive weapon when it comes to money is 'usury'. This is Medieval Latin for 'interest' or 'excessive interest'. There was a ban of usury in the Christian world at one time and there still is within Islam, at least officially. This was a serious piece of 'good fortune' for the former Khazars who made their way north from the Caucasus region and into Europe. They followed the religion of Judaism, which did not ban usury, and to a large extent the field was left open for them to exploit and establish the rules and the way things have been done to the present day. The former Khazars, who we now call 'Jewish', controlled the trade in gold and silver in places like Germany, where a family called the Bauers would change their name to Rothschild, or Red Shield/Sign, the six-pointed star that represents Saturn. 'Goldsmith', or 'Goldschmidt' in German, became a Jewish name because of the association with the trade. Goldsmiths issued paper receipts for the gold and silver that was deposited in their strongrooms, and these receipts began to be exchanged rather than going through the process of exchanging the actual gold or silver. This stayed in the hands of the goldsmiths and silversmiths who realised that with very little of the gold or silver ever being moved they could issue paper receipts to others who didn't own the gold and silver – and charge them interest for doing so. They were lending the wealth of others to make fortunes for themselves, and so long as they didn't issue more paper receipts (loans at interest) than the gold and silver that the true owners would want to withdraw, they could get away with it indefinitely. The banking system that we know today was born, and this is still owned and controlled by the secret society operating within elements of the former Khazar community that I call Rothschild Zionism – Rothschild *Saturnism*.

Money Madness

People know so little about the banking system that controls their lives. How many ask where 'money' actually comes from? Oh, it's the government, isn't it? Well, no, it's not. The vast majority of 'money' is created out of thin air by the private banking system owned by the bloodlines, particularly the Rothschilds, and it is known as 'credit'. Put another way, banks are lending people money that doesn't exist and charging interest on it – just as they were lending paper receipts against gold and silver which did not, in terms of ownership, exist. Humanity is drowning in debt because money is 'created' from the start as a *debt*. Bloodline control of government and banking has allowed them to pass laws through their puppet politicians which make it quite legal for them to lend some ten times what they have on deposit – and in practise, far, far more. The system is called 'fractional reserve lending'. Every time you deposit a pound, a dollar or a euro you are giving the bank the right to lend at least another *ten* and charge interest on it. When you go to a bank to borrow, say £50,000 – what happens? Does the bank print the money or transfer precious metals to you? No, no. It simply types into your account the 'money' that you have theoretically 'borrowed' (although you haven't, because it doesn't exist). Now you are responsible for paying back that 'money' to the bank, plus interest; and if you can't do that when the economy crashes or you lose your job, the banks comes a-calling to take your wealth that *does* exist – your land, property, possessions or business. This has been happening for hundreds of years and it has allowed the bloodlines to accumulate most of the wealth of the world and leave the people with mere pieces of paper or figures on a screen which are backed by *nothing* and

Figure 305: Get them in debt and feed them mind-fodder: *Gotcha*

only have buying power because we *think* they are worth something. Oh, but there's more – much more. When you spend the fresh air 'money' that you have just 'borrowed', let's say £15,000 to buy a car, the seller takes non-existent 'money' from you and deposits the cheque in his or her bank. This second bank can now lend at least *ten times* the £15,000 and charge interest on it! Then the car seller buys something, for say £10,000, and the recipient puts that in his or her bank. Now bank number three can lend at least ten times that figure and charge interest. This all happens from the initial 'loan' of £50,000 that did not exist in the first place. The amount of interest that a single loan generates as it passes through the banking system is simply fantastic. Another thing: when the bank makes a 'loan', it 'creates' the amount that you have agreed – the £50,000 in this case. But you are not paying back £50,000. You are paying back that figure *plus interest,* and the interest is never 'created'. Therefore, and by design, there is never even nearly enough 'money' in circulation at any time for all the principal and interest on outstanding 'loans' to be paid back. This can be hidden better in times of economic expansion as 'Peter pays Paul', but during a slump or depression it is catastrophic for people's lives, as we are seeing now. People losing their homes, businesses and livelihoods is built into the system this way, because there is always far more outstanding debt than there is 'money' in circulation to repay it (Fig 305).

This system gives the bloodlines virtually total control of the game through what is called the 'economic cycle' by ignorant economists and financial 'journalists', as if there is something 'natural' about it. There *isn't*. The 'economic cycle' is callous manipulation. The difference between a boom and a bust is basically the amount of units of exchange – 'money' – in circulation. There can be an expansion in economic activity when a lot of credit money is in circulation. More people are able to buy things and so more things need to be produced to meet demand, and employment is plentiful; but when 'money' in circulation significantly decreases, the opposite happens. People are not able to buy so many things and so less needs to be made. This leads to people losing their jobs and livelihoods, and often their homes, in vast numbers. People and businesses tend to get into more debt during a boom. They are confident about their jobs and the order books and they buy bigger houses and cars, and go on holiday to more expensive locations (Fig 306). Businesses borrow to buy new plant and machinery to meet expanding demand. The amount of 'money' in circulation is crucial to whether we are in an economic boom or depression; and who controls that? *The banks.* The 'economic cycle' goes like this ... Stage 1: Banks stimulate economic activity by making lots of theoretical loans of theoretical 'money' – credit – at low rates of interest to encourage people to borrow. Often you can get a loan in this period to do virtually anything. An economic boom ensues and people and businesses get themselves into staggering amounts of

Figure 306: Keep 'em rolling, Ben, print and be damned

debt. Stage 2: The bloodline bankers start to take money out of circulation at the optimum point when borrowing has reached a peak. This can be done by raising interest rates which suck more 'money' out of circulation to the banks, or by engineering events that lead to a dramatic reduction in the number of loans being made. In current jargon, this is known as a 'credit crunch'. Stage 3: Economic activity plummets, jobs are lost and people and businesses go bankrupt because they can't repay debt, plus interest. Property, businesses and other wealth are then absorbed by the bloodline banks and corporations when people cannot repay 'money' that has never even existed. The reason why the overwhelming majority of people lose their homes and livelihoods isn't because they can't be bothered to work. This nightmare happens when the system stops producing enough employment for those people to earn a living. Even when it does, the system is still insane. Did we really come here to work like slaves most days of our lives only to survive until 'death'? *Look at it.* People are born and then 'educated' just enough to be slaves to work and live in debt until their number is up. The bloodlines are coldly imposing expensive tuition fees for students to go to college and university to force them into ridiculous levels of debt (non-existent 'money' called credit) that they are then committed to paying back for most of their lives. What is debt? *Control.* This has reached the point where young people are borrowing large sums from the bloodline banks to pay for their own indoctrination and preparation for life as a slave in the bloodline system. *What are we doing??* One Scottish 'academic' ... *wait for this* ... has even called for the selling of organs to be made legal so that students can sell their organs to pay to be 'educated' by idiots like this. 'I am just selling a kidney so I can get a degree in medicine and human health.' I can understand why students have taken to the streets to protest at what is being done to them; but what has it changed? *Nothing.* Trying to reason with law-making politicians is a waste of time. They answer to their masters – not to the public. Instead of protesting, just don't go to college and university. Do something else with your life. Is that the only 'choice' that we have within All Possibility? Going to college and university? Don't go until the system is changed, and save yourself from being saddled with extreme levels of perception programming and debt. I left school at 15 and never took a major exam. You can educate yourself, on your terms – not the system's.

Stealing the world

Here's another question about money. Why do governments borrow 'money' from the private bloodline banking cartel and commit the population to paying it back, *plus interest?* They are governments that are supposed to run the country. Why don't they create their own money interest free and put it into circulation interest free? Well, we know why by now. The bloodlines own both governments *and* banks and so the governments do what is best for the banks. American presidents Abraham Lincoln and John F Kennedy both introduced forms of interest-free government money that was not borrowed from the banks. They have one other thing in common. The American government borrows much of its 'money' from the privately-owned cartel of banks known as the Federal Reserve System, created by the Rothschild–Rockefeller networks in 1913 (Fig 307). Most people think that 'the Fed' is part of the government, as I said earlier, because it is called 'Federal' and the 'central bank of

Figure 307: The Federal Reserve was created to destroy America, and that's precisely what it is doing

America'. Doesn't the US president appoint the chairman? The Federal Reserve is a cartel of private banks and the president does not appoint the chairman, except officially. He is told by the bloodlines who it is going to be. They don't hand over multiple millions to secure a president's election with no strings attached. The deal is: We give you multiple millions to finance your El-ection campaign and we tell you who is going to be in your government. The Federal Reserve lends money to the US government and charges interest. The *Fed* owns the dollar, not the government or people. Mayer Amschel Rothschild, founder of the dynasty, said: 'Let me issue and control a nation's money and I care not who writes the laws.' His son, Nathan, who built the Rothschild Empire in Britain, also said:

> I care not what puppet is placed upon the throne of England to rule the empire on which the sun never sets. The man who controls Britain's money supply controls the British Empire, and I control the money supply.

I have heard it said that there is a 'crisis' of 'capitalism' when there *is* no capitalism if we are talking about Big Banking, Big Oil, Big Pharma, Big Biotech, Big Food and all the rest. Capitalism, as in competition, is the last thing they want. The El-lite operate a system that I call 'cartelism'. Oil tycoon John D Rockefeller captured this mind-set when he said: 'Competition is a sin.' What is happening to the United States and Europe today was planned a long, long time ago in an agenda called 'Steal the World'. The poor, or 'Third World', was the first in the line of fire and now it is the turn of the rest of us if we stand by and take it. Third World debt has killed hundreds of millions of people and has devastated the lives of billions, and this is debt on money that does not, and will never, exist. I explain the detailed background to how poor countries were manipulated into shocking levels of debt in ... *And the Truth Shall Set You Free*. Africa, Asia and Central and South America were hijacked through theoretical 'credit' and debt on money which has never, does not, and will never exist. See if you recognise the modus operandi. When the European colonialists apparently dismantled their far-flung empires, the former colonies were said to be 'independent'. But they never were. Physical occupation was replaced by financial occupation in preparation for a new and permanent physical occupation. The Rothschild bloodline network ensured that political leaders of their choosing, and often on their pay-roll, filled the vacuum after the colonialists departed (at least on paper) and bloodline representatives and secret societies ran everything from the shadows. This was the sequence of events that ensnared the poorest people in the world in a trap set by the richest. The Rothschild's' Bilderberg group met in May1973 at Saltsjoebaden, Sweden, hosted by the Rothschild Zionist banking family, the Wallenbergs, the 'Swedish Rothschilds'. Among the Bilderberg attendees were:

Henry Kissinger; Robert Anderson, owner of Atlantic Richfield Oil; Sir Eric Drake, chairman of BP; Sir Dennis Greenhill, a director of BP; Rene Granier de Lilliac, of French Petroleum; Gerrit Wagner, president of Royal Dutch Shell; George Ball of Lehman Brothers; David Rockefeller of Chase Manhattan Bank; Zbigniew Brzezinski, director of the Trilateral Commission, future national security advisor to Jimmy Carter, and now mentor to Barack Obama; and Edmond de Rothschild, Mr 'World Conservation Bank'.

Walter Levy, the US Government's official oil economist for the Marshall Plan (the European Recovery Programme) after the war, presented a proposal to the Bilderbergers to hike the price of oil by 400 per cent. What they needed was an excuse to do this. Five months later came the 'Yom Kippur War' of October, 1973 when Egypt and Syria invaded Israel. America supported Israel and this led to the Arab oil dictators announcing an oil embargo, reduced production and massively inflated prices for the oil that they did produce in protest at America's backing of 'the enemy', which included resupplying weapons during the conflict. But it was all a movie. The world economy was devastated and we had a three-day working week in Britain to 'preserve fuel stocks'. Millions lost their jobs and livelihoods across the world. American oil giants like the Rockefellers' Exxon had been reducing domestic oil stocks to ridiculous levels in the run up to the Yom Kippur War to make the impact even greater. Henry Kissinger, then US Secretary of State and National Security Advisor, had assured President Richard Nixon that reducing domestic oil reserves would not be a problem. It just so happens that Rothschild Zionist Kissinger was the architect of the Yom Kippur War through his 'shuttle diplomacy'. This involved working in league with Israel and lying to Egypt and Syria. The Rothschild Bilderberg Group now had its enormous oil hike and it was time for stage two. Part of the deal between the Rothschild cabal and the Arab oil countries was that they would deposit their vastly increased revenues in a series of designated banks, including Chase Manhattan, Citibank, Manufacturers Hanover Trust, Bank of America, Barclays, Lloyds and Midland. By 1994, 70 per cent of the oil profits from members of the Organisation of Petroleum Exporting Countries (OPEC) were invested in overseas stocks, bonds and land. Sixty per cent of this figure was deposited with financial institutions based in New York and London, and they were able to lend at least ten times what they were receiving because of the scam called fractional reserve landing. Populations across the world were struggling to survive in the wake of the economic crash caused by the oil hike and cuts in production, but the major banks were awash with money. Sound familiar? The banks then sent out streams of representatives across the Third World to offer them as much credit as they were prepared to take, and they were especially looking for corrupt and incompetent politicians that would steal and squander it. They *wanted* these countries to default on their by now extraordinary levels of debt, because the end game was to steal their land and resources. The 'money' was loaned at low, but *variable*, interest rates and once the noose of the debt was in place they opened the trap door with a colossal increase in the rates of interest. This was achieved by the policies of Rothschild partner, Paul Volcker (Rothschild Zionist, Bilderberg Group), then head of the Federal Reserve and later part of 'Obama's' original economic team, and the two stooges, President Ronald Reagan (controlled by vice president father George Bush) and British Prime Minister, Margaret Thatcher, who thought she was 'the boss' when she wasn't. They introduced under different names the same economic 'monetarist' austerity and 'privatisation' programmes – the selling off of state assets to the Rothschild corporations. N M Rothschild in the City of London was the premier 'agency' for privatising British state assets. These identical policies were called 'Reaganomics' and 'Thatcherism' and they had the effect of causing bank interest rates to soar and produce terrible consequences for the poorest countries on the planet. What became known as 'Third World debt' reached such dramatic proportions that they could not even pay back the interest never mind the principal on the illusory figures on a screen.

The Rothschild-created World Bank and the International Monetary Fund (IMF) moved in to offer more loans, this time from public money to pay back the loans to the private banks. But this came, as always, at a price that constitutes a crime against humanity. It also allowed for a fundamental transfer of money from the global population via the World Bank, IMF and the indebted countries themselves to the banking cartel. In this way, the Rothschild corporations seized ownership of these countries, in effect, and untold hundreds of millions suffered and died from the impact of extreme poverty and malnutrition. The World Bank and IMF insisted on the introduction of severe austerity programmes on the target populations in areas like health, education and support for the poorest, and they said that land that was growing food for the people must be turned over to growing 'cash crops' for the bloodline transnational corporations. They insisted on: state assets being sold off to the corporations; removing regulation to allow those corporations to take over and do whatever they like; tax cuts, or no tax at all for the corporations; cuts in wages; tax increases; and the dismantling of human rights and crushing of trade unions. Loans made to Chile in the 1980s came with a demand for wage cuts of 40 per cent; and in Mexico, where wages and spending on health, education and other programmes had to be cut by half, infant mortality tripled. These are the same people who say that children in the poorest countries must be mass- vaccinated to 'save their lives'. There is no contradiction here, though. The financial oppression and the vaccination programmes are both seeking the same end: depopulation. Another consequence of this manipulated Third World debt was the transfer of land from the ownership of the state to a 'World Conservation Bank', now the Global Environment Facility', which I mentioned earlier. This was orchestrated by Edmond de Rothschild who attended the Bilderberg meeting that started the whole sequence. The theme of getting countries into debt they can't repay and telling them what they must do in return for new loans can also be seen in Western countries today. The scam they have played so successfully on the poorest countries in the world has now come to Europe – and it is coming to America, too. In

many ways, it already has. Countries
such as Ireland and Greece are deluged
with debt, and the Rothschild IMF and
European Central Bank are ordering
viciously severe austerity programmes
and the selling off of state assets to the
bloodline corporations. This is being
done systematically as the bloodlines
seek to own the entire planet. The
EU/IMF bailout has forced Greece to
establish a privatisation agency that will
transfer real state assets to bloodline
banks and corporations in return for
nothing more than figures on a screen.
Jean-Claude Juncker, head of the
Eurogroup of finance ministers, said that
the sovereignty of Greece would be

Figure 308: Greenspan – 'The Wizard' makes the
American economy disappear

massively limited and 'experts' were heading for the country to oversee a fire-sale of
state assets to private corporations. The financial catastrophe in Europe is all engineered
to steal assets and end sovereignty and the same is planned for the United States.

I explained earlier how the current economic meltdown was Rothschild-engineered
through their agents in government such as Alan Greenspan (Rothschild Zionist), who
was chairman of the US Federal Reserve through the presidencies of Ronald Reagan,
Father George Bush, Bill Clinton and most of Boy Bush (Fig 308); Ben Bernanke
(Rothschild Zionist), the current 'Fed' chairman; Robert E Rubin (Rothschild Zionist)
and Larry Summers (Rothschild Zionist), Treasury Secretaries to Bill Clinton; and
Timothy Geithner (Rothschild Zionist), who worked with Rubin and Summers in the
Clinton years, and is now US Treasury Secretary. These were the key people that
triggered the crash in 2008. What was done was literally criminal. Banks sold worthless
'toxic assets' to pension funds and others as a solid gold investment when they knew
the opposite was true. But, at the time of writing, only one person in the financial sector
has been held to account and jailed since 2008 and that was Bernard Madoff (Rothschild
Zionist), who stole billions in a Peter-pays-Paul-pays-Peter Ponzi scheme. Madoff said
that the banks he worked with knew what he was doing. The trustee liquidating the
former investment firm of this mega-crook said in early 2011 that he was suing
JPMorgan Chase & Co. for $6.4 billion, alleging that the bank aided and abetted the $65
billion Madoff fraud. Irving H Picard, the lawyer appointed by a New York bankruptcy
court, said he was seeking $1 billion in fees and $5.4 billion in damages. A spokesman
for Picard said: 'JPMorgan Chase & Co. was at the very centre of that fraud, and
thoroughly complicit in it.' The reason Madoff was jailed, as one commentator rightly
said, is that he made the mistake of stealing from the rich. Do the same to the poor and
middle class and you don't go to jail – you get an enormous bonus. Dick Fuld
(Rothschild Zionist), the CEO of Lehman Brothers at the time of its collapse, walked
away with *half a billion* dollars. Others who were fundamentally responsible for the
banking crisis picked up hundreds of millions in 'compensation' while their victims lost
their homes and their pensions. None of them faced charges for their blatant corruption

because the banks have their people in the key positions in the government's financial law and investigation departments, and many of these government 'regulators' end up working later for the very banks they decided not to prosecute. Meanwhile, as this was happening, an Oklahoma mother of four small children was jailed for ten years after selling marijuana worth just $31 to an undercover policeman who set her up. They have a name for when those in authority and influence are not subject to the same laws as the rest of the population: *Fascism*.

Gold-in-sacks

In so many ways, to understand how the present crash came about is to understand the Rothschild-controlled expression of evil known as 'Goldman Sachs'. This was officially founded in 1869 by the Rothschild Zionist, Marcus Goldman, after he emigrated from Bavaria in the Rothschild fiefdom of Germany. He was one of many Rothschild Zionists who went to America from Germany in the 19th and 20th centuries to establish major banks, companies and organisations to serve the bloodline agenda. The 'Sachs' part of the Goldman operation came with the arrival of his son-in-law, Samuel Sachs, a Rothschild Zionist German–American, whose also came parents came from Bavaria. Sachs had a long-time friend in Philip Lehman of the Lehman Brothers banking family. The Lehmans arrived in America, again from Bavaria, in the 19th century. Bavaria was also the birthplace of Henry Kissinger, Pope Benedict and the Rothschild-created Bavarian Illuminati, founded in 1776, and officially headed by Adam Weishaupt, who fits the bill for what I would call today a Rothschild Zionist. Weishaupt was educated by the Jesuit Order, another key strand in the web that includes Rothschild Zionism. The Bavarian Illuminati manipulated wars, revolutions and other society-changing events, including the French Revolution, and was extremely active in the United States. The Rothschild-controlled Goldman Sachs, headed by Lloyd Blankfein (Rothschild Zionist), is a monster dictating US government policy to suit bloodline demands and it is active around the world, too. Goldman Sachs was heavily involved in the financial crash in Greece and so was JP Morgan Chase. Greece mortgaged airports and roads to Goldman Sachs and others to secure loans that gave the government money in the short-term while keeping the loans (debt) off the books to overcome debt limit restrictions. At the same time, Goldman was betting that Greece would default, thus profiting from the Greek tragedy that it helped to create.

The Goldman technique is to ensure that its people are appointed to the major financial posts in government, and this is what other major corporations do. I have detailed in other books how Biotech royalty, Monsanto, has a similar revolving door between itself and government departments and agencies that relate to its areas of operation. Goldman Sachs makes government banking policy as Monsanto makes government biotech policy. Everything else is just detail. *Time* magazine described Goldman Sachs as 'the single largest supplier of financial talent to the government' and never more outrageously so than during the banking bailout. Goldman Sachs also made the biggest single private campaign donation to Barack Obama. Goldman Sachs received $12.9 billion of borrowed taxpayers' money to 'prevent its collapse' and crucially benefited from the initial $85 billion bailout of the insurance giant, AIG, which would have triggered crippling losses for Goldman had it gone under. AIG would later be given tens of billions more to keep it afloat, much to the delight of its long-time chairman, Maurice Greenberg (Rothschild Zionist), who resigned in 2005 over allegations of fraudulent business practice, securities fraud, common law fraud, and other violations of insurance and securities laws. *No*, surely not? Greenberg is a close friend of Rothschild/Rockefeller agent, Henry Kissinger (Rothschild Zionist), who he appointed to chair AIG's advisory board, and AIG was a client of the notorious Kissinger Associates. Greenberg is Honorary Vice Chairman and Director of the Rothschild Council on Foreign Relations and a member of the Rothschild Trilateral Commission; chairman, and currently trustee, of the Asia Society; Trustee Emeritus of the Rockefeller University; and an honorary Trustee of the Museum of Modern Art. All these institutions were established by the Rockefeller family. The Rockefellers and their 'bosses', the Rothschilds, are both closely connected to Goldman Sachs and they dictated

Figure 309: Hank Paulson searches for integrity – in vain.

policy to the Bush administration, and now to Obama. I wonder how AIG managed to get so much bailout money? Must have been luck, I guess. What do you think? The bailouts were instigated after September 2008 by Boy Bush Treasury Secretary, Henry 'Hank' Paulson Jr (Fig 309). He was chairman and CEO of Goldman Sachs before he joined the government in 2006. One article said: 'The Secretary of the Treasury, who used to be the Goldman CEO, just spent $85 billion to buy a failing insurance giant that happened to owe his former firm a lot of money. Does that smell right to you?' It never smells right if Goldman Sachs is involved. Paulson appointed former Goldman Sachs vice president, Neel Kashkari, as head of the Office of Financial Stability to decide who got the bailout money. Kashkari, in turn, appointed Reuben Jeffery, a Managing Partner at Goldman Sachs, as interim chief investment officer. Other important players in the Treasury were Dan Jester, Steve Shafran, Edward C Forst and Robert K Steel – all Goldman people. Goldman executives at the pivotal New York Federal Reserve Bank were involved in the bailout discussions. They included Stephen Friedman (Rothschild Zionist), head of the board of governors, and Robert Rubin (Rothschild Zionist), Bill Clinton's Treasury Secretary who did so much to prepare the ground for the collapse of 2008. He was CEO at Goldman Sachs. Rubin, a co-chairman of the Council on Foreign Relations, is a former student at the Fabian Society's London School of Economics, and so is Peter Orszag (Rothschild Zionist) who became Obama's first Budget Director. Timothy Geithner (Rothschild Zionist) and Larry Summers (Rothschild Zionist) were 'selected' by Obama (were selected for him) to dictate 'his' economic policy. Geithner is a former executive of Kissinger Associates, a member of the Council on Foreign Relations, and President of the New York Federal Reserve which made a significant contribution to causing the crash. He appointed Goldman Sachs lobbyist, Mark Patterson, as his chief of staff at the Treasury. Summers was paid $135,000 by Goldman Sachs for a single day's 'appearance' in 2008. Barney Frank (Rothschild Zionist), Chairman of the House Financial Services Committee, had the job of questioning

Treasury officials and investigating the bailout policy. His top aide was Michael Paese who left to become a lobbyist with Goldman Sachs. Chief of Staff to President Boy Bush was Joshua Brewster Bolten (Rothschild Zionist), who played a major role in the appointment of Goldman Sachs CEO, Henry Paulson, as Treasury Secretary. Bolten was Executive Director for Legal and Government Affairs with Goldman Sachs in London. When AIG hit the rocks in September 2008, a new chief executive was appointed. This was Edward M Liddy, a former Goldman Sachs executive who held $3 million in Goldman shares. He took the job at the request of Paulson, the Treasury Secretary and former Goldman CEO.

Paul Farrell, a columnist with *Marketwatch*, said that Goldman 'rules the world', and an article in *Rolling Stone* magazine described Goldman Sachs as 'a great vampire squid wrapped around the face of humanity'. The article rightly accused the bank of rigging every major market bubble and burst since the Great Depression. This included the Internet bubble, the commodities bubble and the housing/credit bubble. They have done this for the reasons I have described: start a boom and a frenzy to invest and then burst the bubble and pick up assets for cents on the dollar to vastly increase your control and ownership of the financial system and much else. The *Rolling Stone* article was written by the excellent Matt Taibbi, a contributing editor, and exposed the central role that Goldman played in the crash of 2008 and what has followed. He said the 'big scam' was to have 'a whole bunch of crap, slap it with a triple-A rating, and sell it to a whole bunch of institutional investors'. These institutions, using the money of people of modest incomes and pension funds, would then lose their investments and their clients would lose their pension money. The very 'credit ratings agencies' like Moody's Investors Service and Standard & Poor's that gave triple-A ratings to this worthless junk in the run-up to the crash of 2008 are the same ones giving 'junk' credit ratings to countries like Ireland, Greece and Portugal with all the devastating consequences for their economies and people. It is so simple when you control the major credit ratings agencies; and Moody's, Standard and Poor's and the Fitch Group dominate the market. You get them to rate junk as blue chip so you can sell it to a pension fund or other investors and when you want countries to go under you downgrade their credit rating. The mainstream media is incapable or unwilling to highlight this fantastic absurdity. What if you know beforehand that these agencies are going to deliver a 'junk' verdict on a country and when? You bet on them going bankrupt. Someone placed a $1 billion 'trade' (bet) on the US futures market in July 2011 that the United States would lose its triple-A rating. You don't do that unless you know it is going to happen. Standard and Poor's duly dropped the triple-A rating for America in early August 2011. These agencies have no legal or financial penalties to face no matter how wrong they are and what consequences this creates. Matt Taibbi explains how in 2004 the then Goldman CEO, Henry Paulson, asked the Securities and Exchange Commission to relax restrictions, if you can call them that, on Goldman's ability to lend money that it didn't have:

> They felt restrained by certain rules that said they had to have one dollar for every twelve they lent out, so ... then chief Hank Paulson went to the SEC and asked them to basically end those rules, and they did it. There was no Congressional hearing, no vote or anything like that. The SEC granted Goldman and four other banks exemptions to these rules and said you can lend as

much money as you want, you don't really need to have any money.

Within two years, two of those banks went under: Bear Stearns and Lehman Brothers. This is just because they went to the government and asked for a change in the rules and they got it. This is what they do all the time and they also know that if they ever get in serious trouble they could just call up the government and ask them to give them a whole lot of taxpayer cash to bail them out, and that has happened over and over again.

Taibbi also said that he had never covered a story in which so many people had said that he could not use their names for fear of retribution. He said there were people in government who were afraid to 'cross' Goldman Sachs. One Congressman had sent out a letter criticising Goldman and within an hour Richard Gephardt, the former Democratic presidential candidate, was on the phone 'acting as a Goldman Sachs lobbyist' requesting that he take back everything that he wrote in the letter. 'The big threat is that if you cross Goldman Sachs you are never going to get campaign contributions again,' Taibbi said. 'And not only from them, probably anyone else in the Democratic Party.' Goldman Sachs was the biggest single contributor to Barack Obama's campaign fund, as I mentioned earlier. Any Obama groupies still believe that he is acting independently and is not controlled by the El-ite? Goldman Sachs is a tyranny, and for 'Goldman Sachs' read *Rothschild*.

Another major coordinating vehicle in all this has been the Group of Thirty. This was established by the Rockefeller Foundation in 1978. The Rockefellers employed a frontman for this called Geoffrey Bell – yet another graduate from the London School of Economics. The chairman of the Group of Thirty is Paul Adolph Volcker (Rothschild Zionist), a former Chairman of the Federal Reserve, graduate from the London School of Economics, Rothschild partner, and appointed by Obama to be Chairman of the President's Economic Recovery Advisory Board. Other Group of Thirty members have included Obama's Timothy Geithner and Larry Summers. Goldman Sachs is, of course, involved in the Group of Thirty in the form of Managing Director Gerald Corrigan, the former President of the Federal Reserve Bank of New York. The United States is drowning in a tsunami of debt to China, and this has been central to the unfolding plan to destroy the American economy. The father of the Chinese-speaking Timothy Geithner is Peter F Geithner, who serves with Henry Kissinger on the board of the National Committee on US–China Relations. Another member of the Group of Thirty is Dr Zhou Xiaochuan, Governor of the People's Bank of China. Not coincidentally, Peter F Geithner worked for the Ford Foundation and oversaw the work of Ann Dunham, who was paid by the Foundation to develop 'microfinance programmes' in Indonesia. Ann Dunham is the mother of Barack Obama. Mervyn King, the placeman Governor of the Rothschild-controlled Bank of England, is also a member of the Group of Thirty. This former Professor of Economics at the Fabian-controlled London School of Economics was at the centre of British government policy while all this corruption and deceit was going on in the United States. The Group of Thirty is one of many Rothschild organisations that coordinate financial policy and action around the world. One of the most important is the Bank for International Settlements in Basel, Switzerland. This coordinates bloodline policy through the European Central Bank (established in the

Rothschild city of Frankfurt in 1998), World Bank, International Monetary Fund and national central banks.

Orgy of corruption and greed

The outcome of what I have described has been that government debt (the people's debt) has increased by multiple trillions around the world (Fig 310). This money has been given away by the El-ite in government and central banks to the El-ite in private banks and other financial institutions (Fig 311). The policy of the Federal Reserve giving 'bailout' money to people who didn't need it at interest rates so low that they made fortunes lending it to others at higher rates, has now been exposed many times. Matt Taibbi wrote the following in another brilliant *Rolling Stone* article:

> The Fed sent billions in bailout aid to banks in places like Mexico, Bahrain and Bavaria, billions more to a spate of Japanese car companies, more than $2 trillion in loans each to Citigroup and Morgan Stanley, and billions more to a string of lesser millionaires and billionaires with Cayman Islands addresses. 'Our jaws are literally dropping as we're reading this,' says Warren Gunnels, an aide to Sen. Bernie Sanders of Vermont. 'Every one of these transactions is outrageous'...

Figure 310: Ben Bernanke: To put out a fire you pour more petrol on it

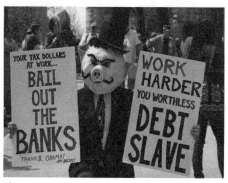

Figure 311: No caption necessary

... thanks to a whole galaxy of obscure, acronym-laden bailout programs, it eventually rivaled the 'official' budget in size – a huge roaring river of cash flowing out of the Federal Reserve to destinations neither chosen by the president nor reviewed by Congress, but instead handed out by fiat [any money declared by a government to be legal tender] by unelected Fed officials using a seemingly nonsensical and apparently unknowable methodology.

Taibbi adds that it was 'as if someone sat down and made a list of every individual on earth who actually did *not* need emergency financial assistance from the United States government, and then handed them the keys to the public treasure'. This included $35 billion in Fed loans to the Arab Banking Corporation of Bahrain at interest rates as low as *a quarter of one per cent* – and 59 per cent of that bank was owned by Colonel Gaddafi's Central Bank of Libya. Even worse, the American government is borrowing money back from the Middle East at interest rates of *three per cent*. This is insane on first hearing, but not, as I have been saying for all these years, if the plan is to bankrupt America and bring it under the control of a world government and central bank. Taibbi highlights one 'bailout' in particular in which a company called Waterfall TALF Opportunity was given nine low-interest 'loans' totalling nearly a quarter of a billion dollars. This was very good news for two of its main investors, Christy Mack and Susan Karches. Christy Mack just so happens to be the wife of John Mack, the chairman of Morgan Stanley, who earned $1,235,097 in 'crash year' 2008 while Morgan Stanley received billions in bailout money. The Macks' close friend, Susan Karches, is the widow of Peter Karches, one-time president of Morgan Stanley's investment-banking division, and the low interest rates from the Fed 'loan' ensured a good profit. Most of it was used to purchase *student loans* and commercial mortgages. What did any of this have to do with 'saving the economy'? *Nothing* – and the same with most of the rest. They were just pouring taxpayers' 'money' (now debt) into the pig trough in which the bloodlines and their associates permanently have their snouts. Government money was not only given with next-to-no interest; the receivers didn't even need to repay the money. They gave the taxpayers, via the Federal Reserve, their toxic assets as 'collateral', yes *collateral*, to be kept if the 'loan' was not repaid. This has morphed the trillions of dollars of bank debt into government debt and so the people's debt – hence that governments are going bankrupt and inflicting draconian austerity measures. But, hey, it gets crazier. *'Emergency' loans made by the Federal Reserve at virtually nil interest were then used to lend back to the government at higher interest rates through buying government bonds!* This was all a scam to ensure an incredible transfer of wealth from government ('the people') to some of the world's richest bankers and others (ultimately the Rothschild network). Matt Taibbi colourfully puts it like this: '... the federal aid they received actually falls under a broader category of bailout initiatives, designed and perfected by Federal Reserve chief Ben Bernanke and Treasury Secretary Timothy Geithner, called "giving already stinking rich people gobs of money for no fucking reason at all".' Or, in the words of Barry Ritholtz, author of *Bailout Nation*: '[It was] ... free money for shit. It turned into "Give us your crap that you can't get rid of otherwise".'

The Federal Reserve was forced kicking and screaming to make public where the money went. Nine trillion dollars of taxpayer debt went in 'short-term loans' to the banking system that caused the crisis – 2.2 trillion to Citigroup; 2.1 trillion to Merrill Lynch; 2 trillion to Morgan Stanley; 600 *billion* to J.P. Morgan; and a fantastic amount was handed over to foreign banks, including 1.2 trillion to British banks. *What?* By the 'central bank' of *America?* The 'Fed' asked for no collateral worth the name against these extraordinary 'loans', and they were given with no conditions such as: we will give you the money, but you must not foreclose on homeowners. It was just handed over; do with it what you like. Why wouldn't they do that when the head of the Fed is the Rothschild Zionist Ben Bernanke whose job has been, along with Rothschild Zionist Alan Greenspan, to destroy the American economy in

Figure 312: Ben Bernanke – destroying America

line with the plan dictated by the Rothschilds (Fig 312). The official United States national debt is heading for $15 trillion at the time of writing, but that is nothing like the true figure. It is rising by about $4 billion a day, and already even the official debt represents nearly $50,000 for every American citizen (Fig 313). It was reported in the summer of 2011 that the Apple corporation had more cash reserves than the United States government – $76.4 billion compared with $73.7 billion (and that was borrowed, anyway). Nearly two million fewer Americans had a job 28 months after Obama's economic 'stimulus' package (more debt) had been passed by Congress and included large sums to fund Smart Meters. This is all being done to a script. The taxpayer bailouts were followed by outrageous bonuses for the bankers; mass home foreclosures; a refusal to lend 'money' to stimulate economic activity; and interest rates for savers of next to nothing while bank fees and overdraft rates are constantly increased and the amount of our own 'money' that we can withdraw continually decreased. London's *Daily Mail* revealed that Lloyds TSB, one of the bailed-out British banks, was charging an annual interest rate of ... wait for it ... *46 million per cent* for people overdrawn 'without authorisation', and other major British banks are close behind. One report explained:

A Lloyds customer who goes £200 into the red without an agreed overdraft for 10 days would rack up charges of £85.95. This breaks down into eight daily charges of £10, a 'usage fee' of £5 and interest of 95p. Annualised, that makes 46,450,869% APR.

Those controlling the banking system, most notably the House of Rothschild and their subordinates like the Rockefeller family, are the world's biggest fraudsters and crooks, and their minute-by-minute exploitation is why the division between the rich and poor has become so shockingly extreme. Inequality between a tiny elite and the rest of the world was breathtaking even before the current crisis broke in 2008, and it's far worse now and getting more so by the day. Senator Bernie Sanders has pointed out that the top one per cent earned more than 23 per cent of all income in America in 2007 and more than the entire combined income of the bottom 50 per cent. The percentage of

income going to that one per cent has nearly tripled since the 1970s; and the top one twelfth of one per cent earns 12 cents of every dollar earned in America. At the same time, 800,000 unemployed American workers lost their only source of income – their average $300 a week unemployment benefit. Another 1.2 million will follow, and millions more in 2012. These are people with children to care for, but they now have no income whatsoever and the chances of getting a job are virtually zero. While charity soup-kitchens and their like are overwhelmed with demand – a need that increases by the day – the Obama administration, supported by the Republican

Figure 313: Americans are suffering the consequences of extraordinary levels of debt

'opposition', are continuing a policy of tax breaks for millionaires and billionaires. In 2011, Senator Bernie Sanders revealed in a speech on Capitol Hill that some of the world's biggest corporations not only paid no tax, they were getting *refunds* from the Internal Revenue Service. He said that ExxonMobil made $19 billion in profit in 2009, paid no tax and received a $156 million tax rebate. Bank of America made $4.4 billion, paid no tax, and received a $1.9 billon rebate. General Electric made $26 billion in profit in the United States, paid no tax and received a $4.1 billion rebate. Sanders went on to name others, such as Boeing and Chevron. At the same time that these giant corporations were paying no tax and collectively receiving billions in rebates, the most vulnerable in America society – children, the poor and the elderly – were being hammered by government spending cuts. Obama is an Obamanation, a bag-carrying 'yessir' fraud beyond words.

Not him again

I said at the time of the crash in 2008 that the plan was threefold: (1) crash the economy; (2) have governments (the people) throw incredible amounts of money at the banks until the coffers were exhausted; and (3) crash the economy again at a time when governments have no means to respond; and then have the bankers and financial crooks step forward as the saviours to offer the solution – *their* solution. This, I said and wrote then, would be a total restructuring of the global financial order based on a world central bank, eventually a single electronic currency, and the control of global finance in fewer hands than ever before. Fast-forward two-and-a-half years to 2011 and the conference at Bretton Woods in New Hampshire hosted by the heartless Rothschild frontman, billionaire financier, George Soros (Rothschild Zionist).The location was chosen because it was at Bretton Woods in July 1944 that the allied countries in World War II gathered to agree a new economic order (one of the endless Problem–Reaction–Solutions made possible by that engineered conflict). This led to the creation of the Rothschild-controlled International Monetary Fund (IMF) and the International Bank for Reconstruction and Development, now part of the World Bank. The Soros conference, at the same Mount Washington Hotel, did not have the power to agree a new economic order; but that was not its aim. The conference was another high-profile stepping stone on the road to that end with Soros calling for ... a world central bank. The conference was co-hosted by Soros and his Institute for New Economic Thinking (we want a world central bank and single world currency) and the Centre for International Governance Innovation (we want a world government). The latter is a 'think tank' established by Canadian billionaire, Jim Balsillie. The big sell is now on to massively centralise world governance and finance and this was the latest throw of the sales pitch by the billionaires to the 'little people', which also include most of the here-today-gone-tomorrow politicians. How apt it was that among the attendees and speakers was Larry Summers offering his solution to the problems he has done so much to create. The same goes for former British Prime Minister, Gordon Brown, a student and follower of Alan Greenspan. Brown mirrored his idol's deregulation policy with the same disastrous consequences during his years as the UK's Chancellor of the Exchequer. People like this should not be let loose on a piggy bank, but here they were in their arrogance telling us how to sort out the mess that they created. The system has always been rigged, but now more so than ever before and growing by the hour. Our world,

Figure 314: Tent city America

our lives and those of our children and grandchildren, are being hijacked before our very eyes. Americans and others all over the planet are suffering terrible consequences from what I have just described with large numbers losing their homes, and either living 'rough' or in the ever-emerging tent cities (Fig 314). A *USA Today* report said that only around 45 per cent of Americans have a job. Meanwhile, caring people feeding the homeless and hungry are being *arrested for doing so*. Fascism is not coming to America; it is *here*.

At a time when payments to the poor and vulnerable are being slashed and the tax burden ever increased, the United States is spending, when all the hidden costs are added in, something like a trillion dollars a year on the military to further the bloodline campaign of killing and acquisition. If the United States' government reduced military spending by *85 per cent* it would still be spending more than any other country on the planet to oppress and kill people. But, of course, it is not the 'American military' protecting Americans; it is the bloodlines' military plundering the world and this is why 'Defence' (attack) spending is so outrageously high. The same money-no-object spending on the military while financially squeezing the population is happening worldwide. Canada is one of the most Rothschild-Zionist-controlled countries on Earth. They run the whole show and own the government of whichever party may be in office. While Canadians are suffering from the world recession, and most want less defence spending, the government announced that it was negotiating to establish military bases in Kuwait, Germany, Jamaica, Senegal, Kenya, Singapore and South Korea. This is being done to expand the reach of the emerging world army – not for the benefit of Canadians. The government has more than doubled 'defence' (war) spending since the year 2000, and Defense Minister Peter MacKay said: 'The focus of the planning, let's be clear, is on our capability for expeditionary participation in international missions – we're big players in NATO, we're a country that has become a go-to nation in response to situations like what we're seeing in Libya, like we saw in Haiti, we are constantly working within that paradigm of countries to see where we can bring that niche capability to bear.' To think these people are in government. Terrifying. But those words 'expeditionary participation in international missions' tell the story of what it is all about. They are already fighting a new world war – it's just not yet official. World War III actually began on September 11th, 2001. Joseph Lie-berman (Rothschild Zionist), chairman of the Senate Committee on Homeland Security and Governmental Affairs, personified the mendacity and lack of compassion of these people when he said that social security payments had to be cut to pay for 'defence' (war): 'Bottom line, we can't protect these entitlements and also have the national defence we need to protect us in a dangerous world while we are at war against Islamist extremists who attacked us on 9/11 and will

for a long time to come.' Oh, go away, you silly man. John Boehner, current Speaker of
the United States House of Representatives, said that the retirement age should be
raised to 70 for the same reason.

The Eurozone – Euro*loan*

The fraudulent bailout of the banks has left most European countries in desperate
financial straits. Irish people are going to be swamped with incredible levels of debt for
generations. And why? It is not that they racked up the debt, or that they are refusing to
work. The demolition of the Irish economy was caused by the sickening greed of the
banks that went under as a result and were bailed out by billions from the Irish
government. Even this was not enough, and the government has borrowed astonishing
amounts of money from the Rothschild European Union, European Central Bank (ECB),
headed by Jean-Claude Trichet (Rothschild Zionist), and the IMF, headed at the time by
Dominique Strauss-Kahn (Rothschild Zionist). The government of the truly useless
Brian Cowen resigned in the face of this catastrophic policy, but Cowen refused to go
until he had negotiated the loans with the IMF and ECB. The obvious and honest thing
to have done would have been to resign immediately and let the incoming government
decide what to do. But Cowen had his orders – don't resign until the deal is done and
the new government handed a fait accompli. This is same Cowen who insisted on
another referendum over centralisation of power in the EU after the public had voted
'no'. The man should be in jail. The Irish government has so far either paid out, or has
secured the borrowing to pay out, some 135 billion euros. This is not to support the Irish
people, but to stop the *banks* from going under and bondholders from losing out.
Targeting funding to keep people in their homes is never an option. Such a people-
based response would have made the banks and bankers pay the price of their greed
and corruption. The same could have been done in America where untold numbers are
losing their homes because they can't pay the very banks that they collectively kept
alive. Greece, Portugal, Spain, Italy and others are also in desperate trouble and this is
playing out to the blueprint of bloodline design as they push on towards total global
control and ownership. George Soros (Rothschild Zionist) fuelled the flames by saying
that an economic collapse in Europe was inevitable. He should know given that he is
trying to make it happen. His mate, Jean-Claude Trichet (Rothschild Zionist), head of
the European Central Bank, has been using the engineered crisis to call for the
appointment of a European Union Treasury Secretary with independent authority over
all European banks. Sources inside the Bilderberg conference in Switzerland in June
2011 said that Trichet made the call in his speech there. Problem–Reaction–Solution.
Trichet then repeated the theme when he accepted the Charlemagne Prize, which is
given to those who do most to enslave Europeans in the iron grip of the European
Union. Previous winners have been Richard Count Coudenhove-Kalergi, founder of the
Pan-European Movement funded by the bloodline Habsburg family that got the
'European project' underway; paedophile and child killer, Edward Heath, the former
British Prime Minister who signed Britain into the EU straightjacket; Henry Kissinger;
King 'Illuminati' Carlos of Spain; Queen 'Bilderberger' Beatrix of the Netherlands; Tony
Blair; and Bill Clinton. Rothschild Zionist Trichet will at least feel right at home. The
prize is named after Charlemagne, ruler of what we now call the region of France and
Germany. He followed the reign of the Merovingian kings and he was a founder of what

became the Holy Roman Empire. Charlemagne is a bloodline hero, and Hitler and the Nazis worshipped him as a god. Trichet told the audience at the award ceremony:

> In this Union of tomorrow, or the day after tomorrow, would it be too bold, in the economic field, with a single market and a single central bank, to envisage a ministry of finance for the Union?

Come on, you bloody liar, you know that's the plan. This is another stepping stone, another Totalitarian Tiptoe, to a world ministry of finance. The introduction of the European single currency, the euro, was introduced to entrap the countries of Europe in a straightjacket of centralised economic dictatorship, and laws were introduced to insist that 'bondholders' in the banks had to be secured by governments against losses. A 'bondholder', a term we have heard a lot about since 2008, is a financial speculator who buys 'bonds' in banks, companies and governments for an agreed period and interest rate. This is speculation – nothing more – in the hope that you will get what you agreed, but when any losses are guaranteed by governments if the investment goes pear-shaped it means that (a) the need to make sensible investments no longer applies because you can't lose; and (b) the taxpayer is stuck with repaying the bondholder any losses on what is a private investment. Crazy – but then the world is. The bondholders in Allied Irish Banks are having their losses covered by Irish and European taxpayers now losing their jobs, homes and services. They include the Rothschild front, Goldman Sachs, and Rothschild & Cie Gestion, an asset management branch of Groupe Rothschild & Cie Banque. No doubt a stream of these other 'bailed out' bondholders will have Rothschild connections. All these financial speculators and manipulators are having their losses repaid by people in Ireland and the wider Europeans who are already in dire straits. They are paying with reduced wages, increased taxation, lost homes and jobs, and severe cutbacks in basic services. The system is rigged from top to bottom, but many still can't see the plainly obvious. I read this comment on a website forum during a discussion about the inequality and unfairness of the economic system:

> This society is very fair. The rich first generation [parents] did not come out of the mountains and become people with money. Every rich person thinks of their next generation, this is normal. I, to, am a poor person, but I am willing to go create opportunities, because to become a rich person requires thinking of a plan ... Don't have this attitude towards society. As long as the first generation's money came cleanly, it should be fine.

Laugh or cry? Difficult choice. A *plan?* Easy. To become rich you just steal money from lots of poor people. Humanity has been a slave race for aeons in which there is one law for the few and another for all the rest; but, even by human standards, we are moving into extreme levels of mass control, oppression and, yes, sheer *slavery*. We slave – they steal. I have been warning about this for so long, and it is here. What we are seeing is the big squeeze in which the Rothschild networks use their governments and banks to squeeze the people until their pips squeak. The less we resist, the harder they squeeze and so events and injustice become ever more extreme. This is what we are seeing now. It is not only that if we'll take this, we'll take anything, but also that if we take this they will give us yet more in the months and years to come. We have to stop being spectators and victims and start running at these people and their evil. This is starting to happen, but it has to be increased dramatically. A major thing that we can do is refuse to leave homes that are foreclosed by banks because of the economic straits of the home 'owner' caused by the banks. The system is terrified of this because it could not cope. If a few individuals do it they can be picked off, but not if hundreds of thousands and more do so. The banks are speeding the process of foreclosure in the United States by issuing fake documents signed by fake people because, insiders say, they cannot deal with so many foreclosures and the time it takes to evict people lawfully. The mortgages have been sold and resold through so many banks and financial institutions that they have no idea much of the time who actually owns the mortgage and the home they are seeking to foreclose. If there was a mass refusal to leave foreclosed homes, the system would be in tatters – it could not cope with the numbers. We need people to focus on organising and coordinating a peaceful rebellion and non-cooperation with our own enslavement. We need to make what would be a tremendous collective statement of intent by refusing to take our families onto the streets because some corrupt and evil bank tells us that we must. When are we going to draw the line en masse? If not now, then probably never. It is time, long past the time, for us to say 'NO MORE!' If we don't, we've seen nothing yet. British wartime Prime Minister, Winston Churchill (Rothschild Zionist), was another pawn in the game, and a willing one; but he was absolutely right when he said this:

> If you will not fight for the right when you can easily win without bloodshed; if you will not fight when your victory will be sure and not too costly; you may come to the moment when you will have to fight with all the odds against you and only a small chance of survival. There may even be a worse case: you may have to fight when there is no hope of victory, because it is better to perish than to live as slaves.

But it is not about *fighting*; it is about ceasing to cooperate with our own enslavement. I'll expand on this in the final chapter.

14

Everything Connects

No-one with a brain in any way generating electrical activity could fail to see how the world has changed dramatically since September 11th, 2001. Tony Blair said that the world changed on 9/11 and, of course, that was the idea. The scale of control and surveillance, the gathering Gestapo employed throughout law enforcement and security, is the bloodline Reptilian Alliance/Saturnian game plan made manifest (Fig 315).

It was so obvious to me many years ago that a new breed was taking over the 'uniform professions' and those in government administration at all levels. My question was how this was being done on such a scale. A significant contribution has been made towards recruiting the 'right people' by targeting a certain type of personality known as 'narcissistic'. This is the same personality trait that they seek out for their 'power' positions in politics, banking, business and media. Barack Obama, David Cameron, Nicolas Sarkozy, Tony Blair and Julia Gillard – I rest my case. The wording and questions on application forms, plus other techniques, are used to sift out the narcissists among the applicants. Narcissism is defined as: 'excessive love or admiration of oneself

Figure 315: The face of Fascism

... a psychological condition characterised by self-preoccupation, lack of empathy [a classic reptilian trait] and unconscious deficits in self-esteem'. In short, they are arrogant and lack empathy on the surface while being emotional cripples underneath. All these traits are used to effect by the bloodline network and they most powerfully lock people into the Saturn–Moon Matrix broadcasts and activate their DNA program. Brian Gerrish, a former British naval officer, has done considerable research into recruiting and 'training' organisations that employ 'headhunting' techniques that identify the narcissists. One in particular stands out in

359

Figure 316: What have we come to?

Britain and operates in many other countries. This is an organisation called 'Common Purpose' which 'trains' the leaders in government, local government and the police – pretty much throughout the entire system, in fact. Brian says of the narcissistic personality:

Their love of themselves and power automatically means that they will crush others who get in their way. I received a major piece of the puzzle when a friend pointed out that when they made public officials re-apply for their own jobs several years ago they were also required to do psychometric tests. This was undoubtedly the start of the screening process to get 'their' sort of people in post.

Psychometrics involves the measurement of knowledge, abilities, attitudes and personality traits, mostly using carefully designed questionnaires and tests. You can clearly see what Brian Gerrish describes happening all over the world as the power-crazy and power-trippers are appointed into law enforcement, security and government administration. The Transportation Security Administration (TSA) in the United States is an outstanding example (Fig 316). So many of them – not all yet, but they're working on it – strut around as if they own the world and treat passengers with contempt. The relationship is akin to a prison warder and a prisoner. It's all 'do this', 'don't do that', with everyone looked upon as a terrorist threat until proven otherwise. They sexually abuse distraught and crying little children, force the elderly and infirm to go through degrading 'checks', and many of them have no sense of reasonableness or common sense whatsoever. They are narcissistic robots in a uniform with a few honourable exceptions. One had to be sacked when he walked through Los Angeles Airport at the end of a shift banging his chest and shouting, 'I have the power.' Well, actually, he *doesn't*. None of them have. The *uniform* has the 'power', not them, because the uniform is an extension of the State. They are just animating it, that's all. The power is in the wardrobe – not in them. This is the case with all people in uniform. I say to them sometimes, 'Take off your uniform and where is your power?' or, 'Get a different job – where is your power?' *Nowhere*, because it was always in the uniform. The sad thing is that while they are imposing the will of the State (the hidden forces that control the State) they are being treated as contemptuously as they treat others. The authorities knew that the full-body radiation scanners would kill staff who worked with them regularly; but who cares when there will always be someone who needs a job? There are so few who are manipulating humanity in full knowledge of what they are doing that they need to recruit from the target population to suppress the target population – hence the TSA, law-enforcement agencies and the military. These people are controlled by the bloodlines, but the great majority are not of the bloodlines. Mind-manipulating techniques are used, too, to develop the 'right type'. A common one is neuro-linguistic programming (NLP) which uses words and phrases to program perception and behaviour. Brian Gerrish again:

> It is interesting that many of the mothers who have had children taken by the State speak of the Social Services people being icily cool, emotionless and, as two ladies said in slightly different words, '... like little robots'. We know that NLP is cumulative, so people can be given small imperceptible doses of NLP in a course here, another in a few months, next year etc. In this way, major changes are accrued in their personality, but the day by day change is almost unnoticeable.

> An example is the policeman who would not get on a bike for a press photo because he had not done the cycling proficiency course. Normal people say this is political correctness gone mad. Nothing could be further from the truth. The policeman has been reframed, and in his reality it is perfect common sense not to get on the bike 'because he hasn't done the cycling course'.

> Another example of this is where the police would not rescue a boy from a pond until they had taken advice from above on the 'risk assessment'. A normal person would have arrived, perhaps thought of the risk for a moment, and dived in. To the police now 'reframed', they followed 'normal' procedure.

There you have the reason why we are seeing the type of personality in so-called 'public service' dramatically changing as the 'old school' make way for the newly-schooled. The whole ridiculous nonsense known as 'Political Correctness' was developed and introduced by a group of Rothschild Zionists known as the 'Frankfurt School' which was established in the city where the House of Rothschild began. The Frankfurt School was an outgrowth of Marxism, yet another Rothschild creation, and promoted by Karl Marx (Rothschild Zionist) who married into the aristocracy. The Frankfurt School was funded into existence by Felix Weil (Rothschild Zionist), and the first director was Carl Grünberg (Rothschild Zionist) followed by Max Horkheimer (Rothschild Zionist). Two of the prime influences on the school's thinking were Theodor W Adorno (Rothschild Zionist) and Herbert Marcuse (Rothschild Zionist). The Frankfurt School relocated to Switzerland before moving to New York in 1935, and six years later settled in California, which, for this reason, became the global capital of political correctness. This Rothschild Zionist centre for social engineering set out to control American social science, and here are just some of the changes that they sought to introduce to American and global society. Perhaps you can recognise them:

- The creation of racism offences.
- Continual change to create confusion.
- The teaching of sex and homosexuality to young children.
- The undermining of schools' and teachers' authority.
- Huge immigration to destroy national identity.
- The promotion of excessive drinking.
- Emptying of churches [targeting anything that brings people together].
- A legal system with bias against victims of crime.

- Dependency on the State or State benefits.
- Control and dumbing down of the media.
- Encouraging the breakdown of family.

None of these goals are to benefit people; they are only to *control* people. National identity is being destroyed by mass immigration and it is clear that this is the real motivation behind the borderless European Union, and the United States failing to adequately police the border with Mexico and making it easier for so-called 'illegal aliens' to be given residency. They want a borderless United States, Canada and Mexico as part of the North American Union and to destroy the self-identity of all three. A sense of nationhood is a big potential block to the acceptance of a single uniform world and so they are working to delete any sense of national identity. The bloodlines don't care about homosexuals any more than they care for the children the bloodline families and their lackeys abuse while claiming to protect them. Rothschild Zionist fronts like the Anti-Defamation League are not concerned with 'racism' or 'minorities'. They merely use these to justify more control, to suppress freedom of speech and to introduce 'hate laws' to make your opinion a criminal offence in which truth is no defence. You can read the detailed story of political correctness in *Human Race Get Off Your Knees* and the same with virtually everything in this book, which is written specifically to present the information crisply with the essential dots connected. Political correctness is a means of censoring the right to free expression by constantly curtailing what is deemed acceptable to say and do. A law passed in Tennessee in 2011 is a perfect example. It makes transmitting or displaying an image online a criminal offence if it is likely to 'frighten, intimidate or cause emotional distress' to anyone who may see it. This means virtually *every* image. You'll always find someone who will be offended by something. The bill was signed into law by Governor Bill Haslam, and this nonsense carries a maximum sentence of a year in prison or a fine of $2,500. Please remember this at the next election anyone from his state. The bloodlines want laws like this to be universal, and this is not to protect people from being frightened, intimidated or emotionally distressed. They use these same laws to stop themselves and what they are doing from being exposed. They are developing another 'front' with regard to this, with 'super injunctions' that prevent information being published about a person or organisation, and to even ban the disclosure that this has been done. Major corporations have taken out these super-gagging orders to block publication of information about their activities.

Anybody home? No? Okay, I'll call back

You constantly see the personality types now being recruited into 'public service' in countless videos posted on *YouTube* by people shocked at how these thugs-in-uniform behave. Two rule-book-for-a-brain police officers were filmed stopping to question a man in a London park who was holding a sign saying: 'Everything is okay'. A long conversation ensued about whether this was in breach of 'royal park' regulations; and one of them pulled out the rule book to see if he could find something that applied. Put 'Everything is OK in Hyde Park (Speakers Corner)' into *Youtube*. There was the shocking video of young people being brutally attacked by police for dancing, without even much animation, at the Thomas Jefferson Memorial in Washington D.C. in May 2011. One man was thrown to the solid floor. They were protesting against a ruling by a

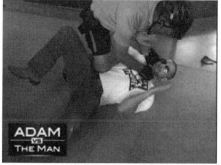

Figs 371 and 318: Dancing is a crime – if you have not got two brain cells to rub together, that is. Truly ludicrous man at work

federal judge that made dancing at the memorial constitute an *illegal demonstration*. Ludicrous laws like this are being introduced by the bucketload and so you need ludicrous and vicious people like the police officers in this case to enforce them (Figs 317 and 318). The authorities want to ban people from filming police on duty to hide their increasingly insane and brutal behaviour from the public. Police in Rochester, New York, arrested a woman for filming them from her own front garden when they stopped a car and questioned the driver outside her home. 28-year-old Emily Good was charged with 'obstructing governmental administration' after she politely refused a police officer's order to stop filming and go back into her house. The narcissistic and brainless police officer said he felt threatened (*aaahhh*, bless him) and she appeared to be 'very anti-police'. When she refused to stop her legal filming of this silly man he arrested her for 'not listening to our orders'. Type the words: 'Rochester Police Arrest Woman in Her Front Lawn for Filming Traffic Stop' into *YouTube* and you will see what she filmed. There is another extraordinary example of this 'new police' mentality with 'Officer Bubbles'. You know how they used to have a 'king of kings'? Well, Officer Bubbles is a Moron of Morons and unfortunately he has unbelievable numbers of people in uniform vying for the title. Put: 'Officer Bubbles – From Bubbles to Bookings' into *YouTube* (a cup of sweet tea is recommended). They even have lower-ranked narcissists policing litter bins now. An 85-year-old New York woman was in the media after a 'sanitation agent' (was he armed?) chased her and threatened her with arrest for putting newspapers in a trash bin. 'I froze,' she said. 'He just frightened the hell out of me, scared me to death, I was terrified.' She said the worker demanded a form of identification and threatened to 'put her away' if she didn't comply. He fined her $100 for putting 'household trash' into the wrong bin, and when she complained at the size of the fine he threatened to make it $300. This is the mentality being specifically employed to control the population down to the finest detail. Some 20 teenagers were arrested by more woodenheads-in-uniform in Oklahoma City for standing outside a cinema in alleged breach of the city's imposed curfew for everyone under 18 years of age. *State curfew??* They were arrested while waiting for adults to collect their cars after watching the movie. Going to a movie theatre exempts you from the 'curfew', but these God's gifts to brain cell activity went ahead with their arrests anyway. One mother called the officers 'thuggish' – exactly the type being recruited today all over the world. The teenagers were taken to a 'Crisis Intervention Center' and kept for at least six hours before even being allowed to see their parents. They were reported to have 'felt violated, harassed and frightened at the

hands of Oklahoma City law enforcement'. Well, get used to it unless we are prepared
to come together and put an end to this. These curfews are becoming more common in
the Totalitarian Tiptoe with British Prime Minister, David Cameron (Rothschild Zionist),
suggesting them as one 'solution' to the manufactured riots in London and other cities
in 2011. Chicago introduced a curfew that means that children under 12 have to be in
their parents' home by 8.30pm every night. The Mayor of Chicago backing this? *Rahm
Emanuel* (Rothschild Zionist), former Israeli soldier and Obama's minder during his
crucial first years in office. Ted Baillieu, Premier of the Australian State of Victoria, has
introduced laws (permanently after a 'trial') that give police the right to issue on-the-
spot fines for language that is 'indecent, disorderly, offensive or threatening'. Who
decides that? The police do. How about on-the-spot fines for police officers and
premiers of Victoria who are 'indecent, disorderly, offensive or threatening'? Then there
is Kelly Morningstar, police chief in Midway, Georgia, who 'closed down' the lemonade
stand of three young girls because they had not obtained $50-a-day business and food
permits – even though the stand was at the home of one of the girls. Kelly Morningstar
explained this victory for neuron deficiency: 'We were not aware of how the lemonade
was made, who made the lemonade, of what the lemonade was made with, so we acted
accordingly by city ordinance.' Well, we could say the same about you, mate. How and
what are you made of, and with what ingredients? They clearly do not include
intelligence or consciousness. If you want to see another absolutely staggering
'lemonade' story put the words 'Children defy police in Washington, purchase
lemonade at Capitol' into *YouTube*. The young girl officer in the peaked cap who keeps
blocking the camera needs some serious help. I do hope she seeks it one day. A
computer store might be the first place to contact – the software department. These
'lemonade raids' are happening so often across America that it is obviously coordinated.

  These arrogant narcissists go particularly apeshit when their power is challenged
and they are questioned or not taken seriously. I pointed out to a security person at
London's Heathrow Airport that it was not the law that I had to remove my belt, as a
security expert had confirmed on television that morning. Well, away she went. 'I know
what the law is,' she shouted, and, don't question me' was the basic response. I asked
her again: 'Is there a law that you have to take your belt off?' Eventually she agreed that
there wasn't, but her ego had been so pricked that she stormed off into the distance not
to return. I did the same with a 'uniform' at London's Gatwick Airport and he nearly
had apoplexy. I had to ask for his supervisor eventually because of his behaviour, and
when the guy arrived he was so young I felt like asking him if his mum knew he was
out. You don't even have the option of a 'pat-down' in Britain if you are selected to go
through a full-body scanner. Refuse, and you don't fly. Hospital consultant Dr Antonio
Aguirre was removed by police from Manchester Airport in England when he declined
to take what he called a 'radiation assault'. He said quite rightly that the scanners can
cause cancer. He said: 'X-rays are known to cause cancer and I think somebody will get
cancer from this body scanner whether it's me or someone else.' It will be lots of people,
especially the staff who operate them. Let's think about this for a second and take in just
how far we have already gone down the road to fascism. You are not allowed to fly
unless you agree to be irradiated at a threat to your health and even life. *Are we standing
for this?* Transportation Security Administration (TSA) staff in the United States are
extraordinary. They grope women and children in 'pat downs' and many of them

specialise in public humiliation. A 95-year-old woman in a wheelchair suffering from leukaemia was forced to remove an adult nappy, or diaper, by the TSA at a Florida airport before leaving on a flight to say goodbye to relatives before she died. A six-year-old girl was given an invasive pat down even after going through the full-body radiation scanner. TSA Administrator, John Pistole, said that it was because the child had moved in the scanner. Pistole is just another bought-and-paid-for gofer who does and says whatever his masters tell him. It goes with the territory. Challenge the behaviour of the TSA personnel in the United States and the police are called, or they make sure you miss your flight. You have to be punished for having the audacity to question their power over you. They express their own sad need for power over others by using the State's power as if it was their own while all the time the State is exposing them to radiation from the scanners in the full knowledge that this is cumulatively killing them. A woman passing through security at Ronald Reagan National Airport in Washington D.C. was viciously attacked, thrown across the room into another passenger and a metal chair, beaten about the face and body and had her head slammed on a metal table causing a permanent traumatic brain injury. Her crime? She had a small container of contact lens solution. Put 'Dr Phil Airport Assault' into *YouTube*. It is extraordinary what happened. The TSA is being expanded into an American version of the Nazi Gestapo or the East German Stasi to operate all over the country, and not only at airports. They are a major part of the domestic security force that Obama promised during his election campaigns when he well knew what the bloodlines funding him were demanding. Obama said that they couldn't rely only on the military for national security: 'We've got to have a civilian national security force that's just as powerful, just as strong, just as well-funded.' The TSA has taken part in 'exercises' covering 5,000 miles and three states in association with other strands in the now vast web of American 'security' (control) agencies.

You see the same TSA attitudes and behaviour when police officers are questioned by the public and out comes the Taser – 55,000 volts of electricity unleashed by a brain-donor with a wounded ego (Fig 319). Many people have been killed by this 'non-lethal' weapon, and this suits the bloodlines because it increases fear of the police and makes people do whatever they are told. Tasers were supposed to be used only by trained firearms officers in dangerous and life-threatening situations. I said at the time that this wouldn't last long, and now they are handed out like confetti and constantly used when there is no danger to anyone or anything except the ego of uniformed narcissists who are so pathetic ('unconscious deficits in self-esteem') that they can't bear to have their perceived omnipotence questioned. Put 'Taser outrageous' into *YouTube*. Police in Dayton, Ohio, Tasered, pepper-sprayed and physically attacked mentally handicapped teenager, Jesse

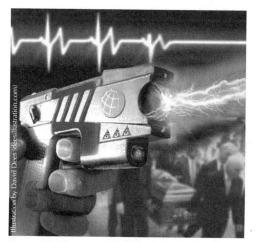

Figure 319: The Taser – weapon of choice for the Battle of Wounded Ego

Kersey, and then charged *him* with assault. His crime? The police officer, another narcissistic moron-for-hire called Willie Hooper, 'mistook' the boy's speech impediment as a sign of disrespect. Willie Wonker, or something close, knew that the 17-year-old was mentally handicapped, but embarked on an extraordinary attack along with fellow moron, Officer John Howard. The teenager rode home on his bicycle because he could not understand what was being said to him when Willie Woodenhead had stopped him. The officers went to the boy's home and, as his mother opened the door, these thugs fired their Tasers hitting the boy in the back with two electrical probes. Jesse's mother told the court hearing the case: 'Once inside the house, defendant Hooper and defendant Howard began to struggle with Jesse, who was standing against the back door with his hands up in front of his face, saying, 'Please quit, please quit'. Officer Howard utilized his Cap-Stun pepper-spray and sprayed Jesse ... [and] struck Jesse with a closed fist in the upper chest area.' They're *real* men, see. Howard continued the beating and then Dumb and Dumber called for backup and another *20 officers* arrived at the house. Jesse was handcuffed, tied up and thrown into a police car. This story would be shocking if it was only a one-off, but police brutality is now becoming the norm across the world and those responsible are being selected, programmed and trained to act like this in a bloodline police state enforced by brainless thugs. There was the man in Loganville – 'Where People Matter' – in Georgia who called the police when he came home to find that his stepson had committed suicide, and when they arrived they beat the living daylights out him while ambulance staff were trying to revive the boy. Ontario police in Canada are securing a gathering and deserved reputation for brutality, sexual assault and wrongful arrest. Sean Salvati was arrested for saying: 'Well, good luck on Saturday' to officers preparing to police the G20 summit in Toronto in 2010. 'One of the officers grabbed my neck and began punching me,' Salvati said. '[He] mentioned something about 'These are your rights'. You know? Like: 'You think you have rights? These are your rights'.' Salvati was taken to the police station, stripped naked, paraded in front of officers – including a woman – and then locked, still naked, in a cage. You can see video of this story if you put these words into *YouTube*: 'Cops Strip Search Man And Leave Him Naked For 10 Hours In Holding Cell'. A woman unlawfully arrested in Ottawa, Ontario, was kicked and beaten by police officers, had her shirt and bra cut off and was left half-naked in a cell for three hours – the *YouTube* headline is 'Ottawa Police Attack and Strip Search Innocent Woman'. The stories of police brutality are now endless because of the specific 'character' type being recruited – and how many others never come to public attention? We have seen nothing yet if we go on taking it. A lot of their arrogance and outrageous behaviour comes from the fact that they know that the system will protect them, because it wants them to behave like that. There will be no shortage of recruits for the guards in the concentration camps already waiting for the 'dissidents'. *Concentration camps??* No, I am not kidding. See some of my other books, or put the words: 'Concentration Camps, America' into a search engine. They are being installed in many countries and in the United States they are the responsibility of the Federal Emergency Management Agency (FEMA). Most people have no idea how far this has already gone. The police are looking ever more like soldiers and the plan is for a global army and police force to implement the dictates of the world government structure as basically one unit. The British government of David Cameron (Rothschild Zionist) is even talking about appointing military officers and

Figure 320: A SWAT team and the Keystone Cops. Spot the difference? Take the guns away and me neither

Intelligence personnel to the highest ranks of the police to establish an 'officer class' in local forces. The US government is supplying police departments with military uniforms, weapons, vehicles (in some cases, including *tanks*) and training. There are 40,000 paramilitary raids on American property every year by Special Weapons and Tactics (SWAT) teams, for which a brain is not essential (Fig 320). A SWAT team threw a flash grenade through the window of a home in Detroit in 2010 while a seven-year-old girl was watching television with her grandmother. The grenade burned the little girl's blanket and the SWAT team then raided the house and shot the child dead. The suspect they were after didn't even live there. They got the wrong apartment. Police in Oakland County, Michigan, raided a medical marijuana dispensary with guns drawn, bulletproof vests and at least one with a mask. They didn't arrest anyone, just cleaned the place out of all cash – including the personal money of staff and patients. Michigan's asset forfeiture law means that 80 per cent of the cash the deputies stole will go to the Oakland County Sheriff's Department and the local prosecutor gets the other 20 per cent. It is armed robbery, nothing less. The Posse Comitatus Act of 1878 bans the use of the military for civilian policing, and to get around that we have people dressed as soldiers, armed like soldiers and acting like soldiers – but they are called 'police'. They are also using real troops in contravention of the act more and more, in a creep to fully militarise control of the United States. Troops have been arresting people in Florida and it will be happening elsewhere, too. The Pentagon announced plans in 2008 to deploy 20,000 troops on duties inside the United States and have them trained by 2011. Martial law is coming unless vast numbers of people wake up and get active. Police are also being exposed ever more often for dressing up as protestors at peaceful demonstrations and engaging in violence that gives their fellow officers the excuse to move in and batter people who are only protesting peacefully. This includes smashing shop windows and burning police cars to discredit peaceful protests. Canadian police have been caught doing this many times, and at the Security and Prosperity Partnership of North America (North American Union) summit in Quebec in 2007 their agents provocateurs were filmed wearing exactly the same boots as the police. I should cancel that application for the undercover squad, chaps. This is happening at peaceful protests all over the world. British police do this as a matter of course at major demonstrations. Can you imagine the scale of character defects necessary to try to discredit people peacefully campaigning for justice by staging violence? How they can look their children in the eyes is beyond me, but I'm sure they have no problem.

How much more will we take?

The level of surveillance is already extraordinary, as I said it would be in my earlier books when people were still laughing at the very suggestion. We have surveillance cameras everywhere, and anyone walking around a town or city in Britain, going in and out of shops and other buildings, will be seen by more than 300 cameras every day. There are cameras all over the road systems that were said to be there to stop speeding, but they record your number plate as you pass. The little town of Royston, in Hertfordshire, England, which has a low level of crime, has had police cameras installed on *every road* leading in and out to record the number plate of every vehicle. The system then checks these against a whole bank of databases. This is what they are planning for everywhere. We are watched by the satellite network in ways that we wouldn't believe possible. British police have introduced radio-controlled flying surveillance cameras – the same as those portrayed in the film, *They Live*, released in 1988. This has all been planned for decades and more. We have face-recognition cameras, iris scanning, full-body radiation scanning and DNA databases. They want everyone's DNA on file for many reasons, and one is that it allows them to access the unique frequency of every individual, and people can then be targeted directly on their specific frequency. There are many scams and laws going on to get DNA samples. I saw a project in South Africa where schoolchildren were being asked to give hair samples, saliva and fingerprints for something called 'Ident-A-Kid'. The scheme is sold as something that would help police find missing children; and I am sure there are some genuine people involved but there is always an ulterior motive with these projects. British police now take and keep DNA from everyone arrested, even when they are found to be innocent. It's just another disingenuous scam to build the database. London's Heathrow Airport announced that it was introducing biometric facial-recognition cameras to 'identify terrorists'. Yawn. The International Criminal Police Organization (Interpol) wants to add a facial recognition database to the ones that it has for DNA and fingerprints. Interpol's multi-faceted databases are planned to retain the records of everyone who has travelled through virtually any airport worldwide. Other plans are for a camera in *every aircraft seat* to 'identify terrorists and other dangers to passengers' – better fit them to the White House, National Security Agency, British Intelligence and Mossad headquarters if they want people to be safe. They also want them on cigarette vending machines ('to stop underage smoking'), at supermarket checkouts ('to stop underage drinking') and at bus and train stations to 'replace tickets'. Tokyo police are asking homeowners to install these cameras on their properties for purposes of 'stopping terrorism and crime'. Many idiots will, too.

Surveillance now includes microchip tags on products that we buy; monitoring of mobile phones, credit card transactions and store 'loyalty' cards; phone-tapping; hidden cameras and bugs; and Internet cookies. There are 'keystroke' programmes that record the keys that you hit on your computer and this gives them passwords and encryption codes. Keystroke can also be used to monitor work rates for computer operators in the openly slave world that is planned. They want to impose compulsory employment with no right to strike, and this is the real reason for moves to make trade unions impotent.

This has happened most famously in Wisconsin where thousands of workers occupied the state's Capitol building in protest in part at draconian trade union laws proposed by the appalling Governor Scott Walker that would end collective bargaining. The United States and the European Union have agreed a scheme to allow check-in data, including credit card details, of all transatlantic flights to be stored for 15 years. Even EU lawyers say that this is illegal under data protection laws, as confirmed by documents passed to London's *The Guardian*. The legal opinion said that allowing US Homeland Security to store personal check-in data was 'not compatible with fundamental rights'; but why would that bother the manipulators when they want to *take away* fundamental rights? The US Department of Homeland Security even announced in 2011 that it believes terrorists intend to bypass the full-body scanners by implanting devices *inside* people – so-called 'belly bombs'. It gets ever more insane. What next, surgical operations before you board your flight? Here is the key line in one report: 'Officials claim that full-body scanners currently being used in airports would not penetrate deep enough to detect such devices.' Oh well, we'd better give every passenger a full-blown X-ray, then, and really zap them with radiation. They're not dying quick enough, see. Technology is being employed to identify faces in crowds and 'suspicious behaviour patterns', with 'lie detectors' being planned for airports. We can be monitored and tracked 24 hours a day and in ways that we don't even know about, with technology supplied by the Reptilian Alliance that most people would not believe possible. They have introduced technology to identify people by their brain patterns and heart rhythms; and a 'sensing seat' fitted to trucks can record each driver's characteristic seated posture 'in an attempt to spot whether commercial vehicles had been hijacked'. This all comes under the heading of 'Humabio', or 'Human Monitoring and Authentication using Biodynamic Indicators and Behavioural Analysis'. American Homeland Security is developing technology called the Future Attribute Screening Technology (FAST) designed to identify people *intending* to commit a crime or terrorist act. FAST monitors heart rate, tone of voice, a person's 'gaze', body temperature and so on, and can create checkpoints, or 'security boundaries' anywhere, including at sporting events and airports. This is the concept of 'pre-crime' technology portrayed in the Tom Cruise film, *Minority Report*. Hollywood is in the control of the bloodlines through the Rothschild Zionists and they are conditioning the public to accept the agenda. Steven Aftergood, a senior research analyst at the Federation of American Scientists, is not impressed with FAST and believes it will produce a lot of 'false positives' to mark innocent people as potential terrorists. I'm sure he's right, but they don't give a damn so long as it adds to the ever-growing tapestry of multi-levelled control and intimidation. The darkest of dark US National Security Agency, the boss of the CIA, awarded a classified $100 million contract to the Illuminati 'defence' giant, Raytheon, to introduce something called 'Perfect Citizen'. Raytheon is the company that once owned the patents for HAARP. Perfect Citizen would use secret technology to monitor Internet communications. *The Wall Street Journal* quoted a Raytheon email as saying that 'Perfect Citizen is Big Brother'. Telephone calls, emails and faxes are being monitored by the Echelon spy network which scans for key words and voice-recognition patterns at establishments like the deeply sinister Menwith Hill in North Yorkshire, England. This is a ground base for satellites operated by the US National Reconnaissance Office and it is run by the US National Security Agency (NSA) on British soil. I am told that Menwith

Hill had a role in the attacks of 9/11. Washington journalist, Bill Blum, who extensively researched Echelon, describes it as a network of massive, highly-automated interception stations which is eavesdropping on the entire world. He said: 'Like a mammoth vacuum cleaner in the sky, the National Security Agency (NSA) sucks it all up: home phone, office phone, cellular phone, email, fax, telex ... satellite transmissions, fibre-optic communications traffic, microwave links, voice, text images [which are] captured by satellites continuously orbiting the Earth and then processed by high-powered computers.' Blum said that Echelon surveillance spied on political leaders, the United Nations, the Pope and groups like Amnesty International. Confidential business information is also being stolen this way and passed to bloodline corporations. 'If God has a phone, it's being monitored,' he said. Other Echelon centres are at Morwenstow (Cornwall, UK); the Australian Defence Satellite Communications Station (Geraldton, Western Australia); Misawa Air Base (Japan); Pine Gap (near Alice Springs, Northern Territory, Australia); Sabana Seca (Puerto Rico, US); Sugar Grove (West Virginia, US); Yakima (Washington, US); and Waihopai (New Zealand). Statewatch, an organisation tracking the assault on civil liberties in Europe, said this:

> Across the EU, governments have, or are, adopting national laws for the mandatory retention of everyone's communications data – all forms of communication (phone calls, faxes, mobile calls including locations) which will be extended to keeping a record of all internet usage from 2009 – even though few are aware this is happening. When traffic data including internet usage is combined with other data held by the state or gathered from non-state sources (tax, employment, bank details, credit card usage, biometrics, criminal record, health record, use of e-government services, travel history etc.) a frightening detailed picture of each individual's everyday life and habits can be accessed at the click of a button.

This was written a few years ago, and it is far more advanced now. The European Union took this on to a still more extreme stage when it announced a new surveillance system that would monitor data taken from countless sources through the continuous monitoring of 'websites, discussion forums, Usenet groups, file servers, P2P networks [and] individual computer systems'. This information is planned to be collated and assessed by the giant computer system to detect 'abnormal behaviour'. The system is called 'Project Indect' and will be used by a European Union police force and the EU equivalent of the CIA. Internet providers have to record our surfing activity and provide this information to MI5 as a result of Tony Blair's Regulation of Investigatory Powers Act. The Rothschild Zionist-controlled Yahoo, the world's largest email provider, has even included in its updated terms and conditions, or Additional Terms of Service, that they have the right to scan private emails. They also make it the customers' responsibility to tell non-Yahoo correspondents that their emails are being scanned. The US Patriot Act co-authored by Michael 'body scanner' Chertoff (Rothschild Zionist) has deleted many basic freedoms in the United States. 'Anti-terrorist' (anti-people) legislation means that Americans can now have their citizenship removed, go to jail without trial, and be flown to another country to be tortured and even executed in secret. These Acts are examples of the Totalitarian Tiptoe in that the legislation is sold and passed on the basis of targeting 'terrorists', but the wording allows them to apply it, as planned, to the domestic population. I said at the time that 'anti-terrorism' laws were not aimed at terrorists. The people *introducing* them are the terrorists. Anti-terrorism laws are actually anti-people laws and now the truth of that is there for all to see. Fascism has reached the point in the United States where Obama has demanded the right to declare war whenever he likes and order any American citizen to be assassinated, with no charge or trial, on the basis of the 'Intelligence and military community' (read bloodlines) *saying* that they are terrorists. No evidence necessary. Admiral Dennis Blair, Obama's Director of National Intelligence, acknowledged in Congressional testimony that they reserve the 'right' to assassinate Americans. The Joint Chiefs of Staff at the Pentagon compile a hit-list for the presidential assassination programme, and when the president gives the nod the American population is reduced by one. This is only where they have reached in their agenda this far. Imagine where they want to go from here. All this is happening to 'stop terrorism'. But how many people does terrorism actually kill? Take away those who die in El-ite-staged terrorism like 9/11, and what is left? Virtually nothing compared, for instance, with the fantastic numbers who die every year in America alone from taking prescribed pharmaceutical drugs; or the millions killed by the bombs of those who say we must 'stop terrorism'. The 'War on Terror' is all a gigantic hoax.

Targeting the Internet

The right to free speech and free association is being shredded by the day. We now have 'free speech zones' well away from the people in power that the 'free speech' is aimed at, and the right to free expression and protest at all will be banned if they get their way (Fig 321). A mountain of so-called 'hate laws' is being introduced to silence anyone exposing the Rothschild Zionists. These are nothing to do with protecting minorities and everything to do with protecting the bloodlines from exposure. The Hidden Hand is now moving in on the Internet. The World Wide Web is a bloodline creation and has endless benefits for them in that it makes tracking communications and gathering personal information child's play. Did you know that anything you post on Rothschild-Zionist Facebook becomes their property? When you sign up you grant Facebook the following:

Figure 321: Use it or lose it

An irrevocable, perpetual, non-exclusive, transferable, fully paid, worldwide license (with the right to sublicense) to (a) use, copy, publish, stream, store, retain, publicly perform or display, transmit, scan, reformat, modify, edit, frame, translate, excerpt, adapt, create derivative works and distribute (through multiple tiers), any User Content you (i) Post on or in connection with the Facebook Service or the promotion thereof subject only to your privacy settings or (ii) enable a user to Post, including by offering a Share Link on your website and (b) to use your name, likeness and image for any purpose, including commercial or advertising, each of (a) and (b) on or in connection with the Facebook Service or the promotion thereof.

Social networking sites are a Rothschild Zionist scam to glean information about people and seize ownership of their photographs, text and creativity. The US Federal Trade Commission has approved a company called Social Intelligence Corporation that performs background checks on job applicants by searching social media accounts and retains what it finds for seven years. Everything you say and do on these sites can be used against you years later. Nor does it matter if you use anonymous names. Social Intelligence Corporation employs software that links nicknames with real names. These lovely people also scour video and picture sharing sites, blogs, eBay, Craiglist and Wikipedia entries. The Internet is also a technological collective mind that can manipulate people's sense of reality. There is so much going on while we are on the Internet that we have no idea about. Susan Greenfield from Oxford University says that the Internet is re-moulding brains to rely on 'associative thinking' which makes people unable to read and write at length. She warned that networking sites such as Facebook and Twitter are giving people 'a lobotomy of empathy'. She said her fear was that 'these technologies are infantilizing the brain into the state of small children who are attracted by buzzing noises and bright lights, who have a small attention span and who live for the moment'. Real conversation may give way to sanitized screen dialogues, she said, and for many it already has. American technologist Nicholas Carr wondered in an article for *Atlantic Magazine* if the Net is remapping neural-circuitry and reprogramming the memory. He said his friends told him that they could no longer absorb information delivered at length. Carr's article was headed: *'Is Google Making Us Stupid?'* So there are many benefits for the bloodlines from the Internet and this is why they created it. But there is one big downside for them. The Internet has allowed for the global communication of information about the conspiracy which would not have been even nearly possible had it not existed. The bloodlines are now manoeuvring to block that flow of information by using a number of excuses, including, of course, the threat of terrorism. They will have their Problem–Reaction–Solutions waiting in the wings to

justify Internet censorship and this will be aimed at people like me, US radio hosts Jeff Rense and Alex Jones, and a great swathe of Internet researchers that have appeared in such large numbers since 9/11 (Fig 322). The Department of Homeland Security (DHS) has been shutting down websites for simply linking to sites accused of copyright infringements. Copyright infringement is another frontline pretext being used to remove websites that the bloodlines wish to delete. There are reports that the Rothschild-Zionist-controlled entertainment industry has 'convinced' corporations including Comcast and AT&T to impose a 'three-strikes rule' on people accused of streaming or

Figure 322: Rothschild Zionist Internet censorship

downloading files alleged to be subject to copyright. The reports say that after the third 'strike', Internet access would be reduced or deleted. I don't think that corporations such as Comcast and AT&T would take much convincing given that they answer to the same masters as the entertainment industry. The US Department of Homeland Security suspended 84,000 websites 'by mistake' in a trawl supposedly aimed at stopping the commnunication of child pornography. There are a list of famous names in political power I could give them if they are serious about stopping the sexual abuse of children; but, of course, they're not. Serial child abusers and killers in power are using the excuse of child pornography to censor the Internet. Ed Vaizey, the UK Minister for Culture, Communications and Creative Industries, is meeting with copyright lobbyists to discuss plans to censor the Internet. They want to establish 'expert bodies' to decide which websites were allowed and which were not. A judge would make the decision in a 'streamlined procedure' to allow for sites to be quickly shut down. The Digital Economy Act includes the power to remove websites, and this was due to a proposal by Liberal Democrats (the 'freedom' party) in the House of Lords that was written by lobbyists for the music industry. Danish police have asked the government for laws to ban anonymous use of the Internet; and Facebook's Randi Zuckerberg (Rothschild Zionist), sister of founder Mark Zuckerberg (Rothschild Zionist), has called for all Internet anonymity to end. Google CEO Eric Schmidt (Rothschild Zionist) agrees. He has said that Internet anonymity was a 'dangerous' precedent and 'predicted' (he knows) that governments would bring about its demise. The US Immigration and Customs Enforcement (ICE) agency announced in 2011 that it was targeting overseas websites for breaching US copyright and would seek to extradite people to stand trial in America. Erik Barnett, the agency's assistant deputy director, outrageously claimed the right to do this because all 'dot com' and 'dot org' domains have all their connections routed through VeriSign, an Internet infrastructure company based in Virginia. He said that this was sufficient to seek a US prosecution. This also means that the American government (Rothschilds) could block all of those websites whenever it wants.

The usual suspects

The White House released a 52-page document in May 2001 that makes the Department of Homeland Security the 'lead agency' for implementing Internet 'countermeasures'. A 'countermeasure' can be defined in translated Orwell-speak as: 'We can do what we bloody like.' Legislation is worded in ways that can be so widely interpreted that a simple 'we can do what we like' would save a whole lot of trees. The pressure for Internet censorship in America is coming from bloodline sources such as 'shapeshifter' Jay Rockefeller (Rothschild Zionist), Chairman of the Senate Committee on Commerce, Science and Transportation; and Joe Lieberman (Rothschild Zionist), Chairman of the Committee on Homeland Security and Governmental Affairs. Jay Rockefeller is the great-grandson of the truly evil J D Rockefeller, and was the force behind the Cybersecurity Act of 2009. This allows the president to 'declare a cybersecurity emergency' whenever he chooses and to either close down or restrict any information network 'in the interest of national security'. They plan to do just this in the final stages of their planned takeover, or when it is vital for them to stop information reaching the public to expose what they are doing. Rothschild gofer Peter Mandelson (Rothschild Zionist) targeted Internet freedom in Britain in the last Labour government from his position as Svengali to prime ministers Tony Blair and Gordon Brown. Another Internet censor is the French President Nicolas Sarkozy (Rothschild Zionist), who hosted an event at the G8 summit in 2011to press for just that. He said that the Internet must have 'values' and 'rules' – his 'values' and his 'rules'. Among those attending the event in Paris were Google executive chairman, Eric Schmidt (Rothschild Zionist); Facebook founder, Mark Zuckerberg (Rothschild Zionist); and media tycoon, Rupert Murdoch (Rothschild Zionist). You can see the pattern as bloodline gofers sing for their supper. Bill 'I did not have sexual relations with that woman' Clinton has been wheeled out to do the honours. This man, who knowingly lied (he never knowingly tells the truth) to the nation on live television at the height of the Monica Lewinsky scandal, called in 2011 for the creation of an Orwellian Internet 'Ministry of Truth'-style organisation that would be run by the federal government or the UN. This would address 'misinformation and rumours floating on the Internet'. In other words, target the people telling the truth about the mob that Clinton answers to. Right okay, Bill, try this: You and your cover-story-on-the-arm wife are responsible for decades of horrors that have maimed and murdered multi-millions worldwide and destroyed the lives of even more. What happened to the two young boys found dead on the railroad track near the Mena Airstrip in Arkansas where you were – in league with the Bush family and others – running drugs as part of Iran–Contra and other deals? What happened to the people who died or went missing because they had information that would have destroyed your political career? And what really happened to Vince Foster who knew symbolically and literally where the bodies were buried, and who was murdered in the most plainly-staged 'suicide' you could imagine. Shall I go on, Slick Will? I could do for days. Put that through your 'Ministry of Truth', Mr Sniff, Sniff. You are just another pathetic gofer licking the backsides of the masters that have controlled you all your life.

'Go and call for a Ministry of Truth, Clinton, the Internet is a danger to our plans.'

'Yessir, master, anything you say, master.'

Drink your milk, Bill, it's time for bed.

(You will find the detailed background to the Clinton stories listed above in ... *And the Truth Shall Set You Free*.)

Chips with everything

The Big Brother technology they are drooling over the most is the microchip (Fig 323). I was told about this plan by a 'patched' CIA scientist in 1997. The term 'patched' refers to a see-through sachet on the skin containing a drug which reluctant servants of the bloodlines are manipulated to need in order to survive. The scientist showed me his patch when I asked why he was using his scientific abilities to serve an agenda that disgusted him. He said that he joined the CIA thinking he was serving his country, but then realised that the conspiracy I am exposing was real. He refused to work for them after his technology – designed to stimulate rapid plant growth with electromagnetic fields – was used to kill a large group of Ethiopians during a famine. Elements within the CIA realised that the technology could be used as a mass-killer through directed

Figure 323: Accept the microchip and it's goodbye freedom in every sense

electromagnetism. They put the word out among starving Ethiopians that food would be dropped at a certain location and they flew over the crowd and unleashed the deadly electromagnetic field. The scientist was in the back of the plane believing this to be an experiment to stimulate crop growth in deserts. He walked to the front of the plane and looked through the window after the technology was activated, and all he could see was dead bodies. He left his home one day, soon after he'd walked out on the CIA, and he remembers nothing until he woke up in a room and realised that something was stuck to his chest – the 'patch'. He opened his shirt when I met him and showed me the sachet containing an orangey-gold liquid. The patch needs to be replaced every 72 hours or he will start to die a very horrible death. He knows this is true, because he tried it. If he doesn't obey orders, the patch is not replaced. He told me there were thousands of 'patched' people working in secret projects against their will; and if you think this is evil beyond words then read some of my other books where I go into everything in great detail. These people are insane. The scientist told me about the human microchipping agenda and he said this was about far more than merely electronic tagging and surveillance. He said that this was part of it, of course, and the chips would send signals to a computer system; but even more important were the signals coming the other way from the computers to the chip. He said that this would allow people to be manipulated mentally, emotionally and 'physically', either individually or en masse, and for anyone to be killed whenever they chose by sending information to the chip. The human body is a biological computer and they know that. The chip would act as a receiver for information to destabilise – even kill – as many people as they want. Think what an internal microchip could do to DNA receiver–transmitters. Quite a weapon for crazies with a depopulation agenda.

We already have people being chipped so they can interact with computers through mind instructions alone; and look how television companies can add a new channel by sending signals to the card in your television box while you are still on the phone placing the order. Scientists at the University of Southern California announced in 2011 that they have developed a chip that controls brain activity and stores long-term memories. These can be downloaded and transferred to other brains implanted with the chip. This would also allow chipped people to have their thoughts, memories and knowledge accessed by the authorities. We are truly in the realms of George Orwell's Thought Police when even our thoughts become a criminal offence. This has been the plan all along and Orwell knew about what was coming through his connections with the Fabian Society and others. The University of Southern California where this chip is being developed is the location of the Department of Homeland Security National Center for Risk and Economic Analysis of Terrorism Events. The CIA scientist told me in 1997 that microchips developed in the secret projects were already so small that they could be inserted by hypodermic needles in vaccination programmes. Today we call what he was talking about 'nanotechnology'. This is so small that the human eye can't even come close to seeing it. Hitachi unveiled a tiny new 'powder' chip measuring 0.05 x 0.05 mm. What we see in the public arena is not the cutting edge, either. Far more advanced technology is waiting to be revealed in the secret projects. We have been prepared for human microchipping by the chipping of animals (which many studies have connected with animal cancers). This was voluntary initially, but that is changing. The same Totalitarian Tiptoe technique is planned for humans. Inside-the-body microchips are being promoted for a variety of uses including the storing of medical records in case you have an accident or are taken ill; and chipping children and people with dementia so they can be found if they go missing. A New Jersey orthopaedic surgeon wants to add a microchip to joint implants that would emit a unique wavelength that could travel through human tissue. The data would be decoded and displayed on a computer screen. I am sure an artificial wavelength resonating inside the body will be very good for your health. One of the stepping-stones or Totalitarian Tiptoes to the fully-fledged microchip are 'electronic tattoos' – micro-thin electrical circuits attached to the skin to monitor a person's heart rate and other vital signs with the potential for much more. The creators say that the 'tattoo', or 'epidermal electronics system' (EES), 'eliminates the distinction between electronics and biology'. In so many ways, they are the same thing, anyway. The 'tattoos' can transmit all kinds of information to those with the technology to decode it – and *receive* information sent the other way (but they don't shout about that bit). Big Brother 'Intelligence' goons must be rubbing their hands with glee. Clothing and other products are increasingly being produced with communication chips.

The late Aaron Russo, the award-winning film producer who produced *Trading Places* with Eddie Murphy, began to alert people to the conspiracy in the years before he died. He said publicly in 2007 that a member of the Rockefeller family, Nick Rockefeller, had told him about the plan for mass microchipping (Fig 324). This happened during a conversation in which Rockefeller attempted to recruit Russo for the Council on Foreign Relations. Rockefeller told him that the goal was to mass-microchip what he called the 'serfs' and to have bankers and the rest of the El-ite control the world. He said that if Russo joined them his chip would be specially coded to avoid unnecessary inspection by the authorities. Rockefeller said to Russo, almost a year *before* 9/11, that there was

going to be an event that would lead to the invasion of Afghanistan to run pipelines through to the Caspian Sea. They were going to invade Iraq to take over the oil fields and establish a base in the Middle East, and 'go after Chávez in Venezuela'. As I write, Hugo Chávez has had a tumour removed and is undergoing chemotherapy. Rockefeller said that Russo would see soldiers looking in caves in Afghanistan and Pakistan for Osama bin Laden. There would be an 'endless war on terror where there's no real enemy', and the whole thing

Figure 324: Aaron Russo and Nick Rockefeller before Rockefeller revealed the game plan

would be a 'giant hoax'. This would allow the government to take over the American people, Rockefeller told him as he cynically laughed and joked. Russo said Rockefeller constantly stressed that 'the people have to be ruled' and the population reduced by at least half. Rockefeller also revealed that the Rockefeller Foundation had created and funded the women's liberation movement to destroy the family. The plan was aimed at getting children into school at an earlier age and indoctrinating them to accept the State as their primary family (straight from the pages of Huxley's *Brave New World*). He said that another reason for creating and funding the 'women's lib' movement

Figure 325: I know, let's put poison in the water supply. Yeah, that's a good idea

was because before then the bankers couldn't tax half of the population. Nick Rockefeller operates out of China plotting with the Chinese Reptilian hybrids for their massive role in what is planned. There is a whole army of computer hackers in China primed to target US and other government computer-systems to justify censorship and information-blocking technology on the Internet.

From all angles

Everything that I am exposing in this book is connected, and the dot-connecting theme is the suppression and control of humanity. The bloodlines are not putting sodium fluoride in public drinking-water supplies and toothpaste to protect people from tooth decay – *it doesn't*. They do this because fluoride is a *brain suppressant* (Fig 325). I have been saying this in my books for two decades and now this fact is being confirmed even by some in the scientific mainstream. A publication of the US National Institute of Environmental Health Sciences, *Environmental Health Perspectives*, published a study revealing that fluoride is already reducing the intelligence of children. More than 500 children, aged between eight and thirteen, were tested in two Chinese villages with high and low levels of fluoride in the water. They found that 28 per cent of children in the low-fluoride village had bright, normal or higher intelligence, but the figure was only *eight per cent* in the high-fluoride community. Paul Connett PhD, director of the Fluoride Action Network, said:

This is the 24th study that has found this association, but this study is stronger than the rest because the authors have controlled for key confounding variables and in addition to correlating lowered IQ with levels of fluoride in the water, the authors found a correlation between lowered IQ and fluoride levels in children's blood. This brings us closer to a cause and effect relationship between fluoride exposure and brain damage in children.

What is also striking is that the levels of the fluoride in the community where the lowered IQs were recorded were lower than the [Environmental Protection Agency's] so-called 'safe' drinking water standard for fluoride of 4 ppm and far too close for comfort to the levels used in artificial fluoridation programs (0.7 – 1.2 ppm).

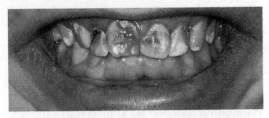

Figure 326: Fluoride is good for teeth

The 'safe' levels they claim for everything, be it fluoride, radiation or whatever, are not 'safe' at all and they know it. You will see from what you have read so far that the bloodlines are not interested in 'safe' levels of anything – it's the dangerous levels they want. They pick a dangerous level and call it safe and then whenever you challenge something for its effect on people the authorities say 'it is within officially agreed safety limits'. But agreed by whom? Precisely. The false 'safe' levels originate with the bloodline networks, and employees of governments and their agencies are told that this is the policy they must sell and implement. Most of them haven't a clue where the policy came from or the motivation behind it. Sodium fluoride was added to the drinking water in the Nazi concentration camps to keep the inmates docile. It is a waste product of the aluminium and phosphate industry and an ingredient in: the mind-altering drug, Prozac, and other hypnotic and psychiatric drugs; Sarin nerve gas; rat and cockroach poisons; and anaesthetic. Fluoride causes cancer, genetic damage, Alzheimer's and calcification of the pineal gland (associated with psychic ability – exactly what the bloodlines and the Reptilian Alliance want to block to entrap people in purely five-sense awareness). Fluoride is also in almost all toothpastes based on the lie (see: global warming, 9/11 and all the rest) that it prevents tooth decay. But it doesn't, and I tell the detailed story of this scam in others books. Fluoride is actually terrible for teeth as the soaring levels of fluorosis can confirm (Fig 326). Communities have voted against having fluoride added to their water, but it has still gone ahead. A study published in the journal Neurologia in 2011 confirmed what other reports have detailed: Fluoride added to drinking water can cause serious brain and other damage. The report said:

> The prolonged ingestion of fluoride may cause significant damage to health and particularly the nervous system. Fluoride is capable of crossing the blood-brain barrier, which may cause biochemical and functional changes in the nervous system during pregnancy, since the fluoride accumulates in brain tissue before birth.

Now they are manoeuvring to add mind-altering lithium to drinking water to make people docile and good little slaves by publishing 'research' that it reduces suicide rates. One of the advocates for this is Dr Jacob Appel (Rothschild Zionist) at Mount Sinai (Moon-god Mountain) Hospital in New York. Appel told the media that the latest studies provided 'compelling' evidence of the 'mood stabilising' benefits of lithium. 'The theory is that lithium in trace amounts enhances the connectivity among neurons, and having exposure over a lifetime makes the brain more happy,' he said. Make them love their servitude. Appel said that it would be relatively easy to add lithium, which is a naturally occurring element: 'People who oppose adding lithium to the drinking water in trace amounts don't go around advocating to strain the lithium from the drinking water from areas where it does exist. Why not give everyone the same benefit?' Oh, please, darling. Cue song sheet, cue Appel. Another major promoter of lithium in drinking water is Dr Gerhard Schauzer (Rothschild Zionist) at the University of California. These people are an open book when you know what is really going on. The widely-used artificial sweetener aspartame is another brain suppressant and it was manipulated through the US government testing procedure by 9/11 US Defense Secretary Donald Rumsfeld (Rothschild Zionist) when he was chief executive, president and chairman of Big Pharma's G D Searle & Company. Rumsfeld was a member of the Rothschild Zionist Project for the New American Century which called for 'advanced forms of biological warfare that can target specific genotypes ...' Searle sold aspartame to Monsanto, who gave the world Agent Orange and genetically-modified food. Enjoy your tea. Two aspartames, please. Watch for it in the lists of ingredients under its own name or 'E951'. Aspartame trade-names include Nutrasweet, Equal and Spoonful.

Killing the children

I have exposed vaccines at great length for the way their cocktail of poisons, including mercury, target the immune system to undermine our natural defences (Fig 327). Children are now having the best part of 30 vaccinations, and combinations of them, by the age of two (Fig 328). What does anyone with a smear of intelligence think this is doing to a still-developing immune system? A child's immune defences will never be what they should be after this bombardment of toxins at such a crucial time. But that's the idea, and the vaccination programme is being orchestrated through the bloodlines' Big Pharma cartel and the Rothschild–Rockefeller-created World Health Organization. Vaccines are also designed to change human DNA – another common theme. We don't need useless vaccines; we need a strong immune system which is being fundamentally undermined by vaccines, by additives in food and drink, and from electromagnetic sources. Who owns the Big Pharma cartel of interconnecting pharmaceutical corporations? *The bloodlines do.* And their drugs and vaccinations are produced for *our* benefit and to keep us *healthy??* Did I mention depopulation? A report in the Human and Experimental Toxicology journal revealed a link between vaccinations and infant

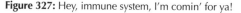
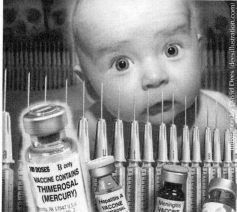

Figure 327: Hey, immune system, I'm comin' for ya!

Figure 328: Vaccination of children at all is appalling, but the scale of it is staggering

mortality. Highly experienced medical researchers, Neil Z Miller and Gary S Goldman, found 'a high statistically significant correlation between increasing number of vaccine doses and increasing infant mortality rates'. The United States vaccinates more children than any other country in the developed world and has the highest number of infant deaths. Japan and Sweden, where children have the fewest vaccinations, have the lowest rates. The polio vaccine given to children since the 1950s was found to contain a cancer causing agent – a virus known as SV40. This was found in kidney cells of rhesus monkeys that are used to make the vaccine, but they kept on giving it to children. A report in the *San Francisco Chronicle* in 2001 said:

> For four decades, government officials have insisted that there is no evidence the simian virus called SV40 is harmful to humans. But in recent years, dozens of scientific studies have found the virus in a steadily increasing number of rare brain, bone and lung-related tumors – the same malignant cancer SV40 causes in lab animals. Even more troubling, the virus has been detected in tumors removed from people never inoculated with the contaminated vaccine, leading some to worry that those infected by the vaccine might be spreading SV40.

The American Childhood Cancer Association says that cancer is now the number one killer of children in America. This is shocking to us, but good news for the bloodlines and Big Pharma in their depopulation programme. The Bill and Belinda Gates Foundation donates billions of dollars for mass vaccination in the Third World with a big chunk of that provided by bloodline billionaire Warren Buffett. Gates has said that he wants to see every child in the world vaccinated in a programme that he calls 'vaccine equity'. He disingenuously tries to sell this nightmare as the 'good guy' ensuring that poor children have what 'rich kids' have – toxins inserted with a needle: 'It's now that we're gonna start to get the last two vaccines that rich kids take for granted, the pneumococcal and rotavirus, and over these next five years, get them out to every child everywhere – that means for the first time ever that we have equity in vaccines.' Hey, that's great. What about equity in food supply, homes, clean water, opportunity? Silence. But poisons? Oh yes, we need 'equity'. Gates has been extremely active in his promotion of the 'global warming' lie, too; and the African Centre for Biosafety claims that Water Efficient Maize for Africa (WEMA), funded into existence by Gates and Buffett, is threatening Africa's food sovereignty and opening new markets for agribusiness giants like Monsanto. Who is 'participating' in the Gates–Buffett WEMA scheme? *Monsanto*. Gates says that biotechnology and genetically-modified crops are needed to feed the world's population (which he wants to dramatically reduce). It seems that anything the bloodlines want, so does Bill Gates, and the world would be a much safer place if he stuck to making billions from computer software. Gates attended a fund-raising conference in London in June 2011 organised by the Global Alliance for Vaccines and Immunisation (GAVI). The Bill and Melinda Gates Foundation is GAVI's main source of funding, but British Prime Minister David Cameron (Rothschild Zionist) also pledged £814 million from British taxpayers for vaccinating children in poor countries (Fig 329). Cameron said that the money would help to vaccinate more than 80 million children, and save 1.4 million lives. He said:

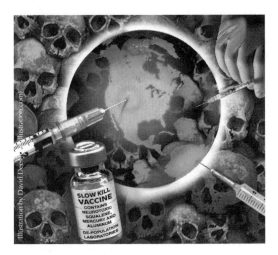

Figure 329: Global genocide

That is one child vaccinated every two seconds for five years. It is one child's life saved every two minutes. That is what the money that the British taxpayer is putting in will give.

Cameron's controllers have a mass depopulation programme. Why would they want to save the lives of poor children if what Cameron and Gates claim is true? GAVI is an 'alliance' of some familiar names ... the World Health Organization (WHO); United Nations Children's Fund (UNICEF); World Bank Group; Bill and Melinda Gates Foundation; governments of donor countries; governments of developing countries; vaccine industry of developing countries and industrialised countries; research and technical health institutes; civil society organisations; and 'independent individuals'. Yep, I'm sure there are lots of 'independent individuals'. GAVI was established in 2000 at the annual meeting of the World Economic Forum in Davos, Switzerland. This is like a more on-the-record version of the Bilderberg Group involving the same people ... you know, the ones who want to see the population massively reduced. The Forum was founded in 1971 by the German economist Klaus Martin Schwab. Another chap connected to the World Economic Forum is Konrad Otto-Zimmermann (Rothschild Zionist), president of the Agenda 21 Local Governments for Sustainability (control and depopulation). Zimmermann's operation is supported by the World Economic Forum and so is the Smart Grid mind-control system that delivers radiation and subliminal messages into every home. Bill Gates (Bilderberg Group) met with the Norwegian Prime Minister Jens Stoltenberg (Bilderberg Group) in 2011, and soon afterwards it was announced that Norway would double its donation to supply vaccines in GAVI's target countries. Norway would also work closely with Bill Gates and Britain on the vaccination programme to 'save nine million children in poor countries'. By the way, Norway has many connections with the global bloodline conspiracy, but if they go 'off-message' over Israel, as they did in the run-up to the 'terrorist bomb' and mass shootings in 2011, then they are given their 'punishment'.

Former insider exposes the scam

While I was writing this chapter, I watched a tremendous interview on the excellent Conscious Media Network (www.consciousmedianetwork.com – highly recommended) with a really gutsy lady – Dr Lorraine Day. She was an orthopaedic surgeon and head of department at San Francisco General Hospital and she saw from the inside the killing machine that is 'modern medicine' and the vaccine fraud. Dr Day said: 'The medical industry in general was developed for control and financial gain. It has no other reason for its existence.' She said that there was a 'sinister plan' to get everyone on drugs because all drugs were mind altering – 'even if it is for your stomach'. They alter your mind and your ability to understand truth, she said. 'When you are on mind-altering drugs, it's like being on street drugs.' She said that disease is caused by the way we eat and live and she gave the example of seeing actor Michael J Fox talking about his Parkinson's disease while drinking a brain-zapping diet soda that was contributing to it. Drugs only covered up the symptoms, she said. 'It never solves the problem; at best it can hide the problem.' Dr Day said that the entire medical industry was based on money made from disease. Would that industry, therefore, want more disease, or less? There are fundraisers for this disease or that disease, charities for this disease or that disease, but nothing really changes. Dr Day said there were more people making their living from the cancer industry than people who have cancer. Sixty-five per cent of the income for the Rockefeller-created American Cancer Society goes to pay executive salaries and other costs and only five per cent funded patient care, she said. 'The American Cancer Society was established by a Rockefeller to control the information that people learn about cancer and to encourage them to go to their doctors.' This is why you rarely see information about alternative ways to treat cancer and, even better, how to avoid it through diet, lifestyle and exercise. Dr Day said that mammograms that check for breast cancer are increasing the chances of getting breast cancer because of the radiation. She also revealed that abortions dramatically increase the chances of breast cancer and that the authorities know this. When a woman is pregnant, her breast cells become unstable as they prepare to produce milk. An abortion terminates this process before completion and the breast cells then remain unstable indefinitely.

Dr Day was one of the first to alert people to the dangers of AIDS, which, she said, was injected into the homosexual community in San Francisco and then into Africa through vaccination programmes. The Big Pharma-controlled Centers for Disease Control (CDC) told her at first that AIDS could not be passed between humans when they knew that it could. They also bizarrely insisted that drug users could contract AIDS from needles, but medical staff could not. It took a member of staff at Dr Day's hospital to acquire AIDS from a needle for the executives at the CDC to accept that they were talking quite obvious nonsense. Dr Day said that the introduction of AIDS to Africa is about depopulation and stealing the resources of the continent. They also infected African monkeys and released them into the wild to spread the disease and give them a fake origin for AIDS when it was probably the creation of the United States biological weapons programme (in truth, if not official) at Fort Detrick in Maryland. This is also home to US Army Medical Command; US Army Medical Research and Materiel Command; US Army Medical Research Institute of Infectious Diseases; and the National Cancer Institute. Good to keep it all in-house. Dr Day said that mandatory vaccinations would cause 'a deterioration and illness and destruction of the human race more rapidly than we're destroying ourselves by the way we are eating and living [and] there will eventually be nothing left if we keep on this tack'. She said that before vaccines there was virtually no autism and virtually no Sudden Infant Death Syndrome. The main cause of Sudden Infant Death Syndrome was vaccines – 'that has been established beyond a shadow of a doubt'. She described an experiment in which babies were connected to sensors to measure their blood pressure, heart rate and breathing rate. They were all fine and stable until they were given vaccines. Then the electrode readings were 'all over the place' for three weeks. Many babies stopped breathing or had slow breathing. There were seizures, and temperature went 'sky high' to the extent that they could cause damage to the brain. 'They don't work, they don't work,' she said. 'Look at the graphs of infectious diseases before and after vaccines and you will see that there was no change.' Polio had already dropped 85 per cent because of improved sanitation and nutrition by the time a vaccine was introduced, she said, and the curve did not change once immunisation began. Dr Day said that after polio vaccination began some 85 to 100 per cent of polio was caused by the live vaccine, and to hide this fact from the public they changed the name of polio to Aseptic Meningitis. A disease was 'eradicated' by changing its name. Dr Day said that mercury in vaccines causes autism which was unknown before vaccination began, and that vaccines are grown in human and animal cells that are contaminated with cancer and other diseases. Vaccines also contain 'a whole bundle of toxins'. The authorities are now talking about 'super vaccines' of six or seven in the same shot. This is insanity, and calculated, like the entire vaccine and Big Pharma medical industry, to kill you and your children and grandchildren. Dr Day told of a study in which a group of animals was injected with one substance and survived; a second group was injected with another substance and survived; but when both substances were injected together into a third group, every animal died. Dr Day has been banned from many radio and television shows for her exposure of Big Pharma from personal experience. Media and medical journals will not quote her or say anything that upsets the pharmaceutical cartel because of the threat to withdraw the advertising that is essential for their survival. You can see Dr Lorraine Day's information on many and various subjects at: www.drday.com.

You are what you eat

Food and drink additives are designed to imbalance the human mind, body and emotions to make our lives as short as possible, and to distort and suppress the way we decode reality (Figs 330). The bloodlines want their slaves to live only as long as they can effectively serve their system; and then who cares about the elderly – deny them treatment, get rid of them. Our intake of chemicals and toxins is also increased by having most food packaged in plastic containers or wrapped in plastic. Toxins in the plastic are absorbed by the food; and I see produce marked 'organic' wrapped in plastic, which, by definition, means that it can't be 'organic'. There is also the point that HAARP transmissions have the potential to increase a thousandfold the strength of toxic substances in toxic human bodies. Food and drink additives target everyone, but especially children and young people generally. They are preparing children to be their adult zombie slaves in their Brave New World (Fig 331). Studies and personal experience have shown that chemical additives cause major changes in the behaviour of children. Their brains are

Figure 330: How can people be mentally, emotionally and physically balanced when they eat and drink this crap?

Figure 331: How is anyone in this physical and mental state going to grasp what is really happening in the world – or care?

Figure 332: Chemical additives in food and drink are rewiring the brains and genetics of people – with children especially targeted

being chemically rewired (Fig 332). When these imbalanced behaviour traits emerge, the kids are given mind-altering drugs like Ritalin to further distort their thinking and emotional processes. Among the physical consequences of Ritalin are heart palpitations and heart attacks. The drugging of children – and the rest of the population come to that – is absolutely fantastic (Fig 333). This has increased with enormous leaps in recent years along with every element of the bloodline conspiracy as they sprint to their line. Here are some figures for Ritalin in the UK: In 1993, doctors issued 3,500 prescriptions for Ritalin; by 1996 it was 26,500; in 2006 the UK National Health Service (not including private medicine) handed out 250,000; and by 2007 the figure was 461,000. There are also similar drugs such as Adderall, Concerta, Metadate CD, Ritalin LA, Focalin XR, Strattera (Atomoxetine) and Risperdal. The latter is a drug used to

extract information from political prisoners in the Soviet Union. Take a deep breath and read that again. They are giving children a truth- extractor drug and it is even being advertised on play bricks for children at paediatricians' offices across America. David Healy, a leading psychopharmacology expert and Professor of Psychiatry at Cardiff University in Wales, said: 'People who took [Risperdal] would tell anything to anyone ... when you think about giving these drugs to kids, it's a whole new ball game.' Maryanne Godboldo, a mother in Detroit, was targeted by an *armed SWAT team* when she refused to give her daughter mind-altering Risperdal for

Figure 333: The bloodlines are drugging their enemy – humanity

alleged 'Attention Deficit Disorder'. This was considered by the now fascist Child 'Protective' Services to be parental neglect and so cue the armed goons in uniform to force their way into the home of Maryanne Godboldo to kidnap her child. A jury, which must surely have been on Risperdal themselves, later found her guilty at a time when federal and multiple state prosecutors were suing producers Johnson & Johnson for deceptive marketing of the drug – including its use by children – and hiding dangerous effects. How do these people remember to breathe? *Unbelievable*. Big Pharma makes nearly $5 billion a year drugging children for invented psychiatric conditions like Attention Deficit Disorder and others that have been 'diagnosed' so far in *20 million* American children. There is a bloodline war on our children and young people, as well as humanity in general, and it was all described in detail by Fabian Society initiate, Aldous Huxley, in his book, *Brave New World*. This is the reason for the dumbing down of education all over the world, and why all the cameras and biometric identity technology are in the schools (Fig 334). They are not there to protect children and students; they are installed to condition them to see as perfectly normal a world in which *everywhere* is like that.

Nor are we only talking about prescribed drugs and chemicals added directly to what we eat and drink. We consume antibiotics in meat from animals given these drugs as a matter of course; we consume growth hormones given to animals to make them fatter quicker to increase profits (one reason why there is so much extreme obesity); and we consume chemical poisons sprayed on crops in the field. Think about that: *People wearing chemical protection suits spray lethal poisons on our food and then we eat the stuff*; but most people still have no problem with that and believe there won't be consequences for health. Plant disease has soared since some of the latest herbicides have been introduced and this is especially true in the case of Monsanto's market leader, Roundup. Their ingredients remove nutrients from the soil, weaken a plant's natural defences, kill beneficial organisms and damage root systems, among a list of other consequences. Herbicides are creating 'superweeds' that have developed a resistance and lead to more and stronger herbicides being used. The combination of crop poisons and genetic modification is one of the prime reasons for the collapse in the vital bee populations that pollinate plants and flowers. We need to understand something big-time and fast. These people, and those that control them, are systematically killing the population and destroying our ability to grow healthy food, or even, in many cases, any food at all. They are planning global famines – yes, in western countries, too. Then we have genetically-modified food which is part of a satanic assault on the human mind and body. Bloodline-funded scientists are genetically modifying nature to produce mice that tweet like birds, cats that glow in the dark and

Figure 334: The 'education' (programming) system turning out the robots of tomorrow. Don't let them do it

Figure 335: Killer 'food'

human genetics mixed with cows, goats, pigs and mice. Crazy South Korean scientists at Seoul National University have genetically engineered a dog that glows 'fluorescent green' in ultraviolet light when given an antibiotic known as doxycycline. Yes, I know. Go figure. Human DNA and plant DNA are being spliced as the whole fabric of nature is rewired. The Defense Advanced Research Projects Agency (DARPA), the driving force behind HAARP, wants to genetically change human DNA to create a breed of mind-controlled soldiers that never disobey orders. Reptilians are obsessed with genetics and technology, which they see as the same thing, and humanity is being enslaved genetically and technologically. The Reptilian Alliance dictates to its bloodline hybrids and they tell their lackeys in government to make it law against all logic and good sense – unless you know what the real intention is. The British government secretly subsidised research to develop a genetically-modified potato resistant to the fungal disease known as 'blight' when there was already a natural potato resistant to blight. Britain doesn't even commercially grow GM crops because of public opposition, but the government secretly uses public funds to develop GM. This would seem crazy until you realise that introducing GM to Britain and destroying natural varieties is the hidden agenda. The US watchdog group, Public Employees for Environmental Responsibility (PEER), revealed, with others, that the Obama administration is supporting genetically-engineered agriculture in more than 50 national wildlife refuges – a fact confirmed by internal emails. This was a 'priority' for the White House, the emails confirmed. PEER Executive Director Jeff Ruch said: 'The White House is engaging in a joint effort with Monsanto.' The White House working in collusion with Monsanto? I don't believe it. Must be a conspiracy theory. Those in the shadows know about the dangers to human health of GM food, but the ignorant gofers in government and administration introduce it because that is what they are told to do. This is how genetically-modified food is allowed against all independent scientific evidence (Fig 335). A study reported in *India Today* found that the Bt toxin widely used in GM crops has turned up in human blood samples. The report said:

> Scientists ... have detected the insecticidal protein ... circulating in the blood of pregnant as well as non-pregnant women. They have also detected the toxin in fetal blood, implying it could pass on to the next generation.

That's the idea. Whenever frontline Illuminati assets like Monsanto tell you that something is safe, you know by definition that it's not. Making something safe for humans is not the motivation (Fig 336). Jeffrey Smith, executive director of the Institute for Responsible Technology, said that mice fed natural Bt toxin showed significant immune responses and they became sensitive to other formerly harmless compounds.

Figure 336: Genetically-modifying the population

Here is the theme again – targeting the *immune system*. Smith said that about 500 people reported reactions, mostly allergy or flu-like symptoms, when natural Bt was sprayed in Vancouver and Washington State to kill gypsy moths. Six people required emergency treatment. They don't do this to kill moths and it's the same with all the other mass spraying of populations under various excuses. It is the *people* they're after. Bt toxin has also started turning up in waterways. They are systematically poisoning our world. The bloodlines can do this and not be exposed and prosecuted because they own and control the Big Food, Big Biotech and Big Pharma corporations; they control the government food, drug and environment agencies which are supposed to protect the public from the 'Bigs'; and they own and control the mainstream media and the reporting, or non-reporting, of these abominations. They are also crucially aided and abetted by the global army of 'repeaters'. These are politicians, scientists, teachers and academics, 'journalists', doctors and the general population who just repeat what they are told without question. 'Journalists' repeat what politicians say. Politicians repeat what their advisors and 'think tanks' say. Scientists repeat what the official song-sheet says. Doctors repeat what Big Pharma and the Big Pharma-funded medical schools say. Teachers and academics repeat what the curriculum, text books and official versions of everything say. Great swathes of the public then repeat what all of those people say. The blind leading the blind is a phrase that could have been invented to describe human society. All these people need to stop repeating and start questioning and thinking for themselves.

Multiple attacks

Small farms and organic alternatives to this toxic diet are being targeted, along with alternatives to the Big Pharma medical system when the third biggest cause of death in America is medical treatment. Small farms are in the bloodline gun-sight along with back-yard food growers (Figs 337 and 338). The idea is that eventually only bloodline corporations will produce food. Did you know that the US Department of Agriculture claims to own the name 'organic'? Put the words: 'Political Control Freaks Take Over Farmers Market' into *YouTube* to see how far this has already gone. Monsanto and other members of Big Biotech are destroying seed variety and patenting the rest for their

Figure 337: Small and independent farmers and growers are on the hit list of Big Pharma-and Big Biotech-controlled governments and law enforcement

Figure 338: Ever more laws and regulations are planned to make life impossible for farmers and growers that are not part of the giant food corporations

exclusive use. They are even patenting natural varieties of seeds that they have had *nothing to do with developing*. I tell this story at length in *The David Icke Guide to the Global Conspiracy*. Big Biotech has introduced what are called 'terminator seeds' that do not flower or grow fruit after the initial planting, therefore requiring customers to repurchase seed for every subsequent planting. This has devastated small and poor farmers around the world who were using seeds from one year's crop to sow the following year. The plan is to make everyone dependent on the Biotech giants for their seeds and then massively increase the price to put the competition for food production out of business. In 2009, Bloomberg reported that Monsanto, the world's biggest seed-maker, was increasing the price of new genetically-modified seeds by a colossal 42 per cent. We will also see Problem–and–No-Problem–Reaction–Solution food scares involving foods that are good for us, especially those produced organically. The e-coli outbreak in Germany in 2011 was an example of this and involved a new 'super strain' of drug-resistant e-coli called 0104:H4. Yes, I bet it did. The 'mystery strain' is resistant to an unprecedented eight major classes of antibiotics and had to be engineered in a laboratory. Humans are becoming more immune to antibiotics in general because they are so over prescribed that the bugs mutate to counter them; and eaters of meat are consuming antibiotics regularly. The e-coli outbreak was exploited to call for all food to be irradiated, and organic and small farmers in Spain were severely affected when they were wrongly blamed as the source. US government communications made public by WikiLeaks revealed that Spain was resisting American pressure to accept genetically-modified food and crops, and that the US pledged retaliation for doing so.

The scale of the deceit can be seen in the way that the Sun has been demonised in recent decades. Oh, you mustn't go out in the sun or you might get skin cancer; and if you do go out in the sun you must use sunscreen. A couple of things here: Firstly, we need the vitamin D that we get from sunlight to be at all healthy; and secondly, it is the toxic sunscreen creams that cause skin cancer – not the Sun. They have also demonised cholesterol as a cause of heart attacks when we need cholesterol to transform ultra-violet light from the Sun into vitamin D. Some sanity was restored in 2010 when the British Association of Dermatologists, Multiple Sclerosis Society, Cancer Research UK, Primary Care Dermatology Society, National Osteoporosis Society, Diabetes UK and National Heart Forum agreed that exposure to sunlight is necessary for the absorption of Vitamin D. A deficiency can damage kidneys and bones, cause diabetes, cancer and mental disorders such as schizophrenia. The sunlight–cholesterol double whammy is part of the depopulation agenda and produces colossal profits for Big Pharma from all the ill health that it generates. They tell people that cholesterol causes heart disease, because they know that suppressed cholesterol will mean less vitamin D is absorbed and a long list of health consequences, especially when combined with using cancer-causing sunscreens to block out the sunlight. You have to take everything the authorities tell us and flip it around. The opposite of what they say is nearly always the truth. Big Pharma came up with 'statins', a drug to reduce cholesterol (and therefore vitamin D absorption), to protect people from heart disease – when statins *increase* the chance of heart disease! Researchers at the Tufts University School of Medicine in the United States also found that 'cholesterol-lowering drugs significantly increased the risk of cancer'. A study involving 350,000 men at high risk of heart disease reduced their cholesterol consumption by 42 per cent, saturated fat consumption by 28 per cent and total calories by 21 per cent ... and it *made no difference whatsoever*. No clinical trial has ever shown that reducing saturated fat intake has produced a reduction in heart disease. Dr Ancel Keys, professor emeritus at the University of Minnesota, rightly said:

> There's no connection whatsoever between cholesterol in food and cholesterol in blood. And we've known that all along. Cholesterol in the diet doesn't matter at all unless you happen to be a chicken or a rabbit.

Dr George Mann, a biochemist and physician at Vanderbilt University in Nashville, wrote an editorial in the *New England Journal of Medicine* calling the cholesterol hoax the 'greatest scam in the history of medicine'. There have been so many. Dr Mann talked of the 'Heart Mafia' and he said that 'it will seem to many that there was an unwholesome conspiracy'. There was, and is. The food and drug industry earns more than $50 billion a year from the low-cholesterol lie. The bloodline-controlled US Food and Drug Administration (FDA) is still saying that 'broad spectrum' sunscreen is the only way to stop skin cancer when the sunscreen is the *cause* of skin cancer, while doing nothing about full-body radiation scanners that blast the skin with radiation. The FDA is owned by Big Pharma and Big Biotech. Dr Michael Holick, Professor of Medicine, Physiology and Biophysics at Boston University School of Medicine, said:

> The population of the world has been brainwashed by the American Academy of Dermatology and the sunscreen industry for thirty years, with the unrelenting message that you should never be exposed to direct sunlight because it is going to cause serious skin cancer and death. People are really quite surprised by the new message that sensible skin exposure in moderation is very important for good health. We should appreciate the sun for its benefits, and not abuse it.

They are surprised because they have been told a deliberate lie for decades. All the legislation and red tape that is drowning small businesses all over the world is also part of the plan. They want an end to all business that isn't done through the world government structure and its corporations and banks. The public, too, is being deluged with laws and regulations, and the scale of legislation over the last 20 years has been incredible. A new law was passed every *three hours* during the ten years that 'shapeshifter' Tony Blair was in Downing Street and 98 per cent of them were not even debated in Parliament. They were imposed through something called 'statutory instruments' that allow the government to dictate what is going to happen. The same can be seen in the United States through Presidential Orders that bypass Congress, and through government agencies that can make their own rules. The constant spraying of

new laws and regulations across society
from all levels of government is part of a
psychological operation aimed at mass
behaviour-modification (Fig 339). This
works in the same way as behaviour
experiments with rats and mice. Scientists
set up a maze of channels for a mouse to
walk down, but some routes produce an
electric shock and the mouse will change
direction. When the mouse has been
shocked a few times you can take the
shock equipment away and it still won't go
down that channel again. The mouse's
behaviour has been modified. The
explosion of laws dictating virtually every
detail of our lives is meant to do the same
to humans. The technique is to ensure that
people constantly face 'shocks' or potential
'shocks' from all the 'dos and don'ts',
'musts and can'ts'; and to bombard us with
so many punishments – big and small – for
not complying, that our behaviour is
modified and we become acquiescent,
unquestioning slaves. Well, I know
someone who won't be.

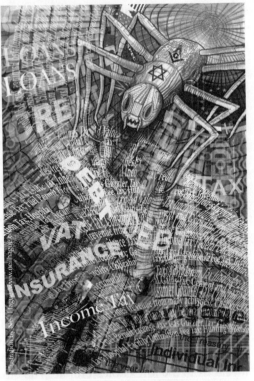

Figure 339: The explosion in Big Brother legislation is the bloodline spider tying humanity to its web

There is no conspiracy?

I included in my last book, the mega work, *Human Race Get Off Your Knees*, the story of a
man called Dr Richard Day, and it is appropriate to repeat what he said in 1969 about
the way the world was going to change in accordance with a hidden plan. For those
new to this information, or those who have not read 'Human Race', it might be a
sobering moment after reading the conspiracy that I have laid out in this book and
which people can see with their own eyes today as the Orwellian world rolls out.
Richard Day (Rothschild Zionist) was the national medical director of the
Illuminati–front, Planned Parenthood, established by the eugenics-funding Rockefeller
family, and he was Professor of Pediatrics at 'Moon-god Mountain' – the Mount Sinai
Medical School in New York. Dr Jacob Appel (Rothschild Zionist), who wants to put
mind-altering lithium into drinking water, also works there. Day made a speech to
about 80 doctors at the Pittsburgh Pediatric Society on March 20th, 1969. He asked
everyone to turn off any recording equipment and stop taking notes, because he wanted
to reveal a coming a new world system and the plan to sabotage American industry.
One doctor in the audience, Lawrence Dunegan, a Pittsburgh paediatrician, *did* take
notes, and before he died in 2004 he made a series of taped interviews about what he
had heard nearly 50 years earlier. Dr Richard Day, a Rockefeller insider, said that
different parts of the world would be assigned different roles of industry and commerce
in a unified global system (the same was planned from the start with the European

Union, as I have exposed in other books). The pre-eminence of the United States and the relative independence and self-sufficiency of America was going to end, Day said. The old structure would have to be destroyed to make way for the new. What did I say? They are using America to destroy America. Every part of the world would have a specialty and so become inter-dependent, Day said. America would remain a centre for agriculture, high tech, communications and education, but heavy industry would be 'transported out'. This is exactly what has happened with the run-down of the American manufacturing industry and the mass outsourcing of jobs to other countries. More than 42,000 American factories closed between 2001 and 2010 with 5.5 million manufacturing jobs lost. China now makes more cars than the US and Japan together. This has also been happening within the European Union as we have witnessed the end of previously diverse economies and their domination by certain specialisations. This makes everyone dependent on everyone else and only the bloodlines would have control of the system as a whole.

Dr Dunegan said that Richard Day revealed the plan to cull and control the population through medicine, food, new laboratory-made diseases and the suppression of the cure for cancer. 'We can cure almost every cancer right now,' he said in 1969. 'Information is on file in the Rockefeller Institute [now the Rockefeller University] if it's ever decided that it should be released.' The El-ite has access to it though, naturally, and this is another reason why so many of them live for so long. The CIA scientist who told me about the microchip programme said that he had been cured of cancer by a serum made available to him only because they wanted to keep him alive to continue his work for them. Day said that letting people die of cancer would slow down population growth. And, charmingly: 'You may as well die of cancer as something else.' Like I say, these people have no empathy and no emotion. Day believed in eugenics and 'survival of the fittest', so long as it didn't apply to him. He said in 1969 that abortion would no longer be illegal and it would be accepted as normal (and provide a constant supply of foetuses for the satanic rituals). The food supply would be monitored so that no-one could give food to a 'fugitive of the system'. He was talking about people challenging the system when it reached its most extreme stages. Growing food privately would be banned by saying it wasn't safe. Young people would spend longer in school, but not learn anything (the dumbing down that we have seen); and family would be manipulated to 'diminish in importance' (hence the endless attacks on family life and the State stealing children). There would be restrictions on travel, and private home–ownership would disappear (this is included in Agenda 21). He said that they would increase violence, pornography and obscenity in the media and movies to desensitise people to violence and porn and make them feel that life is short, precarious and brutish. Music would 'get worse' and be used for programming perception (see: Lady Gaga and so many others). Society would be severely controlled and people would be electronically tagged. Long-established communities would be destroyed by unemployment and mass immigration (one of the goals of the Rothschild Zionist Frankfurt School behind political correctness). Weather modification would be used as a weapon of war and to create drought or famine (HAARP). This was one of Day's specialist fields. He was involved in weather modification during World War II. 'People will have to get used to the idea of change, so used to change that they'll be expecting change [see: Barack Obama]. Nothing will be permanent.' This is a summary of what

Day predicted in 1969 posted at: www.overlordsofchaos.com:

Population control; permission to have babies; redirecting the purpose of sex – sex without reproduction and reproduction without sex; contraception universally available to all; sex education and carnalising of youth as a tool of world government; tax-funded abortion as population control; encouraging anything-goes homosexuality; technology used for reproduction without sex; families to diminish in importance; euthanasia and the 'demise pill'; limiting access to affordable medical care makes eliminating elderly easier; medicine would be tightly controlled; elimination of private doctors; new difficult-to-diagnose and untreatable diseases; suppressing cancer cures as a means of population control; inducing heart attacks as a form of assassination; education as a tool for accelerating the onset of puberty and evolution; blending all religions ... the old religions will have to go; changing the Bible through revisions of key words; restructuring education as a tool of indoctrination; more time in schools, but pupils 'wouldn't learn anything'; controlling who has access to information; schools as the hub of the community; some books would just disappear from the libraries; changing laws to promote moral and social chaos; the encouragement of drug abuse to create a jungle atmosphere in cities and towns; promote alcohol abuse; restrictions on travel; the need for more jails, and using hospitals as jails; no more psychological or physical security; crime used to manage society; curtailment of US industrial pre-eminence; shifting populations and economies – tearing out the social roots; sports as a tool of social engineering and change; sex and violence inculcated through entertainment; implanted ID cards – microchips; food control; weather control; knowing how people respond – making them do what you want; falsified scientific research; use of terrorism; surveillance, implants, and televisions that watch you; the arrival of the totalitarian global system.

Day also said that people who don't want to go along with the new world system would be 'disposed of humanely'. There would be no 'martyrs', he said. 'People will just disappear.' So that is what is 'going on'. Nice isn't it? So are we going to just sit around and wait for our fate? Or, is not time to say, *'ENOUGH – NO MORE!'?*

I think so.

15

Truth Vibrations

The question that I am asked most is 'what can we do?' This is understandable once people realise that we are facing the onslaught of evil which I have been describing in these pages. I will provide answers to that question in this closing chapter, but a key part of the 'solution', or removing the cause of the problem, is to know what is happening and what we are dealing with. We can only find relevant 'answers' when we understand the true nature of the problem.

'Love' is the one-syllable answer to 'what can we do?' I am sure the reaction to this by many people will be: '*Love?* What good will love do against HAARP?' Well, actually, plenty, as I will explain shortly. We have a support system now which I call the Truth Vibrations and there is a terrific challenge to Reptilian/Grey control happening involving benevolent extraterrestrial/interdimensional forces to remove them from Saturn and the Moon and eliminate the Matrix 'hack'. I was told in 1990 that a great awakening was coming in my lifetime that would open human minds to all that had been suppressed and forgotten. Neil Hague and myself symbolise the Truth Vibrations as a lion (Fig 340). I was given the information through Betty Shine and others in the earliest days of my own awakening that humanity had been in a trance, a state of amnesia, and new vibrations – a new waveform information source – were going to symbolically snap their fingers and allow sleeping beauty to awaken. The more open minds would be the first to be touched by this transformation, but eventually vast numbers would be freed from their mental and emotional prison cells. I was told that the Truth Vibrations would also bring to the surface all that has been hidden, and the veil would be lifted on the secrets that have been kept from us. This was more than

Figure 340: The Truth Vibrations are breathing a new awareness into the information fabric of our reality

Illustration by Neil Hague (www.neilhague.com)

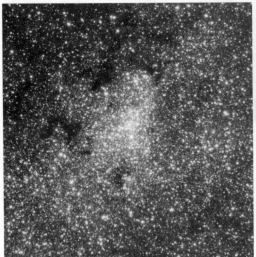

Figure 341: The galactic centre

Figure 342: The galactic centre in infra-red

20 years ago and this is precisely what is happening. Multi-millions are awakening to a new perception of self and the world, and the veil is most certainly being lifted on the conspiracy to enslave us all. This is a moment of great challenge, but also limitless opportunity for those prepared to grasp it. We need to appreciate how we are interacting with the energy field of Planet Earth every moment that we are attached to this reality. Without that interaction, we couldn't be here. The point to emphasise is that the term is *inter-action*, a two-way process. We give and we receive. What we call 'physical' reality is decoded waveform information communicated from the centre of the galaxy where mainstream scientists say there is, to use their term, a 'supermassive black hole' (Fig 341). There is a star right in the centre of it according to some reports, and certainly more sophisticated infra-red cameras have discovered what are described as 'massive' stars and star clusters in the galactic centre (Fig 342). Mainstream science suggests that there are supermassive black holes at the centre of every galaxy, but their description of what 'black holes' are differs fundamentally from my own. The galactic centre is mission control for the galaxy. This is where the power emanates from and the information for the Milky Way expression of the cosmic virtual-reality game. The galaxy is a mass of encoded waveform information fields that we decode into the 'physical' (holographic) galaxy that we see. Well, that is how it is supposed to be without 'The Hack'. Stars like our Sun (and the brown dwarf/sun known as the 'planet' Saturn) receive this information in multiple dimensions of reality and communicate this in their region of the galaxy. Stars are like vast receiver–transmitters and transformers on a galactic waveform/electrical communication grid. Earth, humanity and all life, be they animals, plants or trees, are receiving, transmitting and generally interacting with these galactic/solar/planetary information sources.

What I call the Time Loop *appears* to pass through distinct cycles that provide very different collective 'movies' for Consciousness to experience, and the ancients described this with their concepts of the circular/cyclical nature of 'time'. Ancient India referred to these segments of experience as 'yugas' (cycles). The Ancient Greeks talked of the 'Great Year' of 24,000 years through which we pass from a Golden Age to Silver, Bronze and Iron ages before returning through Bronze and Silver to Golden. Don't confuse this with the Iron Age and Bronze Age taught in the schools about the periods when iron and bronze were discovered. This is not the same thing at all. Ancient Greeks and many

Figure 343: The Dendera Zodiac

others said that it takes 12,000 years to travel through the cycle from the Golden Age of fantastic expansion of Consciousness and Awareness to the Iron Age when the opposite is the case and people are only aware of the five senses and little more. This is also known as the Dark Age. The Greek ages of the Great Year correspond with the Vedic and Hindu yugas – the Kali yuga (Iron Age), Dwapara yuga (Bronze Age), Treta yuga (Silver Age) and Satya yuga (Golden Age). At least 30 ancient societies told the same story. There appear to be several opinions about how long it takes to complete a yuga and which one we are currently experiencing. Some of it is a bit of a 'dog's breakfast' (a mess or a muddle) it seems to me.

Many connect these alleged cycles to the 'Precession of the Equinoxes'. The ancients divided the heavens into astrological sections that together complete a circle, and this is represented in the famous Dendera Zodiac at the Hathor temple at Dendera, near Luxor in Egypt and in many other artefacts left by long-lost civilisations (Fig 343). Mainstream science says that the Earth's 'wobble' causes the planet to move slowly though a cycle of facing different signs, or ages, of the zodiac in the heavens and this is the Precession of the Equinoxes which is estimated to take approximately 25,765 years to complete a full cycle (Fig 344). We are now in the process of moving from the Age of Pisces into the Age of Aquarius, according to that system. The Ancient Greek philosopher, Plato, wrote that he had been told of the Great Year cycle by Egyptian priests who spoke of the four different ages in the Great Year. Plato said that the priests had told him that the Ancient Greeks were like children, because they had forgotten the knowledge from higher ages. Ancient Indian accounts tell of four illusions that cover the infinity of God. Illusions that cover infinity is a very good way of describing the Time Loop reality in general that we currently experience as the 'physical' world. We are now moving through a Bronze Age towards a Silver Age on an upward spiral to the Golden Age if you believe the 'ages' system. There are many myths and legends about highly advanced civilisations known as Atlantis and Mu, or Lemuria, which ended in great Earth upheavals. Plato wrote about Atlantis and said that this existed during the Golden Age. I have already said that Charles Darwin's version of human experience with a constant forward direction of increasing knowledge and intelligence through 'survival of the fittest' and 'natural selection' is nonsense, and this is why the concept dominates mainstream science and 'education'. When the

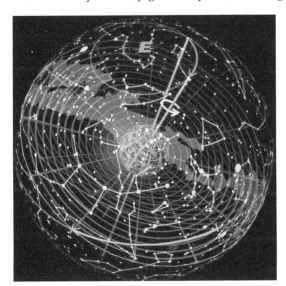

Figure 344: Scientists say that the Earth's 'wobble' is the cause of the 'Precession of the Equinoxes'

consciousness of a planet's inhabitants is suppressed and at other times not suppressed there will be a subsequent difference in their potential to understand and manifest. This has happened many times on Planet Earth and so there have been periods of expanded awareness and others of suppressed awareness. Extraordinary ancient structures that we would struggle to build today were created by high initiates using expanded awareness and the know-how and support of the Reptilian Alliance. It has been pointed out that the Great Pyramid at Giza in Egypt consists of two-and-a-half million stones, each weighing many tonnes which were put together over something like 20 years. This would require between one and two blocks being placed into position approximately every two minutes in that period; and there is a granite block in the King's Chamber that alone weighs 70 tonnes. Scientists and archaeologists produce theories on how the pyramids were built from the perspective of current knowledge and the idea that, because of the Darwin theory, the ancients must have been more primitive than we are. We therefore have the laughable official story that the pyramids were built by constructing ramps alongside them so that slaves could pull the stones up the incline to where they were needed. This is how stones weighing many tonnes were placed in position every two minutes? Yeah, sounds feasible.

The Great Year and 2012

Boris Fritz, an American aerospace engineer, has studied the yuga cycles and the history of India and its ancient Sanskrit language for 40 years. He said in an interview with Regina Meredith on the Conscious Media Network that the most that can be attained in the Iron Age or Dark Age is to explore and be aware of the realm of the five senses. Fritz indicates from Vedic and other sources that the last descending period of a Dark Age was between 700 BC to the zenith at AD 500. He says the ascending Dark Age took us from AD 500 to about AD 1600 when humans began to enter a Bronze Age period. What followed was the intellectual transformation known as the Renaissance and the emergence of literature, science, art, religion and politics, and a focus on classical sources of information. Copernicus published his work on the Earth orbiting the Sun shortly before his death in 1543, and then came Galileo (1564–1642), the Italian physicist, mathematician, astronomer and philosopher who has been described as the 'Father of Modern Science'. Boris Fritz says that we were fully into the Bronze Age by 1900 and that this has been expressed in all the technological discoveries and developments of the 20th and now 21st centuries. The theory says that the early period of a Bronze Age sees the expansion of the intellect, but as the age progresses we begin to break out of mind and into our higher levels of awareness. It is said that we will climb the spiral to the Silver Age about 2,000 years from now when we conquer the illusion of time and communicate through telepathy as a matter of course. The theory says that this is the age of 'wizardry' and that what today we would call miracles would be achieved through manipulating the illusion by *knowing* it is an illusion and how it functions. Finally, comes the Golden Age of fantastic expansions of consciousness that mean technology is no longer needed to do anything, this theory says. Advocates believe that creation in the Golden Age period comes from direct manifestation through consciousness. The Mayan people, in what is now the Yucatan in Mexico from about AD 250 to 900, also believed in the circular nature of time and how the cycle was divided into periods of differing levels of awareness. They measured cycles within larger cycles.

Figure 345: The Truth Vibrations are changing the information that we receive from the Sun

Figure 346: Those who open their hearts and minds to the Truth Vibrations are going to experience a transformation of their perception of self and the 'world'. Those that don't, will not

The 24,000/25,000-year cycle was only one of them. They said there are other cycles that are much longer and others that are much shorter. The Mayans had a 'Grand Cycle' of 25,630 years, which is roughly one complete cycle of the Precession of the Equinoxes, and they divided the Grand Cycle into five 'Great Cycles' or 'World Ages' of 5,125 years. The present Mayan Great Cycle is said to have begun in 3114 BC and will end according to some researchers on December 21st, 2012. Others say it is 2011, or a different date in 2012 such as December 12th. We are in a *period* of change, that's for sure, but there is a 'Big *But*' coming with regard to 2012 and the cycles. We are experiencing a period of fundamental change because of the gathering impact of the Truth Vibrations that I was told about in 1990, and an enormous amount of manipulation that is becoming ever more extreme (Fig 345). The Truth Vibrations are a vast expansion of the information and awareness available to us, and those who connect with their frequency band have the potential to experience an incredibly expanded awareness. Those who keep their minds under lock and key will not be affected at all in a positive way. It's a choice, as always (Fig 346). The Truth Vibrations are seeking out the 'dark' places of density, manipulation and fear, and deleting the power these have over human perception (Fig 347). I am seeing ever more clearly those who are connecting with the Truth Vibrations and those who are desperately clinging to the old ways of thinking and perceiving. Some are opening their minds to a whole new perception of self, life and the world while others are becoming more stressed, anxious and fearful as their energetic environment changes by the hour, but they don't change with it. We are interacting with the 'sea' of energy, and when that changes and we don't, there are obviously going to be consequences mentally, emotionally and 'physically' the more 'out of syc' that people become. There is such a mass of different vibrational states swirling around in the energy 'sea', including many generated by HAARP and other radiation technologies that are there to entrap people in low-vibrational states that will make the Truth Vibrations pass them by. We have to

Figure 347: Humanity emerging from the Matrix as the Truth Vibrations awaken Mind to Consciousness

open our minds to Consciousness to avoid that vibrational entrapment. I don't see 2012 as a special year in the way that is claimed, and I'll explain why when I get to the 'Big *But*'. The perception-changing Truth Vibrations have been having a gathering impact as their power increases and more people beat to their drum. This power will go on increasing through 2012 and onwards for many years yet. 2012 will be further forward than 2011 but not as advanced as 2013, and so on. We are on the cusp of incredible change, one way or the other, and we need to open our minds and hearts to get the full benefit of the positive aspects of what is happening.

I was taken to see a 'channel' only a few months after my visit to Betty Shine in 1990. I had no idea what a 'channel' was, and I am sure many people new to this information would be asking the same. *Channel?* What channel? – the English Channel, television channel, what's he talking about? A channel is somebody who allows themself to be used as a receiver, or vehicle, for another consciousness from another dimension or frequency range of reality to speak through them. The process is similar to that of a psychic, but while a psychic *reports* the words that they decode, a channel speaks the words directly. There are brilliant channels and there are channels who are connecting with nothing and speaking from their own minds, just as there are brilliant psychics and kidding-you-and-themselves 'psychics'. There are also malevolent entities, not least the Reptilians, that speak through channels to mislead; and there are channels who are assets of mind-control programmes who have their 'channelled' information implanted for them to repeat from apparently 'out there'. In other words, you have to be very careful, discerning and streetwise when dealing with such channelled messages. But the information given to me through the channel, or 'sensitive', that I met in the West of England in 1990, has stood the test of events ever since. I was taken aback when the lady went into channel-mode. Her face changed (anyone who doesn't believe in shapeshifting should have been there) and her voice altered. The awareness communicating through her as she decoded a projected electromagnetic field gave the name 'Magnu'. I have used this information in two or three books over the years and every time I do the message becomes ever more relevant and significant to unfolding events. This is what 'Magnu' said in 1990:

I feel you are sensing now the energies coming in, the energies surrounding your planet. This is causing many of you to ask questions. It is causing many of you to re-evaluate completely your way of life, where you feel you wish to go, what you want to do. It is causing tremendous upheavals. Some of these upheavals are very confusing, very distressing, very disturbing. Some people in partnerships are finding they can no longer continue in those partnerships because their partners cannot tune into what they are tuning into. It is causing a great deal of disturbance. And I have said to this sensitive on more than one occasion that you must organise yourselves into groups to support each other.

Now then. My own allegiance with your planet goes back to an Atlantean period ... [when] ... there were many energies being used and information and knowledge being used which were for particular reasons of safety withdrawn, shall we say, to prevent complete catastrophe, to prevent total destruction of your planet. One could say these were sort of emergency measures if you like, to prevent the inhabitants of this planet from an untimely destruction.

Now at that time, shall we say, this knowledge was distributed only to the few; it was taught in what one could call a temple setting, though I am very careful about using this word. It has connotations, maybe. So, let me use that word in the broadest possible sense. There were those initiated into this knowledge. There were grades of initiation and those who passed the full initiation, these were known as the Guardians of the Light and Keepers of the Secret Knowledge. This is the context from which I am coming.

There came a time when this knowledge and the energies were withdrawn. It is very difficult for me to explain to you precisely what I mean by that, so I will let you mull these things over. As the energies around your planet quicken, so these latent energies, these energies which have been withdrawn, will now be phased back in. They will gradually be awakened. As the consciousness level of your planet raises itself, those of you Light Workers who are working together to raise your consciousness, you will be able to hold more and more refined vibrations, and so we will be able to use you as a catalyst to be able to feed in more and more energies.

As more of you raise yourselves to meet the challenge, so we can awaken more of these energies. Now, energy is consciousness and the energies themselves contain the knowledge and the information which is beginning to surface again in your consciousness, so that many of you will remember the Atlantean times. You will remember that you communicated with say, dolphins and whales. You understood these other sentient creatures. You could levitate. You could manifest things. You could cause spontaneous combustion by not miraculous means at all. Once you know what you are doing, these things follow. It is a matter of order.

Now I am looking at a time on your planet when these energies, this knowledge is re-awakened and re-integrated into your consciousness. I am not looking to a time when this knowledge will be for a few, but when your whole planet will be awakened to this understanding which you have simply forgotten. It is not a matter of new information; it is a matter of remembering who you are and where you come from.

So you are being asked to change. You are being asked to change in a total way. It is not a matter of small changes, of a little thing here, a little thing there. You are really being asked to turn yourselves inside out. There is a massive shadow which must be cleared and it is up to Light Workers such as yourself to focus on that challenge.

The Big *But*

What is being described here is the 'Fall of Man' which, in part, was caused by those energies – information – being withdrawn to prevent the Reptilian Alliance from using them for even greater destruction and control. These Truth Vibration energies are now being phased back in to awaken humanity and to allow those in sync with them to remember what they once knew. This is nothing to do with 2012 or any yuga, age, cycle or any of it. The theory of yugas, ages and cycles passed down from ancient societies makes sense, I'll grant you. I have always had a problem with the 2012 belief system, but I went along with most of the 'cycles within cycles' theme for a while on the basis of this is how it looks at the moment; but I am ready to change in the light of new information. I can understand why so many people believe that this is how the world works and how it explains what is happening today at the end of what is claimed to be a Mayan Great Cycle. But it *doesn't*. This 'information' was encoded long ago to divert and confuse us at this very time. I said earlier that the Reptilian 'hijack program' has been running for aeons. It is the same principle as David Rockefeller knowing the fate of the Twin Towers when he was arranging for them to be built. The same thing happens over thousands of years as information traps are primed in one era to go off in another. In fact, you don't even need to do that in the realms of no-time. You just project a

hologram onto our holographic reality and 'hey, we've just discovered information about the Mayan prophecies and their version of time'. Whichever way it was, it is a trap. These yugas, ages and cycles are phenomena within the Time Loop, and the Time Loop *is the hack* (Fig 348). There are energetic cycles in the *un*hacked virtual reality, but they are not *these* cycles. The concept of 2012 and 'moving into a new age' is all part of the Saturn–Moon Matrix illusion. A sense of *time* is a most profound controlling force that holds us fast in the illusion. It makes us age when we are ageless; it makes us serve the clock (Saturn–Moon) and disconnects us from the infinite NOW. The idea of ages following ages is another version of time moving forward. It may be circular, but so is a hamster wheel. Entering a 'new age' confirms a belief in the illusion of moving forward; but there is no forward, as there is no backwards; there is only *NOW*. The Truth Vibrations are not about advancing us into a new age

Figure 348: The perception of Yugas and '2012' cycles are manipulations of the Saturn–Moon Matrix

within the Saturn–Moon Matrix. They are about *breaking the very illusion* of the Saturn–Moon Matrix. This is so clear to me sitting here as my mind continues to open to Consciousness. The Magnu information does not speak about moving into a new age or cycle; it speaks of *returning* energies – information / consciousness – that were *withdrawn* for emergency reasons. This fits with a lot of other information, hints and big pointing fingers that I have been getting in recent years.

The 'End Times' Scam

People will have to use their own intuition on this and I am sure that the advocates of the yuga, New Age and 2012 belief system will dismiss it without a second thought. This is their right and I respect that, but it makes sense of so much. Our reality was not supposed to go through dark ages, war, suffering and deprivation. We are supposed to be living in a world of love, a world without limits. The world is not like that because of the hack. There is no 'Golden Age' within the hack – that is some distant utopia that never comes because it is not meant to come. The Real Golden Age is the one that exists beyond the vibrational prison walls called the 'speed of light' and it is decoded from the pure, unhacked information broadcast from the galactic centre. The Reptilian Alliance cannot completely disconnect us from our true self and reality beyond the Matrix. We feel this through our heart and intuition. The hack has to work to a large extent with what it is hacking into just as a computer hacker has to work with the computer and its software. In the same way they could not create a completely new human body. They had to leave many elements necessary for the human form to function and be 'alive'. They have not created a completely new body as they have not created a completely new reality. What they have done is to hack into both and distort the information fabric within the electromagnetic spectrum and the way the body–computer decodes reality within that band. The wider reality that humans once decoded in the Real Golden Age is denied by genetic manipulation and the blocking frequencies of the Saturn–Moon Matrix. Some of what we see is 'out there', but much of it is manipulated by the transmissions of the Saturn–Moon Matrix and its holographic implants that look real, but aren't. Mayan and Indus Valley societies from where those time cycles came were both dominated by the Reptilians and so were others like the ancient Egyptians and the Hopi, from where the Hopi prophecies came that tell a familiar story about current times. There was much 'channelling' of the Reptilian 'gods' as their sources of information. I have been to Mayan sites in Central America and they were a classic Reptilian 'gods' society that included the calling card of blood sacrifice. How very evolved. Their neighbours, the serpent-worshipping Aztecs, made human sacrifice the national sport. This is what I wrote earlier:

> The Mayan people, in what is now Mexico, say their ancestors were 'the people of the serpent'. They talked about a reptilian race that came from the sky to take over their civilisation and demand human sacrifice. The latter is a common theme. The reptilian race and their other non-human associates were perceived as 'gods' because of their technological capabilities. Hopi Indians in the United States talk of their 'snake brothers', the 'sky gods', who bred with their women. Indian accounts tell of a Reptilian race called the 'Sharpa' that founded civilisation and were the originators of the shockingly racist Hindu caste system.

And look again at what Cathy O'Brien said about her experience with former Mexican President, Miguel de la Madrid:

> De la Madrid had relayed the 'legend of the Iguana' to me, explaining that lizard-like aliens had descended upon the Mayans. The Mayan pyramids, their advanced astronomical technology, including sacrifice of virgins, were supposedly inspired by the lizard aliens. He told me that when the aliens interbred with the Mayans to produce a form of life they could inhabit, they fluctuated between a human and Iguana appearance through chameleon-like abilities – 'a perfect vehicle for transforming into world leaders'. De la Madrid claimed to have Mayan/alien ancestry in his blood, whereby he transformed 'back into an Iguana at will'.

Ancient artefacts and works reflecting the cycles of the Time Loop were inspired by the Reptilian 'gods' running the Saturn–Moon Matrix programme. Were they going to leave the truth for humans to find – humans they wanted to continue to control, exploit and feed off? Or would a colossal diversion be more likely to mislead minds open enough to see beyond the official 'norms'? The Hopi prophecies describe a sequence of events leading to the dawning of the 'fifth world'. These 'worlds' are yugas or Mayan time-cycles under another name. Other ancient peoples have prophecies with the same theme and they are remarkably similar to the biblical *Book of Revelation* with its sequence of seals and trumpets on the road to a 'new heaven and new Earth'. Pat Robertson, the ludicrous American evangelist and friend of the Bush family, said that cracks in the Washington Monument caused by a rare earthquake in 2011 could be 'a sign from God' that 'we're closer to the coming of the Lord'. He said Biblical prophecy about the end of the world predicts that there could be potential devastation from natural disasters leading up to the 'return of Jesus'. Here we go. All over the world people of different beliefs have been caught in this mind-trap. Christians are waiting for Armageddon and the return of Jesus; followers of the Hopi prophecies are ticking them off as they happen; and even some scientists are tracking the cycles to the end of the Mayan Great Cycle alleged to be in 2012. But they are tracking energetic sequences within the Saturn–Moon Matrix frequency band and not in the greater reality beyond its vibrational walls known as 'the speed of light'. Albert Einstein (Rothschild Zionist) said there is no greater speed than the speed of light, and whether by error or manipulation this has helped to underpin the hack by a belief, in effect, that there is nothing *beyond* the hack. We also have the obsession of so many at this time with a '12th planet', called 'Nibiru', made famous by the books of translations from Sumerian clay tablets by 'shapeshifter' Zecharia Sitchin (Rothschild Zionist, London School of Economics). Sitchin did not like me at all because I exposed the Reptilians and their agenda. Nibiru is supposed to be on an elliptical orbit and pass through our part of the solar system every 3,600 years. The Internet is full of websites and postings about the imminent return of Nibiru, with once again the theme of great destruction and possible extinction. We are being given so many reasons to fear a coming global nightmare and even the 'end of the world'. There may well be other planets or dwarf stars connected with this solar system that we don't know about, but I don't buy Nibiru, or Planet X as some call it, in the context of what appears in Sitchin's books. It is so difficult to discern what is 'real' and what is a projection when you are dealing with holographic illusion; but I am sure we are in for some 'surprises' in the heavens in many forms. The coming years could well be *seriously* bumpy to say the least geologically and in terms of extremes of weather, and challenging in every way, as I have been saying for a long time; but this is not the 'end of the world'. It is the end of a human perception program and the old has to go so the new can take its place. The transition between the two is going to be, how can I put it? Well, *interesting*.

The more I know, the deeper the rabbit hole goes; and there is undoubtedly an effort underway by the Reptilians and their cohorts to massively increase the power of the Saturn–Moon Matrix to increase the power of the illusion into *Matrix* movie-type levels of fake perception when virtually nothing that we see is 'real'. This is to block the effect of the returning information source – the Truth Vibrations. A range of prophecies and accounts have laid a trap to allow the Reptilians to make the prophecies appear to be happening. The energetic cycles that have been identified by researchers are cycles within the Matrix programme. One researcher pointed out that a cycle in 1941 was repeated in 2001 and he connected this to the surprise attack on Pearl Harbor in 1941 and the surprise attack on 9/11 in 2001. But neither was a 'surprise' attack. They were both engineered Problem– Reaction–Solutions by the servants of the Matrix following a game plan *encoded* in the Matrix. The bloodlines are surfing these cycles to ensure the greatest chance of success. We have to see through this or we are going to be seriously caught. Look at what is happening. The Christians believe in an unfolding sequence to Armageddon; the New Agers believe in the Hopi prophecies; 2012ers believe in the end of the Mayan Great Cycle; Nibiru believers are waiting for that to destructively arrive. These are all the same basic story regurgitated. They are planning to project holograms into the sky to depict religious figures 'returning', when they have never existed – as with 'Mother Mary' who appeared in the African sky in 2011. An invasion by 'aliens', even whole 'Planet Nibirus', brown dwarfs, comets and other manifestations in the heavens and the sky can be projected holographically by the Saturn–Moon Matrix, HAARP and related technology to look as real as anything else. *Please*; it is a trap. What we believe, we perceive and therefore create. We are giving power to the illusion. If they announce a threat from an alien presence or invasion, *don't believe them*. American aerospace executive, Dr Carol Rosin, worked in the 1970s with Dr Wernher von Braun, the German rocket scientist I mentioned earlier, who was employed by NASA after the Second World War. She said that he told her when he knew that he was dying of cancer that there was a plan to introduce a series of fake enemies to justify the weaponisation of space (and a lot more, in truth). They would be, in order: the Soviet Union; terrorists; Third World country 'crazies' – 'countries of concern' in current parlance; asteroids; and the last one would be the threat of an 'alien' invasion. Von Braun told her not to believe any of this when it happened, because it would all be a lie and a hoax. Note how these themes have manifested in Hollywood movies. You are going to see increasing promotion of 'alien invasion' material in the media and elsewhere as people are conditioned to believe the lie that would be used to 'bring the world together' against a 'common enemy' and justify a world government, world army, etc., etc. The 'aliens' aren't *coming* – they have been here all along, and when benevolent ones involved in removing the Reptilians make themselves known (which they will at some point) they will be cast as the evil threat to human existence. I have noticed already that the possibility of an 'alien invasion', which has always been either laughed at or never discussed, is appearing more often in the mainstream. There was even a joint study on

the subject published in 2011 by Pennsylvania State University and the NASA Planetary
Science Division called *Would Contact with Extraterrestrials Benefit or Harm Humanity? A
Scenario Analysis.* 'ETI could attack and kill us, enslave us, or potentially even eat us',
the study said. 'ETI could attack us out of selfishness or out of a more altruistic desire to
protect the galaxy from us.' We can expect more of this sort of stuff as humanity is
prepared for another Big Lie. The holographic UFO projections are part of a mass mind-
manipulation programme called 'Project Blue Beam', and so too are the holographic
sky-projections of religious figures to be tailored to the dominant religion of the region. I
have explained Project Blue Beam in previous books and it is all part of the fake 'end
times' scenario that includes the Mayan, Hopi and similar information and prophecies.
    Another aspect of this is the changing of the 'heavens'. There are ever-increasing
reports as I write of the Moon being out of phase and changing angle. Moon-watchers
have said that either the Moon has rotated to the right or the Earth has rotated to the
left. They say this began at the time of the lunar eclipse on December 21st, 2010. Note
the date, December 21st, the date that many say is the end of the Mayan Great Cycle on
December 21st, 2012. It was the first lunar eclipse on the winter solstice (summer
solstice in the Southern Hemisphere) since 1638. Constellations such as Orion have been
reported to be moving around; and the Inuit people, or 'Eskimos', like many others,
have reported that the Sun is rising in a different place and stars have changed
positions. Don't let mainstream science tell you differently, as they will. You don't need
a degree in astronomy when you have watched the Sun come up every day of your life
and it is suddenly appearing someplace else to see that there has been a change. The
same with 'sun gazers' who stare at the Sun as it rises or sets every day and say that it
has changed position. It is far more likely, of course, that the Earth has changed position.
The Reptilians are also changing the hologram in the Saturn–Moon Matrix and when
they do that they can change the positions of stars in the projection – just as an operator
can do with the projection of the heavens onto the ceiling of a planetarium. The rabbit
hole is so deep; the scale of the illusion is so vast, and we need to appreciate this to
grasp what is happening. Magnetic north is moving by the day and this, together with
mass bird and fish deaths, is being connected with the 'End Times' prophecies from
various sources that include the same basic themes. The oil disaster in the Gulf of
Mexico has been connected to the Hopi end-times prophecy about the seas turning
black. But the moving magnetic north and the mass die-offs could be the work of
HAARP and connected technologies making the prophecies appear to be coming true.
The Hopi seventh sign is: 'You will hear of the sea turning black, and many living things
dying because of it.' The ninth and final sign is: 'You will hear of a dwelling-place in the
heavens, above the earth, that shall fall with a great crash. It will appear as a blue star.
Very soon after this, the ceremonies of my people will cease.' The 'signs' and prophecies
have been encoded and communicated in the ancient 'past' specifically to make them
appear to be happening now and in the next few years. One reason for this is to, yet
again, manipulate people to give away their powers of critical thinking and intuitive
knowing to what they believe is an unfolding 'God-driven' destiny that is playing out
when it is all manipulation. When people believe this they empower the illusion even
more and help to create an energetically self-fulfilling prophecy. Many Christians and
Jews will stand back and not challenge horrors imposed by the bloodlines because they
believe that it is 'God's will' to fulfil 'His' prophecy for 'Armageddon', the 'final battle'

between 'good' and 'evil'. Where is Armageddon? In *Israel*. It is a place known as 'Har Megiddo'. I have been saying for years that the plan is to trigger a Third World War in the Middle East involving Israel. Armageddon is the time when Christians believe that the Messiah will return to earth and defeat the Antichrist/Devil/Satan/Lucifer, but you can be sure that those promoted as the 'good guys' fighting evil will be the truly evil. It is a movie called 'Claptrap and Bollocks' that they are making happen through calculated manipulation. It is nothing to do with 'God's will'. How many people have asked the question generation after generation: Why would a loving God allow this or that horror to happen and even say that it *should* happen? Answer: A 'loving God' doesn't do that – the *Reptilian* 'gods' do that in league with the 'Greys' and others. *Please, please,* don't buy into it. The themes of where we are today are the same as they always were no matter what the 'yuga'. Yes, the level of sophistication and scientific knowledge has moved on; but has the outcome? In ancient times untold numbers were killed in wars and mass human sacrifice. Today the wars continue with far greater killing potential and mass human sacrifice is now pepper-bombing Baghdad or Tripoli. The Second World War cost 55 million lives only 70 years ago, and now a third one is being manipulated. Is this really an advance on what was happening in the alleged nadir of the 'Dark Age' in AD 500? Only in the number of dead people – there are more now. Oh, I hear, but we are much more compassionate today. So why don't the fundamentals change? I'm sure there were compassionate people in AD 500, too. It is about *Consciousness*, not ages, and of course energetic changes can affect that, but not to the degree that the fundamentals change in society as a whole. Those controlling the Matrix don't *want* those fundamentals to change. Instead of fighting to plunder and slaughter, we now describe the same outcome as fighting for peace or protecting civilians. The Truth Vibrations are impacting upon that perception today – not any yuga or Mayan cycle. Vibrational change is not being directed into our reality by any new age or cycle, but to break the hack and awaken humanity from its mental, emotional and vibrational prison cell.

Reptiles on the barricades

The Reptilians and their human hybrids have been preparing for the challenge of the Truth Vibrations, and that is the major motive behind HAARP. They are seeking to (a) stop the Truth Vibrations penetrating our reality to the extent that they potentially could, and (b) prevent people from tuning into them and being awakened by them. HAARP has the potential of encircling the planet with a 'full-body shield' together with other facilities around the world including the enormous 'American' (Cabal) underground base at Pine Gap in central Australia. Bernard Eastlund, the original patents holder for HAARP technology, said that the shield could be created with 'relativistic particles'. These are charged particles moving at the speed of light. This, together with GWEN-type technology on the ground, Smart Grids in the home and workplace, and so on, comprises a multi-level energetic defence shield to the Truth Vibrations. What was called the 'Star Wars' defence shield, created allegedly to stop incoming missiles, was primarily a front for establishing a planetary defence shield to block incoming information and awareness, and benevolent extraterrestrials/interdimensionals. The Saturn–Moon Matrix operates within a certain frequency band and the more we open our minds beyond that band the less we are influenced by the transmissions. There was little danger of that before the Truth Vibrations began to open minds, and the Reptilian Alliance has been preparing to resist this change that would bring their house down. This is why, at the very point that humans are demonstrably awakening we are being hit by what is described in this book. They needed to increase the level of mind and emotional suppression to stop people expanding awareness beyond the confines of the Saturn–Moon Matrix. HAARP and associated technologies are a Matrix support system on Earth manipulating the energy field with which we interact. CERN's Large Hadron Collider is involved in this, too, along with what is happening in the vast and interconnected underground bases and cites and those inside gouged-out mountains. Rapidly increasing sources of radiation, not least from Fukushima, are also part of this shield, among other things, and the destabilising of the human body receiver–transmitter system together with chemicals in food and drink, fluoride in drinking water (with lithium on the wish-list), toxic vaccinations and genetic modification of food. Metals in chemtrails are also connected and so is the information-distorting pollution of the seas and water sources with chemicals, radiation and what happened with the oil catastrophe in the Gulf of Mexico. This distortion has since been carried on the tidal flows to a much wider expanse of the world's oceans. You don't need to see the oil on the surface to have information distortion by oil in the sea. This is the same principle that I highlighted earlier with regard to homeopathy. The ingredients in homeopathic remedies are diluted and diluted until there is no ingredient left – but the *information* from the ingredient is still there. The entire receiver– transmitter systems and information fields of the planet, humanity and everything else are being attacked from every angle at the moment to block the Truth Vibrations transformation and the demise of the Saturn–Moon Matrix. Nuclear devices exploded in the Van Allen Belts that significantly increased their radiation levels was also part of the multi-faceted defence shield. The satellite network is involved in this, too. There is so much going on that we don't know about – including a challenge being mounted to those controlling Saturn and the Moon. We are not alone. There is an enormous effort underway to set humanity free and it is happening across multiple dimensions from those we would call 'extraterrestrials' to pure awareness.

The Reptilian game plan is this: They establish a vibrational defence shield to maintain the Earth's atmosphere within frequency bands that will cause most of humanity to remain asleep. They know that some will be conscious enough and open-minded enough to awaken and that is the reason for the police state and fine-detail surveillance technology and programmes. They are seeking out those who are breaking free from the mind prison. The DNA database is being created to have everybody's unique frequency on file so they can target the awakening directly on their frequency to either take them out or block their DNA receiver–transmitter systems. They don't want such people in their Brave New World. They plan a mass cull of the global population because the current numbers, or even a significantly large section, could be lethal to their plans, as I will explain in a moment. I have been saying for nearly 20 years that the plan was to microchip every child at birth. This is to externally control their reality and vibrational state from the time they enter this world. Their very thoughts would be controlled throughout their lives and any source of information that could open their minds would be blocked or banned. Dr Richard Day, the Rockefeller insider, said in 1969 that 'books will just disappear from libraries'. The Truth Vibrations would not be able to connect with people in that state and the Earth would be a fully-fledged prison camp serving the interests and demands of the Reptilians. Movement would be severely restricted in line with Agenda 21. Think of Chinese society today and multiply the level of control many, many times and you'll have something like the world they want to impose. China today is the basic blueprint, started by Freemason and Illuminati placeman, Mao Zedong, but the Brave New World version would be far more extreme and severe. The final 'end game' is to change the atmosphere of the planet to better suit the Reptilians so that they can more easily openly manifest once they have a dramatically smaller population that is mind- controlled to the point of being nothing more than robotic slaves in the world of Agenda 21. This is another crucial reason for unleashing all those sources of radiation and punching holes in the ionosphere – changing the atmosphere to suit the Reptilians. They are planning to mutate human genetics to accept a much more irradiated atmosphere for the half a billion to a billion slaves they wish to survive the 'cull'.

We have the power

There is *nothing* more important in anyone's life – I don't care who it is – than to focus on the situation that we are facing and what we can do about it. *Everything* comes from this focus – our own life experience in its entirety and that of our children and grandchildren. I am 59 as I write this. I won't be living in a global prison camp for anything like as long as children and young people today; but I care deeply about what happens to them and every moment of my life in this reality is focused on making sure that the nightmare is avoided and the Matrix dismantled. This is what we have come to do so *let's get on with it.* I cannot emphasise enough that we are not alone in this endeavour and we can make our crucial contribution to this multidimensional effort if we put aside the manufactured fault lines and divisions of race, religion, culture, 'class', politics and income bracket. None of these things matter to the Reptilians and their hybrids. To them, they are only tools to engineer the essential 'divide and rule'. They will enslave Jewish people in the global prison camp as much as they will Christians, Muslims, Hindus and everyone else. They will kill them equally, too, if they think that it benefits the outcome they are seeking. Put these divisions aside before we are divided and ruled into concentration camps and what is left of freedom is dispatched to oblivion. We are so close already. The answer is *energetic,* as the prison is energetic. We have the power, *more* than the power, to dismantle the vibrational prison walls if we understand even the basics of how it all works. The Control System is not structured by accident to generate incoherent heart energy and low-vibrational thought and emotion such as fear, stress, anger, frustration and depression. This is done to maintain humanity in a low-vibrational, incoherent state that generates the energy they want, enslaves people in close-minded ignorance and ... *here's the big one* ... projects a constant supply of low-vibrational electromagnetic energy into the Earth energy 'sea' in which the Truth Vibrations are now circulating ever more powerfully. HAARP and all the connecting radiation technologies are being used to further suppress the vibrational state of that 'sea', because that is vital to their Truth Vibration defence strategy. People would be amazed if they knew the impact that humans are having on the Earth's energy field minute by minute. Technology can now measure this, and great spikes occur in the field"s vibrational state when there is a global reaction to something such as 9/11.

Obviously, the fear and emotion generated by the 9/11 attacks would have suited the goals of the conspirators, and this was another benefit for them; but we can have an incredible impact on opening the Earth field to the Truth Vibrations and scupper the HAARP brigade and other sources of energetic suppression. We all have a significant individual effect, but when we get together in groups and vast numbers the effect is extraordinary. Satanists say that they perform their repetitive rituals at certain points on the Earth because they leave 'strong impressions upon the Morphic Field'. The bloodlines manipulate large gatherings for royal weddings, religious rituals and other events to trawl the energy that is generated. They *know* the collective power of human energy and they are terrified of its potential. We need to use this energy to bring down the house of cards and to do this we have to put aside all non-essentials and *focus*. Another reason that they want a colossal cull of the human population is because they are well aware of the potential collective power of the human heart and Consciousness if enough people wake up sufficiently to understand the power that we have. I have known for many years that the most important contribution of my all-day speaking events around the world is the collective energy that is generated into the Earth's energy field by a gathering of like-minds and like-hearts coming together as One.

The heart is the key. The heart in its hormonal expression connects with the endocrine system that includes the pineal and pituitary glands in the brain which are part of the psychic senses that we call the third eye. The heart projects the body's most powerful electromagnetic field, and when it is in harmony with the brain and nervous system we are transformed to a whole new level of intelligence, love, mental and emotional balance, clarity of thought, intuitive knowing and connection to higher Consciousness. The heart is at the centre of everything. This is why the global conspiracy has systematically targeted the human heart. People have been sent into my life in an attempt to disrupt me in just this way, but ultimately they failed. The manipulators are fearful of the heart's true power and they also know what mayhem is caused mentally, emotionally and 'physically' when the heart is out of sync with the brain and the nervous system. They manipulate events to trigger states of low-vibrational, imbalanced emotion. They want us angry, frustrated, fearful, resentful, depressed and irritable. They want us to close our hearts and make them a bystander in the process of decoding reality and perception. My friend, Mike Lambert, at the Shen Clinic on the Isle of Wight, was telling me about some 'Kirlian' photographs that he saw which capture activity in the human energy-field. He said that so many people were found to have almost no energy activity around the heart when that area should be an electromagnetic power station. This is how the Control System closes people down, disconnects them from their infinite self and enslaves them in the five senses. HAARP and all the connecting radiation technologies are also being used to further suppress the vibrational state of the Earth's energy 'sea' and therefore manipulate the fish – humans – into those same low-vibrational states. This creates a feedback loop as people are influenced into incoherent states by the energy 'sea' and then feed back these patterns into the 'sea' to further empower its negative influence. We have to break that circuit and transform the individual and collective energy-field from the incoherence that the Control System depends upon to the coherence that will set us individually and collectively free. We can manifest energetic harmony from the manipulated chaos by *loving* each other. We *will* do this if enough people will join us in the awakening project that I will describe shortly.

There is a phenomenon known as 'hypercommunication' which means to connect 'individual minds' on a psychic, intuitive level to form a communication network. Bushmen in Africa communicate through hypercommunication and so we have the term 'bush telegraph'. Researchers of hypercommunication say that if enough minds (and I would say *hearts*) connected in this way they would have a 'god-like' power to create and re-shape the world that we live in. This is certainly true, especially when you think that human brain activity operates in the same frequency band as Earth's resonant frequencies. We are One with the Earth and there is two-way communication. The collective power of human hearts and minds could break the spell of the Matrix and overcome the influence of HAARP, GWEN, Smart Grids ... all of them. They are two-stone weaklings compared with the power of the collective human heart and mind/consciousness. This is the power source of change that has the Control System trembling in its boots. Minds and hearts connecting as a single whole produce the power in rain dances that changes the electromagnetic field to make it rain. We can transform the world from a prison to a paradise merely by focusing together in sufficient numbers to release the transformative power of the collective human heart and mind. Author and researcher Bärbel Mohr writes: 'Whenever a great many people focus their attention or consciousness on something similar like Christmas time, football world championship or the funeral of Lady Diana in England, then certain random number generators in computers start to deliver ordered numbers instead of the random ones.' Numbers are digital versions of vibrational waveform states. The Global Consciousness Project was established in 1998 to study the effect of human consciousness on the 'physical' world. The project has a network of random event generators on every continent and in more than 50 locations to measure the effect of human consciousness. Spikes in activity are produced during events of global and national focus. They conclude from the findings so far: 'The results are evidence that the physical world and our mental world of information and meaning are linked in ways that we don't yet understand.' Or maybe we do. Experiments have shown that DNA can imprint information into energy fields, just as flowers and people imprint their information into water. This is called the 'phantom DNA effect'. We can communicate with each other and connect with each other through heart, consciousness and DNA transmissions, and this is how telepathy and remote healing is possible. All this is happening beyond what we call time and space in levels of reality where everything is One. This is the antidote to the Control System and the Reptilian manipulation, but we have to get tens of millions involved.

Awakening the World – Every Heart Makes a difference

This brings me to something that I launched through my website: www.davidicke.com, in July 2011. We need people all over the world in every town, city, village and community to step forward as organisers of groups and gatherings of people willing to come together *regularly* – several times a week – to connect their energy fields and project love, peace and harmony into the atmosphere. *The more that come together the better.* We need massive gatherings organised at known 'sacred sites' which are perceived as 'sacred' because they are located at major vortex points where the planetary impact is so much greater. I have called this project '*Awakening the World –*

Every Heart Makes a Difference'. You will
find a section with that name on my
website where people all over the world
can communicate and organise together.
Every day we bring people together at
specific times for 20 minutes through the
website to connect our hearts and minds,
and focus love and heart coherence either
on the planet in general or a specific
place, person or event. We want tens of
millions coming together as soon as
possible – *hundreds* of millions eventually
– and what a difference this will make to
the world (Fig 349). We are diluting the
energy of fear, anger, hatred and hostility

Figure 349: The collective power of the human heart will
bring an end to the age of enslavement

and replacing it with love, peace and harmony – everything the Control System doesn't
want. Please get involved because this will change the tide in the hearts of human
beings and those that seek to control us. Make a decision to dedicate yourself to this
cause and then follow your intuitive *knowing* and everything will fall into place. The
'Force' will be with you because you have made a decision to connect with the 'Force'.
The transformation in other levels of reality as the Reptilians and Greys are challenged
by benevolent extraterrestrials/interdimensionals is already well advanced. We only
need to ground that energy of transformation and freedom in our reality. This is what
we came here for. The global population is moving past seven billion and this is a latent
force of incredible power. We need to wake up to that truth and harness that power for
the greater good of all. What a transformation there will be if hundreds of millions

awakened to their true
power and embarked
on the work that I am
asking for here (Figs
350 and 351). There is
nothing you have to do
to take part other than
to focus your heart and
connect with others to
send out love, peace
and harmony into the
energetic atmosphere.
Organisers of events at
sacred sites and other
locations just need to
let us know the time
and place and we'll
publicise it on my
website. The world will
benefit in a most

Figure 350: Nothing can escape the
transforming energies and
information of the Truth Vibrations

Figure 351: The Truth Vibrations are
dismantling the energetic foundation
of the Control System

fundamental way from these collective energy transmissions and you will see the world changing for the better as the energetic distortions from hate and fear are dissolved along with the effect of that energy on human perception and behaviour. Wars, engineered catastrophes and financial meltdowns are instigated for many reasons, but the most important one is to produce ever more of that energy from human reactions and responses. This is also another element of the Truth Vibration defence shield, but this can be countered and far more when we gather together and call in the Truth Vibrations. By doing so, you will connect with them and become a conduit and transmitter of them in this reality:

> As the consciousness level of your planet raises itself, those of you Light Workers who are working together to raise your consciousness will be able to hold more and more refined vibrations, and so we will be able to use you as a catalyst to be able to feed in more and more energies ... As more of you raise yourselves to meet the challenge, so we can awaken more of these energies.

This is the profound truth that we need to understand – *and fast* – to be able to bring down the Control System which depends for its survival on the transmission of low-vibrational brain/mind energy that it constantly manipulates humanity to produce. Doing what I am asking for here is not only of crucial benefit to our collective reality; it will make transformative changes in everyone who contributes. Taking the time regularly to sit quietly and focus on heart coherence and send out love, peace and harmony will manifest as love, peace and harmony within you. This will produce coherence in heart electrical and vibrational activity bringing into harmony the trinity of heart, brain and nervous system. This harmony will unleash your fantastic potential for clear thought and inspired knowing that comes when heart, mind and body are working as one unit. Remember that there are more nerves going from the heart to the brain than going the other way, and the electrical and magnetic fields of the heart are 60 times stronger (and potentially much more) than the brain. Love, appreciation and caring are 5,000 times more powerful than fear, hate, anger, resentment, frustration and depression. We clearly have the power to change the nature of the Earth's energy field to create feedback loops of love, peace and harmony to replace the fear, hatred and chaos that we currently have. The 'head' got us into this mess and the heart, in harmony with the 'head', is going to get us out of it. Heart coherence also increases the power of intuition and the immune system. Everyone's a winner here. As you give, so you will receive. Mind has created our prison reality and heart will set us free of that. The heart will always find a way. Mind is supposed to serve heart, not marginalise and suppress it.

Following the script

We live in an illusion within an illusion – the Matrix hack within the virtual-reality Universe. As I have explained, the 'Queen Bee' (Saturn–Moon) broadcasts the waveform information 'hack' that activates, or '*hack*tivates', the Reptilian program within 'junk' DNA and blocks other parts of the DNA and the human decoding system so that we see what they want us to see and don't see what we would otherwise see. We can be completely controlled by the Matrix and be no more than human robots responding to data input, or we can open our hearts and minds and see beyond what others can see. Secret-society rituals are designed to lock their initiates into the Matrix broadcasts even more powerfully, and these are the people who mostly administer the system, run the banks and corporations and end up in political power. If you tap into the program through one of the major secret-society terminals, such as the Fabian Society, you can write incredibly prophetic books like George Orwell and Aldous Huxley did, because the plan has been encoded in the Saturn– Moon Matrix and human DNA for thousands of years. The only way out of this for humanity is to break the hack and deny the system the low-vibrational energy that it needs. Multiple levels of reality are working to this end. We have to play our part from within the hack and that means opening our hearts and minds to the Truth Vibrations and starting again with a blank sheet of paper when it comes to what we *think* that we know. What people 'know' is what the Matrix has *programmed* them to know. Question *everything* no matter how long you have believed it. If it doesn't stand up to examination then ditch it – religious belief, political belief, reality belief; it's all *Matrix* claptrap. We need to start again and this time let the truth in through the heart – intuition, *knowing* – and break free of the head where the Matrix overwhelmingly seizes control. Head domination = Matrix. Heart domination = *freedom* from the Matrix.

The first step is to believe nothing and question everything that you think you know. Question everything that you have read in this book, too. What I have written makes no claim to be definitive, because there is always more to know. Nor will it be 100 per cent accurate in every detail. How could it be in the suppressed and manipulated energetic environment that we experience daily, and when those in control are doing everything they can to block information that would expose them? But I am very confident about the themes, and when it comes to what is happening with the global conspiracy within five-sense reality the truth of this can now be seen in daily events. What I said would happen in books nearly 20 years ago is happening. People will have to use their intuition about the Matrix and the hack. Does it make sense of the world? Does it *feel* right? If not, sling it. We are in the end times of *belief*, or we had better be. People say that we must believe *something*. But *why*? I believe *nothing*. I have a perception of how things are at any point, but I don't *believe* it in the sense of the perception being so immovable that it solidifies into a belief. There is only the way that I see things in any moment, in the full knowledge that there is always, but *always*, more to know. My perception is constantly fluid and moves on with new events, experiences and information. This is what I mean by not believing anything. Current perception and belief are not the same. Fluidity of perception is a manifestation of the heart intuitively dancing with the Universe and beyond seeking out ever more awareness. Dogmatic belief is mind, the head – the Matrix. The head is a good servant, but a terrible master. Breaking out of the prison of belief is essential for another reason – our feedback relationship with the Matrix. If we believe what the Matrix tells us to believe we then communicate that same belief back to the Matrix and empower its effect when it is re-fed back to us. The feedback relationship means that we are mind-controlling ourselves in many ways and empowering the Matrix with belief systems that can be used to influence others to believe the same. You break this cycle when you move from belief into 'this is my perception in this moment, but I know it is nothing like the whole story and I am constantly open to revising my perception in the light of experience and information'. People are held fast in the feedback loops by a belief in religion, politics, science and all the pillars of perception control. Thousands of protesters demanding 'freedom' on the streets of Egypt were on their collective knees several times a day facing Mecca – the Kaaba cube (Saturn). *Freedom?* (Fig 352) They are so confused they don't know what freedom is; and I see the same in America where many Christian patriots demanding freedom are self-enslaved by self-identifying with being both a Christian and a patriot. They have

Figure 352: Many Egyptians who campaigned for 'freedom' broke off from their protests several times a day to get on their knees and face the Kaaba cube (Saturn). They want *'freedom'?*

forgotten that being a 'Christian' and a 'patriot' are *experiences* and not who they are – Consciousness. A self-identity of being a Christian and a patriot is to self-identify with limitation and body–mind. The same applies to all religions and self-identities based on human concepts and experiences.

Who am I?

We need a total transformation in the perception of 'self' to free us from the Matrix programs which feed us the belief that we are only a powerless 'Little Me'. The Matrix wants us to believe that we are only our body, name, job and life story, or that we are answerable to some 'God' that we must serve and please. We must stop giving the Matrix what it wants and start giving it what it *doesn't* want. This means ending our self-identity with the body and Matrix symbols such as name, job and income bracket. They are not who we *are*; they are what we are *experiencing*. What we are is Infinite Consciousness and Awareness *having* those experiences. Our point of observation and awareness moves away from body–mind and into Consciousness when we change our *self- identity* from body–mind to Consciousness. We are then in this world 'physically', but not of this world in terms of the point of awareness from which we observe it. We start to see what we couldn't see before – including how we can best contribute to human freedom. Consciousness speaks to us most powerfully through the heart in our intuition and knowing, and this must be our guide if we are to overcome the prisons and delusions of mind. No matter what you *think*; what do you *feel*? What do you *know*? The system has desensitised people from a connection to heart awareness, because the Reptilians and their hybrids know the consequences of a heart-inspired humanity for their plans for total global control. They must entrap us in mind–head for that collective control to be possible. Turn off the television to stop that fundamental source of subliminal programming; and instead of mind-numbing games shows, reality shows and twisted 'news', spend the time sitting quietly and accessing your true and infinite power. The more you focus on life and self through the heart the more powerful it will become – *you* will become – and the more *intuitive* and *knowing* you will be. The Illuminati say in their own documents that the only danger to their plans is what they call 'maverick people'; and truly maverick people are *heart* people. They are unpredictable, intuitive and inspired. They are guided by Consciousness unmolested by the predictable programs of the 'I can't' mind. Words do not suffice to express the importance of humanity becoming heart-centred and heart-guided. We are being bombarded with reasons to feel fear, worry, anxiety, stress, anger and frustration. All these emotional states close down the heart centre and disturb a coherent energetic and information connection between heart, brain and nervous system. This dilutes the energetic power of the heart and allows the brain to control perception. We need to transform our interaction with the Matrix and what we call Life. We need to remain calm when the mind wants to panic or 'lose it' in the face of events and personal experience. When these things happen, remember that you are Infinite Awareness having an experience. This will help you to be an *observer* of the experience rather than *being* the experience. The emotional impact of the experience will then be so much less traumatic. Those that choose to take part in 'Awakening the World' groups and mass-focus every day will find that their ability to detach will increase all the time. Anyone can sit quietly and move their point of attention to the heart. You will feel such calmness and the intuitive inspiration will flow. We must stay calm through what is coming, because there are going to many challenges, shocks and surprises. The Reptilian Alliance and their bloodline hybrids are going to be pushing on with their Control System for a while yet and they will be orchestrating events to keep people in fear and bewilderment while quite possibly making the prophecies and the 2012 belief system appear to be happening. At the same time we are going to be seeing the gathering impact of the Truth Vibrations on the human awakening and in terms of dramatic solar activity, earthquakes and volcanoes that are not caused by HAARP, but by something changing in the Earth's crystal core as a result of the changing energetic environment. This is what I was told would happen in 1990. We need to be heart-centred enough not to be pulled in by all the reasons to be fearful that will be thrown at us. If we react to what is happening – and planned – with anger, resentment, hatred and fear we will be feeding the Matrix with precisely the energy it requires to pollute the energy 'sea' with those emotional fields that will influence others to feel and react in the same way. I have watched people who were fine and happy go into a room (energy field) filled with anger and hostility and very soon they start reacting in the same way. This is happening to humanity second by second. We are manipulated to fill the energy sea with toxic emotional fields and other people are influenced by that to produce more of the same energy and the downward spiral goes on. *We have to break the circuit.*

Beyond protest – the non-compli-dance

This brings me to protests. They serve a purpose as an expression of public opinion, but how many protests change anything? Upwards of half-a-million people or more protested in the streets of London against the imminent invasion of Iraq in 2003, but Iraq was still invaded. There were mass protests in the same city in 2011 over criminal levels of student fees for college and university courses, but the fees were still raised. How many 'million-people marches' have there been to Washington D.C. and how many changed a thing? Greeks were in the streets in great numbers in 2011 opposing the draconian austerity programmes imposed by their government on the insistence of the European Union and IMF. What happened? The measures were passed into law.

Protests don't frighten the bloodlines. For goodness sake, they have been *manipulating* them in North Africa and the Middle East and earlier in Eastern Europe. They allow the cover of 'people power' to hide their calculated manipulations and when protests become violent, often through bloodlines' agents provocateurs, they have the excuse to further impose a police state. Angry protests also do what? They add still more of that energy to the Earth energy-sea that is already full to overflowing with it. The bloodlines *want* people to protest in this way, as we saw in London and other British cities in 2011. It gives them precisely what they want. Imagine the power of replacing stand-up, angry protests with sit-down silent focus where thousands join their hearts together and send out the energy of love and peace, which is thousands of times more powerful than anger and resentment. Instead of shouting slogans or abuse at the authorities and police, we just sit down in great numbers and silently focus on the heart. The impact of this all over the world day after day, week after week for as long as it takes would be incredible. And that's the point – *as long as it takes*. The only really effective protests are persistent and long-term and not one day and it's over. The protest, as an 'occupation', then becomes a form of non-cooperation with the oppressors and that is precisely what we need (so long as it is genuine and not Cabal-orchestrated for its own ends). I am not saying that everything will change overnight from 'heart gatherings' or from 'Awakening the World'. The Earth's energy field is very polluted and very sick and the effect of what I am asking for is cumulative; but transformation *will* come and ever more powerfully and obviously as we continue day after day, week after week, month after month and the numbers involved increase dramatically. This is what the bloodlines fear – not banner-waving anger. The Chinese government has waged a campaign of grotesque persecution against the Falun Gong movement – which combines meditation with exercises to calm the body and open the heart. Falun Gong also promotes truthfulness, compassion and forbearance. The bloodlines know the potential consequences for the Control System of this becoming widespread and they banned the practice when by 1999 there were 70 million people involved – more than were in the Chinese Communist Party. The sad, sick and ignorant Chinese dictators declared Falun Gong a 'heretical organisation' and practitioners have been jailed and suffered horrific torture and psychiatric abuse. What are they so afraid of? – Heart energy and awakening to Consciousness. This is their worst nightmare, as I said earlier. How about we stop protesting *against* things and start campaigning for things? Instead of being anti-war, let us be pro-peace. Instead of being anti-New World Order or anti-globalisation, let us be *for* freedom and justice for all. This may seem pedantic – but it isn't. A small change in wording and emphasis can mean a fundamental change in perception and energy that is generated for the cause. There is another aspect of 'Awakening the World – Every Heart Makes a Difference' and this is what I call the Non-compli-dance. If you riot and protest with anger, resentment and hostility, the Control System says 'thank you very much'. Let us give them exactly what they *don't* want, what they are terrified of – unleashed collective human energetic power. Instead of angry protest let us quietly focus on the heart and send out love, peace and harmony into the energy field with which we constantly interact – and then let us DANCE together with love, joy and laughter: *the non-compli-dance*. The energetic impact of this on yourself and the world will be amazing (Fig 353). Let us dance with love, joy and laughter and give that energy of love and harmony even more power as we swirl and

Figure 353: The non-compli-dance

twist our electromagnetic fields to whip up the electromagnetic energy-sea and make it dance with electrical power on the vibration of love and harmony. 'Awakening the World – Every Heart Makes a Difference' and the non-compli-dance. Together in love and harmony we are unstoppable. The Rothschilds have already cancelled the laxative order. We need to do this constantly and in our tens of millions – hundreds of millions all over the world.

There is something else that the bloodlines and their masters are terrified of – non-cooperation. I see people marching in protest against something and then they go home and continue to cooperate with the building of their collective prison. What use is that? There are so few controllers in full knowledge of what they are doing compared with the seven billion in the target population. They have to recruit from that population the law enforcement and administrators to impose their agenda. There are simply not enough of them to do it alone. When we stop cooperating with our own enslavement, and those in dark suits and uniforms stop building a prison for themselves and their children and grandchildren, the house of cards will fall. We need to organise people together in large numbers to cease to 'comply' with anything that advances the agenda for mass human control. We have to do this in large numbers or the few will be picked off. *Scale* is what we need. Those who are not directly involved need to support those who are. Here are some examples and there are countless others: When homes are foreclosed by the banks because of the behaviour of the banks in crashing the economy, people refuse to leave and the non-foreclosed support them. If people did this in their hundreds of thousands and millions the system would collapse. It couldn't cope. We refuse to allow Smart Grids to be installed in our homes to bathe us permanently in radiation and control our minds. Don't let anyone into your home from Smart Grids and get together with others to peacefully stop anyone installing anything on the outside. How would the Smart Gridders cope if they faced this at millions of homes? They couldn't. It must be clear from what you have read in this book that debate and dialogue is irrelevant to these bloodline agents and gofers. They have an agenda and nothing is going to stop it unless *we* do. If you are involved in anything connected to these bloodlines and their agents in power, refuse to cooperate. Boycott anything that they are involved with. It is your right to choose what you will and will not do. Don't go to college or university until the fees are vastly reduced or deleted altogether. *This* will impact on the system – not a day on the streets giving them the energy that they want. You might not pass your exams? Well, is this not preferable to a lifetime of debt? Life does not begin and end with a piece of paper confirming your *degree* of programming. Refuse to vote in political El-ections. But the 'other side' might get in? It doesn't *matter* – there is only one side under different names. It doesn't matter who you vote for because the Hidden Hand is always El-ected. You only have to look around to see all the different ways that we can refuse to cooperate, refuse to comply, and send shockwaves through a system that depends for its

Figure 354: What are you doing down there? Human race *get off your knees*

survival on our compliance. We need to dance to a new vibrational beat in the non-compli-dance, which is not only about dancing, but noncompliance. *Come on people*, we need to get this organised; and not tomorrow – *now*. Instead of protesting outside government buildings where the oil rags of the system work, go directly to the engineers of the conspiracy, the Rothschilds, Rockefellers, Soros, Brzezinski, and the others. Find out where they are making public appearances and *peacefully* expose them and send them love to balance their loveless existence. These people are seeking to kill you and your kids and enslave whoever is left in ways that even Orwell understated. *Why are we just leaving them to get on with it?*

Every day you can see hundreds of sheep controlled by a shepherd (authority figure) and a sheep dog (fear). They trot along with a baa, baa, baa, complying with commands, conceding to fear and mostly merely following the one in front because this is what they have been programmed to do. I have, of course, just described how humanity is controlled. We obey authority either mindlessly or through fear of the consequences of not doing so. *ENOUGH!* The shepherd and the sheepdog have no power over the sheep except for the power that the sheep give away to them. What would happen if those sheep went off in any direction they chose and refused to comply with the shepherd and the sheepdog? Very few would have to do this before the perceived power of the shepherd and sheepdog was exposed for what it really is – *non-existent*. Their power to enforce behaviour on the sheep comes not from them, but from the *sheep* conceding their power and uniqueness to them. Human sheep need to stop doing this and everything will change, but don't think about it forever – *do it*. We need to move on this. There is a tidal wave of control about to descend – it is already happening – and we need to smack it straight back at them through exposure, non-compliance and non-cooperation. *Human race get off your knees!* (Fig 354).

Uniforms awaken

All of the above applies even more profoundly to those in uniform and system-administration who are not knowingly seeking to impose mass human enslavement. This means the great majority who follow orders and Matrix DNA impulses who are pawns in a game they don't understand. A message to every soldier in the world: You are not serving your country; you are serving the forces that are in the process of *destroying* your country and establishing a permanent prison state for you, your children and grandchildren. Every time you fire a gun or enforce a freedom-busting law on the system's behalf, you are further condemning your children to a nightmare. How does that feel? This has to be faced, my friends, or you will complete the job. It is time to walk away, to take another path; or stay in your job and do it differently as a public servant, not a bloodline enforcer. You are serving a system that doesn't care any more about you than it does the rest of us. All that 'support the troops' stuff is only to manipulate you and the public into fighting and supporting wars of conquest and slaughter. They hang you out to dry once you are no longer any use to them because of trauma to mind and body. Since 2001, 26,000 American soldiers have been pressured and manipulated into signing a 'personality disorder' discharge when they have been injured in combat. This extraordinary mendacity and callousness saved the US government $14.2 billion in disability and medical benefits. *This is what they really think of you, soldier.* 'Support the troops', eh? Sergeant Chuck Luther told the US Committee of House Veterans Affairs in 2010 about his treatment by the government and military after he was severely wounded and blinded by mortar fire. Sergeant Luther had been serving for 'dozens of years' and won 22 honours, but all that counted for nothing when he was no longer fit to fight for the orchestrators of tyranny. Doctors pressed him to sign documents which said that his blindness was caused by a pre-existing condition – *personality disorder.* Once you sign these forms you will receive no disability benefits or long-term medical care. Luther rightly refused and was then placed in a storage closet for more than a month under enforced sleep deprivation until he signed the documents. This is a man wounded and blinded in action. He told the House Committee:

> I was assaulted, held down, had my pants ripped from the left thigh and given an injection of something that put me to sleep. When I awoke I was strapped down to a combat litter and had a black eye and cuts to my wrist from the zip ties. I was under guard 24/7.

> I was constantly called a piece of crap, a faker and other derogatory things. They kept the lights on and played all sorts of music from rap to heavy metal very loud all night. These were some of the tactics that we would use on insurgents that we captured to break them to get information and confessions.

> I went through this for four weeks and the ... Commander told me to sign this discharge and if I didn't they would keep me there for six more months and then kick me out when we got back to Fort Hood. Anyway, I said I didn't have a personality disorder and he told me if I signed the paperwork that I would get back home and get help and I would have all my benefits. After the endless nights of sleep deprivation, harassment and abuse, I finally signed just to get out of there. I was broken.

Real journalist Joshua Kors featured Chuck Luther's story in *The Nation* magazine under the telling headline: 'Disposable Soldiers'. He told the committee of other such cases. A soldier who was wounded by a rocket and won the Purple Heart was told that his deafness, which wasn't there before the rocket attack, was caused by 'personality disorder'. A sergeant who had his legs and arms punctured by grenade shrapnel was told that the injuries were caused by 'personality disorder' when the only personality disorder in sight applied to the person who was telling him this. A female soldier was told that profuse vaginal bleeding was caused by personality disorder by these military doctors-for-sale. Civilian doctors removed her uterus and appendix, but the military still insisted that everything was caused by 'personality disorder'. This denied her all benefits and she and her daughter ended up homeless. She had called Joshua Kors because she feared that her daughter would be raped at their homeless shelter. The Committee hearing was also treated to the truly despicable behaviour of Republican Steve Buyer who walked out in outrage that the army's reputation was being sullied. Now here is some real personality disorder. He said:

> I also would say this, I would never, even when I was chairman of a sub-committee or a full committee, ever put a reporter on a panel to testify. I would never do that. I think it's pretty shocking that you would even come here and provide testimony with regard to someone's medical condition. You're not a doctor. If you were a doctor they would knock you right upside the head for that. I'm not gonna do this, I can't, my integrity as a gentleman will not permit me to do this ... I will not participate, I'm not gonna do it, I'm not going to do it, it's wrong.

But what the army has done to Chuck Luther and 26,000 other soldiers is not wrong? It certainly wasn't Buyer's 'integrity' that made him walk out, so what could it have been? *Disgusting.* But this is what they think of you, people in uniform, including those at the TSA who are being irradiated to death by full-body scanners. British troops are killing and being killed in now numerous 'theatres of war', bombing civilians and fighting fake 'enemies' while back at home their families live on military bases in often slum accommodation. Henry Kissinger encapsulated what the bloodlines really think of 'the troops' when he said that military men were 'dumb, stupid animals' to be used as pawns for foreign policy. British Prime Minister David Cameron also let the truth slip when he said in response to members of the armed forces questioning his policy: 'You do the fighting and I'll do the talking.' This is how they see 'the troops'. We'll decide who you kill and you just do it without question. *How much longer are you going to take it?* When they try to bring in a compulsory military draft for their expanding wars of conquest, there must be a mass refusal. Cameron is the classic born-into-privilege narcissist who has never seen a bullet fired in anger. He'd probably run home crying to his mum if he ever did. Military and police of the world – *they don't give a shit about you.* You are just their enforcers, and the same with the dark-suits who administer the system for them. You and your families will end up in servitude the same as everybody else if you continue to serve the system that has your families in its sights. You are already enslaved, but too enslaved to see it.

Figure 355: It is time to stand up and look the suppressors in the eye. Enough!

The time is Now

The situation that we face is already dire, but far, far from hopeless. Are you *kidding?* The 'game' has only just *begun* as we at last understand the 'game'. Life is about choice and consequence, choice and consequence. This is the essential experience that gives us the chance to see through the illusion. We make different choices, we have different consequences. We make different *collective* choices, we have different collective consequences. You – *we* – are the key to everything. *We* are the 'world' and the 'world' is us. It is a collective holographic reflection of *us* – and so we can change it anytime we want. What are we waiting for? The Agenda was meant to be much more advanced than it is, but something went badly wrong for them in the unseen realms in the period around the turn of the Millennium. Rituals were happening in concert all over the world at that time to more fiercely enslave the human psyche, but they didn't work as planned. There is also a challenge well advanced to the Reptilian Alliance by other non-human groups both in this reality and others. So all is not lost, quite the opposite, but further prevarication isn't an option. We have to come together, release the lion within us, say 'no more,' and get on with it (Fig 355). We have to take responsibility for our lives and the world that we are helping to create.

People don't like responsibility; they would much rather blame someone else for their plight. But look at what we are doing when we machine-gun blame in all directions. We are saying that we don't have control over our lives – the people we are blaming do. Talk about giving your power away. We take that power back when we take responsibility because that is a statement that says: 'I am in control of my life. I created what I don't like and so I can create something different.' We can do this collectively now to change the world and bring down the Control System. The Reptilians and their bloodline hybrids are not omnipotent and all-powerful. They are in a tiny box of perception called Mind. Their state of being – insecurity, fear, the need to control, a desire for have power over others – will always deny them access to higher levels of awareness. They have had to develop their mind/intellect to an advanced

level, and this is why they impose their control so much through technological means and control of the mind – the same with the Greys. Humans can advance beyond the Control System's potential for perception when we open our minds and hearts to Consciousness. The Reptilians have manipulated humanity into a smaller box than they are in themselves, but we have the potential to escape this suppression if we go back to that blank sheet of paper without belief or preconceived ideas and let the Truth Vibrations fill our hearts and minds. The intent to connect with this transformative energy/information automatically connects you. You then have to decide if you are going to follow the intuitive urgings and knowing that will begin to flow (Fig 356). This is not rocket science or some complicated, complex process. I roll my eyes when I hear these long-drawn-out explanations by gurus of every kind telling people to do this, that and the other to become 'enlightened'. We *are* enlightened; it

Figure 356: Open your heart and you go beyond the Matrix

is our natural state. We only have to remove the barriers of belief and programming that entrap us in Mind and deny access to Consciousness. Free yourself from belief and programmed perceptions with the blank sheet of paper and state the intent to be connected with the Truth Vibrations and your higher levels of awareness. Then follow your intuitive knowing that you feel in your heart and everything else will take care of itself in the synchronistic sequences that follow. Clear your mind of all the clutter that doesn't matter. Imagine that you have ten minutes to live and you are looking back on your life. What really mattered? What was really important? Did it matter that the guy cut you up at the lights and made you get home a minute later than you would have done? Nope. Did it matter what somebody said to you or about you years ago, or even last week? Nope. Did it matter that your football team lost a big game, or even won it? Nope. What matters in that situation is how much you loved and were loved; how much joy and happiness you gave to others and others gave to you. Well, you don't have ten minutes to live, but you will fill your life with a whole lot more joy, contentment, love and happiness if you take that deathbed perception with you from hereon in. We allow ourselves to be constantly diverted into low-vibrational emotional states by things that simply don't matter. Mountains out of molehills, as they say. It's all diversion; the result of programmed responses and the tidal wave of low-vibrational thought and emotion in the energy 'sea'. The reptilian brain is, not surprisingly, a major access point for the Saturn–Moon Matrix and we can dramatically reduce its influence if we stay calm and stop reacting. The lizard brain doesn't think – it reacts; and it triggers actions before rational thought has had time to form. We can break that pattern if we count to 10 or 20, or whatever number it takes until the reactive reptilian-brain response has passed. It doesn't usually take more than a few seconds before the thought process kicks in. Nothing holds the lizard brain in check more than the coherent electrical fields of the heart. Everything comes from moving out of mind into Heart Consciousness. Just as you cannot solve problems with the same level of Consciousness that created them, to change the world we have to transcend the mind that created this cosmic lunatic asylum. We are the world and the world is us. When we change, the world must change – and the heart holds the key. I would also emphasise this: no matter what they do to our food and drink or what they throw at us in terms of HAARP, radiation and all the rest – Consciousness can overcome it all. For, in the end, it is all an illusion and Consciousness can control the illusion. I would also say that you don't have to constantly meditate, practice yoga, Tai Chi, 'breathe properly', go on a fast or whatever to open Mind to Consciousness. *You just do it.* I have never been involved in any of these things and the nearest I ever come to meditation is sitting quietly and 'having a ponder'. I know that their advocates, practitioners and gurus will say no, you must do this or that to 'connect'. That is their right. I am not saying don't do these things if they feel good to you. I am saying it is not necessary. So many people make the process of awakening to our true self sound so complicated. *It isn't.* It is a decision to awaken to Consciousness followed by listening to your intuitive knowing (heart) and letting it guide you through the experiences (not all of them 'nice') that take you home. No crystals or incense necessary. They can be pleasant to have around, but they are not *necessary*. The process is far simpler than so many make out.

It is vital that we don't focus on the Reptilian Control System succeeding in its goal. We will give it more power though the feedback loop if we do. We make prophecies

Figure 357: A new reality and a whole new way of living awaits us – we just have to grasp it

Figure 358: Come on, Control System. It's time to go

Figure 359: Humanity awakens and the Control System is no more

more likely to happen if we believe them. We need to clear our minds of any idea that the Reptilians will succeed; and clear them, too, of Mayan prophecies, Hopi prophecies, Nostradamus prophecies, *Book of Revelation* prophecies – *all of them*. We need to focus our hearts and minds instead on knowing that we are changing the world from the prison that it is to the paradise it once was and will be again. I didn't come here to make a few waves and leave. I came here with others in multiple realities to bring down the Control System and allow freedom and limitless possibility to reign. Millions of children have come here in the last few decades with awakened consciousness. They are often referred to as 'indigo children' and they retained their knowing as they crossed the vibrational divide. Would they be doing that if all that was waiting for them was a global prison camp? They are here to build the new world when the long era of human slavery is no more (Fig 357). The Control System is coming down. It won't seem like that for a while yet, but its time is coming to an end. *Know* it. *Be* it. The energetic schism, or distortion, on which the Control System is founded, is being healed by the Truth Vibrations and so the vibrational sands are shifting under its very foundations (Fig 358). The Reptilians and their hybrids are going to do everything they can to hold on and make their plans succeed, but we must not allow that possibility to manifest in our sense of reality – only that human enslavement ends and humanity awakens to its true and glorious self (Fig 359). There is a scene in one of the *Matrix* movies in which Neo is asking the Oracle about choice. She replied:

> You've already made the choice. Now you have to understand it. You didn't come here to make the choice, you've already made it. You're here to try to understand why you made it.

We all made the choice to be here now. Why? To be part of a peaceful, loving, global revolution of Consciousness that will think and love the prison out of existence and manifest paradise on Earth. How do we do that – as we *WILL*? We remember, remember, *remember.*

Remember who you are. Remember where you are and where you come from. Remember why you are here. Remember, remember, remember.

Remember.

Appendix I

The Bilderberg Group attendees in 2011

This is not necessarily a complete list, because some prefer not to appear on the official paperwork.

Belgium
Coene, Luc, *Governor, National Bank of Belgium*
Davignon, Etienne, *Minister of State* Leysen,
Thomas, *Chairman, Umicore*

China
Ying, Fu, *Vice Minister of Foreign Affairs*
Huang, Yiping, *Professor of Economics, China Center for Economic Research, Peking University*

Denmark
Eldrup, Anders, *CEO, DONG Energy*
Federspiel, Ulrik, *Vice President, Global Affairs,*
Haldor Topsøe *A/S*
Schütze, Peter, *Member of the Executive Management, Nordea Bank AB*

Germany
Ackermann, Josef, *Chairman of the Management Board and the Group Executive Committee, Deutsche Bank*
Enders, Thomas, *CEO, Airbus SAS*
Löscher, Peter, *President and CEO, Siemens AG*
Nass, Matthias, *Chief International Correspondent, Die Zeit*
Steinbrück, Peer, *Member of the Bundestag; Former Minister of Finance*

Finland
Apunen, Matti, *Director, Finnish Business and Policy Forum EVA*
Johansson, Ole, *Chairman, Confederation of the Finnish Industries EK*
Ollila, Jorma, *Chairman, Royal Dutch Shell*
Pentikäinen, Mikael, *Publisher and Senior Editor-in-Chief, Helsingin Sanomat*

France
Baverez, Nicolas, *Partner, Gibson, Dunn & Crutcher LLP*
Bazire, Nicolas, *Managing Director, Groupe Arnault /LVMH*
Castries, Henri de, *Chairman and CEO, AXA*
Lévy, Maurice, *Chairman and CEO, Publicis Groupe S.A.*
Montbrial, Thierry de, *President, French Institute for International Relations*
Roy, Olivier, *Professor of Social and Political Theory, European University Institute*

Great Britain
Agius, Marcus, *Chairman, Barclays PLC*
Flint, Douglas J., *Group Chairman, HSBC Holdings*
Kerr, John, *Member, House of Lords; Deputy Chairman, Royal Dutch Shell*
Lambert, Richard, *Independent Non-Executive Director, Ernst & Young*
Mandelson, Peter, *Member, House of Lords; Chairman, Global Counsel*
Micklethwait, John, *Editor-in-Chief, The Economist*
Osborne, George, *Chancellor of the Exchequer*
Stewart, Rory, *Member of Parliament*
Taylor, J. Martin, *Chairman, Syngenta International AG*

Greece
David, George A., *Chairman, Coca-Cola H.B.C. S.A.*
Hardouvelis, Gikas A., *Chief Economist and Head of Research, Eurobank EFG*
Papaconstantinou, George, *Minister of Finance*
Tsoukalis, Loukas, *President, ELIAMEP Grisons*

International Organizations
Almunia, Joaquín, *Vice President, European Commission*
Daele, Frans van, *Chief of Staff to the President of the European Council*
Kroes, Neelie, *Vice President, European Commission; Commissioner for Digital Agenda*
Lamy, Pascal, *Director General, World Trade Organization*
Rompuy, Herman van, *President, European Council*
Sheeran, Josette, *Executive Director, United Nations World Food Programme*
Solana Madariaga, Javier, *President, ESADEgeo Center for Global Economy and Geopolitics*
Trichet, Jean-Claude, *President, European Central Bank*
Zoellick, Robert B., *President, The World Bank Group*

Ireland
Gallagher, Paul, *Senior Counsel; Former Attorney General*
McDowell, Michael, *Senior Counsel, Law Library; Former Deputy Prime Minister*
Sutherland, Peter D., *Chairman, Goldman Sachs International*

Italy
Bernabè, Franco, *CEO, Telecom Italia SpA*
Elkann, John, Chairman, *Fiat S.p.A.*
Monti, Mario, *President, Univers Commerciale Luigi Bocconi*

Scaroni, Paolo, *CEO, Eni S.p.A.*
Tremonti, Giulio, *Minister of Economy and Finance*

Canada
Carney, Mark J., *Governor, Bank of Canada*
Clark, Edmund, *President and CEO, TD Bank Financial Group*
McKenna, Frank, *Deputy Chair, TD Bank Financial Group*
Orbinksi, James, *Professor of Medicine and Political Science, University of Toronto*
Prichard, J. Robert S., *Chair, Torys LLP*
Reisman, Heather, *Chair and CEO, Indigo Books & Music Inc. Center, Brookings Institution*

Netherlands
Bolland, Marc J., *Chief Executive, Marks and Spencer Group plc*
Chavannes, Marc E., *Political Columnist, NRC Handelsblad; Professor of Journalism*
Halberstadt, Victor, *Professor of Economics, Leiden University; Former Honorary Secretary General of Bilderberg Meetings*
H.M. the Queen of the Netherlands
Rosenthal, Uri, *Minister of Foreign Affairs*
Winter, Jaap W., *Partner, De Brauw Blackstone Westbroek*

Norway
Myklebust, Egil, *Former Chairman of the Board of Directors SAS, sk Hydro ASA*
H.R.H. Crown Prince Haakon of Norway
Ottersen, Ole Petter, *Rector, University of Oslo*
Solberg, Erna, *Leader of the Conservative Party*

Austria
Bronner, Oscar, *CEO and Publisher, Standard Medien AG*
Faymann, Werner, *Federal Chancellor*
Rothensteiner, Walter, *Chairman of the Board, Raiffeisen Zentralbank Osterreich AG*
Scholten, Rudolf, *Member of the Board of Executive Directors, Oesterreichische Kontrollbank AG*

Portugal
Balsemão, Francisco Pinto, *Chairman and CEO, IMPRESA, S.G.P.S.; Former Prime Minister*
Ferreira Alves, Clara, *CEO, Claref LDA; writer*
Nogueira Leite, António, *Member of the Board, José de Mello Investimentos, SGPS, SA*

Sweden
Mordashov, Alexey A., *CEO, Severstal*
Bildt, Carl, *Minister of Foreign Affairs*
Björling, Ewa, *Minister for Trade*
Wallenberg, Jacob, *Chairman, Investor AB*

Switzerland
Brabeck-Letmathe, Peter, *Chairman, Nestlé S.A.*
Groth, Hans, *Senior Director, Healthcare Policy & Market Access, Oncology Business Unit, Pfizer Europe*
Janom Steiner, Barbara, *Head of the Department of Justice, Security and Health, Canton*
Kudelski, André, *Chairman and CEO, Kudelski Group SA*
Leuthard, Doris, *Federal Councillor*
Schmid, Martin, *President, Government of the Canton Grisons*
Schweiger, Rolf, *Ständerat*
Soiron, Rolf, *Chairman of the Board, Holcim Ltd., Lonza Ltd.*
Vasella, Daniel L., *Chairman, Novartis AG*
Witmer, Jürg, *Chairman, Givaudan SA and Clariant AG*

Spain
Cebrián, Juan Luis, *CEO, PRISA*
Cospedal, María Dolores de, *Secretary General, Partido Popular*
León Gross, Bernardino, *Secretary General of the Spanish Presidency*
Nin Génova, Juan María, *President and CEO, La Caixa*
H.M. Queen Sofia of Spain

Turkey
Ciliv, Süreyya, *CEO, Turkcell Iletisim Hizmetleri A.S.*
Gülek Domac, Tayyibe, *Former Minister of State*
Koç, Mustafa V., *Chairman, Koç Holding A.S.*
Pekin, Sefika, *Founding Partner, Pekin & Bayar Law Firm*

USA
Alexander, Keith B., *Commander, USCYBERCOM; Director, National Security Agency*
Altman, Roger C., *Chairman, Evercore Partners Inc.*
Bezos, Jeff, *Founder and CEO, Amazon.com*
Collins, Timothy C., *CEO, Ripplewood Holdings, LLC*
Feldstein, Martin S., *George F. Baker Professor of Economics, Harvard University*
Hoffman, Reid, *Co-founder and Executive Chairman, LinkedIn*
Hughes, Chris R., *Co-founder, Facebook*
Jacobs, Kenneth M., *Chairman & CEO, Lazard*
Johnson, James A., *Vice Chairman, Perseus, LLC*
Jordan, Jr., Vernon E., *Senior Managing Director, Lazard Frères & Co. LLC*
Keane, John M., *Senior Partner, SCP Partners; General, US Army, Retired*
Kissinger, Henry A., *Chairman, Kissinger Associates, Inc.*
Kleinfeld, Klaus, *Chairman and CEO, Alcoa*
Kravis, Henry R., *Co-Chairman and co-CEO, Kohlberg Kravis, Roberts & Co.*
Kravis, Marie-Josée, *Senior Fellow, Hudson Institute, Inc.*
Li, Cheng, *Senior Fellow and Director of Research, John L. Thornton China Center, Brookings Institution*
Mundie, Craig J., *Chief Research and Strategy Officer, Microsoft Corporation*

Orszag, Peter R., *Vice Chairman, Citigroup Global Markets, Inc.*
Perle, Richard N., *Resident Fellow, American Enterprise Institute for Public Policy Research*
Rockefeller, David, *Former Chairman, Chase Manhattan Bank*
Rose, Charlie, *Executive Editor and Anchor, Charlie Rose*
Rubin, Robert E., *Co-Chairman, Council on Foreign Relations; Former Secretary of the Treasury*
Schmidt, Eric, *Executive Chairman, Google Inc.*
Steinberg, James B., *Deputy Secretary of State*
Thiel, Peter A., *President, Clarium Capital Management, LLC*
Varney, Christine A., *Assistant Attorney General for Antitrust*
Vaupel, James W., *Founding Director, Max Planck Institute for Demographic Research*
Warsh, Kevin, Former *Governor, Federal Reserve Board*
Wolfensohn, James D., *Chairman, Wolfensohn & Company, LLC*

Appendix 2

Countries committed to the United Nations Biodiversity Treaty

Afghanistan; Albania; Algeria; Angola; Antigua and Barbuda; Argentina; Armenia; Australia; Austria; Azerbaijan; Bahamas; Bahrain; Bangladesh; Barbados; Belarus; Belgium; Belize; Benin; Bhutan; Bolivia; Bosnia and Herzegovina; Botswana; Brazil; Brunei Darussalam; Bulgaria; Burkina Faso; Burma; Burundi; Cambodia; Cameroon; Canada; Cape Verde; Central African Republic; Chad; Chile; People"s Republic of China; Colombia; Comoros; Democratic Republic of the Congo; Republic of the Congo; Cook Islands; Costa Rica; Côte d"Ivoire; Croatia; Cuba; Cyprus; Czech Republic; Denmark; Djibouti; Dominica; Dominican Republic; Ecuador; Egypt; El Salvador; Equatorial Guinea; Eritrea; Estonia; Ethiopia; European Union; Fiji; Finland; France; Gabon; The Gambia; Georgia; Germany; Ghana; Greece; Grenada; Guatemala; Guinea; Guinea-Bissau; Guyana; Haiti; Honduras; Hungary; Iceland; India; Indonesia; Iran; Iraq; Ireland; Israel; Italy; Jamaica; Japan; Jordan; Kazakhstan; Kenya; Kiribati; Kuwait; North Korea; South Korea; Kyrgyzstan; Laos; Latvia; Lebanon; Lesotho; Liberia; Libya; Liechtenstein; Lithuania; Luxembourg; Republic of Macedonia; Madagascar; Malawi; Malaysia; Maldives; Mali; Malta; Marshall Islands; Mauritania; Mauritius; Mexico; Federated States of Micronesia; Moldova; Monaco; Mongolia; Montenegro; Morocco; Mozambique; Namibia; Nauru; Nepal; Netherlands; New Zealand; Nicaragua; Niger; Nigeria; Niue; Norway; Oman; Pakistan; Palau; Panama; Papua New Guinea; Paraguay; Peru; Philippines; Poland; Portugal; Qatar; Romania; Russia; Rwanda; Saint Kitts and Nevis; Saint Lucia; Saint Vincent and the Grenadines; Samoa; San Marino; São Tomé and Príncipe; Saudi Arabia; Senegal; Serbia; Seychelles; Sierra Leone; Singapore; Slovakia; Slovenia; Solomon Islands; Somalia; South Africa; Spain; Sri Lanka; Sudan; Suriname; Swaziland; Sweden; Switzerland; Syria; Tajikistan; Tanzania; Thailand; Timor-Leste; Togo; Tonga; Trinidad and Tobago; Tunisia; Turkey; Turkmenistan; Tuvalu; Uganda; Ukraine; United Arab Emirates; United Kingdom; Uruguay; Uzbekistan; Vanuatu; Venezuela; Vietnam; Yemen; Zambia; Zimbabwe.

Index

Christ Lion Consciousness

Remember Who You Are - Placing the Stone

Moon Slayer (A3 only)

Original Limited Fine Art Prints by
Neil Hague

Collectors Edition Prints (only 200 in the first series),
each come with a certificate of authentication and signed by Neil.
prints (above) come in two sizes and are available on both paper or canvas.

- A3 (420 x 297) Giclee print on paper **£85** (plus P&P)
- A2 (594 x 420) Giclee print on paper **£160** (plus P&P)
- A2 Limited Edition Canvas Prints (stretched and ready to hang) £300 each

Includes P&P (UK only)

Kokoro is the story of the 'truth vibrations' and the world that exists beyond the illusion of flesh and bone, time and space. It is a narrative that tells of the plight of humanity, from the construction of time to our present 'mind machine' based reality.

In two parts and through his highly individual style of visionary artwork, Neil Hague tells the story of the lion *Kokoro* (which means Heart) and his emergence in a world fashioned by the creator God Naga (the Serpent) and Marduk. - the Puppet Master (Illuminati).

Colour Paperback 32 pages (7 x 10")
£12.50 (Includes p&p in the UK only)

r more information about Neil's books, prints and original paintings please visit

www.neilhague.com

© Neil Hague 2011

Other work by David Icke

Human Race Get Off Your Knees – The Lion Sleeps No More

A monumental work of more than 650 pages, 355,000 words, 325 images and 32 pages of original artwork by Neil Hague. David's biggest and most comprehensive book introducing the 'Moon Matrix' and providing the fine detail about reality, history and present day events. Highly-acclaimed and a 'must have' for anyone interested in David Icke's work.

The David Icke Guide to the Global Conspiracy (and how to end it)

A masterpiece of dot-connecting that is both extraordinary and unique. There is a 'wow', indeed many of them, on every page as Icke lifts the veil on the unseen world.

Infinite Love is the Only Truth, Everything Else is Illusion

Why the 'world' is a virtual-reality game that only exists because we believe it does. Icke explains how we 'live' in a 'holographic internet' in that our brains are connected to a central 'computer' that feeds us the same collective reality that we decode from waveforms and electrical signals into the holographic 3D 'world' that we all think we see.

Alice in Wonderland and the World Trade Center Disaster – Why the Official Story of 9/11 is a Monumental Lie

A shocking exposé of the Ministries of Mendacity that have told the world the Big Lie about what happened on September 11th, who did it, how and why. This 500 page book reveals the real agenda behind the 9/11 attacks and how they were orchestrated from within the borders of the United States and not from a cave in Afghanistan.

Tales from the Time Loop

In this 500-page, profusely-illustrated book, David Icke explores in detail the multi-levels of the global conspiracy. He exposes the five-sense level and demolishes the official story of the invasions of Iraq and Afghanistan; he explains the inter-dimensional manipulation; and he shows that what we think is the 'physical world' is all an illusion that only exists in our mind. Without this knowledge, the true nature of the conspiracy cannot be understood.

The Biggest Secret

An exposé of how the same interbreeding bloodlines have controlled the planet for thousands of years. It includes the horrific background to the British royal family, the murder of Princess Diana, and the true origins of major religions. A blockbuster.

Children of the Matrix

The companion book of The Biggest Secret that investigates the reptilian and other dimensional connections to the global conspiracy and reveals the world of illusion – the 'Matrix' – that holds the human race in daily slavery.

... And The Truth Shall Set You Free (21st century edition)

Icke exposes in more than 500 pages the interconnecting web that controls the world today. This book focuses on the last 200 years and particularly on what is happening around us today. Another highly acclaimed book, which has been constantly updated. A classic in its field.

I Am Me, I Am Free

Icke's book of solutions. With humour and powerful insight, he shines a light on the mental and emotional prisons we build for ourselves ... prisons that disconnect us from our true and infinite potential to control our own destiny. A getaway car for the human psyche.

Earlier books by David Icke include The Robots' Rebellion (Gill & Macmillan), Truth Vibrations (Gill & Macmillan), Heal the World (Gill & Macmillan), Days of Decision (Jon Carpenter) and It Doesn't Have To Be Like This (Green Print). The last two books are out of print and no longer available.

The Lion Sleeps No More

David Icke marks his 20th year of uncovering astounding secrets and suppressed information with this eight-hour presentation before 2,500 people at London's Brixton Academy in May 2010. David has moved the global cutting edge so many times since his incredible 'awakening' in 1990 and here he does it again – and then some.

Beyond the Cutting Edge – Exposing the Dreamworld We Believe to be Real

Since his extraordinary 'awakening' in 1990 and 1991, David Icke has been on a journey across the world, and within himself, to find the Big answers to the Big questions: Who are we? Where are we? What are we doing here? Who really controls this world and how and why? In this seven-hour presentation to 2,500 people at the Brixton Academy in London, David addresses all these questions and connects the dots between them to reveal a picture of life on earth that is truly beyond the cutting edge.

Freedom or Fascism: the time to choose – 3xDVD set

More than 2,000 people from all over Britain and across the world gather at London's famous Brixton Academy to witness an extraordinary event. David Icke weaves together more than 16 years of painstaking research and determined investigation into the Global Conspiracy and the extraordinary 'sting' being perpetrated on an amnesic human race. Icke is the Dot Connector and he uses hundreds of illustrations to reveal the hidden story behind apparently unconnected world events.

Revelations of a Mother Goddess – DVD

Arizona Wilder was mind-programmed from birth by Josef Mengele, the notorious, 'Angel of Death' in the Nazi concentration camps. In this interview with David Icke, she describes human sacrifice rituals at Glamis Castle and Balmoral in England, in which the Queen, the Queen Mother and other members of the Royal Family sacrificed children in Satanic ceremonies.

The Reptilian Agenda – DVD

In this memorable, almost six hours of interview, contained in parts one and two, Zulu shaman, Credo Mutwa, reveals his incredible wealth of knowledge about the black magicians of the Illuminati and how they use their knowledge of the occult to control the world. Sit back and savour this wonderful man. You are in the presence of a genius and a giant.

Other books available

The Medical Mafia

The superb exposé of the medical system by Canadian doctor, Guylaine Lanctot, who also shows how and why 'alternative' methods are far more effective. Highly recommended.

What The Hell Am I Doing Here Anyway?

A second book by Guylaine Lanctot. We thirst for freedom, yet all the while we are imprisoned by conditioned beliefs.

Trance-Formation Of America

The staggering story of Cathy O'Brien, the mind-controlled slave of the US Government for some 25 years. Read this one sitting down. A stream of the world's most famous political names are revealed as they really are. Written by Cathy O'Brien and Mark Phillips.

Access Denied – For Reasons Of National Security

From the authors of Trance-Formation of America, this is the documented journey through CIA mind-control.

All books, DVDs and videos are available from David Icke Books
(contact details on the back page)
or through the website:

www.davidicke.com

Readings by **Carol Clarke**
Readings are sent via audio file over the internet
or can be sent by cd in the post

'Carol Clarke is the most consistently accurate psychic
I have come across anywhere in the world and she has
an eleven year record of remarkable accuracy with me
and many other people that I know.'

David Icke

To contact Carol for a reading,
email: welshseer@hotmail.co.uk

or

email: welshseer@aol.co.uk